IBM PC ASSEMBLY LANGUAGE AND PROGRAMMING

Fifth Edition

Peter Abel

Professor Emeritus
British Columbia
Institute of Technology

Prentice Hall
Upper Saddle River, New Jersey 07458
http:///www.prenhall.com

Library of Congress Cataloging-in-Publication Data
To come

Editor-in-chief: *Alice Dworkin*
Project manager: *Ana Arias Terry*
Editorial assistant: *Toni Holm*
Marketing manager: *Jennie Burger*
Production editor: *Pine Tree Composition*
Executive managing editor: *Vince O'Brien*
Managing editor: *David A. George*
Art director: *Jayne Conte*
Cover design: *John Christiana*
Manufacturing manager: *Trudy Pisciotti*
Manufacturing buyer: *Dawn Murrin*
Assistant vice president of production and manufacturing: *David W. Riccardi*

This book is accompanied by an Instructor's Manual, which contains solutions,
additional questions, and problems. A Prentice Hall Companion Website is also available.

The author and publisher of this book have used their best efforts in preparing
this book. These efforts include the development, research, and testing of the
theories to determine their effectiveness.

Printed in the United States of America
10   9   8   7   6   5   4   3   2

ISBN 0-13-030655-X

Prentice-Hall International (UK) Limited, *London*
Prentice-Hall of Australia Pty. Limited, *Sydney*
Prentice-Hall Canada Inc., *Toronto*
Prentice-Hall Hispanoamericana, S.A., *Mexico*
Prentice-Hall of India Private Limited, *New Delhi*
Prentice-Hall of Japan, Inc., *Tokyo*
Pearson Education Asia Pte. Ltd., *Singapore*
Editora Prentice-Hall do Brasil, Ltda., *Rio de Janeiro*

DR. P. Tang
Dept of CS
UALR

CONTENTS

Contents

PREFACE

The heart of a personal computer is a microprocessor, which handles the computer's requirements for arithmetic, logic, and control. The microprocessor had its origin in the 1960s, when research designers devised the integrated circuit (IC) by combining various electronic components into a single component on a silicon "chip." In the early 1970s Intel introduced the 8008 chip, which ushered in the first generation of microprocessors.

By 1974 the 8008 had evolved into the 8080, a popular second-generation microprocessor with general-purpose use. In 1978 Intel produced the third-generation 8086 processor, which represented a significant advance in its design. The 8088, a variation of the 8086, provided a slightly simpler design and compatibility with then-current input/output devices. The 8088 was selected by IBM in 1981 for its forthcoming personal computer. Enhanced versions of the 8086 include the 80286, 80386, 80486, Pentium, and other more advanced Pentium and Celeron models, each of which provides additional processing power.

Each family of processors has its own unique set of instructions that are used to direct its operations, such as accept input from a keyboard, display data on a screen, and perform arithmetic. This set of instructions (the machine language) is too complex and obscure for use in the development of programs. Software suppliers provide an assembly language for the processor family that represents the various instructions in more understandable symbolic code.

LEVELS OF PROGRAMMING

The levels of programming languages are the following:

- *Machine language* consists of the individual instructions that the processor executes one at a time; these are embedded in the operating system and in the low-level ready-only portions of the machine architecture.

- *Low-level assembly language* is designed for a specific family of processors; the symbolic instructions directly relate to machine language instructions one-for-one and are assembled into machine language.
- *High-level languages* such as C, C++, and Visual BASIC were designed to eliminate the technicalities of a particular computer; statements compiled in a high-level language typically generate many low-level instructions.

ADVANTAGES OF ASSEMBLY LANGUAGE

A knowledge and use of assembly language includes these advantages:

- Shows how programs interface with the operating system, the processor, and BIOS.
- Shows how data is represented and stored in memory and on external devices.
- Clarifies how the processor accesses and executes instructions and how instructions access and process data.
- Clarifies how a program accesses external devices.

As well, reasons for using assembly language include the following:

- A program written in assembly language requires considerably less memory and execution time than one written in a high-level language.
- Assembly language gives a programmer the ability to perform highly technical tasks that would be difficult, if not impossible, in a high-level language.
- Although most software specialists develop new applications in high-level languages, which are easier to write and maintain, a common practice is to recode in assembly language those sections that are time-critical.
- Resident programs (that reside in memory while other programs execute) and interrupt service routines (that handle input and output) are almost always developed in assembly language.

The following material is required for learning PC assembly language:

- Access to an IBM personal computer (any model) or equivalent compatible.
- A copy of the Windows 95/98 or DOS operating system and familiarity with its use. It is much easier to learn the intricacies of assembly language while working within a relatively simple operating system like DOS rather than within the Windows environment. Within DOS, you can freely experiment and can later step up to the Windows environment.
- A copy of an assembler translator program. Common suppliers include Microsoft, Borland, and SLR Systems.

The following are *not* required for learning assembly language:

- Prior knowledge of a programming language, although such knowledge may help you grasp some programming concepts more readily.
- Prior knowledge of electronics or circuitry. This book provides all the information about the PC's architecture that you require for programming in assembly language.

FOCUS OF THIS BOOK

To assist readers in learning assembly language programming, this book first covers the simpler aspects of the hardware and the language and then introduces instructions as they are needed. As well, the text emphasizes clarity in program examples. Thus the examples use those instructions and approaches that are the easiest to understand, even though a professional programmer would often solve similar problems with more sophisticated—but less clear—code.

The programs also omit macro instructions (explained in Chapter 21); although professional programmers use macros extensively, their appearance in a book of this nature would interfere with learning the principles of the language. Once you have learned these principles, you can then adopt the techniques of the professional.

THE APPROACH TO TAKE

This book can act as both a tutorial and a reference. To make the most effective use of your investment in a PC and software, work through each chapter carefully and reread any material that is not immediately clear. Use the program examples and get them to execute (or "run") on your computer. Also, be sure to work through the exercises at the end of each chapter.

The first eight chapters furnish the foundation material for assembly language. After studying these chapters, you can proceed with Chapters 9, 11, 12, 14, 15, 16, 20, 21, or 22. Chapters 24 through 26 are intended as references. Chapters related to each other are:

- 8 through 10 (screen and keyboard operations)
- 12 and 13 (arithmetic operations)
- 16 through 19 (disk processing)
- 22 and 23 (subprograms and overlays)

On completing this book, you will be able to:

- Understand the hardware of the personal computer.
- Understand machine-language code and hexadecimal format.
- Understand the steps involved in assembling, linking, and executing a program.
- Write programs in assembly language to handle the keyboard and screen, perform arithmetic, convert between ASCII and binary formats, perform table searches and sorts, and handle disk input and output.
- Trace machine execution as an aid in program debugging.
- Write your own macro instructions to facilitate faster coding.
- Link separately assembled programs into one executable program.

Learning assembly language and getting your programs to work is an exciting and challenging experience. For the time and effort invested, the rewards are sure to be great.

NOTES ON THE FIFTH EDITION

This fifth edition reflects a considerable number of enhancements to the previous edition, including the following:

- More features of the Intel Pentium processors
- More program examples and exercises
- Earlier introduction to interrupt operations
- Considerable reorganization and revision of explanations throughout the text
- More material on protected mode, passing parameters, the use of the stack, addressing modes, video systems and INT 10H functions, array handling, subprograms, and ports
- Revised and additional questions at the end of each chapter.

Users of the fourth edition should note that the contents of Chapter 7 (.COM Programs) has been combined in this edition with Chapter 5. Also, Chapter 21 has been dispersed in this way: the material on mouse handling to its own chapter (15) and the rest of the chapter (ports, string I/O, and sound) combined with BIOS and program interrupts in Chapter 24.

Note to the Student/Reader: Check out the web site for answers to selected questions, programs from the book for downloading, and questions for trying out. The address is www.prenhall.com/abel

Note to the Instructor: An instructors' CD with software, additional problems, and solutions is available for adopters of the book.

Acknowledgments

The author is grateful for the assistance and cooperation of all those who contributed suggestions for, reviews of, and corrections to earlier editions.

Chapter 1

Basic Features of PC Hardware

Objective: To explain the basic features of microcomputer hardware and program organization.

INTRODUCTION

Writing a program in assembly language requires knowledge of the computer's hardware (or architecture) and the details of its instruction set. This chapter provides an explanation of the basic hardware—bits, bytes, registers, memory, processor, and data bus. The rest of this book develops the instruction set and its uses.

The main internal hardware features of a computer are the processor, memory, and registers. (Registers are special processor components for holding addresses and data.) External hardware features are the computer's input/output devices such as the keyboard, monitor, disk, and CD-ROM. Software consists of the operating system and the various programs and data files stored on disk.

To execute (or run) a program, the system copies it from an external device into internal memory. (Internal memory, or RAM, is what people mean when they claim that their computer has, for example, 64 megabytes of memory.) The processor executes the program instructions, and its registers handle the requested arithmetic, data movement, and addressing.

BITS AND BYTES

The fundamental building block of computer storage is the *bit*. A bit may be *off* so that its value is considered 0, or it may be *on* so that its value is considered 1. A single bit doesn't provide much information, but it is surprising what a bunch of them can do.

Bytes

A group of nine related bits is called a *byte,* which represents a storage location internally in memory and on external devices. Each byte consists of eight bits for data and one bit for parity:

0	0	0	0	0	0	0	0	1

|—————————————————————data bits————————————————————| parity |

The eight data bits provide the basis for binary arithmetic and for representing such characters as the letter A and the asterisk symbol (*). Eight bits in a byte allow 256 (2^8) different combinations of on-off conditions, from all bits off (00000000) through all bits on (11111111). For example, a representation of the bits for the letter A is 01000001 and for the asterisk is 00101010, although you don't have to memorize these bit values.

According to the rule of parity, the number of bits that are on in each byte must always be odd. Because the letter A contains two bits that are on, the processor forces odd parity by automatically setting the parity bit on (01000001-1). Similarly, since the asterisk contains three bits that are on, the processor maintains odd parity by turning the parity bit off (00101010-0). When an instruction references a byte in internal storage, the processor checks its bits for parity. If parity is even, the system assumes that a bit is "lost" and displays an error message. A parity error may be a result of a hardware fault or an electrical disturbance; either way, it is a rare event.

How does a computer "know" that bit value 01000001 represents the letter A? When you key in A on the keyboard, the system delivers a signal from that particular key into memory and sets a byte (in a location in your program) to the bit value 01000001. You can move the contents of this byte about in memory as you will, and you can print it or display it on the screen as the letter A.

Handling the parity bit is an automatic hardware function and we no longer need be concerned with it. The bits in a byte are numbered 0 to 7 from right to left, as shown here for the letter A:

Bit contents (A):	0 1 0 0 0 0 0 1
Bit number:	7 6 5 4 3 2 1 0

Related Bytes. A program can treat a group of one or more related bytes as a unit of data, such as time or distance. A group of bytes that defines a particular value is commonly known as a *data item* or *field.* The processor also supports certain data sizes that are natural to it:

- *Word.* A 2-byte (16-bit) data item.
- *Doubleword.* A 4-byte (32-bit) data item.
- *Quadword.* An 8-byte (64-bit) data item.

- *Paragraph.* A 16-byte (128-bit) area.
- *Kilobyte (KB).* The number 2^{10} equals 1,024, which happens to be the value K, for kilobyte. Thus 640K of memory is $640 \times 1,024 = 655,360$ bytes.
- *Megabyte (MB).* The number 2^{20} equals 1,048,576, or 1 megabyte.

Bits in a word are numbered 0 through 15 from right to left, as shown here for the letters *PC,* with the *P* (01010000) in the leftmost byte and the *C* (01000011) in the rightmost byte:

```
Bit contents (PC):  0  1  0  1  0  0 0 0 │ 0 1 0 0 0 0 1 1

Bit number:        15 14 13 12 11 10 9 8 │ 7 6 5 4 3 2 1 0
```

Each byte in memory has a unique *address.* The first byte in the lowest memory location is numbered 0, the second is numbered 1, and so forth.

THE BINARY NUMBER SYSTEM

Because a computer can distinguish only between 0 and 1 bits, it works in a base-2 numbering system known as *binary.* In fact, the word "bit" is a contraction of "Binary digIT."

A collection of bits can represent any numeric value. The value of a binary number is based on the presence of 1-bits and their relative positions. Just as in decimal numbers, the positions represent ascending powers (but of 2, not 10) from right to left. In the following 8-bit number, all bits are set to 1 (on):

```
Bit value:        1   1  1   1 1 1 1 1

Position value: 128  64 32  16 8 4 2 1

Bit number:       7   6  5   4 3 2 1 0
```

The rightmost bit assumes the value 1 (2^0), the next bit to the left assumes the value 2 (2^1), the next bit the value 4 (2^2), and so forth. The value of the binary number in this case is $1 + 2 + 4 + 8 + 16 + 32 + 64 + 128 = 255$ (or $2^8 - 1$).

Let's examine the value of the binary number 01000001:

```
Bit value:        0   1  0   0 0 0 0 1

Position value: 128  64 32  16 8 4 2 1
```

You calculate its value as 1 plus 64, or 65. But you may recall that bit value 01000001 is also the letter A. Indeed, the bits 01000001 can represent either the number 65 or the letter A, as follows:

- If a program defines and uses the data for arithmetic purposes, then bit value 01000001 represents a binary number equivalent to decimal number 65.
- If a program defines and uses the data for descriptive purposes, such as a heading, then 01000001 represents an alphabetic character.

When you start programming, you will see this distinction more clearly because you define and use each data item for a specific purpose, that is, arithmetic data for arithmetic purposes and descriptive data for displayed output. In practice, the two uses are seldom a source of confusion.

A binary number is not limited to eight bits. A processor that uses 16-bit (or 32-bit) architecture handles 16-bit (or 32-bit) numbers automatically. For 16 bits, $2^{16} - 1$ provides values up to 65,535, and for 32 bits, $2^{32} - 1$ provides values up to 4,294,967,295.

Binary Arithmetic

Because a microcomputer performs arithmetic only in binary format, an assembly language programmer has to be familiar with binary format and binary addition. The following four examples illustrate simple binary addition:

```
    0          0          1          1
  +0         +1         +1         +1
   0          1         10         +1
                                   11
```

The last two examples illustrate a carry of a 1-bit into the next (left) position. Now, let's add the bit values 01000001 and 00101010. Are we adding the letter A and an asterisk? No, this time they represent the decimal values 65 and 42:

```
Decimal        Binary
   65         01000001
  +42        +00101010
  107         01101011
```

To check that the binary sum 01101011 is actually 107, add the values of the 1-bits. As another example, let's add the decimal values 60 and 53 and their binary equivalents:

```
Decimal        Binary
   60         00111100
  +53        +00110101
  113         01110001
```

Again, be sure to check that the binary sum really equals 113.

Negative Binary Numbers.   A signed binary number (that is, one used for arithmetic) is considered to be positive if its leftmost bit is 0, whereas a signed negative binary number contains a 1-bit in its leftmost position. However, representing a binary number as negative is not as simple as setting the leftmost bit to 1, such as converting 01000001 (+65) to 11000001. Instead, a negative binary value is expressed in *two's complement notation;* that is, the rule to represent a binary number as negative is: *Reverse* *the bit values and add 1.* As an example, let's use this rule to find the two's complement of 01000001 (or 65):

```
Number +65:              01000001
Reverse the bits:        10111110
Add 1:                          1
Number -65:              10111111
```

A signed binary number is negative when its leftmost bit is 1 and the processor handles it accordingly. However, if you add the 1-bit values to determine the decimal value of the binary number 10111111, you won't get 65. To determine the absolute value of a negative binary number, apply the two's complement rule; that is, reverse the bits and add 1:

```
Number -65:              10111111
Reverse the bits:        01000000
Add 1:                          1
Number +65:              01000001
```

To illustrate that this procedure works properly, the sum of +65 and −65 should be zero. Let's try it:

```
  +65          01000001
  -65        +10111111
  ──          ─────────
  00        (1)00000000
```

Note the overflow of a 1-bit out of the 8-bit number. In the sum, the 8-bit value is all zeros, and the overflow of the 1-bit on the left is lost. But because there is both a carry into the sign bit and a carry out, the result is considered to be correct.

To handle binary subtraction, convert the number being subtracted to two's complement format and add the numbers. For example, let's subtract 42 from 65. The binary representation for 42 is 00101010 and its two's complement is 11010110; add −42 to 65, like this:

```
    65          01000001
+(-42)        +11010110
  ────         ─────────
    23        (1)00010111
```

The result, 23, is correct. Note that once again there is a valid carry into and out of the sign bit.

If the justification for two's complement notation isn't immediately clear, consider the following question: What value would you have to add to binary 00000001 to make it equal to 00000000? In terms of decimal numbers, the answer would be −1. The two's complement of 00000001 is 11111111, so add +1 and −1 to get zero:

```
      1          00000001
  +(-1)          11111111
                ─────────
Result:        (1)00000000
```

Ignoring the carry of 1, you can see that the binary number 11111111 is equivalent to decimal -1. You can also see a pattern form as the binary numbers decrease in value:

```
+3        00000011
+2        00000010
+1        00000001
 0        00000000
-1        11111111
-2        11111110
-3        11111101
```

In fact, the 0-bits in a negative binary number indicate its (absolute) value: Treat the positional value of each 0-bit as if it were a 1-bit, sum the values, and add 1.

You'll find this material on binary arithmetic and negative numbers particularly relevant when you get to Chapters 12 and 13 on arithmetic.

HEXADECIMAL REPRESENTATION

Although a byte may contain any of the 256 bit combinations, there is no way to display or print many of them as standard ASCII characters. (Examples of such characters include the bit configurations for such operations as Tab, Enter, Form Feed, and Escape.) Consequently, computer designers developed a shorthand method of representing binary data that divides each byte in half and expresses the value of each half-byte.

Imagine that you want to view the contents of a binary value in four adjacent bytes (a doubleword) in memory. Consider the following four bytes, shown in both binary and decimal formats:

Binary:	0101 1001	0011 0101	1010 1001	1100 1110
Decimal:	5 9	3 5	10 9	12 14

Because the decimal numbers 10, 12, and 14 each require two digits, let's extend the numbering system so that 10 = A, 11 = B, 12 = C, 13 = D, 14 = E, and 15 = F. In this way, the numbering system involves the "digits" 0 through F and, since there are 16 such digits, the system is known as *hexadecimal* (or *hex*) representation. Here's the revised shorthand number that represents the contents of the bytes just given:

Binary:	0101 1001	0011 0101	1010 1001	1100 1110
Hexadecimal:	5 9	3 5	A 9	C E

Figure 1-1 shows the decimal numbers 0 through 15 along with their equivalent binary and hexadecimal values.

Binary	Decimal	Hexadecimal	Binary	Decimal	Hexadecimal
0000	0	0	1000	8	8
0001	1	1	1001	9	9
0010	2	2	1010	10	A
0011	3	3	1011	11	B
0100	4	4	1100	12	C
0101	5	5	1101	13	D
0110	6	6	1110	14	E
0111	7	7	1111	15	F

Figure 1-1   Binary, Decimal, and Hexadecimal Representation

Assembly language makes considerable use of hexadecimal format. A listing of an assembled program shows, in hexadecimal, all addresses, machine-code instructions, and the contents of data constants. For debugging programs, you can use the DEBUG program, which also displays the addresses and contents of bytes in hexadecimal format.

You'll soon get used to working in hexadecimal format. Keep in mind that the hex number immediately following hex F is hex 10, which is decimal value 16. Following are some simple examples of hex arithmetic:

```
    7        6        F        F       10       38          FF
   +3       +7       +1       +F      +30       18       +  1
   ──       ──       ──       ──      ───       ──       ─────
    A        D       10       1E       40       50         100
```

Note also that hex 40 equals decimal 64, hex 100 is decimal 256, and hex 1000 is decimal 4,096. For the example 38 + 18 = 50, note that hex 8 + 8 equals 10.

To indicate a hex number in an assembly language program, you code an "H" immediately after the number, such as 25H (decimal 37). An assembly language requirement is that a hex number always begins with a decimal digit 0-9, so you code B8H as 0B8H. In this book, a hexadecimal value is indicated with the word "hex" preceding or an "H" following the number (such as hex 4C or 4CH); a binary value with the word binary preceding or a "B" following the number (such as binary 01001100 or 01001100B); and a decimal value simply by a number (such as 76). An occasional exception occurs where the base is obvious from its context.

Appendix A gives an explanation of how to convert hex numbers to decimal format and vice versa.

ASCII CODE

Data on the PC may be classed as numeric (binary data used for arithmetic) or as alphanumeric (character and descriptive data). The latter type of data is always used for keyboard input and screen and printer output. To standardize the representation of data, microcomputer designers adopted the ASCII (American Standard Code for Information Interchange) code.

Because a byte contains 8 bits, the PC uses an 8-bit ASCII code that the provides 2^8, or 256 characters, many of which are available on the keyboard. For example, you have already seen the ASCII code for the letter A: 01000001 (hex 41). Fortunately, you don't have to memorize the ASCII codes; when necessary, you can refer to Appendix B for a complete list, and Chapter 8 shows how to display most of them on the screen.

PC COMPONENTS

The main component of the PC is its *system board* (or motherboard). It contains the processor, coprocessors, main memory, connectors, and expansion slots for optional cards. The slots and connectors provide access to such components as read-only memory (ROM), random access memory (RAM), hard disk, CD-ROM drives, additional main memory, video units, keyboard, mouse, parallel and serial devices, sound synthesizers, and cache memory. The processor uses the high-speed cache memory to decrease its need to access the slower main memory.

A *bus* with wires attached to the system board connects the components. It transfers data between the processor, memory, and external devices, in effect managing data traffic. When a program, for example, requests reading data from an external storage device, the processor determines the address in memory where it is to be delivered and places the address on an address bus. The memory unit then delivers the data to a data bus and notifies the processor that the data is ready. The processor now delivers the data from the data bus to the addressed location in memory.

The power supply converts the standard 110-volt alternating current into direct current with voltages reduced to the computer's requirements. The power supply is commonly rated about 300 watts.

The Processor

The brain of the PC is a processor (also known as central processing unit, or CPU) based on the Intel 8086 family that performs all executing of instructions and processing of data. Processors vary in their speed and capacity of memory, registers, and data bus. An internal clock synchronizes and controls all the processor's operations. The basic time unit, the clock cycle, is rated in terms of megahertz (millions of cycles per second). Following is a brief description of various Intel processors:

8088. Has 16-bit registers and an 8-bit data bus and can address up to 1 million bytes of internal memory. Although the registers can process two bytes at a time, the data bus can transfer only one byte at a time. This processor runs in what is known as *real mode,* that is, one program at a time, with actual ("real") addresses in the segment registers.

8086. Is similar to the 8088, but has a 16-bit data bus and runs faster.

80286. Runs faster than the preceding processors, has additional capabilities, and can address up to 16 million bytes. This processor and its successors can operate in real mode or in *protected mode,* which enables an operating system like Windows to perform multitasking (running more than one job concurrently) and to protect them from each other.

80386. Has 32-bit registers and a 32-bit data bus and can address up to 4 billion bytes of memory. As well as protected mode, the processor supports *virtual mode,* whereby it can swap portions of memory onto disk; in this way, programs running concurrently have space to operate.

80486. Also has 32-bit registers and a 32-bit data bus. As well, high-speed *cache memory* connected to the processor bus enables the processor to store copies of the most recently used instructions and data. The processor can operate faster when using the cache directly without having to access the slower main memory.

Pentium. Has 32-bit registers, a 64-bit data bus, and separate caches for data and for memory. (Intel adopted the name "Pentium" because, in contrast to numbers, names can be copyrighted.) Its superscalar design enables the processor to decode and execute more than one instruction per clock cycle.

Pentium II and III. Have a Dual Independent Bus design that provides separate paths to the system cache and to memory. Where the previous processors' connection to a storage cache on the system board caused delays, these processors are connected to a built-in storage cache by a 64-bit wide bus.

Processors up through the 80486 have what is known as a *single-stage pipeline,* which restricts them to completing one instruction before starting the next. Pipelining involves the way a processor divides an instruction into sequential steps using different resources. The Pentium has a five-stage pipelined structure, and the Pentium II has a 12-stage superpipelined structure. This feature enables them to run many operations in parallel.

A problem faced by designers is that because the processor runs considerably faster than does memory, it has to wait for memory to deliver instructions. To handle this problem, each advanced processor in turn has more capability in dynamic execution. For example, by means of multiple branch prediction, the processor looks ahead a number of steps to predict what to process next.

Execution Unit and Bus Interface Unit. As illustrated in Figure 1-2, the processor is partitioned into two logical units: an execution unit (EU) and a bus interface

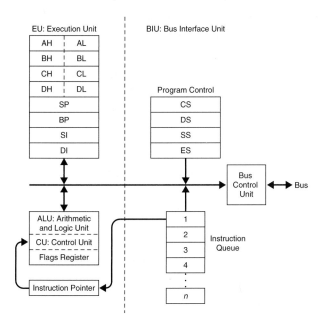

Figure 1-2 Execution Unit and Bus Interface Unit

unit (BIU). The role of the EU is to execute instructions, whereas the BIU delivers instructions and data to the EU. The EU contains an arithmetic and logic unit (ALU), a control unit (CU), and a number of registers. These features provide for execution of instructions and arithmetic and logical operations.

The most important function of the BIU is to manage the bus control unit, segment registers, and instruction queue. The BIU controls the buses that transfer data to the EU, to memory, and to external input/output devices, whereas the segment registers control memory addressing.

Another function of the BIU is to provide access to instructions. Because the instructions for a program that is executing are in memory, the BIU must access instructions from memory and place them in an *instruction queue,* which varies in size depending on the processor. This feature enables the BIU to look ahead and prefetch instructions so that there is always a queue of instructions ready to execute.

The EU and BIU work in parallel, with the BIU keeping one step ahead. The EU notifies the BIU when it needs access to data in memory or an I/O device. Also, the EU requests machine instructions from the BIU instruction queue. The top instruction is the currently executable one and, while the EU is occupied executing an instruction, the BIU fetches another instruction from memory. This fetching overlaps with execution and speeds up processing.

Programmers are not able to access any of these features of the processor.

INTERNAL MEMORY

The two types of internal memory on the PC are *random access memory* (RAM) and *read-only memory* (ROM). Bytes in memory are numbered consecutively, beginning with 00, so that each location has a uniquely numbered address.

Figure 1-3 shows a physical memory map of an 8086-type PC as a simple example. Of the first megabyte of memory, the first 640K is base RAM, most of which is available for your use. The Interrupt Vector Table in lowest memory is described later in this chapter, the BIOS Data Area in Chapters 3 and 24, and the Video Display Area in Chapter 9.

ROM. ROM consists of special memory chips that (as the full name suggests) can only be read. Because instructions and data are permanently "burned into" the chips, they

```
Start Address          Purpose

Dec      Hex
960K     F0000    ┌─────────────────────────┐
                  │   64K base system ROM    │
                  ├─────────────────────────┤
                  │   192K memory expansion  │
768K     C0000    │   area (ROM)             │
                  ├─────────────────────────┤
                  │   128K video display     │
640K     A0000    │   area (RAM)             │
                  ├─────────────────────────┤
                  │                          │
                  │   640K memory (RAM)      │
                  │                          │
                  │   BIOS data area         │
zero     00000    │   Interrupt vector table │
                  └─────────────────────────┘
```

Figure 1-3 Map of Base Memory

cannot be altered. The ROM Basic Input/Output System (BIOS) begins at address 768K and handles input/output devices, such as a hard disk controller. ROM beginning at 960K controls the computer's basic functions, such as the power-on self-test, dot patterns for graphics, and the disk self-loader. When you switch on the power, ROM performs various check-outs and loads special system data from disk into RAM.

RAM. A programmer is mainly concerned with RAM, which would be better named "read-write memory." RAM is available as a "worksheet" for temporary storage and execution of programs. When you turn on the power, the ROM boot-up procedure loads a portion of the operating system into RAM. You then request it to perform actions, such as loading a program from a disk into RAM. Your program executes in RAM and normally produces output on the screen, printer, or disk. When finished, you may ask the system to load another program into RAM, an action that overwrites the previous program.

Turning off the power erases the contents of RAM but does not affect ROM. Consequently, if you have been changing data in a document, you need to save it on disk before shutting down the PC. Further discussions of RAM use the general term *memory*.

Addressing Data in Memory

Depending on model, the processor can access one or more bytes of memory at a time. Consider the decimal number 1,315. The hex representation of this value, 0529H, requires two bytes, or one word, of memory. It consists of a high-order (most significant) byte, 05, and a low-order (least significant) byte, 29. The processor stores the data in memory in *reverse-byte sequence:* the low-order byte in the low memory address and the high-order byte in the high memory address. For example, the processor transfers the value 0529H from a register into memory addresses 04A26H and 04A27H like this:

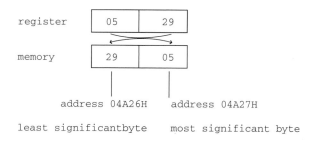

The processor expects numeric data in memory to be in reverse-byte sequence and processes the data accordingly. When the processor retrieves the word from memory, it again reverses the bytes, restoring them correctly in the register as hex 05 29. Although this feature is entirely automatic, you have to be alert to it when programming and debugging assembly language programs.

When programming in assembly language, you have to distinguish clearly between the *address* of a memory location and its *contents*. In the preceding example, the contents of address 04A26H is 29, and the contents of address 04A27H is 05.

There are two types of addressing schemes:

1. An *absolute address,* such as 04A26H, is a 20-bit value that directly references a specific location in memory.

2. A *segment:offset address* combines the starting address of a segment with an offset value. The next section covers this scheme in detail.

SEGMENTS AND ADDRESSING

Segments are special areas defined in a program for containing the code, the data, and what is known as the *stack.* A segment begins on a *paragraph boundary,* that is, at a location evenly divisible by 16, or hex 10. Although a segment may be located almost anywhere in memory and in real mode may be up to 64K bytes, it requires only as much space as the program requires for its use; that is, data and instructions that process the data. When an instruction loads a segment address in a segment register, the operation automatically shifts off the rightmost four 0-bits.

You may define any number of segments; to address a particular segment, it is necessary only to change the address in an appropriate segment register. In real mode, the three main segments are code, data, and stack:

> *Code Segment.* Contains the machine instructions that are to execute. Typically, the first executable instruction is at the start of this segment, and the operating system links to that location to begin program execution. As the name implies, the Code Segment (CS) register addresses the code segment.

> *Data Segment.* Contains a program's defined data, constants, and work areas. The Data Segment (DS) register addresses the data segment.

> *Stack Segment.* Contains any data and addresses that the program needs to save temporarily or for use by your own "called" subroutines. The Stack Segment (SS) register addresses the stack segment.

Segment Boundaries

A segment register is 16 bits in size and contains the starting address of a segment. Figure 1-4 presents a graphic view of the SS, DS, and CS registers and their relationships to the stack, data, and code segments. (The registers and segments are not necessarily in the order shown.) Other segment registers are the ES (Extra Segment) and, on the 80386 and later processors, the FS and GS registers, which provide additional segments for storing data.

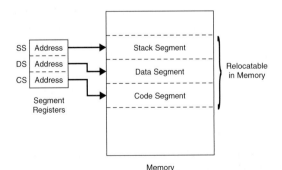

Memory   **Figure 1-4**   Segments and Registers

As mentioned earlier, a segment begins on a paragraph boundary, which is an address evenly divisible by decimal 16, or hex 10. Consider a data segment that begins at memory location 038E0H. Because in this and all other cases the rightmost hex digit is zero, the computer designers decided that it would be unnecessary to store the zero digit in the segment register. Thus 038E0H is stored in the register as 038E, with the rightmost four bits shifted off. Where appropriate, this text uses square brackets to refer to the rightmost hex zero, such as 038E[0].

Segment Offsets

Within a program, all memory locations within a segment are relative to the segment's starting address. The distance in bytes from the segment address to another location within the segment is expressed as an *offset* (or displacement). In real mode, a 2-byte (16-bit) offset can range from 0000H through FFFFH, or zero through 65,535. Thus the first byte of the code segment is at offset 00, the second byte is at offset 01, and so forth, through to offset 65,535. To reference any memory location in a segment, the processor combines the segment address in a segment register with the offset value of that location, that is, its distance in bytes from the start of the segment.

Consider a data segment that begins at location 038E0H. The DS register contains the segment address of the data segment, 038E[0]H, and an instruction references a location with an offset of 0032H bytes from the start of the data segment. To reference the required location, the processor combines the address of the data segment with the offset:

```
DS segment address:        038E0H
Offset:                  +  0032H
Actual address:            03912H
```

The actual memory location of the byte referenced by the instruction is therefore 03912H. Note that a program contains one or more segments, which may begin almost anywhere in memory, may vary in size, and may be in any sequence. You will only occasionally be concerned with segment addresses and offsets because the assembler and the processor take care of them, but you'll need to understand their purposes and uses.

REGISTERS

The processor's registers are used to control instructions being executed, to handle addressing of memory, and to provide arithmetic capability. A program references the registers by name, such as CS, DS, and SS. Bits in a register (like bits in a byte) are conventionally numbered from right to left, beginning with 0, as

```
...15 14 13 12 11 10 9 8 7 6 5 4 3 2 1 0
```

Segment Registers

A *segment register* provides for addressing an area of memory known as the *current segment.* Intel processors used by the PC series provide different addressing capabilities.

8086/8088 Addressing.   The segment registers of the these processors are 16 bits in length and operate in real mode. Because a segment address is on a paragraph boundary (evenly divisible by 16, or hex 10), the rightmost four bits of its address are zero. As discussed earlier, a segment address is stored in a segment register, and the processor shifts off the rightmost four 0-bits, so that hex nnnn0 becomes nnnn. For example, hex address 038E0 is stored in a segment register as 038E. The processor assumes the rightmost four bits, so that effectively, a segment register is 20 bits long.

A maximum value of FFFF[0]H allows addressing up to 1,048,560 bytes. If you are uncertain, decode each hex F as binary 1111, allow for the rightmost four 0-bits, and add the values of the 1-bits.

80286 Addressing.   In real mode, the 80286 processor handles addressing the same as an 8086 does. In protected mode, the 24-bit addressing scheme provides for addresses up to FFFFF[0], or 16 million bytes. The segment registers act as selectors for accessing a 24-bit segment address from memory. Protected mode enables the processor to perform multitasking, where it switches from executing one task (or program) to another. The system must be able to protect each task in memory from each other task.

80386/486/Pentium Addressing.   In real mode, these processors also handle addressing much the same as an 8086 does. In protected mode, the processors use 48 bits for addressing, which allows addressing segments up to 4 billion bytes. The 16-bit segment registers act as selectors for accessing a 32-bit segment address from memory.

The six segment registers are CS, DS, SS, ES, FS, and GS.

CS register.   Contains the starting address of a program's code segment. This segment address, plus an offset value in the Instruction Pointer (IP) register, indicates the address of an instruction to be fetched for execution. For normal programming purposes, you need not directly reference this register.

DS register.   Contains the starting address of a program's data segment. Instructions use this address to locate data; this address, plus an offset value in an instruction, causes a reference to a specific byte location in the data segment.

SS register.   Permits the implementation of a stack in memory, which a program uses for temporary storage of addresses and data. The system stores the starting address of a program's stack segment in the SS register. This segment address, plus an offset value in the Stack Pointer (SP) register, indicates the current word in the stack being addressed. For normal programming purposes, you need not directly reference the SS register.

ES register.   Used by some string (character data) operations to handle memory addressing. In this context, the ES (Extra Segment) register is associated with the DI (Index) register. If a program requires the use of ES, you must initialize it with an appropriate segment address.

FS and GS registers.   Additional extra segment registers introduced by the 80386 for handling storage requirements.

Pointer Registers

The pointer registers are the 32-bit EIP, ESP, and EBP; the rightmost 16-bit portions are IP, SP, and BP, respectively.

Instruction Pointer (IP) register.   The 16-bit IP register contains the offset address of the next instruction that is to execute. IP is associated with the CS register (as CS:IP) in that IP indicates the current instruction within the currently executing code segment. You do not normally reference IP in a program, but you can change its value, for example, when using the DEBUG program to test a program. The 80386 introduced an extended 32-bit IP called EIP.

In the following example, CS contains 39B4[0]H and IP contains 514H. To find the next instruction to be executed, the processor combines the address in CS with the offset in IP:

```
Segment address in CS          39B40H
Plus offset address in IP      +  514H
Address of next instruction    3A054H
```

For each instruction that executes, the processor changes the offset value in IP so that IP in effect directs each step of execution.

The SP (Stack Pointer) and BP (Base Pointer) registers are associated with the SS register and permit the system to access data in the stack segment. The processor automatically handles these registers.

Stack Pointer (SP) register.   The 16-bit SP register provides an offset value, which, when associated with the SS register (SS:SP), refers to the current word being processed in the stack. The 80386 introduced an extended 32-bit stack pointer, the ESP register.

In the following example, the SS register contains segment address 4BB3[0]H and SP contains offset 412H. To find the current word being processed in the stack, the processor combines the address in SS with the offset in SP:

```
Segment address in SS         4BB30H
Plus offset in SP             +  412H
Address in stack:             4BF42H
```

Base Pointer (BP) register.   The 16-bit BP facilitates referencing parameters, which are data and addresses that a program passes via the stack. The processor combines the address in SS with the offset in BP. BP can also be combined with DI and with SI as a base register for special addressing. The 80386 introduced an extended 32-bit BP, the EBP register.

General-Purpose Registers

The general-purpose registers are the 32-bit EAX, EBX, ECX, and EDX; the rightmost 16-bit portions are AX, BX, CX, and DX, respectively. For example, AX is the rightmost 16 bits of EAX. AX itself consists of two portions: the leftmost eight bits, the "high" portion, is known as AH; the rightmost eight bits, the "low" portion, is known as AL. This feature enables you to reference any portion—EAX, AX, AH, or AL—by name for processing doublewords, words, or bytes individually.

The following assembly language instructions illustrate moving zeros to AX, BH, and ECX registers, respectively:

```
MOV AX,00
MOV BH,00
MOV ECX,00
```

AX register. AX, the primary accumulator, is used for operations involving input/output and most arithmetic. For example, the multiply, divide, and translate instructions assume the use of AX. Also, some instructions generate more efficient machine code if they reference AX rather than another register. The 8-bit AH and AL comprise the left and right portions of the 16-bit AX, and AX comprises the rightmost 16 bits of the 32-bit EAX:

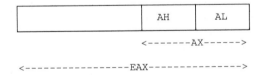

BX register. BX is known as the base register since it is the only general-purpose register that can be used as an index to extend addressing. Another common purpose of BX is for computations. BX can also be combined with DI or SI as a base register for special addressing. The 8-bit BH and BL comprise the left and right portions of the 16-bit BX, and BX comprises the rightmost 16 bits of the 32-bit EBX:

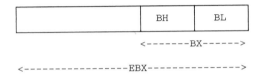

CX register. CX is known as the count register. It may contain a value to control the number of times a loop is repeated or a value to shift bits left or right. You may also use CX for many computations. The 8-bit CH and CL comprise the left and right portions of the 16-bit CX, and CX comprises the rightmost 16 bits of the 32-bit ECX:

<--------CX------>

<----------------ECX------------->

DX register. DX is known as the data register. Some input/output operations require its use, and multiply and divide operations that involve large values assume the use of DX and AX together as a pair. The 8-bit DH and DL comprise the left and right portions of the 16-bit DX, and DX comprises the rightmost 16 bits of the 32-bit EDX:

<--------DX------>

<----------------EDX------------->

The general-purpose registers are available for addition and subtraction of 8-, 16-, or 32-bit values:

```
MOV    EAX,225    ;Move 225 to EAX (doublewords)
ADD    AX,CX      ;Add CX to AX (words)
SUB    BL,AL      ;Subtract AL from BL (bytes)
```

Index Registers

The index registers are the 32-bit ESI and EDI; the rightmost 16-bit portions are SI and DI, respectively. These registers are available for indexed addressing and for some use in addition and subtraction.

SI register. The 16-bit source index register is required for some string (character) handling operations. In this context, SI is associated with the DS register. The 80386 introduced a 32-bit extended register, ESI.

DI register. The 16-bit destination index register is also required for some string operations. In this context, DI is associated with the ES register. The 80386 introduced a 32-bit extended register, EDI.

Flags Register

The 32-bit Eflags contains bits that indicate the status of various activities. The rightmost 16-bit portion of Eflags is the Flags register; nine of its 16 bits indicate the current status of the computer and the results of processing. Many instructions involving comparisons and arithmetic change the status of the flags, which some instructions may test to determine subsequent action.

The following briefly describes the common flag bits:

OF (overflow). Indicates overflow of a high-order (leftmost) bit following arithmetic.

DF (direction). Determines left or right direction for moving or comparing string (character) data.

IF (interrupt). Indicates that all external interrupts, such as keyboard entry, are to be processed or ignored.

TF (trap). Permits operation of the processor in single-step mode. Debugger programs such as DEBUG set the trap flag so that you can step through execution a single instruction at a time to examine its effect on registers and memory.

SF (sign). Contains the resulting sign of an arithmetic operation (0 = positive and 1 = negative).

ZF (zero). Indicates the result of an arithmetic or comparison operation (0 = nonzero and 1 = zero result).

AF (auxiliary carry). Contains a carry out of bit 3 into bit 4 in an arithmetic operation, for specialized arithmetic.

PF (parity). Indicates the number of 1-bits that result from an operation. An even number of bits causes so-called even parity and an odd number causes odd parity.

CF (carry). Contains carries from a high-order (leftmost) bit following an arithmetic operation; also, contains the contents of the last bit of a shift or rotate operation.

The flags are in the Flags register in the following locations (which you need not memorize):

Flag:					O	D	I	T	S	Z		A		P		C
Bit no.	15	14	13	12	11	10	9	8	7	6	5	4	3	2	1	0

The flags most relevant to assembly programming are OF, SF, ZF, and CF for comparisons and arithmetic operations, and DF for the direction of string operations. Some other flags are used for internal purposes, concerned primarily with protected mode. Chapter 7 contains more details about the Flags register.

HARDWARE INTERRUPTS

Certain events cause the processor to suspend the current operation and to act on the reason for the interruption. Usually, the events are normal and expected, such as a request from the keyboard for input. The processor interrupts the current operation, calls a BIOS routine to handle the keyboard request, and then returns to the interrupted program. Other interrupts can be critical, such as an attempt to divide by zero, which causes the system to terminate processing.

Another type of interrupt is a software interrupt, where the program itself issues a request, for example, to display data on the screen. Once again, the system takes control, handles the interrupt, and returns to the interrupted program.

KEY POINTS

- The processor distinguishes only between bits that are 0 (off) and 1 (on) and performs arithmetic only in binary format.
- The value of a binary number is determined by the placement of its bits. For example, the binary value 1101 equals (from right to left) $2^0 + 0^1 + 2^2 + 2^3$, or 13.
- A negative binary number is represented in two's complement notation: Reverse the bits of its positive representation and add 1.
- A single location of memory is a byte, comprised of eight data bits and one parity bit. Two adjacent bytes comprise a word, and four adjacent bytes comprise a doubleword.
- Hexadecimal format is a shorthand notation for representing groups of four bits. Hex digits 0–9 and A–F represent the binary values 0000 through 1111.
- Character format uses ASCII code to represent data.
- The heart of the PC, the processor, stores numeric data in words and doublewords in memory in reverse-byte sequence.
- The two types of internal memory are ROM and RAM.
- An assembly language program consists of one or more segments: a stack segment for maintaining return addresses, a data segment for defined data and work areas, and a code segment for executable instructions. Locations within a segment are expressed as an offset relative to the segment's starting address.
- The CS, DS, and SS registers provide for addressing the code, data, and stack segments, respectively.
- The CS:IP registers contain the segment:offset address of the next instruction that is to execute.
- The SP and BP pointer registers are associated with the SS register and permit the system to access data in the stack.
- The AX, BX, CX, and DX general-purpose registers are the system's workhorses. The leftmost byte is the "high" portion, and the rightmost byte is the "low" portion. AX (primary accumulator) is used for input/output and most arithmetic. BX can also be used as an index to extend addressing. CX is used for calculations and special counts, and DX is also used for calculations. EAX, EBX, ECX, and EDX are 32-bit versions of the general-purpose registers.
- The SI and DI index registers are available for extended addressing and for use in addition and subtraction. These registers are also required for some string (character) operations.
- The Flags register indicates the current status of the processor and the results of executing instructions.

REVIEW QUESTIONS AND EXERCISES

1-1. (a) What is the basic building block of computer storage? (b) What are its two conditions?

1-2. (a) A collection of nine elements mentioned in Question 1-1 is known as what? (b) Eight of the elements are used for what purpose? (c) What is the purpose of the ninth element?

1-3. Provide the length of the following data items: (a) paragraph, (b) word, (c) double-word, (d) byte, (e) kilobyte.

1-4. Convert the following decimal numbers into binary format: (a) 7, (b) 15, (c) 25, (d) 28, (e) 33.

1-5. Add the following 8-bit binary numbers:

(a) 00101101 (b) 00110110 (c) 00101111 (d) 01111111
    00000101   00111001   00000001   01010101

1-6. For Question 1-5, convert each binary number and the sums to their decimal values and check that the sums are valid.

1-7. Provide the two's complement of the following binary numbers: (a) 00110110, (b) 00111101, (c) 01111100, (d) 00000000.

1-8. Convert the following negative binary numbers into positive binary values: (a) 11001100, (b) 10110111, (c) 10101010, (d) 11111111.

1-9. (a) Add the following two 8-bit binary numbers: 11001011 and 01110111. (b) What is the 8-bit sum as a decimal value? (c) Convert the binary values to decimal and show that the sum is correct.

1-10. Provide the hex representation of the following values: (a) ASCII letter R, (b) ASCII number 7, (c) binary 01110101, (d) binary 01110110.

1-11. Add the following hex numbers:

(a) 13B4 (b) 53CD (c) 8798 (d) DCBE (e) FDAC
   +0033   +0004   +0777   +35B5   +0BAF

1-12. Determine the hex representation for the following decimal numbers. Refer to Appendix A for the conversion method. You could also check your result by converting the hex value to binary and adding the 1-bits. (a) 23, (b) 37, (c) 75, (d) 255, (e) 4,095, (f) 56,217.

1-13. Using Appendix B as a guide, provide the bit configuration for the following ASCII characters: (a) G, (b) s, (c) #, (d) 6, (e) *, (f) colon (:).

1-14. What are the main functions of the processor?

1-15. Identify the two main kinds of memory on the PC and give their main purposes.

1-16. Show how the processor stores the following hex values in memory: (a) 2AB5, (b) 0AD4C2.

1-17. Explain each of the following terms: (a) segment, (b) offset, (c) address boundary.

1-18. What are (a) the three kinds of segments, (b) their maximum size, and (c) the address boundary on which they begin?

1-19. What is the purpose of each of the CS, DS, ES, and SS segment registers?

1-20. Show the absolute addresses formed by the following: (a) SS contains 2AB4[0]H and SP contains 24H, (b) CS contains 2BC3[0]H and IP contains 3AH.

1-21. Explain which registers are used for the following purposes: (a) counting for looping, (b) multiplication and division, (c) addressing segments, (d) indication of a zero result, (e) offset address of an instruction that is to execute, (f) addition and subtraction.

1-22. Show the EBX register and the size and position of BH, BL, and BX within it.

1-23. Code the assembly language instructions to move (MOV) the value 50 to each of the following registers: (a) CX, (b) CH, (c) CL, (d) ECX.

1-24. Code the instructions to add (ADD) the value 28 to each of the following registers: (a) CL, (b) CH, (c) CX, (d) ECX.

1-25. Identify the flags affected by each of the following actions: (a) an arithmetic sum is 0, (b) an arithmetic sum is negative, (c) string data is to move left to right.

Chapter 2

INSTRUCTION ADDRESSING AND EXECUTION

Objective: To explain the general requirements for loading and executing programs on the PC.

INTRODUCTION

In this chapter, we describe the PC software environment: the functions of the operating system and its main components. We examine the boot process (how the system loads itself when you power up the computer) and examine how the system loads a program for execution, how the system uses the stack, and how an instruction in the code segment addresses data in the data segment.

The chapter completes the basic explanations of the PC's hardware and software and enables you to proceed to Chapter 3, where you can begin keying simple programs into memory and executing them step by step.

FEATURES OF AN OPERATING SYSTEM

The operating system provides general, device-independent access to the resources of a computer for such devices as keyboards, screens, and disk drives. *Device independence* means that you don't have to address devices specifically because the system can handle input/output (I/O) operations at the device level, independent of the program that requested the operation.

Among the functions that concern us in this book are the following:

- *File management.* The operating system maintains the directories and files on the system's disks. Programs create and update files, but the system is responsible for managing their location on disk.
- *Input/output.* Programs request input data from the system or deliver such data to the system by means of interrupts. The programmer is relieved of coding at the low I/O level.
- *Program loading.* When a user or program requests execution of a program, the program loader handles the steps involved in accessing the program from disk, placing it in memory, and initializing it for execution.
- *Memory management.* When the program loader loads a program from disk into memory for execution, it allocates a large enough space in memory for the program code and its data. Programs can process data within their memory area, can release unwanted memory, and can request additional memory.
- *Interrupt handling.* The system provides means for programs to access external devices by means of interrupts.

THE BIOS BOOT PROCESS

Turning on the computer's power causes the processor to enter a reset state, clear all memory locations to zero, perform a parity check of memory, and set the CS register to segment address FFFF[0]H and the IP register to offset zero. The first instruction to execute, therefore, is at the address formed by the CS:IP pair, which is FFFF0H, the entry point to BIOS in ROM.

BIOS contains a set of routines in ROM to provide device support. The BIOS routine beginning at location FFFF0H checks the various ports to identify and initialize devices that are attached to the computer and provides services that are used for reading to and for writing from the devices. BIOS then establishes two data areas:

1. An *Interrupt Vector Table,* which begins in low memory at location 0 and contains 256 4-byte addresses in the form segment:offset. BIOS and the operating system use these addresss for interrupts that occur.
2. *BIOS Data Areas* beginning at location 40[0], largely concerned with the status of attached devices. This area is described in detail in Chapter 24.

BIOS next determines whether a disk containing the system files is present and, if so, it accesses the bootstrap loader from the disk. This program loads system files from the disk into memory and transfers control to them. The system files contain device drivers and other hardware-specific code. These modules initialize internal system tables and the system's portion of the Interrupt Vector Table.

One task of the operating system is to interface with BIOS when there is a need to access its facilities. When a user program requests an I/O service of the operating system, it transfers the request to BIOS, which in its turn accesses the requested device. Sometimes, however, a program makes requests directly to BIOS, such as for keyboard and screen services. At other times—although rarely and not recommended—a program can bypass both the operating system and BIOS to access a device directly. Figure 2-1 shows these alternative paths.

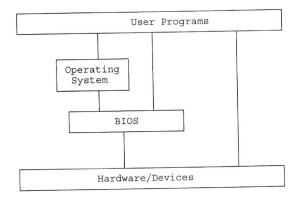

Figure 2-1   Input-Output Interface

THE SYSTEM PROGRAM LOADER

Once BIOS hands control over to the operating system, you may then request execution of a program. The two types of executable programs are .COM and .EXE. A *.COM program* consists of one segment that contains code, data, and the stack. A .COM program is useful as a small utility program or as a resident program (one that is installed in memory and is available while other programs run). In real mode, an *.EXE program* consists of separate code, data, and stack segments and is the method used for more serious programs. This book makes use of both types of programs.

When you request the system to load an .EXE program from disk into memory for execution, the loader performs the following steps:

1. Accesses the .EXE program from disk.
2. Constructs a 256-byte (100H) program segment prefix (PSP) on a paragraph boundary in available internal memory.
3. Stores the program in memory immediately following the PSP.
4. Loads the address of the PSP in the DS and ES registers.
5. Loads the address of the code segment in the CS register and sets the IP register to the offset of the first instruction (usually zero) in the code segment.
6. Loads the address of the stack in the SS register and sets the SP register to the size of the stack.
7. Transfers control to the program for execution, beginning (usually) with the first instruction in the code segment.

In the foregoing way, the program loader correctly initializes CS:IP and SS:SP. But note that the program loader stores the address of the PSP in both DS and ES, although your program normally needs the address of the data segment in these registers. As a consequence, your .EXE programs have to initialize DS with the address of the data segment, as you'll see in Chapter 4.

We'll now examine the stack and the code and data segments.

THE STACK

Both .COM and .EXE programs require an area in the program reserved as a *stack*. The stack has three main uses:

1. The program calls a subroutine for special processing; in so doing, it saves the return address in the stack, which the subroutine later uses for returning.
2. The program that calls the subroutine may also pass data by placing it in the stack, where the subroutine accesses it.
3. The program has to perform calculations that use the registers; it can save the present contents of the registers on the stack, make the calculations, and then restore the data from the stack to the registers.

The program loader automatically defines the stack for a .COM program, whereas you must explicitly define a stack for an .EXE program. In real mode, each data item in the stack is one word (two bytes). The SS register, as initialized by the loader, contains the address of the beginning of the stack. Initially, the SP register contains the size of the stack, a value that points to the byte past the end of the stack. The stack differs from other segments in its method of storing data: It begins storing data at the highest location in the segment and stores data downward (or backward) through memory.

PUSH and POP are two of a number of instructions that modify the contents of the SP register and are used for storing data on the stack and retrieving it. PUSH executes by decrementing SP by 2 to the next lower storage word in the stack and storing (or pushing) a value there. POP executes by returning a value from the stack and incrementing SP by 2 to the next higher storage word.

The portion of the stack that contains all the data pushed onto it for a particular procedure is known as the *stack frame*. The following example illustrates pushing the contents of the AX and BX registers onto the stack and then subsequently popping the data from the stack back to the registers. Assume that AX contains hex 026B, BX contains 04E3, and SP contains 36. (The segment address of the stack in SS does not concern us here.)

1. Initially, the stack is empty and looks like this:

```
      Offset       Stack Frame        SP = 36

        34       ┌──────────────┐
                 │     0000     │
        32       ├──────────────┤
                 │     0000     │
        30       ├──────────────┤
                 │     0000     │
        2E       ├──────────────┤
                 │     0000     │
                 └──────────────┘
```

2. PUSH AX: Decrements SP by 2 (to 34) and stores the contents of AX, 026B, in the stack. Note that the operation reverses the sequence of the stored bytes, so that 026B becomes 6B02:

```
Offset          Stack Frame

  34          ┌──────────┐
              │   6B02   │<-- SP = 34
  32          │   0000   │
  30          │   0000   │
  2E          │   0000   │
              └──────────┘
```

3. PUSH BX: Decrements SP by 2 (to 32) and stores the contents of BX, 04E3, in the stack as E304:

```
Offset          Stack Frame

  34          ┌──────────┐
              │   6B02   │
  32          │   E304   │<-- SP = 32
  30          │   0000   │
  2E          │   0000   │
              └──────────┘
```

4. POP BX: Restores the word from where SP points in the stack (E304) to BX and increments SP by 2 (to 34). BX now contains 04E3, with the bytes correctly restored:

```
Offset          Stack Frame

  34          ┌──────────┐
              │   6B02   │<-- SP = 34
  32          │   E304   │
  30          │   0000   │
  2E          │   0000   │
              └──────────┘
```

5. POP AX: Restores the word from where SP points in the stack (6B02) to AX and increments SP by 2 (to 36). AX now contains 026B, with the bytes correctly restored:

```
Offset          Stack Frame        SP = 36

  34          ┌──────────┐
              │   6B02   │
  32          │   E304   │
  30          │   0000   │
  2E          │   0000   │
              └──────────┘
```

Note that POP instructions are coded in *reverse sequence* from PUSH instructions; the example pushed AX and BX, but popped BX and AX, in that order. Also, the values pushed onto the stack are still there, although SP no longer points to them. Subsequent PUSH operations will replace the old values with new ones.

Ensure that your program coordinates pushing values onto the stack with popping them off of it. Although this is a fairly straightforward requirement, incorrect use can result in a serious program error. Also, for an .EXE program the stack must be large enough to contain all values that could be pushed onto it. Note that when SP = 0, the stack is full.

Other related instructions that push values onto the stack and pop them off are:

- PUSHF and POPF: Save and restore the status of the flags.
- PUSHA and POPA (80286+): Save and restore the contents of all the general-purpose registers (AX, CX, DX, BX, SP, BP, SI, and DI) and increment/decrement SP by 16.
- PUSHAD and POPAD (80386+): Save and restore the contents of all the extended registers (EAX, ECX, EDX, EBX, ESP, EBP, ESI, and EDI) and increment/decrement ESP by 32.

INSTRUCTION EXECUTION AND ADDRESSING

An assembly language programmer writes a program in symbolic code and uses the assembler to translate it into machine code as a .COM or .EXE program. For program execution, the system loads only the machine code into memory. Every instruction consists of at least one operation, such as move, add, or return. Depending on the operation, an instruction may also have one or more operands that reference the data the operation is to process.

The basic steps the processor takes in executing an instruction are:

1. Fetch the next instruction to be executed from memory and place it in the instruction queue.
2. Decode the instruction: calculate addresses that reference memory, deliver data to the arithmetic logic unit, and increment the Instruction Pointer (IP) register.
3. Execute the instruction: perform the requested operation, store the results in a register or memory, and set flags such as Zero or Carry where required.

The Pentium's pipelining capability enables it to overlap operations, as shown by the following simplified example of three instructions:

```
1.  | Fetch | Decode | Execute |
2.          | Fetch | Decode | Execute |
3.                  | Fetch | Decode | Execute |
```

As already discussed, for an .EXE program the CS register provides the address of the beginning of a program's code segment, and DS provides the address of the beginning of the data segment. The code segment contains instructions that are to be executed, whereas the data segment contains data that the instructions reference. The IP register indicates the offset address of the current instruction in the code segment that is to be executed. An instruction operand indicates an offset address in the data segment to be referenced.

Consider an example in which the program loader has determined that it is to load an .EXE program into memory beginning at location 05BE0H. The loader accordingly initializes CS with segment address 05BE[0]H and IP with zero. CS:IP together determine the address of the first instruction to execute: 5BE0H + 0000H = 5BE0H. In this way, the first instruction in the code segment begins execution. If the first instruction is two bytes long, the processor increments IP by 2, so that the next instruction to execute is at 5BE0H + 2 = 5BE2H.

Assume that the program continues executing, and IP currently contains the offset 0023H. CS:IP now determine the address of the next instruction to execute, as follows:

```
CS segment address:       5BE0H
IP offset:              + 0023H
Instruction address:      5C03H
```

Let's say that a MOV instruction beginning at 05C03H copies the contents of a byte in memory into the AL register; the byte is at offset 0016H in the data segment. Here are both the machine code and the symbolic code for this operation:

```
         A01600       MOV AL,[0016]

           |
    Address 05C03H
```

Address 05C03H contains the first byte (A0) of the machine code instruction the processor is to access. The second and third bytes contain the offset value in reversed-byte sequence (0016 is stored as 1600). In symbolic code, the operand [0016] in square brackets (an index operator) indicates an offset value to distinguish it from the actual storage address 16.

Let's say that the program has initialized the DS register with data segment address 05D1[0]H. To access the data item, the processor determines its location from the segment address in DS plus the offset (0016H) in the instruction operand. Because DS contains 05D1[0]H, the actual location of the referenced data item is

```
DS segment address:       5D10H
Segment offset:         + 0016H
Address of data item:     5D26H
```

Assume that address 05D26H contains 4AH. The processor now extracts the 4AH at address 05D26H and copies it into the AL register. See Figure 2-2, which shows CS pointing to the start of the code segment, DS pointing to the start of the data segment, the offsets in the code and data segments, and the value 4A being copied to AL.

As the processor fetches each byte of the instruction, it increments the IP register by 1. Because IP originally contained 23H and the executed machine code was three bytes, IP now contains 0026H, which is the offset for the next instruction. The processor is now ready to execute this instruction, which it locates once again from the segment address in CS (05BE0H) plus the current offset in IP (0026H), in effect, 05C06H.

An instruction may also access more than one byte at a time. For example, suppose an instruction is to store the contents of the AX register (0248H) in two adjacent bytes in

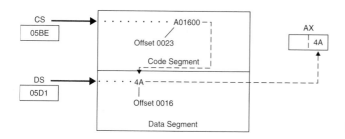

Figure 2-2   Segments and Offsets

the data segment beginning at offset 0016H. The symbolic code is MOV [0016],AX. The processor stores the two bytes in memory in reversed-byte sequence as

```
            Contents of bytes:       48 02
                                      |  |
        Offset in data segment:    0016 0017
```

Another instruction, MOV AX,[0016], subsequently could retrieve these bytes by copying them from memory back into AX. The operation reverses (and corrects) the bytes in AX as 02 48.

INSTRUCTION OPERANDS

An instruction may have no, one, two, or three operands. One feature about operands to get clear is the use of normal names, of names in square brackets, and of numbers. In the following example, a DW defines WORDX as a word (2 bytes):

```
WORDX DW   0              ;Define WORDX as word
      . . .
      MOV CX,WORDX     ;Move contents of WORDX to CX
      MOV CX,25        ;Move value 25 to CX
      MOV CX,BX        ;Move contents of BX to CX
      MOV CX,[BX]      ;Move contents of location addressed by BX
```

- The first MOV transfers data between memory (WORDX) and a register (CX).
- The second MOV transfers immediate data (25) to a register (CX).
- The third MOV transfers data between registers (BX to CX).
- The square brackets in the fourth MOV define an *index operator* that means: Use the offset address in BX (combined with the segment address in DS, as DS:BX) to locate a word in memory and move its contents to CX. Compare the effect of this instruction with that of the third MOV, which simply moves the contents of BX to CX. Chapter 6 covers this indirect addressing in detail.

PROTECTED MODE

Under Window's protected mode, the processor can switch from one task to another. Each program occupies its own area of memory, and the processor must protect each area and preserve the status of each program. In real mode, the segment registers contain the actual segment addresses but are limited to addressing to one megabyte. Protected mode, however, requires much greater addressing capability. To this end, it uses various tables, which include the following:

- Local Descriptor tables. Depending on the system, there is one table for each task. The 16-bit LDT register contains the address of this table for the current task that is executing.
- Interrupt Descriptor table. This table handles interrupt operations; the IDT register contains its address.
- Global Descriptor table. This table contains the address of each Local Descriptor table; the 32-bit GDT register contains the address of this table.

The actual addresses of segments are stored in the Descriptor tables; the segment registers (or selectors) contain pointers to the current Local Descriptor table. The tables provide 32 bits for addressing up to 4.3 gigabytes of memory.

Nominally, the Interrupt Vector Table is (or appears to be) at location 0000:0000, but each task may have its own copy of the table.

KEY POINTS

- Turning on the computer's power causes the processor to enter a reset state, clear all memory locations to zero, perform a parity check of memory, and set the CS and IP registers to the entry point of BIOS in ROM.
- The two types of executable programs are .COM and .EXE.
- For loading an .EXE program for execution, the program loader constructs a 256-byte (100H) PSP on a paragraph boundary in memory and stores the program immediately following the PSP. It then loads the address of the PSP in the DS and ES registers, loads the address of the code segment in CS, sets IP to the offset of the first instruction in the code segment, loads the address of the stack in SS, and sets SP to the size of the stack. Finally, the loader transfers control to the program for execution.
- The purpose of the stack is to provide space for temporary storage of addresses and data items.
- The program loader defines the stack for a .COM program, whereas you must explicitly define a stack for an .EXE program.
- As the processor fetches each byte of an instruction, it increments the IP register so that the CS:IP pair contain the segment:offset address of the next instruction to be executed.

REVIEW QUESTIONS AND EXERCISES

2-1. Identify the five main functions of an operating system.
2-2. Give the steps that the system takes when it is booted up.
2-3. The program loader constructs and stores a data area in front of an executable module when it loads the module for execution. (a) What is the name of this data area? (b) What is its size?

2-4. The program loader performs certain operations when it loads an .EXE program for execution. What values does the loader initialize (a) in SS and SP? (b) in CS and IP? (c) in DS and ES?

2-5. Explain the purpose of the stack.

2-6. Explain how the stack is defined for (a) a .COM program and (b) an .EXE program. (That is, who or what defines the stack?)

2-7. (a) Where initially is the top of the stack, and how is it addressed? (b) What is the size of each entry in the stack?

2-8. Given a stack defined as DW 32H, what are the contents of SP when (a) the stack is empty and (b) the stack is full?

2-9. A stack is defined as 64H bytes in size. (a) What is the initial value in the SP register? (b) CX contains 25A4H. After PUSH CX, show the contents of the stack and SP. (c) DX contains 3B2AH. After PUSH DX, show the contents of the stack and SP. (d) Show the contents of SP after POP DX and POP CX.

2-10. During execution of a program, CS contains 4AB6[0], SS contains 4A82[0], IP contains 36H, and SP contains 28H. (Values are shown in normal, not reversed-byte, sequence.) Calculate the addresses of (a) the top (current location) of the stack and (b) the instruction to execute.

2-11. During execution of a program, CS contains 5C9B[0], SS contains 5C84[0], IP contains 48H, and SP contains 1AH. (Values are shown in normal, not reversed-byte, sequence.) Calculate the addresses of (a) the top (current location) of the stack and (b) the instruction to execute.

2-12. Calculate the memory address of the referenced data for the following. (a) DS contains 7E9B[0] and an instruction that moves data from memory to AX is MOV AX,[24H]. (b) DS contains 43C6[0] and an instruction that moves data from memory to BX is MOV BX,[48H].

Chapter 3

EXAMINING COMPUTER MEMORY AND EXECUTING INSTRUCTIONS

> Objective: To introduce the entering of programs into memory and to trace their execution.

INRODUCTION

This chapter uses a DOS program named DEBUG that allows you to view memory, to enter programs in memory, and to trace their execution. The text describes how you can enter these programs directly into a code segment and provides an explanation of each execution step. Although there are more sophisticated debuggers, such as CODEVIEW and TurboDebugger, we'll use DEBUG because it is simple to use and is universally available.

The initial exercises show how to inspect the contents of particular areas of memory. The first program example uses "immediate" data defined within instructions for loading data into registers and performing arithmetic. The second program example uses data defined separately from the executable instructions. Tracing these instructions as they execute provides insight into the operation of a processor and the role of the registers.

You can start right away with no prior knowledge of assembly language or even of programming. All you need is an Intel-based PC and a copy of the DOS operating system either under Windows or as a standalone product. We do assume, however, that you are familiar with keying in system commands and selecting disk drives and files.

USING THE DEBUG PROGRAM

The DEBUG program is used for testing and debugging executable programs. A feature of DEBUG is that it displays all program code and data in hexadecimal format, and any data that you enter into memory must also be in hex format. DEBUG also provides a single-step mode, which allows you to execute a program one instruction at a time, so that you can view the effect of each instruction on memory locations and registers.

DEBUG Commands

DEBUG's set of commands lets you perform a number of useful operations. The commands of interest at this point are the following:

A   Assemble symbolic instructions into machine code
D   Display the contents of an area of memory in hex format
E   Enter data into memory, beginning at a specific location
G   Run the executable program in memory (G means "go")
H   Perform hexadecimal arithmetic
N   Name a program
P   Proceed, or execute a set of related instructions
Q   Quit the DEBUG session
R   Display the contents of one or more registers in hex format
T   Trace the execution of one instruction
U   Unassemble (or disassemble) machine code into symbolic code

Rules of DEBUG Commands.   Here are some basic rules for using DEBUG:

- DEBUG does not distinguish between lowercase and uppercase letters, so you may enter commands either way.
- DEBUG assumes that all numbers are in hexadecimal format.
- Spaces in commands are used only to separate parameters.
- Segments and offsets are specified with a colon, in the form segment:offset.

Appendix C provides a full description of all the DEBUG commands, including directions on starting it. Let's use it now to prowl about in memory.

The DEBUG Display Command.   The D command displays the contents of a requested data area on the screen. The following three examples use DEBUG's D command to display the same area of memory, beginning at offset 200H in the data segment (DS):

```
D DS:200  (Command in uppercase, space following)
DDS:200   (Command in uppercase, no space following)
dds:200   (Command in lowercase, no space following)
```

The displayed screen consists of three parts:

1. To the left is the hex address of the leftmost displayed byte, in segment:offset format.
2. The wide area in the center is the hex representation of the displayed area.
3. To the right is the ASCII representation of bytes that contain displayable characters, which can help you interpret the hex area.

The D (Display) command displays eight lines of data, each containing 16 bytes (32 hex digits), for 128 bytes in all, beginning with the address that you specify:

```
Address |<---------Hexadecimal representation--------->|<--ASCII-->|

xxxx:xx10 xx ................. xx-xx ............... xx x.........x
xxxx:xx20 xx ................. xx-xx ............... xx x.........x
xxxx:xx30 xx ................. xx-xx ............... xx x.........x
...
xxxx:xx80 xx ................. xx-xx ............... xx x.........x
```

The address to the left refers only to the leftmost (beginning) byte, in segment:offset format; you can count across the line to determine the position of each other byte. The hex representation area shows two hex characters for each byte, followed by a space for readability. Also, a hyphen separates the second eight bytes from the first eight, again for readability. Thus if you want to locate the byte at offset xx13H, start with xx10H, and count three bytes successively to the right.

The D command also lists the contents of the registers and the status of the Flags register.

VIEWING MEMORY LOCATIONS

The first two exercises involve the use of the DEBUG D (Display) command to view the contents of selected memory locations.

Exercise I: Examining the BIOS Data Area

The first exercise examines the contents of the BIOS Data Area in low memory beginning at location 400H, or more precisely, segment address 40[0]. BIOS initializes values in this area when the computer power is turned on and updates them during program execution.

You can view the values by means of a two-part address: 40 for the segment address (technically 400 because the last zero is shifted off) and nn for the offset from the segment address. Interpret the address 40:nn as segment 40[0]H plus offset nnH. In Chapter 24, the section "The BIOS Data Area" explains these data items in detail.

Checking the Serial and Parallel Ports.   The first 16 bytes of the BIOS Data Area contain the addresses of the serial and parallel ports. Key in the following exactly as you see it:

                    D 40:00 (and press <Enter>)

The first four words displayed show serial ports COM1 through COM4. If you have two serial ports, the first two words likely contain F803 and F802 in reversed byte sequence. The ports are at 03F8 and 02F8. The second four words show parallel ports LPT1 through LPT4. For a system with one parallel port, the first word likely contains 7803 for port 0378.

Checking System Equipment.   An equipment status word in the BIOS Data Area provides a primitive indication of installed devices. You can locate this word at locations 410H-411H with the DEBUG command

```
D 40:10 (and press <Enter>)
```

The display should begin like this:

```
0040:0010 xx xx ...
```

Let's say that the two bytes in the equipment status word contain the hex values 23 and 44. To interpret them, reverse the bytes (to 44 23) and convert them to binary format:

```
Binary value:  0  1  0  0  0  1 0 0 0 0 1 0 0 0 1 1
Bit position: 15 14 13 12 11 10 9 8 7 6 5 4 3 2 1 0
```

Here's an explanation of the bits, from left to right:

BITS	DEVICE
15,14	Number of parallel printer ports attached = 1 (binary 01)
11–9	Number of serial ports attached = 2 (binary 010)
7,6	Number of diskette devices = 1 (00 = 1, 01 = 2, 10 = 3, and 11 = 4)
5,4	Initial video mode = 10 (01 = 40 X 25 color, 10 = 80 X 25 color, and 11 = 80 X 25 monochrome)
1	1 = numeric coprocessor is present
0	1 = diskette drive is present

Unreferenced bits are not used.

Checking the Keyboard Shift Status.   The BIOS Data Area at location 417H contains the first byte of the keyboard shift status. First make sure that the NumLock and CapsLock keys are off and then view this location by means of the DEBUG command D 40:17. The display should begin like this:

```
0040:0017 00 00 ...
```

Now turn on the two Lock keys and repeat the display command; the values at 40:17 should now be 60 00.

Checking the Video Status.   The BIOS Data Area at location 449H is the first Video Data Area. Key in the command D 40:49. The first byte contains the current video mode (such as 03 for color) and the second byte is the number of columns on the screen (where 50H = 80). You'll also find the number of rows at location 40:84H.

Exercise II: Examining ROM BIOS

The following exercise examines data in ROM BIOS in high memory.

Checking Copyright Notice and Serial Number. The computer's copyright notice is embedded in ROM BIOS at location FE000H. To view this segment, key in D FE00:0. Depending on the computer make, the operation displays a copyright notice followed, on conventional machines, by a 7-digit serial number. The copyright notice is more viewable from the characters in the ASCII area to the right, whereas the serial number is recognizable as hex numbers. The copyright notice may continue past what is already displayed; to view it, simply press D again followed by <Enter>.

Checking ROM BIOS Date. The date of manufacture of your ROM BIOS, recorded as mm/dd/yy, begins at location FFFF5H. To request this segment, key in D FFFF:5. Knowing this date could be useful in determining a computer's age and model.

Now that you know how to use the display command, you can view the contents of any storage location. You can also step through memory simply by pressing D repeatedly—DEBUG displays eight lines (128 bytes) successively, continuing from the last D operation.

When you've completed probing about, key in Q (for quit) to exit from DEBUG, or continue with the next exercise.

MACHINE LANGUAGE EXAMPLE I: USING IMMEDIATE DATA

Let's now use DEBUG to enter the first of two programs directly into memory and trace its execution. Both programs illustrate simple machine language instructions as they appear in main storage and the effect of their execution. For this purpose, we'll begin with the DEBUG E (Enter) command. Be especially careful in its use, since entering data at a wrong location or entering incorrect data may cause unpredictable results. You are not likely to cause any damage, but you may get a bit of a surprise and may lose data that you entered during the DEBUG session.

The first program uses *immediate data*—data defined as part of an instruction. The following shows both the machine language in hexadecimal format and, for readability, the symbolic code, along with an explanation. For the first instruction, B82301, the symbolic code is MOV AX,0123, which moves (or copies) the value 0123H to AX. (You define an immediate value in normal, not reverse-byte, sequence.) MOV is the instruction, AX is the first operand, and the immediate value 0123H is the second operand.

MACHINE INSTRUCTION	SYMBOLIC CODE	EXPLANATION
B82301	MOV AX,0123	Move value 0123H to AX.
052500	ADD AX,0025	Add value 0025H to AX.
8BD8	MOV BX,AX	Move contents of AX to BX.
03D8	ADD BX,AX	Add contents of AX to BX.
8BCB	MOV CX,BX	Move contents of BX to CX.
2BC8	SUB CX,AX	Subtract contents of AX from CX.
2BC0	SUB AX,AX	Subtract AX from AX (clear AX).
EBEE	JMP 100	Go back to the start.

Note that machine instructions may be one, two, or three bytes in length. The first byte is the actual operation, and any other bytes that are present are *operands*—references to an immediate value, a register, or a memory location. Program execution begins with the first machine instruction and steps through each instruction, one after another, sequentially. At this point do not expect to make much sense of the machine code; for example, in one case the machine code (the first byte) for MOV is hex B8, and in another case the code for MOV is hex 8B.

Keying in Program Instructions

Begin this exercise just as you did the preceding one: Key in the command DEBUG and press <Enter>. When DEBUG is fully loaded, it displays its prompt (-). To key this program directly into memory, just type in the machine instruction portion, but *not* the symbolic code or explanation. Key in the following E command, including the blanks, where indicated:

```
E CS:100 B8 23 01 05 25 00 (and press <Enter>)
```

CS:100 indicates the starting memory address at which the data is to be stored—100H (256) bytes following the start of the code segment (the normal starting address for machine code under DEBUG). The E command causes DEBUG to store each pair of hexadecimal digits into a byte in memory, from CS:100 through CS:105.

The next E command stores 6 bytes, from CS:106 through 10B:

```
E CS:106 8B D8 03 D8 8B CB (followed by <Enter>)
```

The last E command stores 6 bytes, from CS:10C through 111:

```
E CS:10C 2B C8 2B C0 EB EE (followed by <Enter>)
```

If you key in an incorrect command, simply repeat it with the correct values.

Executing Program Instructions

Now it's a simple matter to execute the preceding instructions one at a time. Figure 3-1 shows all the steps, including the E commands used to key in the machine code. Your screen should display similar results as you enter each DEBUG command. You can also view the contents of the registers after executing each instruction. The new commands that concern us here are R (Register) and T (Trace).

To view the initial contents of the registers and flags, key in the R command, followed by <Enter>, as shown in line 4 of Figure 3-1. DEBUG displays the contents of the registers in hexadecimal format as

```
AX=0000 BX=0000 ...
```

Because of differences in computer configurations, some register contents on your screen will differ from those shown in Figure 3-1. DEBUG has initialized DS, ES, SS, and CS all with the same segment address, xxxx[0]. IP should display IP=0100, indicating that instruction execution is to begin 100H bytes past the start of the code segment. (That is why you used E CS:100 for the start of the program.)

The Flags register in Figure 3-1 indicates the following initial settings for the Overflow, Direction, Interrupt, Sign, Zero, Auxiliary Carry, Parity, and Carry flags:

```
NV UP EI PL NZ NA PO NC
```

These settings mean no overflow, up (or right) direction, enable interrupt, plus sign, nonzero, no auxiliary carry, parity odd, and no carry, respectively. At this time, none of these settings is important to us.

Immediately following the registers and also displayed by the R command is the first instruction to be executed. Note that in the figure the CS register contains 21C1. Because your CS segment address is sure to differ from this one, it is shown as xxxx for the instructions:

```
xxxx:0100 B82301 MOV AX,0123
```

```
-E CS:100 B8 23 01 05 25 00
-E CS:106 8B D8 03 D8 8B CB
-E CS:10C 2B C8 2B C0 EB EE
-R
AX=0000  BX=0000  CX=0000  DX=0000  SP=FFEE  BP=0000  SI=0000  DI=0000
DS=21C1  ES=21C1  SS=21C1  CS=21C1  IP=0100   NV UP EI PL NZ NA PO NC
21C1:0100 B82301        MOV     AX,0123
-T

AX=0123  BX=0000  CX=0000  DX=0000  SP=FFEE  BP=0000  SI=0000  DI=0000
DS=21C1  ES=21C1  SS=21C1  CS=21C1  IP=0103   NV UP EI PL NZ NA PO NC
21C1:0103 052500        ADD     AX,0025
-T

AX=0148  BX=0000  CX=0000  DX=0000  SP=FFEE  BP=0000  SI=0000  DI=0000
DS=21C1  ES=21C1  SS=21C1  CS=21C1  IP=0106   NV UP EI PL NZ NA PE NC
21C1:0106 8BD8          MOV     BX,AX
-T

AX=0148  BX=0148  CX=0000  DX=0000  SP=FFEE  BP=0000  SI=0000  DI=0000
DS=21C1  ES=21C1  SS=21C1  CS=21C1  IP=0108   NV UP EI PL NZ NA PE NC
21C1:0108 03D8          ADD     BX,AX
-T

AX=0148  BX=0290  CX=0000  DX=0000  SP=FFEE  BP=0000  SI=0000  DI=0000
DS=21C1  ES=21C1  SS=21C1  CS=21C1  IP=010A   NV UP EI PL NZ AC PE NC
21C1:010A 8BCB          MOV     CX,BX
-T

AX=0148  BX=0290  CX=0290  DX=0000  SP=FFEE  BP=0000  SI=0000  DI=0000
DS=21C1  ES=21C1  SS=21C1  CS=21C1  IP=010C   NV UP EI PL NZ AC PE NC
21C1:010C 2BC8          SUB     CX,AX
-T

AX=0148  BX=0290  CX=0148  DX=0000  SP=FFEE  BP=0000  SI=0000  DI=0000
DS=21C1  ES=21C1  SS=21C1  CS=21C1  IP=010E   NV UP EI PL NZ AC PE NC
21C1:010E 2BC0          SUB     AX,AX
-T

AX=0000  BX=0290  CX=0148  DX=0000  SP=FFEE  BP=0000  SI=0000  DI=0000
DS=21C1  ES=21C1  SS=21C1  CS=21C1  IP=0110   NV UP EI PL ZR NA PE NC
21C1:0110 EB EE         JMP     0100
-
```

Figure 3-1   Tracing Machine Instructions

- xxxx indicates the start of the code segment as xxxx[0]. The value xxxx:0100 means offset 100H bytes following the CS segment address xxxx[0].
- B82301 is the machine code that you entered at CS:100.
- MOV AX,0123 is the symbolic assembly instruction that DEBUG determined from the machine code. This instruction means, in effect, move the immediate value 0123H into AX. DEBUG has "unassembled" the machine instructions so that you may interpret them more easily. After this chapter, you will code symbolic assembly instructions exclusively.

Here's a warning to keep in mind: Before attempting to execute an instruction, make sure that it is *valid.* Even if you type in an incorrect machine code, DEBUG will attempt to execute it, and if the code is invalid, the processor locks up, and it's goodbye DEBUG, hello reboot.

To execute the MOV instruction, key in T (Trace) and press <Enter>. The machine code is B8 (move to AX) followed by 2301. The operation moves the 23 to the low half (AL) of AX and the 01 to the high half (AH) of AX:

```
              AH    AL
      AX:  |  01  |  23  |
```

DEBUG displays the effect of the operation on the registers. The IP register now contains 0103H (the original 0100H plus 3 bytes for the length of the first machine code instruction). The value 0103H indicates the offset location in the code segment of the next instruction to be executed, namely:

```
      xxxx:0103 052500 ADD AX,0025
```

To execute this ADD instruction, enter another T. The instruction adds 25H to the low half (AL) of AX and 00H to the high half (AH), in effect adding 0025H to AX. AX now contains 0148H, and IP contains 0106H for the next instruction to be executed:

```
      xxxx:0106 8BD8 MOV BX,AX
```

Key in another T command. The MOV instruction moves the contents of AX to BX. Note that after the move, BX contains 0148H. AX still contains 0148H because MOV *copies* rather than actually moves the data from one location to another.

Now key in successive T commands to step through the remaining instructions. The ADD instruction adds the contents of AX to BX, giving 0290H in BX. Then the program moves (copies) the contents of BX into CX, subtracts AX from CX, and subtracts AX from itself. The latter operation clears AX to zero and changes the Zero Flag from NZ (nonzero) to ZR (zero), to indicate the result of the operation.

The JMP instruction resets IP to 100 so that processing "jumps" back to the start of the program. It acts here as a precaution because following the last entered instruction is "garbage," which, if you attempted to execute, would cause the processor to lock up. Note that the program as written is an endless loop; that is, it has no way to terminate, although DEBUG lets you work around it. This sort of processing is normally used in special circumstances, such as monitoring systems.

Also, Figure 3-1 shows that DS, ES, SS, and CS all contain the same segment address. This is because DEBUG happens to treat the entire segment as a .COM program, with data, stack, and code all in the same segment, although you keep them separated within the segment. When you write .EXE programs, you keep all three areas in separate segments, each under its own segment address.

To rerun this program, simply press T to execute the JMP, which resets IP to 100H, the start of the program.

Displaying Memory Contents

To view the machine language program in the code segment, request a display as follows:

```
D CS:100
```

Figure 3-2 shows the results of this command, with 16 bytes (32 hex digits) of data displayed on each line. To the right is the ASCII representation (if a standard character) of each byte. In the case of machine code, the ASCII representation is meaningless and may be ignored. Later sections discuss the right side of the display in more detail.

The first line of the display begins at offset 100H of the code segment and represents the contents of locations CS:100 through CS:10F. The second line represents the contents of CS:110 through CS:11F. Although the program actually ends at CS:111, the D command automatically displays eight lines from CS:100 through CS:170. In this example, any data following CS:111 is "garbage." Expect only the machine code from CS:100 through 111 to be identical to that of your own display; the bytes that follow could contain anything.

Enter Q to end the DEBUG session, or continue with the next exercise.

MACHINE LANGUAGE EXAMPLE II: USING DEFINED DATA

The preceding example used immediate values defined directly within MOV and ADD instructions. The next example, however, defines the values (or constants) 0123H and 0025H as separate data items within the program. The program instructions are to access the memory locations that contain these values.

Working through this example should give you an insight into how a computer accesses data by means of an address in the DS register and offset addresses. The example de-

```
-D CS:100
21C1:0100  B8 23 01 05 25 00 8B D8-03 D8 8B CB 2B C8 2B C0  .#..%.......+.+.
21C1:0110  EB EE 8D 46 14 50 51 52-FF 76 28 E8 74 00 8B E5  ...F.PQR.v(.t...
21C1:0120  B8 01 00 50 FF 76 32 FF-76 30 FF 76 2E FF 76 28  ...P.v2.v0.v..v(
21C1:0130  E8 88 15 8B E5 FF 36 18-12 FF 36 16 12 8B 76 28  ......6...6...v(
21C1:0140  FF 74 3A 89 46 06 E8 22-CE 8B E5 30 E4 3D 0A 00  .t:.F.."...0.=..
21C1:0150  75 32 A1 16 12 2D 01 00-8B 1E 18 12 83 DB 00 53  u2...-.........S
21C1:0160  50 8B 76 28 FF 74 3A A3-16 12 89 1E 18 12 E8 FA  P.v(.t:.........
21C1:0170  CD 8B E5 30 E4 3D 0D 00-74 0A 83 06 16 12 01 83  ...0.=..t.......
-
```

Figure 3-2   Dump of the Code Segment

fines the following data items, beginning at offset 0200H, which is clearly separate from the instructions at 0100H:

DS OFFSET	HEX CONTENTS
0200H	2301H
0202H	2500H
0204H	0000H
0206H	2A2A2AH

Remember that a hex digit occupies a half-byte, so that, for example, 23H is stored in off-set 0200H (the first byte) of the data area, and 01H is stored in offset 0201H (the second byte). Here are the machine instructions that process these data items, with the values entered in reverse-byte sequence, for example, 0200 as 0002:

INSTRUCTION	EXPLANATION
A10002	Move the word (two bytes) beginning at DS offset 0200H into AX.
03060202	Add the contents of the word (two bytes) beginning at DS offset 0202H into AX.
A30402	Move the contents of AX to the word beginning at DS offset 0204H.
EBF4	Jump to start of program.

You may have noticed that the two move instructions have different machine codes: A1 and A3. The actual machine code is dependent on the registers that are referenced, the size of data (byte or word), the direction of data transfer (from or to a register), and the reference to immediate data, memory, or register.

Keying in Program Instructions and Data

Again, you can use DEBUG to key in the program and to trace its execution. First, use the E command to key in the instructions, beginning at CS:0100:

```
E CS:100 A1 00 02 03 06 02 02 (press <Enter>)
E CS:107 A3 04 02 EB F4 (press <Enter>)
```

Now use E commands for defining data, beginning arbitrarily at DS:0200:

```
E DS:0200 23 01 25 00 00 00 (press <Enter>)
E DS:0206 2A 2A 2A (press <Enter>)
```

The first E command stores the three words (six bytes) at the start of the data area at offset 0200. You have to key in each of these words with the bytes reversed, so that 0123 is 2301 and 0025 is 2500. When a MOV instruction subsequently accesses these words and loads them into a register, it "unreverses" the bytes so that 2301 becomes 0123 and 2500 becomes 0025.

The second E command stores three asterisks (***), defined as 2A2A2A, so that you can view them later using the D (Display) command. Otherwise, these asterisks serve no particular purpose in the data area.

Figure 3-3 shows all the steps in the program, including the E commands. Your screen should display similar results, although addresses in CS and DS probably differ. To examine the stored data (at DS:200H through 208H) and the instructions (at CS:100H through 10AH), key in the following D commands:

To view the code: D CS:100,10B <Enter>
To view the data: D DS:200,208 <Enter>

Check that the contents of both displayed areas are identical to what is shown Figure 3-3.

Executing the Program Instructions

Having keyed in the instructions, you can now execute them just as you did earlier. First make sure that IP contains 100H. Then press R to view the contents of the registers and flags and to display the first instruction. Although AX may still contain a value from the previous exercise, you'll replace it shortly. The first displayed instruction is

```
xxxx:0100 A10002 MOV AX,[0200]
```

CS:0100 references your first instruction, A10002. DEBUG interprets this instruction as a MOV and has determined that the reference is to the first location [0200H] in the data area. The square brackets tell you that this reference is to a memory address and is not an im-

```
-E CS:100 A1 00 02 03 06 02 02
-E CS:107 A3 04 02 EB F4
-E DS:200 23 01 25 00 00 00
-E DS:206 2A 2A 2A
-D CS:100,10A
21C1:0100  A1 00 02 03 06 02 02 A3-04 02 EB F4             ..........
-D DS:200,208
21C1:0200  23 01 25 00 00 00 2A 2A-2A                      # %...***
-R
AX=0000  BX=0000  CX=0000  DX=0000  SP=FFEE  BP=0000  SI=0000  DI=0000
DS=21C1  ES=21C1  SS=21C1  CS=21C1  IP=0100  NV UP EI PL NZ NA PO NC
21C1:0100 A10002      MOV   AX,[0200]                      DS:0200=0123
-T

AX=0123  BX=0000  CX=0000  DX=0000  SP=FFEE  BP=0000  SI=0000  DI=0000
DS=21C1  ES=21C1  SS=21C1  CS=21C1  IP=0103  NV UP EI PL NZ NA PO NC
21C1:0103 03060202    ADD   AX,[0202]                      DS:0202=0025
-T

AX=0148  BX=0000  CX=0000  DX=0000  SP=FFEE  BP=0000  SI=0000  DI=0000
DS=21C1  ES=21C1  SS=21C1  CS=21C1  IP=0107  NV UP EI PL NZ NA PE NC
21C1:0107 A30402      MOV   [0204],AX                      DS:0204=0000
-T

AX=0148  BX=0000  CX=0000  DX=0000  SP=FFEE  BP=0000  SI=0000  DI=0000
DS=21C1  ES=21C1  SS=21C1  CS=21C1  IP=010A  NV UP EI PL NZ NA PE NC
21C1:010A EB F4       JMP   0100
-D DS:0200,0208
21C1:0000  23 01 25 00 48 01 2A 2A-2A                      #.%.H.***
-Q
```

Figure 3-3   Tracing Machine Instructions

mediate value. (An immediate value for moving 0200H to AX would appear as MOV AX,0200.)

Now key in the T (Trace) command. The instruction MOV AX,[0200] moves the contents of the word at offset 0200H to AX. The contents are 2301H, which the operation reverses in AX as 0123H and replaces any previous contents in AX.

Key in another T command to cause execution of the next instruction, ADD. The operation adds the contents of the word in memory at DS offset 0202 to AX. The result in AX is now the sum of 0123H and 0025H, or 0148H.

The next instruction is MOV [0204],AX. Key in a T command for it to execute. The instruction copies the contents of AX (0148H) to the data area at DS offsets 204H and 205H and is reversed as 4801H. To view the changed contents of the data from 200H through 208H, key in

```
D DS:200,208 <Enter>
```

The displayed values should be:

```
Value in data area:  23  01  25  00  48  01  2A  2A  2A
                      |   |   |   |   |   |   |   |   |
Offset:              200 201 202 203 204 205 206 207 208
```

The left side of the display shows the actual machine code as it appears in memory. The right side simply helps you locate character data more easily. Note that these hex values are represented on the right of the screen by their ASCII equivalents. The 23H and 25H display as a number symbol (#) and a percent symbol (%), respectively, and the three 2AH bytes generate asterisks (*).

You may now enter Q to end the DEBUG session, or continue with the next exercise.

Reexecuting Instructions

There are times when it is necessary to reset the offset value in the IP register. In fact, you'll do this quite often, so here is the procedure:

1. Key in R IP to display the contents of IP, and
2. Type in the value 100 (or address of another instruction), followed by <Enter>.

This procedure returns you to the start of the program (or an instruction within the program), where you can now repeat the previous steps. Key in an R command (without the IP); DEBUG displays the registers, flags, and first instruction to be executed. You can now use T to retrace the instruction steps. If your program accumulates totals, use the E command to clear memory locations and the R command to clear registers. But be sure not to change the contents of CS, DS, SP, and SS, all of which have specific purposes.

Asking DEBUG to Save a Program

You may use DEBUG to save a program on disk under two circumstances:

1. To retrieve an existing program from disk, modify it, and then save it.
2. To use DEBUG to create a very small machine language program that you now want to save.

For details, see the W (Write) command in Appendix C.

At this point, you may find the DEBUG H (Hexadecimal) command useful for adding and subtracting hex values. Maximum field lengths are four hex digits. Key in the command, for example, as H 3443 2A2B. The operation displays the sum on the left and the difference on the right, as 5E6E 0A18.

AN ASSEMBLY LANGUAGE PROGRAM

Although to this point the program examples have been in machine language format, you can also use DEBUG to key in assembly language statements. You may find occasions to use both methods. Let's now examine DEBUG's A and U commands used to enter assembly statements into the computer.

The A (Assemble) Command

The A command tells DEBUG to begin accepting symbolic assembly instructions and to convert them into machine language. Initialize the starting address for your instructions in the code segment at offset 100H as

```
A 100  <Enter>
```

DEBUG displays the address of the code segment and the offset (0100) as xxxx:0100. Type in the following instructions, each followed by <Enter>:

```
MOV   CL,42    <Enter>
MOV   DL,2A    <Enter>
ADD   CL,DL    <Enter>
JMP   100      <Enter>
```

When you've keyed in the program, press <Enter> again to exit from the A command. That's one extra <Enter>, which tells DEBUG you have no more symbolic instructions to enter. On completion, DEBUG displays the offset address of each instruction:

```
xxxx:0100    MOV   CL,42
xxxx:0102    MOV   DL,2A
xxxx:0104    ADD   CL,DL
xxxx:0106    JMP   100
xxxx:0108
```

Before executing the program, let's use DEBUG's U (Unassemble) command to examine the generated machine language.

The U (Unassemble) Command

DEBUG's U command displays the machine code for your assembly language instructions. You can use this command to tell DEBUG the locations of the first and last instructions that you want to see, in this case, 100H and 107H. Key in

```
U 100,107  <Enter>
```

The screen displays columns for the location, machine code, and symbolic code like this:

```
xxxx:0100    B142    MOV CL,42
xxxx:0102    B22A    MOV DL,2A
xxxx:0104    00D1    ADD CL,DL
xxxx:0106    EBF8    JMP 100
xxxx:0108
```

Now trace the machine code execution of the program. Begin by keying in R to display the registers (IP should contain 0100) and the first instruction (MOV CL,42), and then successive T commands to trace subsequent instructions. When you get to the JMP, IP should contain 106H and CL should contain 6CH. Continue with the next exercise or press Q to quit execution.

You have now seen how to key in a program in machine language and in assembly language. However, DEBUG is really intended for what its name implies—debugging programs—and most of your efforts will involve the use of conventional assembly language, which is not associated with DEBUG.

USING THE INT INSTRUCTION

The following four examples show how to request information about the system. To this end, you use the INT (interrupt) instruction, which exits from your program, enters a DOS or BIOS routine, performs the requested function, and returns to your program. There are different types of INT operations, some of which require a *function code* in the AH register to request a specific action. Rather than using the T command for single-stepping, we'll use the P (Proceed) command to execute through the whole interrupt routine. Be sure to reset IP to 100H.

Getting the Current Date and Time

The instruction to access the current date is INT 21H function code 2AH. Once again, type in the DEBUG command A 100 and then the following assembly instructions:

```
MOV    AH,2A <Enter>
INT    21 <Enter>
JMP    100 <Enter>, <Enter>
```

Type in R to display the registers and T to execute the MOV. Then type in P to proceed directly through the interrupt routine; the operation stops at the JMP. The registers contain this information in hex format:

AL: Day of the week, where 0 = Sunday

CX: Year (for example, 07D4H = 2004)

DH: Month (01H through 0CH)

DL: Day of the month (01H through 1FH)

The operation to access the current time is INT 21H function code 2CH. First use R IP to reset IP to 100, and then key in the DEBUG A command and the following assembly instructions:

```
MOV AH,2C <Enter>
INT 21 <Enter>
JMP 100 <Enter>, <Enter>
```

Follow the same procedure as you did for retrieving the date. The operation delivers hours to CH (in 24-hour format, where 00 = midnight), minutes to CL, seconds to DH, and hundredths of a second to DL.

Press Q to quit, or continue with the next exercise (and reset the IP to 100).

Determining Installed Equipment

In an early exercise in this chapter, you checked locations 410H and 411H for the equipment that your computer contains. BIOS also provides an interrupt routine, INT 11H, that delivers the information to AX. Type in the DEBUG command A 100 and then these instructions:

```
INT 11
JMP 100 <Enter>, <Enter>
```

Key in R to display the registers and the first instruction. The instruction, INT 11H, passes control to a routine in BIOS that delivers the equipment data to AX. Press T and <Enter> repeatedly to see each BIOS instruction execute. (Yes, this procedure violates a rule against tracing through an interrupt, but this operation works all right.)

The actual instructions in your BIOS may differ somewhat from these, depending on the version installed (the comments to the right are the author's):

```
JMP   EE53          ;
PUSH  DS            ;Save DS address in stack
MOV   AX,0040       ;Get segment address,
MOV   DS,AX         ;  move it to DS
MOV   AX,[0010]     ;Get data from 40:10 into AX
POP   DS            ;Restore address in DS
IRET                ;Return from interrupt
```

The last T command exits from BIOS and returns to DEBUG. If you survived this adventure into BIOS, AX now contains the record of installed equipment. The displayed instruction is now the JMP that you entered. Press Q to quit, or continue with the next exercise (and reset IP to 100).

Using INT for Displaying

This exercise, which displays data on the screen, introduces a few new features. Type in the DEBUG command A 100 and then these assembly instructions:

```
100    MOV AH,09
102    MOV DX,109
105    INT 21
107    JMP 100
109    DB 'your name', '$' <Enter> <Enter>
```

The two MOV instructions tell INT 21H to display (AH = 09) and from what starting address (DX = 109). Note that offset 109 begins the definition of your name, where DB means "define byte" and the characters are contained in single quotes. Following your name is a dollar sign, also in quotes, which tells INT to end the display.

Key in R to display the registers and the first instruction, and key in T commands for the two MOVs. Key in P to execute INT 21 and you'll see your name displayed. Press Q to quit, or continue with the next exercise (and reset IP to 100).

Using INT for Keyboard Input

This exercise, which accepts characters from the keyboard, also introduces a few new features. Type in the DEBUG command A 100 and then these assembly instructions:

```
100    MOV   AH,10
102    INT   16
104    JMP   100    <Enter> twice
```

The first instruction, MOV, provides function code 10H that tells INT 16H to accept data from the keyboard; the operation delivers the character from the keyboard to the AL register. Key in R to display the registers and the first instruction, and key in a T command to execute the MOV. When you type in P for INT 16H, the system waits for you to press a key. If you press the number 1, you'll see that the operation delivers 31H (hex for ASCII 1) to AL. Key in T to execute the JMP, and you're back at the MOV at 100. Use T to execute the MOV. When you key in P for the INT, the system again waits for you to press a key. If you press 2, you'll see that the operation delivers 32H to AL. You can continue like this indefinitely. You'll find a list of keyboard ASCII codes in Appendix F. Press Q to quit, or continue with the next exercise (and reset IP to 100).

USING THE PTR OPERATOR

The next program example introduces some new features. In this example, you move and add data between registers and memory locations. In earlier programs that move data into a register, DEBUG could tell from the size of the register (AL or AX) how many bytes to move. This program, however, transfers immediate data into memory. Because an instruction like MOV [120],25 does not indicate the number of bytes, you can use the PTR operator for that purpose. Here are the instructions:

```
100    MOV   AX,[11A]
103    ADD   AX,[11C]
107    ADD   AX,25
10A    MOV   [11E],AX
10D    MOV   WORD PTR [120],25
113    MOV   BYTE PTR [122],30
118    JMP   100
11A    DB    14 23
11C    DB    05 00
11E    DB    00 00
120    DB    00 00 00
```

Here is an explanation of the instructions:

100:   Move the contents of memory locations 11AH-11BH to AX. The square brackets indicate a memory address rather than an immediate value.

103:   Add the contents of memory locations 11CH-11DH to AX.

107:   Add the immediate value 25H to AX.

10A: Move the contents of AX to memory locations 11EH-11FH.

10D: Move the immediate value 25H to memory locations 120H-121H. Note the use of the WORD PTR operator, which tells DEBUG that the 25H is to move into a word in memory. If you were to code the instruction as MOV [120],25, DEBUG would have no way of determining what length is intended and would display an ERROR message. Although you will seldom need to use the PTR operator, it's vital to know when it is needed.

113:   Move the immediate value 30H to memory location 122H. This time, use the BYTE PTR operator to indicate a 1-byte length.

11A: Define the byte values 14H and 23H. DB tells DEBUG to "define byte(s)" for data items that your instructions (such as the one at 100) are to reference.

11C, 11E, and 120:   Define other byte values for use in the program.

To key in this program, first type A 100 <Enter>, and then key in each symbolic instruction (but not the location). At the end, key in an additional <Enter> to exit from the A command.

To execute the program, begin by entering R to display the registers and the first instruction, then type in successive T commands. Stop execution when you get to JMP at 118. Key in D 110 to view the changed contents of AX (233E) and of locations 11EH-11FH (3E23), 120H-121H (2500), and 122H (30). Type in T to repeat the program or Q to quit.

You've covered a lot of material in this chapter that will become clearer through repetition.

KEY POINTS

- The DEBUG program is useful for testing and debugging machine language and assembly language programs. Its commands include such useful operations as display, enter, and trace.
- Because DEBUG does not distinguish between lowercase and uppercase letters, you may enter commands either way.
- In DEBUG, all entered and displayed numbers are in hexadecimal format.
- If you enter an incorrect value in the data segment or code segment, reenter the E command to correct it.
- Use the T command to execute a single instruction and the P command to execute right through an INT operation.
- To resume execution at the first instruction, set the Instruction Pointer (IP) to 0100. Key in the R (Register) command, followed by the designated register, as R IP

<Enter>. DEBUG displays the contents of IP and waits for an entry. Key in the value 100, followed by <Enter>.

REVIEW QUESTIONS AND EXERCISES

3-1. Explain the purpose of each of the following DEBUG commands:
(a) A, (b) U, (c) P, (d) T, (e) Q, (f) D, (g) R, (h) E.

3-2. Provide the DEBUG commands for the following unrelated requirements:
  (a) Display the contents of all registers.
  (b) Display the contents of the IP register and change its contents to 100H.
  (c) Display the data beginning at offset 2BCH in the data segment.
  (d) Display the data beginning at location 3AFH. (Note: Separate this address into its segment and offset values.)
  (e) Unassemble the symbolic code in locations 100H through 12BH.
  (f) Key in 24A63BH into the data segment beginning at location 18AH.

3-3. Provide the machine code instructions for the following operations: (a) add the immediate hex value 03A8 to AX, (b) move the hex value 2CA4 to the AX register.

3-4. Assume that you have used DEBUG to enter the following E command:

```
                    E CS:100 B8 45 01 05 25 00
```

The hex value 45 was supposed to be 54. Code another E command to correct only the one byte that is incorrect; that is, change the 45 to 54 directly.

3-5. The Video Display Area for a color monitor in text mode is at address B800[0]. (a) Use the DEBUG D command to display this area. Note that each character in the video area is followed by its attribute (07 if black and white). Use additional single D commands to display further portions. (b) Use the DEBUG F (Fill) command to partially fill the screen with 50 asterisks (2AH). As an example, the following command fills the entire video area with 4,000 (FA0H) hearts (03) and attributes (where 16H is the attribute for brown character on blue background): F B800:0 LFA0 03 16.

3-6. Assume that you have used DEBUG to enter the following E command:

```
                 E CS:100 B8 05 1B 05 00 2C EB F8
```

  (a) What are the three symbolic instructions represented here? (The first program in this chapter gives a clue.)
  (b) On executing this program, you discover that the AX register ends up with 4705 instead of the expected 0547. What is the error, and how would you correct it?
  (c) Having corrected the instructions, you now want to reexecute the program from the first instruction. What DEBUG commands are required?

3-7. Consider the machine language instructions

```
                 B0 1C D0 E0 B3 12 F6 E3 EBF6
```

The instructions perform the following: (a) Move hex value 1C to the AL register, (b) shift the contents of AL one bit to the left (equivalent to multiplying by 2), (c) move hex value 12 to BL, (d) multiply AL by BL.

   Use DEBUG's E command to enter the program beginning at CS:100. (Remember these are hexadecimal values.) Next key in D CS:100 to view it. Then key in R and enough successive T commands to step through the program until reaching the JMP. What is the final product in AX?

3-8. Use DEBUG's E command to enter the following machine language program:

```
Machine code (at 100H): A0 00 02 D0 E0 F6 26 01 02 A3 02 02 90

               Data (at 200H): 1E 16 00 00
```

The program performs the following: (a) Moves the contents of the byte at DS:0200 (1E) to the AL register, (b) shifts AL contents one bit to the left, (c) multiplies AL by the 1-byte contents at DS:0201 (16), (d) moves the product from AX to the word beginning at DS:0202.

Type in D commands to view the code and the data. Then key in R and enough successive T commands to step through the program until reaching the JMP. What is the final product in AX? Key in another D DS:0200 and note how the product at DS:0202 is stored.

3-9. For Question 3-7, code the commands that write the program on disk under the name HEXMULT.COM. (See Appendix C.)

3-10. Use DEBUG's A command to enter the following instructions:

```
MOV    DX,2E
ADD    DX,1F
SHL    DX,01
SUB    DX,BA
JMP    100
```

Unassemble the instructions and trace their execution through to the JMP, and check the value in DX after each instruction.

3-11. What is the purpose of the INT instruction?

3-12. Use DEBUG to create and run a program that displays the phrase "Coffee Break." Start with A 100 for entering the instructions and use A 120 for the phrase (and remember the $ delimiter). Hint: See the section "Using INT for Displaying."

3-13. Use DEBUG to create and run a program that accepts three characters from the keyboard and displays them. (a) Start with A 100. (b) Use INT 16 to accept a character into AL and move the character to location [200]. (c) Use a second INT 16 to accept a character into AL and move it to location [201]. (d) Use a third INT 16 to accept a character into AL and move it to location [202]. (e) Use an E 123 '$' command to define a '$' at the end of the three stored characters. (f) Finally, use INT 21 to display the characters. Hint: See the section "Using INT for Keyboard Input".

Chapter 4

REQUIREMENTS FOR CODING IN ASSEMBLY LANGUAGE

> Objective: To cover the basic requirements for coding an assembly language program and defining data items.

INTRODUCTION

In Chapter 3 you learned how to use DEBUG for keying in and executing machine language programs. No doubt you were very much aware of the difficulty in deciphering the machine code, even for a small program. You also used DEBUG's A command for keying in a small assembly source program, which no doubt you noticed was much easier to understand than machine code. The use of DEBUG's A command is only a convenience because, as of this chapter, you'll start developing larger programs and you'll need far more capability in documenting and revising them.

You write an assembly program according to a strict set of rules, use an editor or word processor for keying it into the computer as a file, and then use the assembler translator program to read the file and to convert it into machine code.

In this chapter, we explain the basic requirements for developing an assembly program: the use of comments, the general coding format, the directives for controlling the assembled program listing, and the requirements for defining segments and procedures. We also cover the general organization of a program, including initializing the program and ending its execution. Finally, we cover the requirements for defining data items.

The two main classes of programming languages are *high-level* and *low-level*. Programmers writing in a high-level language, such as C or BASIC, use powerful commands, each of which may generate many machine language instructions. Programmers writing in a low-level assembly language, on the other hand, code symbolic instructions, each of which generates one machine instruction. Despite the fact that coding in a high-level language is more productive, some advantages to coding in assembly language are that it in general:

- Provides more control over handling particular hardware requirements.
- Generates smaller, more compact executable modules.
- Results in faster execution.

A common practice is to combine the benefits of both programming levels: Code the bulk of a project in a high-level language, and code critical modules (those that cause noticeable delays) in assembly language.

Regardless of the programming language you use, it is still symbolic language that has to be translated into a form the computer can execute. A high-level language uses a *compiler* program to translate the source code into machine code (technically, object code). A low-level language uses an *assembler* program to perform the translation into object code. A *linker* program for both high- and low-levels completes the process by converting the object code into executable machine language.

ASSEMBLY LANGUAGE FEATURES

Certain characteristics of assembly language are first covered: program comments, reserved words, identifiers, statements, and directives. These features provide the basic rules and framework for the language.

Program Comments

The use of comments throughout a program can improve its clarity, especially in assembly language, where the purpose of a set of instructions is often unclear. For example, it is obvious that the instruction MOV AH,10H moves 10H to AH, but the reason for doing this may be unclear. A comment begins with a semicolon (;), and wherever you code it, the assembler assumes that all characters on the line to its right are comments. A comment may contain any printable character, including a blank.

A comment may appear on a line by itself, like this:

```
;Calculate productivity ratio
```

or on the same line following an instruction, like this:

```
ADD AX,BX ;Accumulate total quantity
```

Because a comment appears only on a listing of an assembled source program and generates no machine code, you may include any number of comments without affecting the assembled program's size or execution. In this book, all assembly instructions are in uppercase letters and all comments are in lowercase, only as a convention and to make the programs more readable. Technically, you are free to use either uppercase or lowercase for instructions and comments. Another way to provide comments is by means of the COMMENT directive, described in Chapter 25.

Reserved Words

Certain names in assembly language are *reserved* for their own purposes, to be used only under special conditions. Reserved words, by category, include

- *instructions,* such as MOV and ADD, which are operations that the computer can execute;
- *directives,* such as END or SEGMENT, which you use to provide information to the assembler;
- *operators,* such as FAR and SIZE, which you use in expressions; and
- *predefined symbols,* such as @Data and @Model, which return information to your program during the assembly.

Using a reserved word for a wrong purpose causes the assembler to generate an error message. See Appendix D for a list of reserved words.

Identifiers

An *identifier* (or symbol) is a name that you apply to an item in your program that you expect to reference. The two types of identifiers are name and label:

1. *Name* refers to the address of a data item, such as COUNTER in

```
COUNTER DB 0
```

2. *Label* refers to the address of an instruction, procedure, or segment, such as MAIN and B30: in the following statements:

```
MAIN PROC FAR
B30: ADD  BL,25
```

The same rules apply to both names and labels. An identifier can use the following characters:

CATEGORY	ALLOWABLE CHARACTERS
Alphabetic letters:	A through Z and a through z
Digits:	0 through 9 (not the first character)
Special characters:	question mark (?)
	break, or underline (_)
	dollar ($)
	at (@)
	dot or period (.) (not first character)

The first character of an identifier must be an alphabetic letter or a special character, except for the dot. Because the assembler uses some special words that begin with the @ symbol, you should avoid using it for your own definitions.

By default, the assembler treats uppercase and lowercase letters the same. (The command line has an option that forces the assembler to be case sensitive.) The maximum length of an identifier is 31 characters up to MASM 6.0 and 247 since. Examples of valid names are TOTAL, QTY250, and $P50. Descriptive, meaningful names are recommended.

The names of registers, such as AH, BX, and DS, are reserved for referencing those registers. Consequently, in an instruction such as ADD CX,BX the assembler knows that CX and BX refer to registers. However, in an instruction such as MOV REGSAVE,CX the assembler can recognize the name REGSAVE only if you define it as a data item.

Statements

An assembly program consists of a set of *statements.* The two types of statements are:

1. *instructions,* such as MOV and ADD, which the assembler translates to object code; and
2. *directives,* which tell the assembler to perform a specific action, such as define a data item.

Here is the format for a statement, where square brackets indicate an optional entry:

[identifier]	operation	[operand(s)]	[;comment]

An *identifier* (if any), *operation,* and *operand* (if any) are separated by at least one blank or tab character. There is a maximum of 132 characters on a line up to MASM 6.0 and 512 since, although most programmers prefer to stay within 80 characters because that is the maximum number most screens can accommodate. Two examples of statements are the following:

	IDENTIFIER	OPERATION	OPERAND	COMMENT
Directive:	COUNT	DB	1	;Name, operation, operand
Instruction:	L30:	MOV	AX,0	;Label, operation, 2 operands

The identifier, operation, and operand may begin in any column. However, consistently starting at the same column for these entries makes a more readable program. Also, many editor programs provide tab stops every eight positions to facilitate spacing the fields.

As described earlier under the heading "Identifiers," the term *name* applies to the name of a defined item or directive, whereas the term *label* applies to the name of an instruction; we'll use these terms from now on.

The *operation,* which must be coded, is most commonly used for defining data areas and coding instructions. For a data item, an operation such as DB or DW defines a field, work area, or constant. For an instruction, an operation such as MOV or ADD indicates an action to perform.

The *operand* (if any) provides information for the operation to act on. For a data item, the operand defines its initial value. For example, in the following definition of a data item named COUNTER, the operation DB means "define byte," and the operand initializes its contents with a zero value:

NAME	OPERATION	OPERAND	COMMENT
COUNTER	DB	0	;Define byte with initial 0 value

For an instruction, an operand indicates where to perform the action. An instruction's operand may contain one, two, or even no entries. Here are three examples:

```
OPERATION  OPERAND              COMMENT
   RET                      ;Return from a procedure
   INC      BX              ;Increment BX register by 1
   ADD      CX,25           ;Add 25 to CX register
```

Directives

Assembly language supports a number of statements that enable you to control the way in which a source program assembles and lists. These statements, called *directives,* act only during the assembly of a program and generate no machine-executable code. The most common directives are explained in the next few sections. Chapter 25 covers all of the directives in detail, and is available as a reference any time.

The PAGE and TITLE Listing Directives.   The PAGE and TITLE directives help to control the format of a listing of an assembled program. This is their only purpose, and they have no effect on subsequent execution of the program.

At the start of a program, the PAGE directive designates the maximum number of lines to list on a page and the maximum number of characters on a line. Its format is

```
PAGE [length] [,width]
```

For example, for the directive PAGE 60,132, *length* is 60 lines per page and *width* is 132 characters per line.

Under a typical assembler, the number of lines per page may range from 10 through 255, and the number of characters per line may range from 60 through 132. Omission of a PAGE statement causes the assembler to default to PAGE 50,80.

Suppose that a program defines the maximum line count for PAGE as 60. When the assembler is printing the assembled program and has listed 60 lines, it automatically advances to the top of the next page and increments the page count.

You may also want to force a page to eject at a specific line in the program listing, such as the end of a segment. At the required line, simply code PAGE with no operand. On encountering PAGE, the assembler advances to the top of the next page where it resumes the listing.

You can use the TITLE directive to cause a title for a program to print on line 2 of each page of the program listing. You may code TITLE once, at the start of the program. Its format is

```
TITLE text [comment]
```

For *text,* a common practice is to use the name of the program as cataloged on disk. For example, if you named the program ASMSORT, code that name plus an optional descriptive *comment* (a leading ';' is not required), all up to 60 characters in length, like this:

```
TITLE ASMSORT Assembly program to sort CD titles
```

SEGMENT Directive. As described in Chapter 2, an assembly program in .EXE format consists of one or more segments. In real mode, a stack segment defines stack storage, a data segment defines data items, and a code segment provides for executable code. The directives for defining a segment, SEGMENT and ENDS, have the following format:

NAME	OPERATION	OPERAND		
segment-name	SEGMENT	[*align*]	[*combine*]	['*class*']
	. . .			
segment-name	ENDS			

The SEGMENT statement defines the start of a segment. The *segment-name* must be present, must be unique, and must follow assembly language naming conventions. The ENDS statement indicates the end of the segment and contains the same name as the SEGMENT statement. The maximum size of a segment in real mode is 64K. The operand of a SEGMENT statement may contain three types of options: alignment, combine, and class:

- The *align* option indicates the boundary on which the segment is to begin. The typical requirement is PARA, which causes the segment to align on a paragraph boundary so that the starting address is evenly divisible by 16, or 10H. Omission of the align operand causes the assembler to default to PARA.

- The *combine* option indicates whether to combine the segment with other segments when they are linked after assembly (explained later under "Linking the Program"). Combine types are STACK, COMMON, PUBLIC, and AT *expression.* For example, the stack segment is commonly defined as

```
      segment-name      SEGMENT      PARA STACK
```

- You may use PUBLIC and COMMON where you intend to combine separately assembled programs when linking them. Otherwise, where a program is not to be combined with other programs, you may omit this option or code NONE.

- The *class* option, enclosed in apostrophes, is used to group related segments when linking. This book uses the classes 'code' for the code segment (recommended by Microsoft), 'data' for the data segment, and 'stack' for the stack segment.

The partial program in Figure 4-1 illustrates SEGMENT statements with various options. Note that the program defines a stack segment with alignment (PARA), combine (STACK), and class ('Stack') types.

```
          page    60,132
   TITLE    A04ASM1  Segments for an .EXE Program
; ----------------------------------------------------
   STACK    SEGMENT PARA STACK 'Stack'
            ...
   STACK    ENDS
; ----------------------------------------------------
   DATASEG  SEGMENT PARA 'Data'
            ...
   DATASEG  ENDS
; ----------------------------------------------------
   CODESEG  SEGMENT PARA 'Code'
            MAIN    PROC  FAR
            ...
   MAIN     ENDP                      ;End of procedure
   CODESEG  ENDS                      ;End of segment
            END     MAIN              ;End of program
```

Figure 4-1   Defining Segments for an .EXE Program

PROC Directive.   The code segment contains the executable code for a program, which consists of one or more *procedures,* defined initially with the PROC directive and ended with the ENDP directive. Here is the format:

NAME	OPERATION	OPERAND	COMMENT
procedure-name	PROC	FAR	;Begin procedure
	...		
procedure-name	ENDP		;End procedure

The *procedure-name* must be present, must be unique, and must follow assembly language naming conventions. The operand, FAR in this case, is related to program execution. When you request execution of a program, the program loader uses this procedure as the entry point for the first instruction to execute.

The ENDP directive indicates the end of a procedure and contains the same name as the PROC statement to enable the assembler to relate the end to the start. Because a procedure must be fully contained within a segment, ENDP defines the end of the procedure before ENDS defines the end of the segment, as shown in Figure 4-1.

The code segment may contain any number of procedures used as subroutines, each with its own set of matching PROC and ENDP statements. Each additional PROC is usually coded with (or defaults to) the NEAR operand, as covered in Chapter 7.

END Directive.   As already mentioned, the ENDS directive ends a segment, and the ENDP directive ends a procedure. An END directive ends the entire program and appears as the last statement, as shown in Figure 4-1. Its format (operation and operand) is:

```
END [procedure-name]
```

The operand may be blank if the program is not to execute; for example, you may want to assemble only data definitions, or you may want to link the program with another module. In most programs, the operand contains the name of the first or only PROC designated as FAR, where program execution is to begin.

ASSUME Directive.   An .EXE program uses the SS register to address the stack, DS to address the data segment, and CS to address the code segment. To this end, you have to tell the assembler the purpose of each segment in the program. The required directive is ASSUME, coded in the code segment as follows:

```
ASSUME      SS:stackname,DS:datasegname,CS:codesegname, ...
```

SS:*stackname* means that the assembler is to associate the name of the stack segment with the SS register, and similarly for the other operands shown. The operands may appear in any sequence. ASSUME may also contain an entry for the ES register, such as ES:*dataseg-name*; if your program does not use ES, you may omit its reference or code ES:NOTHING. (Since MASM 6.0, the assembler automatically generates an ASSUME for the code segment.)

Like other directives, ASSUME is just a message to help the assembler convert symbolic code to machine code; you may still have to code instructions that physically load addresses in segment registers when the program begins its execution.

Processor Directives.   Most assemblers assume that the source program is to run on a basic 8086-level computer. As a result, when you use instructions or features introduced by later processors, you have to notify the assembler by means of a processor directive, such as .286, .386, .486, or .586. The directive may appear immediately before the instruction, before the code segment, or even at the start of the source program for protected mode. Also, the use of extended registers, such as EAX, requires the .386 directive. Here are some instructions that require a processor directive:

.286	.386	.486
POPA	MOVSX/MOVZX	CMPXCHG
PUSHA	SHLD/SHRD	XADD

CONVENTIONAL SEGMENT DIRECTIVES

The two basic types of executable programs are .EXE and .COM. We'll develop the requirements for .EXE programs first and leave .COM programs for Chapter 5. Figure 4-2 provides a skeleton of an .EXE program showing the stack, data, and code segments. The following explains the program statements by line number:

LINE	EXPLANATION
1	Uses the PAGE directive to establish 60 lines and 132 columns per page.
2	Uses the TITLE directive to identify the program's name as A04ASM1.

```
 1          page    60,132
 2  TITLE   A04ASM1 Skeleton of an .EXE Program
 3  ; ----------------------------------------------------
 4  STACK   SEGMENT PARA STACK 'Stack'
 5          ...
 6  STACK   ENDS
 7  ; ----------------------------------------------------
 8  DATASEG SEGMENT PARA 'Data'
 9          ...
10  DATASEG ENDS
11  ; ----------------------------------------------------
12  CODESEG SEGMENT PARA 'Code'
13  MAIN    PROC    FAR
14          ASSUME  SS:STACK,DS:DATASEG,CS:CODESEG
15          MOV     AX,DATASEG          ;Set address of data
16          MOV     DS,AX               ;  segment in DS
17          ...
18          MOV     AX,4C00H            ;End processing
19          INT     21H
20  MAIN    ENDP                        ;End of procedure
21  CODESEG ENDS                        ;End of segment
22          END     MAIN                ;End of program
```

Figure 4-2   Skeleton of an .EXE Program

3   Uses comments in lines 3, 7, and 11 that clearly set out the three defined
            segments.

4-6   Define the stack segment, STACK (but not its contents in this example).

8–10   Define the data segment, DATASEG (but not its contents).

12   Define the code segment, CODESEG.

13-20   Define the code segment's only procedure, named MAIN in this example.
            This procedure illustrates common initialization and exit requirements for
            an .EXE program. The two requirements for initializing are (1) notify the
            assembler which segments to associate with segment registers, and (2)
            load DS with the address of the data segment.

14   Uses the ASSUME directive that tells the assembler to associate segments
            with segment registers, in this case, STACK with SS, DATASEG with DS,
            and CODESEG with CS:

```
ASSUME SS:STACK,DS:DATASEG,CS:CODESEG
```

            By associating segments with segment registers, the assembler can deter-
            mine offset addresses for items in the stack, for data items in the data seg-
            ment, and for instructions in the code segment. For example, each machine
            instruction in the code segment is a specific length. The first instruction in
            machine language would be at offset 0 and, if it is two bytes long, the sec-
            ond instruction would be at offset 2, and so forth.

15, 16   Initialize the address of the data segment in DS:

```
MOV AX,DATASEG   ;Get address of data segment
MOV DS,AX        ;Store address in DS
```

The first MOV loads the address of the data segment into the AX register and the second MOV copies the address from AX into DS. Two MOVs are required because the processor allows you to move data only from a general-purpose register to a segment register. Thus the statement MOV DS,DATASEG is invalid because it attempts to move data directly from memory to DS. Chapter 5 discusses initializing segment registers in more detail.

18, 19　　Request an end to program execution and a return to the operating system. A later section discusses them in more detail.

22　　Uses the END directive to tell the assembler that this is the end of the source program. The MAIN operand means that the procedure named MAIN is to be the entry point for subsequent program execution. MAIN could be any other name acceptable to the assembler, as long as PROC, ENDP, and END use the same name.

The sequence in which you define segments is usually unimportant. Figure 4-2 defines them as follows:

```
STACK     SEGMENT     PARA     STACK 'Stack'
DATASEG   SEGMENT     PARA     'Data'
CODESEG   SEGMENT     PARA     'Code'
```

Note that the program in the figure is coded in *symbolic language.* To execute it, you have to use an assembler and a linker to translate it into executable machine code as an .EXE program.

As described in Chapter 2, when the program loader reads an .EXE program from disk into memory for execution, it constructs a 256-byte (100H) PSP (program segment prefix) on a paragraph boundary in available internal memory and stores the program immediately following the boundary. The loader then

- initializes the address of the code segment in CS,
- initializes the address of the stack in SS, and
- initializes the address of the PSP in DS and ES.

The loader initializes the CS:IP and SS:SP registers for the processor to access the code and stack segments, respectively. However, your program normally needs the address of the data segment in DS (and usually in ES as well) rather than the address of the PSP. As a consequence, you have to initialize DS with the address of the data segment, as shown by the two MOV instructions in Figure 4-2.

Now, even if this initialization is not clear at this point, take heart: Every .EXE program has virtually identical initialization steps that you can duplicate every time you code one.

Ending Program Execution

INT 21H is a common DOS interrupt that uses a function code in the AH register to specify an action to be performed. The many functions of INT 21H include keyboard input, screen handling, disk I/O, and printer output. The function that concerns us here is 4CH, which INT 21H recognizes as a request to end program execution. You can also use this operation to pass a return code in AL for subsequent testing in a batch file (via the IF ERRORLEVEL statement), like this:

```
MOV AH,4CH        ;Request end processing
MOV AL,retcode    ;Optional return code
INT 21H           ;Call interrupt service
```

The return code for normal completion of a program is usually 0 (zero). You may also recode the two MOVs as one statement (as shown in Figure 4-2):

```
MOV AX,4C00H      ;Request normal exit
```

Example of a Source Program

Figure 4-3 combines the preceding information into a simple but complete assembly source program that adds two data items in the AX register. The segments are defined in this way:

- STACK contains one entry, DW (Define Word), that defines 32 words initialized to zero, an adequate size for small programs.
- DATASEG defines three words named FLDD (initialized with 215), FLDE (initialized with 125), and FLDF (uninitialized).
- CODESEG contains the executable instructions for the program, although the first two statements, PROC and ASSUME, generate no executable code.

```
          page    60,132
TITLE     A04ASM1 (EXE)  Move and add operations
; ---------------------------------------------------
STACK     SEGMENT PARA STACK 'Stack'
          DW      32 DUP(0)
STACK     ENDS
; ---------------------------------------------------
DATASEG   SEGMENT PARA 'Data'
FLDD      DW      215
FLDE      DW      125
FLDF      DW      ?
DATASEG   ENDS
; ---------------------------------------------------
CODESEG   SEGMENT PARA 'Code'
MAIN      PROC    FAR
          ASSUME  SS:STACK,DS:DATASEG,CS:CODESEG
          MOV     AX,DATASG      ;Set address of data
          MOV     DS,AX          ;  segment in DS
          MOV     AX,FLDD        ;Move 0215 to AX
          ADD     AX,FLDE        ;Add  0125 to AX
          MOV     FLDF,AX        ;Store sum in FLDF
          MOV     AX,4C00H       ;End processing
          INT     21H
MAIN      ENDP                   ;End of procedure
CODESEG   ENDS                   ;End of segment
          END     MAIN           ;End of program
```

Figure 4-3   EXE Program with Conventional Segments

The ASSUME directive tells the assembler to perform these tasks:

- Assign STACK to the SS register so that the processor uses the address in SS for addressing STACK.
- Assign DATASEG to the DS register so that the processor uses the address in DS for addressing DATASEG.
- Assign CODESEG to the CS register so that the processor uses the address in CS for addressing CODESEG.

When loading a program from disk into memory for execution, the program loader sets the correct segment addresses in SS and CS, but, as shown by the first two MOV instructions, the program has to initialize DS (and usually ES).

You'll get to trace the assembly, linkage, and execution of this program in Chapter 5.

SIMPLIFIED SEGMENT DIRECTIVES

The assembler provides some shortcuts in defining segments. To use them, you have to initialize the memory model before defining any segment. The different models tell the assembler how to use segments, to provide enough space for the object code, and to ensure optimum execution speed. The format (including the leading dot) is

```
.MODEL    memory-model
```

The *memory-model* may be Tiny, Small, Medium, Compact, Large, Huge, or Flat. As of MASM 6.0 and TASM 4.0, the Tiny model is intended for the use of .COM programs, which have their data, code, and stack in one 64K segment. The Flat model defines one area up to 4 gigabytes for both code and data; the program uses 32-bit addressing and runs under Windows in protected mode. The requirements for the other models are:

MODEL	NUMBER OF CODE SEGMENTS	NUMBER OF DATA SEGMENTS
Small	1 <= 64K	1 <= 64K
Medium	Any number, any size	1 <= 64K
Compact	1 <= 64K	Any number, any size
Large	Any number, any size	Any number, any size
Huge	Any number, any size	Any number, any size

You may use any of these models for a standalone program (that is, a program that is not linked to another program). The Small model is suitable for most of the examples in this book; the assembler assumes that addresses are near (within 64K) and generates 16-bit offset addresses. In contrast, for the Compact model, the assembler may assume 32-bit addresses, which require more time for execution.

The Huge model is the same as Large, but may contain variables such as arrays greater than 64K. The .MODEL directive automatically generates the required ASSUME statement for all models.

The formats (including the leading dot) for the directives that define the stack, data, and code segments are

```
.STACK [size]
.DATA
.CODE [segment-name]
```

Each of these directives causes the assembler to generate the required SEGMENT statement and its matching ENDS. The default segment names (which you don't have to define) are STACK, _DATA, and _TEXT (the code segment for Tiny, Small, Compact, and Flat models). The break (or underline) character at the beginning of _DATA and _TEXT is intended. The default stack *size* is 1,024 bytes, which you may override. As the coding format indicates, you may also override the default *segment-name* for the code segment. You use these directives to identify where in the program the three segments are to be located. Note, however, that the instructions you now use to initialize the address of the data segment in DS are:

```
MOV   AX,@data  ;Initialize DS with
MOV   DS,AX  ;  address of data segment
```

Figure 4-3 gave an example of a program using conventionally defined segments. Figure 4-4 now provides the same example, but this time using the simplified segment directives .STACK, .DATA, and .CODE. The memory model is specified as Small in the fourth line. The stack is defined as 64 bytes (32 words). Note that the assembler does not gener-

```
      page   60,132
TITLE  A04ASM2 (EXE)  Move and add operations
;------------------------------------------------------
      .MODEL   SMALL
      .STACK   64                  ;Define stack
      .DATA                        ;Define data
FLDD   DW       215
FLDE   DW       125
FLDF   DW       ?
;------------------------------------------------------
      .CODE                        ;Define code segment
MAIN   PROC     FAR
      MOV      AX,@data            ;Set address of data
      MOV      DS,AX               ;  segment in DS

      MOV      AX,FLDD             ;Move 0215 to AX
      ADD      AX,FLDE             ;Add  0125 to AX
      MOV      FLDF,AX             ;Store sum in FLDF

      MOV      AX,4C00H            ;End processing
      INT      21H
MAIN   ENDP                        ;End of procedure
      END      MAIN                ;End of program
```

Figure 4-4 EXE Program with Simplified Segment Directives

ate conventional SEGMENT and ENDS statements, and you also don't code an ASSUME statement.

As you'll see in the next chapter, the assembler handles programs coded with simplified segment directives slightly differently from those using conventional segment directives.

The .STARTUP and .EXIT Directives

MASM 6.0 introduced the .STARTUP and .EXIT directives to simplify program initialization and termination. .STARTUP generates the instructions to initialize the segment registers, whereas .EXIT generates the INT 21H function 4CH instructions for exiting the program. These directives require the .MODEL directive and work for all memory models except Flat. For purposes of learning assembly language, examples in this book use the full sets of instructions and leave shortcuts to more experienced programmers.

INITIALIZING FOR PROTECTED MODE

Programs run under Windows in protected mode and define the Flat memory model. With segment addressing expanded to 32 bits, the single addressable program area may be up to 4 gigabytes in size. A skeleton model of a program is:

```
.386 or .486      ;Processor directive first
.MODEL FLAT, STDCALL
.STACK
.DATA             ;All data follows
.CODE             ;Instruction code follows
END
```

Coding the processor directive before the .MODEL statement causes the assembler to assume 32-bit addressing. The entry STDCALL tells the assembler to use standard conventions for names and procedure calls. The processor operates more efficiently because it does not have to convert segment:offsets to actual addresses. Where in real mode offsets for data and instructions are 16 bits, in protected mode offsets are 32 bits.

The use of DWORD to align segments on a doubleword address speeds up accessing memory for a 32-bit data bus. The USE32 type tells the assembler to generate code appropriate to 32-bit protected mode:

```
segment-name SEGMENT DWORD USE32
```

Initialization of the DS register could look like this, since on these processors, DS is still 16 bits in size:

```
MOV     EAX,DATASEG      ;Get address of data segment
MOV     DS,AX            ;Load 16-bit portion
```

The STI, CLI, IN, and OUT instructions, available in real mode, are not allowed in protected mode.

DEFINING TYPES OF DATA

As already discussed, the data segment in an .EXE program contains constants, work areas, and input/output areas. The assembler provides a set of directives that permits definitions of items by various types and lengths; for example, DB defines byte and DW defines word. A data item may contain an *undefined* (that is, uninitialized) value, or it may contain an initialized *constant,* defined either as a character string or as a numeric value. Here is the format for data definition:

Name.   A program that references a data item does so by means of a *name.* The name is otherwise optional, as indicated by the square brackets. The earlier section "Statements" provides the rules for names.

Directive (Dn).   The directives that define data items are DB (byte), DW (word), DD (doubleword), DF (farword), DQ (quadword), and DT (tenbytes), each of which explicitly indicates the length of the defined item. MASM 6.0 introduced the terms BYTE, WORD, DWORD, FWORD, QWORD, and TWORD, respectively, for these directives. However, the original terms are still in common use among the many versions of assembly language.

Expression.   The *expression* in an operand may specify an uninitialized value or a constant value. To indicate an uninitialized item, define the operand with a question mark, such as

```
        DATAX DB ?      ;Uninitialized item
```

In this case, when your program begins execution, the initial value of DATAX is unknown to you. The normal practice before using this item is to move some value into it, but it must fit the defined size.

You can use the operand to define a constant, such as

```
        DATAY DB 25     ;Initialized item
```

You can freely use this initialized value 25 throughout your program and can even change the value.

An expression may contain multiple constants separated by commas and limited only by the length of the line, as follows:

```
        DATAZ DB 21, 22, 23, 24, 25, 26, ...
```

The assembler defines these constants in adjacent bytes, from left to right. A reference to DATAZ is to the first 1-byte constant, 21 (you could think of the first byte as DATAZ+0), and a reference to DATAZ+1 is to the second constant, 22. For example, the instruction

```
                           MOV AL,DATAZ+3
```

loads the value 24 (18H) into the AL register. The expression also permits duplication of constants in a statement of the format

| [name] | Dn | repeat-count DUP(expression) ... |

The following examples illustrate duplication:

```
DW 10 DUP(?)          ;Ten words, uninitialized
DB 5 DUP(12)          ;Five bytes containing hex 0C0C0C0C0C
DB 3 DUP(5 DUP(4))    ;Fifteen 4s
```

The third example generates five copies of the digit 4 (44444) and duplicates that value three times, giving fifteen 4s in all.

An expression may define and initialize a *character string* or a *numeric constant*.

Character Strings

Character strings are used for descriptive data such as people's names and product descriptions. The string is defined within single quotes, such as 'PC', or within double quotes, such as "PC". The assembler stores the contents of the quotes as object code in normal ASCII format, without the apostrophes.

Oddly, under MASM, DB (or BYTE) is the only format that defines a character string exceeding two characters with the characters stored as left adjusted and in normal left-to-right sequence (like names and addresses). Consequently, DB is the conventional format for defining character data of any length. An example is

```
               DB 'Computer City'
```

If a string must contain a single or double quote, you can define it in one of these ways:

```
DB "Crazy Sam's CD Emporium"   ;Double quotes for string,
                                 single quote for apostrophe
DB 'Crazy Sam''s CD Emporium'   ;Single quotes for string, two
                                 single quotes for apostrophe
```

Numeric Constants

Numeric constants are used to define arithmetic values and memory addresses. The constant is not defined within quotes, but is followed by an optional *radix specifier,* such as H in the hexadecimal value 12H. For most of the data definition directives, the assembler stores the generated bytes in object code in reverse sequence, from right to left. Following are the various numeric formats.

Binary.   Binary format uses the binary digits 0 and 1, followed by the radix specifier B. A common use for binary format is to distinguish values for the bit-handling instructions AND, OR, XOR, and TEST.

Decimal.   Decimal format uses the decimal digits 0 through 9, optionally followed by the radix specifier D, such as 125 or 125D. *Although the assembler allows you to define values in decimal format as a coding convenience, it converts your decimal values to binary object code and represents them in hexadecimal.* For example, a definition of decimal 125 becomes hex 7D.

Hexadecimal.   Hex format uses the hex digits 0 through F, followed by the radix specifier H. Because the assembler expects that a reference beginning with a letter is a symbolic name, the first digit of a hex constant must be 0 to 9. Examples are 3DH and 0DE8H, which the assembler stores as 3D and (with bytes in reverse sequence) E80D, respectively.

Because the assembler converts all numeric values to binary (and represents them in hex), definitions of decimal 12, hex C, and binary 1100 all generate the same value: binary 00001100 or hex 0C, depending on how you view the contents of the byte.

Because the letters D and B act as both radix specifiers and hex digits, they could conceivably cause some confusion. As a solution, MASM 6.0 introduced the use of T (as in ten) and Y (as in binary) as radix specifiers for decimal and binary, respectively.

Real.   The assembler converts a given real value (a decimal or hex constant followed by the radix specifier R) into floating-point format for use with a numeric coprocessor.

Be sure to distinguish between the use of character and numeric constants. For example, a character constant defined as DB '24' generates two ASCII characters, represented as hex 3234. A numeric constant defined as DB 24 generates a binary number, represented as hex 18.

Directives for Defining Data

The conventional directives used to define data, along with the names introduced by MASM 6.0, are the following:

DEFINITION	CONVENTIONAL DIRECTIVE	MASM 6.0 DIRECTIVE
Byte	DB	BYTE
Word	DW	WORD
Doubleword	DD	DWORD
Farword	DF	FWORD
Quadword	DQ	QWORD
Tenbytes	DT	TBYTE

This text uses the conventional directives because of their common usage. The assembled program in Figure 4-5 provides examples of the DB, DW, DD, and DQ directives to define character strings and numeric constants. The generated object code, which you are urged to examine, is listed on the left. Note that the object code for uninitialized values appears as hex zeros. Because this program consists of only a data segment and has no executable instructions, it is not suitable for execution.

DB or BYTE: Define Byte.   A DB (or BYTE) numeric expression may define one or more 1-byte constants, each consisting of two hex digits. For unsigned numeric data, the range of values is 0 to 255; for signed data, the range of values is −128 to +127. The assembler converts numeric constants to binary object code (represented in hex).

In Figure 4-5, the first definition, BYTE1, uses '?' to specify an uninitialized value. Numeric DB constants are BYTE2, BYTE3, BYTE4, and BYTE5. For example, the assembler has converted the defined value 48 to hex 30.

A DB character expression may contain a string of any length up to the end of the line. For examples, see BYTE6 and BYTE7 in the figure. The hex object code shows the

```
                                          page 60,132
                            TITLE     A04DEFIN (EXE)   Define data directives
                                      .MODEL   SMALL
                                      .DATA
                            ;         DB - Define Bytes:
                            ;         ----------------
0000 00                     BYTE1     DB    ?            ;Uninitialized
0001 30                     BYTE2     DB    48           ;Decimal constant
0002 30                     BYTE3     DB    30H          ;Hex constant
0003 7A                     BYTE4     DB    01111010B    ;Binary constant
0004 000A[ 00 ]             BYTE5     DB    10 DUP(0)    ;Ten zeros
000E 50 43 20 45 6D 70      BYTE6     DB    'PC Emporium'
     6F 72 69 75 6D                                      ;Character string
0019 31 32 33 34 35         BYTE7     DB    '12345'      ;Numbers as chars
001E 01 4A 61 6E 02 46      BYTE8     DB    01,'Jan',02,'Feb',03,'Mar'
     65 62 03 4D 61 72                                   ;Table of months

                            ;         DW - Define Words:
                            ;         ----------------
002A FFF0                   WORD1     DW    0FFF0H       ;Hex constant
002C 007A                   WORD2     DW    01111010B    ;Binary constant
002E 001E R                 WORD3     DW    BYTE8        ;Address constant
0030 0002 0004 0006 0007    WORD4     DW    2,4,6,7,9    ;Table of 5 constants
     0009
003A 0008[ 0000 ]           WORD5     DW    8 DUP(0)     ;Six zeros

                            ;         DD - Define Doublewords:
                            ;         ----------------------
004A 00000000               DWORD1    DD    ?            ;Uninitialized
004E 0000A25A               DWORD2    DD    41562        ;Decimal value
0052 00000018 00000030      DWORD3    DD    24, 48       ;Two constants
005A 00000001               DWORD4    DD    BYTE3 - BYTE2 ;Difference
                                                         ;  betw addresses
                            ;         DQ - Define Quadwords:
                            ;         ------------------
005E 0000000000000000       QWORD1    DQ    0            ;Zero constant
0066 395E000000000000       QWORD2    DQ    05E39H       ;Hex constant
006E 5AA2000000000000       QWORD3    DQ    41562        ;Decimal constant
                            END
```

Figure 4-5   Definitions of Character and Numeric Data

ASCII character for each byte in normal left-to-right sequence, where 20H represents a blank character.

BYTE8 shows a mixture of numeric and string constants suitable for defining a table.

DW or WORD: Define Word.   The DW (or WORD) directive defines items that are one word (two bytes) in length. A DW numeric expression may define one or more one-word constants. For unsigned numeric data, the range of values is 0 to 65,535; for signed data, the range of values is −32,768 to +32,767.

The assembler converts DW numeric constants to binary object code (represented in hex), but stores the bytes in reverse sequence. Consequently, a decimal value defined as 12345 converts to hex 3039, but is stored as 3930.

In Figure 4-5, WORD1 and WORD2 define DW numeric constants. WORD3 defines the operand as an address—in this case, the offset address of BYTE8. The generated object code is 001E (the R to the right means relocatable), and a check of the figure shows that the offset address of BYTE8 (the leftmost column) is indeed 001E.

WORD4 defines a table of five numeric constants. Note that the length of each constant is one word (two bytes). WORD5 defines a table initialized with eight zeros.

Because a DW character expression under MASM is limited to two characters, it is of limited use for defining character strings.

DD or DWORD: Define Doubleword.   The DD (or DWORD) directive defines items that are a doubleword (four bytes) in length. A DD numeric expression may define one or more constants, each with a maximum of four bytes (eight hex digits). For unsigned numeric data, the range of values is 0 to 4,294,967,295; for signed data, the range of values is −2,147,483,648 to +2,147,483,647.

The assembler converts DD numeric constants to binary object code (represented in hex), but stores the bytes in *reverse sequence.* Consequently, the assembler converts a decimal value defined as 12345678 to 00BC614EH and stores it as 4E61BC00H.

In Figure 4-5, DWORD2 defines a DD numeric constant, and DWORD3 defines two numeric constants. DWORD4 generates the numeric difference between two defined addresses; in this case, the result is the length of BYTE2, or one byte.

A DD character expression under MASM is limited to two characters and is as trivial as those for DW. The assembler right-adjusts the characters in the 4-byte doubleword.

DQ or QWORD: Define Quadword.   The DQ (or QWORD) directive defines items that are four words (eight bytes) in length. A DQ numeric expression may define one or more constants, each with a maximum of eight bytes, or 16 hex digits. The largest positive quadword hex number is 7 followed by 15 Fs. As an indication of the magnitude of this number, hex 1 followed by 15 zeros equals the decimal number 1,152,921,504,606,846,976.

The assembler handles DQ numeric values and character strings just as it does DD and DW numeric values. In Figure 4-5, QWORD1, QWORD2, and QWORD3 illustrate numeric values.

Display of the Data Segment

There are two steps required to convert a source program into machine code: assembling and linking. Although the assembler generated no error messages for Figure 4-5, the linker displayed "Warning: No STACK Segment" and "There were 1 errors detected." Despite the warning, you can still use DEBUG to view the object code, which is shown in Figure 4-6.

If you want to peek ahead in Chapter 5, you may assemble and link the program. Then use DEBUG to load the .EXE file, and key in D DS:100 for a display of the data. The right side of the display shows the ASCII representation, such as "PC Emporium," whereas the hexadecimal values on the left indicate the actual stored contents. Your display should be identical to Figure 4-6 for offsets 0100 through 019D. Expect your segment address (0D98 in the figure) and data following the end of the program to differ.

The reason you issue DS:100 for the display is because the loader set DS with the address of the PSP, but the data segment for this program begins 100 bytes after that address. Later, when you use DEBUG for .EXE programs that initialize DS to the address of the data segment, you use DS:0 to display it.

EQUATE DIRECTIVES

The assembler provides Equal-Sign, EQU, and TEXTEQU directives for redefining symbolic names with other names and numeric values with names. These directives do not generate any data storage; that is, a program cannot, say, add to an EQU item when it executes. Instead, the assembler uses the defined value to substitute in other statements.

The advantage of equate directives is that many statements may use the assigned value. If the value has to be changed, you need change only the equate statement. The result is a program that is more readable and easier to maintain.

The Equal-Sign Directive. The Equal-Sign directive enables you to assign the value of an expression to a name, and may do so any number of times in a program. The following examples illustrate its use:

```
VALUE_OF_PI = 3.1416
RIGHT_COL = 79
SCREEN_POSITIONS = 80 * 25
```

```
-d ds:100
0D98:0100   00 30 30 7A 00 00 00 00-00 00 00 00 00 00 50 43   .00z.........PC
0D98:0110   20 45 6D 70 6F 72 69 75-6D 31 32 33 34 35 01 4A   .Emporium12345.J
0D98:0120   61 6E 02 46 65 62 03 4D-61 72 F0 FF 7A 00 1E 00   an.Feb.Mar..z...
0D98:0130   02 00 04 00 06 00 07 00-09 00 00 00 00 00 00 00   ................
0D98:0140   00 00 00 00 00 00 00 00-00 00 00 00 00 00 5A A2   ..............Z.
0D98:0150   00 00 18 00 00 00 30 00-00 00 01 00 00 00 00 00   ......0.........
0D98:0160   00 00 00 00 00 00 39 5E-00 00 00 00 00 00 5A A2   ......9^......Z.
0D98:0170   00 00 00 00 00 00 22 DE-42 D9 21 DE 42 D9 21 DE   ......".B.!.B.!.

            <——————— hexadecimal representation ———————>  <——— ASCII ———>
```

Figure 4-6   Displaying the Data Segment

Examples of the use of the preceding directives are:

```
IMUL AX,VALUE_OF_PI        ;Multiply AX by 3.1416
CMP BL,RIGHT_COL           ;Compare BL to 79
MOV CX,SCREEN_POSITIONS    ;Move 2000 to CX
```

When using this directive for defining a doubleword value, first use the .386 directive to notify the assembler:

```
.386
DBLWORD1 = 42A3B05CH
```

The EQU Directive.   Consider the following EQU statement coded in the data segment:

```
FACTOR EQU 12
```

The name, in this case FACTOR, may be any name acceptable to the assembler. Now, whenever the word FACTOR appears in an instruction or another directive, the assembler substitutes the value 12. For example, the assembler converts the directive

```
TABLEX DB FACTOR DUP(?)
```

to its equivalent value

```
TABLEX DB 12 DUP(?)
```

TABLEX may be defined by EQU only once so that it cannot be redefined by another EQU. An instruction may also contain an equated operand, as in the following:

```
RIGHT_COL   EQU 79
            . . .
            MOV CX,RIGHT_COL ;Move 79 to CX
```

You can also equate symbolic names, as in the following code:

```
ANNL_TEMP DW    0
                . . .
AT          EQU ANNL_TEMP
MPY         EQU MUL
```

The first EQU equates the nickname AT to the defined item ANNL_TEMP. For any instruction that contains the operand AT, the assembler replaces it with the address of ANNL_TEMP. The second EQU enables a program to use the word MPY in place of the regular symbolic instruction MUL.

The TEXTEQU Directive.   MASM 6.0 introduced a TEXTEQU directive for redefining text data with the format

| *name* | TEXTEQU | *<text>* |

You can define character *text* within angle brackets, for example, like this:

```
PROMPT_MSSGE TEXTEQU <'Add, Change, or Delete?'>
```

and use it like this:

```
USER_PROMPT DB PROMPT_MSSGE
```

The assembler converts this definition to

```
USER_PROMPT DB 'Add, Change, or Delete?'
```

KEY POINTS

- A semicolon precedes a comment on a line.
- Reserved words in assembly language are used for their own purposes, only under special conditions.
- An identifier is a name that you apply to items in your program. The two types of identifiers are *name*, which refers to the address of a data item, and *label,* which refers to the address of an instruction.
- An operation is commonly used for defining data areas and coding instructions. An operand provides information for the operation to act on.
- A program consists of one or more segments, each of which begins on a paragraph boundary.
- The ENDS directive ends a segment, ENDP ends a procedure, and END ends the program.
- The ASSUME directive associates segment registers CS, DS, and SS with their appropriate segment names.
- For an .EXE program, you normally initialize DS with the address of the data segment.
- For the simplified segment directives, you initialize the memory model before defining any segment.
- INT 21H function 4CH is the standard instruction for exiting a program.
- Names of data items should be unique and descriptive.
- DB (or BYTE) is the preferred format for defining character strings, since it permits strings longer than two bytes and converts them to normal left-to-right sequence.
- Decimal and binary (hex) constants generate different values. Consider the effect of adding decimal 25 versus that of adding hex 25:

```
ADD CX,25     ;Add 25
ADD CX,25H    ;Add 37
```

- For DW, DD, and DQ, the assembler stores numeric values in object code with the bytes in reverse sequence.
- DB items are used for processing half registers (AL, BL, etc.), DW for full registers (AX, BX, etc.), and DD for extended registers (EAX, EBX, etc.). Longer numeric items require special handling.

REVIEW QUESTIONS AND EXERCISES

4-1. Distinguish between a compiler and an assembler.

4-2. What is a reserved word in assembly language? Give two examples.

4-3. What are the two types of identifiers in assembly language?

4-4. For the following items defined in a data segment, determine which are valid: (a) $50, (b) AT&T, (c) @$_A, (d) 23AC, (e) EBX. If invalid, explain.

4-5. Explain the difference between an instruction and a directive, and give two examples of each.

4-6. Give the directives that cause the assembler when listing a program (a) to print a heading at the top of a page, and (b) to advance to a new page.

4-7. In what way, if any, does the assembler treat upper- and lowercase letters differently?

4-8. The format for the SEGMENT directive is

```
name SEGMENT align combine 'class'
```

Explain the purpose of (a) align, (b) combine, (c) 'class'.

4-9. (a) Explain the purpose of a procedure. (b) When do you define a procedure as NEAR? (c) When do you define a procedure as FAR? (d) How do you define the beginning and the end of a procedure?

4-10. What statements are concerned with ending (a) a procedure, (b) a segment, (c) a program?

4-11. Identify the statement that ends an assembly and the statements that end execution.

4-12. Given the names STKSEG, DATSEG, and CODSEG for the stack, data segment, and code segment, respectively, code the required ASSUME statement.

4-13. Consider the instruction MOV AX,4C00H used with INT 21H. (a) Explain what the instruction performs. (b) Explain the purpose of the 4C00H.

4-14. For the simplified segment directives, the .MODEL directive provides for Tiny, Small, Medium, Compact, Large, and Flat models. Under what circumstances would you use each model?

4-15. Give the lengths in bytes generated by the following data directives: (a) DW, (b) DQ, (c) DB, (d) DD.

4-16. Define a character string named CO_NAME containing "Internet Services" as a constant.

4-17. Define the following numeric values in data items named ITEM1 through ITEM5, respectively:
(a) A 1-byte item containing the hex equivalent to decimal 71.
(b) A 2-byte item containing an undefined value.
(c) A 4-byte item containing the hex equivalent to decimal 7524.
(d) A 1-byte item containing the binary equivalent to decimal 47.
(e) An item containing the consecutive word values 6, 9, 14, 18, 23, 29, 31, and 38.

4-18. Show the generated hex object code for (a) DB 82, (b) DB '82', (c) DB 4 DUP('5').

4-19. Determine the hex object code stored by the assembler for (a) DB 72, (b) DW 2ABEH, (c) DD 1EB6C3H, (d) DQ 24C3E29.

4-20. (a) Use an EQU directive to redefine the value 16H as ATTRIBUTE. (b) Use a MOV instruction to move ATTRIBUTE to the BL register.

Chapter 5

ASSEMBLING, LINKING, AND EXECUTING PROGRAMS

Objective: To cover the steps in assembling, linking, and executing assembly language programs.

INTRODUCTION

This chapter explains the procedure for keying in an assembly language program and for assembling, linking, and executing it. The symbolic instructions that you code in assembly language are known as the *source program*. You use an assembler program to translate the source program into machine code, known as the *object program*. Finally, you use a linker program to complete the machine addressing for the object program, generating an *executable module*.

The sections on assembling explain how to request execution of the assembler program, which provides diagnostics (including any error messages) and generates the object program. Also explained are details of the assembler listing and, in general terms, how the assembler processes a source program.

The sections on linking explain how to request execution of the linker program so that you can generate an executable module. Also explained are details of the generated link map, as well as the linker's diagnostics. Finally, a section describes how to request execution of the executable module.

The last section explains how to code, convert, and execute .COM programs.

PREPARING A PROGRAM FOR ASSEMBLING AND EXECUTION

In Chapter 4, Figure 4-3 illustrated only the source code for a program not yet in executable format. For keying in this program, you could use any editor or word processing program that produces a standard unformatted ASCII file. You can gain a lot of productivity by loading your programs and files into a RAM disk. Call up your editor program, key in the statements for the program in Figure 4-3, and name the resulting file A05ASM1.ASM.

Although spacing is not important to the assembler, a program is more readable if you keep the name, operation, operand, and comments consistently aligned on columns. Many editors have tab stops every eight positions to facilitate aligning columns.

Once you have keyed in all the statements for the program, examine the code for accuracy. As it stands, this source program is just a text file that cannot execute—you must first assemble and link it. Figure 5-1 provides a chart of the steps required to assemble, link, and execute a program.

1. The *assembly step* involves translating the source code into object code and generating an intermediate .OBJ (object) file, or module. (You have already seen examples of machine code and source code in earlier chapters.) One of the assembler's tasks is to calculate the offsets for every data item in the data segment and for every instruction in the code segment. The assembler also creates a *header* immediately in front of the generated .OBJ module; part of the header contains

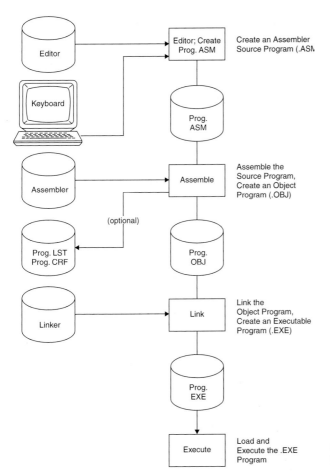

Figure 5-1 Steps in Assembly, Link, and Execute

information about incomplete addresses. The .OBJ module is not quite in executable form.

2. The *link step* involves converting the .OBJ module to an .EXE (executable) machine code module. The linker's tasks include completing any addresses left open by the assembler and combining separately assembled programs into one executable module.

3. The last step is to *load* the program for execution. Because the loader knows where the program is going to load in memory, it is now able to resolve any remaining addresses still left incomplete in the header. The loader drops the header and creates a program segment prefix (PSP) immediately before the program loaded in memory.

Assembling a Source Program

The assembler converts your source statements into machine code and displays any error messages on the screen. Typical errors include a name that violates naming conventions, an operation that is spelled incorrectly (such as MOVE instead of MOV), and an operand containing a name that is not defined. Because there are many possible errors (100 or more) and many different assembler versions, you may refer to your assembler manual for a list. The assembler attempts to correct some errors but, in any event, reload your editor, correct the .ASM source program, and reassemble it.

Optional output files from the assembly step are object (.OBJ), listing (.LST), and cross reference (.CRF or .SBR). You usually request an .OBJ file, which is required for linking a program into executable form. You'll probably often request an .LST file, especially when it contains error diagnostics or you want to examine the generated machine code. A .CRF file is useful for a large program where you want to see which instructions reference which data items. Also, requesting a .CRF file causes the assembler to generate statement numbers for items in the .LST file to which the .CRF file refers. Later sections cover these files in detail.

See Appendix E for details on assembling and linking programs.

Using Conventional Segment Definitions

Figure 5-2 provides the listing that the assembler produced under the name A05ASM1.LST. The line width is 132 positions as specified by the PAGE entry.

Note at the top of the listing how the assembler has acted on the PAGE and TITLE directives. None of the directives, including SEGMENT, PROC, ASSUME, and END, generates machine code, since they are just messages to the assembler. The listing is arranged horizontally according to these sections:

1. At the extreme left is the number for each line listed.

2. The second section shows the hex offset addresses of data items and instructions.

3. The third section shows the generated machine code in hexadecimal format.

4. The section to the right is the original source code.

The program itself is organized vertically into three segments, each with its own offset values for data or instructions. Each segment contains a SEGMENT directive that notifies the assembler to align the segment on an address that is evenly divisible by hex 10—the

```
A05ASM1 (EXE)   Move and add operations                    Page   1-1
 1                                page   60,132
 2                        TITLE   A05ASM1 (EXE)  Move and add operations
 3                        ; ----------------------------------------------
 4 0000            STACK   SEGMENT PARA STACK 'Stack'
 5 0000  0020[             DW      32 DUP(0)
 6        0000
 7            ]
 8
 9 0040            STACK   ENDS
10                        ; ----------------------------------------------
11 0000            DATASEG SEGMENT PARA 'Data'
12 0000  00D7      FLDD    DW      215
13 0002  007D      FLDE    DW      125
14 0004  0000      FLDF    DW      ?
15 0006            DATASEG ENDS
16                        ; ----------------------------------------------
17 0000            CODESEG SEGMENT PARA 'Code'
18 0000            MAIN    PROC    FAR
19                        ASSUME  SS:STACK,DS:DATASEG,CS:CODESEG
20 0000  B8 ---- R        MOV     AX,DATASEG    ;Set address of data
21 0003  8E D8            MOV     DS,AX         ;  segment in DS
22
23 0005  A1 0000 R        MOV     AX,FLDD       ;Move 0215 to AX
24 0008  03 06 0002 R     ADD     AX,FLDE       ;Add  0125 to AX
25 000C  A3 0004 R        MOV     FLDF,AX       ;Store sum in FLDF
26 000F  B8 4C00          MOV     AX,4C00H      ;End processing
27 0012  CD 21            INT     21H
28 0014            MAIN    ENDP                 ;End of procedure
29 0014            CODESEG ENDS                 ;End of segment
30                        END     MAIN          ;End of program
```

```
Segments and Groups:
            N a m e          Length   Align    Combine    Class
CODESEG . . . . . . . . . .  0014     PARA     NONE       'CODE'
DATASEG . . . . . . . . . .  0006     PARA     NONE       'DATA'
STACK   . . . . . . . . . .  0040     PARA     STACK      'STACK'

Symbols:
            N a m e          Type     Value    Attr
MAIN    . . . . . . . . . .  F PROC   0000     CODESEG Length = 0014

FLDD . . . . . . . . . . .  L WORD   0000     DATASEG
FLDE . . . . . . . . . . .  L WORD   0002     DATASEG
FLDF . . . . . . . . . . .  L WORD   0004     DATASEG

0 Warning Errors
0 Severe  Errors
```

Figure 5-2 Assembled Program with Conventional Segments

SEGMENT statement itself generates no machine code. The program loader stores the contents of each segment in memory and initializes its address in a segment register, that is, STACK in SS, DATASEG in DS, and CODESEG in CS. The beginning of the segment is offset zero bytes from that address.

Stack Segment.   The stack segment contains a DW (Define Word) directive that defines 32 words, each generating a zero value designated by (0). This definition of 32 words is a realistic size for a stack because a large program may require many interrupts for input/output and calls to subprograms, all involving use of the stack. The stack segment ends at offset 0040H, which is equivalent to decimal value 64 (32 words X 2 bytes). The assembler shows the generated constant to the left as 0020[0000]; that is, 20H (32) zero words.

If the stack is too small to contain all the items pushed onto it, neither the assembler nor the linker warns you, and the executing program may crash in an unpredictable way.

Data Segment. The program's data segment, DATASEG, contains three defined values, all in DW (Define Word) format:

1. FLDD defines a word (two bytes) initialized with decimal value 215, which the assembler has translated to 00D7H (shown on the left).
2. FLDE defines a word initialized with decimal value 125, assembled as 007DH. The actual stored values of these two constants are, respectively, D700 and 7D00, which you can check with DEBUG.
3. FLDF is coded as a DW with ? in the operand to define a word with an uninitialized constant. The listing shows its contents as 0000.

The offset addresses of FLDD, FLDE, and FLDF are, respectively, 0000, 0002, and 0004, which relate to their field sizes.

Code Segment. The program's code segment, CODESEG, contains the program's executable code, all in one procedure (PROC). Three statements establish the addressability of the data segment:

```
                    ASSUME SS:STACK,DS:DATASEG,CS:CODESEG
0000 B8 —— R        MOV AX,DATASEG
0003 8E D8          MOV DS,AX
```

- The ASSUME directive relates each segment to its corresponding segment register. ASSUME simply provides information to the assembler, which generates no machine code for it.
- The first MOV instruction "stores" DATASEG in the AX register. Now, an instruction cannot actually store a segment in a register—the assembler recognizes the reference to a segment and assumes its address. Note the machine code to the left: B8----R. The four hyphens mean that at this point the assembler cannot determine the address of DATASEG; the system determines this address only when the object program is linked and loaded for execution. Because the loader may locate a program anywhere in memory, the assembler leaves the address open and indicates the fact with an R (for relocatable); the loader is to replace the incomplete address with the actual one.
- The second MOV moves the contents of the AX register to DS. Because there is no valid instruction for a direct move from memory to DS, two instructions are needed to initialize it.

Note that the program does not require the ES register, although many programmers initialize it as a standard practice.

Although the loader automatically initializes SS and CS when it loads a program for execution, it is your responsibility to initialize DS, and ES if required.

While all this business may seem unduly involved, at this point you really don't have to understand it. All programs in this book use a standard definition and initialization, and you simply have to reproduce this code for each of your programs. To this end, store a skeleton assembly program on disk, and for each new program that you want to create, copy the skeleton program into a file under a suitable name and use an editor to complete the additional instructions.

The first instruction after initializing the DS register is MOV AX,FLDD, which begins at offset location 0005 and generates machine code A1 0000. The space in the listing between A1 (the operation) and 0000 (the operand) is only for readability. The next instruction, ADD AX,FLDE, begins at offset location 0008 and generates four bytes of machine code. The instruction, MOV FLDF,AC, copies the sum in AX to FLDF at offset 0004 in the data segment. In this example, machine instructions are two, three, or four bytes in length.

The last statement in the program, END, contains the operand MAIN, which relates to the name of the PROC at offset 0000. This is the location in the code segment where the program loader is to transfer control for starting execution.

Following this program listing are a Segments and Groups table and a Symbols table.

Segments and Groups Table. This table shows any defined segments and groups. Note that segments are not listed in the same sequence as they are coded; the assembler used for this example lists them in alphabetic sequence by name. (This program contains no groups, which is a later topic.) The table provides the length in bytes of each segment, the alignment (all are paragraphs), the combine type, and the class.

Symbols Table. This table provides the names of data fields in the data segment (FLDD, FLDE, and FLDF) and the labels applied to instructions in the code segment. For MAIN (the only entry in the example), Type F PROC means far procedure (far because MAIN, as the entry-point for execution, must be known outside this program). The Value column gives the offset from the beginning of the segment for names, labels, and procedures. The column headed "Attr" (for attribute) provides the segment in which each item is defined.

MASM 6.n also lists a Procedures, Parameters, and Group Table. Appendix E explains these tables in more detail.

Using Simplified Segment Directives

In Chapter 4, Figure 4-4 showed how to code a program using the simplified segment directives. Figure 5-3 now provides the assembled listing of that program. For the simplified segment directives, initialize DS like this:

```
MOV AX,@data
MOV DS,AX
```

The first part of the symbol table under "Segments and Groups" shows the three segments renamed by the assembler and listed alphabetically:

```
A05ASM2 (EXE)   Move and add operations                        Page    1-1
1                                       page  60,132
2                               TITLE   A05ASM2 (EXE)  Move and add operations
3                               ;---------------------------------------------
4                                       .MODEL   SMALL
5                                       .STACK   64              ;Define stack
6                                       .DATA                    ;Define data
7 0000  00D7          FLDD              DW       215
8 0002  007D          FLDE              DW       125
9 0004  0000          FLDF              DW       ?
10                              ;---------------------------------------------
11                                      .CODE                    ;Define code segment
12 0000               MAIN              PROC     FAR
13 0000  B8 ---- R                      MOV      AX,@data        ;Set address of data
14 0003  8E D8                          MOV      DS,AX           ;    segment in DS
15
16 0005  A1 0000 R                      MOV      AX,FLDD         ;Move 0215 to AX
17 0008  03 06 0002 R                   ADD      AX,FLDE         ;Add  0125 to AX
18 000C  A3 0004 R                      MOV      FLDF,AX         ;Store sum in FLDF
19
20 000F  B8 4C00                        MOV      AX,4C00H        ;End processing
21 0012  CD 21                          INT      21H
22 0014               MAIN              ENDP                     ;End of procedure
23                                      END      MAIN            ;End of program
```

```
Segments and Groups:
           N a m e                  Length   Align     Combine   Class
DGROUP . . . . . . . . . . . .      GROUP
  _DATA  . . . . . . . . . . .      0006     WORD      PUBLIC    'DATA'
  STACK  . . . . . . . . . . .      0040     PARA      STACK     'STACK'
_TEXT  . . . . . . . . . . . .      0014     WORD      PUBLIC    'CODE'

Symbols:
           N a m e                  Type     Value     Attr
MAIN   . . . . . . . . . . . .      F PROC   0000      _TEXT   Length = 0014

FLDD . . . . . . . . . . . . .      L WORD   0000      _DATA
FLDE . . . . . . . . . . . . .      L WORD   0002      _DATA
FLDF . . . . . . . . . . . . .      L WORD   0004      _DATA

@CODE  . . . . . . . . . . . .      TEXT     _TEXT
@FILENAME  . . . . . . . . . .      TEXT     a05asm2

       0 Warning Errors
       0 Severe  Errors
```

Figure 5-3   Assembled Program with Simplified Segment Directives

- _DATA, with a length of 6 bytes
- STACK, with a length of 40H (64 bytes)
- _TEXT, for the code segment, with a length of 14H (20 bytes)

Listed under the heading "Symbols" are names defined in the program or default names. The simplified segment directives provide a number of predefined equates, which begin with an @ symbol and which you are free to reference in a program. As well as @data, they are:

```
@CODE       Equated to the name of the code segment, _TEXT
@FILENAME   Name of the program
```

You may use @code and @data in ASSUME and executable statements, such as MOV AX,@data.

TWO-PASS ASSEMBLER

Assemblers typically make two or more passes through a source program in order to resolve forward references to addresses not yet encountered in the program. During pass 1, the assembler reads the entire source program and constructs a symbol table of names and labels used in the program, that is, names of data fields and program labels and their relative locations (offsets) within the segment. You can see such a symbol table immediately following the assembled program in Figure 5-3, where the offsets for FLDD, FLDE, and FLDF are 0000, 0002, and 0004 bytes, respectively. Although the program defines no instruction labels, they would appear in the code segment with their own offsets. Pass 1 determines the amount of code to be generated for each instruction.

During pass 2, the assembler uses the symbol table that it constructed in pass 1. Now that it knows the length and relative position of each data field and instruction, it can complete the object code for each instruction. It then produces, on request, the various object (.OBJ), list (.LST), and cross-reference (.CRF) files.

A potential problem in pass 1 is a *forward reference:* Certain types of instructions in the code segment may reference the label of an instruction, but the assembler has not yet encountered its definition. MASM constructs object code based on what it supposes is the length of each generated machine language instruction. If there are any differences between pass 1 and pass 2 concerning instruction lengths, MASM issues an error message "Phase error between passes." Such errors are relatively rare, but if one appears, you'll have to trace its cause and correct it.

Since version 6.0, MASM handles instruction lengths more effectively, taking as many passes through the file as necessary. TASM can assemble a program in one pass, but you may request that it take more than one if it is having difficulty with forward references.

LINKING AN OBJECT PROGRAM

When your program is free of error messages, the next step is to link the object module, A05ASM1.OBJ, that was produced by the assembler and that contains only machine code. (MASM 6.1 performs assemble and link with the ML command.) The linker performs the following functions:

- Combines, if requested, more than one separately assembled module into one executable program, such as two or more assembly programs or an assembly program with a C program.
- Generates an .EXE module and initializes it with special instructions to facilitate its subsequent loading for execution.

Once you have linked one or more .OBJ modules into an .EXE module, you may execute the .EXE module any number of times. But whenever you need to make a change in the program, you must correct the source program, assemble again into an .OBJ module, and link the .OBJ module into an .EXE module. Even if initially these steps are not entirely clear, you will find that with only a little experience, they become automatic.

The output files from the link step are executable (.EXE), map (.MAP), and library (.LIB). See Appendix E for details on linking programs.

Link Map for the First Program.   For the program A05ASM1, the linker produced this map:

START	STOP	LENGTH	NAME	CLASS
00000H	0003FH	0040H	STACK	STACK
00040H	00045H	0006H	DATASEG	DATA
00050H	00063H	0014H	CODESEG	CODE
Program entry point at 0005:0000				

- The stack is the first segment and begins at offset 0 bytes from the start of the program. Because it is defined as 32 words, it is 64 bytes long, as its length (40H) indicates.
- The data segment begins at the next available paragraph boundary, offset 40H.
- The code segment begins at the next paragraph boundary, offset 50H. (Some assemblers rearrange the segments into alphabetical order.)
- Program entry point 0005:0000, which is in the form segment:offset, refers to the relative address of the first executable instruction. In effect, the relative starting address is at segment location 5[0], offset 0 bytes, which corresponds to the code segment boundary at 50H. The program loader uses this value when it loads the program into memory for execution.

At this stage, the only error that you are likely to encounter is entering a wrong filename. The solution is to restart with the link command.

Link Map for the Second Program.   The link map for the second program, A05ASM2, which uses simplified segment directives, shows a somewhat different setup from that of the previous program. First, the assembler has physically rearranged the segments into alphabetical order; second, succeeding segments are aligned on word (not paragraph) boundaries, as shown by the link map:

START	STOP	LENGTH	NAME	CLASS
00000H	00013H	0014H	_TEXT	CODE
00014H	00019H	0006H	_DATA	DATA
00020H	0005FH	0040H	STACK	STACK
Program entry point at 0000:0000				

- The code segment is now the first segment and begins at offset 0 bytes from the start of the program.
- The data segment begins at the next word boundary, offset 14H.
- The stack begins at the next word boundary, offset 20H.
- The program entry point is now 0000:0000, which means that the relative location of the code segment begins at segment 0, offset 0.

EXECUTING A PROGRAM

Having assembled and linked a program, you can now execute it. If the .EXE file is in the default drive, you could ask the loader to read it into memory for execution by typing

```
A05ASM1.EXE or A05ASM1 (without the .EXE extension)
```

If you omit typing the file extension, the loader assumes it is an executable .EXE or .COM program. However, since this program produces no visible output, it is suggested that you run it under DEBUG and use Trace commands to step through its execution. Key in the following, including the .EXE extension:

```
DEBUG n:A05ASM1.EXE
```

DEBUG loads the .EXE program module and displays its hyphen prompt.

To view the stack segment, key in D SS:0. The stack contains all zeros because it was initialized that way.

To view the code segment, key in D CS:0. Compare the displayed machine code with that of the code segment in the assembled listing:

```
B8----8ED8A10000 ...
```

In this case, the assembled listing does not accurately show the machine code, since the assembler did not know the address for the operand of the first instruction. You can now determine this address by examining the displayed code.

To view the contents of the registers, press R followed by <Enter>. SP (Stack Pointer) should contain 0040H, which is the size of the stack (32 words = 64 bytes = 40H). IP (Instruction Pointer) should be 0000H. SS and CS are properly initialized for execution; their values depend on where in memory your program is loaded.

The first instruction MOV AX,xxxx is ready to execute—it and the following MOV instruction are about to initialize the DS register. To execute the first MOV, press T (for Trace) followed by <Enter> and note the effect on IP. To execute the second MOV, again press T followed by <Enter>. Check DS, which is now initialized with the segment address.

The third MOV loads the contents of FLDD into AX. Press T again and note that AX now contains 00D7. Now press T to execute the ADD instruction and note that AX contains 0154. Press T to cause MOV to store AX in offset 0004 of the data segment.

To check the contents of the data segment, key in D DS:0. The operation displays the three data items as D7 00 7D 00 54 01, with the bytes for each word in reverse sequence.

At this point, you can use L to reload and rerun the program or press Q to quit the DEBUG session.

THE CROSS-REFERENCE LISTING

The assembler generates an optional file that you can use to produce a cross-reference listing of a program's identifiers, or symbols. The file extension is .SBR for MASM 6.1, .CRF for MASM 5.1, and .XRF for TASM. However, you still have to convert the file to a properly sorted cross-reference file. See Appendix E for details on creating this file.

Figure 5-4 shows the cross-reference listing produced for the program in Figure 5-2. The symbols in the first column are in alphabetic order. The numbers in the second column, shown as n#, indicate the line in the .LST file where each symbol is defined. Numbers to the right of this column are line numbers showing where the symbol is referenced by other statements. For example, CODESEG is defined in line 17 and is referenced in lines 19 and 29. FLDF is defined in line 14 and referenced in line 25+, where the "+" means its value is modified during program execution (by MOV FLDF,AX).

Assembling programs generates a lot of redundant files. You can safely delete .OBJ, .CRF, and .LST files. Keep .ASM source programs in case of further changes and .EXE files for executing the programs.

ERROR DIAGNOSTICS

The assembler provides diagnostics for any programming errors that violate its rules. The program in Figure 5-5 is similar to the one in Figure 5-2, except that it has a number of intentional errors inserted for illustrative purposes. The diagnostics will vary by assembler version. Here are the errors:

LINE	EXPLANATION
9	The definition of FLDF requires an operand.
14	DX should be coded as DS, although the assembler does not know that this is an error.
16	AS should be coded as AX.

```
Symbol Cross-Reference   (# definition, + modification)

MAIN . . . . . . . . . . .    18#   28    30

CODE . . . . . . . . . . .    17
CODESEG  . . . . . . . . .    17#   19    29

DATA . . . . . . . . . . .    11
DATASEG  . . . . . . . . .    11#   15    19    20

FLDD . . . . . . . . . . .    12#   23
FLDE . . . . . . . . . . .    13#   24
FLDF . . . . . . . . . . .    14#   25+

STACK. . . . . . . . . . .     4
STACK  . . . . . . . . . .     4#    9    19
```

Figure 5-4   Cross-Reference Table

```
1                                    page 60,132
2                          TITLE     A05ASM3 (EXE)  Coding errors
3                          ; ------------------------------------------------
4                                    .MODEL  SMALL
5                                    .STACK  64
6                                    .DATA
7 0000   00AF         FLDD         DW        175
8 0002   0096         FLDE         DW        150
9 0004                FLDF         DW
a05asm3.ASM(9): error A2027: Operand expected
10                         ; ------------------------------------------------
11                                   .CODE
12 0000               MAIN         PROC      FAR
13 0000   B8 ---- R                MOV       AX,@data     ;Address of data
14 0003   8B D0                    MOV       DX,AX        ;   segment in DS
15
16                                 MOV       AS,FLDD      ;Move 0175 to AX
a05asm3.ASM(16): error A2009: Symbol not defined: AS
17 0005   03 06 0002 R             ADD       AX,FLDE      ;Add  0150 to AX
18 0009   A3 0000 U                MOV       FLDQ,AX      ;Store sum in FLDF
a05asm3.ASM(18): error A2009: Symbol not defined: FLDQ
19 000C   A2 0000 R                MOV       FLDD,AL      ;Store byte value
a05asm3.ASM(19): warning A4031: Operand types must match
20 000F   B8 4C00                  MOV       AX,4C00H     ;End processing
21 0012   CD 21                    INT       21H
22 0014               MAIN         ENDP
a05asm3.ASM(22): error A2006: Phase error between passes
23                                 END       MIAN
a05asm3.ASM(23): error A2009: Symbol not defined: MIAN

1 Warning Errors
5 Severe  Errors
```

Figure 5-5   Assembler Error Diagnostics

18   FLDQ should be coded as FLDF.

19   Field sizes (byte and word) must agree (warning).

22   Correcting the other errors will cause this diagnostic to disappear.

23   MIAN should be coded as MAIN.

Error message 22, "Phase error between passes," occurs when addresses generated in pass 1 of a two-pass assembler differ from those of pass 2. To isolate an obscure error under MASM 5.1, use the /D option to list both the pass 1 and the pass 2 files, and compare the offset addresses.

THE ASSEMBLER LOCATION COUNTER

The assembler maintains a *location counter* that it uses to account for each defined item in the data segment. Figures 5-2 and 5-3 illustrate its effect by means of the three defined data items:

```
0000 ... FLDD DW ...
0002 ... FLDE DW ...
0004 ... FLDF DW ...
```

Initially, the location counter is set at 0, where the assembler establishes the first data item, FLDD. Because FLDD is defined as a word, the assembler advances the location counter by 2, to 0002, where it establishes FLDE. Because FLDE is also defined as a word, the assembler again advances its location counter by 2, to 0004, for the next data item, FLDF, also a word. The location counter is again advanced by 2, to 0006, but there are no further data items.

The assembler provides a number of ways to change the current value in the location counter. For example, you can use EQU to redefine data items with different names (Chapter 4), use the ORG directive to begin a program at a particular offset (the next section), and the EVEN or ALIGN directive to facilitate aligning an address on an even-numbered boundary (see Chapter 6).

WRITING .COM PROGRAMS

For an .EXE program, the linker automatically generates a particular format and, when storing it on disk, precedes it with a special header block that is 512 bytes or more long. (Chapter 23 provides details of header blocks.)

You can also write .COM programs for execution. The advantages of .COM programs are that they are smaller than comparable .EXE programs and are more easily adapted to act as resident programs. The .COM format has its roots in earlier days of microcomputers, when program size was limited to 64K and accordingly somewhat primitive and limited.

Differences between an .EXE and a .COM Program

Significant differences between a program that is to execute as .EXE and one that is to execute as .COM involve the program's size, segmentation, and initialization.

Program Size. A .COM program uses one segment for both instructions and data, basically restricted to a maximum of 64K, including the program segment prefix (PSP). The PSP is a 256-byte (100H) block that the program loader inserts immediately preceding .COM and .EXE programs when it loads them from disk into memory.

A .COM program is always smaller than its counterpart .EXE program; one reason is that a 512-byte header record that precedes an .EXE program on disk does not precede a .COM program. (Don't confuse the header record, covered in Chapter 23, with the PSP.) A .COM program is an absolute image of the executable program, with no relocatable address information.

Segments. The use of segments for .COM programs is significantly different (and easier) than for .EXE programs. A full .COM program combines the PSP, stack, data segment, and code segment into one code segment.

For an .EXE program, you usually define a data segment and initialize DS with the address of that segment. For a .COM program, you define the data within the code segment just as you did when using DEBUG in Chapter 3.

Although you have to define a stack segment for an .EXE program, the assembler automatically generates a stack for a .COM program. Thus, when you write a program that is to be converted to .COM format, omit defining the stack.

If the 64K segment for the program is large enough, the program loader sets the stack at the end of the segment and sets the SP register with the address of the top of the stack. If the 64K segment is not large enough, the assembler establishes the stack after the program, in higher memory. (Most likely, however, a program of that size would be written in .EXE format.)

A number of the smaller programs in this book are in .COM format, and are easily distinguished from .EXE format. Figure 5-6 compares the addressing of segments in .EXE and .COM formats.

Initialization.   When the program loader loads a .COM program for execution, it automatically initializes CS, DS, SS, and ES with the address of the PSP. Because CS and DS now contain the correct initial segment address at execution time, a .COM program does not have to initialize them.

Because the PSP is 100H bytes in size, addressing begins at an offset of 100H bytes. You have to code a directive, ORG 100H, immediately following the code segment's SEGMENT or .CODE statement. The ORG directive tells the assembler to set its location counter at 100H. The assembler then begins generating the object code at an offset of 100H bytes past the start of the PSP, where your coding for the .COM program begins.

Writing a Program in .COM Format

If your source program is already written in .EXE format, you can use an editor to convert the instructions into .COM format.

The program in Figure 5–7 is similar to the one in Figure 5-2, but now revised to conform to .COM requirements. Note the following features:

- There is no defined stack or data segment.
- The ASSUME statement tells the assembler that CS, SS, DS, and ES will contain the starting address of the code segment (where the PSP begins) when the program is loaded for execution.
- The directive ORG 100H tells the assembler to advance its location counter 100H bytes from the beginning of the PSP. The program loader stores the 100H in the IP (Instruction Pointer) register when it loads the .COM program. Because of this feature, the first statement following ORG must be an executable instruction.
- A JMP instruction transfers control of execution around the defined data. Some programmers code data items following the instructions so that no initial JMP instruction is required. Coding data items first may speed up the assembly process slightly,

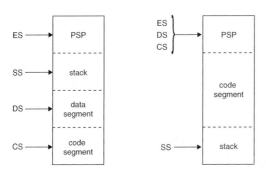

Figure 5-6   .EXE and .COM Segments

```
        TITLE    A05COM1 COM program to move and add
        CODESEG SEGMENT PARA 'Code'
                ASSUME  CS:CODESEG,DS:CODESEG,SS:CODESEG,ES:CODESEG
                ORG     100H                    ;Start at end of PSP
        BEGIN:  JMP     MAIN                    ;Jump past data
        ; -------------------------------------------------------
        FLDD    DW      215                     ;Data definitions
        FLDE    DW      125
        FLDF    DW      ?
        ; -------------------------------------------------------
        MAIN    PROC    NEAR
                MOV     AX,FLDD                 ;Move 0215 to AX
                ADD     AX,FLDE                 ;Add  0125 to AX
                MOV     FLDF,AX                 ;Store sum in FLDF
                MOV     AX,4C00H                ;End processing
                INT     21H
        MAIN    ENDP
        CODESEG ENDS
                END     BEGIN
```

Figure 5-7   .COM Source Program with Conventional Segments

but provides no other advantage. Examples in this book define the data first only as a programming convention.

- The labels BEGIN and MAIN are merely descriptive and are not otherwise meaningful to the assembler. You can use any valid names for these labels.
- The standard INT 21H function 4CH ends processing.

Converting .EXE into .COM Format

The method of generating a .COM file varies by assembler version:

- The Microsoft MASM 6.1 ML command assembles, links, and converts to .COM with the one command if the program specifies the Tiny memory model.
- Microsoft MASM 5.1 produces an .OBJ file, which you then link to produce an .EXE file. To convert the .EXE file to a .COM file, use a program named EXE2BIN. The program name means "convert EXE-to-BIN," where BIN means binary file; but name your output file extension .COM.
- TASM allows you to create the .COM file from its TLINK program.

See Appendix E for details on converting to .COM file format.

When conversion to .COM format is complete, you may delete the generated .OBJ and .EXE files. The .EXE and .COM programs are 792 bytes and 24 bytes in size, respectively. The difference is largely caused by the 512-byte header block stored at the beginning of an .EXE module.

Figure 5-8 shows the use of simplified segment directives for coding a .COM program. Once again, define only a code segment, not a stack or data segment. For MASM 6.1, the program should use the Tiny memory model.

Debugging Tips.   The omission of only one .COM requirement may cause a program to fail. For example, if EXE2BIN finds an error, it simply notifies you that it cannot convert the file, but does not provide a reason. Check the SEGMENT, ASSUME,

```
TITLE     A05COM2  COM program to move and add data
          .MODEL   TINY
          .CODE
          ORG      100H              ;Start at end of PSP
BEGIN:    JMP      MAIN              ;Jump past data
; ------------------------------------------------------
FLDD      DW       215               ;Data definitions
FLDE      DW       125
FLDF      DW       ?
; ------------------------------------------------------
MAIN      PROC     NEAR
          MOV      AX,FLDD           ;Move 0215 to AX
          ADD      AX,FLDE           ;Add  0125 to AX
          MOV      FLDF,AX           ;Store sum in FLDF
          MOV      AX,4C00H          ;End processing
          INT      21H
MAIN      ENDP
          END      BEGIN
```

Figure 5-8   .COM Program with Simplified Segment Directives

and END statements. If you omit ORG 100H, the executing program incorrectly references data in the PSP, with unpredictable results.

If you run a .COM program under DEBUG, use D CS:100 to view the data and instructions.

An attempt to execute the .EXE module of a program written as .COM will fail; be sure to delete this file.

KEY POINTS

- The assembler converts a source program to an .OBJ file and generates an optional listing and cross-reference file.
- The Segments and Groups table following an assembler listing shows any segments and groups defined in the program. The Symbols table shows all symbols (data names and instruction labels).
- The linker program converts an .OBJ file to an executable .EXE file.
- The simplified segment directives generate the names _DATA for the data segment, STACK for the stack segment, and _TEXT for the code segment, as well as a number of predefined equates.
- The cross-reference listing is useful for locating all the references that data items make.
- A .COM program is restricted to one 64K segment and is smaller than its counterpart .EXE program. The program does not define a stack or data segment, nor does it initialize the DS register.
- A program written as .COM requires ORG 100H immediately following the code segment's SEGMENT statement. The statement sets the offset address to the beginning of execution following the PSP.
- The system installs the stack for a .COM program at the end of the program.

REVIEW QUESTIONS AND EXERCISES

5-1. Code the command line to assemble a source program named MONITOR.ASM with listing, object, and cross-reference files.

5-2. Code the command line to link MONITOR.OBJ from Question 5-1, assuming a separate link command.

5-3. Code the commands for MONITOR.EXE from Question 5-2 for the following: (a) direct execution from DOS, (b) execution through DEBUG.

5-4. Explain the purpose of each of the following files: (a) file.ASM, (b) file.LST, (c) file.MAP, (d) file.CRF, (e) file.OBJ, (f) file.EXE.

5-5. Assuming conventional segment definitions and DATASEGM as the name of the data segment, code the two MOV instructions to initialize the DS register.

5-6. Write an assembly program using conventional segment definitions for the following: (a) Move the immediate value hex 40 to the AL register, (b) shift AL contents one bit left (SHL AL,1), (c) move immediate value hex 1A to BL, (d) multiply AL by BL (MUL BL). Remember the instructions required to end program execution. The program does not need to define or initialize the data segment. Copy a skeleton program and use your editor to develop the program. Assemble, link, and use DEBUG to trace and to check the code segment and registers.

5-7. Revise the program in Question 5-6 for simplified segment directives. Assemble and link it, and compare the object code, symbol tables, and link map with those of the original program. Use DEBUG to trace and to check the code segment and registers.

5-8. Add a data segment to the program in Question 5-6 for the following requirements:
- Define a 1-byte item (DB) named ITEMA containing hex 40 and another named ITEMB containing hex 1A.
- Define a 2-byte item (DW) named ITEMC with no constant.
- Move the contents of ITEMA to AL and shift left one bit.
- Multiply AL by ITEMB (MUL ITEMB).
- Move the product in AX to ITEMC.

Assemble, link, and use DEBUG to test the program.

5-9. Revise the program in Question 5-8 for simplified segment directives. Assemble and link it, and compare the object code, symbol tables, and link map with those of the original program. Use DEBUG to test the program.

5-10. For each of the following data items, show the contents of the assembler's location counter:

```
0000 WORD1 DW 0

.... WORD2 DW 0

.... BYTE1 DB 0

             EVEN

.... WORD3 DW 0

.... BYTE2 DB 0
```

5-11. What is the maximum size of a .COM program?

5-12. For a source program to be converted to .COM format, what segment(s) can you define?

5-13. Explain why you code ORG 100H at the beginning of a program to be converted to .COM format.

5-14. Why is it not necessary to define a stack for a .COM program?

5-15. Revise the program in Question 5-8 (conventional segments) for .COM format. Assemble, link, convert it to .COM, and execute it under DEBUG.

5-16. Revise the program in Question 5-9 (simplified segments) for .COM format. Assemble, link, convert it to .COM, and execute it under DEBUG. (Use the Tiny model for MASM 6.x.)

5-17. The following program contains a number of assembly-time errors, as indicated to the right. Correct each error.

```
        TITLE     A04ASM2 (EXE) Program errors
                  .MODEL SMALL
                  .STACK 64
                  .DATA
DATA1   DB        25
DATA2   DB        280        ;1: Value out of range
DATA3   DW        ?
                  .CODE
MAIN    PROC
        MOV       AX,data    ;2: Improper operand type
        MOV       DS,AX
        MOV       AX,DATA1   ;3: Operand types must match
        ADD       AX,DATA2   ;4: Operand types must match
        MOV       DATA3,AX
        MOV       FX,4C00H   ;5: Symbol not defined
        INT       21H
MAIN    ENDP
        END       MAIN
```

The assembler did not locate another error, which concerns the MAIN PROC statement; what is it?

Chapter 6

SYMBOLIC INSTRUCTIONS AND ADDRESSING

> Objective: To provide the basics of the assembly language instruction set and the requirements for addressing data.

INTRODUCTION

This chapter introduces the categories of the processor's instruction set. The instructions formally covered in this chapter are MOV, MOVSX, MOVZX, XCHG, LEA, INC, DEC, ADD, SUB, and INT, as well as the use of constants in instruction operands as immediate values. Finally, the chapter describes the basic addressing formats that are used throughout the rest of the book, and then explains address alignment and the segment override prefix.

THE SYMBOLIC INSTRUCTION SET—AN OVERVIEW

The following is a list of the symbolic instructions for the Intel processor family, arranged by category. Although the list seems formidable, many of the instructions are rarely needed.

ARITHMETIC

ADC: Add with Carry	INC: Increment by 1
ADD: Add Binary Numbers	MUL: Unsigned Multiply
DEC: Decrement by 1	NEG: Negate
DIV: Unsigned Divide	SBB: Subtract with Borrow
IDIV: Signed (Integer) Divide	SUB: Subtract Binary Values
IMUL: Signed (Integer) Multiply	XADD: Exchange and Add

ASCII-BCD CONVERSION

AAA: ASCII Adjust After Addition

AAD: ASCII Adjust Before Division

AAM: ASCII Adjust After Multiplication

AAS: ASCII Adjust After Subtraction

DAA: Decimal Adjust After Addition

DAS: Decimal Adjust After Subtraction

BIT SHIFTING

RCL: Rotate Left Through Carry

RCR: Rotate Right Through Carry

ROL: Rotate Left

ROR: Rotate Right

SAL: Shift Algebraic Left

SAR: Shift Algebraic Right

SHL: Shift Logical Left

SHR: Shift Logical Right

SHLD: Shift Left Double (80386+)

SHRD: Shift Right Double (80386+)

COMPARISON

BSF/BSR: Bit Scan (80386+)

BT/BTC/BTR/BTS: Bit Test (80386+)

CMP: Compare

CMPSn: Compare String

CMPXCHG: Compare and Exchange (80486+)

CMPXCHG8B: Compare and Exchange (Pentium+)

TEST: Test Bits

DATA TRANSFER

LDS: Load Data Segment Register

LEA: Load Effective Address

LES: Load Extra Segment Register

LODS: Load String

LSS: Load Stack Segment Register

MOV: Move Data

MOVS: Move String

MOVSX: Move With Sign-Extend

MOVZX: Move With Zero-Extend

STOS: Store String

XCHG: Exchange

XLAT: Translate

FLAG OPERATIONS

CLC: Clear Carry Flag

CLD: Clear Direction Flag

CLI: Clear Interrupt Flag

CMC: Complement Carry Flag

LAHF: Load AH from Flags

POPF: Pop Flags off Stack

PUSHF: Push Flags onto Stack

SAHF: Store AH in Flags

STC: Set Carry Flag

STD: Set Direction Flag

STI: Set Interrupt Flag

INPUT/OUTPUT

IN: Input Byte or Word

INSn: Input String (80286+)

OUT: Output Byte or Word

OUTSn: Output String (80286+)

LOGICAL OPERATIONS

AND: Logical AND   OR: Logical OR
NOT: Logical NOT   XOR: Exclusive OR

LOOPING

LOOP: Loop until Complete   LOOPNZ: Loop While Not Zero
LOOPE: Loop While Equal   LOOPNEW: Loop While Not Equal (80386+)
LOOPZ: Loop While Zero   LOOPNZW: Loop While Not Zero (80386+)
LOOPNE: Loop While Not Equal

PROCESSOR CONTROL

HLT: Enter Halt State   NOP: No Operation
LOCK: Lock Bus   WAIT: Put Processor in Wait State

STACK OPERATIONS

ENTER: Make Stack Frame   POPA: Pop All General Registers
(80286+)   (80286+)
LEAVE: Terminate Stack Frame   PUSH: Push Word onto Stack
(80286+)   PUSHA: Push All General Registers
POP: Pop Word off Stack   (80286+)
POPF: Pop Flags off Stack   PUSHF: Push Flags off Stack

STRING OPERATIONS

CMPS: Compare String   REPZ: Repeat While Zero
LODS: Load String   REPNE: Repeat While Not Equal
MOVS: Move String   REPNZ: Repeat While Not Zero
REP: Repeat String   SCAS: Scan String
REPE: Repeat While Equal   STOS: Store String

TRANSFER (CONDITIONAL)

INTO: Interrupt on Overflow   JNC: Jump If No Carry
JA: Jump If Above   JNE: Jump If Not Equal
JAE: Jump If Above/Equal   JNG: Jump If Not Greater
JB: Jump If Below   JNGE: Jump If Not Greater/Equal
JBE: Jump If Below/Equal   JNL: Jump If Not Less
JC: Jump If Carry   JNLE: Jump If Not Less/Equal
JCXZ: Jump If CX Is Zero   JNO: Jump If No Overflow
JE: Jump If Equal   JNP: Jump If No Parity
JG: Jump If Greater   JNS: Jump If No Sign
JGE: Jump If Greater/Equal   JNZ: Jump If Not Zero
JL: Jump If Less   JO: Jump If Overflow

JLE: Jump If Less/Equal   JP: Jump If Parity Odd

JNA: Jump If Not Above   JPE: Jump If Parity Even

JNAE: Jump If Not Above/Equal   JPO: Jump If Parity Odd

JNB: Jump If Not Below   JS: Jump If Sign

JNBE: Jump If Not Below/Equal   JZ: Jump If Zero

TRANSFER (UNCONDITIONAL)

CALL: Call a Procedure   JMP: Unconditional Jump

INT: Interrupt   RET: Return

IRET: Interrupt Return   RETN/RETF: Return Near/Return Far

TYPE CONVERSION

CBW: Convert Byte to Word

CDQ: Convert Doubleword to Quadword (80386+)

CWD: Convert Word to Doubleword

CWDE: Convert Word to Extended Doubleword (80386+)

Instructions that indicate a processor, such as (80386+), require the use of a processor directive (covered in Chapter 3) to assemble properly.

DATA TRANSFER INSTRUCTIONS

This section describes some of the commonly-used instructions concerned with data transfer.

The MOV Instruction

MOV transfers (or copies) data referenced by the address of the second operand to the address of the first operand. The sending field is unchanged. The operands that reference memory or registers must agree in size (both must be bytes, both words, or both doublewords). The format for MOV is

| `[label:]` | `MOV` | `register/memory,register/memory/immediate` |

Here are four examples of valid MOV operations by category, given the following data items:

```
BYTEFLD DB ?    ;Define a byte
WORDFLD DW ?    ;Define a word
```

1. Register Moves

```
MOV EDX,ECX            ;Register-to-register
MOV ES,AX              ;Register-to-segment register
MOV BYTEFLD,DH         ;Register-to-memory, direct
MOV [DI],BX            ;Register-to-memory, indirect
```

2. Immediate Moves

```
MOV CX,40H              ;Immediate-to-register
MOV BYTEFLD,25          ;Immediate-to-memory, direct
MOV WORDFLD[BX],16H     ;Immediate-to-memory, indirect
```

3. Direct Memory Moves

```
MOV CH,BYTEFLD          ;Memory-to-register, direct
MOV CX,WORDFLD[BX]      ;Memory-to-register, indirect
```

4. Segment Register Moves

```
MOV AX,DS               ;Segment register-to-register
MOV WORDFLD,DS          ;Segment register-to-memory
```

You can move to a register a byte (MOV CH,BYTEFLD), a word (MOV CX,WORD-FLD), or a doubleword (MOV ECX,DWORDFLD). The operand affects only the portion of the referenced register; for example, moving a byte to CL does not affect CH. *Invalid* MOV operations include the following:

```
MOV DL,WORD_VAL         ;Word-to-byte
MOV CX,BYTE_VAL         ;Byte-to-word
MOV WORD_VAL,EBX        ;Doubleword-to-word
MOV BYTE_VAL2,BYTE_VAL1 ;Memory-to-memory
MOV ES,225              ;Immediate-to-segment register
MOV ES,DS               ;Segment register-to-segment register
```

Performing these operations requires more than one instruction.

Move-and-Fill Instructions: MOVSX and MOVZX

For the MOV instruction, the destination must be the same length as the source, such as byte-to-byte and word-to-word. The MOVSX and MOVZX (move-and-fill) instructions (80386+) facilitate transferring data from a byte or word source to a word or doubleword destination. Here is their format:

[*label:*]	MOVSX/MOVZX	*register/memory,register/memory/immediate*

MOVSX, for use with signed arithmetic values, moves a byte or word to a word or doubleword destination and fills the *sign bit* (the leftmost bit of the source) into leftmost bits of the destination. MOVZX, for use with unsigned numeric values, moves a byte or word to a word or doubleword destination and fills *zero bits* into leftmost bits of the destination. As an example, consider moving a byte containing 10110000 to a word; the result in the destination word depends on the choice of instruction:

```
MOVSX CX,10110000B      ;CX = 11111111 10110000
MOVZX CX,10110000B      ;CX = 00000000 10110000
```

Here are some other examples of using MOVSX and MOVZX:

```
BYTE1   DB 25           ;Byte
WORD1   DW 40           ;Word
```

```
DWORD1 DD 160              ;Doubleword
.386   ...
        MOVSX CX,BYTE1    ;Byte to word
        MOVZX WORD1,BH    ;Byte to word
        MOVSX EBX,WORD1   ;Word to doubleword
        MOVZX DWORD1,CX   ;Word to doubleword
```

The .386 processor directive tells the assembler to accept instructions introduced by the 80386. Chapters 7 and 12 cover signed and unsigned data in detail.

The XCHG Instruction

XCHG performs another type of data transfer, but rather than simply copy the data from one location to another, XCHG *swaps* the two data items. The format for XCHG is

[label:]	XCHG	register/memory,register/memory

Valid XCHG operations involve exchanging data between two registers and between a register and memory. Here are two examples:

```
WORDQ DW ?                ;Word data item
    ...
    XCHG CL,BH            ;Exchange contents of two registers
    XCHG CX,WORDQ         ;Exchange contents of register and memory
```

The LEA Instruction

LEA is useful for initializing a register with an offset address. The format for LEA is

[label:]	LEA	register,memory

A common use for LEA is to initialize an offset in BX, DI, or SI for indexing an address in memory, which is done often throughout this book. Here's an example:

```
DATATBL DB 25 DUP (?)     ;Table of 25 bytes
BYTEFLD DB ?              ;One byte
    ...
    LEA BX,DATATBL        ;Load offset address
    MOV BYTEFLD,[BX]      ;Move first byte of DATATBL
```

An equivalent operation to LEA is MOV with the OFFSET operator, which generates slightly shorter machine code and is used like this:

```
    MOV BX,OFFSET DATATBL ;Load offset address
```

BASIC ARITHMETIC INSTRUCTIONS

This section describes the basic instructions for adding and subtracting: INC, DEC, ADD, and SUB.

The INC and DEC Instructions

INC and DEC are convenient instructions for incrementing and decrementing the contents of registers and memory locations by 1. The format for INC and DEC is

[label:]	INC/DEC	register/memory

Note that INC and DEC require only one operand. Depending on the result, the operations clear or set the OF (carry into the sign bit, no carry out), SF (plus/minus), and ZF (zero/nonzero) flags. Conditional jump instructions may test these conditions.

If a one-byte value contains FFH, INC "increments" it to 00H and sets SF to plus and ZF to zero. DEC "decrements" 00H to FFH and sets SF to plus and ZF to nonzero.

The ADD and SUB Instructions

This section briefly describes ADD and SUB; a more formal explanation is in Chapter 12. Their format is

[label:]	ADD/SUB	register/memory,register/memory/immediate

Valid operations involve register to/from register, register to/from memory, immediate to/from register, and immediate to/from memory. Here are some examples:

```
ADD AX,CX          ;Add register to register
ADD EBX,DBLWORD    ;Add memory doubleword to register
SUB BL,10          ;Subtract immediate from register
```

Flags affected are AF, CF, OF, PF, SF, and ZF. A zero result, for example, sets ZF, and a negative result sets SF.

REPETITIVE MOVE OPERATIONS

The programs to this point have involved moving immediate data into a register, moving data from defined memory to a register, moving register contents to memory, and moving the contents of one register to another. In all cases, the length of the data was limited to one, two, or four bytes, and no operation moved data from one memory area directly to another memory area. This section explains how to move byte-by-byte through a data item. Another method, the use of string instructions, is covered in Chapter 11.

In the program in Figure 6-1, the data segment contains two 9-byte fields defined as HEADNG1 and HEADNG2. The object of the program is to move the contents of HEADNG1 to HEADNG2, from left to right. Because these fields are each nine bytes long, more than a simple MOV instruction is required. The program contains a number of new features.

In order to step through HEADNG1 and HEADNG2, the program initializes CX to 9 (the length of both fields) and uses SI and DI for indexing. Two LEA instructions load the offset addresses of HEADNG1 and HEADNG2 into SI and DI as follows:

```
TITLE     A06MOVE (EXE)   Repetitive move operations
          .MODEL   SMALL
          .STACK   64
;------------------------------------------------------------
          .DATA
HEADNG1 DB         'InterTech'
HEADNG2 DB         9 DUP('*'), '$'
;------------------------------------------------------------
          .CODE
A10MAIN PROC       FAR
          MOV      AX,@data        ;Initialize segment
          MOV      DS,AX           ;  registers
          MOV      ES,AX

          MOV      CX,09           ;Initialize to move 9 chars
          LEA      SI,HEADNG1      ;Initialize offset addresses
          LEA      DI,HEADNG2      ;  of headings
A20:
          MOV      AL,[SI]         ;Get character from HEADNG1,
          MOV      [DI],AL         ;  move it to HEADNG2
          INC      SI              ;Incr next char in HEADNG1
          INC      DI              ;Incr next pos'n in HEADNG2
          DEC      CX              ;Decrement count for loop
          JNZ      A20             ;Count not zero? Yes, loop
                                   ;Finished
          MOV      AH,09H          ;Request display
          LEA      DX,HEADNG2      ;  of HEADNG2
          INT      21H

          MOV      AX,4C00H        ;End processing
          INT      21H
A10MAIN ENDP
          END      A10MAIN
```

Figure 6-1   Repetitive Move Operations

```
LEA SI,HEADNG1    ;Initialize offset addresses
LEA DI,HEADNG2    ; of HEADNG1 and HEADNG2
```

The program uses the addresses in SI and DI to move the first byte of HEADNG1 to the first byte of HEADNG2. The square brackets around SI and DI in the MOV operands mean indirect addressing: the instructions are to use the offset address in the given registers for accessing the memory location. Thus MOV AL,[SI] means "Use the offset address in SI (HEADNG1+0) to move the referenced byte to AL." And the instruction MOV [DI],AL means "Move the contents of AL to the offset address referenced by DI (HEADNG2+0)." The program has to repeat these two MOV instructions nine times, once for each character in the respective fields. To this end, it uses a conditional jump instruction not yet explained: JNZ (Jump if Not Zero).

Two INC instructions increment SI and DI by 1 and DEC decrements CX by 1. DEC also sets or clears the Zero flag, depending on the result in CX; if the result is not zero, there are still more characters to move, and JNZ jumps back to the label A20 to repeat the move instructions. And because SI and DI have been incremented by 1, the next MOVs reference HEADNG1+1 and HEADNG2+1. The loop continues in this fashion until it has moved nine characters in all, up to HEADNG2+8.

As well, the program uses instructions needed to display the contents of HEADNG2 at the end of processing: (1) Load function 09H in AH to request a display; (2) load the address of HEADNG2 in DX; and (3) execute the instruction INT 21H.

The INT operation displays all the characters beginning with the first byte of HEADNG2 up to the terminating '$' sign, which is defined immediately following HEADNG2. Chapter 8 covers this operation in more detail.

As an exercise, key in this program, assemble and link it, and use DEBUG to trace it. Note the effect on the stack, the registers, and IP (particularly after JNZ executes). Use D DS:0 to view the changes to HEADNG2.

THE INT INSTRUCTION

The INT instruction enables a program to interrupt its own processing, for example, to initialize the mouse driver:

```
MOV AX,00H    ;Initialize
INT 33H       ; mouse driver
```

INT exits normal processing and accesses the Interrupt Vector Table in low memory to determine the address of the requested routine. The operation then transfers to BIOS or the operating system for specified action and returns to the program to resume processing. Most often, the interrupt has to perform the complex steps of an input or output operation. An interrupt requires a trail that facilitates exiting a program and, on successful completion, returning to it. For this purpose, INT performs the following:

• Pushes the contents of the Flags register onto the stack. (Push first decrements Stack Pointer by 2.)
• Clears the Interrupt and Trap flags.
• Pushes the CS register onto the stack.
• Pushes Instruction Pointer (containing the address of the next instruction) onto the stack.
• Performs the required operation.

To return from the interrupt, the operation issues an IRET (Interrupt Return), which pops the registers off the stack. The restored CS:IP causes a return to the instruction immediately following the INT.

Because the preceding process is entirely automatic, your only concerns are to define a stack large enough for the necessary pushing and popping and to use the appropriate INT operations.

ADDRESSING MODES

An operand address provides a source of data for an instruction to process. Some instructions, such as CLC and RET, do not require an operand, whereas other instructions may have one, two, or three operands. Where there are two operands, the first operand is the *destination,* which contains data in a register or in memory, and which is to be processed. The second operand is the *source,* which contains either the data to be delivered (immediate) or the address (in memory or of a register) of the data. The source data for most instructions is unchanged by the operation. The three basic modes of addressing are register, immediate, and memory; memory addressing consists of six types, for eight modes in all.

1. Register Addressing

For this mode, a register provides the name of any of the 8-, 16-, or 32-bit registers. Depending on the instruction, the register may appear in the first operand, the second operand, or both, as the following examples illustrate:

```
MOV DX,WORD_MEM        ;Register in first operand
MOV WORD_MEM,CX        ;Register in second operand
MOV EDX,EBX            ;Registers in both operands
```

Because processing data between registers involves no reference to memory, it is the fastest type of operation.

2. Immediate Addressing

An immediate operand contains a constant value or an expression. Here are some examples of valid immediate constants:

```
Hexadecimal: 0148H
Decimal:     328 (which the assembler converts to 0148H)
Binary:      101001000B (which converts to 0148H)
```

For many instructions with two operands, the first operand may be a register or memory location, and the second may be an immediate constant. The destination field (first operand) defines the length of the data. Here are some examples:

```
BYTE_VAL DB 150            ;Define byte
WORD_VAL DW 300            ; word
DBWD_VAL DD 0              ; doubleword
      ...
      SUB BYTE_VAL,50      ;Immediate to memory (byte)
      MOV WORD_VAL,40H     ;Immediate to memory (word)
      MOV DBWD_VAL,0       ;Immediate to memory (doubleword)
      MOV AX,0245H         ;Immediate to register (word)
```

The instruction in the last example moves the immediate constant 0245H to AX. The 3-byte object code is B84502, where B8 means "move an immediate value to AX" and the following two bytes contain the value itself (4502H, in reverse-byte sequence).

The use of an immediate operand provides faster processing than defining a numeric constant in the data segment and referencing it in an operand.

The length of an immediate constant cannot exceed the length defined by the first operand. In the following invalid example, the immediate operand is two bytes, but AL is only one byte:

```
MOV AL,0245H     ;Invalid immediate length
```

However, if an immediate operand is shorter than a receiving operand, as in

```
ADD AX,48H       ;Valid immediate length
```

the assembler expands the immediate operand to two bytes, 0048H, and stores it in object code as 4800H.

3. Direct Memory Addressing

In this format, one of the operands references a memory location and the other operand references a register. (The only instructions that allow both operands to address memory directly are MOVS and CMPS.) DS is the default segment register for addressing data in memory, as DS:offset. Here are some examples:

```
ADD BYTE_VAL,DL     ;Add register to memory (byte)
MOV BX,WORD_VAL     ;Move memory to register (word)
```

4. Direct-Offset Addressing

This addressing mode, a variation of direct addressing, uses arithmetic operators to modify an address. The following examples use these definitions of tables:

```
BYTE_TBL DB 12, 15, 16, 22, ... ;Table of bytes
WORD_TBL DB 163, 227, 485,  ... ;Table of words
DBWD_TBL DB 465, 563, 897,  ... ;Table of doublewords
```

Byte Operations. These instructions access bytes from BYTE_TBL:

```
MOV CL,BYTE_TBL[2]   ;Get byte from BYTE_TBL
MOV CL,BYTE_TBL+2    ;Same operation
```

The first MOV uses an arithmetic operator to access the third byte (16) from BYTE_TBL. (BYTE_TBL[0] is the first byte, BYTE_TBL[1] the second, and BYTE_TBL[2] the third.) The second MOV uses a plus (+) operator for exactly the same effect.

Word Operations. These instructions access words from WORD_TBL:

```
MOV CX,WORD_TBL[4]   ;Get word from WORD_TBL
MOV CX,WORD_TBL+4    ;Same operation
```

The MOVs access the third word of WORD_TBL. (WORD_TBL[0] is the first word, WORD_TBL[2] the second, and WORD_TBL[4] the third.)

Doubleword Operations. These instructions access doublewords from DBWD_TBL:

```
MOV CX,DBWD_TBL[8]   ;Get doubleword from DBWD_TBL
MOV CX,DBWD_TBL+8    ;Same operation
```

The MOVs access the third doubleword of DBWD_TBL. (DBWD_TBL[0] is the first doubleword, DBWD_TBL[4] the second, and DBWD_TBL[8] the third.)

5. Indirect Memory Addressing

Indirect addressing takes advantage of the computer's capability for segment:offset addressing. The registers used for this purpose are base registers (BX and BP) and index registers (DI and SI), coded within square brackets, which indicate a reference to memory. If you code the .386, .486, or .586 directive, you can also use any of the general purpose registers (EAX, EBX, ECX, and EDX) for indirect addressing.

An indirect address such as [DI] tells the assembler that the memory address to use will be in DI when the program subsequently executes. BX, DI, and SI are associated with DS as DS:BX, DS:DI, and DS:SI, for processing data in the data segment. BP is associated with SS as SS:BP, for handling data in the stack.

When the first operand contains an indirect address, the second operand references a register or immediate value; when the second operand contains an indirect address, the first operand references a register. Note that a reference in square brackets to BP, BX, DI, or SI implies an indirect operand, and the processor treats the contents of the register as an off-set address when the program is executing.

In the following example, LEA first initializes BX with the offset address of DATA_VAL. MOV then uses the address now in BX to store CL in the memory location to which it points, in this case, DATA_VAL:

```
DATA_VAL DB 50                  ;Define byte
         ...
         LEA BX,DATA_VAL        ;Load BX with offset
         MOV [BX],CL            ;Move CL to DATA_VAL
```

The effect of the two MOVs is the same as coding MOV DATA_VAL,25, although the uses for indexed addressing are usually not so trivial. Here are a few more examples of indirect operands:

```
      ADD   CL,[BX]             ;2nd operand = DS:BX
      MOV   BYTE PTR [DI],25    ;1st operand = DS:DI
      ADD   [BP],CL             ;1st operand = SS:BP
.386
      MOV   DX,[EAX]            ;2nd operand = DS:EAX
```

The next example uses an absolute value for an offset:

```
      MOV CX,DS:[38B0H]  ;Word in memory at offset 38B0H
```

6. Base Displacement Addressing

This addressing mode also uses base registers (BX and BP) and index registers (DI and SI), but combined with a displacement (a number or offset value) to form an effective address. The following MOV instruction moves zero to a location two bytes immediately following the start of DATA_TBL:

```
DATA_TBL DB   365 DUP(?)           ;Define bytes
         ...
         LEA BX,DATA_TBL           ;Load BX with offset
         MOV BYTE PTR [BX+2],0     ;Move 0 to DATA_TBL+2
```

And here are some additional examples:

```
      ADD   CL,[DI+12]         ;DI offset plus 12 (or 12[DI])
      SUB   DATA_TBL[SI],25    ;SI contains offset (0-364)
      MOV   DATA_TBL[DI],DL    ;DI contains offset (0-364)
.386
      MOV   DX,[EAX+4]         ;EAX offset plus 4
      ADD   DATA_TBL[EDX],CL   ;EDX + offset DATA_TBL
```

7. Base-Index Addressing

This addressing mode combines a base register (BX or BP) with an index register (DI or SI) to form an effective address; for example, [BX+DI] means the address in BX plus the address in DI. A common use for this mode is in addressing a 2-dimensional array, where, say, BX references the row and SI the column. Here are some examples:

```
MOV  AX,[BX+SI]    ;Move word from memory
ADD  [BX+DI],CL    ;Add byte to memory
```

8. Base-Index with Displacement Addressing

This addressing mode, a variation on base-index, combines a base register, an index register, and a displacement to form an effective address. Here are some examples:

```
          MOV  AX,[BX+DI+10]        ;or 10[BX+DI]
          MOV  CL,DATA_TBL[BX+DI]   ;or [BX+DI+DATA_TBL]
     .386
          MOV  EBX,[ECX*2+ESP+4]
```

The last example moves into EBX the contents of (ECX x 2) plus the contents of (ESP + 4).

THE SEGMENT OVERRIDE PREFIX

The processor automatically selects the appropriate segment when addressing: CS:IP for fetching an instruction, DS:offset for accessing data in memory, and SS:SP for accessing the stack. There are occasions, especially for large programs, when you have to handle data that is subject to another segment register, such as the ES, FS, or GS. An example would be a large table of data loaded from external storage into memory in a separate segment of the program.

You can use any instruction to process the data in the other segment, but you must identify the appropriate segment register. Let's say that the address of the other segment is in ES, and BX contains an offset address within that segment. The requirement is to move two bytes (a word) from that location to DX:

```
          MOV DX,ES:[BX] ;Move to DX from ES:[BX]
```

The coding of "ES:" indicates an override operator that means "Replace the normal use of the DS segment register with that of ES." The next example moves a byte value from CL into this other segment, at an offset formed by the value in SI plus 36:

```
          MOV ES:[SI+36],CL ;Move to ES:[SI+36] from CL
```

The assembler generates object code with the override operator inserted as a 1-byte prefix (26H) immediately preceding the instruction, just as if you had coded the two instructions as

```
ES: MOV DX,[BX]          ;Move to DX from ES:[BX]
ES: MOV [SI+36],CL       ;Move to ES:[SI+36] from CL
```

NEAR AND FAR ADDRESSES

An address in a program may be near or far. A *near address* consists of only the 16-bit off-set portion of an address. An instruction that references a near address assumes the current segment—namely, DS for data segment and CS for code segment.

A *far address* consists of both the segment and offset portions in the form of 32-bit segment:offset. An instruction may reference a far address from within the current segment or in another segment.

Almost all assembly programming in real mode makes use of near addresses, which the assembler generates unless instructed otherwise. Large programs that consist of many segments would require far addresses as do programs defined with the Flat memory model.

ALIGNING DATA ADDRESSES

Because the 8086 and 80286 processors have a 16-bit (word) data bus, they execute faster if accessed words begin on an even-numbered (word) address. Consider a situation in which offsets 0012H and 0013H contain the word 63 A7H. The processor can access the full word at offset 0012H directly into, say, AX. But the word could begin on an odd-numbered address, such as 0013H:

In this case, the processor has to perform two accesses. First, it accesses the bytes at 0012H and 0013H and delivers the byte from 0013H (63) to AL. Then, it accesses the bytes at 0014H and 0015H and delivers the byte from 0014H (A7) to AH. AX now contains A763H.

You don't have to perform any special programming for even or odd locations, nor do you have to know whether an address is even or odd.

The 80386+ processors have a 32-bit data bus and, accordingly, prefer alignment of referenced items on addresses evenly divisible by four (a doubleword address). (Technically, 486+ processors prefer alignment on a 16-byte (paragraph) boundary.)

You can use the ALIGN or EVEN directive to force alignment of items on boundaries. For example, either ALIGN 2 or EVEN aligns on a word boundary, and ALIGN 4 aligns on a doubleword boundary. When the assembler adjusts the address of an item according to a boundary, it also advances its location counter accordingly.

Because a data segment defined with PARA begins on a paragraph boundary, you could organize data first with doubleword values, then word values, and, finally, byte values. Alignment could be helpful in time-critical applications.

KEY POINTS

- The MOV instruction transfers (or copies) data referenced by the address in operand 2 to the address in operand 1.
- The LEA instruction is useful for initializing a register with an offset address.
- INC and DEC increment and decrement by 1 the contents of registers and memory locations.
- The INT instruction interrupts processing of a program, transfers to BIOS or DOS for specified action, and IRET returns to the program to resume processing.
- An operand provides a source of data for an instruction. An instruction may have from zero to three operands.
- Where there are two operands, the operand 2 is the source, which references either immediate data or the address (of a register or of memory) of the data. Operand 1 is the destination, which references data to be processed in a register or in memory.
- In immediate format, the second of two operands contains a constant value or an expression. Immediate operands should match the size of the destination, that is, both byte, word, or doubleword.
- In direct memory format, one of the operands references a memory location, and the other operand references a register.
- Indirect addressing takes advantage of the processor's capability for segment:offset addressing. The registers used are BP, BX, DI, and SI, coded within square brackets as an index operator. BP is associated with SS as SS:BP, for handling data in the stack. BX, DI, and SI are associated with DS as DS:BX, DS:DI, and DS:SI, respectively, for processing data in the data segment.
- You may combine registers in an indirect address as [BX+DI], which means the offset in BX plus the offset in DI.

REVIEW QUESTIONS AND EXERCISES

6-1. For an instruction with two operands, (a) which operand is the source, and (b) which is the destination?

6-2. For each of the following unrelated instructions, show the result in the destination operand. Indicate if the instruction is invalid. Assume that BYTE1 is defined as DB 05.

```
    Instruction        Before           After
(a) MOV CX,25H      ;CX = 0000H      CX =
(b) MOV CL,0        ;CX = FFFFH      CX =
(c) MOV AX,BYTE1    ;AX = 1234H      AX =
(d) ADD DL,BYTE1    ;DX = 0120H      DX =
(e) INC DX          ;DX = FFFFH      DX =
(f) INC DL          ;DX = FFFFH      DX =
```

```
            (g)  XCHG AH,AL      ;AX = 1234H       AX =
            (h)  SUB CX,CX       ;CX = 1234H       CX =
            (i)  XCHG CX,CX      ;CX = 1234H       CX =
```

6-3. (a) In what significant way do the following instructions differ in execution?

```
                    MOV DX,AC24H

                    MOV DX,[AC24H]
```

(b) For the second MOV, one operand is in square brackets. What is the name of this feature?

6-4. (a) In what significant way do the following MOV instructions differ in execution?

```
                    MOV BX,WORDA

                    MOV [BX],WORDA
```

(b) For the second MOV, what sort of addressing is involved with the first operand?

6-5. Explain the operation of the instruction

```
                    SUB CX,[BX+DI+4]
```

6-6. For the following statement, (a) identify the error, and (b) explain one way to correct it:

```
                    SUB [SI],[BX]
```

6-7. Given the following data definitions, find the errors in the statements, and code instructions to correct them:

```
            BYTE1    DB   48
            BYTE2    DB   32
            WORD3    DW   216
     (a)             MOV BYTE1,BYTE2
     (b)             SUB CL,WORD3    ;Operand 2 is correct
     (c)             ADD DH,051CH    ;Operand 2 is correct
```

6-8. Code the following as instructions with immediate operands: (a) Add hex 26 to BX, (b) subtract hex 26 from CX, (c) shift CH two bits to the right, (d) shift BYTE1 two bits to the left, (e) store 426 in CX, (f) compare BYTE1 to hex 25.

6-9. Code one instruction that swaps the contents of a word named WORD3 with AX.

6-10. Code the instruction to set SI with the (offset) address of an item named RATE_TBL.

6-11. Explain in general terms the purpose of the INT instruction.

6-12. Explain how (a) the INT instruction affects the stack, and (b) the IRET instruction affects the stack.

6-13. Code, assemble, link, and use DEBUG to test the following program: (a) Define byte items named BYTE1 and BYTE2 (containing any values) and a word item named WORD3 (containing zero), (b) move the contents of BYTE1 to AL, (c) add the contents of BYTE2 to AL, (d) move the immediate value 42H to DL, (e) exchange the contents of AL and DL, (f) multiply the contents of AL by DL (MUL DL), (g) transfer the product from AX to WORD3.

6-14. Explain why the instruction ADD [BX],25 is invalid and correct it.

6-15. Code the instructions to add successively each byte defined in BYTE_TBL to the CL register. Use direct-offset addressing and five ADD instructions.

```
            BYTE_TBL DB 12, 15, 16, 10, 8
```

6-16. Use BYTE_TBL defined in Question 6-15 and code the instructions to move the fourth byte (containing 10) to CL. (a) Use indirect addressing. (b) Use base-displacement addressing.

6-17. Given the following table and initializing instructions, show the effect of the MOVs:

```
        VALUE_TBL DB 1, 2, 3, 4, 5, 6, 7, 8

        . . .

        LEA  BX,VALUE_TBL    ;Initialize BX
        MOV  DI,4            ; and DI
(a)     MOV  CL,[BX]         ;CL =
(b)     MOV  DL,[BX+3]       ;DL =
(c)     MOV  AL,[BX+DI]      ;AL =
(d)     MOV  CH,2[BX+DI]     ;CH =
```

Chapter 7

PROGRAM LOGIC AND CONTROL

> Objectives: To cover the requirements for program control (looping and jumping), for logical comparisons, for logical bit operations, and for program organization.

INTRODUCTION

Up to this chapter, most of the programs have executed in a straight line, with one instruction sequentially following another. Seldom, however, is a programmable problem that simple. Instead, most programs consist of various tests to determine which of several actions to take and a number of loops in which a series of steps repeats until a specific requirement is reached. A common practice, for example, is to test whether a program is supposed to end execution.

Requirements such as these involve a transfer of control to the address of an instruction that does not immediately follow the one currently executing. A transfer of control may be *forward* to execute a new series of steps, or *backward* to reexecute the same steps. Instructions that can transfer control outside the normal sequential flow do so by changing the offset value in IP.

Following are the instructions introduced in this chapter, by category:

Compare Operations	Transfer Operations	Logical Operations	Shift and Rotate
CMP	CALL	AND	SAR/SHR
TEST	JMP	NOT	SAL/SHL
	Jnnn*	OR	RCR/ROR
	LOOP	XOR	RCL/ROL
	RETn		
*Jnnn means all conditional jump instructions such as JNE and JL.			

SHORT, NEAR, AND FAR ADDRESSES

The assembler supports three types of addresses that are distinguished by their distance from the current address:

1. A *short* address, limited to a distance of −128 (80H) to 127 (7FH) bytes.
2. A *near* address, limited to a distance of −32,768 (8000H) to 32,767 (7FFFH) bytes within the same segment.
3. A *far* address, which may be within the same segment at a distance over 32K, or in another segment.

A jump operation reaches a short address by a 1-byte offset and reaches a near address by a one- or two-word offset. A far address is reached by a segment address and an offset; CALL is the normal instruction for this purpose because it facilitates linking to the requested address and the subsequent return.

The following table lists the rules on distances for JMP, LOOP, and CALL operations. There is little need to memorize these rules because normal use of these instructions rarely causes problems.

	Short	Near	Far
Instruction	−128 to 127 Same segment	−32,768 to 32,767 Same segment	Over 32K or in Another segment
JMP	yes	yes	yes
Jnnn	yes	yes (80386+)	no
LOOP	yes	no	no
CALL	N/A	yes	yes

The operand of a JMP, Jnnn (conditional jump), or LOOP instruction refers to the label of another instruction. The following example jumps to L10, which is the label of an INC instruction:

```
        JMP   L10
        . . .
L10:    INC   CX
        . . .
```

The label of an instruction such as L10: is terminated by a colon, which gives it the near attribute—that is, the label is inside a procedure in the same code segment. Omission of the colon is a common error, which the assembler signals. Note that an address label in an instruction operand (such as JMP L10) does not have a colon. You can also code a label on a separate line as

```
L10:
    INC   CX
```

In both cases, the address of L10 references the first byte of the INC instruction.

THE JMP INSTRUCTION

A commonly-used instruction for transferring control is the JMP (Jump) instruction. A jump is unconditional because the operation transfers control under all circumstances. JMP also flushes the processor's prefetch instruction queue so that a program with many jump operations may lose some processing speed. The format for JMP is

[label:]	JMP	short/near/far address

Short and Near Jumps

A JMP operation within the same segment may be short or near (or even far if the destination is a procedure with the FAR attribute). On its first pass through a source program, the assembler generates the length of each instruction. However, a JMP instruction may be two, three, or four bytes long. A JMP operation to a label within −128 (80H) to +127 (7FH) bytes is a *short jump*. The assembler generates one byte for the operation (EB) and one byte for the operand. The operand acts as an offset value that the processor adds to the IP register when executing the program.

A JMP that exceeds −128 to +127 bytes becomes a *near jump* (within 32K), for which the assembler generates different machine code (E9) and a 2-byte operand (8086/80286) or 4-byte operand (80386+). For now, we'll pass on the far jump.

Backward and Forward Jumps

A jump may be backward or forward. The assembler may have already encountered the designated operand (a *backward jump*) within −128 bytes, as in

```
L10:               ;Jump address
      . . .
      JMP L10      ;Backward jump
```

In this case, the assembler generates a 2-byte machine instruction. In a *forward jump,* the assembler has not yet encountered the designated operand:

```
      JMP L20      ;Forward jump
      . . .
L20:               ;Jump address
```

Because the assembler doesn't know at this point whether the forward jump is short or near, some versions assume near and generate a 3-byte instruction EBxx90, where xx is an offset and 90 is machine code for NOP. However, provided that the jump really is short, you can use the SHORT operator to force a short jump and a 2-byte instruction EBxx by coding

```
JMP SHORT L20
```

Program: Using the JMP Instruction

The program in Figure 7-1 illustrates the use of JMP. The program initializes AX and BX to 0 and CX to 1, and a loop performs the following:

- Adds 1 to AX
- Adds AX to BX
- Shifts left one bit (doubles the value in CX).

At the end of the loop (after SHL), the instruction JMP A20 transfers control to the instruction labeled A20. The effect of repeating the loop causes AX to increase as 1, 2, 3, 4, . . .; BX to increase according to the sum of the digits as 1, 3, 6, 10, . . .; and CX to double as 1, 2, 4, 8, ... Because this loop has no exit, processing is endless—usually only a desirable practice for such special applications as monitoring systems.

In the program, A20 is −9 bytes from the JMP. You can confirm this distance by examining the object code for the JMP: EBF7. EB is the machine code for a near JMP and hex F7 is the two's complement notation for −9. Because this is a backward jump, the operand F7 is negative. At this point, IP contains the offset (0112H) of the next instruction to execute. The JMP operation adds the F7 (technically, FFF7 because IP is a word in size) to IP, which contains the offset 0112H of the instruction following the JMP:

```
                     DECIMAL      HEX
IP register:          274         0112
JMP operand:           -9         FFF7  (two's complement)
Jump address:         265        (1)0109
```

The assembler calculates the jump address as 0109H (where the carry out of 1 is ignored) as a check of the program listing for the offset address of A20 shows. The operation changes the offset value in IP, flushes the instruction queue, and proceeds to reexecute the instructions following A20.

```
                    TITLE     A07JUMP (COM)  Using JMP for looping
                              .MODEL SMALL
                              .CODE
0100                          ORG    100H
0100                A10MAIN   PROC   NEAR
0100   B8 0000                MOV    AX,00       ;Initialize AX and
0103   BB 0000                MOV    BX,00       ;  BX to zero,
0106   B9 0001                MOV    CX,01       ;  CX to 01
0109                A20:
0109   05 0001                ADD    AX,01       ;Increment AX
010C   03 D8                  ADD    BX,AX       ;Add AX to BX
010E   D1 E1                  SHL    CX,1        ;Double CX
0110   EB F7                  JMP    A20         ;Repeat
0112                A10MAIN   ENDP
                              END    A10MAIN
```

Figure 7-1 Use of the JMP Instruction

As a useful practice, use DEBUG to trace the program for a number of iterations and observe the effect of execution on AX, BX, CX, and IP. After eight complete iterations, AX contains 08, BX contains 36 (24H) and CX contains 256 (100H). Key in Q to quit DEBUG.

THE LOOP INSTRUCTION

As used in Figure 7-1, the JMP instruction causes an endless loop. But a standard practice is to code a routine that loops a specified number of times or until it reaches a particular condition. The LOOP instruction, which serves this purpose, requires an initial value in CX. For each iteration, LOOP automatically deducts 1 from CX. Once CX reaches zero, control drops through to the following instruction; if CX is nonzero, control jumps to the operand address. The distance to the operand must be a short jump, within −128 to +127 bytes. For an operation that exceeds this limit, the assembler issues a message such as "relative jump out of range." The format for LOOP is

[label:]	LOOP	short-address

The program in Figure 7-2 illustrates the use of LOOP. It performs the same operation as the program in Figure 7-1, except that this one initializes CX with the value 8 and ends after eight loops. Because LOOP requires use of CX, this program uses DX in place of CX for doubling the initial value 1. The LOOP instruction replaces JMP A20 and, for faster processing, INC AX (increment AX by 1) replaces ADD AX,01.

Just as for JMP, the machine code operand for LOOP contains the distance from the end of the instruction to the address of A20, which the operation adds to IP when the program executes.

```
                        TITLE     A07LOOP (COM)    Illustration of LOOP
                        .MODEL SMALL
                        .CODE
0100                    ORG       100H
0100          A10MAIN   PROC      NEAR
0100  B8 0001           MOV       AX,00       ;Initialize AX and
0103  BB 0001           MOV       BX,00       ;  BX to zero,
0106  BA 0001           MOV       DX,01       ;  DX to 01
0109  B9 000A           MOV       CX,8        ;Initialize for
010C          A20:                            ;  8 loops
010C  40                INC       AX          ;Increment AX
010D  03 D8             ADD       BX,AX       ;Add AX to BX
010F  D1 E2             SHL       DX,1        ;Double DX
0111  E2 F9             LOOP      A20         ;Decrement CX,
                                              ;  loop if nonzero
0113  B8 4C00           MOV       AX,4C00H    ;End processing
0116  CD 21             INT       21H
0118          A10MAIN   ENDP
                        END       A10MAIN
```

Figure 7-2 Using the LOOP Instruction

As a useful exercise, use DEBUG to trace through the entire eight loops and observe the effect of execution on AX, BX, CX, DX, and IP. Once CX is reduced to zero, AX, BX, and DX contain, respectively, 0008H, 0024H, and 0100H.

There are two variations on the LOOP instruction, both of which also decrement CX by 1. LOOPE/LOOPZ (loop while equal/zero) continues looping as long as CX is zero or the zero condition is set. LOOPNE/LOOPNZ (loop while not equal/zero) continues looping as long as CX is not zero or the zero condition is not set.

Neither LOOP nor its LOOPxx variants changes the setting of any flags in the Flags register. However, because other instructions within the loop routine do change flags, the program in Figure 7-2 uses LOOP, and not its LOOPxx variants.

THE FLAGS REGISTER

The remaining material in this chapter requires a more detailed knowledge of the Flags register. This register contains 16 bits, which various instructions set to indicate the effect of their operation. In all cases, a flag remains set until another instruction changes it. The Flags register contains the following commonly-used bits:

```
Bit no.:   15  14  13  12  11  10  9  8  7  6  5  4  3  2  1  0

Flag:                          O   D  I  T  S  Z     A     P     C
```

The following section describes the flag bits, from right to left. A reference to "data item" means data in a register or memory.

CF (Carry Flag).   Contains a carry (0 or 1) out of the high-order (leftmost) bit of a data item following an unsigned arithmetic operation and some shift and rotate operations. Some disk operations use the CF to indicate success (0) or failure (1). JC and JNC test this flag.

PF (Parity Flag).   Contains a check of the low-order eight bits of a data item after an arithmetic operation. An even number of 1-bits clears the PF to 0, and an odd number of 1-bits sets it to 1. This flag is not to be confused with the parity bit described in Chapter 1 and is seldom of concern in conventional programming. JP and JPO test this flag.

AF (Auxiliary Carry Flag).   Concerned with arithmetic on ASCII and BCD packed fields, covered in Chapter 13. The AF is set when a 1-byte arithmetic operation causes a carry out of bit 3 (the fourth bit from the right) into bit 4.

ZF (Zero Flag).   Cleared or set as a result of an arithmetic or logical operation. Unexpectedly, a nonzero result clears the ZF to 0, and a zero result sets it to 1. However, the setting, if not apparently correct, is logically correct: 0 means no (the result is not equal to zero), and 1 means yes (the result equals zero). JE and JZ (among other instructions) test the ZF.

SF (Sign Flag). Set according to the sign (high-order or leftmost bit) of a data item following an arithmetic operation: A positive value clears the SF to 0, and negative sets it to 1. JG and JL (among other instructions) test the SF.

TF (Trap Flag). When set, causes the processor to execute in single-step mode, that is, one instruction at a time under user control. Debuggers set the TF for single-step execution, and that's about the only place where you'd expect to find it. The INT 03 operation is used to set the TF.

IF (Interrupt Flag). Disables external interrupts when 0, and enables interrupts when 1. The IF may be set by an STI instruction and cleared by CLI, and is used in critical situations.

DF (Direction Flag). Used by string operations to determine the direction of data transfer. When the DF is 0, the string operation performs left-to-right data transfer; when it is 1, the string operation performs right-to-left data transfer, covered in Chapter 11.

OF (Overflow Flag). Indicates a carry out of the high-order (leftmost) sign bit of a data item following a signed arithmetic operation. JO and JNO test the OF.

THE CMP INSTRUCTION

CMP is used to compare two numeric data fields, one or both of which are contained in a register. Its format is

[label:]	CMP	register/memory,register/memory/immediate

Technically, you may use CMP to compare string (character) data, but CMPS (covered in Chapter 11) is the appropriate instruction for this purpose. The result of a CMP operation affects the AF, CF, OF, PF, SF, and ZF flags, although you do not have to test these flags individually. The following code tests DX for a zero value:

```
        CMP  DX,00              ;DX = zero?
        JE   L10               ;If yes, jump to L10
        .    (action if nonzero)
        .
L10:         ...               ;Jump point if DX = zero
```

If DX contains zero, CMP sets the ZF to 1, and may or may not change the settings of other flags. The JE (Jump if Equal) instruction tests only the ZF. Because ZF contains 1 (meaning a zero condition), JE transfers control (jumps) to the address indicated by operand L10.

In effect, a CMP operation compares the first to the second operand; for example, is the value of the first operand higher than, equal to, or lower than the value of the second operand? (CMP acts like SUB without the additional storage cycle required for execution.) The next section provides the various ways of transferring control based on tested conditions.

CONDITIONAL JUMP INSTRUCTIONS

The processor supports a variety of conditional jump instructions that transfer control depending on settings in the Flags register. For example, you can compare or add two fields and then jump conditionally according to flag values that the compare sets. The format for the conditional jump is

[label:]	Jnnn	short-address

As explained earlier, the LOOP instruction decrements CX; if it is nonzero, control transfers to the operand address. You could replace the LOOP A20 statement in Figure 7-2 with two statements—one that decrements CX and another that performs a conditional jump:

```
DEC CX      ;Equivalent to LOOP
JNZ A20     ;
...
```

DEC decrements CX by 1 and sets or clears the Zero Flag. JNZ then tests the setting of the Zero Flag; if CX is nonzero, control jumps to A20, and if CX is zero, control drops through to the next instruction. (A jump operation that branches also flushes the processor's prefetch instruction queue.) Although LOOP has limited uses, it executes faster and uses fewer bytes than does the use of the DEC and JNZ instructions.

Just as for JMP and LOOP, the machine code operand for JNZ contains the distance from the end of the instruction to the address of A20, which the operation adds to the IP register. For the 8086/286, the distance for a conditional jump must be a short, within -128 to +127 bytes. If the operation exceeds this limit, the assembler issues a message "relative jump out of range." The 80386+ processors provide for 32-bit (near) offsets that allow reaching any address within 32K.

If you code the .386 operator, the assembler automatically generates 4-byte machine code for a forward jump (Example 1); using the SHORT operator causes 2-byte machine code (Example 2):

```
    Example 1              Example 2
.386                   .386
    CMP  BX,CX             CMP  BX,CX
    JE   L20              JE   SHORT L20
```

Signed and Unsigned Data

Distinguishing the purpose of conditional jumps should clarify their use. The type of data (unsigned or signed) on which you are performing comparisons or arithmetic can determine which instruction to use. An *unsigned* numeric item (logical data) treats all bits as data bits; typical examples are numeric values such as customer numbers, phone numbers, and many rates and factors. A *signed* numeric item (arithmetic data) treats the leftmost bit as a sign, where 0 means positive and 1 means negative; typical examples are quantity, bank balance, and temperature, which may be either positive or negative.

In the next example, assume that CX contains 11000110 and DX contains 00010110. The instruction CMP CX,DX compares the contents of CX to the contents of DX. If you treat the data as unsigned, CX is larger; if you treat the data as signed, however, CX is smaller because of the negative sign. The use here of CMP is valid, and you have to select the appropriate conditional jump instruction, such as JB (Jump Below) for unsigned data or JL (Jump Low) for signed data.

Jumps Based on Unsigned (Logical) Data

The following conditional jumps are used for unsigned data:

SYMBOL	DESCRIPTION	FLAGS TESTED
JE/JZ	Jump Equal or Jump Zero	ZF
JNE/JNZ	Jump Not Equal or Jump Not Zero	ZF
JA/JNBE	Jump Above or Jump Not Below/Equal	CF, ZF
JAE/JNB	Jump Above/Equal or Jump Not Below	CF
JB/JNAE	Jump Below or Jump Not Above/Equal	CF
JBE/JNA	Jump Below/Equal or Jump Not Above	AF, CF

You can express each of these conditional jumps in one of the two symbolic operations; choose the one that is clearer and more descriptive.

Jumps Based on Signed (Arithmetic) Data

The following conditional jumps are used for signed data:

SYMBOL	DESCRIPTION	FLAGS TESTED
JE/JZ	Jump Equal or Jump Zero	ZF
JNE/JNZ	Jump Not Equal or Jump Not Zero	ZF
JG/JNLE	Jump Greater or Jump Not Less/Equal	OF, SF, ZF
JGE/JNL	Jump Greater or Equal or Jump Not Less	OF, SF
JL/JNGE	Jump Less or Jump Not Greater/Equal	OF, SF
JLE/JNG	Jump Less/Equal or Jump Not Greater	OF, SF, ZF

The jumps for testing equal/zero (JE/JZ) and not equal/zero (JNE/JNZ) are included in the lists for both unsigned and signed data because the condition exists regardless of the presence or absence of a sign.

Special Arithmetic Tests

The following conditional jump instructions have special uses:

SYMBOL	DESCRIPTION	FLAGS TESTED
JCXZ	Jump if CX is Zero	none
JC	Jump Carry (same as JB)	CF
JNC	Jump No Carry	CF
JO	Jump Overflow	OF
JNO	Jump No Overflow	OF
JP/JPE	Jump Parity or Jump Parity Even	PF
JNP/JPO	Jump No Parity or Jump Parity Odd	PF
JS	Jump Sign (negative)	SF
JNS	Jump No Sign (positive)	SF

JCXZ tests the contents of CX for zero. This instruction need not be placed immediately following an arithmetic or compare operation. One use for JCXZ could be at the start of a loop to ensure that the routine is bypassed if CX is initially zero. JC and JNC are often used to test the success or failure of disk operations.

Now, don't expect to memorize the names of all these instructions or the flags they test. As a reminder, however, note that a jump for *unsigned* data is equal, above, or below, whereas a jump for *signed* data is equal, greater, or less. The jumps for testing the Carry, Overflow, and Parity flags have unique purposes. The assembler translates symbolic to object code, regardless of which instruction you use but, for example, JAE and JGE, although apparently similar, do not test the same flags (because JAE assumes unsigned data and JGE assumes signed data).

The 80386+ processors permit far conditional jumps. You can specify short and far jumps, for example, as

```
JNB     SHORT address
JBE     FAR address
```

Testing Multiple Conditions

For conditional jumps, a true condition causes a jump, whereas a false condition drops through to the next instruction. A program may have to test a series of related conditions. In the following, Example 1 determines if *any* condition is true (OR operation) and Example 2 determines if *all* conditions are true (AND operation):

```
Example 1 Any Condition True      Example 2 All Conditions True
        CMP   AL,BL                       CMP   AL,BL
        JE    equal                       JNE   not_equal
        CMP   AL,BH                       CMP AL,BH
        JE    equal                       JNE not_equal
        CMP   AL,CL                       CMP AL,CL
        JE    equal                       JNE not_equal
not_equal: <processing>               equal: <processing>
        ...                                   ...
equal: <processing>...                not_equal: <processing>
```

In Example 1, the true conditions test as equal, and all jump to the equal label; in Example 2, the true conditions test as not equal, and jump to the not_equal label. In effect, Example 2 (AND operations) reverses the test (JNE) and the jump point (not_equal).

CALLING PROCEDURES

The code segments in examples to now have consisted of only one procedure, coded as

```
proc-name    PROC    FAR
             . . .
proc-name    ENDP
```

The FAR operand in this case informs the assembler and linker that the defined procedure name is the entry point for program execution, whereas the ENDP directive defines the end of the procedure. A code segment, however, may contain any number of procedures, each distinguished by its own PROC and ENDP directives. A called procedure (or subroutine) is a section of code that performs a clearly defined task (such as set cursor or get keyboard input). Organizing a program into procedures provides the following benefits:

- Reduces the amount of code because a common procedure can be called from any number of places in the code segment,
- Encourages better program organization,
- Facilitates debugging of a program because defects can be more clearly isolated,
- Helps in the ongoing maintenance of programs because procedures are readily identified for modification.

A programming convention is to provide comments at the start of each procedure to identify its purpose and registers used and, if necessary, to push changed registers at the start and to pop them on exiting.

CALL and RETn Operations

The purpose of the CALL instruction is to transfer control to a called procedure. (The only examples in this book that *jump* to a procedure are at the beginning of .COM programs.) The RETn instruction, effectively the counterpart of CALL, returns from the called procedure to the original calling procedure. RETn is normally the last instruction in the called procedure. The formats for CALL and RETn are:

[*label:*]	CALL	*procedure-name*
[*label:*]	RET[n]	[*immediate*]

The assembler can tell from the procedure whether RET is near or far and generates the appropriate object code. However, for purposes of clarity, you may code RETN for near returns and RETF for far returns. The particular object code that CALL and RET generate depends on whether the operation involves a NEAR or FAR procedure.

Near Call and Return.   A CALL to a procedure within the same segment is near and performs the following:

- By means of a push operation, decrements SP by 2 (one word) and transfers IP (containing the offset of the instruction following the CALL) onto the stack.
- Inserts the offset address of the called procedure into IP (and also flushes the processor's prefetch instruction queue.)

A RET (or RETN) that returns from a near procedure basically reverses the CALL's steps:

- Pops the old IP value from the stack back into IP (and also flushes the processor's prefetch instruction queue).
- Increments SP by 2.

CS:IP now point to the instruction following the original CALL in the calling procedure, where execution resumes.

Far Call and Return.   A far CALL calls a procedure labeled FAR, possibly in another code segment. A far CALL pushes both CS and IP onto the stack, and RET (or RETF) pops them both from the stack. Far calls and returns are the subject of Chapter 22.

Example of a Near Call and Return.   A typical organization of a program with near calls and returns appears in Figure 7-3. Note the following features:

- The program is divided into a far procedure, A10MAIN, and two near procedures, B10 and C10. Each procedure has a unique name and contains its own ENDP for ending its definition.
- The PROC directive for A10MAIN has the FAR attribute because it is the entry point from the operating system.
- The PROC directives for B10 and C10 have the attribute NEAR to indicate that these procedures are within the current code segment. Because omission of the attribute causes the assembler to default to NEAR, many subsequent examples omit it.
- In procedure A10MAIN, the CALL transfers program control to the procedure B10 and begins its execution.
- In procedure B10, the CALL transfers control to the procedure C10 and begins its execution.
- In procedure C10, the RET causes control to return to the instruction immediately following CALL C10.
- In procedure B10, the RET causes control to return to the instruction immediately following CALL B10.
- Procedure A10MAIN then resumes processing from that point.
- RET always returns to its calling routine. If B10 did not end with RET, processing would continue through B10 and drop directly into C10. In fact, if C10 did not end with RET, the program would execute past the end of C10 into whatever instructions (if any) happen to be there, with unpredictable results.

```
                          TITLE A07CALLP (EXE)  Calling procedures
                               .MODEL SMALL
                               .STACK 64
                               .DATA
                          ;-------------------------------------------------
                               .CODE
0000                      A10MAIN PROC    FAR
0000  E8 0008 R                   CALL    B10          ;Call B10
                          ;          . . .
0003  B8 4C00                     MOV     AX,4C00H     ;End processing
0006  CD 21                       INT     21H
0008                      A10MAIN ENDP
                          ;-------------------------------------------------
0008                      B10     PROC    NEAR
0008  E8 000C R                   CALL    C10          ;Call C10
                          ;       . . .
000B  C3                          RET                  ;Return to
000C                      B10     ENDP                 ;  caller
                          ;-------------------------------------------------
000C                      C10     PROC    NEAR
                          ;       . . .
000C  C3                          RET                  ;Return to
000D                      C10     ENDP                 ;  caller
                          ;-------------------------------------------------
                                  END     A10MAIN
```

Figure 7-3   Calling Procedures

As explained earlier, you can transfer control to a near procedure by normal inline code, and you can also enter a near procedure by means of a jump instruction. However, for clarity and consistency, the practice is to use CALL to transfer control to a procedure, and RET/RETN to end the execution of the procedure.

THE EFFECT OF PROGRAM EXECUTION ON THE STACK

Up to this point, programs have had little need to push data onto the stack and, consequently, had to define only a very small stack. However, as illustrated in Figure 7-3, a called procedure can CALL another procedure, which in turn can CALL yet another procedure, so the stack must be large enough to contain all the pushed addresses. All this turns out to be easier than it first appears, and a stack definition of 32 words is ample for most of our purposes.

CALL and PUSH both store a one-word address or value onto the stack. RET and POP pop the stack and access the previously pushed word. All of these operations increment or decrement the offset address in the SP register for the next word. Because of this feature, RET and POP must match their respective CALL and PUSH operations.

As a reminder, on loading an .EXE program for execution, the program loader initializes the following register values:

- DS and ES: Address of the PSP, a 256-byte (100H) area that precedes an executable program module in memory.
- CS: Address of the code segment, the entry point to the program.
- IP: Zero, if the first executable instruction is at the beginning of the code segment.
- SS: Address of the stack segment.

• SP: Offset to the top of the stack. For example, for a stack defined as .STACK 64 (64 bytes or 32 words), SP initially contains 64, or 40H.

Let's trace the simple program in Figure 7-3 through its execution. In practice, called procedures would contain any number of instructions. You may find it worthwhile to assemble this program and use debugger to trace its execution; also, check the contents of IP, SP, and the stack.

The current available location for pushing is the top of the stack. For this example, the program loader would set SP to the size of the stack, 64 bytes (40H). Words in memory contain bytes in reverse sequence; for example, 0003 becomes 0300. The program performs the following operations:

• CALL B10 decrements SP by 2, from 40H to 3EH. It then pushes IP (containing 0003, the location of the next instruction) onto the top of the stack at offset 3EH. The processor uses the address formed by CS:IP to transfer control to B10, as shown by the following stack frame:

```
CALL B10 (push 0003):   003E   | 0300 |  <--SP = 003E
                        003C   | xxxx |
                        003A   | xxxx |
```

• In procedure B10, CALL C10 decrements SP by 2, to 3CH. It then pushes IP (containing 000B) onto the top of the stack at offset 3CH. The processor uses the CS:IP addresses to transfer control to C10:

```
CALL C10 (push 000B):   003E   | 0300 |
                        003C   | 0B00 |  <--SP = 003C
                        003A   | xxxx |
```

• To return from C10, RET pops the offset (000B) from the top of the stack at 3CH, inserts it in IP, and increments SP by 2 to 3EH. The offset in IP causes an automatic return to offset 000BH in procedure B10:

```
RET (pop 000B):         003E   | 0300 |  <--SP = 003E
                        003C   | 0B00 |
                        003A   | xxxx |
```

- RET at the end of procedure B10 pops the address (0003) from the top of the stack at 003EH into IP and increments SP by 2 to 0040H. The offset in IP causes an automatic return to offset 0003H, where the program ends execution.

```
                                              <--SP = 0040

    RET (pop 0003):        003E    0300

                           003C    0B00

                           003A    xxxx
```

If you use a debugger to view the stack, you may find harmless data left there by a previously executed program.

Overfilling the Stack. Consider a program that defines a stack with only 12 words. When executing, a series of CALL and PUSH operations fill the stack, from higher to lower memory. At that point, SP = 0. With no RET or POP, the next CALL or PUSH decrements SP from 0 to FFFEH and will store the new value outside the defined stack, with unpredictable results.

Passing Parameters

A common practice when calling a procedure is to pass what are called *parameters* (or arguments) that the procedure is to use. A program may pass parameters by *value* (the actual data item) or by *reference* (the address of the data). As well, it may pass parameters in registers or in the stack.

Passing Parameters by Value. Examples 1 and 2 next illustrate passing parameters by value. The program passes multiplicand and multiplier as parameters to a procedure that simply multiplies them. This version of MUL assumes the multiplicand in AX and multiplier in the operand and develops the product in the DX:AX pair.

```
Example 1 Pass Values in Registers    Example 2 Pass Values in Stack
          MOV AX,MULTICAND                       PUSH MULTICAND
          MOV BX,MULTIPLER                        PUSH MULTIPLER
          CALL M30MULT                           CALL M30MULT
          . . .                                   . . .
M30MULT   PROC NEAR                    M30MULT   PROC   NEAR
          MUL   BX                               PUSH   BP
          RET                                    MOV    BP,SP
M30MULT   ENDP                                   MOV    AX,[BP+6]
                                                 MUL    WORD PTR [BP+4]
                                                 POP    BP
                                                 RET    4
                                       M30MULT   ENDP
```

Example 2 merits further study. At the point of entry to M30MULT, SP points to the return address in the stack. Indirect addressing is needed to access the stack; SP cannot do it, but BP can. The procedure performs the following convention:

• Pushes BP onto the stack to save its contents. The stack frame now appears as

```
Multiplicand      [BP+6]

Multiplier        [BP+4]

ReturnAddress     [BP+2]

Bpvalue           <--SP and BP
```

• Copies the SP offset into BP.
• Uses BP for indirect addressing to access the passed parameters at [BP+6] and [BP+4].
• Pops BP (the operation also increments SP by 2 to ReturnAddress).
• Executes RET 4, which performs two functions:
  1. Loads ReturnAddress into IP and increments SP by 2 (it now points to Multiplier in the stack).
  2. Adds the RET immediate value (or pop-value) 4 to SP, effectively "removing" the two parameters from the stack. Note that because the called procedure did not pop the parameters, RET has to adjust SP.

Passing Parameters by Reference.   Examples 3 and 4 next illustrate passing parameters by reference and is the method used by high-level languages for calling subroutines. Passed parameters are the addresses of the multiplier and multiplicand.

```
Example 3 Addresses in Registers    Example 4 Addresses in Stack
        LEA BX,MULTICAND              .386 ;needed for next 2 PUSHes
        LEA SI,MULTIPLER                 PUSH   OFFSET MULTICAND
        CALL M30MULT                     PUSH OFFSET MULTIPLER
        . . .                            CALL   M30MULT
M30MULT    PROC NEAR                     . . .
        MOV AX,[BX]         M30MULT    PROC   NEAR
        MUL WORD PTR [SI]              PUSH   BP
        RET                            MOV    BP,SP
M30MULT    ENDP                        MOV    BX,[BP+6]
                                       MOV    DI,[BP+4]
                                       MOV    AX,[BX]
                                       MUL    WORD PTR [DI]
                                       POP    BP
                                       RET    4
                           M30MULT    ENDP
```

Be sure to use a debugger to examine how these examples work.

The choice of methods of passing parameters depends on circumstances and conventions. For example, passing by value works only for small values; to pass an array as a parameter requires passing by reference. As well, high-level languages use passing by reference.

A common practice for a called procedure is to push one or more registers that it has to use and to pop them prior to returning. When the program uses the stack for passing parameters, the called procedure pushes the registers *after* moving SP to BP:

```
PUSH BP                          ;Push BP
MOV BP,SP
PUSHF                            ;Push flags
PUSHA                            ;  and all registers
...
POPA                             ;Pop all registers,
POPF                             ;  flags,
POP BP                           ;  and BP
```

Chapter 22 covers passing parameters to separately assembled subprograms.

BOOLEAN OPERATIONS

Boolean logic is important in circuitry design and has a parallel in programming logic. The instructions for Boolean logic are AND, OR, XOR, TEST, and NOT, all of which can be used to clear, set, and test bits. The format for the Boolean operations is

[*label:*]	operation	*register/memory, register/memory/immediate*

The first operand references one byte, word, or doubleword in a register or memory and is the only value that is changed. The second operand references a register, memory, or immediate value, but a memory-to-memory operation is invalid. The operation matches the bits of the two referenced operands and sets the CF, OF, PF, SF, and ZF flags accordingly (AF is undefined).

Here's a useful rule to remember: ANDing bits with 0 clears them to 0, whereas ORing bits with 1 sets them to 1.

The AND Instruction.   In the case of AND, if matched bits are both 1, the operation sets the result to 1; all other conditions result in 0:

```
Operand 1:              0101
AND operand 2:          0011
Result in operand 1:   0001
```

For the following unrelated examples, assume that BL contains 0011 1010 and CH contains 1010 0011:

```
1. AND  BL,0FH   ;Sets BL to 0000 1010
```

```
            2. AND   BL,00H   ;Sets BL to 0000 0000
            3. AND   BL,CH    ;Sets BL to 0010 0010
```

Example 2 provides a way of clearing a register to zero.

The OR Instruction.   In the case of OR, if either (or both) of the matched bits is 1,
the operation sets the result to 1; if both bits are 0, the result is 0:

```
            Operand 1:                0101
            OR operand 2:             0011
            Result in operand 1:      0111
```

For the following unrelated examples, assume that BL contains 0011 1010 and CH
contains 1010 0011:

```
            1. OR    CH,BL    ;Sets CH to 1011 1011
            2. OR    CH,CH    ;Sets SF and ZF
```

Although the use of CMP may be clearer, you can use OR for the following purposes:

```
            1. OR    DX,DX    ;Test DX,
               JZ    exit     ;  jump if zero
            2. OR    DX,DX    ;Test DX,
               JS    exit     ;  jump if negative
```

The XOR Instruction.   In the case of XOR, if the matched bits differ, the operation
sets the result to 1. If matched bits are the same (both 0 or both 1), the result is 0.

```
            Operand 1:                0101
            XOR operand 2:            0011
            Result in operand 1:      0110
```

For the following unrelated examples, assume that BL contains 0011 1010 and CH
contains 1010 0011:

```
            1. XOR   BL,0FFH  ;Sets BL to 1100 0101
            2. XOR   BL,BL    ;Sets BL to 0000 0000
```

Example 2 provides another way of clearing a register to zero.

The TEST Instruction.   TEST sets the flags as AND does, but does not change the
bits referenced in the target operand. If any matching bits are both 1, TEST clears the
Zero Flag. Here are some examples:

```
            1. TEST   CX,0FFH        ;Does CX contain
               JZ     exit           ;  a zero value?
            2. TEST   BL,00000001B   ;Does BL contain
```

```
        JNZ     exit                ; an odd number?
    3.  TEST    CL,11110000B        ;Are any of the 4 leftmost
        JNZ     exit                ; bits in CL nonzero?
```

The NOT Instruction. NOT simply reverses the bits in a byte, word, or doubleword in a register or memory so that 0s become 1s and 1s become 0s, in effect, one's complement. The format for NOT is

[label:]	NOT	register/memory

For example, if BL contains 0011 1010, the instruction NOT BL changes BL to 1100 0101. (The effect is exactly the same as that of XOR BL,0FFH in the earlier example.) Flags are unaffected.

NOT differs from NEG in this way: NEG performs two's complement, which changes a binary value from positive to negative and vice versa by reversing the bits and adding 1. Typically, NOT is used on unsigned data and NEG on signed data.

Program: Changing Between Uppercase and Lowercase

There are various reasons for converting between uppercase and lowercase letters. For example, you may have a data file in which all the alphabetic data is in uppercase letters. Or, a program may allow users to enter a value as either uppercase or lowercase (such as "YES" or "yes") and then convert it to uppercase to facilitate testing it. Uppercase letters A through Z are represented by ASCII values as 41H through 5AH, and lowercase letters a through z as 61H through 7AH. The only difference is that bit 5 is 0 for uppercase and 1 for lowercase, as the following shows:

```
                    UPPERCASE                   LOWERCASE
    Letter A:       01000001        Letter a:   01100001
    Letter Z:       01011010        Letter z:   01111010
         Bit:       76543210             Bit:   76543210
```

The program in Figure 7-4 converts the contents of a data item, CONAME, from uppercase to lowercase, beginning at CONAME+1. The program initializes BX with the address of CONAME+1 and uses the address to move each character, starting at CONAME+1, to AH. If the value is between 41H and 5AH, an XOR instruction clears bit 5 to 0:

```
    XOR   AH,00100000B
```

All characters other than A through Z remain unchanged. The program then moves the changed character back to CONAME and increments BX for the next character. The program loops 15 times, once for each character from CONAME+1 on. Used this

```
TITLE      A07CASE (COM)   Change uppercase to lowercase
           .MODEL SMALL
           .CODE
           ORG      100H
BEGIN:     JMP      A10MAIN
; ------------------------------------------------------------
CONAME     DB       'LASER-12 SYSTEMS', '$'
; ------------------------------------------------------------
A10MAIN    PROC     NEAR
           LEA      BX,CONAME+1        ;1st char to change
           MOV      CX,15              ;No. of chars to change
A20:
           MOV      AH,[BX]            ;Character from CONAME
           CMP      AH,41H             ;Is it
           JB       A30                ;  upper
           CMP      AH,5AH             ;  case
           JA       A30                ;  letter?
           XOR      AH,00100000B       ;Yes, convert
           MOV      [BX],AH            ;Restore in CONAME
A30:
           INC      BX                 ;Set for next char
           LOOP     A20                ;Loop 15 times
                                       ;Done,
           MOV      AH,09H             ;  display
           LEA      DX,CONAME          ;  CONAME
           INT      21H
           MOV      AX,4C00H           ;End processing
           INT      21H
A10MAIN    ENDP
           END      BEGIN
```

Figure 7-4   Changing Uppercase Letters to Lowercase

way, BX acts as an index register for addressing memory locations. You may also use SI and DI for the same purpose. At the end, the program displays the changed contents of CONAME.

SHIFTING BITS

The shift instructions, which are part of the computer's logical capability, can perform the following actions:

- Reference a register or memory address.
- Shift bits left or right.
- Shift up to 8 bits in a byte, 16 bits in a word, and 32 bits in a doubleword.
- Shift logically (unsigned) or arithmetically (signed).

SHR/SAR/SHRD: Shifting Bits Right

The SHR (Shift Logical Right), SAR (Shift Arithmetic Right), and SHRD (Shift Right Doubleword) operations shift bits to the right in the designated register or memory location. The format for SHR and SAR is

| [label:] | SHR/SAR | register/memory,CL/immediate |

The second operand contains the shift value, which is an immediate value or a reference to the CL register. For the 8088/8086 processors, the immediate shift value may be only 1; a greater value must be contained in CL; later processors allow immediate shift values up to 31.

Each bit shifted off enters the Carry Flag. SHR (Shift Logical Right) provides for logical (unsigned) data and SAR (Shift Arithmetic Right) for arithmetic (signed) data:

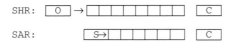

SHRD is covered in the next section. The following related instructions illustrate using SHR to shift unsigned data:

INSTRUCTION	COMMENT	BINARY	DECIMAL	CF
MOV BH,10110111B	;Initialize BH	10110111	183	
SHR BH,01	;Shift right 1	01011011	91	1
MOV CL,02	;Set shift value			
SHR BH,CL	;Shift right 2 more	00010110	22	1
SHR BH,02	;Shift right 2 more	00000101	5	1

The first SHR shifts the contents of BH one bit to the right. The shifted 1-bit now resides in the Carry Flag, and a 0-bit is filled to the left in BH. The second SHR shifts BH two more bits. The Carry Flag contains successively 1 and 1, and two 0-bits are filled to the left in BH. The third SHR shifts BH two more bits.

SAR differs from SHR in one important way: SAR uses the *sign bit* to fill leftmost vacated bits. In this way, positive and negative values retain their signs. The following related instructions illustrate using SAR to shift signed data:

INSTRUCTION	COMMENT	BINARY	DECIMAL	CF
MOV BH,10110111B	;Initialize BH	10110111	-73	
SAR BH,01	;Shift right 1	11011011	-37	1
MOV CL,02	;Set shift value			
SAR BH,CL	;Shift right 2 more	11110110	-10	1
SAR BH,02	;Shift right 2 more	11111101	-3	1

Right shifts are especially useful for *halving* values and execute significantly faster than does a divide operation. In the examples of SHR and SAR, the first right shift of one bit effectively divides by 2, and the second and third right shifts of two bits each divide by 4.

Halving odd numbers such as 5 and 7 generates 2 and 3, respectively, and sets the Carry Flag to 1. After the shift operation, you can use JC (Jump if Carry) to test the status of the Carry Flag (0/1).

Right Shifting in 32-Bit Registers.   Consider a 32-bit value of which the leftmost 16 bits are in DX and the rightmost 16 bits are in AX, as DX:AX. The following example transfers the DX:AX pair to the 32-bit ECX register, where a right shift operation divides the value by 2:

```
MOV CX,DX        ;BX to lower ECX
SHL ECX,16       ;Shift to upper ECX
MOV CX,AX        ;AX to lower ECX
SHR ECX,01       ;Divide ECX by 2
```

For the 80386 and later, SHRD can be used to right shift 16- and 32-bit values. Its format is

[label:]	SHRD	register/memory,register,CL/immediate

The first operand receives the bits that are shifted. The second operand is the same size and contains the bits to be shifted. The third operand (CL or immediate value) contains the shift count. Here are some examples:

```
SHRD   CX,DX,4          ;Right shift 4 bits from DX into CX
SHRD   ECX,EBX,CL       ;Right shift ? bits from EBX into ECX
```

SHL/SAL/SHLR: Shifting Bits Left

The SHL (Shift Logical Left), SAL (Shift Arithmetic Left), and SHLD (Shift Left Doubleword) operations shift bits to the left in the designated register or memory location. Their format is

[label:]	SHL/SAL	register/memory,CL/immediate

The second operand contains the shift value, which is an immediate value or a reference to the CL register. For the 8088/8086 processors, the immediate shift value may be only 1; a greater value must be contained in CL, whereas later processors allow immediate shift values up to 31.

Each bit shifted off enters the Carry Flag. SHL and SAL are identical in operation and both provide for logical (unsigned) and arithmetic (signed) data; that is, there is no difference between left shifting unsigned and signed data:

SHLD is covered in the next section. The following related instructions illustrate the use of SHL to shift unsigned data:

INSTRUCTION	COMMENT	BINARY	DECIMAL	CF
MOV BH,00000101B	;Initialize BH	00000101	5	
SHL BH,01	;Shift left 1	00001010	10	0
MOV CL,02	;Set shift value			
SHL BH,CL	;Shift left 2 more	00101000	40	0
SHL BH,02	;Shift left 2 more	10100000	160	0

The first SHL shifts the contents of BH one bit to the left. The shifted 1-bit now resides in the Carry Flag, and a 0-bit is filled to the right in BH. The second SHL shifts BH two more bits. The Carry Flag contains successively 0 and 0, and two 0-bits are filled to the right in BH. The third SHL shifts BH two more bits

Left shifts always fill 0-bits to the right. As a result, SHL and SAL are identical, so that SAL could be used in the previous example with the same effect. Left shifts are especially useful for doubling values and execute significantly faster than does a multiply operation. In the examples of the shift left operation, the first left shift of one bit effectively multiplies by 2, and the second and third left shifts of three bits each multiply by 8.

After a shift operation, you can use the JC (Jump if Carry) instruction to test the bit shifted into the Carry Flag.

Left Shifting in 32-Bit Registers. Consider a 32-bit value, of which the leftmost 16 bits are in DX and the rightmost 16 bits are in AX, as DX:AX. The following example transfers DX:AX to ECX, where a shift operation doubles the value:

```
MOV   CX,DX      ;DX to lower ECX
SHL   ECX,16     ;Shift to upper ECX
MOV   CX,AX      ;AX to lower ECX
SHL   ECX,01     ;Multiply ECX by 2
```

For the 80386 and later, SHLD can be used to left shift 16- and 32-bit values. Its format is

[label:]	SHLD	register/memory,register,CL/immediate

The first operand receives the bits that are shifted. The second operand is the same size and contains the bits to be shifted. The third operand (CL or immediate value) contains the shift count. Here are some examples:

```
SHLD BX,DX,2       ;Left shift 2 bits from DX into BX

SHLD EAX,EDX,CL    ;Left shift ? bits from EDX into EAX
```

ROTATING BITS

The rotate instructions, which are part of the computer's logical capability, can perform the following actions:

- Reference a register or memory.
- Rotate right or left. The bit that is shifted off rotates to fill the vacated bit position in the register or memory location and is also copied into the Carry Flag.
- Rotate up to 8 bits in a byte, 16 bits in a word, and 32 bits in a doubleword.
- Rotate logically (unsigned) or arithmetically (signed).

The second operand contains the rotate value, which is a constant (an immediate value) or a reference to the CL register. For the 8088/8086 processors, the rotate value may be only 1; a value greater than 1 must be contained in CL; later processors allow immediate rotate values up to 31. The format for rotate is

[label:]	rotate	register/memory,CL/immediate

ROR/RCR: Rotating Bits Right

The ROR and RCR operations rotate the bits to the right in the designated register or memory location. Each bit rotated off enters the Carry Flag. ROR (Rotate Logical Right) provides for logical (unsigned) and RCR (Rotate with Carry Right) for arithmetic (signed) data:

The following related instructions illustrate using ROR:

INSTRUCTION	COMMENT	BINARY	CF
MOV BL,10110111B	;Initialize BH	10110111	–
ROR BL,01	;Rotate right 1	11011011	1
MOV CL,03	;Set shift value		
ROR BL,CL	;Rotate right 3 more	01111011	0
ROR BL,03	;Rotate right 3 more	01101111	0

The first ROR rotates the rightmost 1-bit of BL into the leftmost vacated position and into the CF. The second and third ROR operations rotate the three rightmost bits into the leftmost vacated positions and into the CF.

The following RCR instruction shifts bits in ECX:

```
RCR ECX,6 ;Rotate right 6 bits of doubleword
```

RCR differs from ROR in this way: Each bit that RCR rotates off on the right first moves into the CF, and the CF bit moves into the vacated bit position on the left.

ROL/RCL: Rotating Bits Left

The ROL and RCL operations rotate to the left the bits in the designated register or memory location. Each bit rotated off enters the Carry Flag. ROL (Rotate Logical Left) provides for logical (unsigned) and RCL (Rotate with Carry Left) for arithmetic (signed) data:

The following related instructions illustrate using ROL:

INSTRUCTION	COMMENT	BINARY	CF
MOV BL,10110111B	;Initialize BH	10110111	–
ROL BL,01	;Rotate left	101101111	1
MOV CL,03	;Set shift value		
ROL BL,CL	;Rotate left 3 more	01111011	1
ROL BL,03	;Rotate left 3 more	11011011	1

The first ROL rotates the leftmost 1-bit of BL into the rightmost vacated position and into the Carry Flag. The second and third ROL operations rotate the three leftmost bits into the rightmost vacated positions and into the Carry Flag.

The following RCL instruction shifts bits in the EBX:

```
RCL EBX,4     ;Rotate left 4 bits of doubleword
```

RCL differs from ROL in this way: Each bit that RCL rotates off on the left moves into the CF, and the CF bit moves into the vacated bit position on the right. After an RCL or RCR operation, you can use the JC (Jump if Carry) instruction to test the bit rotated into the CF.

Doubleword Shift and Rotate

You can also use shift and rotate instructions for multiplying and dividing doubleword values by multiples of 2. Consider a 32-bit value, of which the leftmost 16 bits are in DX and the rightmost 16 bits are in AX, as DX:AX. The instructions to "multiply" the value by 2 are:

```
SHL AX,1    ;Use left shift to multiply

RCL DX,1    ; DX:AX pair by 2
```

The SHL operation shifts all bits in AX to the left, and the leftmost bit shifts into the Carry Flag. The RCL rotates DX left and inserts the CF bit into the rightmost vacated bit. To multiply by 4, follow the SHL-RCL pair with an identical pair.

For division, consider again a 32-bit value in DX:AX. Instructions to "divide" the value by 2 are

```
SAR DX,1    ;Use right shift to divide

RCR AX,1    ; DX:AX pair by 2
```

The SAR operation shifts all bits in DX to the right, and the rightmost bit shifts into the Carry Flag. The RCR rotates AX right and inserts the CF bit into the leftmost vacated bit. To divide by 4, follow the SAR-RCR pair with an identical pair.

ORGANIZING A PROGRAM

The following are recommended steps in writing an assembly program:

1. Have a clear idea of the problem that the program is to solve.
2. Sketch your ideas in general terms and plan the overall logic. For example, if a problem is to perform multibyte move operations, start by defining the fields to be moved. Then plan the strategy for the instructions: routines for initialization, for using a con-

ditional jump, and for using a loop. The following, which shows the main logic, is pseudocode that many programmers use to plan a program:

> Initialize segment registers
>
> Call the Jump routine
>
> Call the Loop routine
>
> End processing

The Jump routine could be planned as

> Initialize registers for count, addresses of names Jump1:
>
> Move one character of name
>
> Increment for next characters of names
>
> Decrement count: If nonzero, Jump1
>
> > If zero, Return

The Loop routine could be handled in a similar way.

3. Organize the program into logical units such that related routines follow one another. Procedures that are about 25 lines (the size of the screen) are easier to debug than procedures that are longer.

4. Use other programs as guides. Attempts to memorize all the technical material and code "off the top of the head" often result in even more program bugs.

5. Use comments to clarify what arithmetic and comparison operations are performing and what a seldom-used instruction is doing. (An example of the latter is LOOPNE: Does it loop *while* not equal or *until* not equal?) A useful practice is to provide header comments for each procedure that describes its purpose, inputs and outputs, and registers changed.

6. To facilitate keying in the program, use a saved skeleton program that you can copy into a newly named file.

7. Test modules as you develop them, even if many of them are simply empty procedures. This practice helps to locate and identify faults early.

8. Use numeric data that test for extreme but valid values, including zero and negative cases. Then try some invalid data to see how the program handles it.

The remaining programs in this text make considerable use of JMP, LOOP, conditional jumps, CALL, and called procedures. Having covered the basics of assembly language, you are now in a position for more advanced and realistic programming.

KEY POINTS

- A short address is reached by an offset and is limited to a distance of -128 to 127 bytes. A near address is reached by an offset and is limited to a distance of -32,768 to 32,767 bytes within the same segment. A far address in another segment is reached by a segment address and offset.

- An instruction label such as "L10:" requires a colon to indicate that it is a near label.

- Labels for conditional jump and LOOP instructions must be short. The operand generates 1 byte of object code: 01H to 7FH covers the range from decimal +1 to +127, and FFH to 80H covers the range from -1 to -128.
- When using LOOP, initialize CX with a positive nonzero value because LOOP decrements CX and then checks it for zero.
- When an instruction sets a flag, the flag remains set until another instruction changes it.
- Select the appropriate conditional jump instruction, depending on whether the operation processes signed or unsigned data.
- Use CALL to access a procedure, and include RET/RETN at the end of the procedure for returning. A called procedure may call other procedures, and if you follow the conventions, RET causes the correct address in the stack to pop.
- Use left shift to double a value and right shift to halve a value. Be sure to select the appropriate shift and rotate instructions for unsigned and for signed data.

REVIEW QUESTIONS AND EXERCISES

7-1. Explain these types of addresses: (a) short, (b) near, (c) far.

7-2. (a) What is the maximum number of bytes that a near JMP, a LOOP, and a conditional jump instruction may jump? (b) What characteristic of the machine code operand causes this limit?

7-3. A JMP instruction begins at offset location 02D4H. Determine the transfer offset address based on the following object code for the JMP operand: (a) 2AH, (b) 6EH, (c) B8H.

7-4. Explain how many times each of the following LOOP operations loop:

```
(a) MOV CX,1          (b) L5:MOV CX,10
    L5:                   . . .
    . . .                 LOOP L5
    LOOP L5
(c) MOV CX,0          (d) MOV CX,10
    L5:                   L5:
    . . .                 INC CX
    LOOP L5               LOOP L5
```

7-5. Write a program that calculates the Fibonacci series: 1, 1, 2, 3, 5, 8, 13,. . . . (Except for the first two numbers in the sequence, each number is the sum of the preceding two numbers.) Use LOOP and set the limit for 12 iterations. Assemble, link, and use DEBUG to trace through the routine.

7-6. Write a program that adds each of the values defined in BYTE_TBL and store the sum in BYTE-TOTAL. (Hint: Use indirect addressing, one ADD, INC BX, and LOOP.)

```
BYTE_TBL    DB 5, 6, 4, 9, 7
BYTE-TOTAL DB 0
```

7-7. CHAR_STRING contains uppercase letters that a program is to convert to lowercase. Access each character successively into a register, add 20H to it, and restore it in the string. Use indirect addressing and the LOOP instruction. (Hint: Use indirect addressing and increment BX for each character.)

```
CHAR_STRING  DB  'ABCDEFGHIJ'
```

7-8. Assume that CX and DX contain unsigned data and that AX and BX contain signed data. Determine the CMP (where necessary) and conditional jump instructions for the following: (a) Is AX equal to or smaller than BX? (b) Is CX equal to or smaller than DX? (c) Is AX greater than BX? (d) Is CX greater than DX? (e) Does DX contain zero? (f) Is there an overflow?

7-9. In the following, what flags are affected, and what would they contain? (a) Processing is in single-step mode. (b) A transfer of string data is to be right to left. (c) A result is negative. (d) A result is zero. (e) An overflow occurred.

7-10. Code and test a program that contains the following set of instructions. Determine the value in the destination register and the result in the Flags register for OF, ZF, SF, and CF.

```
(a)  MOV AL,FFH            (b)  MOV BL,24H
     ADD AL,1                   SUB BL,BL
(c)  MOV CL,10101010B       (d)  MOV DL,11001100B
     ADD CL,01010101B           ADD DL,01110011B
```

7-11. Refer to Figure 7-3 and explain the effect on program execution if the procedure B10 does not contain a RET.

7-12. Explain the difference between defining a PROC operand with NEAR and with FAR.

7-13. Identify three ways in which an executing program can enter a procedure.

7-14. Assemble and link the program in Figure 7-3, first as a Small and then as a Medium model. Compare the generated object code and link maps for differences.

7-15. In a program, D10 calls E10, E10 calls F10, and F10 calls G10. As a result of these calls, how many addresses does the stack now contain?

7-16. Assume that DL contains 01111001 and that an item named BOOL_AMT contains 11100011. Determine the effect on DL for the following unrelated operations: (a) AND DL,BOOL_AMT, (b) OR DL,BOOL_AMT, (c) XOR DL,BOOL_AMT, (d) AND DL,00000000B, (e) XOR DL,11111111B.

7-17. Revise the program in Figure 7-4 as follows: Define the contents of CONAME as all lowercase letters and code the instructions that convert all lowercase to uppercase.

7-18. Assume that DX contains binary 10111001 10111001. Determine the binary contents of DX after execution of the following unrelated instructions: (a) SHL DL,1, (b) SHL DX,2, (c) SHR DX,1, (d) SAR DX,2, (e) SAL DH,3, (f) ROR DX,3, (g) ROR DL,3.

7-19. Use move, shift, and add instructions to initialize DX with 24H and to multiply it by 10.

7-20. An example at the end of the section titled "Rotating Bits" multiplies DX:AX by 2. Revise the routine to (a) multiply by 4, (b) divide by 4, (c) multiply the 48 bits in DX:AX:BX by 2.

7-21. Transfer the contents of DX:CX to EBX and use a shift to multiply EBX by 4.

Chapter 8

INTRODUCTION TO VIDEO
AND KEYBOARD PROCESSING

Objective: To introduce the requirements for displaying information on a screen and accepting input from a keyboard.

INTRODUCTION

Up to this chapter, the programs have defined data items either in the data area or as immediate data within an instruction operand. However, most programs require input from an
external source, such as keyboard, disk, mouse, or modem and must provide output in a useful format on a screen, printer, or disk. This chapter covers the basic requirements for displaying information on a screen and for accepting input from a keyboard.

The INT (Interrupt) instruction handles input and output for most purposes. The two
interrupts covered in this chapter are INT 10H functions for screen handling and INT 21H
functions for displaying screen output and accepting keyboard input. These *functions* request a particular action; you insert a function value in the AH register to identify the type
of service the interrupt is to perform.

Low-level BIOS operations such as INT 10H transfer control directly to BIOS. However, to facilitate some of the more complex operations, INT 21H provides an interrupt service that first transfers control to the operating system. For example, input from a keyboard
may involve a count of characters entered and a check against a maximum number. The INT
21H operation handles much of this additional high-level processing and then transfers control automatically to BIOS, which handles the low-level part of the operation.

As a convention, this book refers to the value 0DH as the Enter character for the keyboard and as Carriage Return for the screen and printer.

INT 10H and INT 21H operations introduced in this chapter are:

INT 10H FUNCTIONS	INT 21H FUNCTIONS
02H Set cursor	02H Display character
06H Scroll screen	09H Display string
	0AH Input from keyboard
	3FH Input from keyboard
	40H Display string

Chapters 9 and 10 cover more advanced features for handling the screen and keyboard.

SCREEN FEATURES

A typical video monitor has 25 rows (numbered 0 to 24) and 80 columns (numbered 0 to 79). The rows and columns provide a grid of addressable locations at any one of which the cursor can be set. Here are some examples of cursor locations:

	Decimal Format		Hex Format	
Screen Location	Row	Column	Row	Column
Upper left corner	00	00	00H	00H
Upper right corner	00	79	00H	4FH
Center of screen	12	39/40	0CH	27H/28H
Lower left corner	24	00	18H	00H
Lower right corner	24	79	18H	4FH

The system provides space in memory for a *Video Display Area*, or buffer. The location in BIOS varies according to the mode in which the system is currently operating, such as text or graphics and color or monochrome. In text mode, the Video Display Area requires 4K bytes of memory, 2K of which are available for characters and 2K for an attribute for each character, such as reverse video, blinking, high intensity, and underlining.

The Video Display Area also provides for screen "pages" numbered 0 through 7. Pages and attributes are covered in detail in Chapter 10; for this chapter, we'll assume the default page 0.

The interrupts that handle screen displays transfer your data directly to the Video Display Area. Technically, your programs may transfer data directly to the Video Display Area. However, its memory address varies according to mode and there is no assurance that the addresses will always be the same, so writing data directly to a display area, although fast, can be somewhat risky. A common practice is to use the appropriate INT 10H and INT 21H operations that know the location of the Video Display Areas.

SETTING THE CURSOR

Setting the cursor is a basic requirement because its position determines where the next character is to be displayed or entered. The BIOS operation for screen handling is INT 10H combined with a function code in AH. For example, INT 10H function 02H tells BIOS to set the cursor. You load the required page number, normally 0, in BH, the row in DH, and the column in DL. The contents of the other registers is not important.

The following example sets the cursor to row 08, column 15:

```
MOV AH,02H     ;Request set cursor
MOV BH,00      ;Page number 0
MOV DH,08      ;Row 8
MOV DL,15      ;Column 15
INT 10H        ;Call interrupt service
```

To set the row and column in DX, you could also use one MOV instruction with an immediate hex value:

```
MOV DX,080FH    ;Row 08, column 15
```

CLEARING THE SCREEN

INT 10H function 06H handles screen clearing or scrolling. You can clear all or part of a display beginning at any screen location and ending at any higher-numbered location lower on the screen. Load these registers:

AH = function 06H

AL = number of lines to scroll, or 00H for the full screen

BH = attribute value (color, blinking, etc.)

CX = starting row:column

DX = ending row:column

CX and DX together define the screen area (or window) to be scrolled, and AL provides the number of lines to be scrolled up. To clear the entire screen, specify the starting row:column in CX as 00:00H and the ending row:column in DX as 18:4FH. Attribute 71H in the following example sets the entire screen to white background (attribute 7) with blue foreground (attribute 1):

```
MOV AX,0600H    ;AH = 06 (scroll), AL = 00 (full screen)
MOV BH,71H      ;White background (7), blue foreground (1)
MOV CX,0000H    ;Upper left row:column
MOV DX,184FH    ;Lower right row:column
INT 10H         ;Call interrupt service
```

For example, to scroll a screen window from row 05, column 00 through row 12, column 79, load 0500H in CX and 0C4FH in DX.

Be careful of mistakenly setting the lower right screen location higher than 184FH. The next chapter describes scrolling in more detail.

A program often has to display messages to a user that requests data or an action the user must take. We'll first examine some simple methods, which are useful for exercises and small programs, and later examine methods that involve file handles.

INT 21H FUNCTION 09H FOR SCREEN DISPLAY

The simplicity of the original INT 21H function 09H for displaying makes it convenient for beginners. It requires definition of a display string in the data area, immediately followed by a dollar sign ($ or 24H) delimiter, which the operation uses to end the display. The disadvantage, however, is that you can't use this function to display a $ character on the screen. The following example illustrates:

```
CUST_MSG DB 'Customer name?','$' ;Display string
```

You can code the dollar sign immediately following the display string as just shown, inside the string as 'Customer name?$', or on the next line as DB '$'. Set function 09H in AH, use LEA to load the address of the display string in DX, and issue an INT 21H instruction:

```
MOV     AH,09H          ;Request display
LEA     DX,CUST_MSG     ;Load address of prompt
INT     21H             ;Call interrupt service
```

The INT operation displays the characters from left to right and recognizes the end of data on encountering the dollar sign ($) delimiter. The operation does not change the contents of the registers. A displayed string that exceeds the rightmost screen column automatically continues on the next row and scrolls the screen as necessary. If you omit the dollar sign at the end of the string, the operation continues displaying characters from consecutive memory locations until it encounters one—if there is one.

Displaying ASCII Characters

Most of the 256 ASCII characters are represented by symbols that can be displayed on a video screen. Some values, such as 00H and FFH, have no displayable symbol and appear as blank, although the true ASCII blank character is 20H.

The program in Figure 8-1 displays the entire range of ASCII characters. The procedure A10MAIN calls three procedures:

- B10SCREEN uses INT 10H function 06H to clear the screen.
- C10CURSOR uses INT 10H function 02H to initialize the cursor to 08:00H.
- D10DISPLY uses INT 21H function 09H to display the contents of ASCHAR, which is initialized to 00H and is successively incremented by 1 to display each ASCII character until reaching FFH.

The first displayed line begins with a blank (00H), two "happy faces" (01H and 02H), and then a heart (03H), diamond (04H), club (05H), and spade (06H). ASCII 07H causes the speaker to sound. The program bypasses all characters between 08H and 0DH (08H would have caused a backspace, 09H a tab, 0AH a line feed, and 0DH a "carriage return" to the start of the next line). And, of course, under function 09H the dollar symbol, 24H, is not displayed at all. (As covered in Chapter 9, you can use BIOS services to display proper symbols for these special characters.) The musical note is 0EH, and 7FH through FFH are extended ASCII characters.

Note that displaying the Backspace, Tab, Line Feed, and Carriage Return characters is the normal way to perform these operations.

Suggestion: Reproduce the preceding program, assemble it, link it, and convert it to a .COM file for execution.

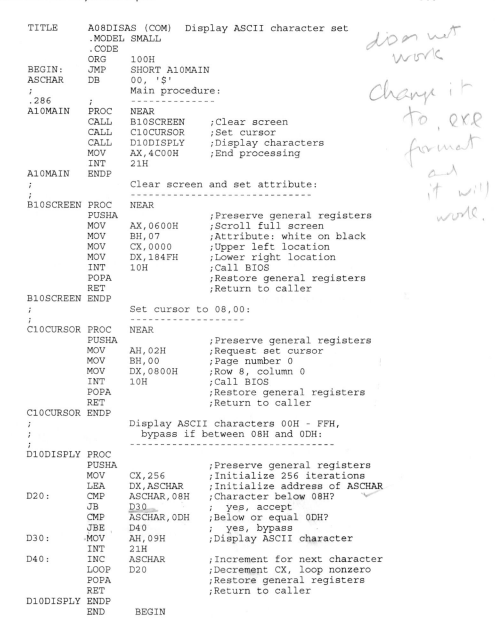

```
TITLE      A08DISAS (COM)   Display ASCII character set
           .MODEL SMALL
           .CODE
           ORG     100H
BEGIN:     JMP     SHORT A10MAIN
ASCHAR     DB      00, '$'
;                          Main procedure:
.286       ;               ----------------
A10MAIN    PROC    NEAR
           CALL    B10SCREEN      ;Clear screen
           CALL    C10CURSOR      ;Set cursor
           CALL    D10DISPLY      ;Display characters
           MOV     AX,4C00H       ;End processing
           INT     21H
A10MAIN    ENDP
;                          Clear screen and set attribute:
;                          -------------------------------
B10SCREEN  PROC    NEAR
           PUSHA                  ;Preserve general registers
           MOV     AX,0600H       ;Scroll full screen
           MOV     BH,07          ;Attribute: white on black
           MOV     CX,0000        ;Upper left location
           MOV     DX,184FH       ;Lower right location
           INT     10H            ;Call BIOS
           POPA                   ;Restore general registers
           RET                    ;Return to caller
B10SCREEN  ENDP
;                          Set cursor to 08,00:
;                          --------------------
C10CURSOR  PROC    NEAR
           PUSHA                  ;Preserve general registers
           MOV     AH,02H         ;Request set cursor
           MOV     BH,00          ;Page number 0
           MOV     DX,0800H       ;Row 8, column 0
           INT     10H            ;Call BIOS
           POPA                   ;Restore general registers
           RET                    ;Return to caller
C10CURSOR  ENDP
;                          Display ASCII characters 00H - FFH,
;                             bypass if between 08H and 0DH:
;                          ----------------------------------
D10DISPLY  PROC
           PUSHA                  ;Preserve general registers
           MOV     CX,256         ;Initialize 256 iterations
           LEA     DX,ASCHAR      ;Initialize address of ASCHAR
D20:       CMP     ASCHAR,08H     ;Character below 08H?
           JB      D30            ;  yes, accept
           CMP     ASCHAR,0DH     ;Below or equal 0DH?
           JBE     D40            ;  yes, bypass
D30:       MOV     AH,09H         ;Display ASCII character
           INT     21H
D40:       INC     ASCHAR         ;Increment for next character
           LOOP    D20            ;Decrement CX, loop nonzero
           POPA                   ;Restore general registers
           RET                    ;Return to caller
D10DISPLY  ENDP
           END     BEGIN
```

Figure 8-1   Displaying ASCII Character Set

INT 21H FUNCTION 0AH FOR KEYBOARD INPUT

INT 21H function 0AH for accepting data from the keyboard is particularly powerful. The input area for keyed-in characters requires a *parameter list* containing specified fields that the INT operation is to process. (The comparable term in a high-level language is *record* or *structure.*) First, the operation needs to know the maximum number of input characters. The purpose is to prevent users from keying in too many characters; if so, the operation sounds the speaker and does not accept further input. Second, the operation delivers to the parameter list the number of bytes actually entered. The parameter list consists of these elements:

1. The first statement provides the name of the parameter list in the form LABEL BYTE. LABEL is a directive with the type attribute of BYTE, which simply causes alignment on a byte boundary. Because that's the normal alignment, the assembler does not advance its location counter. LABEL is used for assigning a name to the parameter list.

2. The first byte of the parameter list contains your limit for the maximum number of input characters. The minimum is 0 and, because this is a 1-byte field, the maximum is FFH, or 255. You decide on the maximum based on the kind of data you expect users to enter.

3. The second byte is for the operation to store in binary format the actual number of characters typed.

4. The third byte begins a field that is to contain the typed characters, from left to right.

The following example defines a parameter list for a keyboard input area:

```
PARA_LIST LABEL BYTE      ;Start of parameter list
MAX_LEN DB 20             ;Maximum number of input characters
ACT_LEN DB ?              ;Actual number of input characters
KB_DATA DB 20 DUP(' ')    ;Characters entered from keyboard
```

In the parameter list, the LABEL directive tells the assembler to align on a byte boundary and gives the location the name PARA_LIST. Because LABEL takes no space, PARA_LIST and MAX_LEN refer to the same memory location. MAX_LEN defines the maximum number of keyboard characters (20), ACT_LEN provides a space for the operation to insert the actual number of characters entered, and KB_DATA reserves 20 spaces for the characters. You may use any valid names for these fields.

To request keyboard input, set function 0AH in AH, load the address of the parameter list (PARA_LIST in the example) into DX, and issue INT 21H:

```
MOV AH,0AH          ;Request keyboard input
LEA DX,PARA_LIST    ;Load address of parameter list
INT 21H             ;Call interrupt service
```

The INT operation waits for a user to type characters and checks that the number does not exceed the maximum of 20. The operation echoes each typed character onto the screen where the cursor is situtated and advances the cursor. The user presses <Enter> to signal the end of a keyboard entry. The operation also transfers the Enter character (0DH) to the input field KB_DATA, but does not count its entry in the actual length. If you key in a name such as Wilson+<Enter>, the parameter list appears like this:

ASCII:	20	6	W	i	l	s	o	n	#				...
Hex:	14	06	57	69	6C	73	6F	6E	0D	20	20	20	...

The operation delivers the length of the input name, 06H, into the second byte of the parameter list, named ACT_LEN in the example. The Enter character (0DH) is at KB_DATA+6. (The # symbol here indicates this character because 0DH has no printable symbol.) Given that the maximum length of 20 includes the 0DH, the user may type only up to 19 characters.

This operation accepts and acts on the Backspace character, but doesn't add it to the count. Other than Backspace, the operation does not accept more than the maximum number of characters. In the preceding example, if a user keys in 20 characters without pressing <Enter>, the operation causes the speaker to beep; at this point, it accepts only the Enter character.

Although the operation is useful for entering data, it bypasses extended function keys such as F1, Home, PgUp, and Arrows. If you expect a user to press any of them, use INT 16H or INT 21H function 01H, both covered in Chapter 10.

Program: Accepting and Displaying Names

The program in Figure 8-2 requests a user to key in a name, and then displays the name at the center of the screen and sounds the speaker. If the user types, for example, the name Dana Wilson, the program performs the following:

1. Divides the length 11 by 2: $11/2 = 5$, with the remainder ignored.
2. Subtracts this value from 40: $40 - 5 = 35$.

In the procedure C10CENTER, the SHR instruction shifts the length of 11 one bit to the right, effectively dividing the length by 2: Bits 00001011 become 00000101, or 5. The NEG instruction reverses the sign, changing +5 to -5. ADD adds the value 40, giving the starting position for the column, 35, in DL. With the cursor set at row 12, column 35, the name appears on the screen beginning at row 12, column 35.

Note the instructions in C10CENTER that insert the Bell (07H) character in the input area immediately following the name:

```
        MOVZX BX,ACTULEN        ;Replace 0DH with 07H in BX
        MOV KBNAME[BX],07H
```

The MOVSX sets BX with the number of characters that were typed. In the MOV, [BX] acts as an index register to facilitate extended addressing. The MOV combines the length in BX with the address of KBNAME and moves the 07H to the calculated address. For a length of 11, the instruction inserts 07H at KBNAME+11 (replacing the Enter character) following the name. The instruction in C10CENTER

```
        MOV     KBNAME[BX+1],'$'     ;Set display delimiter
```

inserts a '$' delimiter following the 07H so that INT 21H function 09H can display the name and sound the speaker.

Procedures C10ENTER, D10DISPLY, and Q20CURSOR indicate register usage by means of comments. In practice, the procedures would push and pop the registers.

Additional Programming Practices

The following sections illustrate a few useful techniques.

```
TITLE      A08CTRNM (EXE)  Accept names from keyboard,
;                          center them on screen, sound bell
           .MODEL SMALL
           .STACK 64
           .DATA
PARLIST    LABEL  BYTE                  ;Name parameter list:
MAXNLEN    DB     20                    ;  maximum length of name
ACTULEN    DB     ?                     ;  no. of characters entered
KBNAME     DB     21 DUP(' ')           ;  entered name
PROMPT     DB     'Name? ', '$'
;---------------------------------------------------------------
           .CODE
.386                                    ;Directive for MOVZX
A10MAIN    PROC   FAR
           MOV    AX,@data              ;Initialize segment
           MOV    DS,AX                 ;  registers
           MOV    ES,AX
           CALL   Q10CLEAR              ;Clear screen
A20:
           MOV    DX,0000               ;Set cursor to 00,00
           CALL   Q20CURSOR
           CALL   B10INPUT              ;Provide for input of name
           CALL   Q10CLEAR              ;Clear screen
           CMP    ACTULEN,00            ;Name entered?
           JE     A30                   ;  no, exit
           CALL   C10CENTER             ;Set bell and '$' and center
           CALL   D10DISPLY             ;Display name
           JMP    A20                   ;Repeat
A30:
           MOV    AX,4C00H              ;End processing
           INT    21H
A10MAIN    ENDP
;                 Display prompt and accept input of name:
;                 -------------------------------------------
B10INPUT   PROC   NEAR
           PUSH   AX                    ;Preserve used
           PUSH   DX                    ;  registers
           MOV    AH,09H                ;Request display
           LEA    DX,PROMPT             ;  of user prompt
           INT    21H
           MOV    AH,0AH                ;Request keyboard
           LEA    DX,PARLIST            ;  input
           INT    21H
           POP    DX                    ;Restore
           POP    AX                    ;  registers
           RET
B10INPUT   ENDP
;                 Set bell and '$' delimiter and
;                    set cursor at center of screen:
;                 -------------------------------
C10CENTER  PROC   NEAR                  ;Uses BX and DX
           MOVZX  BX,ACTULEN            ;Replace 0DH with 07H
           MOV    KBNAME[BX],07
           MOV    KBNAME[BX+1],'$'      ;Set display delimiter
           MOV    DL,ACTULEN            ;Locate center column:
           SHR    DL,1                  ;  divide length by 2,
```

Figure 8-2 Accepting and Displaying Names

Replying with Only the Enter Key. The program in Figure 8-2 continues
accepting and displaying names until the user presses only <Enter> as a reply to a
prompt. INT 21H function 09H accepts the keystroke and inserts a length of 00H in the
parameter list, like this:

Parameter list (hex): | 14 | 00 | 0D | ... |

```
                  NEG     DL              ;  reverse sign,        4
                  ADD     DL,40           ;  add 40
                  MOV     DH,12           ;Center row
                  CALL    Q20CURSOR       ;Set cursor
                  RET
       C10CENTER  ENDP
       ;                   Display centered name:
       ;                   ---------------------
       D10DISPLY  PROC    NEAR
                  MOV     AH,09H
                  LEA     DX,KBNAME       ;Display name
                  INT     21H
                  RET
       D10DISPLY  ENDP
       ;                   Clear screen and set attribute:
       ;                   -------------------------------
       Q10CLEAR   PROC    NEAR
                  PUSHA                   ;Preserve general registers
                  MOV     AX,0600H        ;Request scroll screen
                  MOV     BH,30           ;Color attribute
                  MOV     CX,0000         ;From 00,00
                  MOV     DX,184FH        ;  to 24,79
                  POPA                    ;Restore general registers
                  INT     10H
                  RET
       Q10CLEAR   ENDP
       ;                   Set cursor row, column:
       ;                   -----------------------
                                          ;DX set on entry
       Q20CURSOR  PROC    NEAR            ;Uses AH and BH
                  MOV     AH,02H          ;Request set cursor
                  MOV     BH,00           ;Page #0
                  INT     10H
                  RET
       Q20CURSOR  ENDP
                  END     A10MAIN
```

Figure 8-2 *Continued*

If the length is zero, the program determines that input is ended, as shown by the instruction CMP ACTLEN,00 in A10MAIN.

Clearing the Enter Character. You can use input characters for various purposes, such as printing on a report, storing in a table, or writing on disk. For these purposes, you may have to replace the Enter character (0DH) wherever it is in KBNAME with a blank (20H). The field containing the actual length of the input data, ACTLEN, provides the relative position of the Enter character. For example, if ACTLEN contains 11, then the Enter character is at KBNAME+11. You can move this length into BX for indexing the address of KBNAME as follows:

```
       MOVZX BX,ACTULEN     ;Set BX to 00 0B (11)
       MOV KBNAME[BX],20H   ;Clear Enter character
```

The MOVZX instruction sets BX with the length 11. The MOV moves a blank (20H) to the address specified in the first operand: the address of KBNAME plus the contents of BX—in effect, KBNAME+11.

Clearing the Input Area.   Each character keyed in replaces the previous contents in the input area and remains there until other characters replace them. Consider the following successive input:

	Input			PARLIST (hex)											
1.	Monroe	14	06	4D	6F	6E	72	6F	65	0D	20	20	...	20
2.	Franklin	14	08	46	72	61	6E	6B	6C	69	6E	0D	...	20
3.	Adams	14	05	41	64	61	6D	73	0D	69	6E	0D	...	20

The first name, Monroe, requires only six bytes. The second name, Franklin, fully replaces the shorter name Monroe. But because the third name, Adams, is shorter than Franklin, it replaces only Frank and the Enter character replaces the l. The remaining two letters ("in") still follow Adams. You could also clear KBNAME prior to prompting for a name, like this:

```
        MOV CX,20           ;Initialize for 20 loops
        MOV SI,0000         ;Start position for name
L10:
        MOV KBNAME[SI],20H  ;Move one blank to name
        INC SI              ;Increment for next character
        LOOP L10            ;Repeat 20 times
```

Instead of the SI register, you could use DI or BX. Also, if the routine moves a word of two blanks, it would require only 10 loops. However, because KBNAME is defined as DB (byte), you would have to override its length with a WORD and PTR (pointer) operand, as the following indicates:

```
        MOV CX,10            ;Initialize for 10 loops
        LEA SI,KBNAME        ;Initialize the start of name
L10:
        MOV WORD PTR[SI],2020H  ;Move two blanks to name
        ADD SI,2             ;Increment two positions in name
        LOOP L10             ;Repeat 10 times
```

Interpret the MOV at L10: as "Move a blank word to the memory location where the address in SI points." This example uses LEA to initialize the clearing of KBNAME and uses a slightly different method for the MOV at B30 because you cannot code an instruction such as

```
        MOV WORD PTR[KBNAME],2020H     ;First operand is invalid
```

Clearing the input area solves the problem of short names being followed by previous data. For faster processing, you could clear only positions to the right of the most recently entered name.

Using Control Characters for a Screen Display

One way to make more effective use of displays is to use the Carriage Return, Line Feed, and Tab control characters. You can code them as ASCII or hex values, like this:

CONTROL CHARACTER	ASCII	HEX	EFFECT ON CURSOR
Carriage return	13	0DH	Resets to left position of screen
Line feed	10	0AH	Advances to next line
Tab	09	09H	Advances to next tab stop

You can use these control characters for handling the cursor whenever you display output or accept keyboard input. Here's an example that displays the contents of a character string named REPTITLE, followed by Carriage Return (13) and Line Feed (10) to set the cursor on the next line. Using the EQU directive to redefine the control characters may make a program more readable:

```
CR          EQU  13    ;or EQU 0DH
LF          EQU  10    ;or EQU 0AH
TAB         EQU  09    ;or EQU 09H
REPTITLE    DB   TAB,  'Annual Rainfall Statistics', CR, LF, '$'
            ...
            MOV  AH,09H          ;Request display
            LEA  DX,REPTITLE     ;Load address of title
            INT  21H             ;Call interrupt service
```

INT 21H FUNCTION 02H FOR SCREEN DISPLAY

INT 21H function 02H is useful for displaying single characters. Load in DL the character that is to display at the current cursor position, and request INT 21H. The Tab, Carriage Return, and Line Feed characters act normally, and the operation automatically advances the cursor. The instructions are:

```
MOV AH,02H        ;Request display character
MOV DL,char       ;Character to display
INT 21H           ;Call interrupt service
```

The following example shows how to use this service to display a string of characters. The string to display is defined in CO_TITLE. The example loads the address of CO_TITLE in DI and its length in CX. The loop involves incrementing DI (by INC) for each successive character and decrementing CX (by LOOP) for the number of characters to display. Here are the instructions:

```
CO_TITLE DB 'Intertech Corp.', 13, 10
        ...
        MOV AH,02H            ;Request display character
        MOV CX,17             ;Length of character string
        LEA DI,COTITLE        ;Address of character string
L10:    MOV DL,[DI]           ;Character to display
```

```
INT 21H                  ;Call interrupt service
INC DI                   ;Increment for next character
LOOP L10                 ;Repeat 17 times
...                      ;Finished
```

FILE HANDLES

This section examines the use of *file handles* for screen and keyboard operations. A file handle is simply a number that refers to a specific device. The following standard file handles are preset and do not require defining:

HANDLE	DEVICE
00	Input, normally keyboard (CON), may be redirected
01	Output, normally display (CON), may be redirected
02	Error output, display (CON), may not be redirected
03	Auxiliary device (AUX)
04	Printer (LPT1 or PRN)

As shown, the normal file handles are 00 for keyboard input and 01 for screen display. File handles for disk devices (covered in Chapter 17) have to be set by your program. You can also use these services for redirecting input and output to other devices, although this feature doesn't concern us here.

INT 21H FUNCTION 40H FOR SCREEN DISPLAY

INT 21H function 40H uses file handles to process display operations. To request this service, load the following registers:

AH = Function 40H   CX = Number of characters to display

BX = File handle 01   DX = Address of the display area

A successful INT operation delivers to AX the number of bytes written and clears the Carry Flag (which you may test).

An unsuccessful INT operation sets the Carry Flag and returns an error code in AX: 05H = access denied (for an invalid or disconnected device) or 06H = invalid handle. Because AX could contain either a length or an error code, the only way to determine an error condition is to test the Carry Flag, although display errors are rare:

```
JC error-routine     ;Test for display error
```

The operation acts upon control characters 07H (Beep), 08H (Backspace), 0AH (Line Feed), and 0DH (Carriage Return), just like INT 21H function 09H. The following instructions illustrate function 40H:

```
PROMPT      DB        'Part number?',     0DH, 0AH      ;Display area
            ...
            MOV       AH,40H                ;Request display
            MOV       BX,01                 ;File handle for screen
            MOV       CX,14                 ;14 characters includes 0DH + 0AH
            LEA       DX,PROMPT             ;Display area
            INT       21H                   ;Call interrupt service
```

Exercise: Using Function 40H for Displaying on the Screen

Let's use DEBUG to examine the internal effects of using a file handle to display your name. Load DEBUG and, when its prompt appears, type A 100 to begin keying in the following assembly statements (but not the leftmost numbers) at offset location 100H (remember that DEBUG assumes that entered numbers are in hexadecimal format):

```
100 MOV AH,40
102 MOV BX,01
105 MOV CX,xx (Insert length of your name in hex)
108 MOV DX,10F
10B INT 21
10D JMP 100
10F DB 'x----x' (Insert your name here)
```

The instructions set AH to request a display and set offset 10EH in DX—the location of the DB containing your name.

When you have keyed in the instructions, press <Enter> again. To unassemble the program, use the U command (U 100,10E), and, to trace execution, press R and then repeated T commands. On reaching INT 21, use the P (Proceed) command to execute the interrupt through to the JMP instruction; it should display your name on the screen.

INT 21H FUNCTION 3FH FOR KEYBOARD INPUT

INT 21H function 3FH uses file handles to request keyboard input, although it's a somewhat clumsy operation. Load the following registers:

AH = Function 3FH   CX = Maximum number of characters to accept
BX = File handle 00   DX = Address of area for entering characters

A successful INT operation clears the Carry Flag (which you may test) and sets AX with the number of characters entered.

An unsuccessful INT operation could occur because of an invalid handle; the operation sets the Carry Flag and inserts an error code in AX: 05H = access denied (for an invalid or disconnected device) or 06H = invalid handle. Because AX could contain either a length or an error code, the only way to determine an error condition is to test the Carry Flag, although keyboard errors are rare.

Like INT 21H function 0AH, function 3FH also acts on Backspace, but ignores extended function keys such as F1, Home, and PageUp, seriously limiting its usefulness.

The following instructions illustrate the use of function 3FH:

```
KBINPUT    DB    20 DUP(' ')    ;Input area
           ...
           MOV   AH,3FH          ;Request keyboard input
           MOV   BX,00           ;File handle for keyboard
           MOV   CX,20           ;Maximum 20 characters
           LEA   DX,KBINPUT      ;Input area
           INT   21H            ;Call interrupt service
```

The INT operation waits for you to enter characters, but unfortunately does not check whether the number of characters exceeds the maximum in CX (20 in the example). Pressing <Enter> (0DH) signals the end of an entry. For example, typing the characters "Intertech Corp" delivers the following to KBINPUT:

```
                    |Intertech Corp|0DH|0AH|
```

The typed characters are immediately followed by Enter (0DH), which you typed, and Line Feed (0AH), which you did not type. Because of this feature, the maximum number and the length of the input area that you define should provide for an additional two characters. If you type fewer characters than the maximum, the locations in memory following the typed characters still contain the previous contents.

A successful INT operation clears the Carry Flag and sets AX with the number of characters delivered. In the preceding example, this number is 14, plus 2 for the Enter and Line Feed characters. Accordingly, a program can use the value in AX to determine the actual number of characters typed. Although this feature is trivial for YES and NO type of replies, it is useful for replies with variable length, such as names.

If the number of characters that you key in exceeds the maximum in CX, the operation actually accepts all the characters. Consider a situation in which the maximum in CX is 08 and a user types the characters "PC Exchange". The operation sets the first eight characters in the input area to "PC Excha" with no Enter and Line Feed following and sets AX with a length of 08. Now, watch this—the next INT operation to execute does not accept a name directly from the keyboard because it still has the rest of the previous string in its buffer. It delivers "nge" followed by Enter and Line Feed to the input area and sets AX to 05. Both operations are "normal" and clear the Carry Flag:

```
          First INT:     PC Excha          AX = 08
          Second INT:    nge, 0DH, 0AH     AX = 05
```

A program can tell whether a user has keyed in a "valid" number of characters if (a) the number returned in AX is less than the number in CX, or (b) the number returned in AX is equal to that in CX, and the last two characters in the input area are 0DH and 0AH. If neither condition is true, you have to issue additional INTs to accept the remaining characters. After all this, you may well wonder what is the point of specifying a maximum length in CX.

Exercise: Using Function 3FH for Keying in Data

Here's a DEBUG exercise in which you can view the effect of using INT 21H function 3FH for keying in data. The program allows you to key in up to 12 characters, including a character for Enter and one for Line Feed. Load DEBUG and, when the prompt appears, type A 100 to begin entering the following instructions (but not the numbers) at location 100H:

```
100   MOV AH,3F
102   MOV BX,00
105   MOV CX,0C
108   MOV DX,10F
10B   INT 21
10D   JMP 100
10F   DB 20 20 20 20 20 20 20 20 20 20 20 20
```

When you have keyed in the instructions, press <Enter> again. The program sets AH and BX to request keyboard input and inserts the maximum length in CX. It also sets offset 10FH in DX—the location of the DB where the entered characters are to begin.

Try the U command (U 100,10E) to unassemble the program. Use R and repeated T commands to trace the execution of the four MOV instructions. At location 10BH, use P (Proceed) to execute through the interrupt; the operation waits for you to key in characters followed by <Enter>. Check the contents of AX and the Carry Flag, and use D DS:10F to display the entered characters in memory. You can continue looping indefinitely.

KEY POINTS

- Interrupts that handle screen displays transfer data to the Video Display Area.
- The INT 10H instruction transfers control to BIOS for display operations. Two common operations are function 02H (set cursor) and 06H (scroll screen).
- When using INT 21H function 09H for displaying, define a delimiter ($) immediately following the display area. A missing delimiter can cause spectacular effects on the screen.
- INT 21H function 0AH for keyboard input requires a parameter list. The first byte contains a maximum value and the operation inserts an actual value in the second byte.
- A file handle is a number that refers to a specific device. The numbers for file handles 00 through 04 are preset, whereas others can be set by your program.
- For INT 21H function 40H to display, use handle 01 in BX.
- For INT 21H function 3FH for keyboard input, use handle 00 in BX. The operation inserts Enter and Line Feed characters following the typed characters in the input area, but does not check for characters that exceed your specified maximum.

REVIEW QUESTIONS AND EXERCISES

8-1. On an 80-column screen, what are the locations as hex values for (a) the bottom rightmost location, and (b) the top leftmost location?

8-2. Write the instructions to set the cursor to row 12, column 24.

8-3. Write the instructions to clear the screen, beginning at row 08, column 0, with color attribute 71H.

8-4. Define data items and use INT 21H function 09H to display a message "What is the date (mm/dd/yy)?" Follow the message with a beep.

8-5. Define data items and use INT 21H function 0AH to accept input from the keyboard according to the format in Question 8-4.

8-6. The section titled "Clearing the Input Area" shows how to clear to blank the entire keyboard input area, defined as KBNAME. Change the example so that it clears only the characters immediately to the right of the most recently entered name.

8-7. Revise the program in Figure 8-2 for the following changes: (a) Allow for names up to 25 characters; (b) instead of row 12, set the center at row 07; (c) instead of clearing the entire screen, clear only rows 0 through 07 and use attribute 16H in the operation; (d) for each procedure, push used registers at the start and pop them on exit. Assemble, link, and test the program.

8-8. Identify the standard file handles for (a) the printer, (b) keyboard input, (c) normal screen display.

8-9. Define data items and use INT 21H function 40H to display the message "What is the date (mm/dd/yy)?" Follow the message with a Carriage Return, Line Feed, and Beep.

8-10. In a program, INT 21H function 3FH has set the Carry Flag and returns 06H in AX. What is a possible cause of this error?

8-11. Define data items and use INT 21H function 3FH to accept input from the keyboard according to the format in Question 8-9.

8-12. Revise Question 8-7 for use with INT 21H functions 3FH and 40H for input and display. Assemble, link, and test the program.

Chapter 9

VIDEO SYSTEMS

> Objective: To cover advanced features of screen handling, including scrolling, reverse video, setting modes and attributes, and the use of graphics.

INTRODUCTION

This chapter further advances the material on video operations introduced in Chapter 8. The first section describes the components of a video system: monitor, Video Display Area, and Video Controller. The next sections explain such video features as modes, attributes, and pages. The large section on the BIOS video operation, INT 10H, describes many of the functions involved with such activities as setting mode, setting cursor, scrolling the screen, displaying characters, and setting attributes.

The last few sections explain the various functions used for displaying graphics, as well as direct video display and designing boxes for menus.

This chapter covers the following services offered by BIOS INT 10H:

00H	Set video mode	0BH	Set color palette
01H	Set cursor size	0CH	Write pixel dot
02H	Set cursor position	0DH	Read pixel dot
03H	Return cursor status	0EH	Write in teletype mode
05H	Select active page	0FH	Get current video mode
06H	Scroll up screen	10H	Access palette registers
07H	Scroll down screen	11H	Access character generator
08H	Read character/attribute	12H	Select alternative routine
09H	Display character/attribute	13H	Display character string
0AH	Display character	1BH	Return video information

COMPONENTS OF A VIDEO SYSTEM

The common (or once-common) video adapters include MDA (monochrome display adapter), CGA (color graphics adapter), EGA (enhanced graphics adapter), and VGA (video graphics array). The VGA and its superVGA successors replaced the CGA and EGA video adapters. Because of the prevalence of the VGA system, this book describes only its features.

The basic components of a video system are monitor, Video Display Area, video BIOS, and Video Controller. Other integrated devices include Character Generator, Mode Controller, Video Signal Generator, and Attribute Decoder. Figure 9-1 shows their relationship.

Monitor.   The monitor's screen consists of a group of closely-spaced horizontal lines known as the *raster*. Each line contains hundreds of points called *pixels*, which consist of three luminescent phosphor dots for each of the three primary additive colors: red, green, and blue.

Three electron beams activate the three colors in the pixels. The beams start at the upper left corner of the screen and scan each line successively from left to right. The varying intensity of the beams sets the brightness and color of the pixels. The combinations of red, green, and blue, along with intensity, create the various colors and shades.

Video Display Area.   A program sends data—characters for text mode and pixels for graphics mode—to the Video Display Area (or buffer) in RAM either by means of an INT operation or by transferring directly into the area. The data undergoes a rather complex transformation before it is finally displayed on the screen. The starting address of the Video Area depends on the type of video adapter and the chosen mode. The interrupts that handle screen displays transfer your data directly to this area. Following are the beginning segment addresses for major video modes:

- A000:[0] Used for font descriptors when in text mode and for high-resolution graphics for video modes 0DH through 13H.

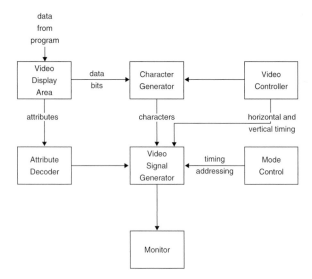

Figure 9-1   Video System Components

- B000:[0] Monochrome text for mode 07H.
- B800:[0] Text and graphics for modes 00H through 06H.

The video circuitry continuously scans the data in the Video Area and refreshes the screen accordingly. Data in the Video Area may be ASCII text (alphanumeric) or graphics format. In text mode, each character in the Video Area requires two bytes: one byte for the character, immediately followed by an attribute byte that determines the character's color and intensity. In graphics mode, the Video Area contains groups of bits that determine the color of each pixel.

The Video Display Area allows you to store data in *pages*. A page stores a screenful of data and is numbered 0 through 7. Page number 0 is the default and, for text modes, begins in the Video Display Area at B800[0]. Page 1 begins at B900[0], page 2 at BA00[0], page 3 at BB00[0], and so forth.

You may format any of the pages in memory, although you can display only one page at a time. In text mode, each character to be displayed on the screen requires two bytes of memory—one byte for the character and a second for its attribute. In this way, a full page of characters for 80 columns and 25 rows requires $80 \times 25 \times 2 = 4,000$ bytes. The amount of memory actually allocated for each page is 4K, or 4,096 bytes, so that a block of 96 unused bytes immediately follows each page.

Video Controller.   The Video Controller generates horizontal and vertical timing signals. It also maintains and increments a counter that indicates the current location in the Video Display Area. The counter tells the video circuitry the current data to access, to decode, and to send to the monitor. The Controller has to synchronize the delivery of the data with the timing signals.

Immediately following its horizontal scanning, the Controller issues a vertical synch signal, which causes the monitor to perform vertical scanning beginning at the top left corner. Both the horizontal and vertical operations perform *overscanning*, which results in a border (the overscan area) around the four sides of the screen.

Other tasks of the Video Controller involve handling the size and location of the cursor and selecting the page to be displayed. The Controller also contains a number of registers that a program can access for both reading and rewriting their contents.

The ASCII (or Alphanumeric) Character Generator shown in Figure 9-1 converts ASCII codes from the Video Display Area into dot patterns that comprise the characters. The Attribute Decoder translates the attribute byte from the Video Display Area into signals that determine the character's color.

Video BIOS.   The video BIOS, which acts as an interface to the video adapter, contains such routines as setting the cursor and displaying characters. Video RAM BIOS supports two Video Data Areas:

1. 40:[49H] contains such data as current mode, number of columns, and size of the Video Display Area.
2. 40:[84H] contains such data as number of rows and character height.

For details about the video BIOS, see Chapter 24. The video ROM BIOS routines for the VGA adapter begin at C000:[0].

VIDEO MODES

The video mode determines such factors as text or graphics, color or monochrome, screen resolution, and the number of colors. BIOS INT 10H function 00H is used to initialize the mode for the currently executing program or to switch between text and graphics. Setting the mode also clears the screen. As an example, mode 03 provides text mode, 25 rows × 80 columns, color, and 720 × 400 dots screen resolution. You can also use INT 10H function 0FH, which returns the current video mode in AL. Both functions are covered later.

Text (or alphanumeric) mode is used for displaying the ASCII 256-character. Processing is similar for both color and monochrome, except that color does not support the underline attribute. Following are common text modes, with the mode number on the left:

Mode	Rows x Cols	Type	Display Area	Pages	Resolution	Colors
00	25 x 40	Color	B800	0-7	360 x 400	16
01	25 x 40	Color	B800	0-7	360 x 400	16
02	25 x 80	Color	B800	0-3	720 x 400	16
03	25 x 80	Color	B800	0-3	720 x 400	16
07	25 x 80	Monochrome	B000	0	720 x 400	

- Text modes 00 and 01: 40-column format; although originally designed for the CGA, also work on VGA systems, but are identical on the VGA.
- Text modes 02 and 03: 80-column format; although originally designed for the CGA, also work on VGA systems, but are identical on the VGA.
- Text mode 07 (mono): standard monochrome mode.

Graphics modes are covered later in the section "Using Graphics Mode."

ATTRIBUTES

The *attribute byte* in text mode determines the characteristics of each displayed character. When a program sets an attribute, it remains set; that is, all subsequent displayed characters have the same attribute until another operation changes it. You can use INT 10H functions to generate a screen attribute and perform such actions as scroll up or down, read attribute or character, or display attribute or character. You can use the DEBUG command D B800:0 to view the Video Display Area to see each 1-byte character, immediately followed by its 1-byte attribute.

The attribute byte has the following format:

	Background			Foreground		
Attribute:	BL	R	G	B	I	R	G	B
Bit number:	7	6	5	4	3	2	1	0

The letters R, G, and B indicate bit positions for red, green, and blue, respectively, for each of the three primary additive colors.

- Bit 7 (BL) sets *blinking* (may be disabled)
- Bits 6–4 determine the character's *background* color
- Bit 3 (I) sets normal (if 0) or high *intensity* (if 1)
- Bits 2–0 determine the character's *foreground* color

The background can display one of eight colors and the foreground characters can display one of 16 colors. Blinking and intensity apply only to the foreground, although you can use INT 10H function 10H to override the blinking feature and enable the foreground to display 16 colors. You can also select one of 16 colors for the border.

You can combine the three basic video colors red (R), green (G), and blue (B) in the attribute byte to form a total of eight colors (including black and white) and can set high intensity (I in the following chart), for a total of 16 colors:

COLOR	I	R	G	B	HEX	COLOR	I	R	G	B	HEX
Black	0	0	0	0	0	Gray	1	0	0	0	8
Blue	0	0	0	1	1	Light blue	1	0	0	1	9
Green	0	0	1	0	2	Light green	1	0	1	0	A
Cyan	0	0	1	1	3	Light cyan	1	0	1	1	B
Red	0	1	0	0	4	Light red	1	1	0	0	C
Magenta	0	1	0	1	5	Light magenta	1	1	0	1	D
Brown	0	1	1	0	6	Yellow	1	1	1	0	E
White	0	1	1	1	7	Bright white	1	1	1	1	F

If the background and foreground colors are the same, the displayed character is invisible. You can also use the attribute byte to cause a foreground character to blink. The video system causes blinking in this way: It substitutes the background attribute for the foreground attribute about every two seconds, so that the normal character alternates with a blank character.

Here are some typical attributes, where BL means blinking:

BACK-GROUND	FORE-GROUND	BACKGROUND				FOREGROUND				
		BL	R	G	B	I	R	G	B	HEX
Black	Blue	0	0	0	0	0	0	0	1	01
Blue	Red	0	0	0	1	0	1	0	0	14
Green	Cyan	0	0	1	0	0	0	1	1	23
White	Light magenta	0	1	1	1	1	1	0	1	7D
Green	Gray (blinking)	1	0	1	0	1	0	0	0	A8

For a monochrome monitor, the attribute byte is used the same way as was shown for a color monitor, except that bit 0 sets the underline attribute. To specify attributes, you may set combinations of bits as follows:

- Normal video (black, white) 0000 0111 (07H)
- Reverse video (white, black) 0111 0000 (70H)

The value of the four bits of the attribute byte relate to one of bits 0–3 of the Controller's Color Plane Enable register, which in turn specifies one of the 16 palette registers. Bits 0–5 of the Palette register then relate to the six RGB signals (three normal and three intense). The bit value in the Palette register specifies one of the 256 DAC (digital-to-analog converter) color registers, which determines the displayed color.

You can generate colors by choosing an attribute for each character. You can also revise the default colors in any or all Palette registers by means of INT 10H function 10H, covered later.

The attribute remains set until another operation changes it. The INT 10H functions (explained later) that set the attribute are:

- 06H   Scroll up screen
- 07H   Scroll down screen
- 09H   Display character with attribute
- 13H   Display character string

As an example, the following INT 10H operation uses function 09H to display 12 brown, blinking (1110) asterisks on a blue (0001) background:

```
MOV   AH,09H   ;Request display
MOV   AL,'*'   ;Asterisk
MOV   BH,00H   ;Page number 0
MOV   BL,1EH   ;Color attribute (0001 1110)
MOV   CX,12    ;12 successive characters
INT   10H      ;Call interrupt service
```

You can use DEBUG to check out this example, as well as trying other color combinations.

BIOS INT 10H OPERATIONS

INT 10H supports many services (available through function codes in AH) to facilitate video operations. Subject to returned values, the INT operation preserves the contents of BX, CX, DX, DI, SI, DS, ES, and BP. Some of the functions return or set bits in fields in the BIOS Video Data Area at 0040:nn, described in Chapter 24.

INT 10H attempts to execute anything you throw at it, and does not return status codes or error flags. Be especially careful matching proper function codes with INT 10H; you cannot cause any permanent harm, but an error may cause the screen to go blank so that you have to reboot the system.

The following sections describe the INT 10H functions.

INT 10H Function 00H: Set Video Mode

The purpose of this function is to set the video mode. Load the function code (00H) in AH and the required mode in AL. The following example sets the video mode for standard color text on any type of color monitor:

```
MOV  AH,00H  ;Request set mode
MOV  AL,03H  ;Standard color text
INT  10H     ;Call interrupt service
```

The operation returns no values. It also clears the screen, although you can override this feature by setting bit 7 of the mode to 1 using MOV AL,83H.

INT 10H Function 01H: Set Cursor Size

The cursor is not part of the ASCII character set and exists only in text mode. The Video Controller handles the cursor size and location, with special INT 10H operations for its use. The default size for color VGA is 13 for the top of the cursor and 14 for the bottom (and 6:7 for monochrome). For function 01H to adjust the cursor size vertically, set these registers:

- CH (bits 4–0) = top of cursor (start scan line)
- CL (bits 4–0) = bottom of cursor (end scan line)

The following code enlarges the cursor to its maximum size (0:14):

```
MOV  AH,01H  ;Request set cursor size
MOV  CH,00   ;Start scan line
MOV  CL,14   ;End scan line
INT  10H     ;Call interrupt service
```

The operation returns no values, and the cursor now blinks as a solid rectangle. You can adjust its size anywhere between the stated limits, such as 04:08, 03:10, and so forth. Setting the value to 20H makes the cursor invisible: MOV CX,20H. The cursor retains these attributes until another operation changes them.

INT 10H Function 02H: Set Cursor Position

This operation in text or graphics mode sets the cursor anywhere on a screen according to row:column coordinates. (Function 13H also sets the cursor). Set these registers: BH = page number (0 is the default), DH = row, and DL = column. This example sets row 12, column 30, for page 0:

```
MOV  AH,02H  ;Request set cursor
MOV  BH,00   ;Page number 0 (normal)
MOV  DH,12   ;Row 12
MOV  DL,30   ;Column 30
INT  10H     ;Call interrupt service
```

The cursor location on each page is independent of its location on the other pages. The operation returns no values. Although in graphics mode the cursor is invisible, you can still set it.

INT 10H Function 03H: Return Cursor Status

You can use function 03H in text or graphics mode to determine the present row, column, and size of the cursor, particularly in situations where a program uses the screen temporarily and has to save and reset the original screen. Set page number in BH, just as for function 02H:

```
MOV  AH,03H ;Request cursor location
MOV  BH,00  ;Page number 0 (normal)
INT  10H    ;Call interrupt service
```

The operation leaves AX and BX unchanged and returns these values:

CH = Starting scan line   CL = Ending scan line
DH = Row   DL = Column

The following example uses function 03H to read the cursor and determine its location and size; it then uses function 02H to advance the cursor to the next column on the screen:

```
MOV  AH,03H  ;Request cursor position
MOV  BH,00   ;Page 0
INT  10H     ;Returns column in DL
MOV  AH,02H  ;Request set cursor
INC  DL      ;  at next column
INT  10H     ;Call interrupt service
```

INT 10H Function 05H: Select Active Page

Function 05H lets you select the page that is to be displayed in text or graphics mode. You can create different pages and request alternating between pages. The operation is simply a request that returns no values:

```
MOV  AH,05H    ;Request active page
MOV  AL,page#  ;Page number
INT  10H       ;Call interrupt service
```

INT 10H Function 06H: Scroll Up Screen

This operation for text or graphics mode performs a scroll upward of lines in a specified area of the screen (the active video page). Displayed lines scroll off at the top and blank lines appear at the bottom.

You already used function 06H in Chapter 8, where setting AL to 0 caused the entire screen to scroll up, effectively clearing it. Setting a nonzero value in AL causes that number of lines to scroll up. Load the following registers:

AL = Number of rows (00 for full screen)   CX = Starting row:column
BH = Attribute or pixel value   DX = Ending row:column

The following example in text mode sets a color attribute and scrolls up the full screen one line:

```
MOV  AX,601H    ;Request scroll up one line (text)
MOV  BH,61H     ;Brown background, blue foreground
MOV  CX,0000    ;From 00:00 through
MOV  DX,184FH   ;  24:79 (full screen)
INT  10H        ;Call interrupt service
```

The operation returns no values. Here's a standard approach for scrolling up one line:

1. For setting the row location of the cursor, define an item named, for example, ROW, initialized to zero.
2. Display a line and advance the cursor to the next line.
3. Test whether ROW is near the bottom of the screen (CMP ROW,22).
4. If yes, scroll one line, use ROW to set the cursor, and clear ROW to 00.
5. If no, increment ROW (INC ROW).

The CX:DX registers permit scrolling any portion of the screen. Be careful to coordinate the AL value with the distance in CX:DX, especially when you reference a partial screen. The following instructions create a window (with its own attributes) of 7 rows and 30 columns, with the top left at 12:25, the top right at 12:54, the bottom left at 18:25 and the bottom right at 18:54:

```
MOV  AX,0607H   ;Request scroll 7 lines (text)
MOV  BH,30H     ;Cyan background, black foreground
MOV  CX,0C19H   ;From row 12, column 25 through
MOV  DX,1236H   ;  row 18, column 54 (window)
INT  10H        ;Call interrupt service
```

This example specifies scrolling 7 lines, which is the same value as the distance between rows 12 and 18 inclusive, so that only the window is cleared. It's a common practice when creating a window to scroll (and clear) all of its rows, and subsequently, say, one row at a time. Because the attribute for a window remains set until another operation changes it, you may set various windows to different attributes at the same time.

In graphics mode, you set a pixel value in BH, rather than an attribute. Here's an example that sets rows to red:

```
MOV  AX,060FH   ;Request scroll 15 lines (graphics)
MOV  BH,0100B   ;Pixel value
MOV  CX,0A00H   ;From row 10, column 00 through
MOV  DX,184FH   ;  row 24, column 79
INT  10H        ;Call interrupt service
```

INT 10H Function 07H: Scroll Down Screen

For text and graphics mode, scrolling down the screen causes the bottom lines to scroll off and blank lines to appear at the top. Other than the fact that this operation scrolls down, it works the same as function 06H, which scrolls up. Load the following registers:

AL = Number of rows (00 for full screen)   CX = Starting row:column

BH = Attribute or pixel value   DX = Ending row:column

INT 10H Function 08H: Read Character and Attribute at Cursor

Function 08H can read both a character and its attribute from the Video Display Area in either text or graphics mode. The position of the cursor determines the character that is read. Set the page number in BH, as follows:

```
MOV   AH,08H   ;Request read character/attribute
MOV   BH,00    ;Page number 0 (normal)
INT   10H      ;Call interrupt service
```

The operation delivers the character to AL and its attribute to AH. In graphics mode, the operation returns 00H for a non-ASCII character. Because the operation reads only one character at a time, you have to code a loop to read successive characters.

INT 10H Function 09H: Display Character and Attribute at Cursor

This useful operation displays a specified number of characters in text or graphics mode according to a given attribute. The position of the cursor determines where the character is to display. Set these registers:

AL = ASCII character   BL = Attribute or pixel value
BH = Page number   CX = Count

The count in CX specifies the number of times the operation is to repetitively display the character in AL. The following example in text mode sets a color attribute and displays 60 "happy faces" (01H):

```
MOV   AH,09H   ;Request display (text)
MOV   AL,01H   ;Happy face for display
MOV   BH,0     ;Page number 0 (normal)
MOV   BL,16H   ;Blue background, brown foreground
MOV   CX,60    ;No. of repeated characters
INT   10H      ;Call interrupt service
```

The operation does not advance the cursor or respond to the Bell, Carriage Return, Line Feed, or Tab characters; instead, it attempts to display them as ASCII characters. In text mode, when the display exceeds the rightmost column, the operation automatically continues the display on the next row at column 00.

For graphics mode, use BL for defining the foreground color. If bit 7 is 0, the defined color replaces present pixel colors; if bit 7 is 1, the defined color is combined (XORed) with them.

The following example in graphics mode displays ten hearts:

```
MOV   AH,09H   ;Request display (graphics)
MOV   AL,03H   ;Heart (to be displayed)
MOV   BH,00    ;Page number 0 (normal)
MOV   BL,04    ;Pixel value
MOV   CX,10    ;Ten times
INT   10H      ;Call interrupt service
```

See function 13H for displaying a string of different characters.

INT 10H Function 0AH: Display Character at Cursor

The only difference between functions 0AH and 09H is that function 09H sets the attribute, whereas function 0AH uses the current value. Here is the code for function 0AH:

```
MOV   AH,0AH            ;Request display
MOV   AL,char           ;Character to display
MOV   BH,page#          ;Page number (0 = normal)
MOV   BL,value          ;Pixel value (graphics mode only)
MOV   CX,repetition     ;Number of repeated characters
INT   10H               ;Call interrupt service
```

The operation returns no values.

INT 10H Function 0BH: Set Color Palette

Use this function to set the color palette in graphics mode. The value in BH (00 or 01) determines the purpose of BL:

- BH = 00. Select the background color, where BL contains the color value in bits 0–3 (any of 16 colors):

```
MOV   AH,0BH   ;Request
MOV   BH,00    ;  background
MOV   BL,04    ;  color red (options are 00 - 0FH)
INT   10H      ;Call interrupt service
```

- BH = 01. Select the palette for graphics, where BL contains the palette (0 or 1):

```
MOV   AH,0BH   ;Request color
MOV   BH,01    ;Select palette
MOV   BL,00    ;  number 0 (green, red, brown)
INT   10H      ;Call interrupt service
```

The operation stores the color value in the Color Select register and modifies the palette value in the BIOS Video Display Area at 40:[66].

Once you set a palette, it remains set, but when you change the palette, the whole screen changes to that color combination.

INT 10H Function 0CH: Write Pixel Dot

Function 0CH is used to display a selected color (background and palette) in graphics mode. Set these registers:

AL = Color of the pixel   CX = Column
BH = Page number   DX = Row

The minimum value for the column or row is 0, and the maximum value depends on the video mode. The following example sets a pixel at column 200, row 50:

```
MOV   AH,0CH   ;Request write dot
MOV   AL,03    ;Color of pixel
MOV   BH,0     ;Page number 0
MOV   CX,200   ;Horizontal x-coordinate (column)
MOV   DX,50    ;Vertical y-coordinate (row)
INT   10H      ;Call interrupt service
```

The value in AL becomes the pixel's row value with this exception: In all graphics modes except 04, setting bit 7 of AL to 1 causes the operation to XOR the AL value with that in the Video Display Area.

INT 10H Function 0DH: Read Pixel Dot

This operation, the opposite of function 0CH, reads a dot to determine its color value. Set page number in BH, column in CX, and row in DX. The minimum value for column or row is 0, and the maximum value depends on the video mode:

```
MOV   AH,0DH   ;Request read pixel dot
MOV   BH,0     ;Page number 0
MOV   CX,80    ;Horizontal x-coordinate
MOV   DX,110   ;Vertical y-coordinate
INT   10H      ;Call interrupt service
```

The operation returns the pixel color in AL.

INT 10H Function 0EH: Display in Teletype Mode

This operation lets you use the monitor as a terminal for simple displays in text and graphics modes, used as follows:

```
MOV   AH,0EH    ;Request display
MOV   AL,char   ;Character to display
MOV   BL,color  ;Foreground color (graphics mode)
INT   10H       ;Call interrupt service
```

Backspace (08H), Bell (07H), Carriage Return (0DH), and Line Feed (0AH) act as commands for screen formatting, but Tab (09H) does not. The operation automatically advances the cursor, wraps characters onto the next line, scrolls the screen, and maintains the present screen attributes. The operation returns no values.

INT 10H Function 0FH: Get Current Video Mode

You can use this function to determine the current video mode. Here's an example:

```
MOV   AH,0FH   ;Request video mode
INT   10H      ;Call interrupt service
CMP   AL,03    ;If mode 3,
JE    ...      ;  jump
```

The operation returns these values from the BIOS Video Data Area: AL = current video mode, AH = number of screen columns, and BH = active video page.

Program: Displaying the ASCII Character Set

The program in Figure 8-1 used INT 21H function 09H to display the ASCII character set, but bypassed the Backspace, Bell, Carriage Return, and Line Feed control characters. The revised program in Figure 9-2 uses INT 10H to display the full character set using the following functions:

OFH Get the current video mode and save it.

00H Set video mode 03 for this program and restore the original mode on exiting.

08H Read the attribute at the current cursor position for use by function 06H.

06H Scroll up the screen to clear the entire screen using the attribute just read. Also, create a 16-line window with brown foreground and blue background for the displayed characters.

02H Set the cursor initially and advance it for each displayed character.

0AH Display each character, including control characters, at the current cursor position.

The characters are displayed in a grid of 16 columns and 16 rows. This program, like others in this book, are written for clarity rather than processing speed. You could revise the program to make it run faster, for example, by using registers for the row, column, and ASCII character value. Also, because INT 10H destroys only the contents of AX, the values in the other registers don't have to be reloaded. However, the program won't run noticeably faster and it would lose some clarity.

INT 10H Function 10H: Access Palette Registers and Video DAC

This operation provides a number of functions concerned with reading and changing the Palette registers, the Overscan (border) register, and Video DAC. Load a subfunction in AL to specify an activity.

Subfunction 00H: Update Palette Register. To change the color displayed by any of the 16 Palette registers, load the color value in BH and Palette register number (00-0FH) in BL:

```
MOV  AX,1000H  ;Request update palette register
MOV  BH,02     ;New color (green)
MOV  BL,01     ;Palette register
INT  10H       ;Call interrupt service
```

Subfunction 01H: Update Border Color. The default border color is black. To change the color, load the new color in BH and request this operation:

```
MOV  AX,1001H  ;Request update border color
MOV  BH,02     ;New color (green)
INT  10H       ;Call interrupt service
```

```
TITLE        A09BIOAS (EXE)  INT 10H to display ASCII character set
             .MODEL SMALL
             .STACK 64
             .DATA
CHAR_CTR  DB    00               ;Counter for ASCII characters
COL       DB    24               ;Column of screen
ROW       DB    04               ;Row of screen
MODE      DB    ?                ;Video mode
.286  ;----------------------------------------------------------------
             .CODE
A10MAIN   PROC  NEAR
          MOV   AX,@DATA     ;Initialize
          MOV   DS,AX        ;  segment
          MOV   ES,AX        ;  registers
          CALL  B10MODE      ;Get/set video mode
          CALL  C10CLEAR     ;Clear screen
A20:
          CALL  D10CURSOR    ;Set cursor
          CALL  E10DISPLY    ;Display characters
          CMP   CHAR_CTR,0FFH ;Last character displayed?
          JE    A30           ;  yes, exit
          INC   CHAR_CTR     ;Increment char. counter
          ADD   COL,02       ;Increment column
          CMP   COL,56       ;At end of column?
          JNE   A20          ;  no, bypass
          INC   ROW          ;  yes, increment row
          MOV   COL,24       ;  and reset column
          JMP   A20
A30:
          MOV   AH,10H       ;Request get character
          INT   16H          ;  from keyboard
          MOV   AH,00H       ;Request reset mode
          MOV   AL,MODE      ;  to original value
          INT   10H
          MOV   AX,4C00H     ;End of processing
          INT   21H
A10MAIN   ENDP
;                 Get and save current mode, set new mode:
;                 ------------------------------------
B10MODE   PROC  NEAR
          MOV   AH,0FH       ;Request get mode
          INT   10H
          MOV   MODE,AL      ;Save mode
          MOV   AH,00H       ;Request set new mode
          MOV   AL,03        ;Standard color
          INT   10H
          RET
B10MODE   ENDP
;                 Clear screen, create window, set attribute:
;                 ------------------------------------
C10CLEAR  PROC  NEAR
          PUSHA              ;Preserve general registers
          MOV   AH,08H       ;Request get current
          INT   10H          ;  attribute in AH
          MOV   BH,AH        ;Move it to BH
```

Figure 9-2   INT 10H to Display the ASCII Character Set

Subfunction 03H: Select Background Intensity.   This operation lets you enable or disable the blinking attribute. Load a code in BL (00H = disable and 01H = enable). The operation accesses the Attribute Controller's Mode Control register. With blinking disabled, all 16 Palette registers are available for background color instead of eight.

```
MOV  AX,1003H  ;Request
MOV  BL,00H    ;  disable blinking
INT  10H       ;Call interrupt service
```

```
                MOV     AX,0600H      ;Scroll whole screen
                MOV     CX,0000       ;Upper left location
                MOV     DX,184FH      ;Lower right location
                INT     10H
                MOV     AX,0610H      ;Create 16-line window
                MOV     BH,16H        ;Blue backgrd, brown foregrd
                MOV     CX,0418H      ;Upper left corner  04:24
                MOV     DX,1336H      ;Lower right corner  19:54
                INT     10H
                POPA                  ;Restore registers
                RET
C10CLEAR   ENDP
;                       Set cursor to row and column:
;                       ----------------------------
D10CURSOR  PROC    NEAR
                PUSHA                 ;Preserve general registers
                MOV     AH,02H        ;Request set cursor
                MOV     BH,00         ;Page 0 (normal)
                MOV     DH,ROW        ;New row
                MOV     DL,COL        ;New column
                INT     10H
                POPA                  ;Restore registers
                RET
D10CURSOR  ENDP
;                       Display ASCII characters one at a time:
;                       -------------------------------------
E10DISPLY  PROC    NEAR
                PUSHA                 ;Preserve general registers
                MOV     AH,0AH        ;Request display
                MOV     AL,CHAR_CTR   ;ASCII character
                MOV     BH,00         ;Page 0
                MOV     CX,01         ;One character
                INT     10H
                POPA                  ;Restore registers
                RET
E10DISPLY  ENDP
                END     A10MAIN
```

Figure 9-2   *Continued*

Subfunction 07H: Read Palette Register.   This operation allows you to determine the color code stored in any of the 16 Palette registers. Request the register number in BL:

```
        MOV   AX,1007H     ;Request color code
        MOV   BL,register  ;  from Palette register
        INT   10H          ;Call interrupt service
```

The operation returns the color code in BH. See subfunction 09H for the different colors in the Palette register.

Subfunction 08H: Read Overscan Register.   This operation returns the color code currently in the Overscan (border) register:

```
        MOV   AX,1008H   ;Read overscan register
        INT   10H        ;Call interrupt service
```

The operation returns the color code in BH.

Subfunction 09H: Read Table of Palette Register Values.   This operation returns all the current Palette and Overscan register values into a 17-byte table. You define the table and send its address in ES:DX. The following example assumes that ES contains the appropriate segment address:

```
REGTABLE  DB  17 DUP(?)       ;17-byte table
          ...
          MOV  AX,1009H        ;Read Palette register values
          LEA  DX,REGTABLE     ; into table (ES:DX)
          INT  10H             ;Call interrupt service
```

The operation returns the contents of the Palette registers into the first 16 bytes and the Overscan register into the 17th. A typical default is 00 01 02 03 04 05 14 07 38 39 3A 3B 3C 3D 3E 3F 00. The last value, 00 for black, is the border color.

Subfunction 10H: Update DAC Color Register.   The Video DAC (digital-to-analog converter) contains 256 3-byte color registers:

00-0FH   Range of default CGA colors

10-1FH   Gray scale of increasing intensity

20-67H   First of three groups; high intensity blue, red, green

68-AFH   Second of three groups; medium intensity blue, red, green

B0-F7H   Third of three groups; low intensity blue, red, green

F8-FFH   Black

The three groups at 20, 68, and B0 each consist of three color ranges of decreasing saturation. Subfunction 10H enables you to update any DAC register with color values:

```
MOV  AX,1010H       ;Update DAC color register
MOV  BX,register    ;DAC register number
MOV  CH,green       ;Values for green,
MOV  CL,blue        ; blue, and
MOV  DH,red         ; red
INT  10H            ;Call interrupt service
```

The operation uses only the low-order six bits of the color code.

Subfunction 12H: Update Block of DAC Registers.   This operation enables you to update a block of DAC registers with color values. You define a table of colors (three bytes per register for red, green, and blue) and send its address in ES:DX. The following example assumes that ES contains the appropriate segment address:

```
DACTABLE  DB  nn DUP(?)        ;Table (3 bytes per register)
          ...
          MOV  AX,1012H        ;Update block of DAC registers
          MOV  BX,register     ;First DAC register of block
          MOV  CX,number       ;Number of DAC registers in block
          LEA  DX,DACTABLE     ; into table (ES:DX)
          INT  10H             ;Call interrupt service
```

Subfunction 15H: Read Video DAC Color Register.   Subfunction 15H enables you to read any DAC register:

```
        MOV  AX,1015H     ;Read video DAC color register
        MOV  BX,register  ;DAC register number
        INT  10H          ;Call interrupt service
```

The operation returns green in CH, blue in CL, and red in DH.

Subfunction 17H: Read Block of DAC Registers.   This operation enables you to
read a block of DAC registers (up to 256) into a table (three bytes per register for red,
green, and blue). Send its address in ES:DX. The following example assumes that ES
contains the appropriate segment address:

```
DACTABLE  DB nn DUP(?)       ;Table (3 bytes per register)
          ...
          MOV AX,1017H       ;Read block of DAC registers
          MOV BX,register    ;First DAC register of block
          MOV CX,number      ;Number of DAC registers in block
          LEA DX,DACTABLE    ;Table (ES:DX)
          INT 10H            ;Call interrupt service
```

Returned values in the table could look like 00 00 00 (register 0), 00 00 2A (register 1), 00
2A 00 (register 2), and so forth.

Subfunction 1BH: Perform Gray Scaling on DAC Registers.   This operation
enables you to perform gray scaling on a block of Video DAC registers:

```
        MOV  AX,101BH     ;Perform gray scaling
        MOV  BX,register  ;First DAC register of block
        MOV  CX,number    ;Number of DAC registers in block
        INT  10H          ;Call interrupt service
```

Try, say, BX = 0 and CX = 10H to see the effect of gray scaling.

INT 10H Function 11H: Access Character Generator

This operation supports a number of subfunctions concerned with text and graphics character generators, which you can use to change the size and shape of displayed characters.
Twelve related subfunctions appear in the following chart:

	User-defined table	8 x 14 size	8 x 8 size	8 x 16 size
Load text-based characters	00H	01H	02H	04H
Load text-based characters and program Video Controller	10H	11H	12H	14H
Load graphics-based characters	21H	22H	23H	24H

Subfunctions 00H, 10H, and 21H.   These operations involving user-defined
characters are outside the scope of this book.

Subfunctions 01H, 02H, and 04H.   These operations support text-based characters in three predefined sizes.

Subfunctions 11H, 12H, and 14H (default).   These operations are similar to 00H, 01H, and 04H, respectively, but also reprogram the Video Controller to handle the height of the character matrix. For these functions, load BL with the code for the Character-Generator table. The following example loads 8×8 text-based characters:

```
MOV  AX,1112H  ;Load 8 x 8 text characters
MOV  BL,0      ;Table codes 0-7
INT  10H       ;Call interrupt service
```

The operation causes the screen to display 43 lines of 8 x 8 size characters.

Subfunctions 22H, 23H, and 24H.   These operations support graphics-based characters. For these, BL indicates the character-rows per screen, where 1 = 14, 2 = 25, 3 = 43, and 0 = value in DL gives character-rows per screen:

```
MOV  AX,1123H   ;Load 8 x 8 graphics characters
MOV  BL,code    ;0, 1, 2, or 3
MOV  DL,number  ;Character-rows when BL = 0
INT  10H        ;Call interrupt service
```

Subfunction 03H: Select Display Character Definition Table.   You load BL with a bit string. Depending on bit 3 of the string's attribute (intensity):

• If 0, bits 0, 1, and 4 indicate using 1 of 8 of the 256 character tables.
• If 1, bits 2, 3, and 5 indicate the character table to use.

Subfunction 30H: Read Character Generator Data.   To get data about the current Character Generator, load BH with one of the following codes:

0 = Contents of INT 1FH vector
1 = Contents of INT 43H vector
2 = Address of BIOS 8 x 14 Character table
3 = Address of first half of BIOS 8 x 8 Character table
4 = Address of second half of BIOS 8 x 8 Character table
5 = Address of BIOS 9×14 Alternate Character table
6 = Address of BIOS 8×16 Character table
7 = Address of BIOS 9×16 Alternate Character table

The operation returns these values: CX = height of character matrix in points, DL = number of rows − 1 (typically 18H), and ES:BP = address of Character Definition table. You can use DEBUG (in text mode) to display each option like this:

```
MOV  AX,1130  ;Request character generator info
MOV  BH,0     ;Code 0, 1, 2, ..., 7
INT  10       ;Call interrupt service
```

```
            INC   BH         ;Next DAC register
            JMP   100        ;Repeat
```

Use DEBUG's D command to display the segment:offset delivered in ES:BP, as D ES: offset.

INT 10H Function 12H: Select Alternative Video Routine

This operation supports a number of subfunctions coded in BL:

- Subfunction 10H: Return video configuration information. The operation returns:

  BH = Video class (0 is color and 1 is monochrome)

  BL = Amount of video RAM (0 = 64K, 1 = 128K, 2 = 192K, and 3 = 256K+)

  CH = Adapter bits

  CL = Configuration switch setting

- Subfunction 30H: Select scan lines for text mode. You can use this operation to change the vertical resolution of scan lines in text modes 0, 1, 2, 3, and 7. Load AL with the number of scan lines: 0 = 200, 1 = 350, and 2 = 400. Follow this operation with function 00H to set mode:

```
            MOV   AX,1202H   ;Request select 400 lines
            MOV   BL,30H     ;  scan lines
            INT   10H        ;Call interrupt service
            MOV   AX,0003H   ;Set text mode 03 (720 x 400)
            INT   10H        ;Call interrupt service
```

- Other subfunctions include enabling and disabling gray-scale summing, cursor emulation, and refresh control.

INT 10H Function 13H: Display Character String

This powerful operation in text or graphics modes displays strings of any length with options for setting the attribute and moving the cursor. Load ES:BP with the segment:offset address of the string to display. The operation acts on the Backspace, Bell, Carriage Return, and Line Feed control characters, but not on Tab.

```
            MOV   AH,13H            ;Request display string
            MOV   AL,subfunction    ;00, 01, 02, or 03 (see below)
            MOV   BH,page#          ;Page number
            MOV   BL,attribute      ;Screen attribute
            LEA   BP,address        ;Address of string in ES:BP
            MOV   CX,length         ;Length of string
            MOV   DH,row            ;Screen row
            MOV   DL,column         ;Screen column
            INT   10H               ;Call interrupt service
```

The four subfunctions that you set in AL are:

    00   Display string and attribute; do not advance cursor

    01   Display string and attribute; advance cursor

    02   Display character and then attribute; do not advance cursor

    03   Display character and then attribute; advance cursor

Subfunctions 02 and 03 require that each character in the display string is immediately followed by an attribute byte. This feature facilitates displaying data with mixed attributes and displaying directly from the Video Display Area.

In graphics modes, setting bit 7 of BL to 1 causes the operation to XOR the string value with that in the Video Area.

Program: Setting Attributes and Scrolling

The program in Figure 9-3 accepts names from the keyboard and displays them on the screen. To make things more interesting, it displays the prompt with reverse video (blue on white), accepts the name normally (white on blue), and displays the name so that it is displayed as right-adjusted at column 70 of same row with reverse video. Here is the format:

```
          Name? Mark Twain ... Mark Twain
              |                      |
          Column 0              Column 70
```

The program consists of the following procedures:

- A10MAIN provides the main logic for accepting any number of keyboard entries and uses INT 10H function 10H to disable the blink attribute.
- B10PROMPT displays a prompt for the user to enter a name.
- C10INPUT uses INT 21H function 0AH for keyboard input.
- D10NAME calculates the starting column so that the entered name is right-adjusted when displayed. Calls E10DISPLY to display down the screen until reaching row 23, and then begins scrolling up one line for each additional prompt.
- E10DISPLY uses INT 10H function 13H for setting the cursor and displaying the entered name.
- Q10SCROLL handles scrolling of the screen, and sets the screen background to gray (1000B), which works because blink has been disabled.

INT 10H Function 1AH: Video Display Combination

This operation supports a number of subfunctions concerned with combinations of video subsystems (for example, both color and monochrome monitors). A discussion is outside the scope of this book.

INT 10H Function 1BH: Return Video BIOS Information

For this operation, you define a 64-byte buffer for dynamic information and send its address in ES:DI. In DEBUG, code the operation like this:

```
MOV  AH,1B    ;Request video BIOS information
MOV  BX,0     ;0 for implementation type
MOV  DI,110   ;Offset for dynamic information (ES:DI)
INT  10       ;Call interrupt service
JMP  100
```

The operation returns the following dynamic information (in this example, at ES:110):

```
TITLE      A09NMSCR (EXE)  Setting attributes and scrolling
           .MODEL  SMALL
           .STACK  64
           .DATA
PARLIST    LABEL   BYTE                ;Name parameter list:
MAX_LEN    DB      20                  ;  maximum length of name
ACT_LEN    DB      ?                   ;  no. of chars entered
KB_NAME    DB      20 DUP(' ')         ;  name

LEFT_COL   EQU     51                  ;Left column for display
BOTT_SCRN  EQU     23                  ;Bottom row for display
ATTRIB     DB      00                  ;Screen attribute
COL        DB      05                  ;Screen column
ROW        DB      00                  ;  and row
PROMPT     DB      'Name? '            ;Prompt for input
.386 ; -------------------------------------------------
           .CODE
A10MAIN    PROC    FAR
           MOV     AX,@data            ;Initialize segment
           MOV     DS,AX               ;  registers
           MOV     ES,AX
           MOV     AX,1003H            ;Disable blink
           MOV     BL,00               ;  attribute
           INT     10H
           MOV     AL,00H              ;Request clear
           CALL    Q10SCROLL           ;  full screen
A20:
           MOV     COL,05              ;Set column to 0
           CALL    B10PROMPT           ;Display prompt
           CALL    C10INPUT            ;Provide for input of name
           CMP     ACT_LEN,00          ;No name? (indicates end)
           JE      A30                 ;  yes, exit
           CALL    D10NAME             ;Display name
           JMP     A20
A30:
           MOV     AL,00H              ;Exit,
           CALL    Q10SCROLL           ;  clear screen,
           MOV     AX,4C00H            ;End of processing
           INT     21H
A10MAIN    ENDP
;                  Display prompt for user:
;                  ------------------------
B10PROMPT  PROC    NEAR                ;Uses BP and CX
           MOV     ATTRIB,71H          ;Set attribute
           LEA     BP,PROMPT           ;Set address of prompt
           MOV     CX,06               ;  and length
           CALL    E10DISPLY           ;Display routine
           RET
B10PROMPT  ENDP
;                  Accept input of name from keyboard:
;                  -----------------------------------
C10INPUT   PROC    NEAR                ;Uses AH and DX
           MOV     AH,0AH              ;Request keyboard
           LEA     DX,PARLIST          ;  input
           INT     21H
           RET
C10INPUT   ENDP
```

Figure 9-3 Reverse Video and Scrolling

```
;                          Set up for displaying name, scroll if
;                          near bottom of the screen:
;                          --------------------------
D10NAME   PROC    NEAR
          PUSHA                       ;Preserve general registers
          MOV     AL,MAX_LEN          ;Calculate screen
          SUB     AL,ACT_LEN          ;   indent,
          ADD     AL,LEFT_COL         ;   add to left column,
          MOV     COL,AL              ;   and store
          MOV     ATTRIB,17H          ;Reverse video
          LEA     BP,KB_NAME          ;Initialize name
          MOVZX   CX,ACT_LEN          ;   and length
          CALL    E10DISPLY           ;Display name
          CMP     ROW,BOTT_SCRN       ;Near bottom of screen?
          JAE     D30                 ;   yes, bypass
          INC     ROW                 ;   no, increment row
          JMP     D90                 ;   and exit
D30:      MOV     AL,01H              ;Scroll screen
          CALL    Q10SCROLL           ;   one line
D90:      POPA                        ;Restore general registers
          RET
D10NAME   ENDP
;                          Display characters and set attribute:
;                          ------------------------------------
E10DISPLY PROC    NEAR                ;BP, CX set on entry
          PUSHA                       ;Preserve general registers
          MOV     AH,13H              ;Request display
          MOV     AL,01               ;   characters
          MOV     BH,00               ;Page number
          MOV     BL,ATTRIB           ;Attribute
          MOV     DH,ROW              ;Screen row
          MOV     DL,COL              ;   and column
          INT     10H
          POPA                        ;Restore general registers
          RET
E10DISPLY ENDP
;                          Scroll screen and set attribute:
;                          --------------------------------
Q10SCROLL PROC    NEAR                ;AL set on entry
          PUSHA                       ;Preserve general registers
          MOV     AH,06H              ;Request scroll
          MOV     BH,86H              ;Gray, brown
          MOV     CX,0000             ;Full
          MOV     DX,184FH            ;   screen
          INT     10H
          POPA                        ;Restore general registers
          RET
Q10SCROLL ENDP
          END     A10MAIN
```

Figure 9-3 *Continued*

OFFSET	SIZE	DESCRIPTION
00H	Dword	Address of Static Functionality table (see below)
04H	Byte	Current video mode
05H	Word	Number of screen columns (5000H = 80)
07H	Word	Size of current video buffer (0010H= 4096)
09H	Word	Address of start of current video buffer
0BH	Array	16-byte array for eight pages of cursor column:rows
1BH	Byte	End of cursor scan line

1CH	Byte	Start of cursor scan line
1DH	Byte	Current video page
1EH	Word	Port for CRTC address register
20H	Byte	Current setting of video mode register
21H	Byte	Current color palette
22H	Byte	Current number of screen rows (19H = 25)
23H	Word	Character height in scan lines (1000H = 16)
25H	Bytes	Active and inactive display combination codes
27H	Word	Number of currently displayed colors
29H	Byte	Number of video pages
2AH	Byte	Scan lines (0 = 200, 1 = 350, 2 = 400, 3 = 480)
2BH	Bytes	Text character tables for normal/high intensity
2DH	Byte	Bits 0–5 indicate enabled/disabled conditions
31H	Byte	Available video memory (3 = 256K+)
32H	Byte	Bits 0–5 indicate active/inactive conditions

The address at the start of the dynamic table points to a 16-byte Static Functionality table. For example, contents 8839 00C0 means offset 3988H and segment C000H, which you use in DEBUG to view the table, as D C000:3988.

OFFSET	SIZE	DESCRIPTION
0H	Byte	Bit 0 = 1 means mode 0 supported, and so forth
01H	Byte	Bit 0 = 1 means mode 8 supported, and so forth
02H	Byte	Bit 0 = 1 means mode 10H supported, and so forth
07H	Byte	Bit = 1 if scan line supported for text mode (bit 0 for 200 lines, 1 for 350, and 2 for 400)
8H	Byte	Maximum number of displayable text character sets
9H	Byte	Number of text character definition tables
0AH	Byte	Bits 0–3 indicate various video capabilities

INT 10H Function 1CH: Save or Restore Video State

This operation supports three subfunctions that return buffer sizes, save requested states, and restore requested states. A discussion is outside the scope of this book.

USING GRAPHICS MODE

Graphics mode uses pixels (picture elements or pels) to generate color patterns. We saw earlier that an attribute in text mode consists of four bits for background and four bits for foreground. The video system interprets pixels in a similar way but, depending on mode, may represent a pixel from one to eight bits.

Setting graphics mode causes the cursor to disappear, although it is still accessible. Following are common graphics modes:

Mode	Type	Display Area	Pages	Resolution	Colors
04H	Color	B800	8	320 x 200	4
05H	Color	B800	8	320 x 200	4
06H	Color	B800	8	640 x 200	2
0DH	Color	B800	8	320 x 200	16
0EH	Color	A000	4	640 x 200	16
0FH	Monochrome	A000	2	640 x 350	1
10H	Color	A000	2	640 x 350	16
11H	Color	A000	1	640 x 480	2
12H	Color	A000	1	640 x 480	16
13H	Color	A000	1	320 x 200	256

- *Graphics modes 04H and 05H.* Original CGA modes also used by VGA for upward compatibility. One byte represents four pixels (two bits per pixel). Two bits can provide 2^2, or four, different colors at the same time.
- *Graphics mode 06H.* Original CGA mode used by VGA for upward compatibility. One byte represents eight pixels (one bit per pixel), giving two colors at one time.
- *Graphics modes 0DH, 0EH, and 10H.* Original EGA modes also used by VGA for upward compatibility. In 16-color graphics mode, each screen character is contained in an 8×8 matrix of pixels. The Video Display Area represents the value with 32 bytes of data; that is, four bits per pixel $\times 8 \times 8 = 256$ bits = 32 bytes.
- *Graphics mode 0FH.* Original EGA monochrome mode also used by VGA for upward compatibility.
- *Graphics modes 11H and 12H.* Modes specifically designed for VGA. These modes are similar to modes 0DH and 0EH in operation. Technically, mode 11H needs only one bit map to represent a screen of pixels. However, where mode 11H has access to two palette colors, mode 12H has access to 16.
- *Graphics mode 13H.* Mode specifically designed for VGA. This mode also uses pixel maps, but represents each pixel by a byte in the video map. The eight bits provide 2^8, or 256, different colors.

Use BIOS INT 10H function 00H to set graphics mode, as the following example shows:

```
MOV  AH,00H    ;Request set mode
MOV  AL,0CH    ;Color graphics
INT  10H       ;Call interrupt service
```

In graphics mode, ROM contains dot patterns for only the first (bottom) 128 ASCII characters. INT 1FH provides access to a 1K area in memory that defines the top 128 characters, eight bytes per character.

Program: Using Functions in Graphics Mode

The program in Figure 9-4 uses the following functions in graphics mode:

```
TITLE      A09GRFX1 (EXE)  Graphics functions for displaying
           .MODEL SMALL
           .STACK 64
           .DATA
STRING     DB     '1234567890'
.286  ; -------------------------------------------------------
           .CODE
A10MAIN    PROC   FAR
           MOV    AX,@data      ;Establish
           MOV    DS,AX         ;  addressability
           MOV    ES,AX
           MOV    AH,0FH        ;Get original
           INT    10H           ;  video mode
           PUSH   AX            ;  and save
           CALL   B10MODE       ;Set graphics mode
           CALL   C10SCROLL     ;Scroll screen
           CALL   D10STRING     ;Function 13H to display
           CALL   E10DISPLY     ;Function 0AH to display
           MOV    AH,10H        ;Request keyboard
           INT    16H           ;  input
           POP    AX            ;Restore original
           MOV    AH,00H        ;  video mode
           INT    10H           ;  (in AL)
           MOV    AX,4C00H      ;End of processing
           INT    21H
A10MAIN    ENDP
;                    Set graphics mode and request palette:
B10MODE    PROC   NEAR          ;Uses AX and BX
           MOV    AH,00H        ;Request graphics mode
           MOV    AL,12H        ;640 cols x 480 rows
           INT    10H
           MOV    AH,0BH        ;Request color palette
           MOV    BH,00         ;Background
           MOV    BL,07H        ;Gray
           INT    10H           ;
           RET
B10MODE    ENDP
;                    Scroll screen, set attributes:
C10SCROLL  PROC   NEAR
           PUSHA                ;Preserve general registers
           MOV    AX,0605H      ;Request scroll 5 rows
           MOV    BH,1110B      ;Yellow color
           MOV    CX,0000H      ;From row:column
           MOV    DX,044FH      ;To row:column
           INT    10H
           POPA                 ;Restore registers
           RET
C10SCROLL  ENDP
;                    Display string, set attribute and cursor:
D10STRING  PROC   NEAR
           PUSHA                ;Preserve general registers
           MOV    AX,1301H      ;Request display
           MOV    BX,00021H     ;Page:attribute
           LEA    BP,STRING     ;Character string
           MOV    CX,10         ;Length
```

Figure 9-4   Graphics Functions for Video Displays

```
              MOV      DX,0815H      ;Row:column
              INT      10H           ;
              POPA                   ;Restore registers
              RET
D10STRING ENDP
;                      Display character repeatedly
E10DISPLY PROC   NEAR
              PUSHA                  ;Preserve general registers
              MOV      AX,0A01H      ;Request display
              MOV      BH,00         ;Happy faces
              MOV      BL,0100B      ;Red color
              MOV      CX,10         ;10 times
              INT      10H           ;
              POPA                   ;Restore registers
              RET
E10DISPLY ENDP
              END      A10MAIN
```

Figure 9-4 *Continued*

- 0FH to get and save the original mode on entry.
- 00H to set graphics mode 12H.
- 0BH to request a color palette.
- 06H to scroll the screen and set five rows to yellow.
- 13H to set the cursor and attribute and display a string of characters.
- 0AH to display a character a repeated number of times.

At the end, the program waits for the user to press a key, and then resets the display to the original mode.

Pixel Example

As a simple example, mode 04H provides 200 rows of 320 pixels. In this mode, each byte represents four pixels (that is, two bits per pixel), numbered 0 through 3, as follows:

```
byte:    C1 C0 C1 C0 C1 C0 C1 C0
pixel:     0    1    2    3
```

At any given time, there are four available colors, numbered 0 through 3. The limitation of four colors is because the 2-bit pixel provides only four bit combinations: 00, 01, 10,

Color		Color	
Black	0000	Gray	1000
Blue	0001	Light blue	1001
Green	0010	Light green	1010
Cyan	0011	Light cyan	1011
Red	0100	Light red	1100
Magenta	0101	Light magenta	1101
Brown	0110	Yellow	1110
Light gray	0111	White	1111

and 11. You can choose pixel 00 for any one of the 16 available colors for the background color.

For mode 04H, palette 0 consists of foreground green, red, and brown, and palette 1 consists of foreground cyan, magenta, and white.

Use INT 10H function 0BH to select a color palette and the background. If you choose background color yellow and palette 0, the available colors are yellow, green, red, and brown. A byte consisting of the pixel value 10101010 displays as all red. If you choose background color blue and palette 1, the available colors are blue, cyan, magenta, and white. A byte consisting of pixel value 00011011 displays blue, cyan, magenta, and white.

Program: Displaying Graphics Pixels

The program in Figure 9-5 includes the following INT 10H functions for a display of graphics:

    0FH = Get the original video mode
    00H = Set graphics mode 12H
    0BH = Select background color green
    0CH = Write pixel dots for 640 columns and 480 rows.

The actual window displayed is 210 rows and 512 columns (columns 64 through 576). Note that rows and columns are in terms of dots, not characters.

The program increments the color for each row (so that bits 0000 become 0001, etc.) and, because only the rightmost four bits are used, the colors repeat after every 16 rows. The display begins 64 columns from the left of the screen and ends 64 columns from the right.

At the end, the program waits for the user to press a key, and then it resets the display to the original mode. You could modify this program for other graphics modes.

DIRECT VIDEO DISPLAY

For some applications, because the video display is routed through the operating system and BIOS, it may be noticeably slow. The fastest way to display text or graphics characters is to transfer them directly to the appropriate Video Display Area. For example, the address of page 0 in the Video Area for mode 03 (color, text) is B800[0]H. Each character requires two bytes of memory—one for the character and one immediately following for its attribute. With a screen size of 80 columns and 25 rows, a page in the Video Area requires 80 × 25 × 2 = 4,000 bytes.

The first two bytes in the Video Display Area represent one screen location for row 00, column 00, and the bytes at offsets F9EH and F9FH represent the location for row 24, column 79. Simply moving a character:attribute into the Video Area of the active page causes the character to appear immediately on the screen. You can use DEBUG commands to check this feature. First, use the command D B800:00 to display the Video Area at B800[0]H. The display shows what was on the screen at the time you typed the command, which is usually a set of bytes containing 20 07H (for blank character, black background, and white foreground). Note that both DEBUG and you are competing for the same display area and screen. Try changing the screen with these commands to display happy faces (01, 02, and 03) with various attributes (25, 36, and 47) on the top and bottom rows:

```
TITLE     A09GRFX2 (EXE)  Display of Pixels
          .MODEL SMALL
          .STACK 64
.286  ; ------------------------------------------------
          .CODE
A10MAIN   PROC    FAR
          MOV     AX,@data       ;Establish
          MOV     DS,AX          ;  addressability
          MOV     ES,AX
          MOV     AH,0FH         ;Get original
          INT     10H            ;  video mode
          PUSH    AX             ;  and save
          CALL    B10MODE        ;Set graphics mode
          CALL    C10DISPLY      ;Display color graphics
          MOV     AH,10H         ;Request keyboard
          INT     16H            ;  response
          POP     AX             ;Restore original
          MOV     AH,00H         ;  video mode
          INT     10H            ;  (in AL)
          MOV     AX,4C00H       ;End of processing
          INT     21H
A10MAIN   ENDP
;                 Set graphics mode and palette:
;                 ----------------------------
B10MODE   PROC    NEAR           ;Uses AX and BX
          MOV     AX,0012H       ;Request graphics mode
          INT     10H            ;640 cols x 480 rows
          MOV     AH,0BH         ;Request color palette
          MOV     BX,0007H       ;Background gray
          INT     10H
          RET
B10MODE   ENDP
;                 Display 210 rows of graphics dots, 512
;                 columns, change color for each row:
;                 ----------------------------------------
C10DISPLY PROC    NEAR
          PUSHA                  ;Preserve general registers
          MOV     BX,00          ;Set initial page,
          MOV     CX,64          ;  column,
          MOV     DX,70          ;  and row
C20:
          MOV     AH,0CH         ;Request pixel dot
          MOV     AL,BL          ;Color
          INT     10H            ;BX, CX, & DX are preserved
          INC     CX             ;Increment column
          CMP     CX,576         ;Column at 576?
          JNE     C20            ;  no, loop
          MOV     CX,64          ;  yes, reset column
          INC     BL             ;Change color
          INC     DX             ;Increment row
          CMP     DX,280         ;Row at 280?
          JNE     C20            ;  no, loop
          POPA                   ;Restore registers
          RET                    ;  yes, ended
C10DISPLY ENDP
          END     A10MAIN
```

Figure 9-5   Graphics Display of Pixels

```
E B800:000 01 25 02 36 03 47
E B800:F90 01 25 02 36 03 47
```

The program in Figure 9-6 gives an example of transferring data directly to the Video Display Area at B900[0]H—that is, page 1, rather than the default page 0. The program uses the SEGMENT AT feature to define the Video Display Area as VID_SEG, in effect as a dummy segment. VID_AREA identifies the location of page 1 at the start of the segment.

```
          TITLE     A09DRVID (EXE)  Direct video display of rows,
          ;            increasing characters A-P) and attributes.
                    .MODEL SMALL
                    .STACK 64
VIDEO_SEG SEGMENT AT 0B900H    ;Page 1 of video area
VID_AREA  DB        1000H DUP(?)
VIDEO_SEG ENDS
.286 ;  --------------------------------------------------
                    .CODE
A10MAIN   PROC      FAR
                    MOV     AX,VIDEO_SEG ;Addressability for
                    MOV     ES,AX        ;  video area
                    ASSUME ES:VIDEO_SEG
                    MOV     AH,0FH       ;Request get
                    INT     10H          ;  and save
                    PUSH    AX           ;  current mode
                    PUSH    BX           ;  and page
                    MOV     AX,0003H     ;Set mode 03,
                    INT     10H          ;  clear screen
                    MOV     AX,0501H     ;Set page #01
                    INT     10H
                    CALL    B10DISPLY    ;Process display area
                    MOV     AH,10H       ;Wait for keyboard
                    INT     16H          ;  response
                    MOV     AH,05H       ;Restore
                    POP     BX           ;  original
                    MOV     AL,BH        ;  page number
                    INT     10H
                    POP     AX           ;Restore video
                    MOV     AH,00H       ;  mode (in AL)
                    INT     10H
                    MOV     AX,4C00H     ;End of processing
                    INT     21H
A10MAIN   ENDP
          ;              Store character + attribute in video area,
          ;              incrementing characters and attributes:
          ;              ---------------------------------------
B10DISPLY PROC      NEAR
                    PUSHA                ;Preserve general registers
                    MOV     AL,41H       ;Character to display
                    MOV     AH,01H       ;Attribute
                    MOV     DI,820       ;Start of display area
B20:                MOV     CX,60        ;Characters per row
B30:                MOV     ES:WORD PTR[DI],AX  ;Character to display
                    ADD     DI,2         ;Next attribute + character
                    LOOP    B30          ;Repeat 60 times
                    INC     AH           ;Next attribute
                    INC     AL           ;  and character
                    ADD     DI,40        ;Indent for next row
                    CMP     AL,51H       ;Last character to display?
                    JNE     B20          ;  no, repeat
                    POPA                 ;  else restore registers
                    RET                  ;  and return
B10DISPLY ENDP
                    END     A10MAIN
```

Figure 9-6 Direct Video Display

The program displays characters in rows 5 through 20 and columns 10 through 69. The first row displays a string of the character A (41H) with an attribute of 01H, the second row displays a string of the character B (42H) with an attribute of 02H, and so forth, with the character and attribute incremented for each row.

The program establishes the starting position of a page in the Video Display Area based on the formula for locating any offset address in the area:

$$\text{Offset address} = [(\text{row} \times 80) + \text{column}] \times 2$$

The starting position, then, for row 05, column 10, is $[(5 \times 80) + 10] \times 2 = 410 \times 2 = 820$. After displaying one row, the program advances 40 positions in the display area for the start of the next line and ends on reaching the letter Q (51H).

The video display segment for page 1 is defined as VIDEO_SEG and the page as VID_AREA. The program establishes ES as the segment register for VIDEO_SEG. At the start, the program saves the current mode and page and then sets mode 03 and page 01.

In the procedure B10DISPLY, the starting character and attribute are initialized in AX and the starting Video Area offset in DI. The instruction MOV ES:WORD PTR [DI],AX moves the contents of AL (the character) to the first byte of the display area and AH (the attribute) to the second byte. The LOOP routine executes this instruction 60 times, displaying the character:attribute across the screen. It then increments the character:attribute and adds 40 to the DI—20 for the end of the current row and 20 for indenting the start of the next row (on the screen, 10 columns each). The routine then repeats the display of the next row of characters.

On completion of the display, the program waits for the user to press a key and then restores the original mode and page before ending.

ASCII CHARACTERS FOR BOXES AND MENUS

Among the extended ASCII characters 128-255 (80H-FFH) are a number of special characters that are useful for displaying prompts, menus, and logos, as shown in Figure 9-7.

The following example uses INT 10H function 09H to draw a solid horizontal line 25 positions long:

CHARACTER	SINGLE LINE		DOUBLE LINE		MIXED LINES			
Straight Lines:								
Horizontal	C4H	-	CDH	=				
Vertical	B3H	|	BAH	||				
Corners:								
Top left	DAH	r	C9H	╔	D6H	╓	D5H	F
Top right	BFH	┐	BBH	╗	B7H	╖	B8H	╕
Bottom left	C0H	L	C8H	╚	D3H	╙	D4H	╘
Bottom right	D9H	╛	BCH	╝	BDH	╜	BEH	╛
Middle:								
Left	C3H	├	CCH	╠	C7H	╟	C6H	╞
Right	B4H	┤	B9H	╣	B6H	╢	B5H	╡
Top	C2H	┬	CBH	╦	D2H	╥	D1H	╤
Bottom	C1H	┴	CAH	╩	D0H	╨	CFH	╧
Center Cross	C5H	+	CEH	╬	D7H	╫	D8H	╪

Blocks:				
One-quarter dots on	B0H	░	Solid shadow, upper half	DFH
One-half dots on	B1H	▒	Solid shadow, left half	DDH
Three-quarter dots on	B2H	▓	Solid shadow, right half	DEH
Solid shadow	DBH	█	Solid shadow, lower half	DCH

Figure 9-7 ASCII Characters for Boxes and Menus

```
MOV   AH,09H   ;Request display
MOV   AL,0C4H  ;Solid single line
MOV   BH,00    ;Page number 0
MOV   BL,1EH   ;Blue background, brown foreground
MOV   CX,25    ;25 repetitions
INT   10H      ;Call interrupt service
```

Remember that although function 09H displays a string of characters, it does not advance the cursor.

The simplest way to display a box is to define it in the data segment and display the whole area. This example defines a menu in a solid single-line box:

```
MENU  DB    0DAH,    17 DUP(0C4H),        0BFH
      DB    0B3H,  ' Add records      ', 0B3H
      DB    0B3H,  ' Delete records   ', 0B3H
      DB    0B3H,  ' Enter orders     ', 0B3H
      DB    0B3H,  ' Print report     ', 0B3H
      DB    0B3H,  ' Update accounts  ', 0B3H
      DB    0B3H,  ' View records     ', 0B3H
      DB    0C0H,    17 DUP(0C4H),        0D9HLF
```

In the next chapter, Figures 10-1 and 10-2 illustrate a similar menu in a double-line box, along with "dots on" characters for a drop shadow to the right and bottom of the box.

KEY POINTS

- The horizontal lines (raster) on the video screen contain hundreds of points (pixels) that consist of phosphor dots for the three primary additive colors red, green, and blue.
- Data in the Video Display Area is stored in adjacent pages. The default is page 0, but you may select any other page for displaying. Its address depends on the current mode.
- The role of the Video Controller includes generating horizontal and vertical signals, tracking the current data in the Video Display Area, horizontal and vertical scanning of the monitor, handling the cursor, and selecting the current page.
- Overscanning causes a border (overscan area) on the screen.
- The attribute byte for text mode provides for blinking, reverse video, high intensity, and RGB bits for selecting colors.
- BIOS INT 10H provides such functions as setting video mode, setting cursor location, scrolling the screen, selecting a color palette, and displaying characters.
- A program that displays lines down the screen may use INT 10H function 06H to scroll up before the display reaches the bottom.
- A pixel (picture element) consists of a specified number of bits, depending on the graphics adapter and resolution.

Chapter 10

KEYBOARD OPERATIONS

> Objectives: To cover all the keyboard operations and advanced features of keyboard input, including the shift status, keyboard buffer, and scan codes.

INTRODUCTION

This chapter describes the many operations for handling keyboard input, some of which have specialized uses. Of these operations, INT 21H function 0AH (covered in Chapter 9), and INT 16H (covered in this chapter) should provide almost all the keyboard operations you'll require.

Other topics in the chapter include the keyboard shift status bytes, scan codes, and the keyboard buffer area. The *shift status* bytes in the BIOS Keyboard Data Area enables a program to determine, for example, whether the Ctrl, Shift, or Alt keys have been pressed. The *scan code* is a unique number assigned to each key on the keyboard that enables the system to identify the source of a pressed key and enables a program to check whether the pressed key is an extended function such as Home, PageUp, or Arrow. And the *keyboard buffer area* provides space in memory for you to type ahead before a program actually requests input.

Operations covered in this chapter are the following:

INT 21H FUNCTIONS	INT 16H FUNCTIONS
07H Direct keyboard input no echo	03H Set typematic rate
08H Keyboard input no echo	05H Keyboard write in buffer
0AH Buffered keyboard input	10H Read keyboard character
0BH Check keyboard status	11H Determine if character present
0CH Clear buffer, invoke function	12H Return keyboard shift status

The keyboard provides three basic types of keys:

1. *Standard characters,* which consist of the letters A through Z, numbers 0 through 9, and such characters as %, $, and #.
2. *Extended function keys,* which consist of:
   • Program function keys, such as F1 and Shift+F1
   • Numeric keypad keys with NumLock toggled off:Home, End, Arrows, Del, Ins, PageUp, and PageUp, and the duplicate keys for them on the extended keyboard
   • Alt+alphabetics and Alt+program-function keys
3. *Special keys Alt, Ctrl, and Shift,* which normally work in association with other keys as well CapsLock, NumLock, and ScrollLock, which indicate a condition. BIOS does not deliver these keystrokes as ASCII characters to the program. Instead, BIOS treats these differently from other keys by updating their current state in the shift status bytes in the BIOS Keyboard Data Area.

The original PC with its 83 keys suffered from a short-sighted design decision that caused keys on the so-called numeric keypad to perform two actions. Thus numbers share keys with Home, End, Arrows, Del, Ins, PageUp, and PageUp, with the NumLock key toggling between them. To overcome problems caused by this layout, designers produced an enhanced keyboard with 101 keys and subsequently 104 keys for Windows. Of the 18 added keys, only F11 and F12 provide a new function; the rest duplicate the functions of keys on the original keyboard.

BIOS KEYBOARD DATA AREAS

The BIOS Data Area at segment 40[0]H in low memory contains a number of useful data items. These include two Keyboard Data Areas that indicate the current status of the control keys. Keyboard Data Area 1 contains two bytes. The first byte is at 40:17H, where bits set to 1 indicate the following:

Bit	Action	Bit	Action
7	Insert active	3	Right Alt pressed
6	CapsLock state active	2	Right Ctrl pressed
5	NumLock state active	1	Left Shift pressed
4	Scroll Lock state active	0	Right Shift pressed

You may use INT 16H function 02H (covered later), to check these values. "Pressed" means that the user is currently holding down the key; releasing the key causes BIOS to clear the bit value.

For the second byte of Keyboard Data Area 1 at 40:18H, bits set to 1 indicate the following:

Bit	Action	Bit	Action
7	Insert pressed	3	Ctrl/NumLock (Pause) active
6	CapsLock pressed	2	SysReq pressed
5	NumLock pressed	1	Left Alt pressed
4	Scroll Lock pressed	0	Left Ctrl pressed

You can test, for example, whether either Ctrl or Alt is pressed, or both.

Keyboard Data Area 2 at 40:80H is used for the keyboard buffer, covered later. Keyboard Data Area 3 resides at 40:96H. Bit 4, when on, indicates that an enhanced keyboard is installed. A full description of the Keyboard Data Areas can be found in Chapter 24.

Exercise: Examining the Shift Status. To see the effect on the shift status bytes of pressing Ctrl, Alt, and Shift, load DEBUG for execution. Type D 40:17 to view the contents of the two status bytes. Press CapsLock, NumLock, and ScrollLock, and type D 40:17 again to see the result on both status bytes. The byte at 40:17H should show 70H (0111 0000), and the byte at 40:18H is probably 00H. The byte at 40:96H (bit 4) shows the presence (1) or absence (0) of an enhanced keyboard.

Try changing the contents of the status byte at 40:17H—type E 40:17 00. If your keyboard Lock keys have indicator lights, they should turn off. Now try typing E 40:17 70 to turn them on again. You could try various combinations, although it's difficult to type a valid DEBUG command while holding down the Ctrl and Alt keys. Key in Q to quit DEBUG.

The Keyboard Buffer

The BIOS Data Area at location 40:1EH contains the *keyboard buffer*. This feature allows you to type up to 15 characters even before a program requests keyboard input. When you press a key, the keyboard's processor automatically generates the key's scan code (its unique assigned number) and requests BIOS INT 09H.

In simple terms, the INT 09H routine gets the scan code from the keyboard, converts it to an ASCII character, and delivers it to the keyboard buffer area. Subsequently, INT 16H (the lowest level keyboard operation) reads the character from the buffer and delivers it to your program. Your program need never request INT 09H because the processor performs it automatically when you press a key. A later section covers INT 09H and the keyboard buffer in detail.

INT 21H OPERATIONS FOR KEYBOARD INPUT

This section covers various INT 21H services that handle keyboard input. All of these operations require a function code in AH and accept only one input character. In the discussion that follows, the term "respond to a Ctrl+Break request" means that the system terminates the program if the user presses the Ctrl+Break or Ctrl+C keys together.

INT 21H Function 01H: Keyboard Input with Echo. This operation accepts a character from the keyboard buffer or, if none is present, waits for keyboard entry:

```
            MOV   AH,01H      ;Request keyboard input
            INT   21H
```

The operation returns one of two status codes to AL. AL = a nonzero value means that a standard ASCII character (such as a letter or number) is present, which the operation echoes on the screen. AL = zero means that the user has pressed an extended function key such as Home or F1, and AH still contains the original function. The operation handles extended functions clumsily, attempting to echo them on the screen. And to get the scan code for the function key in AL, you immediately have to repeat the INT 21H operation. The operation also responds to a Ctrl+Break request.

INT 21H Function 07H: Direct Keyboard Input without Echo. This operation works like function 01H, except that the entered character does not echo on the screen and the operation does not respond to a Ctrl+Break request. It could be used to key in a password that is to be invisible.

INT 21H Function 08H: Keyboard Input without Echo. This operation works like function 01H, except that the entered character does not echo on the screen.

INT 21H Function 0AH: Buffered Keyboard Input. This operation is covered in detail in Chapter 9. However, its inability to accept extended function keys limits its capability.

INT 21H Function 0BH: Check Keyboard Status. This operation returns FFH in AL if an input character is available in the keyboard buffer and 00H if no character is available. Note that the operation does not expect the user to press a key; rather, it simply checks the buffer.

INT 21H Function 0CH: Clear Keyboard Buffer and Invoke Function. You may use this operation in association with function 01H, 06H, 07H, 08H, or 0AH. Load the required function in AL:

```
            MOV   AH,0CH       ;Request keyboard function
            MOV   AL,function  ;Required function
            INT   21H
```

The operation clears the keyboard buffer, executes the function in AL, and accepts (or waits for) a character, according to the function request. This operation could be used for a program that does not allow a user to type ahead.

INT 16H OPERATIONS FOR KEYBOARD INPUT

INT 16H is the basic BIOS keyboard operation used extensively by software developers and provides the following services according to a function code that you load in AH.

INT 16H Function 03H: Set Typematic Repeat Rate

When you hold down a key for more than one-half second, the keyboard enters typematic mode and automatically repeats the character. To change the rate, you can use the function like this:

```
MOV   AH,03H              ;Set typematic repeat rate
MOV   AL,05H              ;Required subfunction
MOV   BH,repeat-delay     ;Delay before start
MOV   BL,repeat-rate      ;Speed of repetition
INT   16H
```

The values for *repeat-delay* in BH are 0 = 1/4 sec., 1 = 1/2 sec. (default), 2 = 3/4 sec., and 3 = 1 sec. The values for *repeat-rate* in BL range from 0 (fastest) through 31 (slowest).

INT 16H Function 05H: Keyboard Write

This operation allows a program to insert characters in the keyboard buffer as if a user had pressed a key. Load the ASCII character into CH and its scan code into CL. The operation allows you to enter characters into the buffer until it is full. If full, the operation sets the Carry Flag and AL to 1.

INT 16H Function 10H: Read Keyboard Character

This standard keyboard operation checks the keyboard buffer for an entered character. If none is present, it waits for the user to press a key. If a character is present, the operation delivers it to AL and its scan code to AH. If the pressed key is an extended function such as Home or F1, the character in AL is 00H. On the enhanced keyboard, F11 and F12 also return 00H to AL, but the other newer (duplicate) control keys, such as Home and PageUp, return E0H. Here are the three possibilities:

Key Pressed	AH	AL
Regular ASCII character	Scan code	ASCII character
Extended function key	Scan code	00H
Extended duplicate control key	Scan code	E0H

The program can test AL for 00H or E0H to determine whether an extended function key was pressed:

```
MOV   AH,10H     ;Request BIOS keyboard input
INT   16H        ;Call interrupt service
CMP   AL,00H     ;Extended function key?
JE    exit       ; yes, exit
CMP   AL,0E0H    ;Extended function key?
JE    exit       ; yes, exit
```

Because the operation does not echo the character on the screen, the program has to request a screen display operation for that purpose.

INT 16H Function 11H: Determine Whether Character is Present

If an entered character is present in the keyboard buffer, the operation clears the Zero Flag and delivers the character to AL and its scan code to AH; the entered character remains in the buffer. If no character is present, the operation sets the Zero Flag and does not wait. Note that the operation provides a look-ahead feature because the character remains in the keyboard buffer until function 10H reads it.

INT 16H Function 12H: Return Keyboard Shift Status

This operation delivers the keyboard status byte from BIOS Data Area 1 at location 40:17H to AL and the byte from 40:18H to AH. The following example tests AL to determine whether the Left Shift (bit 1) or Right Shift (bit 0) keys are pressed:

```
MOV  AH,12H        ;Request shift status
INT  16H           ;Call interrupt service
AND  AL,00000011B  ;Left or right shift pressed?
JZ   exit          ; yes ...
```

For the status byte in AH, 1-bits mean the following:

Bit	Key	Bit	Key
7	SysReq pressed	3	Right Alt pressed
6	Caps Lock pressed	2	Right Ctrl pressed
5	Num Lock pressed	1	Left Alt pressed
4	Scroll Lock pressed	0	Left Ctrl pressed

Keyboard Exercise.   Here's a simple DEBUG exercise that tests function 12H. When in DEBUG, request the command A 100 and enter the following instructions:

```
MOV  AH,12
INT  16
JMP  100
```

Make sure that the Lock keys are all off. Now key in the commands R, T, and P. AL should now contain 00H. Next turn on the NumLock, CapsLock, and ScrollLock keys and repeat the three instructions. This time, AL should contain 7CH (0111 0000) to reflect the keyboard status. Now turn off the Lock keys and repeat the instructions, but this time stop after pressing the P key. Hold down CapsLock while pressing <Enter>; AH and AL should both contain 40H (0100). Check Insert, which acts as a toggle key. Try experimenting with other combinations, although some like Alt+Enter do not work.

EXTENDED FUNCTION KEYS AND SCAN CODES

An extended function key such as F1 or Home requests an action rather than delivers a character. There is nothing in the system design that compels these keys to perform a specific action; as the programmer, you determine, for example, that pressing Home is to set the cursor at the top left corner of the screen or that pressing End sets the cursor at the end of text on the screen. You could as easily program these keys to perform wholly unrelated operations.

Each key has a designated *scan code*, beginning with 01 for Esc. (See Appendix F for a complete list of these codes.) By means of the scan codes, a program may determine the source of any keystroke. For example, a program could issue INT 16H function 10H to request input of one character. The operation responds in one of two ways, depending on whether a character key or an extended function key was pressed. For a character, such as the letter A, the operation delivers two items to AX:

AH = scan code for the letter A, 1EH, and

AL = ASCII character A (41H).

The keyboard contains two keys each for such characters as -, +, and *. Pressing the asterisk key, for example, sets the character code 2AH in AL and one of two scan codes in AH, depending on which key was pressed: 09H for the asterisk above the number 8, or 29H for the asterisk by the numeric keypad. The following example tests the scan code to determine which asterisk was pressed:

```
CMP   AL,2AH   ;Asterisk?
JNE   exit1    ; no, exit
CMP   AH,09H   ;Scan code on #8 key?
JE    exit2    ; yes, exit
```

If you press an extended function key, such as Del, the operation delivers these two items to AX:

AH = scan code for Del, 53H and

AL = 00H for Del on the numeric keypad, or E0H for the duplicate key on the enhanced keyboard.

After an INT 16H operation (and some INT 21H operations), you can test AL. If it contains 00H or E0H, the request is for an extended function; otherwise, the operation has delivered a character. The following example tests for an extended function key:

```
MOV   AH,10H    ;Request keyboard input
INT   16H       ;Call interrupt service
CMP   AL,00H    ;Extended function?
JE    exit      ; yes, exit
CMP   AL,0E0H   ;Extended function?
JE    exit      ; yes, exit
```

In the next example, if a user presses the Home key (scan code 47H), the cursor is set to row 0, column 0:

```
        MOV   AH,10H    ;Request keyboard input
        INT   16H       ;Call interrupt service
        CMP   AL,00H    ;Extended function?
        JE    L30       ; yes, bypass
        CMP   AL,0E0H   ;Extended function?
        JNE   exit      ; no, exit
  L30:  CMP   AH,47H    ;Scan code for Home?
        JNE   exit      ; no, exit
        MOV   AH,02H    ;Request
        MOV   BH,00     ; set cursor
        MOV   DX,00     ; to 00:00
        INT   10H       ;Call interrupt service
```

Function keys F1-F10 generate scan codes 3BH-44H, respectively, and F11 and F12 generate 85H and 86H. The following example tests for function key F10:

```
        CMP   AH,44H   ;Function key F10?
        JE    exit     ; yes, exit
```

Keyboard Exercise.   The following DEBUG exercise examines the effects of keying in various characters. Use the command A 100 to key in these instructions:

```
        MOV   AH,10
        INT   16
        JMP   100
```

Use the P (Proceed) command to execute the INT operation. Enter various normal characters combined with Shift and with Ctrl, and compare the results in AH (scan code) and AL (character) with the list in Appendix F. And then continue with the next exercise.

Keying in the Full ASCII Character Set.   The entire ASCII set consists of 256 characters numbered 0 through 255 (FFH). Many of these are standard displayable characters, from ASCII 20H (space) through ASCII 7EH (the tilde character ~). Because of keyboard limitations, most of the 256 ASCII characters are not represented on it. You can, however, key in any of the ASCII codes 01 through 255 by holding down Alt and keying in the appropriate code as a decimal value on the numeric keypad. The system stores your entered value as two bytes in the keyboard buffer: The first is the generated ASCII character and the second is zero. For example, Alt+001 delivers 01H, and Alt+255 delivers FFH. While still in DEBUG, use INT 16H with DEBUG's A command to examine the effect of entering various values. Check the values returned in AX and see Appendix B for a complete table of ASCII values.

Program: Selecting from a Menu

The next program displays a menu with a drop shadow, as explained in Chapter 9 and shown in Figure 10-1. The menu itself is defined in the data segment within a double-lined box: eight rows of 19 shadow characters (0DBH). A user selects an item from the menu by pressing UpArrow or DownArrow and then Enter. An explanation of the procedures in the program in Figure 10-2 follows:

```
Add records
Delete records
Enter orders
Print report
Update accounts
View records
```

Figure 10-1   Menu with Drop Shadow

```
TITLE      A10SELMU (EXE)  Select item from menu
           .MODEL SMALL
           .STACK 64
;  -------------------------------------------------------
           .DATA
TOPROW     EQU   08                      ;Top row of menu
BOTROW     EQU   15                      ;Bottom row of menu
LEFCOL     EQU   26                      ;Left column of menu
ATTRIB     DB    ?                       ;Screen attribute
ROW        DB    00                      ;Screen row
SHADOW     DB    19 DUP(0DBH)            ;Shadow characters
MENU       DB    0C9H, 17 DUP(0CDH), 0BBH
           DB    0BAH, ' Add records    ', 0BAH
           DB    0BAH, ' Delete records ', 0BAH
           DB    0BAH, ' Enter orders   ', 0BAH
           DB    0BAH, ' Print report   ', 0BAH
           DB    0BAH, ' Update accounts ', 0BAH
           DB    0BAH, ' View records   ', 0BAH
           DB    0C8H, 17 DUP(0CDH), 0BCH
PROMPT     DB    'To select an item, use <Up/Down Arrow>'
           DB    ' and press <Enter>.'
           DB    13, 10, 'Press <Esc> to exit.'
.386  ; -------------------------------------------------------
           .CODE
A10MAIN    PROC  FAR
           MOV   AX,@data               ;Initialize segment
           MOV   DS,AX                  ;  registers
           MOV   ES,AX
           CALL  Q10CLEAR               ;Clear screen
           MOV   ROW,BOTROW+4           ;Set row
A20:
           CALL  B10MENU                ;Display menu
           MOV   ROW,TOPROW+1           ;Set row to top item
           MOV   ATTRIB,16H             ;Set reverse video
           CALL  D10DISPLY              ;Highlight current menu line
           CALL  C10INPUT               ;Provide for menu selection
           CMP   AL,1BH                 ;Escape key pressed?
           JNE   A20                    ;  no, continue
           MOV   AX,0600H               ;  yes, end
           CALL  Q10CLEAR               ;Clear screen
           MOV   AX,4C00H               ;End of processing
           INT   21H
A10MAIN    ENDP
;                    Display shadow box, next menu on top, then prompt
;                    -------------------------------------------------
B10MENU    PROC  NEAR
           PUSHA                        ;Preserve general registers
           MOV   AX,1301H               ;Request display shadow box
           MOV   BX,0060H               ;Page and attribute
           LEA   BP,SHADOW              ;Shadow characters
           MOV   CX,19                  ;19 characters
           MOV   DH,TOPROW+1            ;Top row of shadow
           MOV   DL,LEFCOL+1            ;Left column of shadow
B20:       INT   10H
           INC   DH                     ;Next row
```

Figure 10-2   Selecting an Item from a Menu

```
                 CMP       DH,BOTROW+2        ;All rows displayed?
                 JNE       B20                ;  no, repeat
                 MOV       ATTRIB,71H         ;Blue on white
                 MOV       AX,1300H           ;Request display menu
                 MOVZX     BX,ATTRIB          ;Page and attribute
                 LEA       BP,MENU            ;Menu line
                 MOV       CX,19              ;Length of line
                 MOV       DH,TOPROW          ;Row
                 MOV       DL,LEFCOL          ;Column
      B30:
                 INT       10H
                 ADD       BP,19              ;Next menu line
                 INC       DH                 ;Next row
                 CMP       DH,BOTROW+1        ;All rows displayed?
                 JNE       B30                ;  no, repeat

                 MOV       AX,1301H           ;Request display prompt
                 MOVZX     BX,ATTRIB          ;Page and attribute
                 LEA       BP,PROMPT          ;Prompt line
                 MOV       CX,79              ;Length of line
                 MOV       DH,BOTROW+4        ;Screen row,
                 MOV       DL,00              ;  column
                 INT       10H
                 POPA                         ;Restore registers
                 RET
      B10MENU    ENDP
      ;                    Accept keyboard request, Arrow and Enter
      ;                    to select menu line, Esc to exit:
      ;                    -------------------------------------------
      C10INPUT   PROC      NEAR
                 PUSHA                        ;Preserve general registers
      C20:       MOV       AH,10H             ;Request one character
                 INT       16H                ;  from keyboard
                 CMP       AH,50H             ;Down arrow?
                 JE        C30
                 CMP       AH,48H             ;Up arrow?
                 JE        C40
                 CMP       AL,0DH             ;Enter key?
                 JE        C90
                 CMP       AL,1BH             ;Escape key?
                 JE        C90
                 JMP       C20                ;None, retry
      C30:       MOV       ATTRIB,71H         ;Blue on white
                 CALL      D10DISPLY          ;Set old line to normal video
                 INC       ROW                ;Increment for next row
                 CMP       ROW,BOTROW-1       ;Past bottom row?
                 JBE       C50                ;  no, ok
                 MOV       ROW,TOPROW+1       ;  yes, reset
                 JMP       C50
      C40:       MOV       ATTRIB,71H         ;Blue on white
                 CALL      D10DISPLY          ;Set old line to normal video
                 DEC       ROW
                 CMP       ROW,TOPROW+1       ;Below top row?
                 JAE       C50                ;  no, ok
                 MOV       ROW,BOTROW-1       ;  yes, reset
```

Figure 10-2 *Continued*

- A10MAIN calls Q10CLEAR to clear the screen, calls B10MENU to display the menu and the prompt, calls D10DISPLY to set the first menu item to reverse video, and calls C10INPUT to accept keyboard input.
- B10MENU displays the full set of menu selections. It first uses INT 10H function 09H to display the shadow box. The procedure then uses INT 10H function 13H to display the menu (defined in the data segment as MENU on top of the shadow box

```
C50:       MOV     ATTRIB,17H          ;White on blue
           CALL    D10DISPLY           ;Set new line to reverse video
           JMP     C20
C90:       POPA                        ;Restore registers
           RET
C10INPUT   ENDP
;                  Set menu line to highlight (if
;                  selected) or normal (if not selected):
;                  ------------------------------------
D10DISPLY  PROC    NEAR
           PUSHA                       ;Preserve general registers
           MOVZX   AX,ROW              ;Row tells which line to set
           SUB     AX,TOPROW
           IMUL    AX,19               ;Multiply by length of line
           LEA     SI,MENU+1           ;  for selected menu line
           ADD     SI,AX

           MOV     AX,1300H            ;Request display
           MOVZX   BX,ATTRIB           ;Page and attribute
           MOV     BP,SI               ;Character string
           MOV     CX,17               ;Length of string
           MOV     DH,ROW              ;Row
           MOV     DL,LEFCOL+1         ;Column
           INT     10H
           POPA                        ;Restore registers
           RET
D10DISPLY  ENDP
;                  Clear screen:
;                  ------------
Q10CLEAR   PROC    NEAR
           PUSHA                       ;Preserve general registers
           MOV     AX,0600H
           MOV     BH,61H              ;Blue on brown
           MOV     CX,0000             ;Full screen
           MOV     DX,184FH
           INT     10H
           POPA                        ;Restore registers
           RET
Q10CLEAR   ENDP
           END     A10MAIN
```

Figure 10-2   *Continued*

but offset one row and column), and uses function 13H again to display the prompt below the menu.

- C10INPUT uses INT 16H function 10H for input: DownArrow to move down the menu, UpArrow to move up the menu, Enter to accept a menu item, and Esc to quit. All other keyboard entries are bypassed. The routine wraps the cursor around so that trying to move the cursor above the first menu line sets it to the last line, and vice versa. The routine also calls D10DISPLY to reset the previous menu line to normal video and the new (selected) menu line to reverse video.

- D10DISPLY uses INT 10H function 13H to display the currently selected line according to an attribute (normal or reverse video) that has been provided.

- Q10CLEAR clears the entire screen and sets it to blue foreground and brown background.

The program illustrates menu selection in a simple manner; a full program would execute a routine for each selected item. You'll get a better understanding of this program by assembling, testing, and enlarging it.

BIOS INT 09H AND THE KEYBOARD BUFFER

The keyboard has an 8-bit Intel 8048 processor that senses the pressing and releasing of keys. Based on the key(s) pressed, the keyboard sends codes to another 8-bit processor, an Intel 8042, on the system board. When you press a key, the keyboard's processor generates the key's scan code and requests INT 09H. This interrupt (at location 36 of the Interrupt Vector Table) points to an interrupt-handling routine in ROM BIOS. The routine issues a request for input from port 96 (60H): IN AL,60H. The BIOS routine reads the scan code and compares it with entries in a scan code table for the associated ASCII character (if any). The routine combines the scan code with its associated ASCII character and delivers the two bytes to the keyboard buffer. Figure 10-3 illustrates this procedure.

Note that INT 09H handles the status bytes in the Keyboard Data Area at 40:17H, 40:18H and at 40:96H for Shift, Alt, and Ctrl. Although pressing these keys generates INT 09H, the interrupt routine sets the appropriate bits in the status bytes, but doesn't deliver any characters to the keyboard buffer. Also, INT 09H ignores undefined keystroke combinations, such as Ctrl+/.

When you *press* a key, the keyboard processor automatically generates its scan code and issues INT 09H. When you *release* the key within one-half second, it generates a second scan code (the value of the first code plus 1000 0000B, which sets the leftmost bit) and issues another INT 09H. The second scan code tells the interrupt routine that you have released the key. If you hold the key for more than one-half second, the keyboard process becomes typematic; that is, it automatically repeats the key operation.

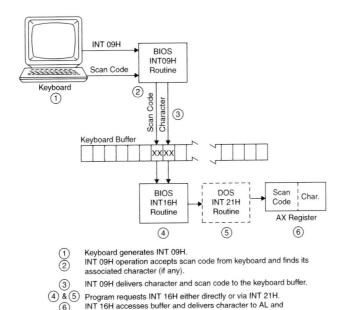

①   Keyboard generates INT 09H.
②   INT 09H operation accepts scan code from keyboard and finds its associated character (if any).
③   INT 09H delivers character and scan code to the keyboard buffer.
④ & ⑤   Program requests INT 16H either directly or via INT 21H.
⑥   INT 16H accesses buffer and delivers character to AL and scan code to AH.

Figure 10-3 Keyboard Buffer

The keyboard buffer requires one address (the head of the buffer) to tell INT 16H from where to read the next character and another address (the tail of the buffer) to tell INT 09H where to store the next character. The two addresses are offset in Keyboard Data Area 1 at 41AH and 41CH, respectively. The following describes the contents of the buffer:

ADDRESS   **EXPLANATION**

41AH   Current head of the buffer, the next position for INT 16H to get a character and send it to the program in AX.

41CH   Current tail of the buffer, the next position for INT 09H to store a character entered from the keyboard.

41EH   Beginning of the keyboard buffer itself. The buffer contains 16 words (32 bytes), although it can be longer, and holds entered keyboard characters and their associated scan codes. Subsequently, INT 16H will read each character and its scan code and deliver them to the program. Two bytes are required for each character and its scan code.

When the user types a character, INT 09H advances the tail in the buffer. When INT 16H reads a character, it advances the head. In this way, the process is circular, with the head continually chasing the tail. When the buffer is *empty* (INT 16H has read all the stored characters), the head and tail are at the same address.

In the following example, both the head and tail initially are at 41EH. A user then keys ahead the characters 'abc<Enter>,' which INT 09H stores as follows:

- 'a' in the buffer at 41EH and its scan code 1EH at 41FH;
- 'b' in the buffer at 420H and its scan code 30H at 421H;
- 'c' in the buffer at 422H and its scan code 2EH at 423H;
- the Enter at 424H and its scan code E0H at 425H.

At this point, INT 09H has advanced the tail to 426H:

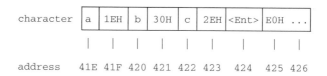

The first time the program issues INT 16H, the operation reads the "a" and its scan code and advances the head to 420H. Once the program has issued INT 16H four times, it has read all the characters and advanced the tail to 426H; because the tail has the same address as the head, the buffer is in effect empty.

When you key in 15 characters, the buffer is *full,* and the tail is immediately behind the head. To see this, suppose you now type ahead 'fghijklmnopqrs<Enter>'. INT 09H stores the characters beginning with the tail at 426H and circles around to store the '<Enter>' at 422H. The tail is now advanced to 424H, immediately before the head at 426H:

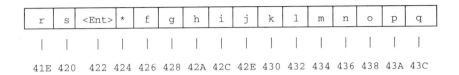

At this point, INT 09H does not accept any more typed characters and, indeed, accepts only 15 at most, although the buffer holds 16. (Can you tell why? If INT 09H were to accept another character, it would advance the tail to the same address as the head, and INT 16H would incorrectly assume that the buffer is empty.)

The Shift, Ctrl, and Alt Keys

INT 09H also handles the keyboard status bytes at 40:17H, 40:18H, and 40:96H in the BIOS Data Area. When you press Shift, Ctrl, or Alt, the BIOS routine sets the appropriate bit to 1, and when you release the key, it clears the bit to 0. Note that just pressing a control key alone does not satisfy INT 16H; you have to press it in common with another key that causes a valid keyboard entry, such as Shift+A, Ctrl+F1, etc. (See Appendix F.) The keyboard status byte reflects the action of the control key. A program may test whether any of the control keys are pressed by means of INT 16H function 12H.

The program in Figure 10-4 illustrates accessing and testing the status byte at 40:17H. As a rule, it is better programming practice to use BIOS interrupts to access BIOS areas, but this program illustrates a number of assembly language techniques. The program contains the following procedures:

- A10MAIN waits for the user to press a key. Pressing Enter tells the program to end; if other than Enter, the program issues INT 16H function 12H to get the keyboard status. If one of the Shift, Ctrl, or Alt keys was pressed along with a valid key, the program calls B10DISPLY.
- B10DISPLY displays the appropriate message for the pressed control key.

You could modify this program to test as well for the keyboard status byte at 40:18H.

KEY POINTS

- The shift status bytes in the BIOS Keyboard Data Area at 40:17H and 40:18H indicate the current status of such keys as Ctrl, Alt, Shift, CapsLock, NumLock, and ScrollLock.
- INT 21H keyboard operations provide a variety of services to echo or not echo characters on the screen, to recognize or ignore Ctrl+Break, and to accept scan codes.

```
TITLE      A10KBSTA (EXE)   Testing Alt, Shift, & Ctrl Status
           .MODEL SMALL
           .STACK 64
           .DATA
BIODATA    SEGMENT AT 40H           ;Locate BIOS data area
           ORG  17H                 ;  and
KBSTATE    DB   ?                   ;  status byte
BIODATA    ENDS
;  ----------------------------------------------------------
CR         EQU  0DH                 ;Carriage return
LF         EQU  0AH                 ;Line feed
ALTKEY     DB   'Alt key pressed  ', CR, LF
CTRLKEY    DB   'Ctrl key pressed ', CR, LF
SHIFTKEY   DB   'Shift key pressed', CR, LF
.286  ;  -------------------------------------------------------
           .CODE
A10MAIN    PROC FAR
           MOV  AX,BIODATA          ;Initialize seg. address
           MOV  ES,AX               ;  of BIODATA in ES
A20:       MOV  AH,10H              ;Request keyboard entry
           INT  16H
           CMP  AL,0DH              ;User requests end?
           JE   A90                 ;  yes, exit
           MOV  BL,ES:KBSTATE       ;Get keyboard status byte
           TEST BL,00000011B        ;Shift+char pressed?
           JZ   A30                 ;  no, bypass
           LEA  BP,SHIFTKEY         ;Request display
           CALL D10DISPLY           ;  shift message
A30:       TEST BL,00000100B        ;Ctrl+char pressed?
           JZ   A40                 ;  no, bypass
           LEA  BP,CTRLKEY          ;Request display
           CALL D10DISPLY           ;  ctrl message
A40:       TEST BL,00001000B        ;Alt+char pressed?
           JZ   A20                 ;  no, bypass
           LEA  BP,ALTKEY           ;Request display
           CALL D10DISPLY           ;  alt message
           JMP  A20                 ;Repeat
A90:       MOV  AX,4C00H            ;End processing
           INT  21H
A10MAIN    ENDP
;                    Display message for Alt, Ctrl, and
;                    Shift if key is pressed.
D10DISPLY  PROC NEAR                ;BP set on entry
           PUSHA                    ;Preserve registers
           PUSH ES
           MOV  AX,@data            ;Set up for ES:BP
           MOV  ES,AX               ;  for address of data
           MOV  AX,1301H            ;Request display
           MOV  BX,0016H            ;Page and attribute
           MOV  CX,17               ;Length of string
           MOV  DX,1008H            ;Row and column
           INT  10H
           POP  ES
           POPA                     ;Restore registers
           RET
D10DISPLY  ENDP
           END  A10MAIN
```

Figure 10-4   Checking the Keyboard Status Byte

- INT 16H function 10H provides the basic BIOS keyboard operation for accepting characters from the keyboard buffer. For a character key, the operation delivers the character to AL and the key's scan code to AH. For an extended function key, the operation delivers 00H or E0H to AL and the key's scan code to AH.

- The scan code is a unique number assigned to each key that enables BIOS to identify the source of a pressed key and enables a program to check for extended function keys such as Home, PageUp, and Arrow.

- The BIOS Keyboard Data Area at 40:1EH contains the keyboard buffer, which allows typing ahead up to 15 characters before a program requests input.

- Pressing a key causes the keyboard's processor to generate the key's scan code and requests INT 09H. Releasing the key causes it to generate a second scan code (the first code plus 10000000B, which sets the leftmost bit) to tell INT 09H that the key is released.

- BIOS INT 09H retrieves a scan code from the keyboard. The operation uses the scan code to generate an associated ASCII character, which it delivers to the keyboard buffer area. BIOS may also set the status for the Ctrl, Alt, and Shift keys.

REVIEW QUESTIONS AND EXERCISES

10-1. (a) What is the location of the first byte of the keyboard shift status in the BIOS Data Area? (b) What does the value 00000010 mean? (c) What does the value 00001100 mean?

10-2. Describe the features of the following functions for INT 21H keyboard input: (a) 01H, (b) 07H, (c) 08H, (d) 0AH.

10-3. Explain how INT 16H function 11H differs from function 10H.

10-4. Provide the scan codes for the following pressed keys: (a) End, (b) PageUp, (c) Up-Arrow, (d) function key F6.

10-5. Use DEBUG to examine the effects of entered keystrokes. To request entry of assembly statements, type A 100 and key in the following instructions:

```
MOV AH,10
INT 16
JMP 100
```

Use U 100,104 to unassemble the program, and use the P command to get DEBUG to execute through the INT. Execution stops, waiting for your input. Press any key and examine AH and AL. Continue typing a variety of keys. Press Q to quit DEBUG.

10-6. Code the instructions for INT 16H function 10H to accept a keystroke; if Page-Down, set the cursor to column 0, row 24.

10-7. Revise the program in Figure 10-2 to provide for the following features: (a) Revise the drop shadow from full shadow to three-quarter dots on (B2H). (b) After the initial clearing of the screen, display a prompt that asks users to press F1 for a menu screen. (c) When F1 is pressed, display the menu. (d) Allow users to select menu items also by pressing the first character (upper- or lowercase) of each item. (e) On request of an item, display a message for that particular selection, such as "Procedure to Delete Records." (f) Add a last line to the menu containing the item "Exit from program" that allows users to end processing. You'll also have to revise the procedure B10MENU to handle the display of another row.

10-8. Under what circumstances does an INT 09H operation occur?

10-9. Explain in simple terms how INT 09H handles the Alt and Ctrl keys differently from how it handles standard keyboard keys.

10-10. (a) Where is the BIOS memory location of the keyboard buffer? (b) What is the buffer's size, in bytes? (c) How many keyboard characters can it contain?

10-11. Explain the effect of the following occurrences in the keyboard buffer: (a) The address of the tail immediately follows the head. (b) The address of the head and tail are the same.

10-12. Revise the program in Figure 10-4 for the following requirements: (a) Transfer the contents of the second byte of the keyboard shift status to BH. (b) Test also for LeftAlt and LeftCtrl pressed, and display an appropriate message.

Chapter 11

PROCESSING STRING DATA

Objective: To explain the special instructions used to process string data.

INTRODUCTION

Up to this chapter, the instructions presented have handled data defined as only one byte, word, or doubleword. It is often necessary, however, to move or compare data fields that exceed these lengths. For example, you may want to compare descriptions or names in order to sort them into ascending sequence. Items of this type are known as *string data* and may be in either character or numeric format. Assembly language provides these string instructions for processing string data:

MOVS   Moves one byte, word, or doubleword from one location in memory to another.

LODS   Loads from memory a byte into AL, word into AX, or doubleword into EAX.

STOS   Stores the contents of AL, AX, or EAX into memory.

CMPS   Compares byte, word, or doubleword items in memory.

SCAS   Compares the contents of AL, AX, or EAX with the contents of an item in memory.

An associated instruction, the REP prefix, causes a string instruction to perform repetitively so that it may process any number of bytes, words, or doublewords a specified number of times. Two other string instructions, INS and OUTS, are covered in Chapter 24.

FEATURES OF STRING OPERATIONS

Each string instruction has a byte, word, and doubleword version for repetitive processing and assumes use of the ES:DI or DS:SI pair of registers. Thus you could select a byte operation for a string with an odd number of bytes and a word operation for a string with an even number of bytes. The use of word and doubleword operations can provide faster processing.

String instructions expect that the DI and SI registers contain valid offset addresses that reference bytes in memory. SI is normally associated with DS (data segment) as DS:SI, whereas DI is always associated with ES (extra segment) as ES:DI. For this reason, MOVS, STOS, CMPS, and SCAS require that an .EXE program initialize ES usually, but not necessarily, with the same address as that in DS:

```
MOV   AX,@data   ;Get address of data segment,
MOV   DS,AX      ; store it in DS
MOV   ES,AX      ; and in ES
```

As shown in Figure 11-1, there are basically two ways to code string instructions:

1. The second column shows the basic format for each operation, which uses the implied operands listed in the third column. (If you code an instruction as MOVS, you include the operands—for example, as MOVS BYTE1,BYTE2, where the definition of the operands indicates the length of the move.) A later section, "Alternative Coding for String Instructions," describes this format in more detail.

2. The second way to code string instructions is the standard practice, as shown in the fourth, fifth, and sixth columns. You load the addresses of the operands in DI and SI and code the instruction without operands, for example, as:

```
LEA   DI,BYTE2   ;Address of BYTE2 (ES:DI)
LEA   SI,BYTE1   ;Address of BYTE1 (DS:SI)
MOVSB            ;Move BYTE1 to BYTE2
```

REP: Repeat String Prefix

The REP prefix immediately before a string instruction, such as REP MOVSB, provides for repeated execution based on an initial count that you set in CX. REP executes the string instruction, decrements CX, and repeats this operation until the count in CX is zero. In this way, you can process strings of virtually any length.

The Direction Flag (DF) determines the direction of a repeated operation:

- To process from left to right, use CLD to clear the DF to 0.
- To process from right to left, use STD to set the DF to 1.

Oper- ation	Basic Instruction	Implied Operands	Byte Operation	Word Operation	Doubleword Operation
Move	MOVS	ES:DI,DS:SI	MOVSB	MOVSW	MOVSD
Load	LODS	AX,DS:SI	LODSB	LODSW	LODSD
Store	STOS	ES:DI,AX	STOSB	STOSW	STOSD
Compare	CMPS	DS:SI,ES:DI	CMPSB	CMPSW	CMPSD
Scan	SCAS	ES:DI,AX	SCASB	SCASW	SCASD

Figure 11-1   Formats for the String Instructions

In the following example, assume that DS and ES are both initialized with the address of the data segment, as shown earlier. A REP MOVSB operation copies the 20 bytes of SEND_STR to RECV_STR:

```
SEND_STR  DB    20 DUP('*')    ;Sending field
RECV_STR  DB    20 DUP(' ')    ;Receiving field
          ...
          CLD                  ;Clear Direction Flag
          MOV   CX,20          ;Initialize for 20 bytes,
          LEA   DI,RECV_STR    ;  receiving address (ES:DI),
          LEA   SI,SEND_STR    ;  sending address (DS:SI)
          REP   MOVSB          ;Copy SEND_STR to RECV_STR
```

MOV, LODS, and STOS always fully repeat the specified number of times. However, CMPS and SCAS make comparisons that set status flags so that the operations can end immediately on finding a specified condition. The variations of REP that CMPS and SCAS use for this purpose are the following:

- REP: Repeat the operation until CX is decremented to zero.
- REPE or REPZ: Repeat the operation while the Zero Flag (ZF) indicates equal/zero. Stop when ZF indicates not equal/zero or when CX is decremented to zero.
- REPNE or REPNZ: Repeat the operation while ZF indicates not equal/zero. Stop when ZF indicates equal or zero or when CX is decremented to zero.

The following sections examine each string operation in detail.

MOVS: MOVE STRING INSTRUCTION

MOVSB, MOVSW, and MOVSD combined with a REP prefix and a length in CX can move a specified number of characters. The segment:offset registers are ES:DI for the receiving string and DS:SI for the sending string. As a result, at the start of an .EXE program, be sure to initialize ES along with DS, and prior to executing the MOVS, also initialize DI and SI. Depending on the Direction Flag, MOVS increments or decrements DI and SI by 1 for byte, 2 for word, and 4 for doubleword. The following example illustrates moving 12 words:

```
MOV   CX,12          ;Number of words
LEA   DI,RECV_STR    ;Address of RECV_STR (ES:DI)
LEA   SI,SEND_STR    ;Address of SEND_STR (DS:SI)
REP MOVSW            ;Move 12 words
```

The instructions equivalent to the REP MOVSW operation are:

```
      JCXZ  L40       ;Bypass if CX initially zero
L30:  MOV   AX,[SI]   ;Get word from SEND_STR
      MOV   [DI],AX   ;Store word in RECV_STR
      ADD   DI,2      ;Increment for next word
      ADD   SI,2      ;
      LOOP  L30       ;Decrement CX and repeat
L40:  ...
```

Earlier, Figure 6-2 illustrated moving a 9-byte field. The program could also have used MOVSB for this purpose. In the partial program in Figure 11-2, ES is initialized because it is required by the MOVS instructions. The program uses MOVSB to move a 12-byte field, STRING1, one byte at a time to STRING2. The first instruction, CLD, clears the Direction Flag so that the MOVSB processes data from left to right. The Direction Flag is normally 0 at the start of execution, but CLD is coded here as a precaution.

A MOV instruction initializes CX with 12 (the length of STRING1 and of STRING2). Two LEA instructions load SI and DI with the offset addresses of STRING1 and STRING2, respectively. REP MOVSB now performs the following:

- Moves the leftmost byte of STRING1 (addressed by DS:SI) to the leftmost byte of STRING2 (addressed by ES:DI);
- Increments DI and SI by 1 for the next bytes to the right;
- Decrements CX by 1;
- Repeats this operation 12 times until CX becomes 0.

Because the Direction Flag is 0 and MOVSB increments DI and SI, each iteration processes one byte farther to the right, as STRING1+1 to STRING2+1, and so on. At the end of execution, CX contains 0, DI contains the address of STRING2+12, and SI contains the address of STRING1+12—both one byte past the end of the name.

To process from *right to left,* set the Direction Flag to 1. MOVSB then decrements DI and SI, but to move the contents correctly, you have to initialize SI with STRING1+11 and DI with STRING2+11.

The program next uses MOVSW to move six words from STRING2 to STRING3. At the end of execution, CX contains 0, DI contains the address of STRING3+12, and SI contains the address of STRING2+12.

Because MOVSW increments DI and SI by 2, the operation requires only six loops. For processing right to left, set the Direction Flag and initialize SI with STRING1+10 and DI with STRING2+10.

```
STRING1 DB      'Interstellar'       ;Data items
STRING2 DB      12 DUP(' ')
STRING3 DB      12 DUP(' ')
        . . .
        MOV     AX,@data             ;Initialize
        MOV     DS,AX                ;  segment
        MOV     ES,AX                ;  registers
                                     ;Use of MOVSB:
        CLD                          ;Left to right
        MOV     CX,12                ;Move 12 bytes,
        LEA     DI,STRING2           ;  STRING1 to STRING2
        LEA     SI,STRING1
        REP MOVSB
                                     ;Use of MOVSW:
        CLD                          ;Left to right
        MOV     CX,06                ;Move 6 words,
        LEA     DI,STRING3           ;  STRING2 to STRING3
        LEA     SI,STRING2
        REP MOVSW
        . . .
```

Figure 11-2   Using MOVS String Operations

LODS: LOAD STRING INSTRUCTION

LODS simply loads AL with a byte, AX with a word, EAX with a doubleword from memory. The memory address is subject to DS:SI registers, although you can override SI. Depending on the Direction Flag, the operation also increments or decrements SI by 1 for byte, 2 for word, and 4 for doubleword.

Because one LODS operation fills the register, there is no practical reason to use the REP prefix with it. For most purposes, a simple MOV instruction is adequate. But MOV generates three bytes of machine code, whereas LODS generates only one, although you have to initialize SI. You could use LODS to step through a string one byte, word, or doubleword at a time, examining successively for a particular character.

The instructions equivalent to LODSB are

```
MOV AL,[SI] ;Transfer byte to AL
INC SI      ;Increment SI for next byte
```

The following example defines a 12-byte field named STRING1 containing the value "Interstellar" and another 12-byte field named STRING2. The objective is to transfer the bytes from STRING1 to STRING2 in reverse sequence, so that STRING2 contains "ralletsretnI." LODSB accesses one byte at a time from STRING1 into AL, and MOV [DI],AL transfers the bytes to STRING2, from right to left.

```
STRING1  DB    'Interstellar' ;Data items
STRING2  DB    12 DUP(20H)
         ...
         CLD                  ;Left to right
         MOV   CX,12
         LEA   SI,STRING1      ;Address of STRING1 (DI:SI)
         LEA   DI,STRING2+11   ;Address of STRING2+11 (ES:DI)
L20:     LODS                 ;Get character in AL,
         MOV   [DI],AL        ;  store in STRING2,
         DEC   DI             ;  right to left
         LOOP  L20            ;12 characters?
         ...
```

STOS: STORE STRING INSTRUCTION

STOS stores the contents of AL, AX, or EAX into a byte, word, or doubleword in memory. The memory address is always subject to ES:DI. Depending on the Direction Flag, STOS also increments or decrements DI by 1 for byte, 2 for word, and 4 for doubleword.

A practical use of STOS with a REP prefix is to initialize a data area to any specified value, such as clearing an area to blanks. You set the number of bytes, words, or doublewords in CX. The instructions equivalent to REP STOSB are:

```
         JCXZ L30     ;Jump if CX zero
L20:     MOV [DI],AL  ;Store AL in memory
         INC/DEC DI   ;Increment or decrement (sets flags)
         LOOP  L20    ;Decrement CX and repeat
L30:     ...          ;Operation complete
```

The STOSW instruction in the following example repeatedly stores a word containing 2020H (blanks) six times through STRING1. The operation stores AL in the first byte and AH in the next byte (that is, reversed). At the end, all of STRING1 is blank, CX contains 00, and DI contains the address of STRING1+12.

```
CLD                     ;Left to right
MOV     AX,2020H    ;Move
MOV     CX,06       ; 6 blank words
LEA     DI,STRING1 ; to STRING1 (ES:DI)
REP STOSW
```

PROGRAM: USING LODS AND STOS TO EDIT DATA

The program in Figure 11-3 illustrates the use of both the LODS and STOS instructions. Its purpose is to allow a user to edit a string of characters. To reduce the space required and the complexity, this is a bare-bones editor. Basically, the program displays a string of 30 characters. The more relevant procedures perform the following:

- A10MAIN initializes addressability, calls Q30DISPLY to display the string, and calls B10KEYBRD to request a keyboard character. The program ends when the user presses <Esc>.
- B10READ accepts a keyboard character: If <RightArrow>, calls C10RTARRW; if <LeftArrow>, calls D10LFARRW; if <Del>, calls E10DELETE; if <Home> calls F10HOME; if <End>, calls G10END; else calls H10CHARS for all other characters.
- C10RTARRW arranges to move the cursor to the right; if already at the right edge, calls F10HOME.
- D10LFARRW arranges to move the cursor to the left; if already at the left edge, calls G10END.
- E10DELETE replaces the current character with the one to its right and shuffles all other rightmost characters to the left. The character farthest to the right is filled with a blank.
- F10HOME sets the cursor at the leftmost edge.
- G10END sets the cursor at the rightmost edge.
- H10CHARS bypasses any character below 20H or above 7EH; if <Home>, sets cursor to the left; if <End>, sets cursor to the right; otherwise replaces the character in the string and screen.

Some ways to enhance this program include:

- Display the string within a boxed window.
- Make <Ins> a toggle key, so that characters replace (as done at present) or insert (bump rightmost characters to the right).

A challenge in this type of program is to coordinate the data on the screen as you change the text. You may want to experiment with transferring the data directly to the Video Display Area.

```
          TITLE    A11EDIT (EXE)  Editing Features
                   .MODEL SMALL
                   .STACK 64
                   .DATA
INDENT    EQU      24                      ;Screen indent
LEFTLIM   EQU      00                      ;Left limit of data
RIGHTLIM  EQU      29                      ;Right limit of data
NOCHARS   EQU      30                      ;Length of data
COL       DB       00                      ;Screen column
ROW       DB       10                      ;Screen row
DATASTR   DB       'abcdefghijklmno' ;Area for editing data
          DB       'pqrstuvwxyzABCD', 20H
.386    ;  ------------------------------------------------
                   .CODE
A10MAIN   PROC     FAR
          MOV      AX,@data                ;Initialize segment
          MOV      DS,AX                   ;  registers
          MOV      ES,AX
          CALL     Q10CLEAR                ;Clear screen
          CALL     Q20CURSOR               ;Set cursor start
          CALL     Q30DISPLY               ;Display string
A30:
          CALL     Q20CURSOR               ;Reset cursor start
          CALL     B10KEYBRD               ;Get KB character
          CMP      AH,01H                  ;Escape key?
          JNE      A30                     ;  no, continue
          MOV      AX,0600H                ;  yes, quit
          CALL     Q10CLEAR                ;Clear screen
          MOV      AX,4C00H                ;End of processing
          INT      21H
A10MAIN   ENDP

;         Get keyboard character and determine action to take:
;         ------------------------------------------------
B10KEYBRD PROC     NEAR                    ;Uses AX only
          MOV      AH,10H                  ;Get
          INT      16H                     ;  character
          CMP      AL,00H                  ;Function/direction key?
          JE       B20                     ;  yes
          CMP      AL,0E0H                 ;Function/direction key?
          JE       B20                     ;  yes
          CALL     H10CHARS                ;Other character
          JMP      B90                     ;Exit
B20:      CMP      AH,4DH                  ;Right arrow?
          JNE      B30                     ;  no
          CALL     C10RTARRW               ;  yes, process
          JMP      B90
B30:      CMP      AH,4BH                  ;Left arrow?
          JNE      B40                     ;  no
          CALL     D10LFARRW               ;  yes, process
          JMP      B90
B40:      CMP      AH,53H                  ;Delete key?
          JNE      B50                     ;  no
          CALL     E10DELETE               ;  yes, process
          JMP      B90
```

Figure 11-3 Simple Editing Instructions

CMPS: COMPARE STRING INSTRUCTION

CMPS compares the contents of one memory location (addressed by DS:SI) with that of another memory location (addressed by ES:DI). Depending on the Direction Flag, CMPS increments or decrements SI and DI, by 1 for byte, 2 for word, and 4 for doubleword. The operation ends on a successful compare or when REP reduces CX to 0. The operation then sets the AF, CF, OF, PF, SF, and ZF flags depending on the result, if any, of the compare.

```
B50:        CMP     AH,47H          ;Home key?
            JNE     B60             ;  no
            CALL    F10HOME         ;  yes, process
            JMP     B90
B60:        CMP     AH,4FH          ;End key?
            JNE     B90             ;  no
            CALL    G10END          ;  yes, process
B90:        RET
B10KEYBRD   ENDP


;           Right arrow.  If at right edge, set cursor
;           to left edge, else increment column:
;           -----------------------------------------
C10RTARRW   PROC    NEAR
            CMP     COL,RIGHTLIM    ;At rightmost edge?
            JAE     C20             ;  yes,
            INC     COL             ;  no, increment col
            JMP     C90             ;  exit
C20:        CALL    F10HOME         ;  cursor to left edge
C90:        RET                     ;
C10RTARRW   ENDP


;           Left arrow.  If at left edge, set cursor
;           to right edge, else decrement column:
;           -----------------------------------------
D10LFARRW   PROC    NEAR
            CMP     COL,LEFTLIM     ;At leftmost edge?
            JBE     D20             ;  yes,
            DEC     COL             ;  no, decrement col
            JMP     D90             ;  exit
D20:        CALL    G10END          ;  cursor to right edge
D90:        RET
D10LFARRW   ENDP


;           Delete key.  Replace current character with one
;           to right, shift rightmost characters to left:
;           -----------------------------------------------
E10DELETE   PROC    NEAR            ;Uses BX, DI, SI
            MOVZX   BX,COL          ;Get column
            PUSH    BX              ;Save for later
            LEA     DI,[DATASTR+BX] ;Init. present col
            LEA     SI,[DATASTR+BX+1] ; and adjacent col
E20:
            LODSB                   ;Store adjacent char
            STOSB                   ;  in present col
            CALL    Q40DISCHR       ;Display the char
            INC     COL             ;Increment next col
            CALL    Q20CURSOR       ;Set cursor
            CMP     COL,RIGHTLIM    ;At right edge?
            JBE     E20             ;  no, repeat
            POP     BX              ;Get saved original
            MOV     COL,BL          ;  column
            RET
E10DELETE   ENDP
```

Figure 11-3 *Continued*

When combined with a REPnn prefix and a length in CX, CMPS can successively compare strings of any length. The three CMPS operations are CMPSB for byte, CMPSW for word, and CMPSD for doubleword.

Note that CMP compares operand 2 to operand 1, whereas CMPS compares operand 1 to 2. Also, CMPS provides an *alphanumeric* comparison, that is, a comparison according to ASCII values. The operation is not suited to algebraic comparisons, which consist of signed numeric values.

```
;               Home key.  Set cursor to left column:
;               ------------------------------------
F10HOME   PROC    NEAR
          MOV     COL,LEFTLIM         ;Set cursor
          CALL    Q20CURSOR           ;  at left edge
          RET
F10HOME   ENDP


;               End key.  Set cursor to right column:
;               ------------------------------------
G10END    PROC    NEAR
          MOV     COL,RIGHTLIM        ;Set cursor
          CALL    Q20CURSOR           ;  at right edge
          RET
G10END    ENDP


;               All other characters.  Bypass characters below
;               20H and above 7EH, else insert at cursor:
;               -----------------------------------------------
H10CHARS  PROC    NEAR                ;Uses BX, DI
          CMP     AL,20H              ;ASCII char below 20H?
          JB      H90                 ;  yes, bypass
          CMP     AL,7EH              ;Above 7EH?
          JA      H90                 ;  yes, bypass
          MOVZX   BX,COL              ;Use COL as index
          LEA     DI,DATASTR          ;Move character to
          MOV     [DI+BX],AL          ;  data string
          CALL    Q40DISCHR           ;Display the character
          CMP     COL,RIGHTLIM        ;At right edge?
          JAE     H90                 ;  yes, exit
          INC     COL                 ;  no, increment column
H90:      RET
H10CHARS  ENDP


;               Clear screen and set attribute:
;               -------------------------------
Q10CLEAR  PROC    NEAR
          MOV     AX,0600H            ;Request scroll
          MOV     BH,61H              ;Blue on brown
          MOV     CX,0000             ;Full screen
          MOV     DX,184FH
          INT     10H
          RET
Q10CLEAR  ENDP


;               Set cursor row:column:
;               ----------------------
Q20CURSOR PROC    NEAR
          MOV     AH,02H              ;Request set cursor
          MOV     BH,00               ;Page 0
          MOV     DH,ROW              ;Row
          MOV     DL,COL              ;Column
          ADD     DL,INDENT           ;Indent on screen
          INT     10H
          RET
Q20CURSOR ENDP
```

Figure 11-3 *Continued*

Consider the comparison of two strings containing "Jean" and "Joan." A comparison from left to right, one byte at a time, results in the following:

J : J   Equal

e : o   Unequal (e is low)

a : a   Equal

n : n   Equal

```
;              Display full data string:
;              --------------------------
Q30DISPLY PROC     NEAR
          MOV      AX,1301H              ;Request display
          MOV      BX,0016H              ;Page, attribute
          LEA      BP,DATASTR            ;Data line
          MOV      CX,NOCHARS+1          ;Length of line
          MOV      DH,ROW                ;
          MOV      DL,COL                ;
          ADD      DL,INDENT             ;Indent on screen
          INT      10H
          RET
Q30DISPLY ENDP

;              Display single character:
;              --------------------------
Q40DISCHR PROC     NEAR                  ;Character in AL
          MOV      AH,0AH                ;  on entry
          MOV      BH,00                 ;Page
          MOV      CX,01                 ;One character
          INT      10H
          RET
Q40DISCHR ENDP
          END      A10MAIN
```

Figure 11-3 *Continued*

A comparison of the entire four bytes ends with a comparison of "n" with "n" (equal). Now since the two names are not identical, the operation should end as soon as it makes a comparison between two different characters. For this purpose, the REP variation, REPE (Repeat on Equal), repeats the operation as long as the comparison is between equal characters, or until CX is decremented to 0. The coding for a repeated one-byte comparison is REPE CMPSB.

Following are two examples that use CMPSB. The first example compares STRING1 with STRING2, which contain the same 12-byte values. The CMPSB operation therefore continues for the entire 12 bytes. At the end of execution, CX contains 0, DI contains the address of STRING2+12, SI contains the address of STRING1+12, the Sign Flag is positive, and the Zero Flag indicates equal/zero.

```
STRING1  DB       'Interstellar'  ;Data items
STRING2  DB       'Interstellar'
STRING3  DB       12 DUP(' ')

         ...
         CLD                      ;Left to right
         MOV      CX,12           ;Initialize for 12 bytes
         LEA      DI,STRING2      ;ES:DI
         LEA      SI,STRING1      ;DS:SI
         REPE CMPSB               ;Compare STRING1 : STRING2
         JNE      exit            ; not equal, bypass
         ...                      ; equal
```

The second example compares STRING2 with STRING3, which contain different values. The CMPSB operation ends after comparing the first byte and results in a high/unequal condition: CX contains 11, DI contains the address of STRING3+1, SI contains the address of STRING2+1, the Sign Flag is positive, and the Zero Flag indicates unequal.

```
        MOV     CX,12               ;Initialize for 12 bytes
        LEA     DI,STRING3
        LEA     SI,STRING2
        REPE CMPSB                  ;Compare STRING2 : STRING3
        JE      exit                ; equal, exit
        ...                         ; not equal
```

Warning! These examples use CMPSB to compare data one byte at a time. If you use CMPSW to compare data a word at a time, you have to initialize CX to 5. But that's not the problem. When comparing words, CMPSW reverses the bytes. For example, let's compare the names SAMUEL and ARNOLD. For the initial comparison of words, instead of comparing SA with AR, the operation compares AS with RA. So, instead of the name SAMUEL indicating a higher value, it incorrectly compares as lower. CMPSW works correctly only if the compared fields contain unsigned numeric data defined as DW, DD, or DQ (that is, with the data stored in reversed-byte sequence). As well, a shorter string value should be filled with blanks to the right.

SCAS: SCAN STRING INSTRUCTION

SCAS differs from CMPS in that SCAS *scans* a string for a specified value. To this end, SCAS compares the contents of a memory location (addressed by ES:DI) with the contents of AL, AX, or EAX. Depending on the Direction Flag, SCAS also increments or decrements DI by 1 for byte, 2 for word, and 4 for doubleword. The operation ends on a successful compare or when REP reduces CX to zero. SCAS then sets the AF, CF, OF, PF, SF, and ZF flags, depending on the result of the compare. When combined with a REPnn prefix and a length in CX, SCAS can scan virtually any string length. The three SCAS operations are SCASB for byte, SCASW for word, and SCASD for doubleword.

SCAS would be particularly useful for a text-editing application in which the program has to scan for punctuation, such as periods, commas, and blanks.

The following example scans STRING1 for the lowercase letter *r*. Because the SCASB operation is to continue scanning while the comparison is not equal or until CX is 0, the operation in this case is REPNE SCASB:

```
    STRING1 DB      'Interstellar'  ;Data item
            ...
            CLD                     ;Left to right
            MOV     AL,'r'          ;Scan STRING1 for 'r'
            MOV     CX,12           ;12 characters
            LEA     DI,STRING1      ;ES:DI
            REPNE SCASB
            JE      exit            ;Found
            ...                     ;Not found
```

When scanning the string "Interstellar" in STRING1, SCASB finds a match on the fifth comparison. Using a debugger to trace the instructions discloses at the end of execution of the REP SCASB operation that the Zero Flag is 0, CX is decremented to 7, and DI is incremented by 5. (DI is incremented 1 byte past the actual location of the matched character.)

For a word operation, SCASW scans a string in memory for a value that matches the word in the AX register. If you used LODSW or MOV to transfer a word into AX, the first byte would be in AL and the second byte in AH. Because SCASW compares the bytes in reversed sequence, the operation works correctly.

Example: Using Scan and Replace

You may also want to replace a specific character with another character, for example, to clear editing characters such as paragraph and end-of-page symbols from a document. The following example scans TESTDATA for an asterisk (*) and replaces it with a blank. If SCASB locates an asterisk, it ends the operation. TESTDATA contains an asterisk at TESTDATA+5, where the blank is to be inserted, although SCASB will have incremented DI to TESTDATA+6. Decrementing DI by 1 [DI-1] provides the correct address for inserting the blank replacement character.

```
DATALEN   EQU 13                        ;Length of TESTDATA
TESTDATA  DB   'Extra*innings'
          ...
          CLD                           ;Set left to right
          MOV  AL,'*'                   ;Search character
          MOV  CX,DATALEN               ;Length of TESTDATA
          LEA  DI,TESTDATA              ;Address of TESTDATA (ES:DI)
          REPNE SCASB                   ;Scan TESTDATA
          JNE  exit                     ;Character found?
          MOV  BYTE PTR[DI-1],20H        ;Yes, replace with blank
          ...
```

ALTERNATIVE CODING FOR STRING INSTRUCTIONS

As discussed earlier, if a string instruction is coded explicitly with a B, W, or D suffix, such as MOVSB, MOVSW, or MOVSD, the assembler assumes the correct length and does not require operands. You can also use the basic instruction formats for the string operations. For an instruction such as MOVS, which has no suffix to indicate byte, word, or double-word, the operands must indicate the length. For example, if CHAR1 and CHAR2 are defined as DB, the instruction

```
REP MOVS CHAR1,CHAR2
```

implies a repeated move of the byte beginning at CHAR2 to the byte beginning at CHAR1.

Another format allows you to refer to the segment registers explicitly and to use the PTR directive. If you load DI and SI registers with the addresses of CHAR1 and CHAR2, you can code the MOVS instruction as

```
LEA DI,CHAR2
LEA SI,CHAR1
REP MOVS ES:BYTE PTR[DI],DS:[SI]
```

Few programs are coded this way, and these formats are covered here just for the record.

REPLICATING A PATTERN

The STOS instruction is useful for setting an area according to a specific byte, word, or doubleword value. However, for repeating a pattern that exceeds these lengths, you can use MOVS with a minor modification. Let's say that you want to set a display line to the following pattern:

|****||****||****||****||****| . . .

Rather than define the entire pattern repetitively, you can define only the first six bytes immediately preceding the display line. Here are the instructions:

```
PATTERN  DB '|****|'        ;Pattern, immediately precedes
DISPAREA DB 42 DUP(?)       ; display area
         . . .
         CLD                ;Left to right operation
         MOV CX,21          ;21 words
         LEA DI,DISPAREA    ;Destination
         LEA SI,PATTERN     ;Source
         REP MOVSW          ;Move characters
```

On execution, MOVSW moves the first word of PATTERN (|*) to the first word of DISPAREA and then moves the second (**) and third (*|) words:

|****| |****|
↑   ↑
PATTERN   DISPAREA

At this point, the DI contains the address of DISPAREA+6, and the SI contains the address of PATTERN+6, which is also the same address as DISPAREA. The operation now automatically replicates the pattern by moving the first word of DISPAREA to DISPAREA+6, DISPAREA+2 to DISPAREA+8, DISPAREA+4 to DISPAREA+10, and so forth. Eventually the pattern is duplicated through to the end of DISPAREA:

You can use this technique to replicate a pattern any number of times. The pattern itself may be any length, but must immediately precede the destination field.

KEY POINTS

- For the string instructions MOVS, STOS, CMPS, and SCAS, an .EXE program must initialize the ES register.
- String instructions use the suffixes B, W, or D to handle byte, word, or doubleword strings.
- The Direction Flag controls the required direction of processing: Clear flag (CLD) for left to right or set flag (STD) for right to left.

- For MOVS, DI and SI control addressing of the operands, whereas for CMPS, SI and DI control addressing.
- CX must contain an initial value for REP to process the specified number of bytes, words, or doublewords.
- For normal processing, REP is used with MOVS and STOS, and a conditional REP (REPE or REPNE) is used with CMPS and SCAS.
- The CMPSW and SCASW operations reverse the bytes in words that are compared.
- To process right to left, addressing begins at the rightmost byte of the field. For example, if a field named COTITLE is 10 bytes long, then for processing bytes, the load address for LEA is COTITLE+9. For processing words, the address is COTITLE+8 because the string operation initially accesses COTITLE+8 and COTITLE+9.

REVIEW QUESTIONS AND EXERCISES

11-1. String operations assume that the operands relate to ES:DI or DS:SI registers. Identify the registers for the following: (a) MOVS (operands 1 and 2), (b) LODS (operand 1), (c) CMPS (operands 1 and 2), (d) STOS (operand 2).

11-2. For a string operation such as REP MOVSB, (a) how do you set the number of repetitions that are to occur? (b) How do you set processing right to left?

11-3. The chapter gives the instructions equivalent to (a) MOVSB, (b) LODSB, and (c) STOSB, each with a REP prefix. For each case, provide the equivalent code for processing words.

11-4. Revise the program in Figure 11-2 to change the MOVSB and MOVSW operations to move data from right to left. Use a debugger to trace through the procedures, and note the contents of the data segment and registers.

11-5. For what conditions do each of the following instructions test? (a) REPNE COMPSW, (b) REPE SCASW.

11-6. Use the following data definitions and for parts (a)–(f) code the instructions for the unrelated string operations:

```
BUS_TITLE DB    'Computer Wizards'
WORK_SPACE DB  16 DUP(20H)
```

(a) Move BUS_TITLE to WORK_SPACE, from left to right.
(b) Move BUS_TITLE to WORK_SPACE, from right to left.
(c) Load the fourth and fifth bytes of BUS_TITLE into AX.
(d) Store AX beginning at WORK_SPACE+12.
(e) Compare BUS_TITLE with WORK_SPACE.
(f) Scan BUS_TITLE for the first blank character and, if found, move it to CH.

11-7. Revise the program fragment in the section "SCAS: Scan String Instruction" so that the operation scans STRING1 for *st* as a pair of characters. A check of STRING1 discloses that *st* does not appear as a word, as shown by the following: /In/te/rs/te/ll/ar/. Two possible solutions are: (a) Use SCASW twice, with the first SCASW beginning at STRING1 and the second SCASW at STRING1+1; (b) or use SCASB and on finding an *s*, compare the byte that follows it for a *t*.

11-8. Define a 5-byte field containing the hex value C9CDCDCDBB. Use MOVSB to duplicate this field 12 times into a 60-byte area, and display the result.

11-9. Code a program for the following requirements. Define NAME1 with the string "Computer Tech" and NAME2 with 13 blanks. Use LODSB to access each character in NAME1 from left to right. Then use STOSB to store each accessed character into NAME2 from right to left so that NAME2 contains the string in reverse sequence. You have to clear and set the Direction Flag for this procedure. Assemble and test.

11-10. Revise Figure 11-3 to check the Ins key. If it is toggled off, the entered character overtypes the present character; if toggled on, the character is inserted so that characters to the right are bumped left to right and the rightmost character is deleted. Assemble and test.

Chapter 12

ARITHMETIC I: PROCESSING BINARY DATA

> Objective: To cover the requirements for addition, subtraction, multiplication, and division of binary data.

INTRODUCTION

This chapter covers addition, subtraction, multiplication, and division and the use of unsigned and signed numeric data. Included as well are many examples and warnings of various pitfalls for the unwary traveler in the realm of computer arithmetic. Chapter 13 covers special requirements involved with conversion between binary and ASCII data formats.

Although we are accustomed to performing arithmetic in decimal (base 10) format, a microcomputer performs its arithmetic only in binary (base 2). Instructions described in this chapter are:

ADC	Add with carry	IDIV	Divide signed
ADD	Add	IMUL	Multiply signed
CBW	Convert byte to word	MUL	Multiply unsigned
CDQ	Convert doubleword to quadword	NEG	Negate
CWD	Convert word to doubleword	SBB	Subtract with borrow
CWDE	Convert word to extended doubleword	SUB	Subtract
DIV	Divide unsigned		

PROCESSING UNSIGNED AND SIGNED BINARY DATA

Some numeric fields—for example, a customer number and the day of the month—are unsigned. Some signed numeric fields—for example, customer's balance owing and a temperature reading—may contain positive or negative values. Other signed numeric fields—for example, a product price and the value of pi—are supposed to be always positive.

The following table gives the maximum values for unsigned and signed data according to register width:

FORMAT	BYTE	WORD	DOUBLEWORD
Unsigned	255	65,535	4,294,967,295
Signed	127	32,767	2,147,483,647

For unsigned data, all bits are intended to be data bits. For signed data, the leftmost bit is a sign bit. But note that the ADD and SUB instructions do not distinguish between unsigned and signed data and, indeed, simply add and subtract bits.

The following example illustrates the addition of two binary numbers, with the values shown as both unsigned and signed. The top number contains a 1-bit to the left; for unsigned data, the bits represent 249, whereas for signed data, the bits represent −7. The addition does not set the Overflow (OF) or Carry (CF) Flags:

	UNSIGNED	SIGNED		
BINARY	DECIMAL	DECIMAL	OF	CF
11111001	249	−7		
+00000010	+ 2	+2		
11111011	251	−5	0	0

The result of this binary addition is the same for both unsigned and signed data. However, the bits in the unsigned field represent decimal 251, whereas the bits in the signed field represent decimal −5. In effect, the contents of a field mean whatever you intend them to mean, and you must handle them accordingly.

Arithmetic Carry. An arithmetic operation transfers the resulting sign bit (0 or 1) to the Carry Flag. If the sign bit is a 1, then, in effect, the Carry Flag is set. Where a carry occurs on unsigned data, the arithmetic result is invalid. The following example of addition causes a carry:

	UNSIGNED	SIGNED		
BINARY	DECIMAL	DECIMAL	OF	CF
11111100	252	−4		
+00000101	+ 5	+5		
(1)00000001	1	1	0	1
	(invalid)	(valid)		

The operation on the unsigned data is invalid because of the carry out of a data bit, whereas the operation on the signed data is valid.

Arithmetic Overflow. An arithmetic operation sets the Overflow Flag when a carry *into* the sign bit does not carry out, or a carry *out* occurs with no carry in. If an overflow occurs on signed data, the arithmetic result is invalid (because of an overflow into the sign bit). The following example of addition causes an overflow:

	UNSIGNED	SIGNED		
BINARY	DECIMAL	DECIMAL	OF	CF
01111001	121	+121		
+00001011	+ 11	+ 11		
10000100	132	-124	1	0
	(valid)	(invalid)		

An add operation may set both Carry and Overflow Flags. In the next example, the carry makes the operation on unsigned data invalid, and the overflow makes the operation on signed data invalid:

	UNSIGNED	SIGNED		
BINARY	DECIMAL	DECIMAL	OF	CF
11110110	246	-10		
+10001001	+137	-119		
(1)01111111	127	+127	1	1
	(invalid)	(invalid)		

The upshot of all this is that you must have a good idea as to the magnitude of the numbers that your program will handle, and you define and process numeric fields accordingly.

ADDITION AND SUBTRACTION OF BINARY DATA

The ADD and SUB instructions perform simple addition and subtraction of binary data in byte, word, and doubleword size. Their formats are:

[label:]	ADD/SUB	register,register
[label:]	ADD/SUB	memory,register
[label:]	ADD/SUB	register,memory
[label:]	ADD/SUB	register,immediate
[label:]	ADD/SUB	memory,immediate

An ADD or SUB operation sets or clears the Overflow and Carry Flags, as described in the previous section. Like most other instructions, there are no direct memory-to-memory operations.

As described in Chapter 1, a negative binary number is represented in two's complement form by reversing the bits of the positive number and adding 1. The following self-explanatory examples of ADD and SUB process byte and word values.

```
BYTE1   DB   24H                 ;Data items
WORD1   DW   4000H
        ...
        MOV  CL,BYTE1            ;Processing bytes:
        MOV  DL,40H
        ADD  CL,DL              ;Register-to-register
        SUB  CL,20H             ;Immediate-to-register
        ADD  BYTE1,BL           ;Register-to-memory
        MOV  CX,WORD1           ;Processing words:
        MOV  DX,2000H
        SUB  CX,DX              ;Register-from-register
        SUB  CX, 124H           ;Immediate-from-memory
        ADD  WORD1,DX           ;Register-from-memory
```

Overflows

Overflows are a concern in arithmetic operations, especially for signed data. Because a byte provides for only a sign bit and seven data bits (from −128 to +127), an arithmetic operation can easily exceed the capacity of a 1-byte register. And a sum in AL register that exceeds its capacity may cause unexpected results. For example, if AL contains 60H, then the instruction ADD AL,20H generates a sum of 80H in AL. Having added two positive values, you may expect the sum to be positive, but the operation sets the Overflow Flag to overflow and the Sign Flag to negative. The reason? The value 80H, or binary 10000000, is a negative number; instead of +128, the sum is −128. The problem is that AL is too small for the sum, which should be in the full AX, as shown in the next section.

Extending Bytes into Words

The previous section showed how adding 20H to the value 60H in AL caused an incorrect sum. A better solution is to perform the arithmetic in AX. One instruction for this purpose is CBW (Convert Byte to Word), which automatically propagates the sign bit of AL (0 or 1) through AH. Note that CBW has no operands and is restricted to the use of AX.

In the next example, CBW extends the sign (0) in AL through AH, which generates 0060H in AX. The example then adds 20H to AX (rather than to AL) and generates the correct result in AX: 0080H, or +128:

```
                                       AH    AL
        ...                            xx    60H
        CBW            ;Extend AL sign into AH  00    60
        ADD  AX,20H    ;Add to AX              00    80
```

This example has the same numeric result as the one in the previous section, but the addition in AX does not treat it as an overflow or as negative. Still, although a full word in AX allows for a sign bit and 15 data bits, AX is limited to values from −32,768 to +32,767.

Other instructions that convert bytes to words are MOVZX (for unsigned data) and MOVSX (for signed data), used like this:

```
        MOVZX CX,BYTEVAL   ;Byte in CL, zeros in CH
        MOVSX WORDVAL,DL   ;Byte into word, fill with sign
```

Extending Words into Doublewords

The CWD (Convert Word to Doubleword) instruction is used to extend a one-word signed value to a doubleword by duplicating the sign bit of AX through DX. Note that CWD has no operands and is restricted to the use of DX:AX. Here is an example:

```
MOV AX,WORD1    ;Move word to AX
CWD             ;Extend word to DX:AX
```

The CWDE (Convert Word to Extended Doubleword) instruction is used to extend a one-word signed value to a doubleword by duplicating the sign bit of AX through EAX. Here is an example:

```
MOV AX,WORD1    ;Move word to AX
CWDE            ;Extend word to EAX
```

MOVZX and MOVSX also convert words into doublewords:

```
MOVZX ECX,WORDVAL   ;Word in CX, fill with zeros
MOVSX DBLWORD,DX    ;Word in DBLWORD, fill with sign
```

The CDQ (Convert Doubleword to Quadword) instruction is used to extend a doubleword signed value to a quadword by duplicating the sign bit of EAX through EDX. Note that CDQ has no operands and is restricted to the use of EDX:EAX. Here is an example:

```
MOV EAX,DBWORD   ;Move doubleword to EAX
CDQ              ;Extend doubleword to EAX:EDX
```

Performing Arithmetic on Doubleword Values

As we have seen, large numeric values may exceed the capacity of a word, in effect requiring multiword capacity. A consideration in multiword arithmetic is reverse-byte and reverse-word sequence. Recall that the assembler automatically converts the contents of defined numeric words into reverse-byte sequence so that, for example, a definition of 0134H is stored as 3401H. The following example adds and stores doubleword values:

```
DBLWORD1  DD  0123BC62H    ;Define doublewords
DBLWORD2  DD  0012553AH
DBLWORD3  DD  0
          ...
          MOV EAX,DBLWORD1  ;Add and store
          ADD EAX,DBLWORD2  ; doubleword
          MOV DBLWORD3,EAX  ; values
```

The assembler automatically arranges the defined data in reverse-byte (and word) sequence. For some applications, however, the data may be defined as *word* values. For DBLWORD1 defined in the previous example, you have to define the words as adjacent but in reverse order:

```
DW   0BC62H
DW   0123H
```

The assembler then converts these definitions into reverse-byte sequence as |62 BC|23 01|, now suitable for doubleword arithmetic. Let's examine two ways to perform arithmetic on these values. The first is simple and specific, whereas the second is more sophisticated and general. Here is the data used by the examples:

```
WORD1A    DW    0BC62H    ;Data items
WORD1B    DW    0123H
WORD2A    DW    553AH
WORD2B    DW    0012H
WORD3A    DW    ?
WORD3B    DW    ?
```

In effect, the program is to add values:

```
WORD1B:WORD1A    0123 BC62H
WORD2B:WORD2A    0012 553AH
WORD3B:WORD3A    0136 119CH
```

Because of reverse-byte sequence in memory, the program defines the values with the words adjacent but reversed: BC62 0123 and 553A 0012, respectively. The assembler then stores these doubleword values in memory in reverse-byte sequence:

```
WORD1A and WORD1B:    62BC 2301
WORD2A and WORD2B:    3A55 1200
```

The first example adds one pair of words (WORD1A and WORD1B) to a second pair (WORD2A and WORD2B) and stores the sum in a third pair (WORD3A and WORD3B):

```
MOV    AX,WORD1A    ;Add leftmost word
ADD    AX,WORD2A
MOV    WORD3A,AX
MOV    AX,WORD1B    ;Add rightmost word
ADC    AX,WORD2B    ; with carry
MOV    WORD3B,AX
```

The example first adds WORD2A to WORD1A in AX (the low-order portions) and stores the sum in WORD3A. It next adds WORD2B to WORD1B (the high-order portions) in AX, along with the carry from the previous addition. It then stores the sum in WORD3B.

Let's examine the operations in detail. The first MOV and ADD operations reverse the bytes in AX and add the leftmost words:

```
WORD1A:      BC62H
WORD2A:     +553AH
Total:      (1)119CH (9C11H is stored in WORD3A)
```

Because the sum of WORD1A plus WORD2A exceeds the capacity of AX, a carry occurs, setting the Carry Flag to 1. Next, the example adds the words at the right, but this time us-

ing ADC (Add with Carry) instead of ADD. ADC adds the two values and, because the
Carry Flag is set, adds 1 to the sum:

```
WORD1B              0123H
WORD2B             +0012H
Plus carry         +   1H
Total               0136H (stored in WORD3B as 3601H)
```

Using a debugger to trace the arithmetic shows the sum 0136H in AX and the reversed values 9C11H in WORD3A and 3601H in WORD3B.

The second example provides a more sophisticated approach to adding values of any
length, although here it adds the same pairs of words as before, WORD1A:WORD1B and
WORD2A:WORD2B:

```
        CLC                     ;Clear Carry Flag
        MOV     CX,02           ;Set loop count
        LEA     SI,WORD1A       ;Leftmost word of pair
        LEA     DI,WORD2A       ;Leftmost word of pair
        LEA     BX,WORD3A       ;Leftmost word of sum
L20:
        MOV     AX,[SI]         ;Move word to AX
        ADC     AX,[DI]         ;Add with carry to AX
        MOV     [BX],AX         ;Store word
        INC     SI              ;Adjust addresses
        INC     SI              ; for next word
        INC     DI              ; to right
        INC     DI
        INC     BX
        INC     BX
        LOOP    L20             ;Repeat for next word
        ...
```

The example uses SI, DI, and BX as index registers for the addresses of WORD1A,
WORD2A, and WORD3A, respectively. It loops once through the instructions for each pair
of words to be added—in this case, two times. The first loop adds the leftmost words, and
the second loop adds the rightmost words. Because the second loop is to process the words
to the right, the addresses in SI, DI, and BX are incremented by 2. Two INC instructions
perform this operation for each register. INC (rather than ADD) is used for a good reason:
The instruction ADD reg,02 would clear the Carry Flag and would cause an incorrect answer, whereas INC does not affect the Carry Flag.

Because of the loop, there is only one add instruction, ADC. At the start, a CLC (Clear
Carry) instruction ensures that the Carry Flag is initially clear. The results in WORD3A,
WORD3B, and AX are the same as the previous example.

To make this method work, be sure to (1) define the words adjacent to each other, (2)
initialize CX to the number of words to be added, and (3) process words from left to right.

For multiword subtraction, the instruction equivalent to ADC is SBB (Subtract with Borrow). Simply replace ADC with SBB. Here are the formats for ADC and SBB:

[*label:*]	ADC/SBB	*register,register*
[*label:*]	ADC/SBB	*memory,register*
[*label:*]	ADC/SBB	*register,memory*
[*label:*]	ADC/SBB	*register,immediate*
[*label:*]	ADC/SBB	*memory,immediate*

For adding quadwords, use the technique covered earlier for adding multiwords; that is, define two pairs of adjacent doublewords and use EAX register.

MULTIPLYING BINARY DATA

For multiplication, the MUL (Multiply) instruction handles unsigned data, and IMUL (Integer Multiply) handles signed data. Both instructions affect the Carry and Overflow Flags. As programmer, you have control over the format of the data you process, and you have the responsibility of selecting the appropriate multiply instruction. The format for MUL and the basic IMUL is

[*label:*]	MUL/IMUL	*register/memory*

The multiplication operations are byte times byte, word times word, and doubleword times doubleword. IMUL provides three additional formats involving doublewords and immediate operands, covered in a later section.

Byte Times Byte

For multiplying two 1-byte values, the multiplicand is in AL register, and the multiplier is a byte in memory or another register. For the instruction MUL DL, the operation multiplies the contents of AL by the contents of DL. The generated product is in AX. The operation ignores and erases any data that may already be in AH.

Word Times Word

For multiplying two one-word values, the multiplicand is in AX, and the multiplier is a word in memory or another register. For the instruction MUL DX, the operation multiplies the contents of AX by the contents of DX. The generated product is a doubleword that requires two registers: the high-order (leftmost) portion in DX and the low-order (rightmost) portion in AX. The operation ignores and erases any data that may already be in DX.

	DX	AX
Before multiplication:	(Ignored)	Multiplicand
After multiplication:	High product	Low product

Doubleword Times Doubleword

For multiplying two doubleword values, the multiplicand is in EAX and the multiplier is a doubleword in memory or another register. The product is generated in the EDX:EAX pair. The operation ignores and erases any data already in EDX.

	EDX	EAX
Before multiplication:	(Ignored)	Multiplicand
After multiplication:	High product	Low product

Field Sizes

The operand of MUL or IMUL references only the multiplier, which determines the field sizes. The instruction assumes that the multiplicand is in AL, AX, or EAX, depending on the size of the multiplier. In the following examples, the multiplier is in a register as byte, word, or doubleword:

INSTRUCTION	MULTIPLIER	MULTIPLICAND	PRODUCT
MUL CL	byte	AL	AX
MUL BX	word	AX	DX:AX
MUL EBX	doubleword	EAX	EDX:EAX

In the next examples, the multipliers are defined in memory:

```
BYTE1    DB    ?    ;Byte value
WORD1    DW    ?    ;Word value
DWORD1   DD    ?    ;Doubleword value
```

INSTRUCTION	MULTIPLIER	MULTIPLICAND	PRODUCT
MUL BYTE1	BYTE1	AL	AX
MUL WORD1	WORD1	AX	DX:AX
MUL DWORD1	DWORD1	EAX	EDX:EAX

Unsigned Multiplication: MUL

The purpose of the MUL instruction is to multiply unsigned data. The following program fragments give four examples of the use of MUL: Byte x byte, word x word, word x byte, and doubleword x doubleword. The data is defined as follows:

```
BYTE1    DB    80H
BYTE2    DB    40H
WORD1    DW    8000H
WORD2    DW    2000H
DWORD1   DD    00018402H
DWORD2   DD    00012501H
```

Example 1 multiplies 80H (128) by 40H (64). The product in AX is 2000H (8,192):

```
MOV   AL,BYTE1    ;Byte x byte
MUL   BYTE2       ;  product in AX
```

Example 2 generates 1000 0000H in the DX:AX pair:

```
MOV   AX,WORD1    ;Word x word
MUL   WORD2       ;  product in DX:AX
```

Example 3 multiplies word x byte and requires extending BYTE1 into a word:

```
MOVZX   AX,BYTE1    ;Byte x word
MUL     WORD1       ;  product in DX:AX
```

Because the values are supposed to be unsigned, the example assumes that bits in AH are to be 0. (The problem with using CBW here is that the leftmost bit of AL could be 1, and propagating 1-bits in AH would result in a larger unsigned value.) The product in DX:AX is 0040 0000H.

Example 4 uses EAX for doubleword multiplication:

```
MOV   EAX,DWORD1    ;Doubleword x
MUL   DWORD2        ;  doubleword
```

The product in EDX:EAX is 00000001 BC17CE02H.

Signed Multiplication: IMUL

The purpose of the IMUL instruction is to multiply signed data. The following program fragments show the same four examples just given, but replace MUL with IMUL.

Example 1 multiplies 80H (a negative number) by 40H (a positive number):

```
MOV    AL,BYTE1    ;Byte x byte
IMUL   BYTE2       ;  product in AX
```

The product in AX is E000H. Using the same data, MUL generates a product of 2000H, so you can see the difference between using MUL and using IMUL. MUL treats 80H as +128, whereas IMUL treats 80H as −128. The product of −128 times +64 is −8192H, which equals E000H. (Try converting E000H to bits, reverse the bits, add 1, and add up the bit values.)

Example 2 multiplies 8000H (a negative value) by 2000H (a positive value). The product in DX:AX is F000 0000H, which is the negative of the product that MUL generated:

```
MOV    AX,WORD1   ;Word x word
IMUL   WORD2      ;  product in DX:AX
```

Example 3 first extends BYTE1 to a word in AX. Because the values are supposed to be signed, the example uses MOVSX to extend the leftmost sign bit into AH: 80H in AL becomes FF80H in AX. Because the multiplier, WORD1, is also negative, the product should be positive. And indeed it is: 0040 0000H in DX:AX—the same result as MUL, which multiplied two unsigned numbers.

```
MOVSX  AX,BYTE1   ;Byte x word
IMUL   WORD1      ;  product in DX:AX
```

Example 4 uses EAX for doubleword multiplication. The product in EDX:EAX is 00000001 BC17CE02H:

```
MOV    EAX,DWORD1   ;Doubleword x
IMUL   DWORD2       ;  doubleword
```

In effect, if the multiplicand and multiplier have the same sign bit, MUL and IMUL generate the same product. But if the multiplicand and multiplier have different sign bits, MUL produces a positive product and IMUL produces a negative product. The upshot is that your program must know the format of the data and use the appropriate instructions.

Try using a debugger to trace through these examples.

Other IMUL Formats

The 80286 and 80386 processors introduced three IMUL formats that provide for immediate operands and for generating products in registers other than AX. You can use these instructions for either signed or unsigned multiplication, since the results are the same. The values must be all the same length: 16 or 32 bits. Here are their formats:

16-Bit Immediate	[label:]	IMUL register,immediate
32-Bit Immediate	[label:]	IMUL register,memory,immediate
16/32-Bit	[label:]	IMUL register,register/memory

16-Bit Immediate IMUL Operation. The first operand (a register) contains the multiplicand, and the second operand (an immediate value) is the multiplier. The product is generated in the first operand. A product that exceeds the register causes the Carry and Overflow Flags to be set.

32-Bit Immediate IMUL Operation. This format has three operands in doubleword format. The second operand (memory) contains the multiplicand, and the third operand (an immediate value) contains the multiplier. The product is generated in the first operand (a register).

16/32-Bit IMUL Operation. The first operand (a register) contains the multiplicand, and the second operand (register/memory) contains the multiplier. The product is generated in the first operand.

Here are examples of these three IMUL instructions:

SIZE	INSTRUCTION	MULTIPLICAND	MULTIPLIER	PRODUCT
16-bit Imm.	IMUL DX,25	DX	25	DX
32-bit Imm.	IMUL ECX,MULTCAND,25	MULTCAND	25	ECX
16/32-bit	IMUL BX,CX	BX	CX	BX
16/32-bit	IMUL EBX,EDX	EBX	EDX	EBX
16/32-bit	IMUL EBX,DWORDVAL	EBX	DWORDVAL	EBX

Performing Doubleword Multiplication

Conventional multiplication involves multiplying byte by byte, word by word, or doubleword by doubleword. As we have already seen, the maximum signed value in a word is +32,767. Multiplying larger values on pre-80386 processors involves additional steps. The approach on these processors is to multiply each word separately and then add each product together. The examples are worth examining because the techniques are applicable to the doubleword registers such as EAX. The following example multiplies a four-digit decimal number by a two-digit number:

$$
\begin{array}{r}
1,365 \\
\times \quad 12 \\
\hline
16,380
\end{array}
$$

What if you could multiply only two-digit numbers? Then you could multiply the 13 and the 65 by 12 separately, like this:

$$
\begin{array}{r}
13 \\
\times\ 12 \\
\hline
156
\end{array}
\qquad
\begin{array}{r}
65 \\
\times\ 12 \\
\hline
780
\end{array}
$$

Next, add the two products; but remember, since the 13 is in the hundreds position, its product is actually 15,600:

$$
\begin{array}{rl}
15,600 & \text{(13 X 12 X 100)} \\
+\quad 780 & \text{(65 X 12)} \\
\hline
16,380 &
\end{array}
$$

An assembly language program can use this same technique, except that the data consists of words (four digits) in hexadecimal format. The next sections examine the requirements for multiplying doubleword by word and doubleword by doubleword.

Doubleword by Word. The following program fragment multiplies a double-word by a word. The multiplicand, MULTCAN, consists of two words containing 3206H and 2521H, respectively. The reason for defining two DWs instead of a DD is to facilitate addressing for MOV instructions that move words to AX. The values are defined in reverse-word sequence, and the assembler stores each word in reverse-byte sequence. Thus MULTCAN, which has a defined value of 32062521H, is stored as 21250632H.

```
MULTCAN   DW    2521H       ;Data items
          DW    3206H
MULTPLR   DW    6400H
PRODUCT   DW    0, 0, 0     ;Three words
```

The multiplier, MULTPLR, contains 6400H. The field for the generated product, PRODUCT, provides for three words. The first MUL operation multiplies MULTPLR2 and the left word of MULTCAN; the product is hex 0E80 E400H, stored in PRODUCT+2 and PRODUCT+4:

```
MOV   AX,MULTCAN      ;Multiply left word
MUL   MULTPLR         ;  of multiplicand
MOV   PRODUCT,AX      ;Store product
MOV   PRODUCT+2,DX
```

The second MUL multiplies MULTPLR and the right word of MULTCAN; the product is 138A 5800H.

```
MOV   AX,MULTCAN+2    ;Multiply right word
MUL   MULTPLR         ;  of multiplicand
ADD   PRODUCT+2,AX    ;Add to second
ADC   PRODUCT+4,DX    ;  and third words
```

At the end, the example adds the two products, like this:

```
Product 1:    0000 0E80 E400
Product 2: +   138A 5800
Total:         138A 6680 E400
```

Because the first ADD may cause a carry, the second add is ADC (Add with Carry). Numeric data is stored in reversed-byte format, so PRODUCT will actually contain 00E4 8066 8A13. The routine requires that the first word of PRODUCT initially contains zero.

Doubleword by Doubleword. Multiplying two doublewords in DX:AX involves four multiplications:

MULTIPLICAND		**MULTIPLIER**
word 2	×	word 2
word 2	×	word 1
word 1	×	word 2
word 1	×	word 1

Add each product in DX and AX to the appropriate word in the final product. The following program fragment gives an example. MULTCAND contains 3206 2521H, MULTPLER contains 6400 0A26H, and PRODUCT provides for four words:

```
MULTCAND   DW      2521H           ;Data items
           DW      3206H
MULTPLER   DW      0A26H
           DW      6400H
PRODUCT    DW      0, 0, 0, 0      ;Four words
```

Although the logic is similar to multiplying doubleword by word, this problem requires an additional feature. Following the ADD/ADC pair is another ADC that adds 0 to PRODUCT. The first ADC itself could cause a carry, which subsequent instructions would clear. The second ADC, therefore, adds 0 if there is no carry and adds 1 if there is a carry. The final ADD/ADC pair does not require an additional ADC; because PRODUCT is large enough for the final generated answer, there is no carry.

```
       MOV   AX,MULTCAND        ;Multiplicand word 1
       MUL   MULTPLER           ; x multiplier word 1
       MOV   PRODUCT+0,AX       ;Store product
       MOV   PRODUCT+2,DX
;
       MOV   AX,MULTCAND        ;Multiplicand word 1
       MUL   MULTPLER+2         ;  x multiplier word 2
       ADD   PRODUCT+2,AX       ;Add to stored product
       ADC   PRODUCT+4,DX
       ADC   PRODUCT+6,00       ;Add any carry
;
       MOV   AX,MULTCAND+2      ;Multiplicand word 2
       MUL   MULTPLER           ;  x multiplier word 1
       ADD   PRODUCT+2,AX       ;Add to stored product
       ADC   PRODUCT+4,DX
       ADC   PRODUCT+6,00       ;Add any carry
;
       MOV   AX,MULTCAND+2      ;Multiplicand word 2
       MUL   MULTPLER+2         ;  x multiplier word 2
       ADD   PRODUCT+4,AX       ;Add to product
       ADC   PRODUCT+6,DX
```

The final product is 138A 687C 8E5C CCE6, stored in PRODUCT with the bytes reversed. Try using a debugger to trace through this example.

Multiplication by Shifting

For multiplying by a power of 2 (2, 4, 8, etc.), shifting left the necessary number of bits may provide faster processing. In the following unrelated examples, the multiplicand is in the first operand and CL contains 2:

```
Multiply by 2 (shift left 1):    SHL AX,01
Multiply by 4 (shift left 2):    SHL DX,CL
Multiply by 8 (shift left 3):    SHL WORDVAL,03
```

The following routine could be useful for left shifting a doubleword value in the DX:AX pair. Although specific to a 4-bit shift, it could be adapted to other values:

```
SHL   DX,04    ;Shift DX to left 4 bits
MOV   BL,AH    ;Store AH in BL
SHL   AX,04    ;Shift AX to left 4 bits
SHR   BL,04    ;Shift BL to right 4 bits
OR    DL,BL    ;Insert 4 bits from BL in DL
```

Be sure to check before shifting off a significant digit.

DIVIDING BINARY DATA

For division, the DIV (Divide) instruction handles unsigned data and IDIV (Integer Divide) handles signed data. You are responsible for selecting the appropriate divide instruction. The format for DIV/IDIV is

[label:]	DIV/IDIV	register/memory

The basic divide operations are byte into word, word into doubleword, and doubleword into quadword.

Byte into Word. To divide byte into word, the dividend is in AX and the divisor is a byte in memory or another register. The operation stores the remainder in AH and the quotient in AL. Note that a 1-byte quotient is very small—a maximum of +255 (FFH) if unsigned and +127 (7FH) if signed.

Before division:	AX	
	<------- Dividend ------->	
After division:	AH Remainder	AL Quotient

Word into Doubleword. To divide word into doubleword, the dividend is in DX:AX and the divisor is a word in memory or another register. The operation stores the remainder in DX and the quotient in AX. The one-word quotient allows a maximum of +32,767 (FFFFH) if unsigned and +16,383 (7FFFH) if signed.

	DX	AX
Before division:	High dividend	Low dividend
After division:	Remainder	Quotient

Doubleword into Quadword. For dividing a doubleword into a quadword, the dividend is in EDX:EAX and the divisor is a doubleword in memory or another register. The operation stores the remainder in EDX and the quotient in EAX.

	EDX	EAX
Before division:	High dividend	Low dividend
After division:	Remainder	Quotient

Field Sizes. The operand of DIV/IDIV references the divisor, which determines the field sizes. In the following DIV examples, the divisors are in a register as byte, word, or doubleword:

INSTRUCTION	DIVISOR	DIVIDEND	QUOTIENT	REMAINDER
DIV CL	byte	AX	AL	AH
DIV CX	word	DX:AX	AX	DX
DIV EBX	doubleword	EDX:EAX	EAX	EDX

In the following DIV examples, the divisors are defined in memory:

```
BYTE1   DB    ?     ;Byte value
WORD1   DW    ?     ;Word value
DWORD1  DD    ?     ;Doubleword value
```

INSTRUCTION	DIVISOR	DIVIDEND	QUOTIENT	REMAINDER
DIV BYTE1	BYTE1	AX	AL	AH
DIV WORD1	WORD1	DX:AX	AX	DX
DIV DWORD1	DWORD1	EDX:EAX	EAX	EDX

Remainder. The result of dividing 13 by 3 is 4 1/3, where the quotient is 4 and the true remainder is 1. Note that a calculator (and a high-level programming language) would deliver a quotient of 4.333, which consists of an integer portion (4) and a fraction portion (.333). The values 1/3 and .333 are fractions, whereas the 1 is a remainder.

Using DIV for Unsigned Division

The purpose of the DIV instruction is to divide unsigned data. The following program fragment gives four examples of DIV: byte into word, byte into byte, word into doubleword, and word into word. Here's the data for the example:

```
BYTE1   DB    80H     ;Data items
BYTE2   DB    16H
WORD1   DW    2000H
WORD2   DW    0010H
WORD3   DW    1000H
```

Example 1 divides 2000H (8092) by 80H (128). The remainder in AH is 00H, and the quotient in AL is 40H (64):

```
          MOV    AX,WORD1    ;Word / byte
          DIV    BYTE1       ; rmdr:quot in AH:AL
```

Example 2 requires extending BYTE1 to a word. Because the value is supposed to be unsigned, the example assumes that bits in AH are to be 0. The remainder in AH is 12H, and the quotient in AL is 05H.

```
          MOVZX  AX,BYTE1    ;Byte / byte
          DIV    BYTE2       ; rmdr:quotient in AH:AL
```

In example 3, the remainder in DX is 1000H, and the quotient in AX is 0080H.

```
          MOV    DX,WORD2    ;Doubleword / word
          MOV    AX,WORD3    ; dividend in DX:AX
          DIV    WORD1       ; rmdr:quotient in DX:AX
```

Example 4 first extends WORD1 to a doubleword in DX. After the division, the remainder in DX is 0000H and the quotient in AX is 0002H:

```
          MOV    AX,WORD1    ;Word / word
          SUB    DX,DX       ; extend dividend in DX
          DIV    WORD3       ; rmdr:quotient in DX:AX
```

Using IDIV for Signed Division

The purpose of the IDIV instruction is to divide signed data. The following program fragments show the same four examples just given, but replace DIV with IDIV.

Example 1 divides 2000H (positive) by 80H (negative). The remainder in AH is 00H, and the quotient in AL is C0H (−64) (using the same data, DIV resulted in a quotient of +64):

```
          MOV    AX,WORD1    ;Word / byte
          IDIV   BYTE1       ; rmdr:quot in AH:AL
```

In example 2, the quotient is FB (−5) and the remainder is EE (−18):

```
          MOVZX  AX,BYTE1    ;Byte / byte
          IDIV   BYTE2       ; rmdr:quotient in AH:AL
```

In example 3, the quotient is 0080 (128) and the remainder is 1000 (4096):

```
          MOV    DX,WORD2    ;Doubleword / word
          MOV    AX,WORD3    ; dividend in DX:AX
          IDIV   WORD1       ; rmdr:quot in DX:AX
```

In example 4, the quotient is 0002 and the remainder is 0000:

```
          MOV    AX,WORD1    ;Word / word
          CWD                ; extend dividend in DX
          IDIV   WORD3       ; rmdr:quot in DX:AX
```

Only example 4 produces the same answer as did DIV. In effect, if the dividend and divisor have the same sign bit, DIV and IDIV generate the same result. But if the dividend and divisor have different sign bits, DIV generates a positive quotient and IDIV generates a negative quotient.

The following example illustrates dividing a quadword by a doubleword. The quotient is DC5CH (56,412):

```
DBLWD1    DD      0
DBLWD2    DD      225648
DBLWD3    DD      4

          . . .

          MOV     EDX,DBLWD1      ;Quadword / doubleword
          MOV     EAX,DBLWD2      ;  dividend in EDX:EAX
          IDIV    DBLWD3          ;  rmdr:quotient in EDX:EAX
```

Try using a debugger to trace through these examples.

Overflows and Interrupts

DIV and IDIV operations assume that the quotient is significantly smaller than the original dividend. As a consequence, the operation can easily cause an overflow; when it does, an interrupt occurs, with unpredictable results. Dividing by zero, for example, always causes an interrupt. But dividing by 1 generates a quotient that is the same as the dividend and could also cause an interrupt.

Here's a useful rule: *If the divisor is a byte, its value must be greater than the left byte (AH) of the dividend; if the divisor is a word, its value must be greater than the left word (DX) of the dividend; if the divisor is a doubleword, its value must be greater than the left doubleword (EDX) of the dividend.*

The following instructions use a divisor of 1, although other values could serve:

Divide Operation	Dividend	Divisor	Quotient
Word by byte:	012A	01	(1)2A
Doubleword by word:	0001 402B	0001	(1)402B
Quadword by doubleword:	00000002 10542EB4	00000001	(2)10542EB4

In each case, the generated quotient exceeds its available space. It is often wise to include a test prior to a DIV or IDIV operation, as shown in the next two examples. In example 1, DIVBYTE is a 1-byte divisor, and the dividend is in AX:

```
          CMP AH,DIVRBYTE     ;Compare AH to divisor (byte)
          JNB L20             ;Bypass if not smaller
          DIV DIVRBYTE        ;Divide word by byte
```

In example 2, DIVRDWD is a doubleword divisor, and the dividend is in EDX:EAX:

```
          CMP   EDX,DIVRDWD    ;Compare EDX to divisor (doubleword)
          JNB   L30            ;Bypass if not smaller
          DIV   DIVRDWD        ;Divide quadword by doubleword
```

For IDIV, the logic should account for the fact that either dividend or divisor could be negative. Because the *absolute value* of the divisor must be the smaller of the two, you could use the NEG instruction to set a negative value temporarily to positive and restore the sign after the division.

Division by Subtraction

If a quotient is too large for the divisor, you could perform division by means of successive subtraction. That is, subtract the divisor from the dividend, increment a quotient value by 1, and continue subtracting until the dividend is less than the divisor. In the following example, the dividend is in AX, the divisor is in BX, and the quotient is developed in CX:

```
        SUB  CX,CX    ;Clear quotient
L20:    CMP  AX,BX    ;If dividend < divisor,
        JB   L30      ; exit
        SUB  AX,BX    ;Subtract divisor from dividend
        INC  CX       ;Add 1 to quotient
        JMP  L20      ;Repeat
L30:    ...           ;Quotient in CX, remainder in AX
```

At the end of the routine, CX contains the quotient and AX contains the remainder. If the quotient is in DX:AX, the routine looks like this:

```
        SUB CX,CX    ;Clear quotient
L20:    CMP DX,0     ;If DX = zero,
        JNE L30      ; bypass
        CMP AX,BX    ;If dividend < divisor,
        JB L40       ; exit
L30:    SUB AX,BX    ;Subtract divisor from dividend
        SBB DX,0     ;Subtract Carry Flag
        INC CX       ;Add 1 to quotient
        JMP L20      ;Repeat
L40:    ...          ;Quotient in CX, remainder in AX
```

Note that a very large quotient and a small divisor may cause thousands of loops at a cost of processing time.

Division by Shifting

For division by a power of 2 (2, 4, 8, and so on), shifting right the required number of bits may provide faster processing. The following unrelated examples assume that the dividend is in BX and CL contains 2:

```
Shift right 1: SHR BX,01    ;Divide by 2
Shift right 2: SHR BX,CL    ;Divide by 4
Shift right 3: SHR BX,03    ;Divide by 8
```

The following routine could be useful for right shifting a doubleword value in DX:AX. Although specific to a 4-bit shift, it could be adapted to other values:

```
SHR  AX,04    ;Shift AX to right 4 bits
MOV  BL,DL    ;Store DL in BL
```

```
SHR   DX,04      ;Shift DX to right 4 bits
SHL   BL,04      ;Shift BL to left 4 bits
OR    DL,BL      ;Insert 4 bits from BL in DL
```

Reversing the Sign

The NEG (negate) instruction reverses the sign of a binary value, from positive to negative and vice versa. In effect, NEG reverses the bits, just like NOT, and then adds 1 for proper two's complement notation. The format for NEG is

[label:]	NEG	register/memory

Here are some unrelated examples:

```
NEG   CL          ;Byte
NEG   BX          ;Word
NEG   EDX         ;Doubleword
NEG   BINVAL      ;Data item in memory
```

Reversing the sign of a 32-bit value in DX:AX involves more steps. NEG cannot act on DX:AX concurrently, and using NEG on both registers would invalidly add 1 to both. Instead, use NOT to flip the bits, and use ADD and ADC to add the 1 for two's complement:

```
NOT   DX          ;Flip bits in DX
NOT   AX          ;Flip bits in AX
ADD   AX,1        ;Add 1 to AX
ADC   DX,0        ;Add carry to DX
```

One minor problem remains: It is all very well to perform arithmetic on binary data that the program itself defines or on data already in binary form on an external file. However, data that enters a program from a keyboard is in ASCII format. Although ASCII data is suitable for displaying and printing, it requires special adjusting for arithmetic—a topic discussed in the next chapter.

THE NUMERIC DATA PROCESSOR

This section provides a general introduction to the numeric data processor; a full discussion is outside the scope of the book. The Intel Numeric Data Processor, or coprocessor, has its own instruction set and floating-point hardware for performing such operations as exponentiation and logarithmic and trigonometric operations. The eight 80-bit floating-point registers can represent numeric values up to 10 to the 400th power and execute considerably faster than a regular processor.

The coprocessor contains eight 80-bit registers, R1-R8, in the following format:

S	exponent	significand
79	78 64	63 0

Each register has an associated 2-bit tag that indicates its status:

00   Contains a valid number   10   Contains an invalid number
01   Contains a zero value   11   Is empty

The coprocessor recognizes seven types of numeric data:

1. *Word integer:* 16 bits of binary data.

S	number
15	14 0

2. *Short integer:* 32 bits of binary data.

S	number
31	30 0

3. *Long integer:* 64 bits of binary data.

S	number
63	62 0

4. *Short real:* 32 bits of floating-point data.

S	exponent	significand
31	30 23	22 0

5. *Long real:* 64 bits of floating-point data.

S	exponent	significand
63	62 52	51 0

6. *Temporary real:* 80 bits of floating-point data.

S	exponent	significand
79	78 64	63 0

7. *Packed decimal:* 18 significant decimal digits.

S	zeros	significand
79 78	72	71 0

Types 1, 2, and 3 are common binary two's-complement formats. Types 4, 5, and 6 represent floating-point numbers. Type 7 contains 18 4-bit decimal digits. You can load any of these formats from memory into a coprocessor register and can store the register contents into memory. However, for its calculations, the coprocessor converts all formats in its registers into temporary real. Data is stored in memory in reverse-byte sequence.

The processor requests a specific operation and delivers numeric data to the coprocessor, which performs the operation and returns the result.

KEY POINTS

- The maximum signed values for 1-byte accumulators are +127 and −128.
- For multiword addition, use ADC to account for any carry from a previous ADD. If the operation is performed in a loop, use CLC to clear the Carry Flag.
- MUL is used for unsigned data and IMUL for signed data.
- For MUL, if a multiplier is defined as a byte, the multiplicand is AL; if the multiplier is a word, the multiplicand is AX; if the multiplier is a doubleword, the multiplicand is EAX.
- The shift left instructions (SHL or SAL) may be used for multiplying by powers of 2.
- DIV is used for unsigned data and IDIV for signed data.
- For division, if the divisor is defined as a byte, the dividend is AX; if the divisor is a word, the dividend is DX:AX; if the divisor is a doubleword, the dividend is EDX:EAX.
- The divisor must be greater than the contents of AH if the divisor is a byte, DX if the divisor is a word, or EDX if the divisor is a doubleword.
- The shift right instructions may be used for dividing by powers of 2—SHR for unsigned fields and SAR for signed fields.

REVIEW QUESTIONS AND EXERCISES

12-1. For both unsigned and signed data, what are the maximum values in (a) a byte, (b) a word, (c) doubleword?

12-2. Distinguish between a carry and an overflow as a result of an arithmetic operation.

12-3. For the following binary additions, show the sums as binary numbers and as unsigned and signed decimal numbers, plus show the settings of the Overflow and Carry Flags:

```
    (a) 00010011   (b) 01010110   (c) 11010101   (d) 11011011
        +00111000       +00111001       +01011010       +11010110
```

12-4. The section "Performing Arithmetic on Doubleword Values" contains two program fragments that add pairs of word values (the first is WORD1A). Revise both examples so that they add three pairs of words instead of two. Define the additional words as WORD3A and WORD3B and change the old WORD3A and WORD3B to WORD4A and WORD4B.

For Questions 12-5 through 12-8, refer to the following data, with words properly defined in reverse sequence:

```
BIN_AMT1   DW  0147H
           DW  139AH
BIN_AMT2   DW  02B3H
           DW  2D41H
CAL_AMT    DW  0
           DW  0
           DW  0
```

12-5. Code the instructions to add the following: (a) the word BIN_AMT1 to the word BIN_AMT2, and (b) the doubleword beginning at BIN_AMT1 to the doubleword at BIN_AMT2.

12-6. Explain the effect of the following related instructions:

```
STC
MOV  BX,BIN_AMT1
ADC  BX,BIN_AMT2
```

12-7. Code the instructions to multiply (MUL) the following: (a) the word BIN_AMT1 by the word BIN_AMT2, and (b) the doubleword beginning at BIN_AMT1 by the word BIN_AMT2. Store the product in CAL_AMT.

12-8. Code the instructions to divide (DIV) the following: (a) the word BIN_AMT1 by 24H, and (b) the doubleword beginning at BIN_AMT1 by the word BIN_AMT2. Store the quotient in CAL_AMT.

12-9. What divisors other than zero cause overflow errors?

12-10. Refer to the section "Multiplication by Shifting," which illustrates shifting left four bits in the DX:AX pair. Revise the example for a left shift of two bits.

12-11. Refer to the section "Division by Shifting," which illustrates shifting right four bits in the DX:AX pair. Revise the example for a right shift of two bits.

Chapter 13

ARITHMETIC II: PROCESSING ASCII AND BCD DATA

> Objective: To examine ASCII and BCD data formats, to perform arithmetic in these formats, and to cover conversions between these formats and binary.

INTRODUCTION

The natural data format for arithmetic on a computer is binary. As seen in Chapter 12, binary format causes no major problems as long as the program itself defines the data. However, much of the numeric data that a program must process is in a form other than binary. For example, numeric data enters a program from a keyboard as ASCII characters in base-10 format. Similarly, the display of numeric values on a screen is in ASCII format.

A related numeric format, *binary-coded decimal (BCD)*, has occasional uses and appears as unpacked and as packed. The PC provides a number of instructions that facilitate simple arithmetic and conversion between formats. This chapter also covers techniques for converting ASCII data into binary format to perform arithmetic, as well as techniques for converting the binary results back into ASCII format for viewing. The program at the end of the chapter combines much of the material covered in Chapters 1 through 12.

In a high-level language such as C, the compiler accounts for the radix (decimal or binary) point. However, neither the computer nor the assembler recognizes a radix point in an arithmetic field, so that an assembly language programmer has to account for its position.

Instructions introduced in this chapter are:

AAA	ASCII Adjust After Addition	AAD	ASCII Adjust for Division
AAS	ASCII Adjust After Subtraction	DAA	Decimal Adjust After Addition
AAM	ASCII Adjust After Multiplication	DAS	Decimal Adjust After Subtraction

DATA IN DECIMAL FORMAT

To this point, program examples have handled numeric values in binary and in ASCII formats. The processor also supports binary-coded decimal (BCD) format, which allows for some limited arithmetic operations. Two uses for BCD format are:

1. Permits proper rounding of numbers with no loss of precision, a feature that is particularly useful for handling dollars and cents. (Rounding of binary numbers that represent dollars and cents may cause a loss of precision.)
2. Is often a simpler format for performing arithmetic on small values entered from a keyboard or for output on the screen or printer.

A BCD digit consists of four bits that represent the decimal digits 0 through 9:

Binary	BCD digit	Binary	BCD digit
0000	0	0101	5
0001	1	0110	6
0010	2	0111	7
0011	3	1000	8
0100	4	1001	9

You can store BCD digits as unpacked or as packed:

1. *Unpacked BCD* contains a single BCD digit in the lower (rightmost) four bits of each byte, with zeros in the upper four bits. Note that although numbers in ASCII format are also in a sense "unpacked," they aren't called that.
2. *Packed BCD* contains two BCD digits, one in the upper four bits and one in the lower four bits. This format is commonly used for arithmetic using the numeric coprocessor, defined by the DT directive as 10 bytes.

Here's the representation of decimal number 1,527 in the three formats:

Format	Length	Contents
ASCII	Four bytes	31 35 32 37
Unpacked BCD	Four bytes	01 05 02 07
Packed BCD	Two bytes	15 27

The processor performs arithmetic on ASCII and BCD values one digit at a time. You have to use special instructions for converting between the two formats.

PROCESSING ASCII DATA

Because data entered from a keyboard is in ASCII format, the representation in memory of an entered decimal value such as 1234 is 31323334H. Performing arithmetic on the ASCII value involves the AAA and AAS instructions:

[label:]	AAA	;ASCII Adjust After Addition
[label:]	AAS	;ASCII Adjust After Subtraction

These instructions are coded without operands and automatically adjust an ASCII value in AX register. The adjustment occurs because an ASCII value represents an unpacked base-10 number, whereas the processor performs base-2 arithmetic.

Adding ASCII Numbers

Consider the effect of the following three examples of adding ASCII numbers:

```
        Ex. 1    35H      Ex. 2    38H      Ex. 3   39H
                +32H              +34H              +39H
        Total    67H               6CH               72H
```

In Example 1, the rightmost digit, 7, is the correct sum, although the leftmost digit needs correcting. In Example 2, 6CH is not the correct ASCII sum because of a carry from decimal into hex digits. Example 3 is incorrect because of the carry from the units to the tens position.

To correct an ASCII sum, the AAA operation checks the rightmost hex digit of AL register. If the digit is between A and F or the Auxiliary Carry flag (AF) is 1, the operation adds 6 to AL, adds 1 to AH, and sets the Carry (CF) and Auxiliary Carry flags to 1. In all cases, AAA clears the leftmost hex digit of AL to zero. (Why add 6? Because that's the difference between hexadecimal (16) and decimal (10).)

Let's see how AAA handles the three previous examples. Assuming the ASCII numbers in AL and BL, the instructions are:

```
        ADD    AL,BL    ;Add ASCII numbers
        AAA             ;Adjust for ASCII addition
```

Example 1. The sum of 35H and 32H is 67H. AAA checks the rightmost digit (7). Because it is not between A and F, nor is the AF flag set, AAA simply clears the leftmost digit (6) to 0.

Example 2. The sum of 38H and 34H is 6CH. Because the rightmost digit (C) is between A and F, AAA performs the following:

```
                                        AH    AL
                                        00    0C
        Adds 6 to AL                    00    72
        Adds 1 to AH                    01    72
        Clears leftmost digit of AL     01    02    (sum = 12)
```

Example 3. The sum of 39H and 39H is 72H. Although the rightmost digit (2) is not between A and F, the AF flag is set because of the carry into the tens position. AAA performs the following:

```
                                        AH    AL
                                        00    72
        Adds 6 to AL                    00    78
        Adds 1 to AH                    01    78
        Clears leftmost digit of AL     01    08    (sum = 18)
```

The sums 0006, 0102, and 0108 are technically BCD numbers. To restore the ASCII representation, simply insert 3s in the leftmost hex digits of AH and AL:

```
OR AX,3030H ;Convert BCD to ASCII
```

All that is very well for adding 1-byte ASCII numbers. Adding multibyte ASCII numbers, however, requires a loop that processes from right to left (low order to high order) and accounts for carries. The partial program in Figure 13-1 adds two 3-byte ASCII numbers, ASCVALUE1 and ASCVALUE2, and produces a 4-byte sum, ASCTOTAL. Note the following points:

- A CLC instruction at the start zeros the CF flag.
- Following A20, the MOVZX instruction loads successive ASCII characters into AL. It also clears AH because the following AAA may add 1 to AH, which would still be present on the next loop. Note that the use of XOR or SUB to clear AH would change the CF flag.
- ADC is used for addition because it automatically adds any carry from AL to AH.
- The MOV stores each ASCII "sum" in successive bytes of ASCTOTAL.
- When looping is complete, the program moves AH (containing either a final 00 or 01) to the leftmost byte of ASCTOTAL.

At the end, ASCTOTAL contains 01020702H. To insert ASCII 3 in each byte, the program steps through ASCTOTAL and ORs each byte with 30H. The result is 31323732H, or decimal 1272, which the program displays before ending.

```
ASCVALUE1   DB      '548'               ;ASCII items
ASCVALUE2   DB      '724'
ASCTOTAL    DB      '0000'
.386   ;    ...
            CLC                         ;Add ASCII values:
            LEA     SI,ASCVALUE1+2      ;Initialize addresses
            LEA     DI,ASCVALUE2+2      ;  of ASCII numbers
            LEA     BX,ASCTOTAL+3
            MOV     CX,03               ;Initialize 3 loops
A20:
            MOVZX   AX,[SI]             ;Load ASCII byte in AX
            ADC     AL,[DI]             ;Add (with carry)
            AAA                         ;Adjust for ASCII
            MOV     [BX],AL             ;Store sum
            DEC     SI
            DEC     DI
            DEC     BX
            LOOP    A20                 ;Loop 3 times
            MOV     [BX],AH             ;At end, store carry
            LEA     BX,ASCTOTAL+3       ;Convert ASCTOTAL
            MOV     CX,04               ;  to ASCII format
A30:
            OR      BYTE PTR[BX],30H
            DEC     BX
            LOOP    A30                 ;Loop 4 times
            MOV     AX,1300H            ;Request display
            MOV     BX,0031H            ;Page and attribute
            LEA     BP,ASCTOTAL         ;ASCII line
            MOV     CX,04               ;Length of line
            MOV     DX,0824H            ;Row and column
            INT     10H
            ...
```

Figure 13-1　Adding ASCII Numbers

The program did not use OR after AAA to insert leftmost 3s because OR sets the Carry Flag and changes the effect for the ADC instructions. A solution that saves the flag settings is to push (PUSHF) the Flags register, execute the OR, and then pop (POPF) the flags to restore them:

```
ADC     AL,[DI]     ;Add with carry
AAA                 ;Adjust for ASCII
PUSHF               ;Save flags
OR      AL,30H      ;Insert ASCII 3
POPF                ;Restore flags
MOV     [BX],AL     ;Store sum
```

Subtracting ASCII Numbers

The AAS instruction works much like AAA. AAS checks the rightmost hex digit (four bits) of AL. If the digit is between A and F or the auxiliary carry is 1, the operation subtracts 6 from AL, subtracts 1 from AH, and sets the Auxiliary (AF) and Carry (CF) flags. In all cases, AAS clears the leftmost hex digit of AL.

The next two examples assume that ASCVALUE1 contains 39H and ASCVALUE2 contains 35H. The first example subtracts ASCVALUE2 (35H) from ASCVALUE1 (39H). AAS does not need to make an adjustment because the rightmost hex digit is less than hex A:

```
                        AX      AF   CF
MOV   AL,ASCVALUE1     ;0039
SUB   AL,ASCVALUE2     ;0004    0    0
AAS                   ;0004    0    0
OR    AL,30H          ;0034
```

The second example subtracts ASCVALUE1 (39H) from ASCVALUE2 (35H). Because the rightmost digit of the result is hex C, AAS subtracts 6 from AL, subtracts 1 from AH, and sets the AF and CF flags:

```
                        AX      AF   CF
MOV   AL,ASCVALUE2     ;0035
SUB   AL,ASCVALUE1     ;00FC    1    1
AAS                   ;FF06    1    1
```

The answer, which should be −4, is FF06H, its ten's complement; that is, decimal −10 + 6 = −4.

Multiplying ASCII Numbers

Multiplication and division of ASCII numbers require first converting them into unpacked BCD format. You can then use the AAM and AAD instructions to perform arithmetic directly on unpacked BCD numbers:

```
[label:]    AAM     ;ASCII Adjust After Multiplication
[label:]    AAD     ;ASCII Adjust Before Division
```

The AAM instruction corrects the result of multiplying ASCII data in AX register. However, you must first clear the 3 in the leftmost hex digit of each byte, thus converting the value to unpacked BCD, so that AAM really corrects BCD, not ASCII, data. For example, the ASCII number 31323334H becomes 01020304H as unpacked BCD. Also, because the adjustment is only one byte at a time, you can multiply only 1-byte fields and have to perform the operation repetitively in a loop. Use only the MUL (unsigned multiplication), not the IMUL, operation.

AAM divides AL by 10 (0AH) and stores the quotient in AH and the remainder in AL. For example, suppose that AL contains ASCII 35H and CL contains 39H. The following code multiplies the contents of AL by CL and converts the result to ASCII format:

INSTRUCTION	COMMENT	AX	CL
...	;Initial values	0035	39
AND CL,0FH	;Convert CL to 09	0035	09
AND AL,0FH	;Convert AL to 05	0005	09
MUL CL	;Multiply AL by CL	002D	09
AAM	;Convert AX to unpacked BCD	0405	
OR AX,3030H	;Convert AX to ASCII	3435	

The MUL operation generates 002DH (45) in AX. AAM divides this value by 0AH, generating a quotient of 04 in AH and a remainder of 05 in AL. The OR instruction then converts the unpacked BCD value to ASCII format.

The partial program in Figure 13-2 depicts multiplying a 4-byte ASCII multiplicand by a 1-byte ASCII multiplier. Because AAM can accommodate only 1-byte operations, the program steps through the multiplicand one byte at a time, from right to left. At the end, the unpacked BCD product is 0108090105, which a loop at A30 converts to true ASCII format as 3138393135, or decimal 18,915. The program displays the product before it ends processing.

If the multiplier is greater than one byte, you have to provide yet another loop that steps through the multiplier. In that case, it may be simpler to convert the ASCII data to binary format, as covered in a later section.

Dividing ASCII Numbers

The AAD instruction provides a correction of an ASCII dividend prior to dividing. Just as with AAM, you first clear the leftmost 3s from the ASCII bytes to create unpacked BCD format. AAD allows for a 2-byte dividend in AX. The divisor can be only a single byte containing 01 to 09.

Assume that AX contains the ASCII value 28 (3238H) and CL contains the divisor, ASCII 7 (37H). The following instructions perform the adjustment and division:

INSTRUCTION	COMMENT	AX	CL
...	;Initial values	3238	37
AND CL,0FH	;Convert to unpacked BCD	3238	07
AND AX,0F0FH	;Convert to unpacked BCD	0208	
AAD	;Convert to binary	001C	
DIV CL	;Divide by 7	0004	

AAD multiplies AH by 10 (0AH), adds the product 20 (14H) to AL, and clears AH. The result, 001CH, is the hex representation of decimal 28.

```
MULTCAND    DB      '3783'              ;ASCII items
MULTPLER    DB      '5'
ASCPROD     DB      5 DUP(0)
            . . .
            MOV     CX,04               ;Initialize 4 loops
            LEA     SI,MULTCAND+3
            LEA     DI,ASCPROD+4
            AND     MULTPLER,0FH        ;Clear ASCII 3
A20:
            MOV     AL,[SI]             ;Load ASCII character
            AND     AL,0FH              ;Clear ASCII 3
            MUL     MULTPLER            ;Multiply
            AAM                         ;Adjust for ASCII
            ADD     AL,[DI]             ;Add to
            AAA                         ;   stored
            MOV     [DI],AL             ;   product
            DEC     DI
            MOV     [DI],AH             ;Store product carry
            DEC     SI
            LOOP    A20                 ;Loop 4 times
            LEA     BX,ASCPROD+4        ;Convert product to ASCII:
            MOV     CX,05               ;Right to left, 5 bytes
A30:
            OR      BYTE PTR[BX],30H
            DEC     BX
            LOOP    A30                 ;Loop 5 times
            MOV     AX,1300H            ;Request display
            MOV     BX,0031H            ;Page and attribute
            LEA     BP,ASCPROD          ;ASCII line
            MOV     CX,05               ;Length of line
            MOV     DX,0824H            ;Row
            INT     10H
            . . .
```

Figure 13-2   Multiplying ASCII Numbers

The partial program in Figure 13-3 divides a 1-byte divisor into a 4-byte dividend. The program steps through the dividend from left to right. LODSB gets a byte from DIVIDEND into AL (via SI), and STOSB stores bytes from AL into ASCQUOT (via DI). The remainder stays in AH so that AAD can adjust it in AL. At the end, the quotient, in unpacked BCD format, is 00090204, and the remainder in AH is 02. The program converts the quotient to ASCII format as 30393234 (from left to right this time) and displays the ASCII quotient, 0924.

If the divisor is greater than one byte, you have to provide yet another loop to step through the divisor. Better yet, see the later section "Conversion of ASCII to Binary Format."

PROCESSING PACKED BCD DATA

In the preceding example of ASCII division, the quotient was 00090204. If you compress this value, keeping only the right digit of each byte, the result is 0924, now in packed BCD format. You can perform addition and subtraction on packed BCD data using the two decimal adjustment instructions, DAA and DAS:

| [*label*:] | DAA | ;Decimal Adjustment After Addition |
| [*label*:] | DAS | ;Decimal Adjustment After Subtraction |

```
DIVIDEND   DB       '3698'                ;ASCII items
DIVISOR    DB       '4'
ASCQUOT    DB       4 DUP(0), '$'
           ...
                                          ;Divide ASCII numbers:
           MOV      CX,04                  ;Initialize 4 loops
           SUB      AH,AH                  ;Clear left byte of dividend
           AND      DIVISOR,0FH            ;Clear divisor of ASCII 3
           LEA      SI,DIVIDEND
           LEA      DI,ASCQUOT
A20:
           LODSB                           ;Load ASCII byte
           AND      AL,0FH                 ;Clear ASCII 3
           AAD                             ;Adjust for divide
           DIV      DIVISOR                ;Divide
           STOSB                           ;Store quotient
           LOOP     A20                    ;Loop 4 times
                                           ;Convert product to ASCII:
           LEA      BX,ASCQUOT             ;Leftmost byte,
           MOV      CX,04                  ;   4 bytes
A30:
           OR       BYTE PTR[BX],30H       ;Clear ASCII 3
           INC      BX                     ;Next byte
           LOOP     A30                    ;Loop 4 times
           MOV      AH,09H                 ;Display
           LEA      DX,ASCQUOT             ;   quotient
           INT      21H
           ...
```

Figure 13-3   Dividing ASCII Numbers

DAA corrects the result of adding two packed BCD values in AL, and DAS corrects the result of subtracting them. Once again, you have to process the BCD fields one byte (two digits) at a time.

The BCD sum in AL consists of two 4-bit digits. If the value of the rightmost digit exceeds 9 or the AF flag is set, DAA adds 6 to AL and sets the AF. If the value in AL now exceeds 99H or the CF is set, DAA adds 60H to AL and sets the CF. Otherwise, it clears the AF and CF. The following example should clarify this procedure.

Consider adding the BCD values 057836 and 069427. With the CF flag cleared to 0, start the addition with the rightmost pair of digits, 36 + 27, in AL:

	BCD	HEX	BINARY	STORED BCD
First ADC, clears CF	36	36	0011 0110	
	27	27	0010 0111	
	63	5D	0101 1101	
DAA adds 06H, sets AF			0000 0110	
			0110 0011	63
Second ADC, sets CF	78	78	0111 1000	
	94	94	1001 0100	
	(1)72	(1)0C	(1)0000 1100	
DAA adds 06H, sets AF			0000 0110	
			0001 0010	
DAA adds 60H (because			0110 0000	
CF set), sets CF			0111 0010	72
Third ADC, adds 1	05	05	0000 0101	
(because CF set),	06	06	0000 0110	
clears CF	1	1	0000 0001	
	12	0C	0000 1100	

DAA adds 06H, sets AF

$$
\begin{array}{r}
0000\ 0110 \\
\underline{0001\ 0010} \\
\end{array} \quad 12
$$

The BCD sum is now correctly stored as 127263.

The partial program in Figure 13-4 illustrates the foregoing example of BCD addition. The procedure B10CONVRT converts the ASCII values ASCVALUE1 and ASC-VALUE2 to the packed BCD values BCDVALUE1 and BCDVALUE2, respectively. Processing, which is from right to left, could just as easily be from left to right. Also, processing words is easier than processing bytes because you need two ASCII bytes to generate one packed BCD byte. However, the use of words does require an even number of bytes in the ASCII field.

The program performs a loop three times to add the packed BCD numbers to BCDSUM. The final total is 00127263H, which you can confirm with DEBUG. A useful exercise is to convert the BCD total to ASCII and display it.

```
ASCVALUE1    DB      '057836'         ;ASCII data items
ASCVALUE2    DB      '069427'
BCDVALUE1    DB      '000'            ;BCD data items
BCDVALUE2    DB      '000'
BCDSUM       DB      4 DUP(0)
.386  ;         ...
             LEA     SI,ASCVALUE1+4   ;Initialize ASCII
             LEA     DI,BCDVALUE1+2   ;  and BCD values
             CALL    B10CONVRT        ;Call convert routine
             LEA     SI,ASCVALUE2+4   ;Initialize ASCII
             LEA     DI,BCDVALUE2+2   ;  and BCD values
             CALL    B10CONVRT        ;Call convert routine
                                      ;Add BCD numbers:
             XOR     AH,AH            ;Clear AH
             LEA     SI,BCDVALUE1+2   ;Initialize
             LEA     DI,BCDVALUE2+2   ;  BCD
             LEA     BX,BCDSUM+3      ;  addresses
             MOV     CX,03            ;3-byte fields
             CLC
A20:
             MOV     AL,[SI]          ;Get BCDVALUE1
             ADC     AL,[DI]          ;Add BCDVALUE2
             DAA                      ;Decimal adjust
             MOV     [BX],AL          ;Store in BCDSUM
             DEC     SI
             DEC     DI
             DEC     BX
             LOOP    A20              ;Loop 3 times
             ...
;              Convert ASCII to BCD:
;              --------------------
B10CONVRT    PROC
             MOV     CX,03            ;Words to convert
B20:         MOV     AX,[SI]          ;Get ASCII pair
             XCHG    AH,AL
             SHL     AL,04            ;Shift off
             SHL     AX,04            ;  ASCII 3s
             MOV     [DI],AH          ;Store BCD digits
             DEC     SI
             DEC     SI
             DEC     DI
             LOOP    B20              ;Loop 3 times
             RET
B10CONVRT    ENDP
```

Figure 13-4   Converting and Adding BCD Numbers

CONVERTING ASCII DATA TO BINARY FORMAT

Performing arithmetic in ASCII or BCD format is suitable only for short fields. For most arithmetic purposes, it is more practical to convert such numbers into binary format. In fact, it is easier to convert from ASCII directly to binary than to convert from ASCII to BCD to binary.

Conversion from ASCII to binary is based on the fact that an ASCII number is in base 10 and the computer performs arithmetic in base 2. Here is the procedure:

1. Start with the rightmost byte of the ASCII field and process from right to left.
2. Strip the 3 from the left hex digit of each ASCII byte, thereby forming a packed BCD number.
3. Multiply the first (rightmost) BCD digit by 1, the second by 10 (0AH), the third by 100 (64H), and so forth, and sum the products.

The following example converts ASCII number 3569 to binary from right to left

	Decimal			Hexadecimal	
Step	Product		Step	Product	
9 × 1 =	9		9 × 01H =	9H	
6 × 10 =	60		6 × 0AH =	3CH	
5 × 100 =	500		5 × 64H =	1F4H	
3 × 1000 =	3000		3 × 3E8H =	668H	
Total:	3569			0DF1H	

Try checking that the sum 0DF1H actually equals decimal 3569.

The partial program in the next example converts ASCII number 1234 to its binary equivalent:

```
ASCLENTH   EQU     4                 ;ASCII length
ASCVALUE   DB      '3569'            ;ASCII value
BINVALUE   DW      0                 ;Binary sum
MULTFACT   DW      1                 ;1, 10, 100, ...
           ...
           MOV     CX,ASCLENTH       ;Count for loop
           LEA     SI,ASCVALUE+3     ;Address of ASCVALUE
L10:
           MOV     AL,[SI]           ;Select ASCII character
           AND     AX,000FH          ;Remove 3-zone
           MUL     MULTFACT          ;Multiply by 10 factor
           ADD     BINVALUE,AX       ;Add to binary
           MOV     AX,MULTFACT       ;Calculate next
           IMUL    AX,10             ;   10 factor
           MOV     MULTFACT,AX
           DEC     SI                ;Last ASCII character?
           LOOP    L10               ;   no, continue
```

An LEA instruction initializes the address of the rightmost byte of the ASCII field, ASC-VALUE+3, in SI. The instruction at A20 that moves the ASCII byte to AL is MOV

AL, [SI]. The operation uses the address of ASCVALUE+3 to copy the rightmost byte of ASCVALUE into AL. Each iteration of the loop decrements SI by 1 and references the next byte to the left. The loop repeats for each of the four bytes of ASCVALUE. Also, each iteration multiplies MULTFACT by 10 (0AH), giving multipliers of 1, 10, 100, and 1,000. At the end, BINVALUE contains the correct binary value, F10DH, in reverse-byte sequence.

The program in the next section converts the binary value back to its decimal format.

CONVERTING BINARY DATA TO ASCII FORMAT

To print or display the result of binary arithmetic, you have to first convert it into ASCII format. The operation involves reversing the previous steps: Instead of multiplying, repetitively divide the binary number by 10 (0AH) until the quotient is less than 10. Each remainder, which can be only 0 through 9, successively generates the ASCII number. As an example, let's convert 0DF1H back into decimal format:

```
Divide by 0AH      Quotient      Remainder
DF1 ÷ A              164              9
164 ÷ A               23              6
23  ÷ A                3              5
```

Because the quotient (3) is now less than the divisor (0AH), the operation is complete. The remainders from right to left, along with the last quotient, form the BCD result: 3569. All that remains is to store these digits in memory with ASCII 3s, as 31323334.

The following example converts binary number 0DF1H to ASCII format:

```
ASCVALUE    DB   4 DUP(' ')          ;Data items
BINVALUE    DW   0DF1H
            ...
            MOV CX,0010               ;Division factor
            LEA SI,ASCVALUE+3         ;Address of ASCVALUE
            MOV AX,BINVALUE           ;Get binary amount
L20:
            CMP AX,CX                 ;Value < 10?
            JB  L30                   ;  yes, exit
            XOR DX,DX                 ;Clear upper quotient
            DIV CX                    ;Divide by 10
            OR  DL,30H
            MOV [SI],DL               ;Store ASCII character
            DEC SI
            JMP L20
L30:
            OR  AL,30H                ;Store last quotient
            MOV [SI],AL               ;  as ASCII character
```

The example divides the binary number successively by 10 (0AH) until the remaining quotient is less than 10, and stores the generated hex digits in ASCII format as 33353639. You may find it useful to reproduce this program and trace its execution step by step.

SHIFTING AND ROUNDING A PRODUCT

Suppose a product contains three decimal places and you have to round it and reduce it to two decimal places. As an example, if the product is 17.385, add 5 to the rightmost (unwanted) decimal position, and shift right one digit:

```
Product:            17.385
Add 5:            +  0.005
Rounded product:    17.390 = 17.39
```

If (a) the product is 17.3855, add 50 and shift two digits, and if (b) the product is 17.38555, add 500 and shift three digits:

```
(a)  17.3855           (b)  17.38555
   +  0.0050              +  0.00500
     17.3905 = 17.39         17.39055 = 17.39
```

Further, a number with six decimal places requires adding 5000 and shifting four digits, and so forth. Now, because a computer normally processes binary data, 17.385 appears as 43E9H. Adding 5 to 43E9H gives 43EEH, or 17390 in decimal format. So far, so good. But shifting one binary digit results in 21F7H, or 8695—indeed, the shift simply halves the value. You require a shift that is equivalent to shifting right one decimal digit. You can accomplish this shift by dividing the rounded binary value by 10, or hex A: Hex 43EE divided by hex A = 6CBH. Conversion of 6CBH to a decimal number gives 1739. Now just insert a decimal point in the correct position, and you can display the rounded, shifted value as 17.39.

By this method, you can round and shift any binary number. For three decimal places, add 5 and divide by 10; for four decimal places, add 50 and divide by 100. Perhaps you have noticed a pattern: The rounding factor (5, 50, 500, etc.) is always one-half of the value of the shift factor (10, 100, 1,000, etc.).

Of course, the radix point in a binary number is implied and is not actually present.

Program: Converting between ASCII and Binary Data

The program in Figure 13-5 allows a user to enter quantities and rates, and displays the calculated values. Quantities could be, for example, kilowatt hours or gallons. For brevity, the program omits some error checking that would otherwise be included. Also, each procedure indicates the registers used rather than pushing and popping them. The procedures are as follows:

- A10MAIN handles initialization and invokes the procedures for entering data and calculating values.
- B10INPUT accepts quantity and rate in ASCII format from the keyboard. These values may contain a decimal point.
- C10QTY initializes conversion of ASCII quantity to binary.
- D10RATE initializes conversion of ASCII rate to binary.
- E10MULT performs the multiplication, and rounds and shifts any product with three or more decimal places.
- F10PROD inserts the decimal point, determines the rightmost position to begin storing ASCII characters, and converts the binary product to an ASCII value.

```
            TITLE      A13CALC (EXE)  Enter qty. and rate as ASCII values,
            ;                determine number of decimal places, convert to
            ;                binary, calculate product, display as ASCII.
                       .MODEL SMALL
                       .STACK 64
                       .DATA
LEFTCOL     EQU        28                    ;Equates for screen
RIGHTCOL    EQU        52                    ;  locations
TOPROW      EQU        10
BOTROW      EQU        14
QTYPARAM    LABEL      BYTE                  ;Quantity parameter list:
MAXQLEN     DB         6                     ;  for keyboard input
ACTQLEN     DB         ?                     ;
QTYFLD      DB         6 DUP(?)              ;
RATEPAR     LABEL      BYTE                  ;Rate parameter list:
MAXRLEN     DB         6                     ;  for keyboard input
ACTRLEN     DB         ?                     ;
RATEFLD     DB         6 DUP(?)              ;

PROMPT1     DB         'Quantity?        '
PROMPT2     DB         'Rate?        '
PROMPT3     DB         'Product = '
ASCPROD     DB         10 DUP(30H)
PROMPT4     DB         'Press any key to continue or Esc to quit'
ADJUST      DW         ?                     ;Data items
BINPROD     DW         00
BINQTY      DW         00
BINRATE     DW         00
COL         DB         00
DECIND      DB         00
MULT10      DW         01
NODECIMS    DW         00
ROW         DB         00
SHIFT       DW         ?
TENWD       DW         10
.386   ;-----------------------------------------------------
            .CODE
A10MAIN     PROC       FAR
            MOV        AX,@data              ;Initialize DS
            MOV        DS,AX                 ;  and ES registers
            MOV        ES,AX
            MOV        AX,0003H              ;Set video mode
            INT        10H                   ;  and clear screen
A20:        CALL       Q10WINDOW             ;Clear window
            CALL       B10INPUT              ;Accept quantity & rate
            CALL       C10QTY                ;Convert qty to binary
            CALL       D10RATE               ;Convert rate to binary
            CALL       E10MULT               ;Calculate product, round
            CALL       F10PROD               ;Convert product to ASCII
            CALL       G10FORMAT             ;Display product
            CALL       H10PAUSE              ;Pause for user
            CMP        AL,1BH                ;Esc pressed?
            JNE        A20                   ;  no, continue
            MOV        AX,4C00H              ;End processing
            INT        21H
A10MAIN     ENDP
```

Figure 13-5   Processing ASCII and Binary Data

- G10FORMAT clears leading zeros to blanks and calls K10DISPLY to display the value.
- H10PAUSE prompts for keyboard input. (Pressing <Esc> at the end tells the program to discontinue processing.)
- J10ASCBIN converts ASCII to binary (a common routine for quantity and rate) and determines the number of decimal places in the entered data.

```
                 LEA    SI,ASCPROD          ;Clear
        G20:     CMP    BYTE PTR[SI],30H    ;  leading zeros
                 JNE    G30                 ;  in ASCPROD
                 MOV    BYTE PTR[SI],20H    ;  to blanks
                 INC    SI
                 LOOP   G20
        G30:     LEA    BP,PROMPT3          ;Prompt for product
                 MOV    CX,20               ;No. of characters
                 CALL   K10DISPLY           ;Display prompt
                 RET
        G10FORMAT ENDP
        ;                   Pause for user, press any key to quit:
        ;                   -----------------------------------------
        H10PAUSE  PROC   NEAR                ;Uses AX, CX, BP
                 MOV    COL,20              ;Set cursor
                 MOV    ROW,22              ;  positions
                 LEA    BP,PROMPT4          ;Prompt for user
                 MOV    CX,40               ;No. of characters
                 CALL   K10DISPLY           ;Display message
                 MOV    AH,10H              ;Request reply
                 INT    16H                 ;  from keyboard
                 RET
        H10PAUSE  ENDP


        ;                   Convert ASCII quantity and rate to binary
        ;                   SI set with address of qty/rate on entry:
        ;                   -----------------------------------------
        J10ASCBIN PROC   NEAR                ;Uses AX, BX, SI
                 MOV    MULT10,0001         ;Initialize
                 MOV    BINPROD,00
                 MOV    DECIND,00
                 XOR    BX,BX               ;Clear BX
        J20:     MOV    AL,[SI]             ;Get ASCII character
                 CMP    AL,'.'              ;Decimal point?
                 JNE    J30                 ;  no
                 MOV    DECIND,01           ;  yes, set indicator
                 JMP    J40
        J30:     AND    AX,000FH            ;Force AH = 0
                 MUL    MULT10              ;Multiply by factor
                 ADD    BINPROD,AX          ;Add to binary value
                 MOV    AX,MULT10           ;Calculate next
                 IMUL   AX,10               ;  factor x 10
                 MOV    MULT10,AX
                 CMP    DECIND,00           ;Reached decimal point?
                 JNZ    J40                 ;  no
                 INC    BX                  ;  yes, add to count
        J40:     DEC    SI                  ;Next character
                 LOOP   J20
                 CMP    DECIND,00           ;End of loop
                 JZ     J90                 ;Any decimal point?
                 ADD    NODECIMS,BX         ;  yes, add to total
        J90:     RET
        J10ASCBIN ENDP


        ;                   Display characters, set attribute:
        ;                   --------------------------------
```

Figure 13-5 *Continued*

other character, the program should display a message and redisplay the input prompt. A useful instruction for validating is XLAT, covered in Chapter 14.

In practice, test your program thoroughly for all possible conditions, such as zero values, extremely high and low values, and negative values.

Negative Values.   Some applications involve negative amounts, especially for reversing and correcting entries. You could allow a minus sign following a value, such as

```
K10DISPLY PROC     NEAR                ;BP, CX set on entry
          MOV      AX,1301H            ;Request display line
          MOV      BX,0016H            ;Page and attribute
          MOV      DH,ROW              ;Screen row
          MOV      DL,COL              ;   and column
          INT      10H
          RET
K10DISPLY ENDP

;                   Scroll display window, set attribute:
;                   -------------------------------------
Q10WINDOW PROC     NEAR
          MOV      AX,0605H            ;Five rows
          MOV      BH,16H              ;Attribute
          MOV      CH,TOPROW           ;Top-left
          MOV      CL,LEFTCOL          ;   corner
          MOV      DH,BOTROW           ;Bottom-right
          MOV      DL,RIGHTCOL         ;   corner
          INT      10H
          RET
Q10WINDOW ENDP
          END      A10MAIN
```

Figure 13-5 *Continued*

12.34–, or preceding the value, as –12.34. The program could then check for a minus sign during conversion to binary. On the other hand, you may want to leave the binary number positive and simply set an indicator to record the fact that the amount is negative. When the arithmetic is complete, the program, if required, can insert a minus sign to the left or right of the ASCII field.

To make the binary number negative, convert the ASCII input to binary as usual. (See the section "Reversing the Sign" in Chapter 12 for changing the sign of a binary field.) And watch out for using IMUL and IDIV to handle signed data. For rounding a negative amount, subtract 5 instead of adding 5.

KEY POINTS

- An ASCII field requires one byte for each character. For a numeric field, the rightmost half-byte contains the digit, and the leftmost half-byte contains 3.
- Clearing the leftmost 3s of an ASCII number to 0s converts it to unpacked binary-coded decimal (BCD) format.
- Compressing ASCII characters to two digits per byte converts the field to packed binary-coded decimal (BCD) data.
- After an ASCII add, AAA is used to adjust the answer; after an ASCII subtract, AAS is used to adjust the answer.
- Before an ASCII multiplication, the multiplicand and multiplier should be converted to unpacked BCD by clearing the leftmost hex 3s to 0s. After the multiplication, AAM is used to adjust the product.
- Before an ASCII division, the dividend and divisor should be converted to unpacked BCD by clearing the leftmost hex 3s, and AAD is used to adjust the dividend.
- For most arithmetic purposes, ASCII numbers should be converted to binary. Valid ASCII characters for this purpose are 30H though 39H, decimal point, and possibly minus sign.

REVIEW QUESTIONS AND EXERCISES

13-1. Assume that BX contains ASCII 9 (0039H) and DX contains ASCII 5 (0035H). Explain the results of each of the following unrelated operations:

(a) `ADD BX,34H`   (b) `ADD BX,DX`   (c) `SUB BX,DX`   (d) `SUB BX,0CH`

    AAA   AAA   AAS   AAS

13-2. Use hex notation to show the decimal value 4127 in the following formats: (a) ASCII, (b) unpacked BCD, (c) packed BCD.

13-3. An unpacked BCD field named BCDVAL contains 01060803H. Code a loop that causes its contents to be proper ASCII 31363833H.

13-4. A field named ASCVAL1 contains the ASCII decimal value 174, and another field named ASCVAL2 contains ASCII 4. Code the instructions to multiply the ASCII numbers and to store the product in ASCPROD.

13-5. Use the same fields as in Question 13-4 to divide ASCVAL1 by ASCVAL2 and store the quotient in ASCQUOT.

13-6. Provide the manual calculations for the following: (a) Convert ASCII decimal value 29765 to binary, and show the result in hex format, and (b) convert the hex value back to ASCII.

13-7. Code and test a program that (a) inserts binary values in EAX, EBX, ECX, and EDX, and (b) displays each register value in ASCII format.

13-8. Code and test a program that (a) accepts two numeric values from the keyboard, (b) converts the two ASCII values to binary, (c) adds the binary values, (d) converts the binary sum to ASCII, (e) displays the ASCII sum. Allow for any number of pairs of entries. The user presses just <Enter> for a value to indicate no more data.

Chapter 14

DEFINING AND PROCESSING TABLES

> Objective: To cover the requirements for defining tables, performing searches of tables, and sorting table entries.

INTRODUCTION

Many program applications require *tables* or *arrays* containing such data as names, descriptions, quantities, and rates. This chapter begins by defining some conventional tables and then covers methods for searching through them. Techniques for searching tables are subject to the way in which the tables are defined, and many methods of defining and searching other than those given here are possible. The definition and use of tables largely involves applying what you have already learned. Other commonly-used features are the use of sorting, which rearranges the sequence of data in a table, and the use of address tables and spreadsheets.

The only instruction introduced in this chapter is XLAT (Translate).

DEFINING TABLES

To facilitate searching through them, most tables are arranged in a consistent manner, with each entry defined with the same format (character or numeric), with the same length, and in either ascending or descending order.

A table that you have been using throughout this book is the definition of the stack, which in the following is a table of 64 uninitialized words, where the name STACK refers to the first word of the table, as STACK DW 64 DUP(?).

The following two tables, MONTH_TBL and CUST_TBL, initialize character and numeric values, respectively. MONTH_TBL defines alphabetic abbreviations of the months, whereas CUST_TBL defines a table of customer numbers:

```
MONTH_TBL   DB   'Jan',  'Feb',  'Mar', ..., 'Dec'
CUST_TBL    DB   205, 208, 209, 212, 215, 224, ...
```

All entries in MONTH_TBL are three characters. However, although all entries in CUST_TBL are defined as three digits, the assembler converts the decimal numbers to binary format and, provided that they don't exceed the value 255, stores them each in one byte.

A table may also contain a mixture of numeric and character values, provided that their definitions are consistent. In the following table of stock items, each numeric entry (stock number) is two digits (one byte), and each character entry (stock description) is nine bytes:

```
STOCK_TBL DB 12, 'Computers', 14, 'Paper....', 17, 'Diskettes', ...
```

The four dots following the description "Paper" are to show that spaces should be present; that is, spaces, not dots, are to follow the description. For clarity, you may code each pair of table entries on a separate line:

```
STOCK_TBL   DB   12,   'Computers'
            DB   14,   'Paper....'
            DB   17,   'Diskettes'
                 ...
```

The next example defines a table with 100 entries, each initialized to 15 blanks (1,500 bytes in all):

```
STORE_TBL DB 100 DUP(15 DUP(' '))
```

A program could use this table to store up to 100 values that it has generated internally, or it could use the table to store the contents of up to 100 entries that it accepts from a keyboard or reads from a disk file.

In real-world situations, many programs are *table driven*. That is, tables are stored as disk files, which any number of programs may require for processing. To this end, a program can read a table file from disk into an "empty" table defined for that purpose. The reason for this practice is that the contents of tables change over time. If each program defines its own tables, any changes require redefining the tables and reassembling the programs. With table files on disk, a change to a table may simply involve changing the contents of the file. Chapter 17 gives an example of a table file.

The TYPE, LENGTH, and SIZE Operators

The assembler supplies a number of special operators that you may find useful. For example, the length of a table may change over time and you may have to modify a program to account for the new definition and add routines that check for the end of the table. The use of the TYPE, LENGTH, and SIZE operators can help reduce the number of instructions that have to be changed.

Consider this definition of a table with 12 words:

```
RAIN_TBL DW 12 DUP(?)    ;Table with 12 words
```

The program can use the TYPE operator to determine the definition (DW in this case), the LENGTH operator to determine the DUP factor (12), and the SIZE operator to determine the number of bytes ($12 \times 2 = 24$). The following examples illustrate the three operators:

```
MOV   AX,TYPE RAIN_TBL      ;AX = 0002H  (2 bytes)
MOV   BX,LENGTH RAIN_TBL    ;BX = 000CH  (12 bytes)
MOV   CX,SIZE RAIN_TBL      ;CX = 0018H  (24 bytes)
```

You may use the values that LENGTH and SIZE return to end a search or a sort of a table. For example, if SI register contains the incremented offset address of a search, you may test this offset using

```
CMP SI,SIZE RAIN_TBL
```

Chapter 25 describes the TYPE, LENGTH, and SIZE operators in detail. Let's now examine different ways to use tables in programs.

DIRECT ADDRESSING OF TABLE ENTRIES

Suppose that a user enters a numeric month such as 03 and that a program is to convert it to alphabetic format—in this case, March. The routine to perform this conversion involves defining a table of alphabetic months, all of equal length. The length of each entry should be that of the longest name, September, in this format:

```
MONTH_TBL   DB   'January..'
            DB   'February.'
            DB   'March....'
            ...
            DB   'December.'
```

The entry 'January' is at MONTH_TBL+00, 'February' is at MONTH_TBL+09, 'March' is at MONTH_TBL+18, and so forth. Let's say that a user keys in *3* (for March), which the program is to locate in the table. The program has to perform the following steps:

1. Convert the entered month from ASCII 33 to binary 3.
2. Deduct 1 from this number: $3 - 1 = 2$ (because month 01 is at MONTH_TBL+00).
3. Multiply the new number by 9 (the length of each entry): $2 \times 9 = 18$.
4. Add this product (18) to the address of MONTH_TBL; the result is the address of the required description: MONTH_TBL+18, where the entry "March" begins.

This technique is known as *direct table addressing.* Because the algorithm calculates the required table address directly, you don't have to define the numeric months in the table and the program doesn't have to search successively through the table.

Direct Addressing, Example 1: Table of Months

The partial program in Figure 14-1 provides an example of direct access of a table with the names of the months. The program assumes 12 (December) as input and converts the month from ASCII to binary format (according to the conversion method described in Chapter 13):

```
LEN_ENTRY   EQU   9                        ;Length of table entries
MONTH_IN    DB    '12'                     ;ASCII '3132'
MONTH_TBL   DB    'January   ', 'February ', 'March     '
            DB    'April     ', 'May      ', 'June      '
            DB    'July      ', 'August   ', 'September'
            DB    'October   ', 'November ', 'December '
    .386          ;...
;                       Convert ASCII month to binary:
            XOR   WORD PTR MONTH_IN,3030H ;Clear ASCII 3s
            MOVZX AX,MONTH_IN              ;Mult left digit
            IMUL  AX,10                    ;  by 10 and add
            ADD   AL,MONTH_IN+1            ;  right digit
;                       Locate month in table:
            DEC   AL                       ;Correct for table
            IMUL  AX,LEN_ENTRY             ;Multiply AL by 9
            LEA   BP,MONTH_TBL             ;Add offset to
            ADD   BP,AX                    ;  address of table
    ;                   Display alpha month:
    ;                                      ;ES:BP already loaded
            MOV   AX,1301H                 ;Request display
            MOV   BX,0016H                 ;Page:attribute
            MOV   CX,LEN_ENTRY             ;9 characters
            MOV   DX,0812H                 ;Row:column
            INT   10H
            . . .
```

Figure 14-1   Direct Table Addressing: Example 1

```
Original input month (12) =            3132H
XOR using 3030H =                      0102H
Multiply left byte of month by 10 =    0AH
Add right byte of month =              0CH (decimal 12)
```

The program determines the actual location of the month in the table:

```
Deduct 1 from month in AX =                 000BH (decimal 11)
Multiply by 9 (length of entries) =         0063H (decimal 99)
Add address of table =            MONTH_TBL+63H
```

One way to improve this program is to accept numeric months from the keyboard and to verify that the values are between 01 and 12, inclusive.

Direct Addressing, Example 2: Tables of Months and Days

The partial program in Figure 14-2 retrieves today's date from the system and displays it. INT 21H function 2AH delivers the following binary values:

AL = Day of week (where Sunday = 0)   DH = Month (01–12)
CX = Year (not used by this program)   DL = Day of month (01–31)

The program uses these returned values to display the alphabetic day of the week and the month in the form "Wednesday," "September," and "12." To this end, the program defines a table of days of the week named DAYS_TBL, beginning with Sunday, and a table of months named MONTH_TBL, beginning with January.

Entries in DAYS_TBL and in MONTH_TBL are nine bytes long, with each description padded with blanks to the right. The program multiplies the day of the week by 9 (the

```
LEN_ENTRY  EQU    9                  ;Length of table entries
DAYOFMON   DW     00                 ;
SAVEDAY    DB     ?                  ;
SAVEMON    DB     ?                  ;
TEN        DB     10
ROW        DB     10                 ;Screen row
COLUMN     DB     30                 ; and column
DAYS_TBL   DB     'Sunday   ', 'Monday   '
           DB     'Tuesday  ', 'Wednesday'
           DB     'Thursday ', 'Friday   '
           DB     'Saturday '
MONTH_TBL  DB     'January  ', 'February ', 'March    '
           DB     'April    ', 'May      ', 'June     '
           DB     'July     ', 'August   ', 'September'
           DB     'October  ', 'November ', 'December '
.386 ;     ...    --------------------------------------
           MOV    AH,2AH             ;Get today's date
           INT    21H
           MOV    SAVEMON,DH         ;Save month
           MOV    SAVEDAY,DL         ;Save day of month
                                     ;Display day of week:
           MOV    AH,0               ;------------------
           IMUL   AX,LEN_ENTRY       ;Day x entry length
           LEA    BP,DAYS_TBL        ;Address of table
           ADD    BP,AX              ; plus offset
           MOV    CX,LEN_ENTRY       ;Length
           CALL   B10DISPLY          ;
                                     ;Display month:
           MOVZX  AX,SAVEMON         ;;-------------
           DEC    AX                 ;Decrement month by 1
           IMUL   AX,LEN_ENTRY       ;Month x entry length
           LEA    BP,MONTH_TBL       ;Address of table
           ADD    BP,AX              ; plus offset
           MOV    CX,LEN_ENTRY       ;Length
           CALL   B10DISPLY          ;
                                     ;Display day of month:
           MOVZX  AX,SAVEDAY         ;--------------------
           DIV    TEN                ;Convert day from
           OR     AX,3030H           ; binary to ASCII
           MOV    DAYOFMON,AX        ;Save ASCII day
           LEA    BP,DAYOFMON        ;
           MOV    CX,2               ;No. of characters
           CALL   B10DISPLY          ;
           ...
                                     ;Common display routine:
B10DISPLY  PROC   NEAR               ;BP, CX set on entry
           PUSHA                     ;Preserve registers
           MOV    AX,1301H           ;Request display
           MOV    BX,0016H           ;Page:attribute
           MOV    DH,ROW             ;Screen row
           MOV    DL,COLUMN          ; and column
           INT    10H
           INC    ROW                ;Next row
           POPA                      ;Restore registers
           RET
B10DISPLY  ENDP
```

Figure 14-2   Direct Table Addressing: Example 2

length of each entry in DAYS_TBL). The product is an offset into the table where, for example, Sunday is at DAYS_TBL+0, Monday is at DAYS_TBL+9, and so forth. The day is displayed directly from the table.

The program decrements the month by 1 so that, for example, month 01 becomes entry zero in MONTH_TBL. It then multiplies the month by 9 (the length of each entry in MONTH_TBL). The program displays the month directly from the table.

The program divides the day of the month by 10 to convert it from binary to ASCII format. Because the maximum value for day is 31, the quotient and the remainder can each be only one digit. (For example, 31 divided by 10 gives a quotient of 3 and a remainder of 1.) The program displays each of the two characters, including the leading zero for days less than 10; suppressing the leading zero involves some minor program changes.

Although direct table addressing is very efficient, it works best when entries are in sequence and in a predictable order. Thus it would work well for entries that are in the order 01, 02, 03, . . . , or 106, 107, 108, . . . , or even 05, 10, 15, ... However, few applications provide such a neat arrangement of table values. The next section examines tables with values that are sequential, but not in a predictable order.

SEARCHING A TABLE

Some tables consist of unique numbers with no apparent pattern. A typical example is a table of stock items with nonconsecutive numbers such as 034, 038, 041, 139, and 145. Another type of table—such as an income tax table—contains ranges of values. The following sections examine both of these types of tables and the requirements for searching them.

Tables with Unique Entries

The stock item numbers for most businesses are usually not in consecutive order. Rather, they tend to be grouped by category, perhaps with a leading number to indicate furniture or appliance or to indicate that it is located in a certain department. Also, over time, some items are deleted from stock and other items are added. As an example, let's define a table with stock numbers and their related descriptions. These could be defined in separate tables, such as

```
STOCK_NO   DB '05','10','12', ...
STOCK_DESC DB 'Excavators', 'Lifters...', 'Presses...' , ...
```

Each step in a search could increment the address of the first table by 2 (the length of each entry in STOCK_NO) and the address of the second table by 10 (the length of each entry in STOCK_DESC). Or, a procedure could keep a count of the number of loops executed and, on finding a match with a certain key stock number, multiply the count by 10, and use this product as an offset to the address of STOCK_DESC.

On the other hand, it may be clearer to define stock numbers and descriptions in the same table, with one line for each pair of items:

```
STOCK_TBL  DB    '05','Excavators'
           DB    '10','Lifters...'
           DB    '12','Presses...'
                 ...
```

The partial program in Figure 14-3 defines this table with six pairs of stock numbers and descriptions. The search routine begins comparing the first byte of the input stock number, STOCKN_IN, with the first byte of stock number in the table. The results of the comparison can be low, high, or equal.

```
LEN_STKNO    EQU   02                              ;Length stock no.
LEN_DESCR    EQU   10                              ;  and description
STOCKN_IN    DB    '12'                            ;Input stock no.
STOCK_TBL    DB    '05','Excavators'               ;Start of table
             DB    '10','Lifters    '              ;
             DB    '12','Presses    '              ;
             DB    '15','Valves     '              ;
             DB    '23','Processors'               ;
             DB    '27','Pumps      '              ;End of table
;  ----------------------------------------------------------------
             ...
             MOV   CX,06                            ;Initialize
             LEA   SI,STOCK_TBL                     ;  compares
A20:
             MOV   AL,STOCKN_IN
             CMP   AL,[SI]                          ;Stock#(1) : table
             JNE   A30                              ;Not equal, exit
             MOV   AL,STOCKN_IN+1                   ;Equal:
             CMP   AL,[SI+1]                        ;   stock#(2):table+1
             JE    A50                              ;   equal, found
A30:         JB    A40                              ;Low, not in table
             ADD   SI,LEN_STKNO                     ;High, get
             ADD   SI,LEN_DESCR                     ;  next entry
             LOOP  A20
A40:                                                ;Not in table,
;            ...                                    ;  display error
             JMP   A90                              ;  message and exit
A50:
             INC   SI
             INC   SI                               ;Extract description
             MOV   AX,1301H                         ;Request display
             MOV   BP,SI                            ;Stock description
             MOV   BX,0061H                         ;Page:attribute
             MOV   CX,LEN_DESCR                     ;10 characters
             MOV   DX,0812H                         ;Row:column
             INT   10H
A90:         ...
```

Figure 14-3   Searching a Table Using CMP

1. *Low.* If the comparison of the first or second bytes is low, the program determines that the stock number is not in the table and at A40 could display an error message (not coded). For example, the program compares input stock item 01 with table item 05; the first byte is equal, but because the second byte is low, the program determines that the item is not in the table.

2. *High.* If the comparison of the first or second bytes is high, the program has to continue the search; to compare the input stock item with the next stock item in the table, it increments SI, which contains the table address. For example, the program compares input stock item 06 with table item 05. The first byte is equal, but the second byte is high, so it compares the input with the next item in the table: stock item 06 with table item 10. The first byte is low, so the program determines that the item is not in the table.

3. *Equal.* If both the first and second bytes are equal, the stock number is found. For example, the program compares input stock item 10 with table item 05. The first byte is high, so it compares the input with the next item in the table: Stock item 10 with

table item 10. Because the first byte is equal and the second is equal, the program has found the item; at A50 it displays the description directly from the table.

The search loop performs a maximum of six comparisons. If the number of loops exceeds six, the stock number is known to be not in the table.

The table could also define unit prices. The user keys in stock number and quantity sold. The program could locate the stock item in the table, calculate amount of sale (quantity sold times unit price), and display description and amount of sale.

In Figure 14-3, the stock number is 2 characters and the description is 10. Programming details would vary for different numbers of entries and different lengths of entries. For example, to compare 3-byte fields, you could use REPE CMPSB, although REPE involves the CX register, which LOOP already uses.

Tables with Ranges

Income tax provides a typical example of a table with ranges of values. Consider the following hypothetical table of taxable income, tax rates, and adjustment factors:

TAXABLE INCOME($)	RATE	ADJUSTMENT FACTOR
0-1,000.00	.10	000.00
1,000.01-2,500.00	.15	050.00
2,501.01-4,250.00	.18	125.00
4,250.01-6,000.00	.20	260.00
6,000.01 and over	.23	390.00

In the tax table, rates increase as taxable income increases. The adjustment factor compensates for our calculating tax at the high rate, whereas lower rates apply to lower levels of income. Entries for taxable income contain the maximum income for each step:

```
TAXTBL  DD 100000, 10, 00000
        DD 250000, 15, 05000
        DD 425000, 18, 12500
        DD 600000, 20, 26000
        DD 999999, 23, 39000
```

To perform a search of the table, the program compares the taxpayer's actual taxable income starting with the first entry in the table and does the following, according to the results of the comparison:

- High: Not yet found; increment for the next entry in the table.
- Low or equal: Found; use the associated rate and adjustment factor. Calculate the tax deduction as (taxable income × table rate) − adjustment factor. Note that the last entry in the table contains the maximum value (999999), which always correctly forces an end to the search.

Searching a Table Using String Comparisons

REPE CMPS is useful for comparing item numbers that are two or more characters long. The partial program in Figure 14-4 defines STOCK_TBL, but this time revised as a 3-byte stock number. The last entry in the table contains stock item '999' (the highest possible

```
          LEN_STKNO  EQU  03              ;Length stock no.
          LEN_DESCR  EQU  10              ;  and description
   0000  STOCKN_IN  DB   '123'
   0003  STOCK_TBL  DB   '035','Excavators'   ;Table
   0010             DB   '038','Lifters    '
   001D             DB   '049','Presses    '
   002A             DB   '102','Valves     '
   0037             DB   '123','Processors'
   0044             DB   '127','Pumps      '
   0051             DB   '999', 10 DUP(' ')
   ; -------------------------------------------------------
   ;          ...
             CLD
             LEA   DI,STOCK_TBL         ;Init'ze table address
   A20:      MOV   CX,LEN_STKNO         ;Set to compare 3 bytes
             LEA   SI,STOCKN_IN         ;Init'ze stock# address
             REPE  CMPSB                ;Stock# : table
             JE    A30                  ;  equal, exit
             JB    A40                  ;  low, not in table
             ADD   DI,CX                ;Add CX value to offset
             ADD   DI,LEN_DESCR         ;Next table item
             JMP   A20
   A30:
             MOV   AX,1301H             ;Request display
             MOV   BP,DI                ;Stock description
             MOV   BX,0061H             ;Page:attribute
             MOV   CX,LEN_DESCR         ;10 characters
             MOV   DX,0812H             ;Row:column
             INT   10H
             JMP   A90
   A40:      ...
   ;                      <Display error message>
   A90:      ...
```

Figure 14-4   Searching a Table Using CMPSB

stock number) to force the search to end. The program could have used LOOP to force an end of search, but REPE makes CX unavailable for LOOP. The search routine compares STOCKN_IN (arbitrarily defined to contain 123) with each table entry, as follows:

STOCKN_IN	TABLE ENTRY	RESULT OF COMPARISON
123	035	High, check next entry
123	038	High, check next entry
123	049	High, check next entry
123	102	High, check next entry
123	123	Equal, entry found

The program first initializes DI to the offset address of STOCK_TBL (003), CX to the length (03) of each stock item, and SI to the offset of STOCKN_IN (000). As long as the compared bytes contain equal values, the CMPSB operation compares byte for byte, and automatically increments DI and SI for the next pair of bytes. A comparison with the first table entry (123:035) ends with a high comparison after the first byte; DI contains 004, SI contains 001, and CX contains 02.

For the second comparison, DI should contain 010 and SI should contain 000. Correcting SI simply involves reloading the address of STOCKN_IN. To correct the address of the table entry that should be in DI, however, the increment depends on whether the comparison ended after one, two, or three bytes. CX contains the number of the remaining un-compared bytes, in this case, 02. Adding the CX value plus the length of the stock description (that of the previously compared stock item) gives the offset of the next table item, as follows:

```
Address in DI after CMPSB:            004H
Add remaining length in CX:         + 02H
Add length of stock description:    + 0AH
Next offset address in table:        010H
```

Because CX contains the number of the remaining uncompared bytes (if any), the arithmetic works for all cases and ends after one, two, or three comparisons. On an equal comparison, CX contains 00, and DI is already incremented to the address of the required description. The program displays the description directly from the table.

Tables with Variable-Length Entries

It is possible to define a table with variable-length entries. A special delimiter character such as 00H could follow each table entry, and FFH could mark the end of the table. The SCAS instruction is suitable for scanning for the delimiters. However, you must be sure that no byte within an entry contains the bit configuration of a delimiter; for example, an arithmetic binary amount may contain any possible bit configuration, including 00H and FFH.

THE XLAT (TRANSLATE) INSTRUCTION

The XLAT instruction translates the bit configuration of a byte into another predefined configuration. You could use XLAT, for example, to validate the contents of data items or to encrypt data. The format for XLAT is

| [label:] | XLAT | ;no operand |

To use XLAT, you define a translation table that accounts for all 256 possible characters. XLAT requires that the address of the table is in BX and the byte to be translated is in AL.

The following example converts ASCII numbers 0–9 into EBCDIC format, suitable for an IBM mainframe computer. Because the representation of 0–9 in ASCII is 30–39 and in EBCDIC is F0–F9, you could use an OR operation to make the change. However, let's arbitrarily convert ASCII minus sign (2D) and decimal point (2E) to EBCDIC (60 and 4B, respectively) and all other characters to blank, which is 40H in EBCDIC. In the translation table, EBCDIC codes are defined in the ASCII positions; that is, the EBCDIC characters in ASCII locations and EBCDIC minus sign, decimal point, and blanks in the other locations. Because the number 0 is ASCII 30H, the EBCDIC numbers begin in the table at location 30H, or decimal 48:

```
XLAT_TBL   DB   45 DUP(40H)    ;Translate table
           DB   60H, 4BH
           DB   40H
```

```
DB   0F0H,0F1H,0F2H,0F3H,0F4H
DB   0F5H,0F6H,0F7H,0F8H,0F9H
DB   198 DUP(40H)
```

Note that the first DB in XLAT_TBL defines 45 bytes, addressed as XLAT_TBL+00 through XLAT_TBL+44. The second DB defines data beginning at XLAT_TBL+45, and so forth.

XLAT uses the AL value as an offset address; in effect, BX contains the starting address of the table, and AL contains an offset within the table. If the AL value is 00, for example, the table address would be XLAT_TBL+0 (the first byte of XLAT_TBL containing 40H). XLAT would replace the 00 in AL with 40H from the table. If the AL value is 32H (decimal 50), the table address is XLAT_TBL+50; this location contains F2 (EBCDIC 2), which XLAT would insert in AL.

The following program fragment loops through a 6-byte ASCII field, ASC_NO, using XLAT_TBL to translate it into EBCDIC format. Initially, ASC_NO contains −31.5 followed by a blank, or hex 2D33312E3520. At the end of the loop, EBC_NO contains hex 60F3F14BF540, which you can verify by means of DEBUG.

```
ASC_NO  DB    '-31.5 '          ;ASCII item to convert
EBC_NO  DB    6 DUP(' ')        ;Converted EBCDIC item
        ...
        LEA   SI,ASC_NO         ;Address of ASCII number
        LEA   DI,EBC_NO         ;Address of EBCDIC number
        MOV   CX,06             ;Length of items
        LEA   BX,XLAT_TBL       ;Address of table
L10:
        LODSB                   ;Get ASCII char in AL
        XLAT                    ;Translate character
        STOSB                   ;Store AL in EBC_NO
        LOOP  L10               ;Repeat 6 times
```

Program: Displaying Hex and ASCII Characters

The partial program in Figure 14-5 displays all 256 hex values (00-FF), including most of their related ASCII symbols, for example, both the ASCII symbol S and its hex representation, 53. The full display appears on the screen as a 16-by-16 matrix:

```
00 01 02 03 04 05 06 07 08 09 0A 0B 0C 0D 0E 0F
 .  .  .  .  .  .  .  .  .  .  .  .  .  .  .  .
 .  .  .  .  .  .  .  .  .  .  .  .  .  .  .  .
 .  .  .  .  .  .  .  .  .  .  .  .  .  .  .  .
F0 F1 F2 F3 F4 F5 F6 F7 F8 F9 FA FB FC FD FE FF
```

As was shown in Figure 7-1, displaying ASCII characters causes no serious problem. However, displaying the hex representation of an ASCII value is more involved. For example, you have to convert 00H to 3030H, 01H to 3031H, and so forth. That is, 01H is to display as two characters, 01.

```
ROW         DB      02
DISPROW     DB      16 DUP(5 DUP(' '))
HEXCTR      DB      00
XLATAB      DB      30H,31H,32H,33H,34H,35H,36H,37H,38H,39H
            DB      41H,42H,43H,44H,45H,46H
.386   ;    ...
            CALL    clear_screen        ;Standard procedure
            LEA     SI,DISPROW          ;Init'ze display row
A20:        CALL    B10HEX              ;Translate
            CALL    C10DISPLY           ;  and display
            CMP     HEXCTR,0FFH         ;Last hex value (FF)?
            JE      A90                 ;  yes, exit
            INC     HEXCTR              ;  no,  incr next hex
            JMP     A20
            ...
;                   Convert ASCII to hex:
B10HEX      PROC    NEAR
            MOVZX   AX,HEXCTR           ;Get hex pair in AX
            SHR     AX,04               ;Shift off right hex digit
            LEA     BX,XLATAB           ;Set table address
            XLAT                        ;Translate hex
            MOV     [SI],AL             ;Store left character
            MOV     AL,HEXCTR           ;  in display row
            AND     AL,0FH              ;Clear left hex digit
            XLAT                        ;Translate hex
            MOV     [SI]+1,AL           ;Store right character
            RET
B10HEX      ENDP
;                   Display as hex characters:
C10DISPLY   PROC    NEAR
            MOV     AL,HEXCTR           ;Get character
            MOV     [SI]+3,AL
            CMP     AL,07H              ;Lower than 7?
            JB      C20                 ;  yes, ok
            CMP     AL,10H              ;Higher/equal 16?
            JAE     C20                 ;  yes, ok
            MOV     BYTE PTR [SI]+3,20H  ;Else force blank
C20:        ADD     SI,05               ;Next location in row
            LEA     DI,DISPROW+80
            CMP     DI,SI               ;Filled up row?
            JNE     C90                 ;  no, exit
            MOV     AX,1300H            ;Request display
            MOV     BX,0031H            ;Page and attribute
            LEA     BP,DISPROW          ;Data
            MOV     CX,80               ;Length of line
            MOV     DH,ROW              ;Row
            MOV     DL,00               ;Column
            INT     10H
            INC     ROW                 ;Next row
            LEA     SI,DISPROW          ;Reinitialize
C90:        RET
C10DISPLY   ENDP
```

Figure 14-5   Displaying ASCII and Hex Values

The program defines HEXCTR initially with 00H and subsequently increments it by 1 for each of the 256 ASCII characters. The procedure B10HEX splits HEXCTR into its two hex digits. For example, if HEXCTR contains 4FH, the routine would extract the hex 4, which XLAT uses for the translation. The value returned to AL is 34H. The routine then extracts the F and translates it to 46H. The result, 3446H, is displayed on the screen as 4F.

The procedure C10DISPLY converts non-ASCII characters to blanks. Because INT 10H function 13H acts on Backspace and other control characters, the program changes them to blank. The procedure displays a full row of 16 characters and ends after displaying the 16th row.

There are many other ways of converting hex digits to ASCII characters; for example, you could experiment with shifting and comparing.

SORTING TABLE ENTRIES

Often, an application requires *sorting* data in a table into ascending or descending sequence. For example, a user may want a list of stock descriptions in ascending sequence or a list of sales agents' total sales in descending sequence. There are a number of table sort routines, varying from relatively slow processing but clear, to fast processing but obscure. The routine presented in this section is fairly efficient and could serve for most table sorting.

A general approach to sorting a table is to compare a table entry with the entry immediately following it. If the comparison is high, exchange the entries. Continue in this fashion, comparing entry 1 with entry 2, entry 2 with entry 3, and so on to the end of the table, exchanging where necessary. If you made any exchanges, repeat the entire process from the start of the table, comparing entry 1 with entry 2 again, and so forth. At any point, if you proceed through the entire table without making an exchange, you know that the table is sorted into sequence.

In the following pseudocode, SWAP is an item that indicates whether an exchange was made (YES) or not made (NO).

```
L10:    Initialize address of last entry in the table
L20:    Set SWAP to NO
        Initialize address of start of the table
L30:    Table entry > next entry?
            Yes: Exchange entries
                 Set SWAP to YES
        Increment for next entry in the table
        At end of the table?
            No: Jump to L30
            Yes: Does SWAP = YES?
                 Yes: Jump to L20 (repeat sort)
                 No:  End of sort
```

The program in Figure 14-6 allows a user to key in up to 30 names from the keyboard, which the program stores in a table named NAMETABLE. It contains the following procedures:

- A10MAIN calls B10ENTER to accept a name from the keyboard, calls C10STORE to store the name in a table and, when all the names are keyed in, calls D10SORT and F10NAMES.
- B10ENTER prompts the user to key in a name, accepts it, and fills it to the right with blanks. When all the names are keyed in, the user just presses <Enter>, with no name.
- C10STORE stores each name successively in the table.
- D10SORT and E10XCHNG sort the table of names into ascending sequence.
- F10NAMES displays the sorted table.

Note that the table entries are all fixed-length 20 bytes; a routine for sorting variable-length data would be more complicated.

```
TITLE      A14NMSRT (EXE)   Sort names entered from keyboard
           .MODEL SMALL
           .STACK 64
           .DATA
LEN_NAME   EQU     20                      ;Length of name
ENDADDR    DW      ?
MESSG1     DB      'Name? '
NAMECTR    DB      00
NAMESAVE   DB      20 DUP(?)
NAME_TBL   DB      30 DUP(20 DUP(' ')) ;Name table
ROW        DB      00                  ;Screen row
SWAPPED    DB      00
NAMEPAR    LABEL   BYTE                    ;Name parameter list:
MAXNLEN    DB      21                      ;   maximum length
NAMELEN    DB      ?                       ;   no. of chars entered
NAMEFLD    DB      21 DUP(' ')             ;   input name
.386   ; ----------------------------------------------
           .CODE
A10MAIN    PROC    FAR
           MOV     AX,@data                ;Initialize DS and
           MOV     DS,AX                   ;  ES registers
           MOV     ES,AX
           CLD
           CALL    Q10CLEAR                ;Clear screen
           LEA     DI,NAME_TBL             ;Initialize table address
A20:
           CALL    B10ENTER                ;Accept name from KB
           CMP     NAMELEN,00              ;Any more names?
           JE      A30                     ;   no, go to sort
           CMP     NAMECTR,30              ;30 names entered?
           JE      A30                     ;   yes, go to sort
           CALL    C10STORE                ;Store entered name in table
           JMP     A20                     ;Repeat
A30:
                                           ;End of input
           CALL    Q10CLEAR                ;Clear screen
           CMP     NAMECTR,01              ;One or no name entered?
           JBE     A90                     ;   yes, exit
           CALL    D10SORT                 ;Sort stored names
           CALL    F10NAMES                ;Display sorted names
A90:       MOV     AX,4C00H                ;End processing
           INT     21H
A10MAIN    ENDP
;                  Accept name as input, clear to right:
;                  -----------------------------------
                                           ;DI set on entry
B10ENTER   PROC    NEAR                    ;Uses AH, BP, BX, CX, DX
           LEA     BP,MESSG1               ;Prompt
           MOV     CX,06                   ;No. of characters
           CALL    G10DISPLY               ;Call display routine
           INC     ROW                     ;Next row
           MOV     AH,0AH
           LEA     DX,NAMEPAR              ;Accept name
           INT     21H
           MOVZX   BX,NAMELEN              ;Get count of characters
           MOVZX   CX,MAXNLEN              ;Maximum length - actual
           SUB     CX,BX                   ;   = remaining length
```

Figure 14-6   Sorting a Table of Names

```
B20:        MOV     NAMEFLD[BX],20H    ;Clear rest of name
            INC     BX                 ;  to blank
            LOOP    B20
            RET
B10ENTER    ENDP
;                   Store entered name in table:
;                   ---------------------------
;                                      ;DI for table set on entry
C10STORE    PROC    NEAR               ;Uses AH, BP, BX, CX
            INC     NAMECTR            ;Add to number of names
            CLD
            LEA     SI,NAMEFLD         ;Transfer
            MOV     CX,LEN_NAME        ;  name (SI)
            REP MOVSB                  ;  to table (DI)
            RET
C10STORE    ENDP
;                   Sort names in table in ascending sequence:
;                   -----------------------------------------
;                                      ;DI for table set on entry
D10SORT     PROC    NEAR               ;Uses AX, BX, CX, DI, SI
            SUB     DI,40              ;Set up stop address for
            MOV     ENDADDR,DI         ;  last name in table
D20:        MOV     SWAPPED,00         ;Set up start
            LEA     SI,NAME_TBL        ;  of table
D30:
            MOV     CX,LEN_NAME        ;Length of compare
            MOV     DI,SI
            ADD     DI,LEN_NAME        ;Next name for compare
            MOV     AX,DI              ;Save
            MOV     BX,SI              ;  addresses
            REPE CMPSB                 ;Compare name to next
            JBE     D40                ;  no exchange
            CALL    E10XCHNG           ;  exchange
D40:
            MOV     SI,AX
            CMP     SI,ENDADDR         ;End of table?
            JBE     D30                ;  no, continue
            CMP     SWAPPED,00         ;Any swaps?
            JNZ     D20                ;  yes, continue
            RET                        ;  no, end of sort
D10SORT     ENDP
;                   Exchange table entries:
;                   ----------------------
;                                      ;BX set on entry
E10XCHNG    PROC    NEAR               ;Uses CX, DI, SI
            MOV     CX,LEN_NAME        ;Number of characters
            LEA     DI,NAMESAVE        ;Save lower
            MOV     SI,BX              ;  item
            REP MOVSB                  ;  temporarily

            MOV     CX,LEN_NAME        ;Move
            MOV     DI,BX              ;  higher item
            REP MOVSB                  ;  to lower
            MOV     CX,LEN_NAME        ;Move
            LEA     SI,NAMESAVE        ;  saved item to
            REP MOVSB                  ;  higher item
```

Figure 14-6 *Continued*

```
            MOV     SWAPPED,01          ;Signal exchange made
            RET
E10XCHNG    ENDP
;                   Display sorted names in table:
;                   ------------------------------
F10NAMES    PROC    NEAR                ;Uses BP, CX
            MOV     ROW,00              ;Initialize row
            LEA     BP,NAME_TBL         ;Init'ze start of table
F20:        MOV     CX,LEN_NAME         ;No. of characters
            CALL    G10DISPLY           ;Call display routine
            INC     ROW                 ;Next row
            ADD     BP,LEN_NAME         ;Next name in table
            DEC     NAMECTR             ;Is this last one?
            JNZ     F20                 ;  no, repeat
            RET                         ;  yes, exit
F10NAMES    ENDP
;                   Common display routine:
;                   -----------------------
                                        ;BP, CX set on entry
G10DISPLY   PROC    NEAR                ;Uses AX, BX, DX
            MOV     AX,1301H            ;Request display
            MOV     BX,0016H            ;Attribute
            MOV     DH,ROW              ;Row
            MOV     DL,10               ;Column
            INT     10H
            RET
G10DISPLY   ENDP
;                   Clear screen, set attribute:
;                   ----------------------------
Q10CLEAR    PROC    NEAR                ;Uses AX, BH, CX, DX
            MOV     AX,0600H
            MOV     BH,61H              ;Attribute
            MOV     CX,00               ;Full screen
            MOV     DX,184FH
            INT     10H
            RET
Q10CLEAR    ENDP
            END     A10MAIN
```

Figure 14-6 *Continued*

ADDRESS TABLES

A program may have to test a number of related conditions, each requiring a jump to another routine. Consider, for example, the following program fragment that tests codes 1, 2, 3, 4, and so forth, assumed in a data item named CODE. A conventional way of handling codes is to compare each code successively:

```
CODE    DB    ?            ;Data item for code
        . . .
        CMP   CODE,1       ;Code = 1?
        JE    CODE1_RTNE
        CMP   CODE,2       ;Code = 2?
        JE    CODE2_RTNE
        CMP   CODE,3       ;Code = 3?
        JE    CODE3_RTNE
        . . .
```

With this approach, the opportunity for errors is great because of the need for matching the correct codes and jumping to the correct routine. A more elegant solution involves a table of addresses as shown next:

```
ADDRTBL    DW    CODE1_RTNE      ;Table
           DW    CODE2_RTNE      ; of
           DW    CODE3_RTNE      ; addresss
           DW    CODE4_RTNE      ;
           DW    CODE5_RTNE      ;
           . . .
           MOVZX BX,CODE         ;Code into index register
           DEC   BX              ;Decrement by 1
           SHL   BX,1            ; and double
           JMP   [ADDRTBL+BX]    ;Use table address for jump
           . . .
```

The example moves the code to BX and decrements it by 1. The value is then doubled, so that 0 stays 0, 1 becomes 2, 2 becomes 4, and so forth. The doubled value provides an offset into the table: ADDRTBL+0 is the first address (for code 1), ADDRTBL+2 is the second (for code 2), ADDRTBL+4 is the third, and so forth. The operand of the JMP instruction [ADDRTBL+BX] forms an indirect address based on the start of the table plus an offset into the table. The operation then jumps directly to the appropriate routine.

The example could also use a CALL instruction in place of JMP, where the table addresses are procedure names:

```
CALL  [ADDRTBL+BX]  ;Use table address for call
```

An important constraint in the example is that the codes may be only hex values 1—*max;* any other value may cause dire results, and the program should check for this possibility.

TWO-DIMENSIONAL ARRAYS

A two-dimensional array consists of *y* rows and *x* columns, as the following example of 3 rows and 5 columns shows:

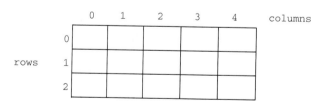

The array is of the form [row, column] and contains $3 \times 5 = 15$ cells, or elements. In memory, each row of data be can considered a one-dimensional array; that is, each row successively follows the other. However, it helps to think of the array as being two-dimensional and could be defined like this:

```
DATA_ARRAY DW 3 DUP(5 DUP(?))
```

Accessing an element in the array, such as [2, 3], that is, row 2, column 3, involves the following steps:

1. Multiply row by number of elements in a column: $2 \times 5 = 10$.

2. Add the column: $10 + 3 = 13$.

In this case, the required element is the 13th (where row and column begin with 0). Note that the elements in the table are words, but addressing is based on byte values, so that it is necessary to double the values for row and column, to 20 and 6, respectively. The 13th element is at the 26th byte and is accessible by base:index addressing in this manner:

```
TITLE        A14SPRED (EXE)   Spreadsheet arithmetic
             .MODEL SMALL
             .STACK 64
             .DATA
SPRD_TBL DW      05, 03, 06, 04, 10, 00    ;Data rows
         DW      04, 05, 01, 09, 06, 00
         DW      06, 02, 00, 10, 11, 00
         DW      10, 07, 03, 05, 02, 00
         DW      00, 00, 00, 00, 00, 00    ;Total row

COUNT    DB      ?
COLS     EQU     12                        ;6 cols x 2 bytes
ROWS     EQU     10                        ;5 rows x 2 bytes
NOCOLS   EQU     06                        ;No. of columns
NOROWS   EQU     05                        ;No. of rows
COLTOT   EQU     NOCOLS*(NOROWS-1)*2       ;6 cols x 4 rows x 2
; ----------------------------------------------------------
.386
             .CODE
A10MAIN  PROC    FAR
         MOV     AX,@data                  ;Initialize
         MOV     DS,AX                     ;  segment
         MOV     ES,AX                     ;  registers
         CALL    B10HORZL                  ;Call horizontal addition
         CALL    C10VERTL                  ;Call vertical addition
;            ...
         MOV     AX,4C00H                  ;End processing
         INT     21H
A10MAIN  ENDP

;                    Add horizontal totals (rows):
;                    ---------------------------
B10HORZL PROC    NEAR
         PUSHA                             ;Preserve registers
         MOV     COUNT,NOROWS-1            ;Count to add row cells
         LEA     DI,SPRD_TBL               ;Initialize table
         LEA     SI,SPRD_TBL               ;  addresses
         ADD     SI,ROWS
B10:
         MOV     CX,NOCOLS-1               ;Count for columns
B20:
         MOV     AX,[DI]                   ;Get amount from cell
         ADD     [SI],AX                   ;Add it to row total
         ADD     DI,02                     ;Next cell in row
         LOOP    B20                       ;Repeat thru all cells in row
         ADD     DI,02                     ;First cell in next row
         ADD     SI,COLS                   ;Next row total
         DEC     COUNT                     ;Repeat thru all rows
         JNZ     B10
         POPA                              ;Restore registers
         RET
B10HORZL ENDP
```

Figure 14-7 Spreadsheet Arithmetic

```
;                       Add vertical totals (columns):
;                       -------------------------------
C10VERTL  PROC    NEAR
          PUSHA                          ;Preserve registers
          MOV     COUNT,NOCOLS-1         ;Count to add column cells
          MOV     BX,00
          LEA     SI,[SPRD_TBL+COLTOT]   ;Initialize column total
C10:
          LEA     DI,SPRD_TBL            ;Initialize top cell
          ADD     DI,BX
          MOV     CX,NOROWS-1            ;Count for rows
C20:
          MOV     AX,[DI]                ;Get amount from cell
          ADD     [SI],AX                ;Add it to column total
          ADD     DI,COLS                ;Next cell in column
          LOOP    C20                    ;Repeat thru all cells in col
          ADD     BX,02                  ;Next cell in row
          ADD     SI,02                  ;Next column total
          DEC     COUNT                  ;Repeat thru all cols
          JNZ     C10
          POPA                           ;Restore registers
          RET
C10VERTL  ENDP
          END     A10MAIN
```

Figure 14-7 *Continued*

```
          MOV  BX,20                 ;Row is base
          MOV  DI,6                  ;Column is index
          ADD  DATA_ARRAY[BX+DI],AX  ;Add to array
```

Rarely, however, does a program know the exact element to address, because row and column values normally result from computations.

Sometimes it is simpler to treat an array as one-dimensional, as in the following example that zeros each element of DATA_ARRAY:

```
          MOV CX,15                  ;Number of elements
          MOV BX,0                   ;Offset of first element
L10:      MOV DATA_ARRAY[BX],0       ;Clear an element
          ADD BX,2                   ;Next word in array
          LOOP L10                   ;Repeat 15 times
```

Spreadsheet Arithmetic

This section covers techniques for performing spreadsheet arithmetic. In simple terms, a spreadsheet is a two-dimensional array consisting of horizontal and vertical cells. Total cells for rows are at the right edge (the last column) and for columns are across the bottom edge (the last row).

The program in Figure 14-7 defines a spreadsheet table and performs horizontal and vertical addition of the cells. For illustration's sake, the table is intentionally small and contains predefined values. The table contains five rows of doublewords, each with six columns. The fifth row and the sixth column are total cells.

The program performs horizontal addition of rows first: Add each cell in a row, from left to right, to the row total. Advance to the next row and repeat the horizontal addition until all the rows are added. Vertical addition follows a similar approach, which you can better understand by examining the instructions and their comments. Horizontal addition can treat each row as one-dimensional, and vertical addition can treat each column as one-dimensional.

KEY POINTS

- For most purposes, a table contains related entries with the same length and data format.
- A table is based on its data format; for example, entries may be character or numeric, typically each the same length.
- If a table is subject to frequent changes, or if several programs reference the table, it could be stored on disk. An updating program can handle changes to the table. Any program can then load the table from disk, and the programs need not be changed.
- Under direct table addressing, the program calculates the address of a table entry and accesses that entry directly.
- When searching a table, a program successively compares a data item against each entry in the table until it finds a match. CMP and CMPSW assume that words contain bytes in reverse sequence.
- The XLAT instruction facilitates translating data from one format to another.

REVIEW QUESTIONS AND EXERCISES

14-1. Distinguish between processing a table by direct addressing and by searching.

14-2. Define a table named ANNUAL_TBL with 365 words, initialized to (a) blanks for character data, (b) zeros for binary data.

14-3. Define three separate related tables that contain the following data: (a) ASCII item numbers 04, 07, 14, 17, and 24, (b) item descriptions of DVDs, receivers, modems, keyboards, and diskettes, (c) item prices 22.20, 95.75, 47.45, 49.35, and 12.95.

14-4. Revise Question 14-3 so that all the data is in the same table. For the first item, define its number and description on the first line and its price on the second line; for the second item, define them on lines three and four, and so forth.

14-5. Revise Figure 14-1 so that it accepts the month from the keyboard in numeric (ASCII) format. If the entry is valid (01-12), locate and display the alphabetic month; otherwise, display an error message. Allow for any number of keyboard entries; end processing when the user replies to the prompt with only <Enter>.

14-6. Code a program that allows a user to enter item numbers and quantities from the keyboard. Use the table defined in Question 14-4 and include a search routine that uses the input item number to locate it in the table. Extract the description and price from the table. Calculate the value (quantity × price) of each sale, and display description and value on the screen. End processing when the user replies to the prompt with only <Enter>.

14-7. Using the description table defined in Question 14-3, write a program that (a) moves the contents of the table to another (empty) table, (b) sorts the contents of this new table into ascending sequence, and (c) displays each description on successive rows of the screen. Provide for scrolling the screen.

14-8. The program fragment in the section "The XLAT Instruction" translates ASCII characters into EBCDIC format. Revise the example to reverse the process—that is, translate EBCDIC data to ASCII format. EBCDIC characters to translate are minus sign (60H), decimal point (4BH), numbers 0–9 (F0H–F9H), and all other characters to ASCII blank. For data, use a string of EBCDIC hex characters containing F0F0F1F24BF5F060 (defined as 0F0H, 0F1H, etc.), which are to be translated to ASCII format and displayed. The hex result should be 303031322E35302D.

14-9. Write a program to provide simple encryption of data. Define an 80-byte data area named CRYPTDATA containing any ASCII data. Arrange a translation table to convert the data somewhat randomly, for example, A to M, B to R, C to X, and so forth. Provide for all 256 possible byte values. Arrange a second translation table that reverses (decrypts) the data. The program should perform the following actions: (a) Display the original contents of CRYPTDATA on a line, (b) encrypt CRYPTDATA and display the encrypted data on a second line, and (c) decrypt CRYPTDATA and display the decrypted data on a third line (which should be identical to the first line).

14-10. Revise the program in Figure 14-7 (two-dimensional table) so that it adds the totals at the right of each row (vertically) and adds the totals at the bottom of each column (horizontally).

Chapter 15

FACILITIES FOR USING THE MOUSE

Objective: To describe the programming requirements for using the mouse.

INTRODUCTION

This chapter describes the use of the mouse: initializing it, displaying and concealing the mouse pointer, setting the pointer's location and limits, and getting button information. Two program examples illustrate the use of mouse handling. The only new instruction introduced is INT 33H for mouse handling.

The mouse is a commonly used pointing device controlled by a software interface known as a device driver that is normally installed by an entry in the CONFIG.SYS or AUTOEXEC.BAT file. The driver must be installed so that a program can recognize and respond to the mouse's actions.

Some basic mouse definitions follow:

- *Pixel:* The smallest addressable element on a screen. For text mode 03, for example, there are eight pixels per byte.
- *Mouse pointer:* In text mode, the pointer is a flashing block in reverse video; in graphics mode, the pointer is an arrowhead.
- *Mickey:* A unit of measure for movement of the mouse, approximately 1/200 of an inch.
- *Mickey count:* The number of mickeys the mouse ball rolls horizontally or vertically. The mouse driver uses the mickey count to move the pointer on the screen a certain number of pixels.
- *Threshold speed:* The speed in mickeys per second that the mouse must move to double the speed of the pointer on the screen. The default is 64 mickeys per second.

All mouse operations within a program are performed by standard INT 33H functions of the form

```
MOV   AX, function        ;Request mouse function
...                       ;Parameters (if any)
INT   33H                 ;Call mouse driver
```

Note that unlike other INT operations that use the AH register, INT 33H functions are loaded in the *full AX register.*

The first mouse instruction that a program issues should be function 00H, which simply initializes the interface between the mouse driver and the program. Typically, you need issue this command just once, at the start of the program. Following function 00H, the program should execute function 01H, which causes the mouse pointer to appear on the screen. After that, you have a choice of a wide range of mouse operations.

The following are the mouse functions available for INT 33H, of which relatively few are commonly used:

00H	Initialize the mouse
01H	Display the mouse pointer
02H	Conceal the mouse pointer
03H	Get button status and pointer location
04H	Set pointer location
05H	Get button-press information
06H	Get button-release information
07H	Set horizontal limits for pointer
08H	Set vertical limits for pointer
09H	Set graphics pointer type
0AH	Set text pointer type
0BH	Read mouse-motion counters
0CH	Install interrupt handler for mouse events
0DH	Turn on light pen emulation
0EH	Turn off light pen emulation
0FH	Set mickey-to-pixel ratio
10H	Set pointer exclusion area
13H	Set double-speed threshold
14H	Swap mouse-event interrupt
15H	Get buffer size for mouse driver state
16H	Save mouse driver state
17H	Restore mouse driver state
18H	Install alternative handler for mouse events
19H	Get address of alternative handler
1AH	Set mouse sensitivity
1BH	Get mouse sensitivity

1CH	Set mouse interrupt rate
1DH	Select display page for pointer
1EH	Get display page for pointer
1FH	Disable mouse driver
20H	Enable mouse driver
21H	Reset mouse driver
22H	Set language for mouse driver messages
23H	Get language number
24H	Get mouse information

BASIC MOUSE OPERATIONS

The following sections describe the basic INT 33H operations required for programs that use a mouse.

Function 00H: Initialize the Mouse. This is the first command that a program issues for handling a mouse and needs to be executed only once. Load AX with function 00H with no other input parameters, and issue INT 33H. The operation returns these values:

- AX = 0000H if no mouse support is available or FFFFH if support is available
- BX = the number of mouse buttons if support is available.

If mouse support is available, the operation initializes the mouse driver as follows:

- Sets the mouse pointer to the center of the screen
- Conceals the mouse pointer if it is visible
- Sets the mouse pointer's display page to zero
- Sets the mouse pointer according to the screen mode: rectangle and inverse color for text or arrow shape for graphics
- Sets the mickey-to-pixel ratio, where horizontal ratio = 8 to 8 and vertical ratio = 16 to 8
- Sets the horizontal and vertical limits for the pointer to their minimum and maximum values
- Sets the double-speed threshold to 64 mickeys per second, which you can change.

Function 01H: Display the Mouse Pointer. This operation, used after function 00H, causes the mouse pointer to be displayed on the screen. The operation requires no input parameters and returns no values.

The mouse driver maintains a *pointer flag* that determines whether or not to display the pointer. It displays the pointer if the flag is 0 and conceals it for any other value. Initially, the value is −1; function 01H increments the flag to 0, thus causing the pointer to be displayed. (See also function 02H.)

Function 02H: Conceal the Mouse Pointer.   The standard practice is to issue this function at the end of a program's execution to cause the pointer to be concealed. The operation requires no input parameters and returns no values.

The pointer flag is displayed when it contains a 0 and is concealed for any other value. This function decrements the flag from 0 to −1 to cause it to be concealed.

Function 03H: Get Button Status and Pointer Location.   This function requires no input parameters and returns this information about the mouse:

- BX = Status of buttons, according to bit location, as follows:
    Bit 0   Left button (0 = up, 1 = pressed down)
    Bit 1   Right button (0 = up, 1 = pressed down)
    Bit 2   Center button (0 = up, 1 = pressed down)
    Bits 3–15   Reserved for internal use
- CX = Horizontal (x) coordinate
- DX = Vertical (y) coordinate

The horizontal and vertical coordinates are expressed in terms of *pixels*, even in text mode (eight per byte for video mode 03). The values are always within the minimum and maximum limits for the pointer.

Function 04H: Set Pointer Location.   This operation sets the horizontal and vertical coordinates for the mouse pointer on the screen (the values for the location are in terms of pixels—eight per byte for video mode 03):

```
MOV  AX,04H         ;Request set mouse pointer
MOV  CX,horizontal  ;Horizontal location
MOV  DX,vertical    ;Vertical location
INT  33H            ;Call mouse driver
```

The operation sets the pointer at the new location, adjusted as necessary if outside the minimum and maximum limits.

PROGAM: DISPLAYING THE MOUSE LOCATION

The program in Figure 15-1 illustrates the basic mouse operations covered to this point. It displays the horizontal and vertical coordinates of the pointer as a user moves, but does not press, the mouse. The main procedures are:

- A10MAIN initializes the program, calls B10INITZ, C10POINTR, D10CONVRT, and E10DISPLY. When the user presses the left button, the program uses function 02H to hide the pointer and ends processing.
- B10INITZ issues INT 33H function 00H to initialize the mouse (or to indicate that no mouse driver is present) and issues function 01H to cause the mouse pointer to display.

```
TITLE       A15MOUSE (EXE)   Handling the mouse
            .MODEL SMALL
            .STACK 64
            .DATA
LEN_DATA    EQU    14                    ;Display length
XCOORD      DW     0                     ;Binary X coordinate
YCOORD      DW     0                     ;Binary Y coordinate
ASCVAL      DW     ?                     ;ASCII field

DISPDATA    LABEL  BYTE                  ;Screen display fields:
XMSG        DB     'X = '                ;X message
XASCII      DW     ?                     ;X ASCII value
            DB     ' '                   ;
YMSG        DB     'Y = '                ;Y message
YASCII      DW     ?                     ;Y ASCII value
.386   ; --------------------------------------------------
            .CODE
A10MAIN     PROC   FAR
            MOV    AX,@data              ;Initialize
            MOV    DS,AX                 ;   DS and ES
            MOV    ES,AX                 ;   addressability
            CALL   Q10CLEAR              ;Clear screen
            CALL   B10INITZ              ;Initialize mouse
            CMP    AX,00                 ;Mouse installed?
            JE     A90                   ;   no, exit
A20:        CALL   C10POINTR             ;Get mouse pointer
            CMP    BX,01                 ;Button pressed?
            JE     A80                   ;   yes, exit
            MOV    AX,XCOORD             ;Convert
            CALL   D10CONVRT             ;   X to ASCII
            MOV    AX,ASCVAL             ;
            MOV    XASCII,AX             ;
            MOV    AX,YCOORD             ;Convert
            CALL   D10CONVRT             ;   Y to ASCII
            MOV    AX,ASCVAL             ;
            MOV    YASCII,AX             ;Display
            CALL   E10DISPLY             ;   X and Y values
            JMP    A20                   ;Repeat
A80:        MOV    AX,02H                ;Request hide pointer
            INT    33H
A90:        CALL   Q10CLEAR              ;Clear screen
            MOV    AX,4C00H              ;End processing
            INT    21H
A10MAIN     ENDP
;                  Initialize mouse pointer:
;                  -------------------------
B10INITZ    PROC   NEAR                  ;Uses AX
            MOV    AX,00H                ;Request initialize
            INT    33H                   ;   mouse
            CMP    AX,00                 ;Mouse installed?
            JE     B90                   ;   no, exit
            MOV    AX,01H                ;Show pointer
            INT    33H
B90:        RET                          ;Return to caller
B10INITZ    ENDP
```

Figure 15-1   Using the Mouse

- C10POINTR issues function 03H to check and to exit if the user has pressed the left button. If not pressed, the program converts the horizontal and vertical coordinates from pixel values to binary numbers (by shifting the values three bits to the right, effectively dividing by 8). If the location is the same as when it was previously checked, the routine repeats issuing function 03H; if the location has changed, control returns to the calling procedure.

```
;                    Get mouse pointer location:
;                    ---------------------------
C10POINTR PROC       NEAR              ;Uses AX, BX, CX, DX
C20:      MOV        AX,03H            ;Get pointer location
          INT        33H
          CMP        BX,00000001B      ;Left button pressed?
          JE         C90               ;  yes, means exit
          SHR        CX,03             ;Divide pixel
          SHR        DX,03             ;  coordinates by 8
          CMP        CX,XCOORD         ;Has pointer location
          JNE        C30               ;  changed?
          CMP        DX,YCOORD         ;
          JE         C20               ;  no, repeat operation
C30:      MOV        XCOORD,CX         ;  yes, save new locations
          MOV        YCOORD,DX         ;
C90:      RET                          ;Return to caller
C10POINTR ENDP
;                    Convert binary X or Y location to ASCII:
;                    ----------------------------------------
                         ;AX set on entry = binary X or Y
D10CONVRT PROC       NEAR              ;Uses CX, SI
          MOV        ASCVAL,2020H      ;Clear ASCII field
          MOV        CX,10             ;Set divide factor
          LEA        SI,ASCVAL+1       ;Load ASCVAL address
          CMP        AX,CX             ;Compare location to 10
          JB         D20               ;  lower, bypass
          DIV        CL                ;  higher, divide by 10
          OR         AH,30H            ;Insert ASCII 3s
          MOV        [SI],AH           ;Store in rightmost byte
          DEC        SI                ;Decr address of ASCVAL
D20:      OR         AL,30H            ;Insert ASCII 3s
          MOV        [SI],AL           ;Store in leftmost byte
          RET                          ;Return to caller
D10CONVRT ENDP
;                    Display X, Y locations:
;                    -----------------------
E10DISPLY PROC       NEAR              ;Uses AX, BX, BP, CX, DX
          MOV        AX,1300H          ;Request display
          MOV        BX,0031H          ;Page:attribute
          LEA        BP,DISPDATA       ;Address of string
          MOV        CX,LEN_DATA       ;No. of characters
          MOV        DX,0020H          ;Screen row:column
          INT        10H
          RET                          ;Return to caller
E10DISPLY ENDP
;                    Clear screen, set attribute:
;                    ----------------------------
Q10CLEAR  PROC       NEAR              ;Uses AX, BH, CX, DX
          MOV        AX,0600H          ;Request clear screen
          MOV        BH,30H            ;Colors
          MOV        CX,00             ;Full
          MOV        DX,184FH          ;  screen
          INT        10H
          RET                          ;Return to caller
Q10CLEAR  ENDP
          END        A10MAIN
```

Figure 15-1 *Continued*

- D10CONVRT converts the binary values for horizontal and vertical screen locations to displayable ASCII characters. Note that with eight pixels per byte, the horizontal value returned at screen column 79 (the rightmost location) is $79 \times 8 = 632$. The procedure divides this horizontal value by 8 to get, in this case, 79, the maximum value. Consequently, the conversion ensures that values returned are within 0 through 79.

- E10DISPLY displays the horizontal and vertical coordinates at the center of the screen as X = *col* and Y = *row*.

One way to improve this program would be to issue function 0CH to set an interrupt handler. In this way, the required instructions are automatically invoked whenever the mouse is active.

MORE ADVANCED MOUSE OPERATIONS

This section covers the remaining mouse operations and the following section provides another program example.

Function 05H: Get Button-Press Information. This function returns information about button presses. Set BX with the button number, where 0 = left, 1 = right, and 2 = center:

```
MOV  AX,05H          ;Request press information
MOV  BX,button-no    ;Button number
INT  33H             ;Call mouse driver
```

The operation returns the up/down status of all buttons and the press count and location of the requested button:

- AX = Status of buttons, according to bit location, as follows:

    Bit 0   Left button (0 = up, 1 = pressed down)

    Bit 1   Right button (0 = up, 1 = pressed down)

    Bit 2   Center button (0 = up, 1 = pressed down)

    Bits 3–15   Reserved for internal use
- BX = Button-press counter
- CX = Horizontal (x) coordinate (pixel value) of last button press
- DX = Vertical (y) coordinate (pixel value) of last button press

The operation resets the button-press counter to 0.

Function 06H: Get Button-Release Information. This function returns information about button releases. Set BX with the button number (0 = left, 1 = right, and 2 = center):

```
MOV  AX,06H          ;Request release information
MOV  BX,button-no    ;Button number
INT  33H             ;Call mouse driver
```

The operation returns the up/down status of all buttons and the release count and location of the requested button, as follows:

- AX = Status of buttons, according to bit location, as follows:

    Bit 0   Left button (0 = up, 1 = pressed down)

    Bit 1   Right button (0 = up, 1 = pressed down)

Bit 2   Center button (0 = up, 1 = pressed down)

Bits 3–15   Reserved for internal use

- BX = Button release counter
- CX = Horizontal (x) coordinate (pixel value) of last button release
- DX = Vertical (y) coordinate (pixel value) of last button release

The operation resets the button release counter to 0.

Function 07H: Set Horizontal Limits for Pointer.   This operation sets the minimum and maximum horizontal limits (pixel values) for the pointer:

```
MOV   AX,07H       ;Request set horizontal limit
MOV   CX,minimum   ;Minimum limit
MOV   DX,maximum   ;Maximum limit
INT   33H          ;Call mouse driver
```

If the minimum value is greater than the maximum, the operation arbitrarily exchanges the values. If the pointer is outside the defined area, the operation moves it inside the area. See also functions 08H and 10H.

Function 08H: Set Vertical Limits for Pointer.   This operation sets minimum and maximum vertical limits (pixel values) for the pointer:

```
MOV   AX,08H       ;Request set vertical limit
MOV   CX,minimum   ;Minimum limit
MOV   DX,maximum   ;Maximum limit
INT   33H          ;Call mouse driver
```

If the minimum value is greater than the maximum, the operation arbitrarily exchanges the values. If the pointer is outside the defined area, the operation moves it inside the area. See also functions 07H and 10H.

Function 0BH: Read Mouse-Motion Counters.   This operation returns the horizontal and vertical mickey count (within the range −32,768 to +32,767) since the last request to the function. Returned values are:

- CX = Horizontal count (a positive value means travel to the right, negative means to the left)
- DX = Vertical count (a positive value means travel downwards, negative means upwards)

Function 0CH: Install Interrupt Handler for Mouse Events.   A program may need to respond automatically when a mouse-related activity (or event) has occurred. The purpose of function 0CH is to provide an *event handler* whereby the mouse software interrupts your program and calls the event handler, which performs its required function and returns to your program's point of execution on completion of the task.

Load CX with an event mask to indicate the actions for which the handler is to respond and ES:DX with the segment:offset address of the interrupt handler routine:

```
MOV   AX,0CH           ;Request interrupt handler
LEA   CX,mask          ;Address of event mask
LEA   DX,handler       ;Address of handler (ES:DX)
INT   33H              ;Call mouse driver
```

Define the event mask with bits set as required:

0 = mouse pointer moved	4	= right button released
1 = left button pressed	5	= center button pressed
2 = left button released	6	= center button released
3 = right button pressed	7–15	= reserved, define as 0

Define the interrupt handler as a FAR procedure. The mouse driver uses a far call to enter the interrupt handler with these registers set:

- AX = The event mask as defined, except that bits are set only if the condition occurred
- BX = Button state (if set, bit 0 means left button down, bit 1 means right button down, and bit 2 means center button down)
- CX = Horizontal (x) coordinate
- DX = Vertical (y) coordinate
- SI = Last vertical mickey count
- DI = Last horizontal mickey count
- DS = Data segment for the mouse driver

On the program's entry into the interrupt handler, push all registers and initialize DS to the address of your data segment. Within the handler, use only *BIOS*, not DOS, interrupts. On exit, pop all registers.

Function 10H: Set Pointer Exclusion Area.   This operation defines a screen area in which the pointer is not displayed:

```
MOV   AX,10H           ;Request set exclusion area
MOV   CX,upleft-x      ;Upper left x-coordinate
MOV   DX,upleft-y      ;Upper left y-coordinate
MOV   SI,lowright-x    ;Lower right x-coordinate
MOV   DI,lowright-y    ;Lower right y-coordinate
INT   33H              ;Call mouse driver
```

To replace the exclusion area, call the function again with different parameters, or reissue function 00H or 01H.

Function 13H: Set Double-Speed Threshold.   This operation sets the threshold speed at which the pointer motion on the screen is doubled. Load DX with the new value (the default is 64 mickeys per second). (See also function 1AH.)

Function 1AH: Set Mouse Sensitivity.   Sensitivity concerns the number of mickeys that the mouse needs to move before the pointer is moved. This function sets the horizontal and vertical mouse motion in terms of the number of mickeys per eight pixels, as well as the threshold speed at which the pointer motion on the screen is doubled (see also functions 0FH, 13H, and 1BH):

```
MOV  AX,1AH          ;Request set mouse sensitivity
MOV  BX,horizontal   ;Horizontal mickeys (default = 8)
MOV  CX,vertical     ;Vertical mickeys (default = 16)
MOV  DX,threshold    ;Threshold speed (default = 64)
INT  33H             ;Call mouse driver
```

Function 1BH: Get Mouse Sensitivity.   This operation returns the horizontal and vertical mouse motion in terms of number of mickeys per eight pixels as well as the threshold speed at which the pointer motion on the screen is doubled. (See function 1AH for the returned registers and values.)

Function 1DH: Select Display Page for Pointer.   The page for video display is set with INT 10H function 05H. For mouse operations, set the page number in BX and issue this function.

Function 1EH: Get Display Page for Pointer.   This operation returns the current video display page in BX.

Function 24H: Get Mouse Information.   This operation returns information about the version and type of mouse that is installed:

BH = Major version number

BL = Minor version number

CH = Mouse type (1 = bus mouse, 2 = serial mouse)

PROGRAM: USING THE MOUSE WITH A MENU

Earlier, the program in Figure 10-2 used the cursor keys for selecting an item from a menu. The program in Figure 15-2 is similar, but now allows the user to move the mouse pointer up and down the menu and to select an entry by pressing the left button. Also, there is now an entry at the bottom of the menu for "Exit Program." The major procedures are the following:

- A10MAIN calls B10INITZ to initialize the mouse, calls C10MENU to display the menu, calls E10DISPLY to highlight the current menu line, calls D10POINTR to respond to mouse actions, and ends processing when the user requests "Exit Program."
- B10INITZ initializes the mouse, displays the pointer, and sets horizontal and vertical limits to the pointer area.
- C10MENU displays the full set of menu selections.
- D10POINTR checks for the left button pressed; if so, calls E10DISPLY to set the old menu line to normal video and the selected line to reverse video.
- E10DISPLY displays menu lines according to given attributes.

```
TITLE     A15SELMU (EXE) Select item from menu
          .MODEL SMALL
          .STACK 64
          .DATA
TOPROW    EQU    08              ;Top row of menu
BOTROW    EQU    16              ;Bottom row of menu
LEFTCOL   EQU    26              ;Left column of menu
LEN_LINE  EQU    19              ;Length of menu line
ATTRIB    DB     ?               ;Screen attribute
COL       DB     00              ;Screen column
ROW       DB     00              ;Screen row
SHADOW    DB     19 DUP(0DBH)    ;Shadow characters
MENU      DB     0C9H, 17 DUP(0CDH), 0BBH
          DB     0BAH, ' Add records    ', 0BAH
          DB     0BAH, ' Delete records ', 0BAH
          DB     0BAH, ' Enter orders   ', 0BAH
          DB     0BAH, ' Print report   ', 0BAH
          DB     0BAH, ' Update accounts ', 0BAH
          DB     0BAH, ' View records   ', 0BAH
          DB     0BAH, ' Exit program   ', 0BAH
          DB     0C8H, 17 DUP(0CDH), 0BCH
PROMPT    DB     'To select an item, press left '
          DB     'button of mouse pointer.'
.386 ;  -----------------------------------------------
          .CODE
A10MAIN   PROC   FAR
          MOV    AX,@data        ;Initialize segment
          MOV    DS,AX           ;  registers
          MOV    ES,AX
          CALL   Q10CLEAR        ;Clear screen
          CALL   B10INITZ        ;Initialize mouse
          CMP    AX,00           ;Mouse installed?
          JE     A90             ;  no, exit
          CALL   C10MENU         ;Display menu
A20:
          MOV    ROW,TOPROW+1    ;Set row to top item
          MOV    ATTRIB,16H      ;Set reverse video
          CALL   E10DISPLY       ;Highlight current menu line
          CALL   D10POINTR       ;Call mouse routine
          CMP    DX,BOTROW-1     ;Exit requested?
          JNE    A20             ;  no, continue
          MOV    AX,02H          ;Hide mouse pointer
          INT    33H
          MOV    AX,0600H        ;Clear
          CALL   Q10CLEAR        ;  screen
A90:      MOV    AX,4C00H        ;End of processing
          INT    21H
A10MAIN   ENDP
;                Initialize mouse pointer, set
;                horizontal and vertical limits:
;                ----------------------------
B10INITZ  PROC   NEAR            ;Uses AX, CX, DX
          MOV    AX,00H          ;Request initialize
          INT    33H             ;  mouse
          CMP    AX,00           ;Mouse installed?
          JE     B90             ;  no, exit
```

Figure 15-2 Selecting from a Menu

```
                    MOV     AX,01H              ;Show pointer
                    INT     33H
                    MOV     AX,04H              ;Set pointer
                    MOV     CX,256
                    MOV     DX,108
                    INT     33H
                    MOV     AX,07H              ;Horizontal limits
                    MOV     CX,LEFTCOL+1        ;  left column
                    MOV     DX,LEFTCOL+17       ;  right column
                    SHL     CX,03               ;Multiply by 8 for
                    SHL     DX,03               ;  pixel value
                    INT     33H
                    MOV     AX,08H              ;Vertical limits
                    MOV     CX,TOPROW+1         ;  top row
                    MOV     DX,BOTROW-1         ;  bottom row
                    SHL     CX,03               ;Divide by 8
                    SHL     DX,03
                    INT     33H
B90:                RET
B10INITZ    ENDP
;                           Display shadow box and full menu:
;                           --------------------------------
C10MENU     PROC    NEAR                ;Uses AX, BP, BX, CX, DX
                    MOV     AX,1301H            ;Request display
                    MOV     BX,0060H            ;Black on brown
                    LEA     BP,SHADOW           ;Address of shadow
                    MOV     CX,LEN_LINE         ;Length of line
                    MOV     DH,TOPROW+1         ;Screen row
                    MOV     DL,LEFTCOL+1        ;  and column
C20:                INT     10H
                    INC     DH                  ;Next row
                    CMP     DH,BOTROW+2         ;All rows displayed?
                    JNE     C20                 ;  no, repeat
                    MOV     ATTRIB,71H          ;Blue on white
                    MOV     AX,1300H            ;Request display
                    MOV     BH,00               ;Page 0
                    MOV     BL,ATTRIB           ;Attribute
                    LEA     BP,MENU             ;Address of menu
                    MOV     CX,LEN_LINE         ;Length of line
                    MOV     DH,TOPROW           ;Screen row,
                    MOV     DL,LEFTCOL          ;  column
C30:                INT     10H
                    ADD     BP,LEN_LINE         ;Next menu line
                    INC     DH                  ;Next row
                    CMP     DH,BOTROW+1         ;All rows displayed?
                    JNE     C30                 ;  no, repeat
                    MOV     AX,1300H            ;Request display
                    MOV     BH,00               ;Page 0
                    MOV     BL,ATTRIB           ;Attribute
                    LEA     BP,PROMPT           ;Prompt line
                    MOV     CX,45               ;Length of prompt
                    MOV     DH,BOTROW+4         ;Screen row,
                    MOV     DL,15               ;  column
                    INT     10H
                    RET
C10MENU     ENDP
```

Figure 15-2   *Continued*

```
;                       If left button pressed, set old menu line to
;                       normal video, new line to reverse video:
;                       -------------------------------------------
D10POINTR PROC     NEAR                    ;Uses AX, BX, DX
D20:      MOV      AX,03H                   ;Get button status
          INT      33H
          CMP      BX,00000001B             ;Left button pressed?
          JNE      D20                      ;  no, repeat
          SHR      DX,03                    ;Divide vertical by 8
          CMP      DX,BOTROW-1              ;Request for exit?
          JE       D90                      ;  yes, exit
          PUSH     DX                       ;  no, save row
          MOV      ATTRIB,71H               ;Blue on white
          CALL     E10DISPLY                ;Set old line to normal video
          POP      DX                       ;Get row
          MOV      ROW,DL
          MOV      ATTRIB,17H               ;White on blue
          CALL     E10DISPLY                ;Set new line to reverse video
          JMP      D20                      ;Repeat
D90:      RET
D10POINTR ENDP
;                       Set menu line to normal or highlight:
;                       -------------------------------------
E10DISPLY PROC     NEAR                    ;Uses AX, BX, BP, CX, DX
          MOVZX    AX,ROW                   ;Row tells which menu line
          SUB      AX,TOPROW
          IMUL     AX,LEN_LINE              ;Multiply by length of line
          LEA      SI,MENU+1                ;  for selected menu line
          ADD      SI,AX
          MOV      AX,1300H                 ;Request display
          MOV      BH,00                    ;Page
          MOV      BL,ATTRIB                ;New attribute
          MOV      BP,SI                    ;Menu line
          MOV      CX,LEN_LINE-2            ;Length of string
          MOV      DH,ROW                   ;Row
          MOV      DL,LEFTCOL+1             ;Column
          INT      10H
          RET
E10DISPLY ENDP
;                       Clear screen, set attribute:
;                       ----------------------------
Q10CLEAR  PROC     NEAR                    ;Uses AX, BH, CX, DX
          MOV      AX,0600H                 ;Request scroll
          MOV      BH,61H                   ;Blue on brown
          MOV      CX,0000                  ;Full screen
          MOV      DX,184FH
          INT      10H
          RET
Q10CLEAR  ENDP
          END      A10MAIN
```

Figure 15-2 *Continued*

KEY POINTS

- In text mode, the mouse pointer is a flashing block in reverse video; in graphics mode, the pointer is an arrowhead.
- Mouse operations use INT 33H with a function code loaded in the full AX.
- The first mouse operation to execute should be INT 33H function 00H, which initializes the mouse driver.

- INT 33H Function 01H is required to display the mouse pointer, 03H to get the button status, 04H to get the pointer location, 05H to get button-press information, and 06H to get button-release information.
- The horizontal and vertical coordinates for the mouse location are in terms of pixels.

REVIEW QUESTIONS AND EXERCISES

15-1. Explain these terms: (a) mickey, (b) mickey count, (c) mouse pointer.

15-2. Provide the INT 33H function for each of the following mouse operations:
- (a) Conceal the mouse pointer
- (b) Get button-press information
- (c) Set pointer location
- (d) Install interrupt handler for mouse events
- (e) Get button-release information
- (f) Read mouse-motion counters

15-3. Explain the purpose of the mouse pointer flag.

15-4. Code the instructions for the following requirements:
- (a) Initialize the mouse
- (b) Display the mouse pointer
- (c) Get mouse information
- (d) Set the mouse pointer on row 22 at the center column
- (e) Get mouse sensitivity
- (f) Get button status and pointer location
- (g) Conceal the mouse pointer.

15-5. Combine the requirements in Question 15-4 into a full program. You can run the program under DEBUG, although at times DEBUG may scroll the pointer off the screen.

15-6. Code instructions for setting the pointer exclusion area to (a) upper left: x = 40, y = 40, (b) lower right: x = 160, y = 80.

Chapter 16

DISK STORAGE I:
ORGANIZATION

Objective: To examine the basic formats for hard disk and diskette storage, the boot record, directory, and file allocation table.

INTRODUCTION

A professional programmer has to be familiar with the technical details of disk organization, particularly for developing utility programs that examine the contents of diskettes, hard disks, and CD-ROMs.

This chapter explains the concepts of tracks, sectors, and cylinders and gives the capacities of some commonly used devices. Also covered is the organization of important data recorded at the beginning of a disk, including the boot record (which helps the system load the operating system from disk into memory), the directory (which contains the name, location, and status of each file on the disk), and the file allocation table (or FAT, which allocates disk space for files).

Where a reference to a disk or diskette is required, this text uses the general term *disk*.

CHARACTERISTICS OF A DISK STORAGE DEVICE

For processing records on disks, you need some familiarity with the terms and characteristics of disk organization. A diskette has two sides (or surfaces), whereas a hard disk contains a number of two-sided disks on a spindle.

Tracks and Sectors

Each side of a diskette or hard disk contains a number of concentric *tracks*, numbered beginning with 00, the outermost track. Each track is formatted into *sectors* of 512 bytes, where the data is stored.

Both diskettes and hard disk devices are run by a *controller* that handles the placement of the read-write heads on the disk surface and the transfer of data between disk and memory. There is a read-write head for each disk surface. For both diskette and hard disk, a request for a read or write operation causes the disk drive controller to move the read-write heads (if necessary) to the required track. The controller then waits for the required sector on the spinning surface to reach the head, at which point the read or write operation takes place. For a read operation, for example, the controller reads each bit from the sector as it passes the read-write head. Figure 16-1 illustrates these features.

A hard disk and a diskette drive differ in two main ways. For hard disk, the read-write head rides just above the disk surface without ever touching it, whereas for diskette, the read-write head actually touches the surface. Also, a hard disk device rotates constantly, whereas a diskette device starts and stops for each read/write operation.

Cylinders

A *cylinder* is a vertical set of all of the tracks with the same number on each surface of a diskette or hard disk. Thus cylinder 0 is the set of all tracks numbered 0 on every side, cylinder 1 is the set of all tracks numbered 1, and so forth. For a diskette, then, cylinder 0 consists of track 0 on side 1 and track 0 on side 2; cylinder 1 consists of track 1 on side 1 and track 1 on side 2; and so forth. Side number and head are the same; for example, disk head 1 accesses the data on side 1.

When writing a file, the controller fills all the tracks on a cylinder and then advances the read-write heads to the next cylinder. For example, the system fills all of diskette cylinder 0 (all the sectors on track 0, sides 1 and 2), and then advances to cylinder 1, side 1.

As seen, a reference to disk sides (heads), tracks, and sectors is by number. Side and track numbers begin with 0, but sectors may be numbered in one of two ways:

1. By *physical sector*, sector numbers on each track begin with 1, so that the first sector on the disk is addressed as cylinder 0, head/side 0, sector 1, the next as cylinder 0, head/side 0, sector 2, and so forth.

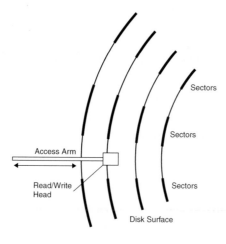

Access Arm

Read/Write Head

Sectors

Sectors

Sectors

Disk Surface

Figure 16-1   Disk Surface and Read/Write Head

2. By *relative sector*, sectors are numbered relative to the start of the disk, so that the first sector on the disk, on cylinder 0, track 0, is addressed as relative sector 0, the next one as relative sector 1, up to the last sector on the disk.

Different disk operations may use one or the other method, depending on how accessing is to be performed.

Disk Controller

The disk controller, which is located between the processor and the disk drive, handles all communication between them. The controller accepts data from the processor and converts the data into a form that is usable by the device. For example, the processor may send a request for data from a specific cylinder-head-sector. The role of the controller is to provide the appropriate commands to move the access arm to the required cylinder, select the read/write head, and accept the data from the sector when the data reaches the read-write head.

While the controller is performing its work, the processor is freed for other tasks. Under this approach, the controller handles only one bit at a time. However, the controller can also perform faster I/O by bypassing the processor entirely and transferring data directly to and from memory. The method of transferring a large block of data in this manner is known as *direct memory access (DMA)*. To this end, the processor provides the controller with the read or write command, the address of the I/O buffer in memory, the number of sectors to transfer, and the numbers of the cylinder, head, and starting sector. With this method, the processor has to wait until the DMA is complete, because only one component at a time can use the memory path.

Two factors govern the data transfer rate, the speed with which the disk drive delivers data to the computer: access time and rotation rate.

1. Access (or seek) time is concerned with the movement required for the read/write heads to reach the required cylinder/track. For sequential processing, the heads move at most one cylinder; for random processing, head movement may involve many cylinders.

2. The rate of rotation determines the time taken for the required sector to reach the head and to transfer the data from the sector to the computer's memory. The *average* time for this operation is, of course, a half revolution, and is known as *latency*. For a rotation rate of 6,000 rpm, the speed per second is 6,000 / 60 = 100 revolutions. A single rotation requires 1/100 seconds, which equals 10 milliseconds. Latency is therefore 5 milliseconds.

Clusters

A *cluster* is a group of sectors that the system treats as a unit of storage space. A cluster size is always a power of 2, such as 1, 2, 4, or 8 sectors. On a diskette device that supports one sector per cluster, sector and cluster are the same. A diskette with two sectors per cluster looks like this:

And a diskette with four sectors per cluster looks like this:

A hard drive may be divided into more than one partition, each identified by a drive number, the first being C. The two types of FAT (file allocation table) on a hard disk, FAT16 and FAT32, determine the size of clusters for a hard disk according to the following rules:

FAT16			FAT32		
Partition	Cluster size	No. of sectors	Partition	Cluster size	No. of sectors
Less than 128MB	2KB	4	260MB – 8GB	4KB	8
128 – 255MB	4KB	8	8MB – 16GB	8KB	16
256 – 511MB	8KB	16	16GB – 32GB	16KB	32
512 – 1,023MB	16KB	32	More than 32GB	32KB	64
1,024 – 2,047MB	32KB	64			

A file begins on a cluster boundary and requires a minimum of one cluster, even if the file occupies only one of the sectors. A 400-byte file (small enough to fit on one sector) stored on disk with 64 sectors per cluster occupies $64 \times 512 = 32,768$ bytes of storage, although only one sector actually contains data. The unused (and for now unusable) disk space is known as slack.

For each file, the FAT stores its clusters in ascending sequence, although a file may be fragmented so that it resides, for example, in clusters 8, 9, 10, 14, 17, and 18. A cluster may also overlap from one track to another.

Disk Capacity.   Here are storage capacities for two types of 3.5″ diskettes:

Capacity	Tracks per Side (Cylinders)	Sectors per Track	Bytes per Sector	Total, Two Sides	Sectors per Cluster
3.5″ 720KB	80	9	512	737,280	2
3.5″ 1.44MB	80	18	512	1,474,560	1

For hard disks, capacities vary considerably by device and by partition. Useful operations for determining the number of cylinders, sectors per track, or read-write heads include INT 21H functions 1FH and 440DH with minor code 60H, both covered in Chapter 18.

THE DISK SYSTEM AREA AND DATA AREA

Certain sectors are reserved for the purpose of supplying information about the files on the disk. The organization of diskettes and hard disks varies according to their capacity. A hard disk and some diskettes are formatted as self-booting—that is, they enable processing to start when the power is turned on or when a user presses the Ctrl+Alt+Del keys. The general organization of a disk consists of a system area, followed by a data area that comprises the rest of the disk.

System Area

The *system area* is the first area of a disk, on the outermost track(s) beginning with side 0, track 0, sector 1. The information that the system stores and maintains in its system area is used to determine, for example, the starting location of each file stored on the disk. The three components of the system area are (1) the boot record, (2) the file allocation table (FAT), and (3) the directory.

The system area and the data area are organized like this:

```
 --------------------------------------------------------------
| Boot   |     |           | System  | User       |
| record | FAT | Directory | files   | files ...  |
 --------------------------------------------------------------
 <-------System area------->|<-----Data area----->
```

The following list gives the organization of 3.5″ diskette devices, showing the starting and ending sector numbers for the boot record, FAT, and directory. Sectors are identified by relative sector number, where relative sector 0 is cylinder 0, track 0, sector 1, the first sector on the device (explained earlier in the section "Cylinders"):

Device	Boot	FAT	Directory	Sectors/Cluster
3.5″ 720KB	0	1-6	7-13	2
3.5″ 1.44MB	0	1-18	19-32	1

For hard disk, the locations of the boot record and the FAT are usually the same as for diskette, whereas the size of the FAT and the location of the directory vary by device.

A formatted diskette contains the following information in terms of beginning physical and relative sectors:

File	720K (9 sectors/track)				1.44MB (18 sectors/track)			
	Cyl.	Side	Sector	Relative Sector	Cyl.	Side	Sector	Relative Sector
Boot record	0	0	1	0	0	0	1	0
FAT1	0	0	2	1	0	0	2	1
FAT2	0	0	4	4	0	0	11	10
Directory	0	0	8	7	0	1	2	19
Data area	0	1	6	1	0	1	16	33

Data files on 720K diskettes begin on cylinder 0, side 1, sectors 6 through 9. The system stores records next on cylinder 1, side 0, then cylinder 1, side 1, then cylinder 2, side 0, and so forth. This feature of filling data on opposite sides (in the same cylinder) before proceeding to the next cylinder reduces the motion of the disk head and is the method used on both diskettes and hard disks.

Data Area

The *data area* for a bootable disk or diskette begins with two system files named IO.SYS and MSDOS.SYS. When you use FORMAT /S to format a disk, DOS copies its system files onto the first sectors of the data area. User files either immediately follow the system files or, if there are no system files, begin at the start of the data area.

The next sections explain the boot record, directory, and FAT.

THE BOOT RECORD

The boot record contains the instructions that load (or "boot") system files (if present) from disk into memory. All formatted disks contain a boot record even if the system files are not stored on it. The boot record contains the following information, in order of offset address:

00H	Jump to bootstrap routine at offset 3EH in the boot record
03H	Name or DOS version number when boot created
0BH	Bytes per sector, usually 200H (512)
0DH	Sectors per cluster (1, 2, 4, or 8)
0EH	Number of reserved sectors
10H	Number of copies of FAT (1 or 2)
11H	Number of root directory entries
13H	Number of disk sectors if volume less than 32MB
15H	Media descriptor byte (same as first byte of FAT, described later)
16H	Number of sectors for FAT
18H	Number of sectors per track
1AH	Number of read-write heads (sides or surfaces)
1CH	Number of hidden sectors
1EH	Reserved by the system
20H	Total number of sectors if volume is greater than 32MB
24H	Physical drive number (for diskette, A = 0; for hard disk, 80H = drive C, etc.)
25H	Reserved by the system
26H	Extended boot sector signature (contains 29H)
27H	Volume ID
2BH	Volume label
36H	Reserved by the system
3EH-1FFH	Bootstrap loader begins here

THE DIRECTORY

All files on a disk begin on a cluster boundary, which is the first sector of the cluster. For each file, the system creates a 32-byte (20H) directory entry that describes the name of the file, the date of creation, its size, and the location of its starting cluster. Directory entries have the following format:

BYTE	PURPOSE
00H-07H	*Filename*, as defined in the program that created the file. The first byte can also indicate the file status:

           00H   File has never been used

           05H   First character of filename is actually E5H

           2EH   File is a subdirectory

           E5H   File has been deleted

BYTE	PURPOSE
08H-0AH	*Filename extension*, such as EXE or ASM
0BH	*File attribute*, defining the type of file (note that a file may have more than one attribute):

           00H   Normal file

           01H   File that can only be read (read-only)

           02H   Hidden file, not displayed by a directory search

           04H   System file, not displayed by a directory search

           08H   Volume label (if this is a volume label record, the label itself is in the filename and extension fields)

           10H   Subdirectory

           20H   Archive file, which indicates whether the file was rewritten since the last update.

                  (For example, code 07H means system file (04H) that is read-only (01H) and hidden (02H).)

BYTE	PURPOSE
0CH-15H	Reserved by the system.
16H-17H	*Time of day* when the file was created or last updated; stored as 16 bits in binary format as hhhhhmmmmmmssssss.
18H-19H	*Date* when the file was created or last updated, stored as 16 bits in binary format as yyyyyyymmmmddddd. Year can be 000–119 (with 1980 as the starting point), month can be 01–12, and day can be 01–31.
1AH-1BH	*Starting cluster* of the file. The number is relative to the last two sectors of the directory. Where there are no system files, the first data file begins at relative cluster 002. The actual side, track, and cluster depend on disk capacity. A zero entry means that the file has no space allocated to it.
1CH-1FH	*Size of the file* in bytes. When a file is written, the system calculates and stores its size in this field.

For numeric fields that exceed one byte in the directory, data is stored with the bytes in reverse sequence.

THE FILE ALLOCATION TABLE

The purpose of the FAT is to allocate disk space for files. The FAT contains an entry for each cluster on the disk. When you create a new file or revise an existing file, the system revises the associated FAT entries according to the location of the file on disk. The FAT begins at sector 2, immediately following the boot record. On a disk where a cluster consists of four sectors, the same number of FAT entries can reference four times as much data as disks where a cluster consists of one sector. Consequently, the use of clusters with multiple sectors reduces the number of entries in the FAT and enables the system to address a larger disk storage space.

The original designers provided for two copies of the FAT (FAT1 and FAT2), presumably because FAT2 could be used if FAT1 became corrupted. However, although FAT2 is still maintained, its use has never been implemented. The earlier section "Disk System Area and Data Area" includes both FAT1 and FAT2 in the FAT storage requirements. All other discussions in this book concern FAT1.

First Entry in the FAT

The first byte of the FAT, the media descriptor, indicates the type of device (similar to byte 15H in the boot record), including the following:

F0H   3.5", two-sided, 18 sectors/track (1.44MB) and 3.5", two-sided, 36 sectors/track (2.88MB)

F8H   Hard disk (including RAM disk)

F9H   3.5", two-sided, nine sectors/track (720KB) and 5.25", two-sided, 15 sectors/track (1.2MB)

Note that F0H and F9H each identify two different disk formats.

Second Entry in the FAT

The second entry contains FFFFH for diskette FATs that support 12-bit FAT entries and FFFFFFH for hard disks that support 16-bit FAT entries. The first two FAT entries look like this:

```
1.44MB diskette   |F0|FF|FF|..|..|..|..|..|...|..|

Hard disk         |F8|FF|FF|FF|..|..|..|..|...|..|
```

As already described, the first field on a disk is the boot record, followed by the FAT and then the directory. The data area is next. The entire picture is as follows:

```
|cluster 0|cluster 1|cluster 2|cluster 3|...|cluster n|
|<---directory area--->|<------------data area------------>|
```

You may expect that the data area would be the starting point for clusters; however, the first two cluster numbers (0 and 1) point to the directory, so the data area for stored data files begins with cluster number 2.

Pointer Entries in the FAT

Following the first two FAT entries are *pointer entries* that relate to every cluster in the data area. The directory (at 1AH-1BH) contains the location of the first cluster for a file, and the FAT contains a chain of pointer entries for each succeeding cluster.

The entry length for diskettes is three hex digits (1 1/2 bytes, or 12 bits), and for hard disk it is four hex digits (two bytes, or 16 bits). Windows also offers 32-bit FAT entries. Each FAT pointer entry indicates the use of a particular cluster according to the following format:

12 BITS	16 BITS	EXPLANATION
000	0000	Referenced cluster is currently unused
nnn	nnnn	Relative number of next cluster for a file
FF0–FF6	FFF0–FFF6	Reserved cluster
FF7	FFF7	Unusable (bad track)
FFF	FFFF	Last cluster of a file

The first two entries for a 1.44MB diskette (a 12-bit FAT) contain F0F and FFn, respectively, and represent clusters 0 and 1:

```
FAT entry:        F0F FF. ... ... ... ... ... ... ...
Relative cluster:  0   1   2   3   4   5   6  ... end
```

F0 at the start indicates a two-sided, nine-sectored (1.44MB) diskette, followed by FFFFH. The term "relative cluster" means, for example, that the third pointer entry in the FAT points to relative cluster 2, the fourth entry points to relative cluster 3, and so forth. In a sense, the first two FAT entries (relative clusters 0 and 1) point to the last two clusters in the directory, which have been assigned as the start of clusters; the directory indicates the size and starting cluster for files.

The directory contains the starting cluster number for each file and a chain of FAT pointer entries that indicate the location of the next cluster, if any, at which the file continues. A pointer entry containing (F)FFFH indicates the last cluster for the file.

Sample FAT Entries. The following examples should help clarify the FAT structure. Suppose a diskette contains only one file, named TEMPSTAT.FIL, that is fully stored on clusters 2, 3, and 4. The directory entry for this file contains the filename TEMPSTAT, the extension FIL, 00H to indicate a normal file, the creation date, 0002H for the location of the first relative cluster of the file, and an entry for the size of the file

in bytes. The 12-bit FAT entry would appear as follows, except that pairs of bytes would
be reversed:

FAT entry: | F0F | FFF | 003 | 004 | FFF | ... | ... | ... | ... |

Relative cluster: 0   1   2   3   4   5   6   ... end

    For a program to read TEMPSTAT.FIL sequentially from diskette into memory, the
system takes the following steps:

- For the first cluster, searches the disk directory for the filename TEMPSTAT and
  extension FIL, extracts from the directory the location of the first relative cluster (2)
  of the file, and delivers its contents (data from the sectors) to the program in main
  memory.
- For the next cluster, accesses the FAT pointer entry that represents relative cluster 2.
  From the diagram, this entry contains 003, meaning that the file continues on relative
  cluster 3. The system delivers the contents of this cluster to the program.
- For the last cluster, accesses the FAT pointer entry that represents relative cluster 3.
  This entry contains 004, meaning that the file continues on relative cluster 4. The system delivers the contents of this cluster to the program.
- The FAT entry for relative cluster 4 contains FFFH to indicate that no more clusters
  are allocated for the file. The system has now delivered all the file's data, from
  clusters 2, 3, and 4.

    We've now seen how FAT entries work in principle; now let's see how they work in
terms of reversed-byte sequence, where a little more ingenuity is required.

Handling 12-Bit FAT Entries

Following is the same example of FAT entries for TEMPSTAT.FIL just covered, but now
with pointer entries in reversed-byte sequence. The 12-bit FAT for this file looks like this:

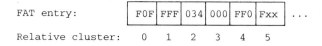

FAT entry: | F0F | FFF | 034 | 000 | FF0 | Fxx | ... |

Relative cluster: 0   1   2   3   4   5

But what's needed now to decipher the entries is to represent them according to *relative byte*
rather than cluster:

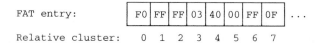

FAT entry: | F0 | FF | FF | 03 | 40 | 00 | FF | 0F | ... |

Relative cluster: 0   1   2   3   4   5   6   7

    Here are the steps used to access the clusters:

- To process the first FAT entry, multiply 2 (the file's first cluster as recorded in the
  directory) by 1.5 (the length of FAT entries) to get 3. (For programming, multiply

by 3 and shift right one bit.) Access the word at bytes 3 and 4 in the FAT. These bytes contain 03 40, which, when reversed, are 4003. Because cluster 2 was an even number, use the last three digits so that 003 is the second cluster for the file.

- For the third cluster, multiply cluster number 3 by 1.5 to get 4. Access FAT bytes 4 and 5. These contain 40 00, which, when reversed, are 0040. Because cluster 3 was an odd number, use the first three digits so that 004 is the third cluster for the file.

- For the fourth cluster, multiply cluster 4 by 1.5 to get 6. Access FAT bytes 6 and 7. These contain FF 0F, which, when reversed, are 0FFF. Because cluster 4 was an even number, use the last three digits, FFF, which mean that this is the last entry.

Handling 16-Bit FAT Entries

As mentioned earlier, the first byte of the FAT for hard disk contains the media descriptor. Following this byte is FFFFFFH, as shown in the chart below. FAT pointer entries are 16 bits long and begin with words 3 and 4, which represent cluster 2. The directory entry provides the starting clusters for files. Determining the cluster number from each FAT entry is simple, although the bytes in each entry are in reverse sequence.

As an example of 16-bit FAT entries, suppose the only file on a particular hard disk occupies four clusters (at four sectors per cluster, or 16 sectors in all). According to the directory, the file starts at cluster 2. Each FAT pointer entry is a full word, so that reversing the bytes involves only the one entry. Here is the FAT, with pointer entries in reversed-byte sequence:

```
FAT entry:           F8FF FFFF 0300 0400 0500 FFFF  ...

Relative cluster:     0    1    2    3    4    5
```

The FAT entry for relative cluster 2, 0300, reverses as 0003 for the next cluster. The FAT entry for relative cluster 3, 0400, reverses as 0004 for the next cluster. Continue with the chain of remaining entries in this fashion through to the entry for cluster number 5. Pointer entry FFFFH indicates end-of-file. FATs with 32-bit entries use doublewords with bytes in reverse sequence.

If a program has to determine the type of disk that is installed, it can check the media descriptor in the boot sector directly or can use INT 21H function 36H.

Exercise: Examining the FAT

Let's use DEBUG to examine the FAT for a diskette. For this exercise, you'll need one formatted blank 3.5″ diskette with 1.44MB capacity, without the system files copied on it. Copy two files onto the disk. The first file should be larger than 512 bytes and smaller than 1,024 bytes, to fit onto two sectors; A04ASM1.ASM is suggested. The second file should be larger than 1,536 bytes and smaller than 2,048 bytes to fit onto four sectors; A09DRVID.ASM is suggested. Because the file is stored beginning at offset 100H, you can locate the records this way:

1. The boot record is at the start, at 100H.

2. The FAT follows the boot sector: 100H + 200H (1 sector, 512 or 200H bytes) = 300H.

3. The directory follows the FAT: 300H + [18 (12H) sectors × 200H] = 2700H.

First insert the diskette in drive A. Load DEBUG and key in the L (load) command (more fully explained in Appendix E):

```
L 100 0 0 30 (for drive B, use L 100 1 0 30)
```

The L command entries are:

- 100H is the starting offset in DEBUG's segment where the data is to be read in.
- The first 0 means use drive A.
- The second 0 means read data beginning with relative sector 0.
- 30 means 30H (48) sectors to read.

To start the display, key in the command D 100. You can now examine the boot record, directory, and FAT for this diskette.

The Boot Record.   Some of the fields on the boot record are:

- Segment offset 103H shows the DOS version when the FAT was created.
- Offset 10BH shows the number of bytes per sector (0002H reverses as 0200H, or 512 bytes).
- Offset 115H is the media descriptor F0H for this diskette. Check out the other fields.

The Directory.   For the directory, key in the command D 2700, where:

- Offset 2700H contains the filename for the first file, A04ASM1.ASM.
- Offset 271AH gives the starting cluster number (0200, or 0002) for this file.
- Offset 271CH-271FH gives the size of the file (27030000, or 327H bytes).
- Offset 2720H begins the entry for the second file, A10DRVID.ASM. Note that 273AH shows its starting cluster as 0400, or 0004. File size is 673H bytes.

The FAT.   For the FAT, key in the command D 300, which should display:

FAT entry:	F0	FF	FF	03	F0	FF	05	60	00	07	F0	FF	. . .
Relative byte:	0	1	2	3	4	5	6	7	8	9	10	11	

- F0 is the media descriptor.
- FF FF at bytes 1 and 2 is the contents of the second field.

The pointer entries beginning at byte 3 can be calculated like this:

- For the first file, multiply 2 (its first cluster according to the directory) by 1.5 to get relative byte 3. Access offset bytes 3 and 4 in the FAT, which contain 03 F0, and reverse the bytes to get F003. Because cluster 2 was an even number, use the last three digits, 003, the next cluster in the series. Cluster 3 × 1.5 is 4; relative bytes 4 and 5 contain F0 FF, which reverse as FFF0. Because cluster 3 was an odd number, use the first three digits, FFF, which indicate the end of the file. You know that the file resides on clusters 2 and 3.

- For the second file, the first cluster is 4:

Cluster	FAT Offsets	FAT value	Cluster	Digits	Next Cluster
4 x 1.5	6 & 7	60 05	even	last	005
5 x 1.5	7 & 8	00 60	odd	first	006
6 x 1.5	9 & 10	F0 07	even	last	007
7 x 1.5	10 & 11	FF F0	odd	first	FFF

FFF indicates the end of the data.

INT 21H provides some supporting services for programs to access information about the directory and the FAT, including function 47H (Get Current Directory), described in Chapter 18.

PROCESSING FILES ON DISK

Data on disk is stored in the form of a *file*, just as you have stored your programs. Although there is no restriction on the kind of data that you may keep in a file, a typical user file would consist of *records* for customers, inventory supplies, or name-and-address lists. Each record contains information about a particular customer or inventory item. Within a file, all records are usually (but not necessarily) the same length and format. A record contains one or more fields that provide information about the record. Records for a customer file, for example, could contain such fields as customer number, name, address, and amount owing. The records could be in ascending sequence by customer number.

Processing for files on hard disk is similar to that for diskette; for both, you have to supply a path name to access files in subdirectories.

A number of special interrupt services support disk input/output. A program that writes (or *creates*) a file first causes the system to generate an entry for it in the directory. When all the file's records have been written, the program *closes* the file so that the system can complete the directory entry for the size of the file.

A program that is to read a file first *opens* the file to ensure that it exists. Once the program has read all the records, it should close the file, making it available to other programs. Because of the directory's design, you may process records in a disk file either sequentially (one record after another, successively) or randomly (records retrieved as requested, throughout the file).

The *highest level* of disk processing is via INT 21H, which supports disk accessing by means of a directory and "blocking" and "unblocking" of records. This method performs

```
MOV   AH,3EH          ;Request close file
MOV   BX,FILHAND1     ;File handle
INT   21H             ;Call interrupt service
JC    error           ;Test for error
```

A successful close operation writes any remaining records still in the memory buffer and updates the FAT and the directory with the date and file size. An unsuccessful operation sets the Carry Flag and returns in AX the only possible error code, 06 (invalid handle).

Program: Creating a Disk File

The program in Figure 17-2 creates a file from names that a user keys in. Its major procedures are the following:

- A10MAIN calls B10CREATE, C10PROC and, if at the end of input, calls E10CLOSE.
- B10CREATE uses INT 21H function 3CH to create the file and saves the handle in a data item named FILEHAND.
- C10PROC accepts input from the keyboard and clears positions from the end of the name to the end of the input area.
- D10WRITE uses INT 21H function 40H to write records.
- E10CLOSE uses INT 21H function 3EH at the end of processing to close the file in order to create a proper directory entry.
- F10DISPLY displays data on the screen.

The input area is 30 bytes, followed by two bytes for the Enter (0DH) and Line Feed (0AH) characters, for 32 bytes in all. The program writes the 32 bytes as a fixed-length record. You could omit the Enter/Line Feed characters, but include them if you want to sort the records in the file, because the SORT program requires these characters to indicate the end of each record.

Note two points. (1) The Enter/Line Feed characters are included after each record only to facilitate the sort, and could otherwise be omitted. (2) Each record could be in variable-length format, only up to the end of the name; this would involve some extra programming, as you'll see later.

READING DISK FILES

This section covers the requirements for opening and reading disk files using file handles. The procedure for reading a disk file is the following:

1. Use an ASCIIZ string to get a file handle from the system;
2. Use INT 21H function 3DH to open the file;
3. Use INT 21H function 3FH to read records from the file; and
4. At the end, use INT 21H function 3EH to close the file.

```
        TITLE     A17CRFIL (EXE)   Create disk file of names
                  .MODEL   SMALL
                  .STACK   64
                  .DATA
NAMEPAR   LABEL    BYTE                  ;Parameter list:
MAXLEN    DB       30                    ;Maximum length
NAMELEN   DB       ?                     ;Actual length
NAMEREC   DB       30 DUP(' '), 0DH, 0AH ;Entered name,
                                         ;  CR/LF for writing
ERRCODE   DB       00                    ;Error indicator
FILEHAND  DW       ?                     ;File handle
PATHNAME  DB       'C:\NAMEFILE.DAT', 0
PROMPT    DB       'Name? '
OPENMSG   DB       '*** Open error  ***'
WRITEMSG  DB       '*** Write error ***'
ROW       DB       0                     ;Screen row
.386  ; -----------------------------------------------
                  .CODE
A10MAIN   PROC     FAR
                  MOV      AX,@data      ;Initialize
                  MOV      DS,AX         ;  segment
                  MOV      ES,AX         ;  registers
                  MOV      AX,0003H      ;Set video mode
                  INT      10H           ;  and clear screen
                  CALL     B10CREATE     ;Create file
                  CMP      ERRCODE,00    ;Create caused error?
                  JNZ      A90           ;  yes, exit
A20:              CALL     C10PROC       ;Get filename
                  CMP      NAMELEN,00    ;End of input?
                  JNE      A20           ;  no, continue
                  CALL     E10CLOSE      ;  yes, close,
A90:              MOV      AX,4C00H      ;End processing
                  INT      21H
A10MAIN   ENDP
;                          Create disk file, test if valid:
;                          -------------------------------
B10CREATE PROC     NEAR                  ;Uses AX, BP, CX, DX
                  MOV      AH,3CH        ;Request create
                  MOV      CX,00         ;Normal file
                  LEA      DX,PATHNAME
                  INT      21H
                  JC       B20           ;Error?
                  MOV      FILEHAND,AX   ;  no, save handle
                  JMP      B90
B20:              LEA      BP,OPENMSG    ;  yes, error,
                  MOV      CX,19         ;    length of message
                  CALL     F10DISPLY
                  MOV      ERRCODE,01    ;Set error code
B90:              RET
B10CREATE ENDP
;                          Accept name from keyboard:
;                          --------------------------
C10PROC   PROC     NEAR                  ;Uses AX, BP, CX, DI, DX
                  MOV      CX,06         ;Length of prompt
                  LEA      BP,PROMPT     ;Display prompt
                  CALL     F10DISPLY
```

Figure 17-2 Creating a Disk File

```
                 MOV       AH,0AH            ;Request input
                 LEA       DX,NAMEPAR        ;Accept name
                 INT       21H
                 CMP       NAMELEN,00        ;Is there a name?
                 JE        C90               ;  no, exit
                 MOV       AL,20H            ;Blank for storing
                 MOVZX     CX,NAMELEN        ;Length
                 LEA       DI,NAMEREC
                 ADD       DI,CX             ;Address + length
                 NEG       CX                ;Calculate
                 MOVZX     DX,MAXLEN         ;  remaining
                 ADD       CX,DX             ;  length
                 REP STOSB                   ;Set to blank
                 CALL      D10WRITE          ;Write disk record
C90:             RET
C10PROC  ENDP
;                          Write disk record, test if valid:
;                          --------------------------------
D10WRITE PROC    NEAR                        ;Uses AH, BP, BX, CX, DX
                 MOV       AH,40H            ;Request write record
                 MOV       BX,FILEHAND
                 MOVZX     CX,MAXLEN         ;30 for name plus
                 ADD       CX,2              ;  2 for CR/LF
                 LEA       DX,NAMEREC
                 INT       21H
                 JNC       D20               ;Valid write?
                 LEA       BP,WRITEMSG       ;  error message,
                 MOV       CX,19             ;  length
                 CALL      F10DISPLY         ;  call error routine
                 MOV       ERRCODE,01        ;Set error code
                 MOV       NAMELEN,00
D20:             RET
D10WRITE ENDP
;                          Close disk file:
;                          ---------------
E10CLOSE PROC    NEAR                        ;Uses AH, BX
                 MOV       NAMEREC,1AH       ;Set EOF mark
                 CALL      D10WRITE          ;  at end of file
                 MOV       AH,3EH            ;Request close
                 MOV       BX,FILEHAND       ;  disk file
                 INT       21H
                 RET
E10CLOSE ENDP
;                          Display data on screen:
;                          ----------------------
F10DISPLY PROC   NEAR                        ;Uses AX, BX, DX
                 MOV       AX,1301H          ;BP and CX set on entry
                 MOV       BX,0016H          ;Page:attribute
                 MOV       DH,ROW            ;Row
                 MOV       DL,00             ;  and column
                 INT       10H
                 INC       ROW               ;Next row
                 RET
F10DISPLY ENDP
                 END       A10MAIN
```

Figure 17-2 *Continued*

INT 21H Function 3DH: Open File

A program that has to read a file first uses INT 21H function 3DH to open it. The operation checks that a file by the given name actually exists and, if so, makes it available to the program. Load DX with the address of the required ASCIIZ string, and AL with an 8-bit access code:

BITS	REQUEST	BITS	REQUEST
0-2	000 = read only	3	1 = reserved
	001 = write only	4-6	Sharing mode
	010 = read/write	7	Inheritance

Before reading a file, a program should use function 3DH to open the file, not function 3CH to create it. The following example opens a file for reading:

```
FILEHAND  DW  ?                      ;File handle
          . . .
          MOV  AH,3DH                ;Request open file
          MOV  AL,00                 ;Access code = read only
          LEA  DX,PATHNM1            ;ASCIIZ string
          INT  21H                   ;Call interrupt service
          JC   error                 ;Special action if error
          MOV  FILEHAND,AX           ;Save file handle
```

If a file with the given name exists, the operation sets the record length to 1 (which you can override), assumes the file's current attribute, sets the file pointer to 0 (the start of the file), clears the Carry Flag, and returns a handle for the file in AX. Use this file handle for all subsequent accesses of the file.

If the file does not exist, the operation sets the Carry Flag and returns an error code in AX: 02, 03, 04, 05, or 12 (see Figure 17-1). Be sure to check the Carry Flag first. For example, creating a file probably delivers handle 05 to AX, which could easily be confused with error code 05, access denied. The program could be modified by scrolling the screen.

INT 21H Function 3FH: Read Record

INT 21H function 3FH is used to read records. Load the file handle in BX, the number of bytes to read in CX, and the address of the input area in DX. The following example uses the file handle from the preceding example to read a 512-byte record:

```
FILEHAND  DW  ?
INAREA    DB  512 DUP(' ')
          . . .
          MOV  AH,3FH                ;Request read record
          MOV  BX,FILEHAND           ;File handle
          MOV  CX,512                ;Record length
          LEA  DX,INAREA             ;Address of input area
```

```
        INT 21H           ;Call interrupt service
        JC error          ;Special action if error
        CMP AX,00         ;Zero bytes read?
        JE endfile        ; yes, end of file
```

A valid operation delivers the record to the program, clears the Carry Flag, and sets AX to the number of bytes actually read. Zero in AX means an attempt to read from the end of the file; this is a warning, not an error. An invalid read sets the Carry Flag and returns to AX error code 05 (access denied) or 06 (invalid handle).

Because the system limits the number of files open at one time, a program that successively reads a number of files should close them as soon as it is through with them.

Program: Reading a Disk File Sequentially

The program in Figure 17-3 reads the file created by the program in Figure 17-2 and sorted by the DOS SORT command. For this example, the command to sort the records from NAMEFILE.DAT into ascending sequence in NAMEFILE.SRT could be

```
        SORT n:<NAMEFILE.DAT >NAMEFILE.SRT
```

(SORT processes from NAMEFILE.DAT to NAMEFILE.SRT.)

Here are the main procedures:

- A10MAIN calls B10OPEN, C10READ, D10DISPLY and, if at the end, closes the file and ends processing.
- B10OPEN uses INT 21H function 3DH to open the file and saves the handle.
- C10READ issues INT 21H function 3FH, which uses the handle to read the records.
- D10DISPLY displays the records and advances the cursor.

RANDOM PROCESSING

The preceding discussion on processing disk files sequentially is adequate for creating a file, for printing its contents, and for making changes to small files. Many applications, however, involve accessing a particular record on a file, such as information from a few customers or inventory parts.

To update a file with new data, a program that is restricted to sequential processing may have to read every record in the file up to the one that is required. For example, to access the 300th record in a file, sequential processing could involve reading through the preceding 299 records before delivering the 300th (although the system could begin at a specific record number).

The solution is to use *random processing,* in which a program can directly access any given record in a file. Although a program creates a file sequentially, it may access the records sequentially or randomly.

When a program first requests a record randomly, the read operation uses the directory to locate the sector in which the record resides, reads the entire sector from disk into a buffer, and delivers the required record to the program.

```
TITLE        A17RDFIL (EXE)   Read disk records sequentially,
;                                             display on the screen
             .MODEL    SMALL
             .STACK    64
             .DATA
RECD_LEN     EQU       32
ENDCODE      DB        00                     ;End process indicator
FILEHAND     DW        ?                      ;File handle
RECAREA      DB        32 DUP(' ')            ;Record area
OPENMSG      DB        '*** Open error ***'
PATHNAME     DB        'C:\NAMEFILE.SRT',0
READMSG      DB        '*** Read error ***'
ROW          DB        00
.386   ;------------------------------------------------------
             .CODE
A10MAIN      PROC      FAR
             MOV       AX,@data               ;Initialize
             MOV       DS,AX                  ;  segment
             MOV       ES,AX                  ;  registers
             MOV       AL,00H                 ;Clear full
             CALL      Q10SCROLL              ;  screen
             CALL      B10OPEN                ;Open file
             CMP       ENDCODE,00             ;Valid open?
             JNZ       A90                    ;  no, exit
A20:
             CALL      C10READ                ;Read disk record
             CMP       ENDCODE,00             ;Normal read?
             JNZ       A80                    ;  no, exit
             LEA       BP,RECAREA             ;  yes, display name
             MOV       CX,RECD_LEN            ;  length
             CALL      D10DISPLY              ;
             JMP       A20                    ;  continue
A80:         MOV       AH,3EH                 ;Request close file
             MOV       BX,FILEHAND            ;
             INT       21H
A90:         MOV       AX,4C00H               ;End processing
             INT       21H
A10MAIN      ENDP
;
;                       Open file, test if valid:
;                       -------------------------
B10OPEN      PROC      NEAR                   ;Uses AX, BP, CX, DX
             MOV       AH,3DH                 ;Request open
             MOV       AL,00                  ;Normal file
             LEA       DX,PATHNAME
             INT       21H
             JC        B20                    ;Error?
             MOV       FILEHAND,AX            ;  no, save handle
             JMP       B90
B20:         LEA       BP,OPENMSG             ;  yes, message
             MOV       CX,18                  ;  length
             CALL      D10DISPLY              ;  error message
             MOV       ENDCODE,01             ;  yes,
B90:         RET
B10OPEN      ENDP
```

Figure 17-3   Reading Records Sequentially

In the next example, records are 128 bytes long and four to a sector. A request for random record number 21 causes the following four records to be read from the sector into the buffer:

record #20	record #21	record #22	record #23

```
;                         Read disk record, test if end of file:
;                         --------------------------------------
C10READ    PROC    NEAR               ;Uses AX, BP, BX, CX, DX
           MOV     AH,3FH             ;Request read
           MOV     BX,FILEHAND
           MOV     CX,RECD_LEN        ;32 for name and CR/LF
           LEA     DX,RECAREA
           INT     21H
           JC      C20                ;Error on read?
           CMP     AX,00              ;End of file?
           JE      C30
           CMP     RECAREA,1AH        ;EOF marker?
           JE      C30                ;  yes, exit
           JMP     C90
C20:       LEA     BP,READMSG         ;  no, message
           MOV     CX,18              ;  length
           CALL    D10DISPLY          ;  error message
C30:       MOV     ENDCODE,01         ;Force end
C90:       RET
C10READ    ENDP
;                         Display routine, test for bottom of screen:
;                         -------------------------------------------
D10DISPLY  PROC    NEAR               ;Uses AX, BX, DX
           MOV     AX,1301H           ;BP and CX set on entry
           MOV     BX,0016H           ;Page:attribute
           MOV     DH,ROW             ;Row
           MOV     DL,10              ;Column
           INT     10H
           CMP     ROW,23             ;Bottom of screen?
           JAE     D80                ;  yes, bypass
           INC     ROW                ;  no, increment row
           JMP     D90
D80:       MOV     AL,01H             ;Scroll
           CALL    Q10SCROLL          ;  one line
D90:       RET
D10DISPLY  ENDP
;                         Scroll screen:
;                         --------------
Q10SCROLL  PROC    NEAR               ;Uses AX, BH, CX, DX
           MOV     AH,06H             ;AL set on entry
           MOV     BH,1EH             ;Set attribute
           MOV     CX,0000
           MOV     DX,184FH           ;Request scroll
           INT     10H
           RET
Q10SCROLL  ENDP
           END     A10MAIN
```

Figure 17-3 *Continued*

When the program requests the next record randomly, such as number 23, the operation first checks the buffer. Because the record is already there, it is transferred directly to the program. If the program requests a record number that is not in the buffer, the operation uses the directory to locate the sector containing the record, reads the entire sector into the buffer, and delivers the record to the program. In this case, requesting random record numbers that are close together in the file results in fewer disk accesses.

INT 21H Function 42H: Move File Pointer

The open operation initializes the file pointer to 0, and subsequent sequential reads and writes increment it for each record processed. You can use function 42H (Move File Pointer) to set the file pointer anywhere within a file and then use other services for random retrieval or updating of records.

To request function 42H, set the file handle in BX and the required offset as bytes in CX:DX. For an offset up to 65,535 bytes, set 0 in CX and the offset value in DX. Also, set a *method code* in AL that tells the operation the point from which to take the offset:

00   Take the offset from the start of the file.

01   Take the offset from the current location of the file pointer, which could be any-where within the file, including at the start.

02   Take the offset from the end-of-file. You can use this method code for adding records to the end-of-file. Or, to determine the file size, clear CX:DX to 0 and then use method code 02.

The following example moves the pointer 1,024 bytes from the start of a file:

```
MOV   AH,42H        ;Relocate pointer
MOV   AL,00         ; from start of file
MOV   BX,HANDLE1    ;Set file handle
MOV   CX,00         ;Upper portion of offset
MOV   DX,1024       ;Lower portion of offset
INT   21H           ;Call interrupt service
JC    error         ;Special action if error
```

A valid operation clears the Carry Flag and delivers the new pointer address in DX:AX. The program may use this address to perform a read or write operation for random processing. An invalid operation sets the Carry Flag and returns in AX code 01 (invalid method code) or 06 (invalid handle).

Program: Reading a Disk File Randomly

The program in Figure 17-4 reads the file created in Figure 17-2. By keying in a relative record number that is within the bounds of the file, a user can request any record in the file to be displayed on the screen. If the file contains 24 records, then valid record numbers are 01 through 24. A number entered from the keyboard is in ASCII format and in this case should be only one or two digits.

The program is organized as follows:

- A10MAIN calls B10OPEN, C10RECNO, D10READ, and E10DISPLY; ends when the user has no more requests.
- B10OPEN opens the file and gets the file handle.
- C10RECNO accepts a record number from the keyboard and checks its length in the parameter list. A detailed description follows this section.
- D10READ uses function 42H and the relative record location from RECINDX to set the file pointer and issues function 3FH to deliver the required record to the program in IOAREA.
- E10DISPLY displays the retrieved record.

For the length of the record number, there are three possible lengths: 00 = end of pro-cessing requested, 01 = one-digit request, stored in AL, and 02 = two-digit request, stored in AX. The procedure has to convert the ASCII number to binary. Because the number is in AX, the AAD instruction handles this problem. For example, assume that the entered num-ber is ASCII 14, and AX now contains 3134:

```
        TITLE      A17RDRAN (EXE)   Read disk records randomly
                   .MODEL  SMALL
                   .STACK  64
                   .DATA
        BOTT_ROW   EQU     22                    ;Bottom of screen
        RECD_LEN   EQU     32                    ;Length of disk record
        FILEHAND   DW      ?                     ;File handle
        RECINDEX   DW      ?                     ;Record index
        ERRCODE    DB      00                    ;Read error indicator
        PROMPT     DB      'Record number? '
        RECAREA    DB      32 DUP(' ')           ;Disk record area
        PATHNAME   DB      'C:\NAMEFILE.SRT',0
        OPENMSG    DB      '*** Open error ***'
        READMSG    DB      '*** Read error ***'
        ROW        DB      00
        COL        DB      10

        RECDPAR    LABEL   BYTE                  ;Input parameter list:
        MAXLEN     DB      3                     ;  maximum length
        ACTLEN     DB      ?                     ;  actual length
        RECDNO     DB      3 DUP(' ')            ;  record number
        .386  ; -------------------------------------------------
                   .CODE
        A10MAIN    PROC    FAR
                   MOV     AX,@data              ;Initialize
                   MOV     DS,AX                 ;  segment
                   MOV     ES,AX                 ;  registers
                   MOV     AL,00H                ;Clear
                   CALL    Q10SCROLL             ;  full screen
                   CALL    B10OPEN               ;Open file
                   CMP     ERRCODE,00            ;Valid open?
                   JNZ     A90                   ;  no, exit
        A20:
                   MOV     COL,10                ;Reset column
                   CALL    C10RECNO              ;Request record #
                   CMP     ACTLEN,00             ;Any more requests?
                   JE      A90                   ;  no, exit
                   CALL    D10READ               ;Read disk record
                   CMP     ERRCODE,00            ;Normal read?
                   JNZ     A90                   ;  no, exit
                   LEA     BP,RECAREA            ;  yes, display name,
                   MOV     CX,RECD_LEN           ;  length
                   CALL    E10DISPLY
                   CMP     ROW,BOTT_ROW          ;Bottom of screen?
                   JAE     A30                   ;  yes, bypass
                   INC     ROW                   ;  no, increment row
                   JMP     A20
        A30:
                   MOV     AL,01H                ;Scroll
                   CALL    Q10SCROLL             ;  one line,
                   JMP     A20                   ;  continue
        A90:       MOV     AX,4C00H              ;End processing
                   INT     21H
        A10MAIN    ENDP
```

Figure 17-4   Reading Disk Records Randomly

- AND converts this value to 0104;
- AAD further converts it to 000E (14);
- DEC deducts 1 (because the system recognizes location 0 as the beginning of a file), giving 000D (13); and
- SHL shifts left five bits, effectively multiplying the number by 32 (the length of records in the file) to get 1A0 (416), which is stored in a field called RECINDX.

An improvement on the program would be for it to validate the input number (01–24).

```
;              Open file, test if valid:
;              -------------------------
B10OPEN  PROC   NEAR                    ;Uses AX, BP, CX, DX
         MOV    AX,3D00H                ;Request open
         LEA    DX,PATHNAME             ;  normal file
         INT    21H
         JC     B20                     ;Error?
         MOV    FILEHAND,AX             ;  no, save handle
         JMP    B90
B20:     MOV    ERRCODE,01              ;  yes,
         LEA    BP,OPENMSG              ;  display message,
         MOV    CX,18                   ;  length
         CALL   E10DISPLY
B90:     RET
B10OPEN  ENDP
;              Get record number from user, check length,
;              convert number to binary, multiply by 32 for index:
;              ----------------------------------------------------
C10RECNO PROC   NEAR                    ;Uses AX, BP, CX, DX
         LEA    BP,PROMPT               ;Display prompt,
         MOV    CX,15                   ;  length
         CALL   E10DISPLY
         MOV    AH,0AH                  ;Request input
         LEA    DX,RECDPAR              ;  of record number
         INT    21H
         CMP    ACTLEN,01               ;Check length 0, 1, 2
         JB     C40                     ;Length = 0, terminate
         JA     C20
         XOR    AH,AH                   ;Length = 1 character
         MOV    AL,RECDNO
         JMP    C30
C20:
         MOV    AH,RECDNO
         MOV    AL,RECDNO+1             ;Length = 2 characters
C30:     AND    AX,0F0FH                ;Clear ASCII 3s
         AAD                            ;Convert to binary
         DEC    AX                      ;Adjust (1st record is 0)
         SHL    AX,05                   ;Multiply by 32
         MOV    RECINDEX,AX             ;Save index
C40:     MOV    COL,30
         RET
C10RECNO ENDP
;              Read disk record randomly based on record index,
;              test if a valid operation:
;              -------------------------------------------------
D10READ  PROC   NEAR                    ;Uses AX, BP, BX, CX, DX
         MOV    AH,42H                  ;Request set file pointer
         MOV    AL,00                   ;  to start of file
         MOV    BX,FILEHAND             ;File handle
         MOV    CX,00                   ;Upper portion of offset
         MOV    DX,RECINDEX             ;Lower portion of offset
         INT    21H
         JC     D20                     ;Error condition?
                                        ;  yes, bypass
```

Figure 17-4 *Continued*

Program: Reading an ASCII File

The preceding examples created files and read them, but you may also want to process
ASCII files created by an editor or word processing program. You need to know the organization of the directory and FAT and the way in which the system stores data in a sector.
The data in an .ASM file, for example, is stored exactly the way you key it in, including the
characters for Tab (09H), Enter (0DH), and Line Feed (0AH). To conserve disk space, the
spaces that appear on the screen immediately preceding a Tab character or spaces on a line

```
              MOV    AH,3FH              ;Request read
              MOV    BX,FILEHAND
              MOV    CX,RECD_LEN         ;32 for name and CR/LF
              LEA    DX,RECAREA
              INT    21H
              JC     D20                 ;Error on read?
              CMP    RECAREA,1AH         ;EOF marker?
              JE     D30                 ;  yes, exit
              JMP    D90
D20:                                     ;  no,
              LEA    BP,READMSG          ;  display message,
              MOV    CX,18               ;  length
              CALL   E10DISPLY
D30:          MOV    ERRCODE,01          ;Force end
D90:          RET
D10READ   ENDP
;
;                     Display routine:
;                     ---------------
E10DISPLY PROC    NEAR                   ;Uses AX, BX, DX
              MOV    AX,1301H            ;BP, CX set on entry
              MOV    BX,0016H            ;Page and attribute
              MOV    DH,ROW              ;Row
              MOV    DL,COL              ;Column
              INT    10H
              RET
E10DISPLY ENDP
;                     Scroll screen, set attribute:
;                     -----------------------------
Q10SCROLL PROC    NEAR                   ;Uses BH, CX, DX
              MOV    AH,06H              ;AL set on entry
              MOV    BH,1EH              ;Set attribute
              MOV    CX,0000
              MOV    DX,184FH            ;Request scroll
              INT    10H
              RET
Q10SCROLL ENDP
              END    A10MAIN
```

Figure 17-4 *Continued*

to the right of an Enter character are not stored. The following illustrates an instruction as entered from a keyboard:

<Tab>MOV<Tab>AH,09<Enter>

The hex representation for this ASCII data is

094D4F560941482C30390D0A

where hex 09 is Tab, 0D is Enter, and 0A is Line Feed. When an editor or word processing program reads the file, the Tab, Enter, and Line Feed characters automatically adjust the cursor on the screen.

Let's now examine the program in Figure 17-5, which reads and displays the file A17RDRAN.ASM (from Figure 17-3), one sector at a time. The program displays each line up to the Enter/Line Feed characters.

- A10MAIN calls B10OPEN, C10READ to read the first sector, and D10XFER, and closes the file at the end.
- B10OPEN opens the file, saves the file handle, and determines the size of the file (based on the low-order portion of the file size in AX).

```
TITLE       A17RDASC (EXE)  Read/display an ASCII file
            .MODEL SMALL
            .STACK 64
            .DATA
DISPAREA    DB      80 DUP(' ')         ;Display area
ENDCODE     DW      00                  ;End process indicator
FILESIZE    DW      0                   ;File size (low-order)
FILEHAND    DW      0                   ;File handle
OPENMSG     DB      '*** Open error ***'
PATHNAME    DB      'C:\A17RDRAN.ASM', 0
ROW         DB      00
SECTOR      DB      512 DUP(' ')        ;Input area
; -------------------------------------------------------------
            .CODE
A10MAIN     PROC    FAR                 ;Main procedure
            MOV     AX,@data            ;Initialize
            MOV     DS,AX               ;  segment
            MOV     ES,AX               ;  registers
            MOV     AX,0003H            ;Set mode and
            INT     10H                 ;  clear screen
            CALL    B10OPEN             ;Open file
            CMP     ENDCODE,00          ;Valid open?
            JNE     A90                 ;  no, exit
            CALL    C10READ             ;Read 1st disk sector
            CMP     ENDCODE,00          ;End-file, no data?
            JE      A90                 ;  yes, exit
            CALL    D10XFER             ;Display/read
A90:
            MOV     AH,3EH              ;Request close file
            MOV     BX,FILEHAND
            INT     21H
            MOV     AX,4C00H            ;End processing
            INT     21H
A10MAIN     ENDP
;                   Open disk file; if valid, calc file size:
;           -----------------------------------------------
B10OPEN     PROC    NEAR                ;Uses AX, BX, CX, DX
            MOV     AX,3D00H            ;Request open, read only
            LEA     DX,PATHNAME
            INT     21H
            JNC     B20                 ;Carry flag set?
            CALL    F10ERROR            ;  yes, error
            JMP     B90
B20:
            MOV     FILEHAND,AX         ;Save handle
            MOV     AX,4202H            ;Set pointer
            MOV     BX,FILEHAND         ;  to end of file
            MOV     CX,0                ;  to determine
            MOV     DX,CX               ;  file size
            INT     21H
            MOV     FILESIZE,AX         ;Save size (low-order)
            MOV     AX,4200H            ;Reset file pointer
            MOV     DX,CX               ;  to start of file
            INT     21H
B90:        RET
B10OPEN     ENDP
```

Figure 17-5   Reading an ASCII File

- C10READ reads a full sector of data into SECTOR.
- D10XFER transfers data from the sector to a display line, calls E10DISPLY to display it, calls C10READ for the next sector, and continues processing until reaching the end of the file. A detailed description of this procedure follows this section.
- E10DISPLY displays the data in the display line up to and including the Line Feed. Because lines in an ASCII file are in variable-length format, you have to scan for the

```
;                        Read disk sector:
;                        -----------------
C10READ   PROC    NEAR                  ;Uses AH, BX, CX, DX
          MOV     AH,3FH                ;Request read
          MOV     BX,FILEHAND           ;Device
          MOV     CX,512                ;Length of sector
          LEA     DX,SECTOR             ;Buffer
          INT     21H
          MOV     ENDCODE,AX            ;Save status
          RET
C10READ   ENDP
;                        Transfer data to display line:
;                        ------------------------------
D10XFER   PROC    NEAR                  ;Uses AL, DI, DX, SI
          CLD                           ;Set left-to-right
          LEA     SI,SECTOR
D20:      LEA     DI,DISPAREA
D30:      LEA     DX,SECTOR+512
          CMP     SI,DX                 ;End of sector?
          JNE     D40                   ;  no,  bypass
          CALL    C10READ               ;  yes, read next
          CMP     ENDCODE,00            ;End of file?
          JE      D80                   ;  yes, exit
          LEA     SI,SECTOR
D40:
          LEA     DX,DISPAREA+80
          CMP     DI,DX                 ;End of DISPAREA?
          JB      D50                   ;  no, bypass
          CALL    E10DISPLY             ;  yes, display
          LEA     DI,DISPAREA
D50:
          LODSB                         ;[SI] to AL, INC SI
          STOSB                         ;AL to [DI], INC DI
          DEC     FILESIZE              ;All chars processed?
          JZ      D80                   ;  yes, exit
          CMP     AL,0AH                ;Line feed?
          JNE     D30                   ;  no,  loop
          CALL    E10DISPLY             ;  yes, display
          JMP     D20
D80:      CALL    E10DISPLY             ;Display last line
D90:      RET
D10XFER   ENDP
;                        Display line, test for bottom of screen:
;                        ----------------------------------------
E10DISPLY PROC    NEAR                  ;Uses AX, BP, BX, CX, DX
          MOV     AX,1301H              ;Request display
          MOV     BX,0061H              ;Page and attribute
          LEA     BP,DISPAREA
          LEA     CX,DISPAREA           ;Calculate
          NEG     CX                    ;  length of
          ADD     CX,DI                 ;  line
          MOV     DH,ROW
          MOV     DL,10
          INT     10H
          CMP     ROW,24                ;Bottom of screen?
          JAE     E20                   ;  no, exit
```

Figure 17-5 *Continued*

end of each line before displaying it. (The screen operation, INT 10H function 13H, does not act on Tab characters, but displays them as a circle.)

- F10ERROR displays a message for a disk error.

The procedure E10DISPLY transfers one byte at a time from SECTOR to DISPAREA, where the characters are to be displayed. It has to check for end of a sector (to

```
                INC   ROW                ;Next row
                JMP   E90
        E20:    MOV   ROW,00
                MOV   AH,10H             ;Wait for keyboard
                INT   16H                ;  entry
                MOV   AX,0003H           ;Set mode and
                INT   10H                ;  clear screen
        E90:    RET
        E10DISPLY ENDP
        ;             Display disk error message:
        ;             --------------------------
        F10ERROR PROC  NEAR              ;Uses AX, BP, BX, CX, DX
                MOV   AX,1301H           ;Request display
                MOV   BX,0031H           ;Page and attribute
                LEA   BP,OPENMSG
                MOV   CX,18              ;Length
                MOV   DX,1020H           ;Row : column
                INT   10H
                MOV   ENDCODE,01         ;Error indicator
                RET
        F10ERROR ENDP
                END   A10MAIN
```

Figure 17-5 *Continued*

read another sector) and end of the display area. For conventional ASCII files, such as .ASM files, each line is relatively short and is sure to end with Enter/Line Feed. Non-ASCII files, such as .EXE and .OBJ files, do not have lines, so the program has to check for the end of DISPAREA to avoid moving data into the area that follows. The program is intended to display only ASCII files, but the test for the end of DISPAREA is insurance against unexpected file types. These are the steps:

1. Initialize the addresses of SECTOR and DISPAREA.
2. If at the end of SECTOR, read the next sector. If at the end-of-file, exit; otherwise initialize the address of SECTOR.
3. If at the end of DISPAREA, display the line and initialize DISPAREA.
4. Get a character from SECTOR and store it in DISPAREA.
5. If all the characters have been processed, exit.
6. If the character is Line Feed (0AH), display the line and go to step 2; otherwise go to step 3.

Try running this program under DEBUG with an appropriate drive number and ASCII file. After each disk input, display the contents of the input area and see how your records are formatted. Enhancements to this program would be to prompt a user to key in the filename and extension and to use the DX:AX pair for the file size.

KEY POINTS

• Many of the INT 21H disk services reference an ASCIIZ string that consists of a directory path followed by a byte of hex zeros.
• On errors, many of the disk functions set the Carry Flag and return an error code in AX.

- The system maintains a file pointer for each file that a program is processing. The create and open operations set the value of the file pointer to 0, the file's starting location. Read and write operations cause the pointer to advance.
- INT 21H function 3CH is used to create a file prior to writing a record, and function 3DH opens the file prior to reading it. Both operations return a file handle that the program uses for subsequent file accessing.
- A program that has completed writing a file should close it so that the system may update the directory.
- INT 21H function 42H (Move File Pointer) is used for random retrieval and updating of disk records.

REVIEW QUESTIONS AND EXERCISES

17-1. What are the error return codes for (a) access denied, (b) file not found, (c) write-protected disk, (d) invalid function number?

17-2. Define an ASCIIZ string named ASCSTRING for a file named MONITOR.FIL on drive C.

17-3. For the file in Question 17-2, write the instructions to (a) create the file as normal and save the handle if valid, (b) use the handle and a 100-byte record to write the file, (c) close the file.

17-4. Revise the program in Figure 17-5 so that a user at a keyboard can key in a filename, which the program uses to locate the file and to display its contents. Provide for any number of requests and for pressing only <Enter> to cause processing to end.

17-5. Write a program that allows a user to key in part numbers (three characters), part descriptions (12 characters), and unit prices (xxx.xx). The program is to create a disk file of records containing this information. Remember to convert the price from ASCII to binary. Following is sample input data:

Part Description	Price	Part Description	Price
|023|Assemblers	|00525|	|122|Lifters	|12320|
|024|Linkages	|00630|	|124|Processors	|12535|
|027|Compilers	|00725|	|127|Labelers	|01560|
|049|Compressors	|01020|	|232|Bailers	|07345|
|114|Extractors	|11750|	|237|Grinders	|09760|
|117|Haulers	|01530|	|999|	|00000|

17-6. Write a program that displays the contents of the file created in Question 17-5. It will have to convert the binary value for the price to ASCII format.

17-7. Using the file created in Question 17-5, write a program for the following requirements: (a) Read all the records into a table in memory, (b) request a user to key in part number and quantity, (c) search the table for part number, (d) if the part number is found, use the table price to calculate the value of the part (quantity x price), (e) display description and calculated value. Allow any number of keyboard requests.

17-8. A file consists of 100 records each 256 bytes long. Write the instructions to set the file pointer to (a) the start of the file, (b) the 20th record, (c) the end of the file.

17-9. Code the instructions for a program to determine the size of a file.

17-10. Revise the program in Question 17-6 so that it does random disk processing. Define a table of the valid part numbers with an offset value. Request a user to key in a part number, which the program locates in the table. Use the offset in the table to calculate the offset in the file, and use INT 21H function 42H to set the file pointer. Display description and price. Request the user to enter quantity sold; then calculate and display amount of sale (quantity × price).

Chapter 18

DISK STORAGE III: INT 21H FUNCTIONS FOR SUPPORTING DISKS AND FILES

Objective: To examine the various INT 21H operations involved in supporting the use of disk drives and files.

INTRODUCTION

This chapter introduces a number of useful operations organized into three sections: those involved with handling disk drives, those involved with handling the directory and the FAT, and those involved with handling disk files. Within each section, functions are described in order of function code.

OPERATIONS HANDLING DISK DRIVES

0DH: Reset disk drive

0EH: Select default drive

19H: Get default drive

1FH: Get default drive parameter block (DPB)

2EH: Set/reset disk verify

32H: Get drive parameter block (DPB)

36H: Get free disk space

4400H: Get device information

4401H: Set device information

4404H: Read control data from drive

4405H: Write control data to drive

4406H: Check input status

4407H: Check output status

4408H: Determine if removable media for device

440DH minor code 41H: Write disk sector

440DH minor code 61H: Read disk sector

440DH minor code 42H: Format track

440DH minor code 46H: Set media ID

440DH minor code 60H: Get device parameters

440DH minor code 66H: Get media ID

440DH minor code 68H: Sense media type

54H: Get verify state

59H: Get extended error

OPERATIONS HANDLING DISK FILES

1AH: Set disk transfer address

29H: Parse filename

41H: Delete file

43H: Get/set file attribute

45H, 46H: Duplicate file handle

4EH, 4FH: Find matching file

56H: Rename file

57H: Get/set file date/time

5AH, 5BH: Create temporary/new file

OPERATIONS HANDLING THE DIRECTORY AND FAT

39H: Create subdirectory

3AH: Remove subdirectory

3BH: Change current directory

47H: Get current directory

Error codes cited in this chapter refer to the list in Figure 17-1.

OPERATIONS HANDLING DISK DRIVES

INT 21H Function 0DH: Reset Disk Drive

Normally, closing a file causes the operation to write all remaining records and update the directory. Under special circumstances, such as between program steps or on an error condition, a program may use function 0DH to reset a disk drive:

```
MOV  AH,0DH  ;Request reset disk
INT  21H     ;Call interrupt service
```

The operation flushes all file buffers and resets the read/write heads to cylinder 0; it does not automatically close the files and it returns no values.

INT 21H Function 0EH: Select Default Disk Drive

The main purpose of function 0EH is to select a drive as the current default. To use it, set the drive number in DL, where 0 = drive A, 1 = B, and so forth:

```
MOV   AH,0EH   ;Request set default
MOV   DL,02    ; drive C
INT   21H      ;Call interrupt service
```

The operation delivers the number of drives (all types, including RAM disks) to AL. Because even the most minimal system requires at least two logical drives A and B, it returns the value 02 for a one-drive system. (Use INT 11H for determining the actual number of drives.)

INT 21H Function 19H: Get Default Disk Drive

This function determines the default disk drive:

```
MOV   AH,19H   ;Request default drive
INT   21H      ;Call interrupt service
```

The operation returns a drive number in AL, where 0 = A, 1 = B, and so forth. You could move this number directly into your program for accessing a file from the default drive, although some disk operations assume that 1 = drive A and 2 = drive B.

INT 21H Function 1FH: Get Default Drive Parameter Block (DPB)

The drive parameter block (DPB) is a data area containing the following low-level information about the data structure of the drive:

OFFSET	SIZE	CONTENTS
00H	Byte	Drive number (0 = A, etc.)
01H	Byte	Logical unit for driver
02H	Word	Sector size in bytes
04H	Byte	Sectors per cluster minus 1
05H	Byte	Sectors per cluster (power of 2)
06H	Word	First relative sector of the FAT
08H	Byte	Number of copies of the FAT
09H	Word	Number of root directory entries
0BH	Word	First relative sector of first cluster
0DH	Word	Highest cluster number plus 1
0FH	Word	Sectors occupied by each FAT
11H	Word	First relative sector of the directory
13H	Dword	Address of device driver
17H	Byte	Media descriptor
18H	Byte	Access flag (0 if disk was accessed)
19H	Dword	Pointer to next parameter block
1DH	Word	Last allocated cluster
1FH	Word	Number of free clusters

A valid operation clears AL and returns an address in DS:BX that points to the DPB for the default drive. For an error, AL is set to FFH. PUSH the DS register before issuing this function, and POP it after using DS to access the DPB. See also function 32H.

INT 21H Function 2EH: Set/Reset Disk Write Verification

This function allows a program to verify disk write operations, that is, whether the data was properly written. The operation sets a switch that tells the system to verify the disk controller's cyclical redundancy check (CRC, a form of parity checking). Loading 00 in AL sets verify off and 01 sets verify on. The switch stays set until another operation changes it. Here is an example:

```
MOV  AH,2EH  ;Request verify (or MOV AX,2E01H)
MOV  AL,01   ;Set verify on
INT  21H     ;Call interrupt service
```

The operation does not return any value. The system subsequently responds to invalid write operations. Because a disk drive rarely records data incorrectly and the verification causes some delay, the operation is most useful where recorded data is especially critical. A related function, 54H, returns the current setting of the verify switch.

INT 21H Function 32H: Get Drive Parameter Block (DPB)

To get the DPB, load the drive number in DX (where 0 = default, 1 = A, etc.). (See function 1FH; other than requesting a specific drive, this function is identical.)

INT 21H Function 36H: Get Information on Free Disk Space

This function delivers information about the space on a disk device. Load the drive number (0 = default, 1 = A, 2 = B, etc.) in DL:

```
MOV  AH,36H  ;Request free disk space
MOV  DL,0    ;  for default drive
INT  21H     ;Call interrupt service
```

A successful operation returns the following: AX = number of sectors per cluster; BX = number of available clusters; CX = number of bytes per sector; DX = total number of clusters on the disk partition. The product of AX, CX, and DX gives the capacity of the partition. For an invalid device number, the operation returns FFFFH in AX. The operation does not set or clear the Carry Flag.

INT 21H Function 44H: I/O Control for Devices

This elaborate service, IOCTL, communicates information between a program and an open device. To use it, load a subfunction value in AL to request one of a number of actions. A valid operation clears the Carry Flag. An error, such as invalid file handle, sets the CF and returns a standard error code to AX. The major IOCTL subfunctions follow.

INT 21H Function 4400H: Get Device Information. This operation returns information about a file or device:

```
MOV  AX,4400H   ;Request device information
MOV  BX,handle  ;Handle of file or device
INT  21H        ;Call interrupt service
```

A valid operation clears the Carry Flag and returns a value in DX, where bit 7 = 0 means that the handle indicates file, and bit 7 = 1 means device. The other bits have this meaning for file or device:

FILE (BIT 7 = 0):

0–5   Drive number (0 = A, 1 = B, etc.)

6   1 = file not written to

DEVICE (BIT 7 = 1):

0	Standard console input	4	Special device
1	Standard console output	5	0 = ASCII mode, 1 = binary mode
2	Null device	6	For input, 0 = end file returned
3	Clock device		

An error sets the Carry Flag and returns code 01, 05, or 06 in AX.

INT 21H Function 4401H: Set Device Information. This operation sets device information, as shown for function 4400H. To use it, load the file handle in BX and the bit setup in DL for bits 0-7. An error sets the Carry Flag and returns code 01, 05, 06, or 0DH in AX.

INT 21H Function 4404H: Read Control Data from Drive. This operation reads control data from a block-device driver (disk drive). To use it, load the drive (0 = default, 1 = A, etc.) in the BL, the number of bytes to read in CX, and the address of the data area in DX. A successful operation returns to AX the number of bytes transferred. An error sets the Carry Flag and returns code 01, 05, or 0DH in AX.

INT 21H Function 4405H: Write Control Data to Drive. This operation writes control data to a block-device driver. The setup is otherwise the same as for function 4404H.

INT 21H Function 4406H: Check Input Status. This service checks whether a file or device is ready for input. Load the handle in BX. A valid operation returns one of the following codes in AL:

Device: 00H = not ready or FFH = ready

File: 00H = EOF reached or FFH = EOF not reached

An error sets the Carry Flag and returns code 01, 05, or 06 in AX.

INT 21H Function 4407H: Check Output Status. This service determines whether a file or device is ready for output. A valid operation returns one of the following codes in AL:

Device: 00H = not ready or FFH = ready

File: 00H = ready or FFH = ready

An error sets the Carry Flag and returns code 01, 05, or 06 in AX.

INT 21H Function 4408H: Determine if Removable Media for Device. This service determines whether the device contains removable media, such as diskette. To use it, load BL with the drive number (0 = default, 1 = A, etc.). A valid operation clears the Carry Flag and returns one of the following codes in AX: 00H = removable device or 01H = fixed device. An error sets the CF and returns code 01 or 0FH (invalid drive number) in AX.

INT 21H Function 440DH, Minor Code 41H: Write Disk Sector. This operation writes data from a buffer to one or more sectors on disk. To use it, load these registers:

```
MOV   AX,440DH      ;Request write disk sector
MOV   BX,drive      ;Drive (0 = default, 1 = A, etc.)
MOV   CH,08H        ;Device category = 08H
MOV   CL,41H        ;Minor code = write track
LEA   DX,devblock   ;Address of device block
INT   21H           ;Call interrupt service
```

The address returned in DX points to a device block with the following format:

```
devblock  LABEL BYTE          ;Device block:
specfunc  DB    0             ; Special functions (zero)
rwhead    DW    head          ; Read/write head
rwcyl     DW    cylinder      ; Cylinder
rwsect1   DW    sector        ; Starting sector
rwsects   DW    number        ; Number of sectors
rwbuffer  DW    buffer        ; Offset address of buffer
          DW    SEG _DATA     ; Address of data segment
```

The entry *rwbuffer* provides the address of the buffer in segment:offset (DS:DX) format, stored in reverse-word sequence. The SEG operator indicates the definition of a segment, in this case the data segment, _DATA. The buffer identifies the data area to be written and should be the length of the number of sectors × 512, such as

```
WRBUFFER DB 1024 DUP (?)  ;Output buffer (2 sectors x 512)
```

A successful operation clears the Carry Flag and writes the data. Otherwise, the operation sets the CF and returns error code 01, 02, or 05 in AX.

INT 21H Function 440DH, Minor Code 42H: Format Track. To use this function to format tracks, set these registers:

```
MOV   AX,440DH   ;Request format track
MOV   BX,drive   ;Drive (0 = default, 1 = A, etc.)
MOV   CH,08      ;Device category (08)
MOV   CL,42H     ;Minor code = format track
LEA   DX,block   ;Address of block (DS:DX)
INT   21H        ;Call interrupt service
```

The address returned in DX points to a block with the following format:

```
blockname LABEL BYTE   ;Disk information block:
specfun   DB    0      ;  Special function, code 0
diskhead  DW    ?      ;  Disk head
cylinder  DW    ?      ;  Cylinder
tracks    DW    ?      ;  Number of tracks
```

A successful operation clears the Carry Flag and formats the tracks. Otherwise, the operation sets the CF and returns error code 01, 02, or 05 in AX.

INT 21H Function 440DH, Minor Code 46H: Set Media ID. For using this function to set the media ID, set these registers:

```
MOV   AX,440DH   ;Request set media ID
MOV   BX,drive   ;Drive (0 = default, 1 = A, etc.)
MOV   CH,08      ;Device category (08)
MOV   CL,46H     ;Minor code = set media ID
LEA   DX,block   ;Address of block (DS:DX)
INT   21H        ;Call interrupt service
```

The address returned in DX points to a media block with the following format:

```
blockname LABEL BYTE       ;Media block:
infolevel DW    0          ;  information level = 0
serialno  DD    ??         ;  serial number
vol_label DB    11 DUP (?) ;  volume label
filetype  DB    8 DUP (?)  ;  type of FAT
```

The entry *filetype* contains the ASCII value FAT12 or FAT16, with trailing blanks. A successful operation clears the Carry Flag and sets the ID. Otherwise, the operation sets the CF and returns error code 01, 02, or 05 in AX. (See also function 440DH, minor code 66H.)

INT 21H Function 440DH, Minor Code 60H: Get Device Parameters. For using this function to get device parameters, set these registers:

```
MOV   AX,440DH   ;Request get device parameters
MOV   BX,drive   ;Drive (0 = default, 1 = A, etc.)
MOV   CH,08      ;Device category (08)
MOV   CL,60H     ;Minor code = get parameters
LEA   DX,block   ;Address of block (DS:DX)
INT   21H        ;Call interrupt service
```

The address returned in DX points to a device parameter block (DPB) with the following format:

```
specfunct  DB  ?   ;Special functions (0 or 1)
devicetype DB  ?   ;Device type
devattrib  DW  ?   ;Device attribute
cylinders  DW  ?   ;Number of cylinders
mediatype  DB  ?   ;Media type
bytesects  DW  ?   ;Bytes per sector
seccluster DB  ?   ;Sectors per cluster
ressectors DW  ?   ;Number of reserved sectors
fats       DB  ?   ;Number of FATs
rootentry  DW  ?   ;Number of root directory entries
sectors    DW  ?   ;Total number of sectors
mediadescs DB  ?   ;Media descriptor
fatsectors DW  ?   ;Number of sectors per FAT
sectrack   DW  ?   ;Sectors per track
heads      DW  ?   ;Number of heads
hiddensect DD  ?   ;Number of hidden sectors
exsects    DD  ?   ;Number of sectors if sectors field = 0
```

If the field named *specfunct* is 0, the information is about the default medium in the drive; if 1, the information is about the current medium. A successful operation clears the Carry Flag and delivers the data. Otherwise, the operation sets the CF and returns error code 01, 02, or 05 in AX.

INT 21H Function 440DH, Minor Code 61H: Read Disk Sector.   This operation reads data from one or more sectors on disk to a buffer. Set CL with minor code 61H; otherwise, technical details for the operation are identical to those for minor code 41H, which writes sectors. Figure 18-1, covered later, illustrates the function.

INT 21H Function 440DH, Minor Code 66H: Get Media ID.   This function is used to get the media ID:

```
MOV  AX,440DH  ;Request media ID
MOV  BX,drive  ;Drive (0 = default, 1 = A, etc.)
MOV  CH,08     ;Device category (08)
MOV  CL,66H    ;Minor code = get media ID
LEA  DX,block  ;Address of block (DS:DX)
INT  21H       ;Call interrupt service
```

The address returned in DX points to a media block:

```
blockname LABEL BYTE       ;Media block:
infolevel DW  0            ;  information level = 0
serialno  DD  ?            ;  serial number
vol_label DB  11 DUP (?) ;  volume label
filetype  DB  8 DUP (?)  ;  type of FAT
```

A successful operation clears the Carry Flag and sets the ID. The field *filetyp* contains the ASCII value FAT12 or FAT16, with trailing blanks. Otherwise, the operation sets the CF and returns error code 01, 02, or 05 in AX. (See also function 440DH, minor code 46H.)

INT 21H Function 440DH, Minor Code 68H: Sense Media Type.   To use this
function to request the media type, set these registers:

```
MOV  AX,440DH  ;Request media type
MOV  BX,drive  ;Drive (0 = default, 1 = A, etc.)
MOV  CH,08     ;Device category (08)
MOV  CL,68H    ;Minor code = get media type
LEA  DX,block  ;Address of block (DS:DX)
INT  21H       ;Call interrupt service
```

The address returned in DX points to a 2-byte media block to receive data:

```
defaultval  DB ?  ;01 for default value, 02 for other
mediatype   DB ?  ;02 = 720K, 07 = 1.44MB, 09 = 2.88MB
```

A successful operation clears the Carry Flag and sets the type. Otherwise, the operation sets
the CF and returns error code 01 or 05 in AX.

Other IOCTL operations for function 44H, not covered here, are concerned with file
sharing.

INT 21H Function 54H: Get Verify State

This service determines the status of the disk write-verify flag. (See function 2EH for setting the switch.) The operation returns 00H to AL for verify off or 01H for verify on. There
is no error condition.

INT 21H Function 59H: Get Extended Error

This operation provides additional information about errors after execution of INT 21H
services that set the Carry Flag and INT 24H error handlers. The operation returns the following:

```
AX = Extended error code    BL = Suggested action
BH = Error class            CH = Location
```

Also, the operation clears the Carry Flag and destroys the contents of CL, DI, DS, DX, ES,
and SI. PUSH all required registers prior to this interrupt, and POP them afterward. The following sections explain the errors:

AX = Extended Error Code. Provides some 90 or more error codes; 00 means that
the previous INT 21H operation caused no error.

BH = Error Class. Provides the following information:

01   Out of resource, such as storage channel

02   Temporary situation (not an error), such as a locked file condition that should
go away

03   Lack of proper authorization

04   System software error, not this program

05   Hardware failure

06   Serious system error, not this program

07 Error in this program, such as inconsistent request
08 Requested item not found
09 Improper file or disk format
0A File or item is locked
0B Disk error, such as CRC error or wrong disk
0C File or item already exists
0D Unknown error class

BL = Action. Provides information on the action to take:

01 Retry a few times; may have to ask user to terminate.
02 Pause first and retry a few times.
03 Ask user to reenter proper request.
04 Close files and terminate the program.
05 Terminate the program immediately; do not close files.
06 Ignore the error.
07 Request user to perform an action (such as change diskette) and retry the operation.

CH = Location. Provides additional information on locating an error:

01	Unknown situation, can't help	04	Serial device problem
02	Disk storage problem	05	Memory problem
03	Network problem		

Program: Reading Data From Sectors

The program in Figure 18-1 illustrates the use of IOCTL function 44H subfunction 0DH minor code 61H. The program reads data from a sector into a buffer in memory and displays each input byte as a pair of hex characters, as was done in Figure 15-6. The block structure in the data segment, RDBLOCK, arbitrarily specifies a head, cylinder, and starting sector, which you can change for your own purposes. RDBUFFR defines two addresses:

1. IOBUFFER is the offset address of the input buffer, which provides for one sector (512 bytes) of data.
2. SEG _DATA uses the SEG operator to identify the address of the data segment for the IOCTL operation.

Major procedures in the code segment are:

• A10MAIN calls B10READ and, if a valid operation, calls C10CONVRT.
• B10READ uses the IOCTL operation to read the data from the sector into IOBUFFER. (The test for a valid read is made on returning from the procedure.)
• C10CONVRT uses XLAT instructions to convert each half-byte in IOBUFFER into one hex character, which it stores successively in DISAREA. On completion, it calls D10DISP.

```
        TITLE     A18RDSCT (EXE)   Read disk sector, convert hex to
        ;                          to ASCII and display
                  .MODEL   SMALL
                  .STACK   64
                  .DATA
        XLATAB    DB      30H,31H,32H,33H,34H,35H,36H,37H,38H,39H
                  DB      41H,42H,43H,44H,45H,46H
        READMSG   DB      '*** Read error ***'

        RDBLOCK   DB      0                    ;Block
        RDHEAD    DW      0                    ;  structure
        RDCYLDERR DW      0                    ;
        RDSECTOR  DW      12                   ;
        RDNOSEC   DW      1                    ;
        RDBUFFER  DW      IOBUFFER             ;
                  DW      SEG _DATA            ;
        IOBUFFER  DB      512 DUP(' ')         ;Disk sector area
        DISPAREA  DB      1024 DUP(' ')        ;Display area
        .386   ;-------------------------------------------------------
                  .CODE
        A10MAIN   PROC    FAR
                  MOV     AX,@data             ;Initialize
                  MOV     DS,AX                ;  segment
                  MOV     ES,AX                ;  registers
                  MOV     AX,0003H             ;Set video mode
                  INT     10H                  ;  and clear screen
                  CALL    B10READ              ;Get sector data
                  JC      A80                  ;If invalid read, bypass
                  CALL    C10CONVRT            ;If valid, convert
                  JMP     A90                  ;  and display
        A80:
                  LEA     BP,READMSG           ;Invalid, display
                  MOV     CX,18                ;  error message
                  CALL    D10DISPLY
        A90:      MOV     AX,4C00H             ;End processing
                  INT     21H
        A10MAIN   ENDP
        ;                  Read contents of disk sector:
        ;                  -----------------------------
        B10READ   PROC    NEAR                 ;Uses AX, BX, CX, DX
                  MOV     AX,440DH             ;IOCTL for block device
                  MOV     BX,01                ;Drive A
                  MOV     CH,08                ;Device category
                  MOV     CL,61H               ;Read sector
                  LEA     DX,RDBLOCK           ;Address of block structure
                  INT     21H
                  RET
        B10READ   ENDP
        ;                  Convert sector data from hex (one byte)
        ;                  to ASCII (two bytes):
        ;                  ---------------------------------------
        C10CONVRT PROC    NEAR                 ;Uses AL, BP, CX, DI
                  LEA     DI,DISPAREA          ;Initialize addresses of
                  LEA     SI,IOBUFFER          ;  data areas
```

Figure 18-1   Reading Disk Sectors

- D10DISPLY displays the hex characters from DISPAREA. INT 10H function 13H automatically wraps data onto the next row when it reaches the rightmost column of the screen.

One way to enhance this program is to allow a user at the keyboard to request any starting sector and any number of sectors.

```
            C20:       MOV     AL,[SI]            ;Get a byte
                       SHR     AL,04              ;Shift off right hex digit
                       LEA     BX,XLATAB          ;Set table address
                       XLAT                       ;Translate hex
                       STOSB                      ;Store AL in DISPAREA
                       MOV     AL,[SI]            ;Get other half of byte
                       AND     AL,0FH             ;Clear left hex digit
                       XLAT                       ;Translate hex
                       STOSB                      ;Store AL in DISPAREA
                       INC     SI                 ;Incr address of IOBUFFER
                       LEA     BX,IOBUFFER+512    ;
                       CMP     SI,BX              ;End of IOBUFFER?
                       JB      C20                ;  If no, repeat
                       LEA     BP,DISPAREA        ;  If yes, display
                       MOV     CX,1024            ;  hex characters
                       CALL    D10DISPLY
                       RET
            C10CONVRT ENDP
            ;                   Display data:
            ;                   ------------       ;Uses AX, BX, DX
            D10DISPLY PROC      NEAR               ;BP, CX set on entry
                       MOV     AX,1301H           ;Request display
                       MOV     BX,0016H           ;Page:attribute
                       MOV     DX,0500H           ;Row:column
                       INT     10H
                       RET
            D10DISPLY ENDP
                       END     A10MAIN
```

Figure 18-1 *Continued*

OPERATIONS HANDLING THE DIRECTORY AND THE FAT

INT 21H Function 39H: Create Subdirectory

This service creates a subdirectory, just as does the system command MKDIR. To use it, load DX with the address of an ASCIIZ string containing the drive and directory pathname:

```
            ASCstrg DB    'n:\pathname',00H  ;ASCIIZ string
                    ...
                    MOV   AH,39H                 ;Request create subdirectory
                    LEA   DX,ASCstrg             ;Address of ASCIIZ string (DS:DX)
                    INT   21H                    ;Call interrupt service
```

A valid operation clears the Carry Flag; an error sets the CF and returns code 03 or 05 in AX.

INT 21H Function 3AH: Remove Subdirectory

This service deletes a subdirectory, just as does the system command RMDIR. Note that you cannot delete the current (active) directory or a subdirectory containing files. Load DX with the address of an ASCIIZ string containing the drive and directory pathname:

```
            ASCstrg DB    'n:\pathname',00H  ;ASCIIZ string
                    ...
                    MOV   AH,3AH                 ;Request delete subdirectory
                    LEA   DX,ASCstrg             ;Address of ASCIIZ string (DS:DX)
                    INT   21H                    ;Call interrupt service
```

INT 21H Function 29H: Parse Filename

This service converts a command line containing a file specification (filespec) of the form *n:filename.ext* into FCB format. FCB (File Control Block) is an obsolete disk accessing method replaced by the file handle method. All that you need to know about FCBs is the layout of the filespec, which consists of 11 bytes:

1–8 Filename. Name of the file, left adjusted, with trailing blanks, if any.

9–11 Filename extension. Left adjusted, with trailing blanks, if any.

The function can accept a filespec from a user, for example, for copying and deleting files. To use it, load SI (used as DS:SI) with the address of the filespec to be parsed, DI (used as ES:DI) with the address of an area where the operation is to generate the FCB format, and AL with a bit value that controls the parsing method:

```
MOV  AH,29H        ;Request parse filename
MOV  AL,code       ;Parsing method
LEA  DI,FCBname    ;Address of FCB (ES:DI)
LEA  SI,filespec   ;Address of filespec (DS:SI)
INT  21H           ;Call interrupt service
```

The codes for the parsing method from right to left are:

BIT	VALUE	ACTION
0	0	Means that filespec begins in the first byte.
0	1	Scan past separators (such as blanks) to find the filespec.
1	0	Set drive ID byte in the generated FCB: missing drive = 00, A = 01, B = 02, and so forth.
1	1	Change drive ID byte in the generated FCB only if the parsed filespec specifies a drive. In this way, an FCB can have its own default drive.
2	0	Change filename in the FCB as required.
2	1	Change filename in the FCB only if the filespec contains a valid filename.
3	0	Change filename extension as required.
3	1	Change extension only if filespec contains a valid extension.
4–7	0	Must be zero.

For valid data, function 29H creates a standard FCB format for the filename and extension, with an eight-character filename filled out with blanks if necessary, a three-character extension filled out with blanks if necessary, and no dot between them.

The operation recognizes standard punctuation and converts the wild cards * and ? into a string of one or more characters. For example, PROG12.* becomes PROG12bb??? (2 blanks to fill out filename and ??? for the extension). AL returns one of the following codes: 00H = no wild cards encountered; 01H = wild cards converted; or FFH = invalid drive specified.

After the operation, DS:SI contains the address of the first byte after the parsed file-spec, and ES:DI contains the address of the first byte of the FCB. For a failed operation, the byte at DI+1 is blank, although the operation attempts to convert almost anything you throw at it.

To make this operation work with file handles, further editing includes deleting blanks and inserting a period between filename and extension.

INT 21H Function 41H: Delete File

This function deletes a file (but not read-only) from within a program. Load the address in DX of an ASCIIZ string containing the device path and filename, with no wild-card references:

```
ASCstrng DB   'n:\pathname',00H  ;ASCIIZ string
         ...
         MOV  AH,41H             ;Request delete file
         LEA  DX,ASCstrng        ;Address of ASCIIZ string (DS:DX)
         INT  21H                ;Call interrupt service
```

A valid operation clears the Carry Flag, marks the filename in the directory as deleted, and releases the file's allocated disk space in the FAT. An error sets the CF and returns code 02, 03, or 05 in AX.

INT 21H Function 43H: Get/Set File Attribute

You can use this operation either to get or set a file attribute in the directory. The operation requires the address of an ASCIIZ string containing the drive, path, and filename for the requested file. (Or use the default directory if no path is given.)

Get File Attribute. To get the file attribute, load AL with code 00, as shown by the following example:

```
ASCstrng DB   'n:\pathname',00H  ;ASCIIZ string
         ...
         MOV  AH,43H             ;Request
         MOV  AL,00              ;  get attribute
         LEA  DX,ASCstrng        ;ASCIIZ string (DS:DX)
         INT  21H                ;Call interrupt service
```

A valid operation clears the Carry Flag, clears CH, and returns the current attribute to CL:

BIT	ATTRIBUTE	BIT	ATTRIBUTE
0	Read-only file	3	Volume label
1	Hidden file	4	Subdirectory
2	System file	5	Archive file

An error sets the CF and returns code 02 or 03 to AX.

Set File Attribute. To set the file attribute, load AL with code 01 and attribute bit(s) in CX. You may change read-only, hidden, system, and archive files, but not volume label or subdirectory. The following example sets hidden and archive attributes for a file:

```
MOV   AH,43H        ;Request
MOV   AL,01         ;  set attributes,
MOV   CX,22H        ;  hidden and archive
LEA   DX,ASCstrng   ;ASCIIZ string (DS:DX)
INT   21H           ;Call interrupt service
```

A valid operation clears the Carry Flag and sets the directory entry to the attribute in CX. An invalid operation sets the CF and returns code 02, 03, or 05 to AX.

INT 21H Function 45H: Duplicate a File Handle

The purpose of this service is to give a file more than one handle. The uses of old versus new handles are identical—the handles reference the same file, file pointer, and buffer area. One use is to request a file handle and use that handle to close the file. This action causes the system to flush the buffer and update the directory. You can then use the original file handle to continue processing the file. Here is an example of function 45H:

```
MOV   AH,45H       ;Request duplicate handle
MOV   BX,handle    ;Current handle to be duplicated
INT   21H          ;Call interrupt service
```

A successful operation clears the Carry Flag and returns the next available file handle in AX. An error sets the CF and returns error code 04 or 06 to AX. (See also function 46H.)

INT 21H Function 46H: Force Duplicate of a File Handle

This service is similar to function 45H, except that this one can assign a specific file handle. You could use the service to redirect output, for example, to another path. To use it, load BX with the original handle and CX with the second handle. A successful operation clears the Carry Flag. An error sets the CF and returns error code 04 or 06 to AX. Some combinations may not work; for example, handle 00 is always keyboard input, 04 is printer output, and 03 (auxiliary) cannot be redirected. (See also function 45H.)

INT 21H Function 4EH: Find First Matching File

You can use function 4EH to begin a search in a directory for the first of (probably) related files and use function 4FH to continue searching for succeeding files of the group. You have to define a 43-byte buffer for the operation to return the located directory entry and issue function 1AH (set DTA) before using this service. DTA (Disk Transfer Address) is simply an area in memory that you define for receiving data from disk. Setting the DTA tells function 4EH where to deliver the requested data.

To begin the search, set CX with the file attribute of the filename(s) to be returned—any combination of read-only (bit 0), hidden (bit 1), system (bit 2), volume label (bit 3), directory (bit 4), or archive (bit 5). Load DX with the address of an ASCIIZ string containing the filespec; the string may (and probably would) contain the wild-card characters ? and *. For example, a request for filespec n:\ASMPROGS\A12*.ASM causes the operation to begin with the first file that matches the string. Here's an example:

```
ASCstrng  DB   'ASCIIZ string', 00H
          ...
          MOV AH,4EH        ;Request first match
          MOV CX,00H        ;Normal attribute
          LEA DX,ASCstrng   ;ASCIIZ string (DS:DX)
          INT 21H           ;Call interrupt service
```

An operation that locates a match clears the Carry Flag and fills the 43-byte (2BH) DTA with the following data:

```
FILEDTA   LABEL  BYTE            ;File DTA:
          DB     21 DUP(20H)     ; Reserved for subsequent search
FILEATTR  DB     0               ; File attribute
FILETIME  DW     0               ; File time
FILEDATE  DW     0               ; File date
LOWSIZE   DW     0               ; File size: low word
HIGHSIZE  DW     0               ; File size: high word
FILENAME  DB     13 DUP(20H)     ; Name and extension as an ASCIIZ
                                 ; string, followed by hex 00
```

An error sets the Carry Flag and returns code 02, 03, or 12H. If you plan to use function 4FH subsequently, do not change the contents of the DTA.

A unique use for function 4EH is to determine whether a reference is to a filename or to a subdirectory. For example, if the returned attribute is 10H, the reference is to a subdirectory. The operation also returns the size of the file, which is illustrated in Figure 23-3. You may use function 4EH to determine the size of a file and function 36H to check the space available for writing it.

INT 21H Function 4FH: Find Next Matching File

Before using this service, issue function 4EH to begin the search in a directory and then function 4FH to continue searching:

```
          MOV  AH,4FH ;Request next match
          INT  21H    ;Call interrupt service
```

A successful operation clears the Carry Flag and returns to AX codes 00 (filename found) or 18 (no more files). An error sets the CF and returns code 02, 03, or 12H to AX.

Figure 18-3 later illustrates functions 4EH and 4FH.

INT 21H Function 56H: Rename File or Directory

This service can rename a file or directory from within a program. Load DX with the address of an ASCIIZ string containing the old drive, path, and name of the file or directory to be renamed. Load DI (combined as ES:DI) with the address of an ASCIIZ string containing the new drive, path, and name, with no wild cards. Drive numbers, if used, must be the same in both strings. Because the paths need not be the same, the operation can both re-name a file and move it to another directory on the same drive:

```
oldstrng  DB 'n:\oldpath\oldname', 00H
newstrng  DB 'n:\newpath\newname', 00H

     ...
     MOV AH,56H          ;Request rename file/directory
     LEA DX,oldstrng     ;DS:DX
     LEA DI,newstrng     ;ES:DI
     INT 21H             ;Call interrupt service
```

A successful operation clears the Carry Flag; an error sets the CF and returns in AX code 02, 03, 05, or 11H.

INT 21H Function 57H: Get/Set a File's Date and Time

This service enables a program to get or set the date and time for an open file. The formats for time and date are the same as those in the directory:

BITS FOR TIME	BITS FOR DATE
0BH-0FH Hours	09H-0FH Year (relative to 1980)
05H-0AH Minutes	05H-08H Month
00H-04H Seconds	00H-04H Day of month

Seconds are in the form of the number of two-second increments, 0–29. Load the request (0 = get or 1 = set) in AL and the file handle in BX. For requesting set date/time, load the time in CX and date in DX. Following is an example:

```
     MOV  AH,57H      ;Request set
     MOV  AL,01       ;  file's date and time
     MOV  BX,handle   ;File handle
     MOV  CX,time     ;New time (hours|mins|secs)
     MOV  DX,date     ;New date (year|month|day)
     INT  21H         ;Call interrupt service
```

A valid operation clears the Carry Flag; a get operation returns the time in CX and date in DX, whereas a set operation changes the date and time entries for the file. An invalid oper-ation sets the CF and returns in AX error code 01 or 06.

INT 21H Function 5AH: Create a Temporary File

A program that creates temporary files could use this service, especially in networks, where the names of other files may be unknown and the program is to avoid accidentally over-writing them. The operation creates a file with a unique name within the path.

Load CX with the required file attribute—any combination of read-only (bit 0), hid-den (bit 1), system (bit 2), volume label (bit 3), directory (bit 4), and archive (bit 5). Load DX with the address of an ASCIIZ path—drive (if necessary), the subdirectory (if any), a backslash, and 00H, followed by 13 blank bytes for the new filename:

```
ASCpath  DB    'n:\pathname\', 00H, 13 DUP(20H)
         ...
         MOV   AH,5AH          ;Request create file
         MOV   CX,attribute    ;File attribute
         LEA   DX,ASCpath      ;ASCIIZ path
         INT   21H             ;Call interrupt service
```

A successful operation clears the Carry Flag, delivers the file handle to AX, and appends the new filename to the ASCIIZ string beginning at the 00H byte. An invalid operation sets the CF and returns code 03, 04, or 05 in AX.

INT 21H Function 5BH: Create a New File

This service creates a file only if the named file does not already exist; otherwise it is identical to function 3CH (Create File). You could use function 5BH whenever you don't want to overwrite an existing file. A valid operation clears the Carry Flag and returns the file handle in AX. An invalid operation (including finding an identical filename) sets the CF and returns code 03, 04, 05, or 50H in AX.

Program: Selectively Deleting Files

The program in Figure 18-3 illustrates the use of functions 4EH and 4FH to find all filenames in the directory and function 41H to delete selected files. The program assumes drive A and consists of the following procedures:

- A10MAIN calls procedures B10FIRST, C10NEXT, D10MESSG, and E10DELETE.
- B10FIRST sets the DTA for function 4EH and finds the first matched entry in the directory.
- C10NEXT finds succeeding matched entries in the directory.
- D10MESSG displays the names of the files and asks whether they are to be deleted.
- E10DELETE accepts a reply Y (yes) to delete the file, N (no) to keep it, or <Enter> to end processing, and deletes the file if requested.

As a precaution during testing, use temporary copied files. You could enhance the program by adding screen scrolling.

KEY POINTS

- Operations involved with handling disk drives include reset, select default, get drive information, get free disk space, and the extensive operation I/O control for devices.
- Operations involved with handling the directory and FAT include create subdirectory, remove subdirectory, change current directory, and get current directory.
- Operations involved with handling disk files (other than create, open, read, and write) include rename file, get/set attribute, find matching file, and get/set date/time.

```
        TITLE    A18SELDL (EXE)  Select and delete files
        CODESG   SEGMENT PARA 'Code'
                 .MODEL SMALL
                 .STACK 64
                 .DATA
MSSG_LEN  EQU    32
ROW       DB     00               ;Screen row
COL       DB     10               ;  and column
PATHNAME  DB     'A:\*.*', 00H
DELMSG    DB     'Delete? '
ENDMSG    DB     'No more directory entries          '
ERRMSG1   DB     'Invalid path/file                  '
ERRMSG2   DB     'Write-protected disk               '
PROMPT    DB     'Y = Delete, N = Keep, Ent = Exit'
DISKAREA  DB     43 DUP(20H)
; --------------------------------------------------------------
                 .CODE
A10MAIN   PROC   NEAR             ;Main procedure
          MOV    AX,@data         ;Initialize
          MOV    DS,AX            ;  segment
          MOV    ES,AX            ;  registers
          MOV    AX,0003H         ;Set video mode
          INT    10H              ;  and clear screen
          CALL   B10FIRST         ;  directory entry
          CMP    AX,00H           ;If no entries,
          JNE    A90              ;  exit
          MOV    CX,MSSG_LEN      ;Length of prompt
          LEA    BP,PROMPT        ;Display initial prompt
          CALL   F10DISPLY
          INC    ROW
A20:
          CALL   D10MESSG         ;Display filename
          CALL   E10DELETE        ;Delete if requested
          CMP    AL,0FFH          ;Request for finish?
          JE     A90              ;  yes, exit
          INC    ROW              ;Set next row
          CALL   C10NEXT          ;Get next directory entry
          CMP    AX,00H           ;Any more entries?
          JE     A20              ;  yes, continue
A90:      MOV    AX,4C00H         ;  no, end processing
          INT    21H
A10MAIN   ENDP
;                 Find first entry in directory:
;                 ------------------------------
B10FIRST  PROC   NEAR             ;Uses AX, BP, CX, DX
          MOV    AH,1AH           ;Get DTA for function
          LEA    DX,DISKAREA      ;  calls
          INT    21H
          MOV    AH,4EH           ;Locate first directory
          MOV    CX,00            ;  entry
          LEA    DX,PATHNAME      ;Address of ASCIIZ string
          INT    21H
          JNC    B90              ;Valid operation?
          PUSH   AX               ;  no,
          MOV    CX,MSSG_LEN      ;  display ending
          LEA    BP,ERRMSG1       ;  message
```

Figure 18-3 Selectively Deleting Files

```
            CALL   F10DISPLY          ;
            POP    AX
B90:        RET
B10FIRST    ENDP
;                  Find succeeding entries in directory:
;                  -------------------------------------
C10NEXT     PROC   NEAR               ;Uses AX, BP, CX
            MOV    AH,4FH             ;Read next
            INT    21H                ;  directory entry
            CMP    AX,00H             ;More entries?
            JE     C90                ;  yes, bypass
            PUSH   AX                 ;  no,
            MOV    CX,MSSG_LEN        ;  display ending
            LEA    BP,ENDMSG          ;  message
            CALL   F10DISPLY          ;
            POP    AX
C90:        RET
C10NEXT     ENDP
;                  Calculate length of filename and display:
;                  -----------------------------------------
D10MESSG    PROC   NEAR               ;Uses AL, BP, CX, DI
            MOV    COL,10
            MOV    CX,08              ;Length of message
            LEA    BP,DELMSG          ;Display delete message
            CALL   F10DISPLY
            MOV    COL,18
            LEA    DI,DISKAREA+30     ;Filename in DTA
            MOV    AL,00H             ;Scan for 13 bytes
            MOV    CX,13              ;  for hex 00s
            REPNE  SCASB              ;  in disk area
            NEG    CX                 ;Calc. length
            ADD    CX,13              ;  of filename
            LEA    BP,DISKAREA+1EH    ;Display
            CALL   F10DISPLY          ;  filename
            RET
D10MESSG    ENDP
;                  Delete record if requested:
;                  ---------------------------
E10DELETE   PROC   NEAR               ;Uses AX, BP, CX, DX
            MOV    AH,10H             ;Accept character
            INT    16H                ;  reply (y/n)
            CMP    AL,0DH             ;Enter character?
            JE     E80                ;  yes, exit
            OR     AL,00100000B       ;Force lowercase
            CMP    AL,'y'             ;Delete requested?
            JNE    E90                ;  no, bypass
            MOV    AH,41H                     MOV    AH,41H
            LEA    DX,DISKAREA+1EH    ;  address of filename
            INT    21H                ;  delete entry
            JNC    E90                ;Valid delete?
            MOV    CX,MSSG_LEN        ;  no, display
            LEA    BP,ERRMSG2         ;  warning message
            CALL   F10DISPLY          ;
E80:        MOV    AL,0FFH            ;End-of-process indicator
E90:        RET
E10DELETE   ENDP
```

Figure 18-3 *Continued*

```
;                       Display routine:
;                       ---------------     ;Uses AX, BX, DX
F10DISPLY PROC          NEAR                ;BP, CX set on entry
          MOV           AX,1301H            ;Request display line
          MOV           BX,0016H            ;Page:attribute
          MOV           DH,ROW
          MOV           DL,COL
          INT           10H
          RET
F10DISPLY ENDP
          END           A10MAIN
```

Figure 18-3 *Continued*

REVIEW QUESTIONS AND EXERCISES

Use DEBUG (or other debugger) for these questions. Key in the A 100 command and the required assembler instructions. Examine any values returned in the registers.

18-1. The following questions involve disk drives:

    (a) Function 19H to determine the current default disk drive.

    (b) Function 1FH for information about the default DPB.

    (c) Function 36H to determine the amount of free disk space.

    (d) Function 4400H to get information on the device in use.

    (e) Function 4406H to check input status.

    (f) Function 4408H to determine whether any media in use are removable.

    (g) Function 440DH minor code 60H to get the device parameters.

    (h) Function 440DH minor code 66H to get the media ID.

18-2. The following questions involve directories:

    (a) Function 39H to create a subdirectory. For safety, you could create it on a diskette or RAM disk. Use any valid name.

    b) Function 56H to rename the subdirectory.

    (c) Function 3AH to remove the subdirectory.

18-3. The following questions involve disk files (use a copied file for this exercise):

    (a) Function 43H to get the attribute from a file on a diskette.

    (b) Function 56H to rename the file.

    (c) Function 43H to set the attribute to hidden.

    (d) Function 57H to get the file's date and time.

    (e) Function 41H to delete the file.

18-4. Write a small program from within DEBUG that simply executes INT 21H function 29H (Parse Filename). Provide for the filespec at 81H and the FCB at 5CH; both are in the PSP immediately before the program. Enter various filespecs, such as n:ASMPRO1.DOC, ASMPRO2, ASMPRO3.*, and n:*.ASM. Check the results at offset 5CH after each execution of the parse.

Chapter 19

Disk Storage IV: INT 13H Disk Functions

Objective: To examine the basic requirements for using the BIOS INT 13H functions to format, verify, read from, and write to disks.

INTRODUCTION

In Chapters 17 and 18, we examined the use of the INT 21H services for disk processing. You can also use INT 13H to process directly at the BIOS level, although BIOS supplies no automatic use of the FAT, directory, or blocking and deblocking of records. BIOS disk operation INT 13H treats data as the size of a sector and handles disk addressing in terms of actual track and sector numbers. INT 13H disk operations involve resetting, reading, writing, verifying, and formatting the drive.

Most of the INT 13H operations are for experienced software developers who are aware of the potential danger in their misuse. Also, BIOS versions may vary according to the processor used and even by computer model.

This chapter covers the following INT 13H functions:

00H	Reset disk/diskette system	0CH	Seek cylinder
01H	Read disk/diskette status	0DH	Alternate disk reset
02H	Read sectors	0EH	Read sector buffer
03H	Write sectors	0FH	Write sector buffer
04H	Verify sectors	15H	Get disk/diskette type
05H	Format tracks	16H	Change of diskette status
08H	Get drive parameters	17H	Set diskette type
09H	Initialize drive	18H	Set media type for format
0AH	Read extended sector buffer	19H	Park disk heads
0BH	Write extended sector buffer		

BIOS STATUS BYTE

Most of the INT 13H functions clear or set the Carry Flag on success or failure and return a status code to the AH register. BIOS maintains information in its data area about each device and its status. The *status byte* shown in Figure 19-1 reflects the indicator bits to be found in the BIOS data area at 40:41H for the Diskette Drive Data Area and at 40:74H for the Hard Disk Data Area. (See Chapter 24 for details.)

If a disk operation returns an error, a program's usual action is to reset the disk (function 00H) and to retry the operation three times. If the error persists, the program could display a message and give the user a chance to change the diskette, if that's the solution to the problem.

BASIC INT 13H DISK OPERATIONS

This section covers the basic INT 13H disk operations, each requiring a function code in AH.

INT 13H Function 00H: Reset Disk System

A program may use this operation after a preceding disk operation has reported a serious error. The operation performs a hard reset on the diskette or hard drive controller; that is, the next time the drive is accessed, it first resets to cylinder 0. For a diskette, set DL to the drive number (0 = drive A, etc.), and for hard disk, set DL to a value of 80H or higher (80H = drive C, 81H = D, etc.). An example of the use of function 00H is as follows:

```
MOV   AH,00H   ;Request reset disk
MOV   DL,80H   ;Disk drive C
INT   13H      ;Call interrupt service
```

Code	Status
00H	No error
01H	Bad command, not recognized by the controller
02H	Address mark on disk not found
03H	Writing on protected disk attempted
04H	Invalid track/sector
05H	Reset operation failed
06H	Diskette removed since last access
07H	Drive parameters wrong
08H	Direct memory access (DMA) overrun (data accessed too fast to enter)
09H	DMA across a 64K boundary attempted on read/write
10H	Bad CRC on a read encountered (error check indicated corrupted data)
20H	Controller failed (hardware failure)
40H	Seek operation failed (hardware failure)
80H	Device failed to respond (diskette: drive door open or no diskette; hard disk: time out)
AAH	Drive not ready
BBH	Undefined error
CCH	Write fault

Figure 19-1 INT 13H Status Codes

A valid operation clears the Carry Flag; an error sets the CF and returns a status code in AH. Function 0DH is a related operation.

INT 13H Function 01H: Read Disk Status

This operation gives another chance to examine the status of the most recent disk operation. (See BIOS status byte in Figure 19-1.) Set DL to the usual code (0 = drive A, etc.) for diskette and a value of 80H or higher (80H = the first drive, etc.) for hard disk. This operation returns to AL the status code that the last disk operation would have returned to AH. The operation, which should always be valid, clears the Carry Flag and returns its own status code, 00H, in AH.

INT 13H Function 02H: Read Disk Sectors

This operation reads a specified number of sectors on the same track directly into memory. Note that cylinder/track numbers begin with 0, whereas sector numbers begin with 1. Initialize these registers:

AL	Number of sectors, up to the maximum for a track
CH	Cylinder/track number (low-order eight bits)
CL	Bits 7-6 Cylinder/track number (high-order two bits)
	Bits 5-0 Starting sector number
DH	Head/side number (0 or 1 for diskette)
DL	Drive number for diskette (0 = A) or hard drive (80H = C)
ES:BX	Address of an I/O buffer in the data area, which should be large enough for all the requested sectors to be read. (BX is subject to ES.)

The next example reads one sector into an area named SECTOR:

```
SECTOR   DB  512 DUP(?)   ;Area for input
         . . .
         MOV AH,02H        ;Request read sector
         MOV AL,01         ;One sector
         LEA BX,SECTOR     ;Input buffer (ES:BX)
         MOV CH,05         ;Track 05
         MOV CL,03         ;Sector 03
         MOV DH,00         ;Head 00
         MOV DL,00         ;0 = drive A, 80H = C, etc.
         INT 13H           ;Call interrupt service
```

A valid operation clears the Carry Flag and returns to AL the number of sectors that the operation has actually read. The contents of DS, BX, CX, and DX are preserved. An error sets the CF and returns the status code in AH; reset the drive (function 00H) and retry the operation.

For most situations, you specify only one sector or all sectors for a track. Initialize CH and CL, and increment them to read the sectors sequentially. Once the sector number exceeds the maximum for a track, reset it to 01 and either increment the track number on the same side of the disk or increment the head number for the next side.

Testing Whether a Diskette Is Ready. A program may issue a request for accessing a diskette that has not yet been inserted. A standard practice is to attempt the operation three times before displaying a message to the user. The example that follows uses INT 13H function 02H in an attempt to read a sector of data. Try using DEBUG to enter the instructions (but not statement numbers or comments) and test the code with and without a diskette present in drive A. For an installed diskette, the operation should read the contents of the disk's boot record, 512 (200H) bytes, beginning at location DS:200H. The code is:

```
0100    MOV CX,03        ;Count for loop
0103    PUSH CX          ;Save count
0104    MOV AX,0201       ;Request read one sector
0107    MOV BX,0200       ;Input address
010A    MOV CX,0001       ;Track and sector numbers
010D    MOV DX,0000       ;Head and drive numbers
0110    INT 13           ;Call interrupt service
0112    POP CX            ;Restore count
0113    JNC 118          ;If no error, exit
0115    CLC              ;If error,
0116    LOOP 103         ;  try 3 times
0118    JMP 100          ;That's it
```

INT 13H Function 03H: Write Sectors

This operation, the opposite of function 02H, writes a specified area from memory (512 bytes or a multiple of 512) onto designated formatted sectors. Load the registers and handle processing just as for function 02H. A valid operation clears the Carry Flag and delivers to AL the number of sectors written; the contents of DS, BX, CX, and DX are preserved. An error sets the CF and returns a status code in AH; reset the drive and retry the operation.

Program: Using INT 13H to Read Sectors

The program in Figure 19-2 uses INT 13H to read sectors from disk into memory. Note that there is no open operation or file handle. The major data areas are:

- BEGINADR contains the beginning track (03) and sector (01), which the program increments.
- ENDADR contains the ending track (04) and sector (01). The total number of sectors is 9 (for track 3) x 2 (for two sides) = 18. One way to enhance the program would be to prompt the user for the starting and ending track and sector.
- SECTORIN defines 512 bytes as an area for reading in a sector.
  The main procedures are:
- A10MAIN calls B10ADDR, C10READ, and D10DISPLY, and ends after reading the last requested sector.
- B10ADDR calculates each disk address in terms of side, track, and sector. When the sector number reaches 19, the routine resets the sector to 01. If the side is 1, the program increments the track number; the side number is then changed, from 0 to 1 or

```
TITLE       A19BIORD (EXE)  Read disk sectors via BIOS
            .MODEL  SMALL
            .STACK  64
            .DATA
BEGINADR  DW        0301H              ;Beginning track-sector
ENDADR    DW        0401H              ;Ending track-sector
ENDCODE   DB        00                 ;End process indicator
READMSG   DB        '*** Read error ***'
SECTORIN  DB        512 DUP(' ')       ;Input area for sector
SIDE      DB        00
; -------------------------------------------------------------
            .CODE
A10MAIN   PROC      FAR
          MOV       AX,@data           ;Initialize
          MOV       DS,AX              ;   segment
          MOV       ES,AX              ;   registers
A20:
          MOV       AX,0003H           ;Set mode and
          INT       10H                ;   clear screen
          CALL      B10ADDR            ;Calculate disk address
          MOV       CX,BEGINADR        ;Start and end
          MOV       DX,ENDADR          ;   addresses
          CMP       CX,DX              ;At ending sector?
          JE        A90                ;   yes, exit
          CALL      C10READ            ;Read disk record
          CMP       ENDCODE,00         ;Normal read?
          JNZ       A90                ;   no, exit
          LEA       BP,SECTORIN        ;Address of sector
          MOV       CX,512             ;   and length
          CALL      D10DISPLY          ;Display sector
          JMP       A20                ;Repeat operation
A90:      MOV       AX,4C00H
          INT       21H                ;End processing
A10MAIN   ENDP
;                   Calculate next track/sector:
;                   ----------------------------
B10ADDR   PROC      NEAR               ;Uses CX register
          MOV       CX,BEGINADR        ;Get track/sector
          CMP       CL,19              ;Past last sector (18)?
          JNE       B90                ;   no, exit
          MOV       CL,01              ;   yes, set sector to 1
          CMP       SIDE,00            ;Bypass if side 0
          JE        B20
          INC       CH                 ;Increment track
B20:      XOR       SIDE,01            ;Change side
          MOV       BEGINADR,CX
B90:      RET
B10ADDR   ENDP
;                   Read contents of disk sector:
;                   -----------------------------
C10READ   PROC      NEAR               ;Uses AX, BP, BX, CX, DX
          MOV       AH,02H             ;Request read
          MOV       AL,01              ;Number of sectors
          LEA       BX,SECTORIN        ;Address of buffer
          MOV       CX,BEGINADR        ;Track/sector
```

Figure 19-2   Using INT 13H to Read Disk Sectors

```
                MOV     DH,SIDE            ;Side
                MOV     DL,00              ;Drive A
                INT     13H
                JNC     C90                ;If normal read, exit
                MOV     ENDCODE,01         ;Else
                LEA     BP,READMSG         ;  display error
                MOV     CX,18              ;  message
                CALL    D10DISPLY          ;
        C90:    INC     BEGINADR           ;Increment sector
                RET
        C10READ ENDP
        ;               Display routine:
        ;               --------------     ;Uses AX, BX, DX
        D10DISPLY PROC  NEAR               ;BP, CX set on entry
                MOV     AX,1301H           ;Request display
                MOV     BX,0016H           ;Page and attribute
                MOV     DX,0300H           ;Row : column
                INT     10H
                MOV     AH,10H             ;Wait for keyboard
                INT     16H                ;  entry
                RET
        D10DISPLY ENDP
                END     A10MAIN
```

Figure 19-2   *Continued*

from 1 to 0. This process works only for diskettes (because they are two-sided) that contain 18 sectors per track.

- C10READ reads a disk sector from drive A into SECTORIN and increments the sector number for a valid read operation.
- D10DISPLY displays the contents of the currently read sector (INT 10H function 13H acts on CR and LF), and waits for the user to press a key before continuing.

Try running this program under DEBUG and trace through the instructions that initialize the segment registers. For the input operation, adjust the starting and ending sectors to the location of the disk's FAT. (See Chapter 16.) Use G (Go) to execute the program, and examine the FAT and directory entries in SECTORIN.

A program could also convert the ASCII characters in the input area to their hex equivalents and display the hex values just as DEBUG does. (See the program in Figure 14-5.) In this way, you could examine the contents of any sector—even hidden ones—and could allow a user to enter changes and write the changed sector back onto disk.

When INT 21H writes a file, it inserts records in available clusters, which may not be contiguous on disk. For that reason, you can't expect INT 13H to read such a file sequentially, although you could access FAT entries for the location of the next cluster.

OTHER INT 13H DISK OPERATIONS

The following sections describe additional INT 13H disk services.

INT 13H Function 04H: Verify Sectors

This operation simply checks that the specified sectors can be read and performs a cyclical redundancy check (CRC). When an operation writes data to a sector, the disk controller calculates and writes a CRC checksum immediately following the sector, based on the bits that are set. You can use function 04H to read the sector, recalculate the checksum, and compare it with the stored value. The verification consists only of recalculating the checksum; it does not check that byte values in the sector agree with the data in memory. You could use this function after a write (function 03H) to ensure more reliable output, at a cost of more processing time.

Load the registers just as for function 02H, but since the operation does not perform true verification of the written data, there is no need to set an address in ES:BX. A successful operation clears the Carry Flag and returns to AL the number of sectors actually verified; the contents of DS, BX, CX, and DX are preserved. An error sets the CF and returns a status code in AH; reset the drive and retry the operation.

INT 13H Function 05H: Format Tracks

Read/write operations require information on track formatting to locate and process a requested sector. This operation formats tracks according to one of four different sizes. Prior to execution of the operation, use function 17H to set the diskette type and function 18H to set the media type. For formatting diskettes, initialize these registers:

AL   Number of sectors to format

CH   Cylinder/track number (numbers begin with 0)

DH   Head/side number (0 or 1 for diskette)

DL   Drive number for diskette (0 = A) or hard drive (80H = C)

ES:BX Segment:offset address that points to a group of address fields for a track. For each sector on a track, there must be one 4-byte entry of the form T/H/S/B, where

Byte 0 T = Cylinder/track number

1 H = Head/side number

2 S = Sector number

3 B = Bytes per sector (00H = 128, 01H = 256, 02H = 512, 03H = 1024)

For example, if you format track 03, head 00, and 512 bytes per sector, the first entry for the track is hex 03000102, followed by one entry for each remaining sector.

The operation clears (if valid) or sets (if invalid) the Carry Flag and returns the status code in AH.

INT 13H Function 08H: Get Disk Drive Parameters

This useful function returns information about a disk drive. Load the drive number in DL (0 = A, 1 = B for diskette and 80H or higher for hard disk). A successful operation returns the following:

BL   Diskette type (01H = 360K, 02H = 1.2M, 03H = 720K, 04H = 1.44M)

CH   High cylinder/track number

CL   Bits 7–6 = high-order 2 bits of cylinder number

Bits 5–0 = high sector number

DH	High head number
DL	Number of drives attached to the controller
ES:DI	For diskettes, the segment:offset address of an 11-byte diskette drive parameter table. Two relevant fields are:

Offset 3 gives bytes per sector (00H = 128, 01H = 256, 02H = 512, 03H = 1024)

Offset 4 gives sectors per track

The operation clears (if valid) or sets (if invalid) the Carry Flag and returns the status code in AH. Try using the DEBUG command D ES:offset (the offset returned in DI) to display the values.

INT 13H Function 09H: Initialize Drive

BIOS performs this function when you boot up your computer according to its own hard disk table. DL contains the drive number (80H or higher). The operation clears (if valid) or sets (if invalid) the Carry Flag and returns the status in AH. BIOS INT 41H and INT 46H are related operations.

INT 13H Function 0AH: Read Extended Sector Buffer

The sector buffer on hard disks includes the 512 bytes of data plus four bytes for an error correction code (ECC), used for error checking and correcting the data. This function can read the whole sector buffer rather than just the data portion. To read an extended buffer, load these registers:

AL	Number of sectors (up to the maximum for the drive)
ES:BX	Segment:offset address of the input buffer
CH	Cylinder/track number
CL	Bits 7–6 = high-order two bits of cylinder number
	Bits 5–0 = high sector number
DH	Head/side number
DL	Drive number (80H or higher)

A successful operation returns to AL the number of sectors transferred. The operation clears (if valid) or sets (if invalid) the Carry Flag and returns a status code in AH.

INT 13H Function 0BH: Write Extended Sector Buffer

This function is similar to function 0AH except that, rather than read the sector buffer, it writes the buffer (including the ECC code) onto disk.

INT 13H Function 0CH: Seek Disk Cylinder

This function positions the read/write head on a hard disk at a specified cylinder (track), but does not transfer any data. To seek a cylinder, load these registers:

CH   Cylinder/track number

CL   Bits 7-6 = high-order two bits of cylinder/track number

      Bits 5-0 = sector number

DH   Head/side number

DL   Drive (80H = C)

The operation clears (if valid) or sets (if invalid) the Carry Flag and returns a status code in AH.

INT 13H Function 0DH: Alternate Disk Reset

This operation is similar to function 00H except that this one is restricted to hard disks. Load the drive (80H or higher) in DL. The operation resets the read/write access arm to cylinder 0. It clears (if valid) or sets (if invalid) the Carry Flag and returns a status code in AH.

INT 13H Function 0EH: Read Sector Buffer

This operation is similar to function 0AH except that this one reads only the 512-byte data portion of the sector and not the ECC bytes.

INT 13H Function 0FH: Write Sector Buffer

This operation is similar to function 0BH except that this one writes only the 512-byte data portion of the sector and not the ECC bytes.

INT 13H Functions 10H: Test for Drive Ready; 11H: Recalibrate Hard Drive; 12H: ROM Diagnostics; 13H: Drive Diagnostics; and 14H: Controller Diagnostics

These functions perform internal diagnostics and report specified information for BIOS and for advanced utility programs. The operations clear (if valid) or set (if invalid) the Carry Flag and return a status code in AH.

INT 13H Function 15H: Get Disk Type

This function returns information about a disk drive. Load DL with the drive (0 = A, etc. for diskette or 80H or higher for hard disk). A valid operation returns one of the following codes in AH:

00H   No drive/disk present

01H   Diskette drive that does not sense a change of diskette

02H   Diskette drive that senses a change of diskette

03H   Hard disk drive

For return code 03 in AH, CX:DX contain the total number of disk sectors on the drive. The operation clears or sets the Carry Flag and returns error codes in AH.

INT 13H Function 16H: Change of Diskette Status

This function checks for a change of diskette for systems that can sense a change (see also function 15H). Load DL with the drive number (0 = A, etc.). The operation returns one of the following codes in AH:

    00H   No change of diskette (Carry Flag = 0)

    01H   Invalid diskette parameter (Carry Flag = 1)

    06H   Diskette changed (Carry Flag = 1)

    80H   Diskette drive not ready (Carry Flag = 1)

Status codes 01H and 80H are errors that set the Carry Flag, whereas 06H is a valid status that also sets the CF—a potential source of confusion.

INT 13H Function 17H: Set Diskette Type

This operation sets up the combination of drive and diskette. Use function 17H along with function 05H for disk formatting. Load the drive number (0 = A, etc.) in DL and the diskette type in AL. Diskette types include the following: 01H = 360K diskette in 360K drive; 02H = 360K diskette in 1.2M drive; 03H = 1.2M diskette in 1.2M drive; 04H = 720K diskette in 720K drive; and 05H = 1.44M diskette in 1.44M drive. The operation clears (if valid) or sets (if invalid) the Carry Flag and returns the status in AH.

INT 13H Function 18H: Set Media Type for Format

Use this operation immediately before executing function 05H. To set the media type, load these registers:

    CH   Number of tracks (low-order eight bits)

    CL   Number of tracks (high two bits in bits 7-6), sectors per track (bits 5-0)

    DL   Drive (0 = A, etc.)

A valid operation returns in ES:DI a pointer to an 11-byte diskette parameter table. (See function 08H.) The operation clears (if valid) or sets (if invalid) the Carry Flag and returns the status in AH.

INT 13H Function 19H: Park Disk Heads

Older disk drives left read/write heads positioned over the drive surface when the system was powered off so that parking the heads into a safe area was recommended; more recent drives automatically park themselves. This operation requires drive number in DL (80H and higher for hard disk). The operation clears (if valid) or sets (if invalid) the Carry Flag and returns the status in AH.

KEY POINTS

- BIOS INT 13H provides direct access to tracks and sectors. Operations include reset/read disk status, read/write sectors, and format tracks.
- INT 13H does not supply automatic directory handling, end-of-file operations, or blocking and deblocking of records.

- The verify sector operation performs an elementary check of data written at some cost of processing time.
- A program should check for the status byte after each INT 13H disk operation.

REVIEW QUESTIONS AND EXERCISES

19-1. What are the two major disadvantages of using BIOS INT 13H? That is, why is the use of INT 21H usually preferred?

19-2. Under what circumstances would a programmer use INT 13H?

19-3. Most INT 13H operations return a status code. (a) Where is the code returned? (b) What does code 00H mean? (c) What does code 03H mean?

19-4. What is the standard procedure for an error returned by INT 13H? That is, how do you check for an error and what action do you take?

19-5. Code the instructions to reset the diskette controller.

19-6. Code the instructions to read the diskette status.

19-7. Using drive A, head 0, track 4, and sector 6, code the instructions for INT 13H to read four sectors into a data area named SECTORS.

19-8. Using memory address SECTOR, drive A, head 0, track 6, and sector 4, code the instructions for INT 13H to write one sector. Be sure to use a spare diskette for this exercise.

19-9. After the write operation in Question 19-8, how would you check for an attempt to write on a protected disk?

19-10. Based on Question 19-8, code the instructions to verify the write operation.

Chapter 20

FACILITIES FOR PRINTING

Objective: To describe the requirements for printing using the various interrupt operations.

INTRODUCTION

Compared to screen and disk handling, printing appears to be a relatively simple process. There are only a few operations involved, all done either through INT 21H or BIOS INT 17H instructions. Special commands to the printer include Form Feed, Line Feed, Tab, and Carriage Return.

A printer must understand a signal from the processor, for example, to eject to a new page, to feed one line down a page, or to tab across a page. The processor also must understand a signal from a printer indicating that it is busy or out of paper. Unfortunately, many types of printers respond differently to signals from a processor, and one of the tasks for software specialists is to interface their programs to such printers.

This chapter introduces the following interrupt operations for handling the printer:

INT 21H FUNCTIONS	INT 17H FUNCTIONS
40H Print characters	00H Print character
	01H Initialize port
	02H Get printer port status

COMMON PRINTER CONTROL CHARACTERS

Standard characters that control printing on all common printers for the PC include the following:

DECIMAL	HEX	FUNCTION
09	09H	Horizontal Tab
10	0AH	Line Feed (advance one line)
12	0CH	Form Feed (advance to next page)
13	0DH	Carriage Return (return to left margin)

Horizontal Tab. The Horizontal Tab (09H) control character causes the printer to advance the current print position to the next tab stop (usually, if set, every eight positions). The command works only on printers that have the feature and when the printer tabs are set up. You can issue a string of blank characters to get around a printer's inability to tab.

Line Feed. The Line Feed (0AH) control character advances the printer by a single line and two successive line feeds cause a double space.

Form Feed. Initializing the paper when you power up a printer determines the starting position for the top of a page. The default length for a page is 11 inches, which provides 66 lines at six lines per inch. Neither the processor nor the printer automatically checks for the bottom of a page. Whether you use cut sheets on a laser printer or continuous forms, as programmer you are responsible for directing the printer to begin printing on the next page. To control paging, count the lines as they print, and on reaching the maximum for the page (such as 60 lines), issue a Form Feed (0CH) command, and then reset the program's line count to 0 or 1.

At the end of printing, deliver a Line Feed or Form Feed command to force the printer to print the last line still in its buffer. Issuing a form feed at the end of printing ensures that the last sheet feeds out of the printer.

Carriage Return. The Carriage Return (0DH) control character, normally accompanied with a Line Feed, resets the printer to its leftmost margin. This character is known as <Enter> or <Return> on the keyboard and as CR on the screen.

INT 21H FUNCTION 40H: PRINT CHARACTERS

We have already used file handles in the chapters on screen handling and disk processing. For printing with INT 21H function 40H, load these registers:

AH = function 40H   CX = number of characters to print
BX = file handle 04   DX = address of the data to be printed

The following example prints 27 characters from a data item named HEADING beginning at the leftmost margin. The Carriage Return (0DH) and Line Feed (0AH) characters immediately following the text in HEADING cause the printer to reset to column 0 and advance one line:

```
CR  EQU  0DH      ;Carriage Return
LF  EQU  0AH      ;Line Feed
```

```
HEADING   DB 'Mountain Outfitting Corp.', CR, LF
          ...
      MOV AH,40H        ;Request printing
      MOV BX,04         ;Handle 04 for printer
      MOV CX,27         ;Send 27 characters
      LEA DX,HEADING    ;Address of data to print
      INT 21H           ;Call interrupt service
```

A successful operation prints the text, clears the Carry Flag, and returns in AX the number of characters printed. An unsuccessful operation sets the Carry Flag and returns in AX error code 05 (access denied) or 06 (invalid handle). An end-of-file marker (Ctrl-Z or 0AH) in the transmitted data also causes the operation to end.

Two conditions that intercept an attempt to print are:

1. The printer power is not turned on. The system displays
   ```
   "Write Fault Error Writing Device PRN"
   "Abort Retry Ignore Fail"
   ```
2. Out of paper or a paper jam. The system displays
   ```
   "Printer out of paper error writing device PRN"
   ```

Program: Printing with Page Overflow and Headings

The earlier program in Figure 8-2 accepts names from a user at the keyboard and displays them down the screen. The program in Figure 20-1 is similar to that one but instead directs the names to the printer. Each printed page contains a heading followed by a double space and the entered names in the following format:

```
List of Customer Names    Page 01
Annie Hall
Fanny Hill
Danny Rose
   ...
```

The program counts each line printed and, on nearing the bottom of a page, ejects the form to the top of the next page. The major procedures are the following:

- A10MAIN calls B10INPUT and C10PRINT and ends processing when the user presses only <Enter>.
- B10INPUT prompts for and accepts a name from the keyboard.
- C10PRINT calls D10PAGE (if at the end of a page) and prints the name (its length is based on the actual length in the keyboard input parameter list).
- D10PAGE advances to a new page, prints the heading, resets line count, and adds to page count.
- P10OUT handles requests to print.

At the beginning of execution, the program must print a heading, but not eject to a new page. To this end, D10PAGE bypasses the form feed if PAGECTR contains 01, its ini-

```
TITLE        A20PRTNM (EXE)   Accept entered names and print
             .MODEL  SMALL
             .STACK  64
             .DATA
NAMEPAR  LABEL   BYTE              ;Keyboard parameter list:
MAXNLEN  DB      20                ;   maximum length of name
NAMELEN  DB      ?                 ;   actual length entered
NAMEFLD  DB      20 DUP(' ')       ;   name entered
HEAD_LEN EQU     37                ;Heading line:
HEADING  DB      'List of Customer Names    Page  '
PAGECTR  DB      '01', 0DH, 0AH, 0AH

BOTTPAGE EQU     60
FORMFEED DB      0CH               ;Form feed
LINEFEED DB      0DH, 0AH          ;CR, line feed
LINECTR  DB      01                ;Count for lines printed
PROMPT   DB      'Name? '
ROW      DB      00                ;Screen row
.386     ;------------------------------------------------
             .CODE
A10MAIN  PROC    FAR
         MOV     AX,@data          ;Initialize
         MOV     DS,AX             ;   segment
         MOV     ES,AX             ;   registers
         MOV     AX,0003H          ;Set mode and
         INT     10H               ;   clear screen
         CALL    D10PAGE           ;Page heading
A20:
         CALL    B10INPUT          ;Accept input of name
         CMP     NAMELEN,00        ;Name entered?
         JE      A30               ;   no, exit
         CALL    C10PRINT          ;   yes, prepare printing
         JMP     A20
A30:     MOV     CX,01             ;End of processing:
         LEA     DX,FORMFEED       ;   one character
         CALL    P10OUT            ;   for form feed,
         MOV     AX,4C00H          ;   exit
         INT     21H
A10MAIN  ENDP
;
;                    Accept input of name from keyboard:
;                    --------------------------------
B10INPUT PROC    NEAR              ;Uses AX, BP, BX, CX, DX
         MOV     AX,1301H          ;Display prompt
         MOV     BX,0016H          ;Page and attribute
         LEA     BP,PROMPT         ;Address of prompt
         MOV     CX,06             ;Length of line
         MOV     DH,ROW            ;Row
         MOV     DL,10             ;Column
         INT     10H
         INC     ROW               ;Set next row
         MOV     AH,0AH            ;Request keyboard
         LEA     DX,NAMEPAR        ;   input
         INT     21H
         RET
B10INPUT ENDP
```

Figure 20-1   Printing with Page Overflow and Headings

tial value. PAGECTR is defined as DB '01', which generates an ASCII number, 3031H. The procedure increments PAGECTR by 1 so that it becomes, progressively, 3032, 3033, and so forth. The value is valid up to 3039 and then becomes 303A, which would print as a zero and a colon. At this point, the procedure resets the units position, 3AH to 30H, and adds 1 to the tens position, so that 303AH becomes 3130H, or decimal value 10. The capacity of PAGECTR is 99.

```
;                       Prepare name for printing:
;                       --------------------------
C10PRINT  PROC     NEAR
          CMP      LINECTR,BOTTPAGE  ;End of page?
          JB       C20               ;  no, bypass
          CALL     D10PAGE           ;  yes, print heading
C20:
          MOVZX    CX,NAMELEN        ;Set no. of characters
          LEA      DX,NAMEFLD        ;Set address of name
          CALL     P10OUT            ;Print name
          MOV      CX,02             ;Request CR,
          LEA      DX,LINEFEED       ;  line feed
          CALL     P10OUT
          INC      LINECTR           ;Add to line count
          RET
C10PRINT  ENDP
;                       Print heading and page number:
;                       ------------------------------
D10PAGE   PROC     NEAR                    ;Uses CX, DX
          CMP      WORD PTR PAGECTR,3130H  ;First page?
          JE       D30               ;  yes, bypass
          MOV      CX,01             ;
          LEA      DX,FORMFEED       ;  no, perform
          CALL     P10OUT            ;  form feed,
          MOV      LINECTR,03        ;  reset line count
D30:
          MOV      CX,HEAD_LEN       ;Length heading, page
          LEA      DX,HEADING        ;Address of heading
          CALL     P10OUT
          INC      PAGECTR+1         ;Add to page count
          CMP      PAGECTR+1,3AH     ;Units position = 10?
          JNE      D90               ;  no, bypass
          MOV      PAGECTR+1,30H     ;  yes, zero units,
          INC      PAGECTR           ;  increment tens
D90:      RET
D10PAGE   ENDP
;                       Print routine:
;                       --------------          ;Uses AH, BX
P10OUT    PROC     NEAR                    ;CX and DX set on entry
          MOV      AH,40H            ;Request print
          MOV      BX,04             ;File handle
          INT      21H
          RET
P10OUT    ENDP
          END      A10MAIN
```

Figure 20-1   *Continued*

Placing a test for the end of the page *before* (rather than after) printing a name ensures that the last page has at least one name under the title. You could enhance the program by adding scrolling.

Program: Printing ASCII Files and Handling Tabs

A common procedure, performed, for example, by the video system, is to replace a Tab character (09H) with blanks through to the next location evenly divisible by 8. Thus tab stops could be at locations 8, 16, 24, and so forth, so that all locations between 0 and 7 tab to 8, those between 8 and 15 tab to 16, and so forth. Some printers, however, ignore Tab characters. A program that prints ASCII files (such as assembly source programs) may check each character it sends to the printer; if the character is a Tab, the program inserts blanks up to the next tab position.

The program in Figure 20-2 requests a user to key in the name of a file and prints the contents of the file. The program is similar to the one in Figure 17-3 that displays records, but goes a step further in replacing tab stops for the printer with blanks. Following are three examples of tab stops, for print positions 1, 9, and 21, and the logic for setting the next tab position:

```
Present print location:      1          9          21
Binary value:            00000001   00001001   00010101
Clear rightmost 3 bits:  00000000   00001000   00010000
Add 8:                   00001000   00010000   00011000
New tab location:             8         16          24
```

The program is organized as follows:

- A10MAIN. Calls B10PROMPT, C10OPEN, D10READ, and E10XFER.
- B10PROMPT. Requests the user to key in a filename. Pressing only <Enter> indicates that the user is finished entering data.
- C10OPEN. Opens the requested disk file for input. If the operation is valid, the procedure uses INT 21H function 42H to determine the file size (uses only the low-order portion, with a maximum of 65,535 bytes).
- D10READ. Reads a sector from the file.
- E10XFER. Checks the input data for end of sector, end of file, end of display area, Line Feed, and Tab. Basically, the procedure sends regular characters to the print area and handles the logic for handling tab stops. The procedure also determines the end-of-file by decrementing the stored file size by 1 for each character processed.
- P10PRINT. Prints the output line and clears it to blanks.

You could modify the program to count the lines printed and force a form feed when near the bottom of a page, at line 60 or so. You could also use an editor program to embed Form Feed characters directly in your ASCII files at the exact location for a page break, such as at the end of a procedure; the usual method is to hold down the Alt key and press numbers on the numeric keypad, such as 012 for Form Feed.

SPECIAL PRINTER CONTROL CHARACTERS

An earlier section described the use of the basic printer control characters: Tab, Line Feed, Form Feed, and Carriage Return. Other commands suitable for most printers are the following:

DECIMAL	HEX	ACTION
08	08	Backspace
11	0B	Vertical Tab
14	0E	Turn on expanded mode
15	0F	Turn on condensed mode
18	12	Turn off condensed mode
20	14	Turn off expanded mode

```
TITLE      A20PRTAS (EXE)  Read and print ASCII records
           .MODEL SMALL
           .STACK 64
           .DATA
NAMEPAR    LABEL  BYTE                     ;Parameter list for
MAXLEN     DB     32                       ;  input of
NAMELEN    DB     ?                        ;  filename
FILENAME   DB     32 DUP(' ')

FILEDTA    LABEL  BYTE                     ;Disk file DTA
           DB     26 DUP(20H)              ;Reserved
FILESIZE   DW     0                        ;File size (low-order)
           DW     0                        ;File size (high-order
           DB     13 DUP(20H)              ;Rest of file DTA
PRINT_LEN  EQU    120
COUNT      DW     00
ENDCODE    DW     00                       ;End process indicator
FORMFEED   DB     0CH
HANDLE     DW     0
OPENMSG    DB     '*** Open error ***'
PRNTAREA   DB     120 DUP(' ')             ;Print area
PROMPT     DB     'Name of file? '
ROW        DB     0                        ;Screen row
SECTOR     DB     512 DUP(' ')             ;Input area for file
.386   ;-------------------------------------------------------
           .CODE
A10MAIN    PROC   FAR                      ;Main procedure
           MOV    AX,@data                 ;Initialize
           MOV    DS,AX                    ;  segment
           MOV    ES,AX                    ;  registers
           MOV    AX,0003H                 ;Set mode,
           INT    10H                      ;  clear screen
A20:
           MOV    ENDCODE,00               ;Initialize
           CALL   B10PROMPT                ;Request filename
           CMP    NAMELEN,00               ;Any request?
           JE     A90                      ;  no, exit
           CALL   C10OPEN                  ;Open file, get handle
           CMP    ENDCODE,00               ;Valid open?
           JNE    A20                      ;  no, request again
           CALL   D10READ                  ;Read 1st disk sector
           CMP    ENDCODE,00               ;End-of-file, no data?
           JE     A80                      ;  yes, request next
           CALL   E10XFER                  ;Print/read
A80:
           MOV    AH,3EH                   ;Close file
           MOV    BX,HANDLE
           INT    21H
           JMP    A20                      ;Repeat processing
A90:       MOV    AX,4C00H                 ;End processing
           INT    21H
A10MAIN    ENDP
;          Request file name from user:
;          ---------------------------
B10PROMPT  PROC   NEAR                     ;Uses AH, BP, BX, CX, DX
           LEA    BP,PROMPT                ;Address of prompt
           MOV    CX,13                    ;Length of line
```

Figure 20-2   Printing an ASCII File

```
              CALL     F10DISPLY
              MOV      AH,0AH             ;Accept filename
              LEA      DX,NAMEPAR         ;  from keyboard
              INT      21H
              MOVZX    BX,NAMELEN         ;Insert zero at end
              MOV      FILENAME[BX],00H   ;  of filespec
              RET
B10PROMPT ENDP
;                      Open disk file:
;                      -------------
C10OPEN    PROC        NEAR               ;Uses AX, BP, CX, DX
           MOV         AX,3D00H           ;Open, read only
           LEA         DX,FILENAME
           INT         21H
           JNC         C20                ;Test carry flag,
           LEA         BP,OPENMSG         ;  error if set
           MOV         CX,18              ;  display error
           CALL        F10DISPLY          ;  message
           MOV         ENDCODE,01         ;  and exit
           JMP         C90
C20:       MOV         HANDLE,AX          ;Save handle
           MOV         AH,1AH             ;Set DTA
           LEA         DX,FILEDTA         ;
           INT         21H                ;
           MOV         AH,4EH             ;Find file
           MOV         CX,0               ;  and get
           LEA         DX,FILENAME        ;  file size
           INT         21H
C90:       RET
C10OPEN    ENDP
;                      Read disk sector:
;                      ---------------
D10READ    PROC        NEAR               ;Uses AH, BX, CX, DX
           MOV         AH,3FH             ;Request read
           MOV         BX,HANDLE          ;Device
           MOV         CX,512             ;Length
           LEA         DX,SECTOR          ;Buffer
           INT         21H
           MOV         ENDCODE,AX
           RET
D10READ    ENDP
;                      Transfer data to print line:
;                      ----------------------------
E10XFER    PROC        NEAR               ;Uses AL, BX, DI, DX, SI
           CLD                            ;Set left-to-right
           LEA         SI,SECTOR          ;Initialize
E20:       LEA         DI,PRNTAREA
           MOV         COUNT,00
E30:       LEA         DX,SECTOR+512
           CMP         SI,DX              ;End of sector?
           JNE         E40                ;  no,  bypass
           CALL        D10READ            ;  yes, read next
           CMP         ENDCODE,00         ;End of file?
           JE          E90                ;  yes, exit
           LEA         SI,SECTOR
E40:       MOV         BX,COUNT
           CMP         BX,PRINT_LEN       ;At end of print area?
```

Figure 20-2 *Continued*

```
               JB     E50                    ;  no,  bypass
               MOV    [DI+BX],0D0AH          ;  yes, set CR/LF
               CALL   P10PRINT
               LEA    DI,PRNTAREA            ;Reinitialize
               MOV    COUNT,00
E50:           LODSB                         ;[SI] to AL, INC SI
               MOV    BX,COUNT
               MOV    [DI+BX],AL             ;Character to print line
               INC    BX
               DEC    FILESIZE               ;All chars processed?
               JZ     E90                    ;  yes, exit
               CMP    AL,0AH                 ;Line feed?
               JNE    E60                    ;  no,  bypass
               CALL   P10PRINT               ;  yes, call print
               JMP    E20
E60:           CMP    AL,09H                 ;Tab character?
               JNE    E70                    ;  no, bypass
               DEC    BX                     ;  yes, reset BX
               MOV    BYTE PTR [DI+BX],20H   ;Clear tab to blank
               AND    BX,0FFF8H              ;Clear rightmost 3 bits,
               ADD    BX,08                  ;  add 8 for tab stop
E70:           MOV    COUNT,BX
               JMP    E30
E90:           MOV    BX,COUNT               ;End of file
               MOV    BYTE PTR [DI+BX],0CH   ;Form feed
               CALL   P10PRINT               ;Print last line
               RET
E10XFER        ENDP
;                     Display routine:
;                     ---------------        ;Uses AX, BX, DX
F10DISPLY PROC        NEAR                    ;BP, CX set on entry
               MOV    AX,1301H               ;Request display
               MOV    BX,0016H               ;Page:attribute
               MOV    DH,ROW                 ;Row
               MOV    DL,10                  ;Column
               INT    10H
               INC    ROW                    ;Next screen row
               RET
F10DISPLY ENDP
;                     Print line and clear to blanks:
;                     -------------------------------
P10PRINT  PROC        NEAR                    ;Uses AX, BX, CX, DI, DX
               MOV    AH,40H                 ;Request print
               MOV    BX,04
               MOV    CX,COUNT               ;Length of line
               INC    CX
               LEA    DX,PRNTAREA
               INT    21H
               MOV    AL,20H                 ;Clear print line
               MOV    CX,PRINT_LEN
               LEA    DI,PRNTAREA
               REP STOSB
               RET
P10PRINT  ENDP
               END    A10MAIN
```

Figure 20-2 *Continued*

Some print commands require a preceding Esc (escape) character (1BH):

1B 30 Set line spacing to eight lines per inch
1B 32 Set line spacing to six lines per inch
1B 45 Set on emphasized printing mode
1B 46 Set off emphasized printing mode

You can send control characters to the printer in two ways:

1. Define control characters in the data area. The following sets condensed mode, sets eight lines per inch, prints a title, and causes a carriage return and line feed:

```
HEADING DB 0FH, 1BH, 30H, 'Mountain Outfitting Corp.', 0DH, 0AH
```

2. Use function 40H to send control characters to the printer:

```
CONDMODE DB   0FH           ;Condensed mode
         . . .
         MOV  AH,40H        ;Request print
         MOV  BX,04         ;File handle
         MOV  CX,01         ;No. of characters
         LEA  DX,CONDMOD    ;Condensed mode
         INT  21H           ;Call interrupt service
```

All subsequent characters print in condensed mode until the program sends another command that resets the mode.

BIOS INT 17H FUNCTIONS FOR PRINTING

INT 17H provides facilities for printing at the BIOS level. Valid printer ports for LPT1, LPT2, and LPT3 are 0 (the default), 1, and 2, respectively. INT 17H provides three functions, as specified in the AH register:

1. First issue function 02H to determine the printer's status, via a selected port number. Include this status test before every attempt to print. If the printer is available, then

2. Issue function 01H to initialize the printer port, and

3. Issue function 00H operations to send characters to the printer.

The operations return the printer status to AH, with one or more bits set to 1:

BIT	CAUSE	BIT	CAUSE
0	Time out	5	Out of paper
3	Input/output error	6	Acknowledged from printer
4	Selected	7	Not busy

If the printer is already switched on and ready, the operation returns 90H (binary 10010000): The printer is not busy and is selected, a valid condition. Printer errors are bit 5 (out of paper) and bit 3 (output error). If the printer is not switched on, the operation returns B0H, or binary 10110000, indicating "out of paper."

INT 17H Function 00H: Print a Character.   This operation causes printing of one character and allows for printer ports 0, 1, or 2. Load the character in AL and the printer port number in DX:

```
MOV  AH,00H    ;Request print
MOV  AL,char   ;Character to be printed
MOV  DX,00     ;Select printer port 0
INT  17H       ;Call interrupt service
```

The operation returns the status to AH. The recommended practice is to use function 02H first to check the printer status.

INT 17H Function 01H: Initialize the Printer Port.   This operation selects a port, resets the printer, and initializes it for data. The following example selects port 0:

```
MOV  AH,01H  ;Request initialize port
MOV  DX,00   ;Select printer port 0
INT  17H     ;Call interrupt service
```

Because the operation sends a Form Feed character to the printer, you can use it to set the forms to the top-of-page position, although most printers do this automatically when turned on. The operation returns a status code in AH.

INT 17H Function 02H: Get Printer Port Status.   The purpose of this operation is to determine the status of the printer. The following example selects port 0:

```
MOV   AH,02H          ;Request read port
MOV   DX,00           ;Select printer port 0
INT   17H             ;Call interrupt service
TEST  AH,00101001B    ;Ready?
JNZ   errormsg        ; no, display message
```

The operation returns the same printer port status as function 01H. When the program runs, if the printer is not initially turned on, BIOS is unable to return a message automatically—the program is supposed to test and act upon the printer status. If the program does not check the status, the only indication is the cursor blinking. If you turn on the printer at this point, some of the output data is lost. Consequently, before executing any BIOS print operations, check the port status; if there is an error, display a message. (INT 21H performs this checking automatically, although its message, "Out of paper," applies to various conditions.) When the printer is switched on, the message no longer appears and printing begins normally with no loss of data.

At any time, a printer may run out of forms or may be inadvertently switched off. If you are writing a program for others to use, include a status test (function 02H) before every attempt to print.

KEY POINTS

- The standard printer control characters are horizontal tab, carriage return, line feed, and form feed.

- After printing is completed, use a Line Feed or Form Feed command to clear the printer buffer.
- INT 21H function 40H prints strings of characters, whereas BIOS INT 17H prints a single character at a time.
- The system displays a message if there is a printer error, although BIOS returns only a status code. When using BIOS INT 17H, use function 02H to check the printer status before printing.

REVIEW QUESTIONS AND EXERCISES

20-1. Provide the printer control characters for (a) Carriage Return, (b) Line Feed, (c) Form Feed, (d) Horizontal Tab.

20-2. Code a program using INT 21H function 40H for the following requirements: (a) Eject the forms to the next page, (b) define and print your name, (c) perform a carriage return and a line feed, and print your street address, (d) perform a carriage return and line feed, and print your city and state, (e) eject the forms.

20-3. Revise the program in Question 20-2 so that the name is printed in expanded mode, street and address in condensed mode, and city and state are in normal size but emphasized mode.

20-4. Revise Question 20-3 so that the program performs parts (b), (c), and (d) five times.

20-5. Revise Figure 20-3 so that it also displays the printed lines.

20-6. Define a heading line that provides for a carriage return and form feed operation, sets condensed mode, defines a title (any name), and turns off condensed mode.

20-7. INT 17H for printing returns an error code in AH. What do the following codes mean? (a) 08H, (b) 10H, (c) 90H.

20-8. Revise Question 20-2 to use INT 17H. Include a test for the printer status.

Chapter 21
Defining and Using Macros

Objective: To explain the definition and use of macro instructions.

INTRODUCTION

For each symbolic instruction that you code, the assembler generates one machine-language instruction. On the other hand, for each coded statement in a high-level language such as C or BASIC, the compiler may generate many machine-language instructions. In this regard, you can think of a high-level language as consisting of a set of *macro* statements.

The assembler has facilities that you can use to define macros. You define a unique name for the macro, along with the set of assembly language instructions that the macro is to generate. Then, wherever you need to code the set of instructions, simply code the name of the macro, and the assembler automatically generates your defined instructions.

Macros are useful for the following purposes:

- To simplify and reduce the amount of repetitive coding.
- To reduce errors caused by repetitive coding.
- To make an assembly language program more readable.

Examples of functions that may be implemented by macros are input/output operations that load registers and perform interrupts, conversions of ASCII and binary data, multiword arithmetic operations, mouse initialization, and string-handling routines.

You may catalog macros in a library where they are available to every program. A program may use a macro once (such as initializing segment addresses) or many times (such as displaying data). A library typically also contains cataloged procedures.

The choice of coding an operation as a macro or as a procedure depends largely on these factors: A macro generally executes faster because there is no need to call and return. A procedure, on the other hand, generally results in a smaller program because the code appears only once. In general, a macro is used where it is not coded many times in a program and the requirement is fairly simple.

Here is the basic format of a *macro definition*:

macroname	MACRO [*parameter-list*]	;Define macro
	[instructions]	;Body of macro
	ENDM	;End of macro

The MACRO directive on the first line tells the assembler that the instructions that follow, up to ENDM, are to be part of a macro definition. The ENDM ("end macro") directive ends the macro definition. The instructions between MACRO and ENDM comprise the body of the macro definition.

To include a macro within a program, you first define it or copy it from a macro library. The macro definition appears before the coding of any segment.

SIMPLE MACRO DEFINITIONS

Let's first examine a simple macro definition that initializes segment registers for an .EXE program:

```
INITZ   MACRO           ;Define macro
        MOV AX,@data    ;   } Body of
        MOV DS,AX        ;   } macro
        MOV ES,AX        ;   } definition
        ENDM            ;End of macro
```

The name of this macro is INITZ. The data items referenced in the macro definition—@data, AX, DS, and ES—must be defined elsewhere in the program or must otherwise be known to the assembler.

You may subsequently use the macro instruction INITZ in the code segment where you want to initialize the registers. When the assembler encounters the macro instruction INITZ, it scans its table of symbolic instructions and, failing to find an entry, checks for macro instructions. Because the program contains a definition of the macro INITZ, the assembler substitutes the body of the definition, generating the instructions—the *macro expansion*. A program would use the macro instruction INITZ only once, although other macros are designed to be used any number of times, and each time the assembler generates the macro expansion.

As well, here's the definition of a second macro named FINISH that handles normal exiting from a program:

```
FINISH  MACRO           ;Define macro
        MOV AX,4C00H    ;Request
        INT 21H         ;end of processing
        ENDM            ;End of macro
```

```
                    TITLE    A21MACR1 Simple macro definitions
                    INITZ    MACRO             ;Define macro
                             MOV     AX,@data  ;Initialize
                             MOV     DS,AX     ;  segment
                             MOV     ES,AX     ;  registers
                             ENDM              ;End macro
                    FINISH   MACRO             ;Define macro
                             MOV     AX,4C00H  ;End processing
                             INT     21H
                             ENDM              ;End macro
                    ;  --------------------------------------------
                             .MODEL SMALL
                             .STACK 64
                             .DATA
0000 54 65 73 74 20 6F  MESSGE  DB    'Test of macro', 13, 10, '$'
     66 20 6D 61 63 72
     6F 0D 0A 24
                             .CODE
0000                     BEGIN  PROC  FAR
                                INITZ            ;Macro instruction
0000 B8 ---- R   1              MOV   AX,@data   ;Initialize segment
0003 8E D8       1              MOV   DS,AX      ;  registers
0005 8E C0       1              MOV   ES,AX
0007 B4 09                      MOV   AH,09H     ;Request display
0009 8D 16 0000 R               LEA   DX,MESSGE  ;Message
000D CD 21                      INT   21H
                                FINISH
000F B8 4C00    1               MOV   AX,4C00H   ;End processing
0012 CD 21      1               INT   21H
0014                     BEGIN  ENDP
                                END   BEGIN
```

Figure 21-1   Simple Assembled Macro Instructions

Figure 21-1 provides a listing of an assembled program that defines and uses both INITZ and FINISH. This particular assembler version lists the macro expansion with the number 1 to the left of each instruction to indicate that a macro instruction generated it.

Note that macro definitions, when assembled, do not generate any object code; it is the macro expansions that generate object code. As well, a macro expansion does not print directives like ASSUME or PAGE that are coded in the macro definition.

It's hardly worth bothering to define a macro that is to be used only once, but you could catalog the macro in a library for use with all programs. A later section explains how to catalog macros in a library and how to include them automatically in a program.

USING PARAMETERS IN MACROS

To make a macro more flexible, you can define parameters in the operand as *dummy arguments*. The following macro definition named PROMPT provides for the use of INT 21H function 09H to display messages:

```
        PROMPT   MACRO   MESSGE        ;Dummy argument
                 MOV     AH,09H
                 LEA     DX,MESSGE
                 INT     21H
                 ENDM                  ;End of macro
```

When using this macro instruction, you have to supply the name of the message, which references a data area terminated by a dollar sign. Also, the macro could contain instructions that push and pop the used registers AH and DX.

A dummy argument in a macro definition tells the assembler to match its name with any occurrence of the same name in the macro body. For example, the dummy argument MESSGE is also an operand in the LEA instruction. Suppose that the program defines a prompt named MESSAGE2 as

```
MESSAGE2 DB 'Enter the date as mm/dd/yy', '$'
```

You now want to use the macro instruction PROMPT to display MESSAGE2. To this end, supply the name MESSAGE2 as a parameter:

```
PROMPT MESSAGE2
```

The parameter (MESSAGE2) in the macro instruction matches the dummy argument (MESSGE) in the original macro definition:

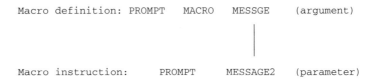

```
Macro definition: PROMPT    MACRO    MESSGE     (argument)



Macro instruction:     PROMPT    MESSAGE2   (parameter)
```

The assembler has already matched the argument in the original macro definition with operand in the LEA statement. It now substitutes the parameter(s) of the macro instruction MESSAGE2 with the dummy argument, MESSGE, in the macro definition. The assembler substitutes MESSAGE2 for the occurrence of MESSGE in the LEA instruction and would substitute it for any other occurrence of MESSGE.

The macro definition and its expansions are shown in full in Figure 21-2. The program also defines the macros INITZ and FINISH at the start and uses them in the code segment.

A dummy argument may contain any valid name, including a register name such as CX. You may define a macro with any number of dummy arguments, separated by commas, up to column 120 of a line (depending on the assembler version). The assembler substitutes parameters of the macro instruction for dummy arguments in the macro definition, entry for entry, from left to right.

USING COMMENTS IN MACROS

You may code comments in a macro definition to clarify its purpose. A semicolon or a COMMENT directive indicates a comment line. The following example of a comment uses semicolons:

```
PROMPT   MACRO    MESSGE
;          This macro permits a display of messages
         MOV  AH,09H        ;Request display
         LEA  DX,MESSGE      ; prompt
         INT  21H
         ENDM
```

```
      TITLE   A21MACR2 (EXE)  Use of parameters
      INITZ   MACRO                    ;Define macro
              MOV     AX,@data         ;Initialize segment
              MOV     DS,AX            ;  registers
              MOV     ES,AX
              ENDM                     ;End macro

      PROMPT  MACRO   MESSGE           ;Define macro
              MOV     AH,09H           ;Request display
              LEA     DX,MESSGE        ;  prompt
              INT     21H
              ENDM                     ;End macro

      FINISH  MACRO                    ;Define macro
              MOV     AX,4C00H         ;End processing
              INT     21H
              ENDM                     ;End macro
      ; ---------------------------------------------------
              .MODEL  SMALL
              .STACK  64
              .DATA
      MESSG1  DB      'Name? ', '$'
      MESSG2  DB      'Address? ', '$'
              .CODE
      BEGIN   PROC    FAR
              INITZ
              PROMPT  MESSG1
              PROMPT  MESSG2
              FINISH
      BEGIN   ENDP
              END     BEGIN
```

Figure 21-2 Using Macro Parameters

Because the default is to list only instructions that generate object code, the assembler does not automatically display a comment when it expands a macro definition. To get a comment to appear within an expansion, use the listing directive .LALL ("list all," including the leading period) prior to requesting the macro instruction:

```
            .LALL
            PROMPT    MESSAGE1
```

A macro definition could contain a number of comments, but you may want to list some and suppress others. Still use .LALL to list them, but code double semicolons (;;) before comments that are always to be suppressed. (The assembler's default is .XALL, which causes a listing only of instructions that generate object code.)

On the other hand, you may not want to list any of the source code of a macro expansion, especially if the macro instruction is used several times in a program. In that case, code the listing directive .SALL ("suppress all"), which reduces the size of the printed program, although it has no effect on the size of the generated object program.

A listing directive holds effect throughout a program until another listing directive is encountered. You can place them in a program to cause some macros to list only the generated object code (.XALL), some to list both object code and comments (.LALL), and some to suppress listing both object code and comments (.SALL). MASM 6.0 introduced the

```
        TITLE   A21MACR3 (EXE)   Use of .LALL & .SALL
        INITZ   MACRO                    ;Define macro
                MOV     AX,@data         ;Initialize segment
                MOV     DS,AX            ;  registers
                MOV     ES,AX
                ENDM                     ;End macro


        PROMPT  MACRO   MESSGE
        ;       This macro displays any message
        ;;              Data requires $ delimiter
                MOV     AH,09H           ;Request display
                LEA     DX,MESSGE        ;  prompt
                INT     21H
                ENDM


        FINISH  MACRO                    ;Define macro
                MOV     AX,4C00H         ;End processing
                INT     21H
                ENDM                     ;End macro
        ; ---------------------------------------------
                .MODEL SMALL
                .STACK 64
                .DATA
        MESSG1  DB      'Name? ', '$'
        MESSG2  DB      'Address? ', '$'
        ; ---------------------------------------------
                .CODE
        BEGIN   PROC    FAR
                .SALL
                INITZ
                PROMPT MESSG1
                .LALL
                PROMPT MESSG2
                .SALL
                FINISH
        BEGIN   ENDP
                END     BEGIN
```

Figure 21-3   List and Suppress Macro Expansions

terms .LISTMACROALL, LISTMACRO, and .NOLISTMACRO for .LALL, .XALL, and .SALL, respectively.

The program in Figure 21-3 illustrates the preceding features. It contains the macros INITZ, FINISH, and PROMPT, described earlier. The code segment contains the listing directive .SALL to suppress listing the expansion of INITZ and FINISH and the first expansion of PROMPT. For the second use of PROMPT, the listing directive .LALL causes the assembler to list the comment and the expansion of the macro. But note that in the macro definition for PROMPT, the comment in the macro expansion containing a double semicolon (;;) is not listed.

NESTED MACROS

A macro definition may contain a reference to one or more other defined (nested) macros. Consider the following two macro definitions, SET_CURSOR and DISPLAY:

```
SET_CURSOR  MACRO  ROW,  COL      DISPLAY  MACRO    MESSGE
            MOV    AH,02H                  MOV      AH,09H
```

```
MOV    BX,0              LEA    DX,MESSGE
MOV    DH,ROW            INT    21H
MOV    DL,COL            ENDM
INT    10H
ENDM
```

A third macro named CURS_DISPLAY could request the SET_CURSOR and DISPLAY macros. CURS_DISPLAY defines the parameters for both nested macros in this way:

```
CURS_DISPLAY   MACRO M_ROW, M_COL, MESSGE
               PUSHA
               SET_CURSOR M_ROW, M_COL
               DISPLAY MESSGE
               POPA
               ENDM
```

You may code CURS_DISPLAY with constants, variables, or registers for row and column, as

```
CURS_DISPLAY 6, 15, ERROR_MSSGE        ;Constants
CURS_DISPLAY ROW, COLUMN, ERROR_MSSGE  ;Variables
CURS_DISPLAY CH, CL, ERROR_MSSGE       ;Registers
```

MACRO DIRECTIVES

The assembler supports a number of useful directives, including LOCAL, PURGE, repetition, and conditional.

The LOCAL Directive

Some macros require the definition of data items and instruction labels within the macro definition itself. However, if you use the macro more than once in the same program, and the assembler defines the data item or label for each occurrence, the duplicate names cause the assembler to generate an error message. To ensure that each generated name is unique, code the LOCAL directive immediately after the MACRO statement, even before comments. Its format is

```
LOCAL    localname-1,  localname-2,  ...
```

The partial program Figure 21-4 illustrates the use of LOCAL. The purpose of the DIVIDE macro is to perform division by successive subtraction. The macro subtracts the divisor from the dividend and adds 1 to the quotient until the dividend is less than the divisor. The macro requires two labels: COMP for the loop address and OUT for exiting the procedure on completion. Both COMP and OUT are defined as LOCAL and may have any valid names.

The program uses DIVIDE twice. In the first macro expansion, the generated symbolic label for COMP is ??0000 and for OUT is ??0001. In the second expansion, the sym-

```
        TITLE    A21MACR4 (EXE)   Use of LOCAL
        DIVIDE   MACRO    DIVIDEND,DIVISOR,QUOTIENT
                 LOCAL    COMP
                 LOCAL    OUT
        ;        AX = div'd, BX = divisor, CX = quotient
                 MOV      AX,DIVIDEND      ;Set dividend
                 MOV      BX,DIVISOR       ;Set divisor
                 SUB      CX,CX            ;Clear quotient
        COMP:
                 CMP      AX,BX            ;Dividend < divisor?
                 JB       OUT              ;  yes, exit
                 SUB      AX,BX            ;Dividend - divisor
                 INC      CX               ;Add to quotient
                 JMP      COMP
        OUT:
                 MOV      QUOTIENT,CX      ;Store quotient
                 ENDM                      ;End macro
        ; -----------------------------------------------
                 .  DATA
        DIVDND1  DW       150              ;Dividend
        DIVSOR1  DW       27               ;Divisor
        QUOTNT1  DW       ?                ;Quotient
        DIVDND2  DW       265              ;Dividend
        DIVSOR2  DW       34               ;Divisor
        QUOTNT2  DW       ?                ;Quotient
                 .CODE
                 . . .
                 DIVIDE DIVDND1,DIVSOR1,QUOTNT1
                 DIVIDE DIVDND2,DIVSOR2,QUOTNT2
                 . . .
```

Figure 21-4   Using the LOCAL Directive

bolic labels are ??0002 and ??0003, respectively. In this way, the feature ensures that each label generated within a program is unique.

Including Macros from a Library

A programming practice is to define macros such as INITZ, FINISH, and PROMPT and use them any number of times. The standard approach is to catalog macros in a disk library under a descriptive name, such as MACRO.LBY. Simply gather all your macro definitions into one or more files that you store on disk:

```
        INITZ    MACRO
                 . . .
                 ENDM
        PROMPT   MACRO    MESSGE
                 . . .
                 ENDM
```

You can use an editor or word processor to write the file, but be sure it is an unformatted ASCII file. The following examples assume that the file is stored under the name MACRO.LBY. Your programs can now use any of the cataloged macros, but instead of coding MACRO definitions at the start of the program, use an INCLUDE directive like this:

```
        INCLUDE path:\MACRO.LBY
```

The assembler accesses the file named MACRO.LBY: and includes *all* the cataloged macro definitions into the program, although your program may need only some of them. The assembled listing will contain a copy of the macro definitions, indicated by the letter C in column 30 of the .LST file for some assembler versions.

For an assembler that involves a two-pass operation, you can use the following statements to cause INCLUDE to occur only during pass 1 (instead of both passes):

```
        IF1
                        INCLUDE path:\MACRO.LBY
        ENDIF
```

IF1 and ENDIF are conditional directives. IF1 tells the assembler to access the named library only on pass 1 of the assembly. ENDIF terminates the IF logic. A copy of the macro definition no longer appears on the listing—a saving of both time and space. However, MASM as of version 6.0 does not need directives that refer to two passes.

The placement of INCLUDE is not critical, but must appear before any macro instruction that references an entry in the library.

The PURGE Directive.   Execution of an INCLUDE statement causes the assembler to include all the macro definitions that are in the specified library. Suppose, however, that the library contains the macros INITZ, FINISH, PROMPT, and DIVIDE, but a program requires only INITZ and FINISH. The PURGE directive enables you to delete the unwanted macros PROMPT and DIVIDE from the current assembly:

```
        IF1
                INCLUDE path:\MACRO.LBY      ;Include full library
        ENDIF
        PURGE    PROMPT,DIVIDE               ;Delete unneeded macros
        ...
        INITZ    ...                         ;Use remaining macros
```

The PURGE operation facilitates only the assembly of a program and has no effect on the macros stored in the library.

Concatenation

The ampersand (&) character tells the assembler to join (concatenate) text or symbols. In the following macro, an ampersand facilitates generating a MOVSB, MOVSW, or MOVSD instruction:

```
            STRMOVE   MACRO    TAG
                      REP MOVS&TAG
                      ENDM
```

A user could code this macro instruction as STRMOVE B, STRMOVE W, or STRMOVE D. The assembler then concatenates the parameter B, W, or D with the MOVS instruction to produce REP MOVSB, REP MOVSW, or REP MOVSD, respectively. (This somewhat trivial example is offered for illustrative purposes.)

Repetition Directives

The repetition directives REPT, IRP, and IRPC cause the assembler to repeat a block of statements up to the directive's terminating ENDM statement. (MASM 6.0 introduced the terms REPEAT, FOR, and FORC for REPT, IRP, and IRPC, respectively.) These directives do not have to be contained in a MACRO definition, but if they are, you code an ENDM to end each repetition directive and another ENDM to end the MACRO definition.

REPT: Repeat Directive.   The REPT (or REPEAT) directive causes the assembler to repeat a block of statements up to ENDM according to the number of times in the *expression* entry:

REPT	expression

The first example generates the DEC instruction four times:

```
REPT   4
       DEC   SI
ENDM
```

The second example initializes the value N to 0 and then repeats the generation of DB N five times:

```
N =      0
REPT    5
    N =    N + 1
    DB     N
ENDM
```

The operation generates five DB statements: DB 1, DB 2, DB 3, DB 4, and DB 5. A use for REPT could be to define a table or part of a table. The next example defines a macro that uses REPT for beeping the speaker five times:

```
BEEPSPKR   MACRO
           MOV    AH,02H  ;Request output
           MOV    DL,07   ;Beep character
           REPT   5       ;Repeat five times
              INT   21H   ;Call interrupt service
           ENDM           ;End of REPT
           ENDM           ;End of MACRO
```

IRP: Indefinite Repeat Directive.   The IRP directive causes the assembler to repeat a block of statements up to ENDM. Its format is

```
IRP   parameter,<arguments>
      statements
ENDM
```

The *arguments*, contained in angle brackets, consist of any number of valid symbols, including string, numeric, or arithmetic constants. The assembler replaces the *parameter* with a *statement* for each argument. For the first example,

```
IRP     N,<3,9,17,25,28>
    DB    N
ENDM
```

the assembler generates DB 3, DB 9, DB 17, DB 25, and DB 28.
        For the second example,

```
IRP   REG <AX, BX, CX, DX>
    PUSH REG
ENDM
```

the assembler generates a PUSH statement for each of the specified registers.

IRPC: Indefinite Repeat Character Directive. The IRPC (or FORC) directive causes the assembler to repeat a block of statements up to ENDM. Its format is

```
IRPC   parameter,string
        statements
ENDM
```

The assembler generates a *statement* for each character in the *string*. In the following example,

```
IRPC  N,345678
    DW    N
ENDM
```

the assembler generates DW 3 through DW 8.

Conditional Directives

An earlier example of conditional directives used IF1 to include a library entry only during pass 1 of an assembly. Conditional directives are most useful within a macro definition, but are not limited to that purpose. Every IFnn directive must have a matching ENDIF to terminate a tested condition. One optional ELSE may provide an alternative action. The treatment of conditions is much like that of the C language. Here is the format for the IF family of conditional directives:

```
IFxx    (condition)
...                     } conditional
ELSE    (optional) }
...                     } block
ENDIF   (end of IF)
```

Omission of ENDIF causes the error message "Undetermined conditional." If the assembler finds that a *condition* is true, it executes the conditional block up to the ELSE or, if no ELSE is present, up to the ENDIF. If the condition is false, the assembler executes the conditional block following the ELSE; if no ELSE is present, it does not generate any of the conditional block.

The following explains how the assembler handles the conditional directives:

- IF *expression*: If the expression evaluates to true (nonzero value), assemble the statements within the conditional block.
- IFE *expression*: If the expression evaluates to false (zero), assemble the statements within the conditional block.
- IF1 (*no expression*): If processing pass 1, act on the statements in the conditional block.
- IF2 (*no expression*): If processing pass 2, act on the statements in the conditional block.
- IFDEF *symbol*: If the symbol is defined in the program or is declared as EXTRN, process the statements in the conditional block.
- IFNDEF *symbol*: If the symbol is not defined or is not declared as EXTRN, process the statements in the conditional block.
- IFB <*argument*>: If the argument is blank, process the statements in the conditional block. The argument is enclosed in angle brackets.
- IFNB <*argument*>: If the argument is not blank, process the statements in the conditional block. The argument is enclosed in angle brackets.
- IFIDN <*arg-1*>,<*arg-2*>: If the arguments are equal, process the statements in the conditional block. The arguments are enclosed in angle brackets.
- IFDIF <*arg-1*>,<*arg-2*>: If the arguments are unequal, process the statements in the conditional block. The arguments are enclosed in angle brackets.

IF and IFE can use the relational operators EQ (equal), NE (not equal), LT (less than), LE (less than or equal), GT (greater than), and GE (greater than or equal) as, for example, in the statement

```
IF expression1 EQ expression2
```

Here's a simple example of the use of IFNB (if not blank). INT 21H function 4CH enables a program to end processing and to deliver a return code in AL. The following example revises the FINISH macro used earlier to provide for a return code:

```
FINISH  MACRO    RETCODE
        MOV      AH,4CH              ;Request end processing
        IFNB     <RETCODE>
            MOV      AL,RETCODE      ;Return code
        ELSE
            MOV AL,00H               ;Default exit code
        ENDIF
        INT      21H                 ;Call interrupt service
        ENDM
```

Here's another example of the use of IFNB. A standard practice is for a procedure to preserve the registers that it has to use by means of PUSH instructions on entry and POP on exit. The number and type of registers vary according to the procedures. The following macros, PUSHMAC and POPMAC, provide for handling one or two registers, but could easily be expanded to include any number:

```
PUSHMAC  MACRO   REG1, REG2     POPMAC   MACRO   REG1, REG2
         IFNB    <REG1>                   IFNB    <REG1>
            PUSH REG1                         POP REG1
         ENDIF                            ENDIF
         IFNB    <REG2>                   IFNB    <REG2>
            PUSH REG2                         POP REG2
         ENDIF                            ENDIF
         ENDM                             ENDM
```

The macros are used in this way:

```
PUSHMAC AX, BX
POPMAC  BX, AX
```

The EXITM Directive

A macro definition may contain a conditional directive that tests for a serious condition. If the condition is true, the assembler is to exit from any further expansion of the macro by means of the EXITM directive:

```
IFxx   [condition]
...    (invalid condition)
EXITM
...
ENDIF
```

If the assembler encounters EXITM in an expansion of a macro instruction, it discontinues the macro expansion and resumes processing after ENDM. You can also use EXITM to end REPT, IRP, and IRPC directives, even if they are contained within a macro definition.

Macro Using IF and IFNDEF Conditions

The partial program in Figure 21-5 contains a macro definition named DIVIDE that generates a routine to perform division by successive subtraction. A user has to code the DIVIDE macro instruction with parameters for the dividend, divisor, and quotient, in that order. The macro uses IFNDEF to check whether these data items are actually defined in the program. For any item not defined, the macro increments a field arbitrarily named COUNTER. (COUNTER could have any valid name and is for temporary use within the macro definition.) After checking the three parameters, the macro checks COUNTER for nonzero:

```
IF    COUNTER
;   Macro expansion terminated
EXITM
ENDIF
```

If COUNTER has been set to a nonzero value, the assembler generates the comment shown in the preceding code and exits (EXITM) from any further expansion of the macro. Note that an initial instruction clears COUNTER to 0 and also that the IFNDEF blocks need only to set COUNTER to 1 rather than increment it.

   If the conditions pass all the tests safely, the assembler generates the macro expansion. In the code segment, the second DIVIDE macro instruction contains an invalid divi-

```
TITLE    A21MACR5 (EXE)   Test of IF and IFNDEF
DIVIDE   MACRO    DIVIDEND,DIVISOR,QUOTIENT
         LOCAL    COMP
         LOCAL    OUT
         CNTR     = 0
;        AX = div'nd, BX = div'r, CX = quot't
         IFNDEF DIVIDEND
;                Dividend not defined
         CNTR     = CNTR +1
         ENDIF
         IFNDEF DIVISOR
;                Divisor not defined
         CNTR     = CNTR +1
         ENDIF
         IFNDEF QUOTIENT
;                Quotient not defined
         CNTR     = CNTR + 1
         ENDIF
         IF       CNTR
;                Macro expansion terminated
         EXITM
         ENDIF
         PUSHA                      ;Preserve registers
         MOV      AX,DIVIDEND       ;Set dividend
         MOV      BX,DIVISOR        ;Set divisor
         SUB      CX,CX             ;Clear quotient
COMP:
         CMP      AX,BX             ;Dividend < divisor?
         JB       OUT               ;  yes, exit
         SUB      AX,BX             ;Dividend - divisor
         INC      CX                ;Add to quotient
         JMP      COMP
OUT:
         MOV      QUOTIENT,CX       ;Store quotient
         POPA                       ;Restore registers
         ENDM
.286     ; ------------------------------------------
         .DATA
DIVDEND  DW       150               ;Dividend
DIVISOR  DW       27                ;Divisor
QUOTENT  DW       ?                 ;Quotient
         .CODE
         ...
         .LALL
         DIVIDE DIVDEND,DIVISOR,QUOTENT
         DIVIDE DIDND,DIVISOR,QUOT
         ...
```

Figure 21-5   Using the IF and IFNDEF Directives

dend and quotient and generates only comments. A way to improve the macro would be to test whether the divisor is nonzero and whether the dividend and divisor have the same sign. For these purposes, use assembly instructions rather than conditional directives because the conditions occur when the program is executed, not when it is assembled.

Macro Using IFIDN Condition

The partial program in Figure 21-6 contains a macro definition named MOVIF that generates MOVSB or MOVSW, depending on the parameter supplied. A user has to code the macro instruction with the parameter B (byte) or W (word) to indicate whether MOVS is to become MOVSB or MOVSW. The two occurrences of IFIDN in the macro definition are

```
TITLE    A21MACR6 (EXE)   Tests of IFIDN
MOVIF    MACRO   TAG              ;Define macro
         IFIDN   <&TAG>,<B>
         REP MOVSB                ;Move bytes
         EXITM
         ENDIF
         IFIDN   <&TAG>,<W>
         REP MOVSW                ;Move words
         ELSE
;        No B or W tag, default to B
         REP MOVSB                ;Move bytes
         ENDIF
         ENDM                     ;End of macro
; ------------------------------------
         .CODE
         ...
         MOVIF   B
         MOVIF   W
         MOVIF
         ...
```

Figure 21-6   Using the IFIDN Directive

```
IFIDN   <&TAG>,<B>     IFIDN <&TAG>,<W>
REP   MOVSB            REP MOVSW
    . . .                  . . .
```

The first IFIDN generates REP MOVSB if you code MOVIF B as a macro instruction, and the second IFIDN generates REP MOVSW if you code MOVIF W. If a user does not supply B or W, the assembler generates a comment and default to MOVSB. (The normal use of the ampersand (&) operator is for concatenation.)

The three examples of MOVIF in the code segment test for B, for W, and for an invalid condition. Don't attempt to execute the program as it stands because DI and SI have to contain proper values for the MOVS instructions. Admittedly, this macro is not very useful, since its purpose is to illustrate the use of conditional directives in a simple manner. By now, however, you should be able to develop some meaningful macros of your own.

KEY POINTS

- A macro definition requires a MACRO directive, a block of one or more statements known as the body that the macro definition is to generate, and an ENDM directive to end the definition.
- A macro instruction is the use of the macro in a program. The code that a macro instruction generates is the macro expansion.
- The .SALL, .LALL, and .XALL directives control the listing of comments and the object code generated in a macro expansion.
- The LOCAL directive facilitates using names within a macro definition and must appear immediately after the macro statement.
- The use of dummy arguments in a macro definition allows a user to code parameters for more flexibility.
- A macro library makes cataloged macros available to other programs.
- Conditional directives enable a program to validate macro parameters.

REVIEW QUESTIONS AND EXERCISES

21-1. Under what circumstances would you use (a) a macro, and (b) a called procedure?

21-2. Code the first and last lines for a simple macro definition named MACARONI.

21-3. Distinguish between the body of a macro definition and the macro expansion.

21-4. What is a dummy argument?

21-5. Code the directives for the following statements: (a) List only instructions that generate object code. (b) Suppress all instructions that a macro generates.

21-6. Code two macro definitions that perform multiplication: (a) MPYBYTE is to generate code that multiplies byte x byte; (b) MPYWORD is to generate code that multiplies word x word. Include the multiplicands and multipliers as dummy arguments in the macro definition. Test the execution of the macros with a small program that also defines the required data fields.

21-7. Store the macros defined in Question 21-6 in a macro library. Revise the program to INCLUDE the library entries during pass 1 of the assembly.

21-8. Write a macro named BIOSPRINT that uses INT 17H to print. The macro should include a test for the status of the printer and should provide for any defined print line with any length.

21-9. Revise the macro in Figure 21-4 so that it generates code to bypass the division if the divisor is zero when the program executes.

21-10. Write, assemble, and test a program that uses the macros named MPYBYTE, MPYWORD, and BIOSPRINT. (a) Define two one-byte fields and two one-word fields, all containing numeric data. (b) Use MPYBYTE to multiply the one-byte fields and use MPYWORD to multiply the one-word fields. (c) Convert the products into ASCII format and use BIOSPRINT to print them.

21-11. Identify the conditional directives for the given requirements. Process statements in the conditional block only if (a) the argument is blank, (b) the expression is zero, (c) the two arguments are equal, (d) the expression is nonzero.

Chapter 22

Linking to Subprograms

> Objective: To cover the programming techniques involved in assembling, linking, and executing separate programs.

INTRODUCTION

Up to this chapter, all of the programs have consisted of one standalone assembled module. It is possible, however, to develop a program that consists of a main program linked with one or more separately assembled subprograms. The following are reasons for organizing a program into subprograms:

- To link between languages—for example, to combine the ease of coding in a high-level language with the processing efficiency of assembly language.
- To facilitate the development of large projects in which different teams produce their modules separately.
- To overlay parts of a program during execution because of the program's large size.

Each program is assembled separately and generates its own unique object (.OBJ) module. The linker then links the object modules into one combined executable (.EXE) module. Typically, the main program is the one that begins execution, and it calls one or more subprograms. Subprograms in turn may call other subprograms.

Figure 22-1 shows two examples of a hierarchy of a main program and three subprograms. In part (a), the main program calls subprograms 1, 2, and 3. In part (b), the main program calls subprograms 1 and 2, and only subprogram 1 calls subprogram 3.

There are numerous ways to organize subprograms, but the organization has to make sense to the assembler and linker. You also have to watch out for situations in which, for example, subprogram 1 calls subprogram 2, which calls subprogram 3, which in turn calls sub-

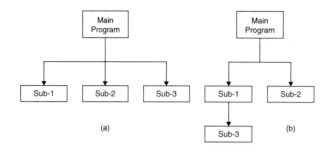

Figure 22-1   Program Hierarchy

program 1. This process, known as *recursion*, can be made to work but, if not handled carefully, can cause interesting execution bugs.

THE SEGMENT DIRECTIVE

This section covers a number of options used for coding the SEGMENT directive. The format for the full SEGMENT directive is

segment-name	SEGMENT	[*align*] [*combine*] ['*class*']

The align, combine, and class types are described next.

Align Type

The *align* operator (if coded) tells the assembler to align the named segment beginning on a particular storage boundary:

- BYTE. Byte boundary, for a segment of a subprogram that is to be combined with that of another program.
- WORD. Word boundary, for a segment of a subprogram that is to be combined with that of another program.
- DWORD. Doubleword boundary, normally for the 80386 and later processors.
- PARA. Paragraph boundary (divisible by 16, or 10H), the default and the most commonly used alignment for both main programs and subprograms.
- PAGE. Page boundary (divisible by 256, or 100H).

Omitting the align operator from the first segment causes a default to PARA. Omitting it from succeeding segments also causes a default to PARA if the name is unique; if it is not unique, the default is the alignment type of the previously defined segment of the same name.

Combine Type

The *combine* operator (if coded) tells the assembler and linker whether to combine segments or to keep them separate. (You have already used the STACK combine type for .EXE programs.) Other combine types relevant to this chapter are NONE, PUBLIC, and COMMON:

- NONE. The segment is to be logically separate from other segments, although they may all end up as physically adjacent. This type is the default for full segment directives.

- PUBLIC. The linker is to combine the segment with all other segments that are defined as PUBLIC and have the same segment name and class. The assembler calculates offsets from the beginning of the first segment. In effect, the combined segment contains a number of sections, each beginning with a SEGMENT directive and ending with ENDS. PUBLIC type is the default for simplified segment directives.
- COMMON. If COMMON segments have the same name and class, the linker gives them the same base address. During execution, the second segment overlays the first one. The largest segment determines the length of the common area.

Class Type

You have already used the *class* names 'Stack,' 'Data,' and 'Code.' You can assign the same class name to related segments so that the assembler and linker group them together. That is, they are to appear as segments one after the other, but are not combined into one segment unless the PUBLIC combine option is also coded. The class entry may contain any valid name, contained in single quotes, although the name 'Code' is recommended for the code segment.

The following two unrelated SEGMENT statements generate identical results, namely, an independent code segment aligned on a paragraph boundary:

```
CODESG1 SEGMENT PARA NONE 'Code'
CODESG2 SEGMENT 'Code' (defaults to PARA and NONE)
```

Fully defined segment directives were explained in Chapter 4, but subsequent chapters have used the simplified segment directives. Because full segment directives can provide tighter control when assembling and linking subprograms, most examples in this chapter use them.

Program examples in this and later chapters illustrate many of the Align, Combine, and Class options.

INTRASEGMENT CALLS

CALL instructions used to this point have been *intrasegment* calls; that is, the called procedure is in the same code segment as that of the calling procedure. An intrasegment CALL is *near* if the called procedure is defined as or defaults to NEAR (that is, within 32K). Programs defined with memory models Tiny, Small, and Compact default to near calls to internal procedures.

A near CALL pushes the IP register onto the stack and replaces IP with the offset of the destination address. Thus a near CALL references a (near) procedure within the same segment:

```
          CALL nearproc    ;Near call: push IP,
          ...              ;  link to nearproc
nearproc  PROC NEAR
          ...
          RET/RETN         ;Near return: pop IP,
nearproc  ENDP             ;  return to caller
```

Now consider a near intrasegment CALL statement that consists of object code E8 2000, where E8 is the operation code for CALL and 2000 (0020) is the offset of a called procedure. The operation pushes the IP onto the stack and stores the 2000 as 0020 in the IP. The processor then combines the current segment address in CS with the offset in IP (CS:IP) for the next instruction to execute. On exit from the called procedure, a (near) RET pops the stored IP off the stack and into IP so that the combined segment:offset address causes a return to the instruction following the CALL.

An intrasegment call may be near, as described, or far if the call is to a procedure defined as far within the same segment. RET is near if it appears in a NEAR procedure and far if it appears in a FAR procedure. You can code these instructions as RETN or RETF, respectively.

INTERSEGMENT CALLS

A CALL is classed as *far* if the called procedure is defined as FAR or as EXTRN, often but not necessarily in another code segment. Programs that are defined with Medium and Large memory models default to far calls.

A far CALL first pushes the contents of CS onto the stack and inserts the new segment address in CS. It then pushes IP onto the stack and inserts a new offset address in IP. (The pushed CS:IP values provide the address of the instruction immediately following the CALL.) In this way, both addresses of the code segment and the offset are saved for the return from the called procedure. A call to another segment is always an *intersegment* far call:

```
            CALL farproc   ;Far call: push CS and IP,
            ...            ;  link to farproc
   farproc  PROC FAR
            ...
            RET/RETF       ;Far return: pop IP and CS,
   farproc  ENDP           ;  return to caller
```

Consider an intersegment CALL statement that consists of object code 9A 0002 AF04. Hex 9A is the operation code for a far CALL, 0002 (or 0200) is the offset, and AF04 (or 04AF) is the new segment address. The operation pushes the current IP onto the stack and stores the new offset 0002 as 0200 in IP. It next pushes the current CS onto the stack and stores the new segment address AF04 as 04AF in CS. The processor then combines the current segment address in CS with the offset in IP (CS:IP) for the effective address of the first instruction to execute in the called subprogram:

```
   Address in code segment:   04AF0H
   Offset in IP:             + 0200H
   Effective address:         04CF0H
```

On exit from the called procedure, an intersegment (far) RET reverses the CALL operation, popping both the original IP and CS addresses back into their respective registers. The CS:IP pair now points to the address of the instruction following the original CALL, where execution resumes.

The basic difference then between a near and a far CALL is that a near CALL replaces only the IP offset, whereas a far CALL replaces both the CS segment address and the IP offset. A near RET/RETN is associated with a near CALL and a far RET/RETF with a far CALL.

THE EXTRN AND PUBLIC ATTRIBUTES

In Figure 22-2, the main program (MAINPROG) calls a subprogram (SUBPROG). The two modules are assembled separately. The requirement here is for an intersegment CALL.

The CALL in MAINPROG has to know that SUBPROG exists outside MAINPROG (or else the assembler generates an error message that SUBPROG is an undefined symbol). The directive EXTRN SUBPROG:FAR notifies the assembler that any reference to SUBPROG is to a FAR label that in this case is defined externally in another assembly. Because the assembler has no way of knowing what the address will be at execution time, it generates "empty" object code operands in the far CALL (the assembled .LST listing shows zeros for the offset and hyphens for the segment), which the linker subsequently is to fill:

```
9A 0000 ---- E          ;E = external
```

SUBPROG in its turn contains a PUBLIC directive that tells the assembler and linker that another module has to know the address of SUBPROG. In a later step, when both MAIN-PROG and SUBPROG are successfully assembled into separate object modules, they may be linked as follows:

```
LINK n:MAINPROG+n:SUBPROG,n:,CON
```

The linker matches EXTRNs in one object module with PUBLICs in the other and inserts any required offset addresses. It then combines the two object modules into one executable module. If unable to match references, the linker supplies error messages, which you should watch for before attempting to execute the linked module.

The EXTRN/EXTERN Directive

The EXTRN directive tells the assembler that the named item—a data item, procedure, or label—is defined in another assembly. (MASM 6.0 introduced the term EXTERN.) It has the following format:

```
          EXTRN   SUBPROG:FAR
MAINPROG  PROC    FAR
          . . .
          CALL    SUBPROG
          . . .
MAINPROG  ENDP
- - - - - - - - - - - - - - - - - - - - - - -
          PUBLIC  SUBPROG
SUBPROG   PROC    FAR
          . . .
          . . .
          RETF
SUBPROG   ENDP
```

Figure 22-2 Intersegment Call

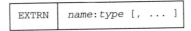

You can define more than one *name* up to the end of the line or code additional EXTRN statements. The other assembly module in its turn must define the name and identify it as PUBLIC. The *type* entry must be valid in terms of the actual definition of a name:

- ABS identifies a constant value.
- BYTE, WORD, and DWORD identify data items that one module references but another module defines.
- NEAR and FAR identify a procedure or instruction label that one module references but another module defines.
- A name defined by an EQU.

THE PUBLIC Directive

The PUBLIC directive tells the assembler and linker that the address of a specified symbol defined in the current assembly is to be available to other modules. The format for PUBLIC is

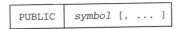

You can define more than one symbol up to the end of the line or code additional PUBLIC statements. The *symbol* entry can be a label (including PROC labels), a variable, or a number. Invalid entries include register names and EQU symbols that define values greater than two bytes.

The calling of far procedures and the use of EXTRN and PUBLIC, should offer little difficulty, although some care is required for making data defined in one module known in other modules.

The next sections examine two different ways of making data known between programs: using EXTRN and PUBLIC, and passing parameters.

USING EXTRN AND PUBLIC FOR AN ENTRY POINT

The program in Figure 22-3 consists of a main program, A22MAIN1, and a subprogram, A22SUB1, both using full segment directives. The main program defines segments for the stack, data, and code. The data segment defines QTY and PRICE. The code segment loads AX with PRICE and BX with QTY and then calls the subprogram. An EXTRN in the main program identifies the entry point to the subprogram as A22SUB1:FAR.

The subprogram A22SUB1 contains a PUBLIC statement (after the ASSUME) that makes its name known to the linker as the entry point for execution. This subprogram simply multiplies the contents of AX (price) by BX (quantity) and develops the product in the DX:AX pair as 002E 4000H.

```
                              TITLE      A22MAIN1 (EXE)  Call subprogram
                                         EXTRN   A22SUB1:FAR
         0000                 STACKSEG   SEGMENT PARA STACK 'Stack'
         0000  0040[????]                DW      64 DUP(?)
         0080                 STACKSEG   ENDS
                              ; --------------------------------------------------
         0000                 DATASEG    SEGMENT PARA 'Data'
         0000  0140           QTY        DW      0140H
         0002  2500           PRICE      DW      2500H
         0004                 DATASEG    ENDS
                              ; --------------------------------------------------
         0000                 CODESEG    SEGMENT PARA 'Code'
         0000                 BEGIN      PROC    FAR
                                         ASSUME  CS:CODESEG,DS:DATASEG,SS:STACKSEG
         0000  B8 ---- R                 MOV     AX,DATASEG
         0003  8E D8                     MOV     DS,AX
         0005  A1 0002 R                 MOV     AX,PRICE        ;Set up price
         0008  8B 1E 0000 R              MOV     BX,QTY          ;  and quantity
         000C  9A 0000 ---- E            CALL    A22SUB1         ;Call subprogram
         0011  B8 4C00                   MOV     AX,4C00H        ;End processing
         0014  CD 21                     INT     21H
         0016                 BEGIN      ENDP
         0016                 CODESEG    ENDS
                                         END     BEGIN
```

```
Segments and Groups:
    N a m e             Length   Align    Combine    Class
CODESEG   . . . . .     0016     PARA     NONE      'CODE'
DATASEG   . . . . .     0004     PARA     NONE      'DATA'
STACKSEG  . . . . .     0080     PARA     STACK     'STACK'
Symbols:
    N a m e             Type     Value    Attr
A22SUB1   . . . . . .   L FAR    0000     External
BEGIN     . . . . . .   F PROC   0000     CODESEG    Length = 0016
PRICE     . . . . . .   L WORD   0002     DATASEG
QTY       . . . . . .   L WORD   0000     DATASEG
```

```
                              TITLE      A22SUB1 Called subprogram
                              ; --------------------------------
         0000                 CODESG     SEGMENT PARA 'Code'
         0000                 A22SUB1    PROC    FAR
                                         ASSUME  CS:CODESG
                                         PUBLIC  A22SUB1
         0000  F7 E3                     IMUL    BX         ;AX = price, BX = qty
         0002  CB                        RETF               ;DX:AX = product
         0003                 A22SUB1    ENDP
         0003                 CODESG     ENDS
                                         END     A22SUB1
```

```
Segments and Groups:
    N a m e             Length   Align    Combine    Class
CODESG  . . . . . .     0003     PARA     NONE      'CODE'
Symbols:
    N a m e             Type     Value    Attr
A22SUB1   . . . .       F PROC   0000     CODESG    Global Length = 0003
```

Figure 22-3   Calling a Subprogram: EXTRN and PUBLIC

Because the subprogram does not define any data, it does not need a data segment; it could, but only the subprogram would recognize the data.

The subprogram uses the addresses in SS and SP that were delivered by the main program. As a result, the subprogram does not define a stack because it references the one defined in the main program. Because the linker requires the definition of at least one stack for an .EXE program, the stack in the main program serves this purpose.

Now let's examine the symbol tables following each assembly. Note that the symbol table for the main program shows A22SUB1 as Far and External. The symbol table for the subprogram shows A22SUB1 as F (for Far) and Global. The term *global* implies that the name is known to other subprograms outside A22SUB1.

Here is the link map of the linked modules showing the organization of the program in memory. Note that there is one stack and one data segment, but two code segments (one for each assembly) at different starting addresses because their combine types are NONE. These segments appear in the sequence that they are entered in the LINK command. In this example, the code segment for the main program (normally first) starts at offset 00090H and the code segment for the subprogram at offset 000B0H:

```
      Object modules: A22MAIN1+A22SUB1
 Start      Stop     Length    Name           Class
 00000H     0007FH   00080H    STACKSEG       STACK
 00080H     00083H   00004H    DATASEG        DATA
 00090H     000A5H   00016H    CODESEG        CODE
 000B0H     000B2H   00003H    CODESG         CODE
       Program entry point at 0009:0000
```

A trace of program execution disclosed that CS for A22MAIN1 contained 0F20[0] and the instruction CALL A22SUB1 generated 9A 0000 220F (your segment value likely differs). The machine code for an intersegment CALL is 9AH. The operation pushes IP onto the stack and loads 0000 (the first operand of the CALL) in IP. It then pushes CS containing 0F20[0] onto the stack and loads 0F22[0] (the second operand) in CS. (Register contents are shown here in normal, not reversed, byte order.)

The CS:IP pair direct the next instruction to execute at 0F22[0] plus 0000. What is at 0F220? It's the entry point to A22SUB1 at its first executable instruction, which you can calculate. The main program began with CS containing 0F20[0]. According to the map, the main code segment offset begins at offset 00090H and the subprogram offset begins at offset 000B0H, 20H bytes apart. Adding the main program's CS value plus 20H supplies the effective address of the subprogram's code segment:

```
      CS address for A22MAIN1:   0F200H
      Size of A22MAIN1:         +00020H
      CS address for A22SUB1:    0F220H
```

The program loader determines this address just as we have and substitutes it in the CALL operand. A22SUB1 multiplies the two values in AX and BX, generates the product in DX:AX, and makes a far return (RETF) to A22MAIN1 (because the return is to a far procedure).

DEFINING THE CODE SEGMENT AS PUBLIC

Figure 22-4 provides a variation of Figure 22-3. There is one change in the main program, A22MAIN2, and one change in the subprogram, A22SUB2, both involving the use of PUBLIC in the SEGMENT directive for both code segments:

```
CODESG SEGMENT PARA PUBLIC 'Code'
```

```
                            TITLE       A22MAIN2 (EXE)  Call subprogram
                                        EXTRN   A22SUB2:FAR
0000                        STACKSEG  SEGMENT PARA STACK 'Stack'
0000    0040[????]                    DW      64 DUP(?)
0080                        STACKSEG  ENDS
            ;  -------------------------------------------------------
0000                        DATASEG   SEGMENT PARA 'Data'
0000    0140                QTY       DW      0140H
0002    2500                PRICE     DW      2500H
0004                        DATASEG   ENDS
            ;  -------------------------------------------------------
0000                        CODESEG   SEGMENT PARA PUBLIC 'Code'
0000                        BEGIN     PROC    FAR
                                      ASSUME  CS:CODESEG,DS:DATASEG,SS:STACKSEG
0000    B8 ---- R                     MOV     AX,DATASEG
0003    8E D8                         MOV     DS,AX
0005    A1 0002 R                     MOV     AX,PRICE        ;Set up price
0008    8B 1E 0000 R                  MOV     BX,QTY          ; and quantity
000C    9A 0000 ---- E                CALL    A22SUB2         ;Call subprogram
0011    B8 4C00                       MOV     AX,4C00H        ;End processing
0014    CD 21                         INT     21H
0016                        BEGIN     ENDP
0016                        CODESEG   ENDS
                                      END     BEGIN
-----------------------------------------------------------------------------
Segments and Groups:
    N a m e             Length  Align    Combine    Class
CODESEG  . . . . .      0016    PARA     PUBLIC     'CODE'
DATASEG  . . . . .      0004    PARA     NONE       'DATA'
STACKSEG . . . . .      0080    PARA     STACK      'STACK'
Symbols:
    N a m e             Type    Value    Attr
A22SUB2  . . . . .      L FAR   0000     External
BEGIN  . . . . . . .    F PROC  0000     CODESEG    Length = 0016
PRICE  . . . . . . .    L WORD  0002     DATASEG
QTY  . . . . . . .      L WORD  0000     DATASEG
-----------------------------------------------------------------------------
                            TITLE       A22SUB2 Called subprogram
                            ;  ----------------------------------------
0000                        CODESEG   SEGMENT PARA PUBLIC 'Code'
0000                        A22SUB2   PROC    FAR
                                      ASSUME  CS:CODESEG
                                      PUBLIC A22SUB2
0000    F7 E3                         IMUL    BX         ;AX = price, BX = qty
0002    CB                            RETF               ;DX:AX = product
0003                        A22SUB2   ENDP
0003                        CODESEG   ENDS
                                      END     A22SUB2
-----------------------------------------------------------------------------
Segments and Groups:
    N a m e             Length  Align    Combine    Class
CODESEG  . . . . .      0003    PARA     PUBLIC     'CODE'
Symbols:
    N a m e             Type    Value    Attr
A22SUB2  . . . .        F PROC  0000     CODESEG    Global Length = 0003
-----------------------------------------------------------------------------
```

Figure 22-4   Calling a Subprogram: PUBLIC Code Segment

Interesting results appear in the link map and the CALL object code. In the symbol table following each assembly, the combine type for CODESG is PUBLIC, whereas in Figure 22-3 it was NONE. Also, the link map at the end now shows only one code segment. The fact that both segments have the same name (CODESEG), class ('Code'), and PUBLIC attribute caused the linker to combine the two logical code segments into one physical code segment. Here is the link map:

```
       Object modules: A22MAIN2+A22SUB2
Start    Stop    Length    Name         Class
00000H   0007FH  00080H    STACKSEG     STACK
00080H   00083H  00004H    DATASEG      DATA
00090H   000B2H  00023H    CODESEG      CODE
       Program entry point at 0009:0000
```

Further, a trace of machine execution showed that the CALL is far. That is, although CALL is within the same segment, it is to a FAR procedure, with object code 9A 2000 200F (your segment address likely differs). This far CALL stores 2000H in IP as 0020H and 200FH in CS as 0F20[0]. Because the subprogram shares a common code segment with the main program, CS is set to the same starting address, 0F20H. But CS:IP for A22SUB2 now provides the following effective address:

```
CS address for A22MAIN2 and A22SUB2:    0F200H
IP offset for A22SUB2:                + 0020H
Effective address of A22SUB2:           0F220H
```

The code segment of the subprogram therefore presumably begins at 0F220H. Is this correct? The link map doesn't make the point clear, but you can infer the address from the listing of the main program, which ends at offset 0015H. (The map shows 16H, which is the next available location.) Because the code segment for the subprogram is defined as PARA, it begins on a paragraph boundary (evenly divisible by 10H, so that the rightmost digit is 0):

The linker sets the subprogram at the first paragraph boundary immediately following the main program, at offset 00020H. Therefore, just as was calculated, the code segment of the subprogram begins at 0F200H plus 0020H, or 0F220H.

The next section examines this same program defined with simplified segment directives.

USING SIMPLIFIED SEGMENT DIRECTIVES

Figure 22-5 shows the previous program now defined with simplified segment directives. Figure 22-4 defined the code segments as PUBLIC, whereas Figure 22-5 defaults to PUBLIC, so that both examples generate one code segment. However, the use of simplified segment directives causes some significant differences. First, the segments (as shown in the map) are now rearranged in sequence of code, data, and stack, although this has no effect on program execution. Second, according to the Segments and Groups table, the subprogram's code segment (_TEXT) aligns on a word (rather than paragraph) boundary.

A trace of machine execution showed the object code for the CALL as 9A 1600 170F (your segment address likely differs). This time, the new offset value is 16H, and the segment address is 0F17H. Because the subprogram shares a common code segment with the

```
                          TITLE     A22MAIN3 (EXE)  Call subprogram
                                    .MODEL   SMALL
                                    .STACK   64
                                    EXTRN    A22SUB3:FAR
                          ; --------------------------------------------
                                    .DATA
0000 0140                 QTY       DW       0140H
0002 2500                 PRICE     DW       2500H
                          ; --------------------------------------------
                                    .CODE
0000                      BEGIN     PROC     FAR
0000 B8 ---- R                      MOV      AX,@data
0003 8E D8                          MOV      DS,AX
0005 A1 0002 R                      MOV      AX,PRICE      ;Set up price
0008 8B 1E 0000 R                   MOV      BX,QTY        ;  and quantity
000C 9A 0000 ---- E                 CALL     A22SUB3       ;Call subprogram
0011 B8 4C00                        MOV      AX,4C00H      ;End processing
0014 CD 21                          INT      21H
0016                      BEGIN     ENDP
                                    END      BEGIN
--------------------------------------------------------------------
Segments and Groups:
     N a m e              Length    Align    Combine    Class
DGROUP . . . . . . GROUP
_DATA  . . . . . . 0004             WORD     PUBLIC     'DATA'
STACK  . . . . . . 0040             PARA     STACK      'STACK'
_TEXT  . . . . . . 0016             WORD     PUBLIC     'CODE'
Symbols:
     N a m e              Type      Value    Attr
A22SUB3  . . . .   L FAR            0000     External
BEGIN  . . . . .   F PROC           0000     _TEXT  Length = 0016
PRICE  . . . . .   L WORD           0002     _DATA
QTY  . . . . . .   L WORD           0000     _DATA
```

```
                          TITLE     A22SUB3 Called subprogram
                                    .MODEL SMALL
                                    .CODE
0000                      A22SUB3   PROC     FAR
                                    PUBLIC A22SUB3
0000 F7 E3                          MUL      BX        ;AX = price, BX = qty
0002 CB                             RETF               ;DX:AX = product
0003                      A22SUB3   ENDP
                                    END      A22SUB3
--------------------------------------------------------------------
Segments and Groups:
     N a m e              Length    Align    Combine    Class
DGROUP . . . . . . GROUP
_DATA  . . . . . . 0000             WORD     PUBLIC     'DATA'
_TEXT  . . . . . . 0003             WORD     PUBLIC     'CODE'
Symbols:
     N a m e              Type      Value    Attr
A22SUB3  . . . .   F PROC           0000     _TEXT Global Length = 0003
```

Figure 22-5   Calling a Subprogram: Simplified Segment Directives

main program, CS is set to the same starting address, 0F17(0), for both. You may calculate the effective address of A22SUB3 as follows:

```
        CS address for A22MAIN3 and A22SUB3:  F170H
        IP offset for A22SUB3:                + 016H
        Effective address of A22SUB3:         F186H
```

You can infer the address from the listing of the main program, which ends at offset 0015H. (The map shows 16H, which is the next available location.) Because the map shows the main code segment beginning at 00000H, the next word boundary following 0015H is at 00016H, where A22SUB3 begins, aligned properly on a word boundary. Here is the link map:

```
        Object modules: A22MAIN3+A22SUB3
   Start    Stop    Length Name           Class
   00000H   00018H  00019H _TEXT          CODE
   0001AH   0001DH  00004H _DATA          DATA
   00020H   0005FH  00040H STACK          STACK
           Program entry point at 0000:0000
```

PASSING PARAMETERS TO A SUBPROGRAM

A common way of making data known to a called subprogram is by *passing parameters,* in which a program passes parameters via the stack frame. In this case, ensure that each PUSH references a word (or doubleword), in either memory or a register. As described in Chapter 7, a program may pass parameters by value (the actual data item) or by reference (the address of the data item). This section gives an example of both methods.

The stack frame is the portion of the stack that the calling program uses to pass parameters and that the called subprogram uses for accessing the parameters. The called subprogram may also use the stack frame for temporary storage of local data. The BP register acts as a frame pointer, and the subprogram makes use of both BP and SP.

Passing Parameters by Value

In Figure 22-6, the calling program A22MAIN4 pushes both values PRICE and QTY onto the stack prior to calling the subprogram A22SUB4. Initially, SP contained the size of the stack, 80H. Each word pushed onto the stack decrements SP by 2.

1. The first PUSH stores PRICE (2500H) in the stack frame at offset 7EH.
2. The second PUSH stores QTY (0140H) in the stack frame at offset 7CH.
3. CALL pushes the contents of CS (0F20H for this execution) onto the stack frame at 7AH. Because the subprogram is PUBLIC, the linker combines the two code segments, and the CS address is the same for both.
4. CALL also pushes the contents of IP, 0012H, onto the stack frame at 78H. SP now contains 78H and the stack frame appears as follows:

```
Offset 7EH | 0025H |   (PRICE)
       7CH | 4001H |   (QTY)
       7AH | 200FH |   (contents of CS)
       78H | 1200H |   (contents of IP)
```

The called program requires the use of BP to access the parameters in the stack frame. Its first action is to save the contents of BP for the calling program, so it pushes BP onto the stack. In this example, BP happens to contain zero, which PUSH stores in the stack frame

```
TITLE      A22MAIN4 (EXE)  Passing parameters
           EXTRN   A22SUB4:FAR
; ----------------------------------------------------
STACKSEG SEGMENT PARA STACK 'Stack'
         DW      64 DUP(?)
STACKSEG ENDS
; ----------------------------------------------------
DATASEG  SEGMENT PARA 'Data'
QTY      DW      0140H
PRICE    DW      2500H
DATASEG  ENDS
; ----------------------------------------------------
CODESEG  SEGMENT PARA PUBLIC 'Code'
BEGIN    PROC    FAR
         ASSUME  CS:CODESEG,DS:DATASEG,SS:STACKSEG
         MOV     AX,DATASEG
         MOV     DS,AX
         PUSH    PRICE        ;Save price
         PUSH    QTY          ; and quantity
         CALL    A22SUB4      ;Call subprogram
         MOV     AX,4C00H     ;End processing
         INT     21H
BEGIN    ENDP
CODESEG  ENDS
         END     BEGIN
----------------------------------------------------
TITLE      A22SUB4 Called subprogram
CODESEG  SEGMENT PARA PUBLIC 'Code'
A22SUB4  PROC    FAR
         ASSUME  CS:CODESEG
         PUBLIC  A22SUB4
         PUSH    BP
         MOV     BP,SP
         MOV     AX,[BP+8]    ;Get price
         MOV     BX,[BP+6]    ;Get quantity
         MUL     BX           ;DX:AX = product
         POP     BP
         RETF    4            ;Return to caller
A22SUB4  ENDP
CODESEG  ENDS
         END
```

Figure 22-6   Passing Parameters by Value

at offset 76H. The program then inserts the contents of SP (0076H) into BP because BP (but not SP) is usable as an index register. Because BP now contains 0076H, PRICE is in the stack at BP + 8 (offset 7EH), and QTY is at BP + 6 (offset 7CH). We know these relative locations because three words (six bytes) were pushed onto the stack after QTY was pushed. The routine transfers PRICE and QTY from the stack to AX and BX, respectively, and performs the multiplication.

Before returning to the calling program, the subprogram pops BP (returning the zero address to BP), which increments SP by 2, from 76H to 78H.

The last instruction, RETF, is a far return to the calling program, which performs the following:

- Pops the word now at the top of the stack frame (1200H) to IP and increments SP by 2, from 78H to 7AH.
- Pops the word now at the top (0F20) onto CS and increments SP by 2, from 7AH to 7CH.

Because of the two passed parameters at offsets 7CH and 7EH, the return instruction is coded as RETF 4. The immediate value 4 contains the number of bytes in the passed parameters (two one-word parameters in this case). RETF adds the pop-value to the SP, correcting it to 80H. In effect, because the parameters in the stack are no longer required, the operation "discards" them and returns correctly to the calling program. Note that although the POP and RET operations increment SP, they don't actually erase the contents of the stack.

Here is the link map:

```
      Object modules: A22MAIN4+A22SUB4
   Start    Stop    Length   Name          Class
   00000H   0007FH  00080H   STACKSEG      STACK
   00080H   00083H  00004H   DATASEG       DATA
   00090H   000BEH  0002FH   CODESEG       CODE
      Program entry point at 0009:0000
```

Passing Parameters by Reference

The program in Figure 22-7 passes parameters by reference, in this case, the addresses of QTY and PRICE. The main difference in the called subprogram, A22SUB5, is that it gets the address of PRICE into DI and the address of QTY into BX:

```
        MOV    DI,[BP+8]   ;Address of price
        MOV    BX,[BP+6]   ; and quantity
```

It then uses the address now in DI to get PRICE into AX:

```
        MOV    AX,[DI]    ;Get price
```

and uses the address in BX for QTY, which it multiplies by PRICE in AX:

```
        IMUL   WORD PTR [BX]   ;Mult by qty
```

The program is otherwise self-explanatory.

THE ENTER AND LEAVE INSTRUCTIONS

The ENTER instruction (introduced by the 80826) is used to create a temporary stack frame for a called procedure that is to receive passed parameters. The LEAVE instruction, the counterpart of ENTER, terminates the stack frame. Their formats are

[label:]	ENTER	*size, nest-level*
[label:]	LEAVE	*[no operand]*

- The *size* operand specifies the number of bytes that the operand is to allocate for the stack frame. Although a stack normally consists of word or doubleword values, ENTER permits the passing of byte-sized parameters.
- The *nest-level* operand identifies the nesting level for the operation. For the BASIC, C, and Fortran compilers, the level is always 0.

```
TITLE     A22MAIN5 (EXE)  Passing parameters
          EXTRN   A22SUB5:FAR
STACKSEG SEGMENT PARA STACK 'Stack'
          DW    64 DUP(?)
STACKSEG ENDS
; --------------------------------------------------
DATASEG   SEGMENT PARA 'Data'
QTY       DW      0140H
PRICE     DW      2500H
DATASEG   ENDS
; --------------------------------------------------
CODESEG   SEGMENT PARA PUBLIC 'Code'
BEGIN     PROC    FAR
          ASSUME  CS:CODESEG,DS:DATASEG,SS:STACKSEG
          MOV     AX,DATASEG
          MOV     DS,AX
          LEA     CX,PRICE
          LEA     DX,QTY
          PUSH    CX              ;Save address of
          PUSH    DX              ;  price, quantity
          CALL    A22SUB5         ;Call subprogram
          MOV     AX,4C00H        ;End processing
          INT     21H
BEGIN     ENDP
CODESEG   ENDS
          END     BEGIN
--------------------------------------------------
TITLE  A22SUB5 Called subprogram
CODESEG   SEGMENT PARA PUBLIC 'Code'
A22SUB5   PROC    FAR
          ASSUME  CS:CODESEG
          PUBLIC A22SUB5
          PUSH    BP
          MOV     BP,SP
          MOV     DI,[BP+8]       ;Address of price
          MOV     BX,[BP+6]       ;  and quantity
          MOV     AX,[DI]         ;Get price
          IMUL    WORD PTR [BX]   ;Mult by qty
          POP     BP
          RETF    4               ;Return to caller
A22SUB5   ENDP
CODESEG   ENDS
          END
```

Figure 22-7   Passing Parameters by Reference

As an example, the instruction ENTER 4,0 is equivalent to

```
PUSH   BP
MOV    BP,  SP
SUB    SP,  4
```

The effect of the operation is to create a stack frame in which BP points to its top and SP to the bottom. The program is to pass parameters within this stack frame to a called procedure.

The LEAVE instruction terminates the stack frame by reversing the action of the ENTER. The LEAVE operation is equivalent to

```
MOV  SP, BP
POP  BP
```

The operation restores SP and BP to their original values.

```
TITLE   A22ENTER (EXE)   Use of ENTER/LEAVE
        .MODEL   SMALL
        .STACK   64
        .DATA
ROW            EQU    5
COL            EQU    8
.286    ; --------------------------------------------------
        .CODE
BEGIN   PROC    FAR
        MOV     AX,@data
        MOV     DS,AX           ;SP = 40. BP = 0
        ENTER   2,0             ;SP = 3C, BP = 3E
        MOV     BYTE PTR [BP-1],ROW   ;Row and column
        MOV     BYTE PTR [BP-2],COL   ; to stack frame
        CALL    SET_CURSOR      ;SP = 3A, BP = 3E
        LEAVE                   ;SP = 40, BP = 0
        MOV     AX,4C00H        ;End processing
        INT     21H
BEGIN   ENDP
SET_CURSOR PROC   NEAR
        PUSHA                   ;SP = 2A, BP = 3E
        MOV     AH,02H          ;Set cursor:
        MOV     BX,0            ;  page
        MOV     DH,[BP-1]       ;  row
        MOV     DL,[BP-2]       ;  column
        INT     10H             ;
        POPA                    ;SP = 3A, BP = 3E
        RET                     ;SP = 3C, BP = 3E
SET_CURSOR ENDP
        END     BEGIN
```

Figure 22-8   Using ENTER and LEAVE

In the program in Figure 22-8, ENTER creates a 2-byte stack frame for passing two parameters (row and column) to a procedure, SET_CURSOR. Note that the program moves the parameters to and from the stack, rather than using PUSH and POP. The comments show the SP and BP contents, assumed to begin with 40H and 00H, respectively.

If you follow the general rules discussed in this chapter, you should be able to link a program consisting of more than two assembly modules. But watch out for the size of the stack: For large programs with many PUSH and CALL operations, defining 64 words could be a wise precaution.

Chapter 23 covers some important concepts on managing memory and executing overlay programs. Chapter 25 provides additional features of segments, including defining more than one code or data segment in the same assembly module and the use of GROUP to combine these into a common segment.

LINKING A C/C++ PROGRAM WITH AN ASSEMBLY LANGUAGE PROGRAM

Although a C/C++ program can perform much of an assembly language's capabilities, there are a number of features that only assembly language can do:

- Execute PUSH and POP operations.
- Access the BP and SP registers.

- Initialize certain segment registers.
- Execute routines that are time-critical, such as displaying video graphics and performing I/O via the ports.

The following sections describe the requirements for interfacing C/C++ programs with assembly language modules. The material is based on the Microsoft C and C++ compilers.

Memory Models. Both the caller and the called assembly programs must be defined with the same memory model. Programs defined with Tiny, Small, and Compact models make near calls to the external module, which push only IP onto the stack. Medium and Large memory models make far calls, which push CS and IP. Flat models, which run in protected mode under Windows, make near calls.

The assembly .MODEL statement indicates the C/C++ convention, such as .MODEL SMALL,C.

Naming conventions. The assembly modules must use a naming convention for segments and variables that is compatible with that in C/C++. All external names in the C/C++ program contain a leading underscore character, such as _column. Assembler references to functions and variables in the C/C++ module must also begin with an underscore (_).

Further, because C/C++ is *case sensitive*, the assembly module should use the same case (upper or lower) for any variable names in common with the C/C++ module. You can force the assembler to maintain case sensitivity with the following command line options:

/mx Microsoft 5.0 and Borland 4.0

/Cx Microsoft 6.0

Registers. The assembly module must preserve the original values in BP, SP, CS, DS, SS, DI, and SI; that is, PUSH them on entry and POP them on exit.

Passing parameters. There are three methods of passing parameters:

1. By *value*. The C/C++ caller passes a copy of the variable on the stack. The called assembly module can alter the passed value, but has no access to the caller's original value. If there is more than one parameter, C/C++ pushes them onto the stack starting with the rightmost parameter.
2. By *near reference*. The caller passes an offset address of a data item value. The called assembly module is assumed to share the same data segment as the caller.
3. By *far reference*. The caller passes both segment and offset addresses (segment first, then offset). The called assembly module is assumed to use a different data segment from the caller. The called program may use the LDS or LES instructions to initialize segment addresses.

C/C++ programs pass parameters onto the stack in a sequence that is the *reverse* of that of other languages. Consider, for example, the statement

```
Adds (value_1, value_2);
```

The statement pushes value_1 and then value_2 onto the stack in that order and calls Adds. On return from the called module, the C/C++ module (not the assembly module) increments SP to discard the passed parameters. A typical procedure in the called assembly module for accessing the two passed parameters is as follows:

```
PUSH  BP              ;Save BP
MOV   BP,SP           ;Use SP address as base pointer
MOV   DH,[BP+4]       ;Get values from
MOV   DL,[BP+6]       ; the stack
...
POP   BP              ;Restore BP
RET
```

After the PUSH BP instruction, the stack frame appears as

value_2	BP + 6
value_1	BP + 4
caller's return address	BP + 2
BP offset	BP + 0

On return from the called module, issue RET with no immediate operand because the C/C++ caller assumes responsibility for clearing up the stack.

Compatibility of Data Types.   The following list shows the types of C/C++ variables and their equivalent assembler types:

C DATA TYPE	MASM 5.X TYPE	MASM 6.X TYPE
char	DB	BYTE
unsigned short/int	DW	WORD
int, short	DW	SWORD
unsigned long	DD	DWORD
long	DD	SDWORD

Returned Values.   The called assembly module uses the following registers for any returned values:

C DATA TYPE	REGISTER
char	AL
short, near int (16 bit)	AX
short, near int (32 bit)	EAX
long, far (16 bit)	DX:AX
long, far (32 bit)	EDX:EAX

Program Example: Linking C with Assembly Language

The simple example in Figure 22-9 links a C program to an assembly subprogram whose sole purpose is to set the cursor. The C/C++ program is compiled to produce an .OBJ module, and the assembly program is assembled to produce an .OBJ module. The linker then combines these two .OBJ modules into one .EXE executable module.

The C program defines two items named temp_row and temp_col and accepts entries for row and column from the keyboard into these variables. The program defines the name of the assembly subprogram as set_curs. It sends the addresses of temp_row and temp_col as parameters to the subprogram for setting the cursor. The C statement that calls the subprogram and passes the parameters is

```
set_curs (temp_row, temp_col);
```

```
#include <stdio.h>
int main (void)
{
    int temp_row, temp_col;

    printf ("Enter cursor row: ");
    scanf ("%d", &temp_row);

    printf ("Enter cursor column: ");
    scanf ("%d", &temp_col);

    set_curs (temp_row, temp_col);
    printf ("New cursor location\n");
}
----------------------------------------------------------
;
; Use small memory model for C: near code, near data
; Use 'standard' segment names, and group directive

_DATA      segment word 'DATA'
row        equ     [bp+4]        ;Parameters
col        equ     [bp+6]        ;  (arguments)
_DATA      ends


_TEXT      SEGMENT BYTE PUBLIC 'CODE'
DGROUP     GROUP   _DATA
           ASSUME  CS:_TEXT, DS:DGROUP, SS:DGROUP
           PUBLIC  _set_curs
_set_curs PROC     NEAR
           PUSH    BP            ;Caller's BP register
           MOV     BP,SP         ;Point to parameters

           MOV     AH,02H        ;Request set cursor
           MOV     BX,0          ;Video page 0
           MOV     DH,ROW        ;Row from BP+4
           MOV     DL,COL        ;Column from BP+6
           INT     10H           ;Call interrupt

           POP     BP            ;Restore BP
           RETF                  ;Return to caller
_set_curs ENDP
_TEXT      ENDS
           END
```

Figure 22-9 Linking C to Assembler

Values pushed onto the stack are the calling program's SP, the return offset address, and the addresses of the two passed parameters.

The first passed parameter, temp_row, is at offset 04H in the stack frame and is accessed by BP + 04H. The second passed parameter, temp_col, is at offset 06H and is accessed by BP + 06H. The subprogram uses row and column in DX for INT 10H to set the cursor. On exit, the subprogram pops BP. The RET instruction transfers control back to the calling program, which clears up the stack frame.

This trivial program produces a module larger than 20K bytes. A compiler language typically generates considerable overhead regardless of the size of the source program.

Other C/C++ versions do not necessarily follow the conventions used here. For particulars, see the compiler manual, usually in a section whose title begins with "Interfacing . . ." or "Mixed Languages. . . ."

KEY POINTS

- The align operator tells the assembler to align the named segment beginning on a particular storage boundary.
- The combine operator tells the assembler and linker whether to combine segments or to keep them separate.
- Assigning the same class name to related segments causes the assembler and linker to group them together.
- An intrasegment CALL is near if the called procedure is defined as or defaults to NEAR (within 32K). An intrasegment call may be far if the call is to a far procedure within the same segment.
- An intersegment CALL calls a procedure in another segment and is defined as FAR or as EXTRN.
- In a main program that calls a subprogram, the entry point is defined as EXTRN; in the subprogram, the entry point is PUBLIC.
- For linking two code segments into one segment, both are defined with the same name, the same class, and the PUBLIC combine type.

REVIEW QUESTIONS AND EXERCISES

22-1. Give four reasons for organizing a program into subprograms.
The next three questions refer to the format for the SEGMENT directive:

```
segment-name SEGMENT [align] [combine] ['class']
```

22-2. (a) What is the default for the SEGMENT directive's align option? (b) What is the effect of the BYTE option? (That is, what action does the assembler take?)

22-3. (a) What is the default for the SEGMENT directive's combine option? (b) Why would you use its PUBLIC option? (c) Why would you use its COMMON option?

22-4. (a) What is normally the code segment's class option for the SEGMENT directive? (b) If two segments have the same class but not the PUBLIC combine option, what is the effect? (c) If two segments have the same class and both have the PUBLIC combine option, what is the effect?

22-5. Explain the difference between an intrasegment call and an intersegment call.

22-6. A program named MAINPROG is to call a subprogram named SUBCALC. (a) What statement in MAINPROG informs the assembler that the name SUBCALC is defined outside its own assembly? (b) What statement in SUBCALC is required to make its name known to MAINPROG?

22-7. Write and test a program based on Question 22-6. Define three data items in MAIN-PROG as DWs: STOCK_QTY (stock quantity on hand), UNITCOST, and STOCK-VALUE. MAINPROG passes all three data items as parameters to SUBCALC. SUBCALC in turn is to divide STOCKVALUE by STOCK_QTY and is to store the quotient in UNITCOST. Note that SUBCALC is to return the calculated price intact in its parameter.

22-8. Revise the program in Question 22-8 so that it uses the ENTER and LEAVE instructions for the stack frame.

22-9. Expand Question 22-8 so that MAINPROG accepts stock quantity and value from the keyboard, subprogram SUBBINRY converts the ASCII amounts to binary, subprogram SUBCALC calculates the price, subprogram SUBASCII converts the binary price to ASCII, and MAINPROG displays the result.

Chapter 23

PROGRAM LOADING AND OVERLAYS

> Objective: To explain how the system loads programs and overlays modules for execution.

INTRODUCTION

This chapter describes the program segment prefix, program loader, program overlays, and resident programs. The operations introduced are INT 2FH function 4A01H Multiplex Interrupt and these INT 21H functions:

25H	Set interrupt vector	4AH	Modify allocated memory block
31H	Keep program	4BH	Load or execute a program
35H	Get interrupt vector	51H	Get address of current PSP
48H	Allocate memory	58H	Get/set memory allocation strategy
49H	Free allocated memory		

THE PROGRAM SEGMENT PREFIX

The program loader loads .COM and .EXE programs for execution into a program segment and creates a PSP at offset 00H and the program itself at offset 100H of the segment. The PSP contains the following fields of interest, according to relative position:

00–01H	An INT 20H instruction (CD20H) to facilitate a return to the system
02–03H	The segment address of the last paragraph of memory allocated to the program, as xxxx0. For example, 640K is indicated as 00A0H, meaning A0000[0].
0A–0DH	Terminate address (segment address for INT 22H)

0E–11H   Ctrl+Break exit address (segment address for INT 23H)

12–15H   Critical error exit address (segment address for INT 24H)

18–2BH   Default file handle table

2C–2DH   Segment address of program's environment

32–33H   Length of the file handle table

34–37H   Far pointer to the handle table

50–51H   Call to INT 21H function (INT 21H and RETF)

5C–6BH   First command-line argument (FCB #1)

6C–7FH   Second command-line argument (FCB #2)

80–FFH   Buffer for a default DTA (disk transfer area)

FCB (File Control Block) is an obsolete method of accessing disk files. The term as used in PSPs simply involves the way filespecs are formatted: *n:filename.ext,* where *filename* is eight characters and *ext* is three.

The following sections describe relevant fields in the PSP.

PSP 18-2BH: Default File Handle Table.   Each byte in the 20-byte default file handle table refers to an entry in a system table that defines the related device or driver. Initially, the table contains 0101010002FF . . . FF, where the first 01 refers to the keyboard, the second 01 to the screen, and so forth:

TABLE TERM	HANDLE DEVICE
01 Console	0 Keyboard (standard input)
01 Console	1 Screen (standard output)
01 Console	2 Screen (standard error)
00 COM1	3 Auxiliary (serial port)
02 LPT1	4 Standard printer
FF Unassigned	5 Unassigned

Normally, the word at PSP offset 32H contains the length of the table (14H, or 20), and 34H contains its segment address in the form IP:CS, where IP is 18H (the offset in the PSP) and CS is the segment address of the PSP.

Programs that need more than 20 open files have to release memory (INT 21H function 4AH) and use function 67H (set maximum handle count):

```
MOV    AH,67H       ;Request more handles
MOV    BX,count     ;New number (20 to 65,535)
INT    21H          ;Call interrupt service
```

The amount of memory required is one byte per handle, rounded up to the next byte paragraph plus 16 bytes. The operation creates the new handle table outside the PSP and updates PSP locations 32H and 34H. An invalid operation sets the Carry Flag and sets an error code in AX.

PSP 2C-2DH: Segment Address of Environment.   Programs loaded for execution have a related environment that the system stores in memory, beginning on a paragraph boundary before the program segment. The default size is 160 bytes, with a maximum of 32K. The environment contains such system commands as COMSPEC, PATH, PROMPT, and SET that are applicable to the program.

PSP 80-FFH: Default DTA Buffer.   The program loader initializes this area with the full text (if any) keyed in after the requested program name, such as MASM or COPY. The first byte contains the number of keys (if any) pressed immediately *after* the program name that is keyed in. Following the number are the characters (if any) keyed in, and then any "garbage" left in memory from a previous operation.

The following four examples should clarify the contents and purpose of the DTA.

Example 1: Command with No Operand.   Suppose that you request a program named CALCIT.EXE to execute by keying in CALCIT <Enter>. When the program loader constructs the PSP, it sets up the default DTA as 00 0D. . . . The first byte contains the number of bytes keyed in after the name CALCIT, not including the <Enter> character. Because no keys other than <Enter> were pressed, the number is zero. The second byte contains 0DH, for <Enter>.

Example 2: Command with Text Operand.   Suppose that you want to execute a program named COLOR and pass a parameter "BY" that tells the program to set the foreground color to blue (B) and background to yellow (Y). Type the program name followed by the parameter COLOR BY. The program loader then formats the DTA as:

```
                         03 20 42 59 0D ...
```

The bytes mean a length of 3 followed by a space, "BY," and 0DH for <Enter>. Other than the length, this field contains exactly what was typed after the program name COLOR.

Example 3: Command with a Filename Operand.   Many programs allow you to type a filename after the program name. If you key in, for example, DEL A:CALCIT.OBJ <Enter>, the DTA contains the following:

```
          0D 20 41 3A 43 41 4C 43 49 54 2E 4F 42 4A 0D ...
             A  :  C  A  L  C  I  T  .  O  B  J
```

The length of 13 (0DH) is followed by exactly what was typed, including 0DH for <Enter>.

Example 4: Command with Two Filename Operands.   Consider entering a command followed by two operands, such as

```
          COPY A:FILEA.ASM C:FILEB.ASM
```

The program loader sets the DTA with the following:

```
80H DTA: 10 20 41 3A 46 49 4C 45 41 2E 41 53 4D 20 etc...
          A  :  F  I  L  E  A  .  A  S  M     etc...
```

The DTA contains the number of characters keyed in (10H), a space (20H), A:FILEA.ASM
C:FILEB.ASM, and 0DH for <Enter>.

Accessing the PSP.   By determining the address of the PSP, you can access it in
order to process specified files or to take special action. To locate the DTA for a .COM
program, simply set 80H in BX, DI, or SI and access the contents:

```
MOV  SI,80H            ;Address of DTA
CMP  BYTE PTR[SI],0    ;Check buffer (DS:SI)
JE   EXIT              ; zero, no data
```

An .EXE program, however, can't always assume that its code segment immediately
follows the PSP. You can request INT 21H function 51H to deliver to BX the segment address of the current PSP.

The partial program in Figure 23-1 sets the attribute of a requested file to hidden
(02H). A user would key in the program name followed by the name of the file, such as
A23ATTRB n:filename.ext. The program first determines the address of the PSP. Next, it
scans the DTA for the <Enter> character and replaces it with a byte of hex zeros, creating
an ASCIIZ string. INT 21H function 43H then uses the ASCIIZ string in the DTA to change
the attribute of the file in the directory.

For a more flexible program, a user could type in the directory path and the required
file attribute.

```
           PUSH   ES              ;Save ES
           PUSH   DS              ;  and DS
           MOV    AH,51H          ;Request address of PSP,
           INT    21H             ;  delivered to BX
           MOV    ES,BX           ;PSP address into ES
           MOV    DS,BX           ;  and DS
           MOV    AL,0DH          ;Search character <Enter>
           MOV    CX,21           ;Number of bytes
           MOV    DI,82H          ;Start address in PSP
           REPNZ  SCASB           ;Scan for <Enter>
           JNZ    exit            ;Not found, error
           DEC    DI              ;Found,
           MOV    ES:BYTE PTR [DI],0 ;  replace with 00H
           MOV    AH,43H          ;Request
           MOV    AL,01           ;  set file attribute
           MOV    CX,02           ;  to hidden
           MOV    DX,82H          ;ASCIIZ string in PSP,
           INT    21H             ;  addressed by DS:DX
           POP    DS
           POP    ES
           JC     exit            ;Error caused by INT?
;          ...
exit:                             ;  yes, display message
;          ...
A10MAIN ENDP
        END    A10MAIN
```

Figure 23-1   Setting the File Attribute

THE HIGH-MEMORY AREA

The processor uses a number of address lines to access memory. Line number A20 can address a 64K space known as the *high-memory area (HMA),* from FFFF:10H through FFFF:FFFFH, just above the 1-megabyte address. When the processor runs in real (8086) mode, it normally disables the A20 line so that addresses that exceed this limit wrap around to the beginning of memory. Enabling the A20 line permits addressing locations in the HMA. You can ask CONFIG.SYS to relocate system files from low memory to the HMA, thereby freeing space for user programs.

INT 2FH (Multiplex Interrupt), among its many services, provides a check (via function 4A01H) for available space in the HMA:

```
MOV  AX,4A01H  ;Request space in HMA
INT  2FH       ;Call multiplex interrupt
```

The operation returns the following values in registers:

BX   = Number of free bytes available in the HMA (zero if COMMAND.COM is not loaded high)

ES:DI = Address of the first free byte in the HMA (FFFF:FFFF if system modules are not loaded high)

MEMORY ALLOCATION STRATEGY

INT 21H function 58H provides a number of strategies to determine where in memory to load a program.

Function 5800H: Get Memory Allocation Strategy

This operation allows queries to the memory allocation strategy:

```
MOV  AX,5800H  ;Request get strategy
INT  21H        ;Call interrupt service
```

The operation clears the Carry Flag and returns the strategy in AX:

- 00H = First fit (the default): Search from the lowest address in conventional memory for the first available block that is large enough to load the program.
- 01H = Best fit: Search for the smallest available block in conventional memory that is large enough to load the program.
- 02H = Last fit: Search from the highest address in conventional memory for the first available block.
- 40H = First fit, high only: Search from the lowest address in upper memory for the first available block.
- 41H = Best fit, high only: Search for the smallest available block in upper memory.
- 42H = Last fit, high only: Search from the highest address in upper memory for the first available block.
- 80H = First fit, high: Search from the lowest address in upper memory for the first available block. If none is found, search conventional memory.

- 81H = Best fit high: Search for the smallest available block in upper memory. If none is found, search conventional memory.
- 82H = Last fit, high: Search from the highest address in upper memory for the first available block. If none is found, search conventional memory.

Best fit and last fit strategies are appropriate to multitasking systems, which could have fragmented memory because of programs running concurrently. When a program finishes processing, its memory is released to the system.

Function 5801H: Set Memory Allocation Strategy

This operation allows changes to the memory allocation strategy. To set a strategy, set AL with code 01 and BX with the strategy code. An error sets the Carry Flag and returns 01 (invalid function) in AX.

Function 5802H: Get Upper Memory Link

This operation indicates whether a program can allocate memory from the upper memory area (above 640K). The operation clears the Carry Flag and returns one of the following codes to AL: 00H means the area is not linked and you cannot allocate, and 01H means the area is linked, you can allocate.

Function 5803H: Set Upper Memory Link

This operation can link or unlink the upper memory area and, if the area is linked, can allocate memory from it:

```
MOV  AX,5803H      ;Request
MOV  BX, linkflag  ;  link/unlink
INT  21H           ;  upper memory area
```

The *linkflag* operand has the following meaning: 00H = unlink the area and 01H = link the area. A successful operation clears the Carry Flag and allows a program to allocate memory from it. An error sets the Carry Flag and returns to AX code 01 (CONFIG.SYS did not contain DOS=UMB) or 07 (memory links damaged).

THE PROGRAM LOADER

On loading .COM and .EXE programs, the program loader creates a program segment prefix at location 00H of the program segment in memory and loads the program at 100H. Other than this step, the load and execute steps differ for .COM and .EXE programs. A major difference is that the linker inserts a special header record in an .EXE file when storing it on disk, and the program loader uses this record for loading.

Loading and Executing a .COM Program

On loading a .COM program, the program loader

- Installs a PSP preceding the program in memory.
- Sets the four segment registers with the address of the first byte of the PSP.

- Sets Stack Pointer (SP) to the end of the 64K segment, offset FFFEH (or to the end of memory if the segment is not large enough), and pushes a zero word on the stack.
- Sets Instruction Pointer (IP) to 100H (the size of the PSP) and allows control to proceed to the address generated by CS:IP, the first location immediately following the PSP. This is the first byte of the program, and it should contain an executable instruction.

Loading and Executing an .EXE Program

As stored on disk by the linker, an .EXE module consists of two parts: a *header record* containing control and relocation information, and the actual *load module*.

The header is a minimum of 512 bytes and may be longer if there are many relocatable items. The header contains information about the size of the executable module, where it is to be loaded in memory, the address of the stack, and relocation offsets to be inserted into incomplete machine addresses. In the following list, the term *block* refers to a 512-byte area in memory:

00–01H	Hex 4D5A ('MZ') identifies an .EXE file.
02–03H	Number of bytes in the last block of the .EXE file.
04–05H	Size of the file including the header in 512-byte block increments. For example, if the size is 1,025, this field contains 2 and field 02-03H contains 1.
06–07H	Number of relocation table items (see 1CH).
08–09H	Size of the header in 16-byte (paragraph) increments, to help the program loader locate the start of the executable module following the header. The minimum number is 20H (32) (32 x 16 = 512 bytes).
0A–0BH	Minimum count of paragraphs that must reside above the end of the program when it is loaded.
0C–0DH	High/low loader switch. When linking, you decide whether the program is to load for execution at a low (the usual) or a high memory address. The value 0000H indicates high. Otherwise, this location contains the maximum count of paragraphs that must reside above the end of the loaded program.
0E–0F	Offset location in the executable module of the stack segment.
10–11H	The defined size of the stack as an offset that the loader is to insert in SP when transferring control to the executable module.
12–13H	Checksum value—the sum of all the words in the file (ignoring overflows), used as a validation check for possible lost data.
14–15H	Offset (usually, but not necessarily, 00H) that the loader is to insert in the IP register when transferring control to the executable module.
16–17H	Offset of the code segment within the executable module that the loader inserts in CS. The offset is relative to the other segments, so that if the code segment is first, the offset would be zero.
18–19H	Offset of the relocation table (see the item at 1CH).

1A–1BH   Overlay number, where zero (the usual) means that the .EXE file contains the main program.

1CH–end Relocation table containing a variable number of relocation items, as identified at offset 06-07H. Positions 06-07H of the header indicate the number of items in the executable module that are to be relocated. Each relocation item, beginning at header 1CH, consists of a 2-byte offset value and a 2-byte segment value.

The system constructs memory blocks for the environment and the program segment. Following are the steps that the program loader performs when loading and initializing an .EXE program:

- Reads the formatted part of the header into memory.
- Calculates the size of the executable module (total file size in position 04H minus header size at position 08H) and reads the module into memory at the start of the segment.
- Reads the relocation table items into a work area and adds the value of each item to the start segment value.
- Sets DS and ES to the segment address of the PSP.
- Sets SS to the address of the PSP, plus 100H (the size of the PSP), plus the SS offset value (at 0EH). Also, sets SP to the value at 10H, the size of the stack.
- Sets CS to the address of the PSP plus 100H (the size of the PSP), plus the CS offset value in the header (at 16H) to CS. Also, sets IP with the offset at 14H. The CS:IP pair provides the starting address of the code segment and, in effect, program execution.

After the preceding steps, the loader is finished with the .EXE header and discards it. CS and SS are set correctly, but the program has to set DS and ES for its own data segment:

```
MOV   AX,datasegname   ;Set DS and ES
MOV   DS,AX            ;  to address
MOV   ES,AX            ;  of data segment
```

Example: Loading an .EXE Program

Consider the following Link Map that the linker generated for an .EXE program:

Start	Stop	Length	Name	Class
00000H	0003AH	003BH	CODESEG	Code
00040H	0005AH	001BH	DATASEG	Data
00060H	0007FH	0020H	STACK	Stack

Program entry point at 0000:0000

The map provides the *relative* (not actual) location of each of the three segments. (Some systems arrange these segments in alphabetic sequence by name.) According to the map, the code segment (CODESEG) is to start at 00000H—its relative location is the beginning of the executable module, and its length is 003BH bytes. The data segment, DATASEG, begins at 00040H and has a length of 001BH. The 00040H is the first address following

CODESEG that aligns on a paragraph boundary (a boundary evenly divisible by 10H). The stack segment, STACK, begins at 00060H, the first address following DATASEG that aligns on a paragraph boundary.

DEBUG can't display a header record after a program is loaded for execution because the loader replaces the header record with the PSP. However, you can use DEBUG's L command to load a sector from disk and the D command to display it. For example, load beginning at CS:100 from drive A: (0), relative sector 3, and one sector (512 bytes): L 100 0 3 1. The header for the program we are examining contains the following relevant information, according to hex location (numeric data is in reverse-byte sequence):

00H	Hex 4D5A ("MZ")
02H	Number of bytes in last block: 5B00H (or 005BH)
04H	Size of file, including header, in 512-byte blocks: 0200H (0002 x 512 = 1,024 bytes)
06H	Number of relocation table items following formatted portion of header: 0100H (that is, 0001)
08H	Size of header in 16-byte increments: 2000H (0020H = 32, and 32 x 16 = 512 bytes)
0CH	Load in low memory: FFFFH
0EH	Offset location of stack segment: 6000H, or 0060H
10H	Offset to insert in SP: 2000H, or 0020H
14H	Offset for IP: 0000H
16H	Offset for CS: 0000H
18H	Offset for the relocation table: 1E00H, or 001EH

When DEBUG loaded this program, the registers contained the following values:

```
SP = 0020   DS = 138F   ES = 138F
SS = 13A5   CS = 139F   IP = 0000
```

For .EXE modules, the loader sets DS and ES to the address of the PSP and sets CS, IP, SS, and SP to values from the header record. Let's see how the loader initializes these registers.

CS:IP Registers.   According to the DS register, when the program loaded, the address of the PSP was 138F[0]H. Because the PSP is 100H bytes long and the code segment is first (at offset 0), the code segment follows the PSP immediately at 139F[0]H. You can see the offset at location 16H in the header. The loader uses these values to initialize CS:

```
Start address of PSP (see DS):   138F0H
Length of PSP:                 +  100H
Offset of code segment             0H
Address of code segment          139F0H
```

CS now provides the starting address of the code portion (CODESEG) of the program. You can use the DEBUG display command D CS:0000 to view the machine code of a program in memory. The code is identical to the hex portion of the assembler's .LST printout, other than operands that .LST tags as R. Also, the loader sets IP with 0000H, the offset from 14H in the header.

SS:SP Registers. The loader used the value 60H in the header (at 0EH) for setting the address of the stack in SS:

```
Start address of PSP (see DS):                      138F0H
Length of PSP:                                    +   100H
Offset of stack (see location 0EH in header):     +    60H
Address of stack:                                   13A50H
```

The loader used 20H from the header (at 10H) to initialize the stack pointer to the length of the stack. In this example, the stack was defined as DW 16 DUP(?), that is, 16 2-byte fields = 32, or 20H. SP points to the current top of the stack.

DS Register. The loader uses DS to establish the starting point for the PSP at 138F[0]. Because the header does not contain the program's segment address for DS, the program has to initialize it:

```
0004 B8 ---- R      MOV AX,DATASEG
0007 8E D8          MOV DS,AX
```

The assembler leaves unfilled the machine address of DATASEG, which has become an entry in the header's relocation table (which begins at 1EH). The loader calculates the DS address as follows:

```
CS address:                   139F0H
Offset for data segment +       40H  (see Link Map)
DS address:                   13A30H
```

DEBUG shows the completed instruction as B8 A313. The loader loads A313 in DS as 13A3. These values at the start of execution are:

REGISTER	ADDRESS	MAP OFFSET
CS	139F[0]H	00H
DS	13A3[0]H	40H
SS	13A5[0]H	60H

As an exercise, trace any of your linked .EXE programs with DEBUG and note the changed values in the registers:

INSTRUCTION	REGISTERS CHANGED
MOV AX,DATASEG	IP and AX
MOV DS,AX	IP and DS
MOV ES,AX	IP and ES

DS now contains the correct address of the data segment. Try using D DS:00 to view the data segment and D SS:00 to view the stack.

ALLOCATING AND FREEING MEMORY

INT 21H services allow you to *allocate, release,* and *modify* the size of an area of memory. You most likely would use these services for resident programs and programs that load other programs for execution. Because DOS was designed as a single-user environment, a program that needs to load another program for execution has to release some of its memory space.

INT 21H Function 48H: Allocate Memory

To allocate memory for a program, request function 48H, and set BX with the number of required paragraphs:

```
MOV  AH,48H          ;Request allocate memory
MOV  BX,paragraphs   ;Number of paragraphs
INT  21H             ;Call interrupt service
```

The operation begins at the first memory block and steps through each block until it locates a space large enough for the request, usually at the high end of memory.

     A successful operation clears the Carry Flag and returns in AX the segment address of the allocated memory block. An unsuccessful operation sets the Carry Flag and returns in AX an error code (07 = memory block destroyed or 08 = insufficient memory) and in BX the size, in paragraphs, of the largest block available. A memory block destroyed means that the operation found a block in which the first byte was not 'M' or 'Z'.

INT 21H Function 49H: Free Allocated Memory

Function 49H frees allocated memory; it is commonly used to release a resident program. Load in ES the segment address of the block to be returned:

```
MOV  AH,49H          ;Request free allocated memory
LEA  ES,seg-address  ;Address of block for paragraphs
INT  21H             ;Call interrupt service
```

A successful operation clears the Carry Flag and stores 00H in the second and third bytes of the memory block, meaning that it is no longer in use. An unsuccessful operation sets the Carry Flag and returns in AX an error code (07 = memory block destroyed and 09 = invalid memory block address).

INT 21H Function 4AH: Modify Allocated Memory Block

Function 4AH can increase or decrease the size of a memory block. Initialize BX with the number of paragraphs to retain for the program and ES with the address of the PSP:

```
MOV  AH,4AH          ;Request modify allocated memory
MOV  BX,paragraphs   ;Number of paragraphs
LEA  ES,PSP-address  ;Address of PSP
INT  21H             ;Call interrupt service
```

A program can calculate its own size by subtracting the end of the last segment from the address of the PSP. You'll have to ensure that you use the last segment if the linker rearranges segments in alphabetic sequence.

A successful operation clears the Carry Flag. An unsuccessful operation sets the Carry Flag and returns in AX an error code (07 = memory block destroyed, 08 = insufficient memory, and 09 = invalid memory block address) and returns in BX the maximum possible size (if an attempt to increase the size was made). A wrong address in ES can cause error 07.

LOADING OR EXECUTING A PROGRAM FUNCTION

Let's now examine how to get an executing program to load and, in turn, to execute a subprogram. Function 4BH enables a program to load a subprogram into memory for execution. Load these registers:

AL = Function code for one of the following: 00H = load and execute, 01H = load program, 03H = load overlay, 05H = set execution state (not covered in this text).
ES:BX = Address of a parameter block.
DS:DX = Address of the path name for the called subprogram, an ASCIIZ string in uppercase letters.

Here are the instructions to load the subprogram:

```
MOV   AH,4BH          ;Request load subprogram
MOV   AL,code         ;Function code (load only)
LEA   BX,para-block   ;Address of parameter block
LEA   DX,path         ;Address of path name
INT   21H             ;Call interrupt service
```

An invalid operation sets the Carry Flag and returns an error code in AX, described in Figure 18-1.

AL = 00H: Load and Execute

This operation loads an .EXE or .COM program into memory, establishes a program segment prefix for it, and transfers control to it for execution. Because all registers, including SS, are changed, the operation is not for novices. The parameter block addressed by ES:BX has the following format:

OFFSET	PURPOSE
00H	Address of environment-block segment to be passed at PSP+2CH. A zero address means that the loaded program is to inherit the environment of its parent.
02H	Doubleword pointer to command line for placing at PSP+80H.
06H	Doubleword pointer to FCB #1 for passing at PSP+5CH.
0AH	Doubleword pointer to FCB #2 for passing at PSP+6CH.

The doubleword pointers have the form offset:segment address.

AL = 01H: Load Program

The operation loads an .EXE or .COM program into memory and establishes a program segment prefix for it, but does not transfer control to it for execution. The parameter block addressed by ES:BX has the following format:

OFFSET	PURPOSE
00H	Address of environment-block segment to be passed at PSP+2CH. If the address is zero, the loaded program is to inherit the environment of its parent.
02H	Doubleword pointer to command line for placing at PSP+80H.
06H	Doubleword pointer to FCB #1 for passing at PSP+5CH.
0AH	Doubleword pointer to FCB #2 for passing at PSP+6CH.
0EH	Starting stack address
12H	Starting code segment address

The doubleword pointers are addressed in the form offset:segment.

AL = 03H: Load Overlay

This operation loads a program or block of code, but does not establish a PSP or begin execution of the program or block. Thus the requested program could be overlaid on all or part of a program already in memory. The parameter block addressed by ES:BX has the following format:

Offset 00H   Word segment address where file is to be loaded

Offset 02H   Word relocation factor to apply to the image

An error sets the Carry Flag and returns an error code in AX, described in Figure 18-1.

Program: Load and Execute

The program in Figure 23-2 requests the system to perform the DIR command for the specified drive. The program first uses function 4AH to reduce its memory requirements to its actual size in paragraphs. The program uses simplified segment directives and the assembler has arranged segments in sequence of code, data, and stack. Note also that at the start of execution, ES contains the segment address of the PSP. The steps in calculating program size for INT 21H function 4AH are:

1. Set the segment address of the stack (the last segment) in BX.
2. Add the size of the stack (in paragraphs) to BX.
3. Subtract the segment address of the PSP from BX.

Other assemblers may arrange segments in a different sequence, so it is advised to check the link map before executing this program.

```
TITLE      A23EXDIR (EXE)  Executing the DIR Command
           .MODEL SMALL
           .STACK 64
           .DATA
PARAREA    LABEL  BYTE              ;Parameter block:
           DW    0                  ;  address of envir. string
           DW    OFFSET DIRCOM      ;  pointer to command line
           DW    @data
           DW    OFFSET FCB1        ;  pointer to default FCB1
           DW    @data
           DW    OFFSET FCB2        ;  pointer to default FCB2
           DW    @data
DIRCOM     DB    17,'/C DIR C:',13,0  ;Command line
FCB1       DB    16 DUP(0)
FCB2       DB    16 DUP(0)
PROGNAME   DB    'C:\COMMAND.COM',0    ;Location of COMMAND.COM
.286 ; -----------------------------------------------------
           .CODE
A10MAIN    PROC FAR
           MOV   AH,4AH             ;Reduce memory space
           MOV   BX,STACK           ;Segment address of stack
           ADD   BX,04              ;Add size in paragraphs
           MOV   CX,ES              ;Segment address of PSP
           SUB   BX,CX              ;Subtract from total
           INT   21H
           JC    A20ERR             ;Not enough space?
           MOV   AX,@data           ;OK,
           MOV   DS,AX              ;  set DS and ES
           MOV   ES,AX
           MOV   AH,4BH             ;Request load
           MOV   AL,00              ;  and execute
           LEA   BX,PARAREA         ;  COMMAND.COM
           LEA   DX,PROGNAME
           INT   21H
           JC    A30ERR             ;Execute error?
           MOV   AL,00              ;OK, no error code
           JMP   A90XIT
A20ERR:
           MOV   AL,01              ;Error code 1
           JMP   A90XIT
A30ERR:
           MOV   AL,02              ;Error code 2
A90XIT:
           MOV   AH,4CH             ;Request
           INT   21H               ;  end processing
A10MAIN    ENDP
           END   A10MAIN
```

Figure 23-2   Executing DIR from within a Program

INT 21H function 4BH with code 00 in AL handles the loading and execution of
COMMAND.COM. The program displays the directory entries for the specified drive.

INT 21H Function 4DH: Get Subprogram Return Value

This operation retrieves the return value that the last subprogram delivered when it terminated by function 4CH or 31H. The returned values are:

AH contains the subprogram's termination method, where 00H = normal
termination, 01H = terminated by Ctrl+C, 02H = critical device error, and 03H =
terminated by function 31H (keep program).

AL contains the return value from the subprogram.

PROGRAM OVERLAYS

The program in Figure 23-3 uses the same service (4BH) as that in Figure 23-2, but this time just to load a program into memory without executing it. The process consists of a main program, A23CALLV, and two subprograms, A23SUB1 and A23SUB2. A23CALLV contains these segments:

```
TITLE     A23CALLV (EXE)  Call subprogram and overlay
          EXTRN   A23SUB1:FAR
STACK     SEGMENT PARA STACK 'Stack1'
          DW      64 DUP(?)
STACK     ENDS
; --------------------------------------------------
DATASEG   SEGMENT PARA 'Data1'
PARABLOK  LABEL   WORD                  ;Parameter block
          DW      0                     ;
          DW      0                     ;
FILENAME  DB      'C:\A23SUB2.EXE',0
ERRMSG1   DB      'Modify mem error'
ERRMSG2   DB      'Allocate error  '
ERRMSG3   DB      'Seg call error  '
DATASEG   ENDS
.286   ; --------------------------------------------------
CODESEG   SEGMENT PARA 'Code1'
A10MAIN   PROC    FAR
          ASSUME  CS:CODESEG,DS:DATASEG,SS:STACK
          MOV     AX,DATASEG
          MOV     DS,AX
          MOV     AX,0003H              ;Set mode and
          INT     10H                   ; clear screen
          CALL    A23SUB1               ;Call subprogram 1

          MOV     AH,4AH                ;Shrink memory:
          MOV     BX,CS                 ;Seg address of CS
          MOV     CX,OFFSET B90END      ;Offset of end program
          SHR     CX,04                 ;Convert to paragraph
          INC     CX                    ; and add 1 more
          ADD     BX,CX                 ;Add to total paragraphs
          MOV     CX,ES                 ;Subtract segment
          SUB     BX,CX                 ; address of PSP
          INT     21H                   ;Size of this program
          JC      A20ERROR              ;If error, exit

          MOV     AX,DS                 ;Initialize ES for
          MOV     ES,AX                 ; overlay service
          MOV     AH,48H                ;Allocate memory
          MOV     BX,40                 ;40 paragraphs
          INT     21H
          JC      A30ERROR              ;If error, exit
          MOV     PARABLOK,AX           ;Save segment address

          MOV     AH,4BH                ;Load subprogram 2
          MOV     AL,03                 ; with no execute
          LEA     BX,PARABLOK
          LEA     DX,FILENAME
          INT     21H
          JC      A50ERROR              ;If error, exit

          MOV     AX,PARABLOK           ;Exchange two words
          MOV     PARABLOK+2,AX         ; of PARABLOK
          MOV     PARABLOK,20H          ;Set CS offset to 20H
          LEA     BX,PARABLOK
          CALL    DWORD PTR [BX]        ;Call subprogram 2
```

Figure 23-3 Calling a Subprogram and Overlay

```
                JMP     A90

A20ERROR: LEA   BP,ERRMSG1
          CALL  B10DISPLY              ;Display message
          JMP   A90
A30ERROR: LEA   BP,ERRMSG2
          CALL  B10DISPLY              ;Display message
          JMP   A90
A50ERROR: LEA   BP,ERRMSG3
          CALL  B10DISPLY              ;Display message
          JMP   A90
A90:      MOV   AX,4C00H               ;End processing
          INT   21H
A10MAIN   ENDP

B10DISPLY PROC  NEAR                   ;BP set on entry
          MOV   AX,DS                  ;Initialize ES for
          MOV   ES,AX                  ;  this service
          MOV   AX,1301H               ;Request display
          MOV   BX,001EH               ;Page:attribute
          MOV   CX,16                  ;Length
          MOV   DX,1510H               ;Row:column
          INT   10H
          RET
B90END:   NOP                          ;End offset of program
B10DISPLY ENDP
CODESEG   ENDS
          END   A10MAIN
```

```
TITLE     A23SUB1  Called subprogram
DATASEG   SEGMENT PARA 'Data2'
SUBMSG    DB      'Subprogram 1 reporting'
DATASEG   ENDS

CODESEG   SEGMENT PARA 'Code2'
A23SUB1   PROC    FAR
          ASSUME  CS:CODESEG,DS:DATASEG
          PUBLIC  A23SUB1
          PUSH    DS                   ;Save caller's DS
          PUSH    ES                   ;  and ES
          MOV     AX,DATASEG
          MOV     DS,AX                ;Initialize DS
          MOV     ES,AX                ;  and ES
          MOV     AX,1301H             ;Request display
          MOV     BX,001EH             ;Page and attribute
          LEA     BP,SUBMSG            ;Message
          MOV     CX,22                ;Length
          MOV     DX,0810H             ;Row : column
          INT     10H
          POP     ES                   ;Restore caller's ES
          POP     DS                   ;  and DS
          RET
A23SUB1   ENDP
CODESEG   ENDS
          END
```

Figure 23-3 *Continued*

```
TITLE      A23SUB2 Called overlay subprogram
DATASEG    SEGMENT PARA 'Data'
SUBMSG     DB        'Subprogram 2 reporting'
DATASEG    ENDS

CODESEG    SEGMENT PARA 'Code'
A23SUB2    PROC      FAR
           ASSUME    CS:CODESEG,DS:DATASEG
           PUSH      DS              ;Save caller's DS
           MOV       AX,CS           ;Set address of first
           MOV       DS,AX           ;  segment in DS
           MOV       ES,AX
           MOV       AX,1301H        ;Request display
           MOV       BX,001EH        ;Page:attribute
           LEA       BP,SUBMSG       ;Message
           MOV       CX,22           ;Length
           MOV       DX,1010H        ;Row:column
           INT       10H
           POP       DS              ;Restore caller's DS
           RET
A23SUB2    ENDP
CODESEG    ENDS
           END
```

Figure 23-3 *Continued*

```
STACK      SEGMENT PARA STACK 'Stack1'
DATASEG    SEGMENT PARA 'Data1'
CODESEG    SEGMENT PARA 'Code1'
```

A23SUB1 is linked with and called by A23CALLV. Its segments are:

```
DATASEG    SEGMENT PARA 'Data2'
CODESEG    SEGMENT PARA 'Code2'
```

A23CALLV's segments are linked first—that's why their class names differ: 'Data1', 'Data2', 'Code1', 'Code2', and so forth. Here's the link map for A23CALLV+A23SUB1:

Start	Stop	Length	Name	Class
00000H	0007FH	00080H	STACK	Stack1
00080H	000C2H	00043H	DATASEG	Data1
000D0H	0015FH	00090H	CODESEG	Code1
00160H	00175H	00016H	DATASEG	Data2
00180H	0019DH	0001EH	CODESEG	Code2

A23SUB2 is also called by A23CALLV, but is linked separately. Its segments are:

```
DATASEG    SEGMENT    PARA    'Data'
CODESEG    SEGMENT    PARA    'Code'
```

A23SUB2's link map looks like this (along with a warning about no stack segment):

Start	Stop	Length	Name	Class
00000H	00015H	00016H	DATASEG	Data
00020H	0003AH	0001BH	CODESEG	Code

This program, unlike that in Figure 23-2, contains conventional segment directives, which the assembler has left in their origianl sequence. The code segment therefore has the last and highest address.

When the program loader transfers A23CALLV+A23SUB1 into memory for execution, A23CALLV calls and executes A23SUB1 in normal fashion. The near CALL initializes IP correctly, but because A23SUB1 has its own data segment, it has to push A23CALLV's DS and establish its own DS address. A23SUB1 sets the cursor, displays a message, pops DS, and returns to A23CALLV.

To overlay A23SUB2 on A23SUB1, A23CALLV has to shrink its own memory space because the system has given it all available memory. The steps in calculating program size for INT 21H function 4AH are:

1. Set the segment address of the code segment in BX.
2. Add the size of the code segment (in paragraphs) to BX.
3. Subtract the segment address of the PSP from BX.

INT 21H function 48H then allocates memory to allow space for A23SUB2 to be loaded (overlaid) on top of A23SUB1, arbitrarily set to 40H paragraphs. The operation returns the loading address in AX, which A23CALLV stores in PARABLOK. This is the first word of a parameter block to be used by function 4BH.

Function 4BH with code 03 in AL loads A23SUB2 into memory. Note the definition in the data segment: C:\A23SUB2.EXE,0. Function 4BH references CS and PARA-BLOK—the first word contains the segment address where the overlay is to be loaded and the second word is an offset, in this case, zero. A diagram may help make these steps clearer:

After initial load	After function 4AH shrinks memory	After function 48H allocates memory
000 PSP	000 PSP	000 PSP
100 A23CALLV	100 A23CALLV	100 A23CALLV
260 A23SUB1		260 A23SUB2

The far CALL to A23SUB2 requires a reference defined as IP:CS, but PARABLOK is in the form CS:IP. The CS value is therefore moved to the second word, and 20H is stored in the first word for IP because the link map shows that value as the offset of A23SUB2's code segment. The next instructions load the address of PARABLOK in BX and call A23SUB2:

```
LEA   BX,PARABLOK    ;Address of PARABLOK
CALL  DWORD PTR [BX] ;Call A23SUB2
```

Note that A23CALLV doesn't reference A23SUB2 by name in its code segment and so doesn't require an EXTRN statement specifying A23SUB2. Because A23SUB2 has its own data segment, it first pushes DS onto the stack and initializes its own address. But A23SUB2 wasn't linked with A23CALLV. As a result, the instruction MOV AX,DATASEG would set AX with only the offset address of DATASEG, 0[0]H, and not its segment address. We do know that the CALL set CS with the address of the first segment, which (according to the

Link Map) happens to be the address of the data segment. Copying CS to DS gives the correct address in DS. Note that if A23SUB2's code and data segments are arranged in a different sequence, the coding has to be revised accordingly.

A23SUB2 displays a message, pops DS, and returns to A23CALLV.

RESIDENT PROGRAMS

A number of programs are designed to reside in memory while other programs run, and you can activate their services through special keystrokes. You load resident programs before activating other normal processing programs. They are almost always .COM programs and are also known as "terminate but stay resident" (TSR) programs.

The easy part of writing a resident program is getting it to reside. Instead of normal termination, you cause it to exit by means of INT 21H function 31H (Keep Program). The operation requires the size of the program in DX:

```
MOV   AH,31H          ;Request TSR
MOV   DX,prog-size    ;Size of program
INT   21H             ;Call interrupt service
```

When you execute the initialization routine, the system reserves the memory block where the program resides and loads subsequent programs higher in memory.

The not-so-easy part of writing a resident program involves activating it after it is resident because it is not a program internal to the system, as are CLS, COPY, and DIR. A common approach is to modify the Interrupt Vector Table so that the resident program interrupts all keystrokes, acts on a special keystroke or combination, and passes on all other keystrokes. The effect is that a resident program typically, but not necessarily, consists of the following parts:

1. A section that redefines locations in the Interrupt Vector Table.
2. An initialization procedure that executes only the first time the program runs and that performs the following:
   • replaces the address in the interrupt vector table with its own address,
   • establishes the size of the portion of the program that is to remain resident, and
   • uses an interrupt that tells the system to end executing the current program and to attach the specified portion of the program in memory.
3. A procedure that remains resident and that is activated, for example, by such actions as special keyboard input or the timer clock.

In effect, the initialization procedure sets up all the conditions to make the resident program work and then allows itself to be erased.

A resident program may use two INT 21H functions for accessing the Interrupt Vector Table because there is no assurance that more advanced computers will have the table located beginning at location 0000H.

INT 21H Function 35H: Get Interrupt Vector

To retrieve the address in the Interrupt Vector Table of a particular interrupt, load AL with the required interrupt number:

```
MOV   AH,35H        ;Request get vector
MOV   AL,int#       ;Interrupt number
INT   21H           ;Call interrupt service
```

The operation returns the address of the interrupt in ES:BX as segment:offset. For conventional memory, a request for the address of INT 09H, for example, returns 00H in ES and 24H (36) in BX.

INT 21H Function 25H: Set Interrupt Vector

To set a new interrupt address, load the required interrupt number in AL and the new address in DX:

```
MOV   AH,25H        ;Request set interrupt vector
MOV   AL,int#       ;Interrupt number
LEA   DX,newaddr    ;New address for interrupt
INT   21H           ;Call interrupt service
```

The operation replaces the present address of the interrupt with the new address. In effect, then, when the specified interrupt occurs, processing links to the resident program rather than to the normal interrupt address.

Example of a Resident Program

The resident program in Figure 23-4 named A23RESID beeps if you press the ESC key. The program's only practical purpose is to illustrate the technical details of a resident program in the simplest way possible so that you may attempt other types of perhaps more useful programs.

The following points about the resident program are of interest:

CODESEG begins the code segment of A23RESID. The first executable instruction, JMP B10INIT, transfers execution past the resident portion to the B10INIT procedure near the end. This routine first uses CLI to prevent any further interrupts that may happen to occur at this time. It then uses INT 21H function 35H to locate the address of INT 09H in the interrupt vector table. The operation returns the address in ES:BX, which the B10INIT routine stores in SAVEINT9. Next, function 25H sets the program's own address for INT 09H in the interrupt table, A10TEST, the entry point to the resident program. In effect, the program saves INT 09H's address and replaces it with its own address. The last step establishes the size of the resident portion (all the code up to B10INIT) in DX and uses INT 21H function 31H (Terminate but Stay Resident) to exit. The code from B10INIT to the end gets overlaid by the next program that is loaded for execution.

A10TEST is the name of the resident procedure that is activated when a user presses a key. The system transfers execution to the address of INT 09H in the Interrupt Vector Table, which has been changed to the address of A10TEST. Because the interrupt may happen, for example, while the user is performing any kind of operation, A23RESID has to save the registers that it uses. The program accesses the keyboard flag to determine whether the Esc key was pressed (scan code 01). If so, the program beeps the speaker. (The use of the speaker is explained in Chapter 24, under the section "Generating Sound.") Final instructions involve restoring the pushed registers—in reverse sequence—and jumping to

```
TITLE      A23RESID (COM)   Resident program: Beep if use
;                           Esc key
CODESEG  SEGMENT PARA
         ASSUME  CS:CODESEG
         ORG     100H
BEGIN:   JMP     B10INIT                 ;Jump to initialization
SAVEINT9 DD      ?                       ;INT 09H address
DURATION DW      100H                    ;
A10TEST: PUSH    AX                      ;Save registers
         PUSH    CX
         IN      AL,60H                  ;Get keystroke from port
         CMP     AL,01                   ;Scan code 01 (Esc)?
         JNE     A50EXIT                 ;  no, exit
         IN      AL,61H                  ;Get port status
         PUSH    AX                      ;  and save
         OR      AL,00000011B            ;Turn on speaker
         OUT     61H,AL
         MOV     CX,512H                 ;Length
A20:     LOOP    A20                     ;
         OR      AL,00000010B            ;Set bit 1 on
         MOV     CX,512H                 ;
A30:     LOOP    A30                     ;
         POP     AX                      ;Port status
         AND     AL,11111100B            ;Turn off speaker
         OUT     61H,AL
A50EXIT: POP     CX                      ;Restore registers
         POP     AX
         JMP     CS:SAVEINT9             ;Resume INT 09H
                                         ;Initialization:
B10INIT:                                 ;---------------
         CLI                             ;Prevent interrupts
         MOV     AH,35H                  ;Get address of INT 09H
         MOV     AL,09H                  ;  in ES:BX
         INT     21H
         MOV     WORD PTR SAVEINT9,BX ;  and save it
         MOV     WORD PTR SAVEINT9+2,ES
         MOV     AH,25H
         MOV     AL,09H                  ;Set new address for
         MOV     DX,OFFSET A10TEST       ;  INT 09H in A10TEST
         INT     21H
         MOV     AH,31H                  ;Request stay resident
         MOV     DX,OFFSET B10INIT       ;Set size
         STI                             ;Restore interrupts
         INT     21H
CODESEG  ENDS
         END     BEGIN
```

Figure 23-4   Resident Program

SAVEINT9, which contains the original INT 09H address. Control is now released back to the interrupt.

The next example should help make the procedure clear. First, here's an explanation of a conventional operation without a TSR intercepting the interrupt:

1. A user presses a key, and the keyboard sends INT 09H to BIOS.

2. BIOS uses the address of INT 09H in the Interrupt Vector Table to locate its BIOS routine.

3. Control then transfers to the BIOS routine.

4. The routine gets the character and, if a standard character, delivers it to the keyboard buffer.

Next is the procedure for the resident program:

1. A user presses a key, and the keyboard sends INT 09H to BIOS.
2. BIOS uses the address of INT 09H in the Interrupt Vector Table to locate its BIOS routine.
3. But the table now contains the address of A10TEST in the resident program, to which control transfers.
4. If the character is Esc, the program beeps the speaker.
5. A10TEST exits by jumping to the original saved INT 09H address, which transfers control to the BIOS routine.
6. The BIOS routine gets the character and, if a standard character, delivers it to the keyboard buffer.

Try using DEBUG to examine the results of executing this program. Use D 0:20 to display the contents of the Interrupt Vector Table at 20H (36), where the interrupt address for INT 09H is stored. The first word is the offset and the second word is the segment address, both in reverse-byte sequence. For example, if the stored address is 0701 EF05, then use D 107:05EF to view the contents of the stored address. The display should begin with 50511EB8, which is the start of the machine code for A10TEST in the resident program.

Some programs that also replace the table address of INT 09H do not allow concurrent use of a resident program such as this one.

KEY POINTS

- The .EXE module that the linker creates consists of a header record containing control and relocation information and the actual load module.
- On loading a .COM program, the loader sets the segment registers with the address of the PSP, sets the stack pointer to the end of the segment, pushes a zero word onto the stack, and sets the Instruction Pointer to 100H (the size of the PSP). Control then proceeds to the address generated by CS:IP, the first location immediately following the PSP.
- On loading an .EXE program, the loader reads the header record into memory, calculates the size of the executable module, and reads the module into memory at the start segment. It adds the value of each relocation table item to the start segment value. It sets DS and ES to the segment address of the PSP; sets SS to the address of the PSP plus 100H plus the SS offset value; sets SP to the size of the stack, and sets CS to the address of the PSP, plus 100H, plus the CS offset value in the header. The loader also sets IP with the offset at 14H. The CS:IP pair provide the starting address of the code segment for program execution.
- Fields within the PSP include parameter area 1 at 5CH, parameter area 2 at 6CH, and default disk transfer area at 80H.
- Load a resident program before activating other normal processing programs. Exit by means of INT 21H function 31H, which requires the size of the program in DX and reserves the block of memory where the program resides.

REVIEW QUESTIONS AND EXERCISES

23-1. (a) Where does the system store the program segment prefix? (b) What is its size?

23-2. What is the purpose of these fields in the program segment prefix? (a) The first byte, which contains CD20H, (b) 18-2BH, the default file handle table, (c) 2C-2DH, the segment address of the program's environment, (d) 80-FFH, the default DTA.

23-3. A .COM program is loaded for execution with its PSP beginning at location 3AB6[0]H. What address does the program loader store in each of the following registers: (a) CS, (b) DS, (c) ES, (d) SS.

23-4. A link map for an .EXE program shows the following:

Start	Stop	Length	Name	Class
00000H	0004FH	00050H	STACK	STACK
00050H	0007BH	0002CH	CODESEG	CODE
00080H	000ACH	0002DH	DATASEG	DATA

The loader loads the program with the PSP beginning at location 2AC6[0]H. Showing calculations where appropriate, determine the contents of each of the registers at the time of loading: (a) SS, (b) SP, (c) CS, (d) DS, (e) ES.

23-5. Resident programs commonly intercept keyboard input. Where and what exactly is this intercepted address?

23-6. In what two significant ways does the coding for terminating a resident program differ from terminating a normal program?

Chapter 24

BIOS DATA AREAS, INTERRUPTS, AND PORTS

> Objective: To describe the BIOS data areas, interrupt services, and port operations.

INTRODUCTION

BIOS contains an extensive set of input/output routines and tables that indicate the status of the system's devices. Both operating system and user programs can request BIOS routines for communication with devices attached to the system. The method of interfacing with BIOS is by means of software interrupts. This chapter examines the data areas that BIOS supports, the interrupt procedure, and BIOS interrupts 00H through 1BH, DOS interrupt 21H, and the system's ports.

THE BOOT PROCESS

On the PC, ROM resides beginning at location FFFF0H. Turning on the power causes the processor to enter a reset state, set all memory locations to zero, perform a parity check of memory, and set CS to FFFF[0]H and IP to zero. The first instruction to execute is therefore at FFFF:0, the entry point to BIOS. BIOS also stores the value 1234H at 40[0]:72H to signal a subsequent Ctrl+Alt+Del (reboot) not to perform the preceding power-on self-test.

BIOS checks the various ports to identify and initialize devices that are attached, including INT 11H (Equipment Determination) and INT 12H (Memory Size Determination). Then, beginning at location 0 of conventional memory, BIOS establishes the Interrupt Vector Table that contains addresses of interrupt routines.

Next, BIOS determines whether a disk containing the system files is present and, if so, it executes INT 19H to access the first disk sector containing the bootstrap loader. This program is a temporary operating system to which the BIOS routine transfers control after loading it into memory. The bootstrap has only one task: to load the first part of the operating system into memory.

THE BIOS DATA AREA

BIOS maintains its own 256-byte (100H) data area in lower memory beginning at segment address 40[0]H, with fields containing data in reverse-byte sequence, and which are listed next by offset.

Serial Port Data Area

00H–07H Four words, addresses of up to four serial ports, COM1-COM4.

Parallel Port Data Area

08H–0FH Four words, addresses of up to four parallel ports, LPT1-LPT4.

System Equipment Data Area

10H–11H Equipment status, a primitive indication of the status of installed devices. You can issue INT 11H, which returns the following in AX:

BIT	DEVICE
15,14	Number of parallel ports attached
11–9	Number of RS232 serial ports attached
7,6	Number of diskette devices, where bit 00 = 1, 01 = 2, 10 = 3, and 11 = 4
5,4	Initial video mode. Bit values are 00 = unused, 01 = 40 × 25 color, 10 = 80 × 25 color, 11 = 80 × 25 monochrome
2	Pointing device (mouse), where 1 = installed
1	1 = numeric coprocessor is present
0	1 = diskette drive is present

Miscellaneous Data Area

12H Manufacturer's test flags

Memory Size Data Area

13H–14H Amount of memory on system board, in kilobytes
15H–16H Amount of expansion memory, in kilobytes

Keyboard Data Area 1

17H First byte of the current shift status:

BIT	ACTION	BIT	ACTION
7	Insert active	3	Right Alt pressed
6	CapsLock active	2	Right Ctrl pressed
5	NumLock active	1	Left shift pressed
4	Scroll Lock active	0	Right shift pressed

"Active" means that the key was already pressed and set on. "Pressed" means that the key was being held down when BIOS stored the status.

18H Second byte of the current shift status:

BIT	ACTION	BIT	ACTION
7	Insert pressed	3	Ctrl/NumLock pressed
6	CapsLock pressed	2	SysReq pressed
5	NumLock pressed	1	Left Alt pressed
4	Scroll Lock pressed	0	Left Ctrl pressed

19H Alternate keyboard entry for ASCII characters.

1AH–1BH Pointer to keyboard buffer head

1CH–1DH Pointer to keyboard buffer tail

1EH–3DH Keyboard buffer (32 bytes)

Diskette Drive Data Area

3EH Disk seek status. Bit number 0 refers to drive A, 1 to B, 2 to C, and 3 to D. A bit value of 0 means that the next seek is to reposition to cylinder 0 to recalibrate the drive.

3FH Disk motor status. If bit 7 = 1, a write operation is in progress. Bit number 0 refers to drive A, 1 to B, 2 to C, and 3 to D.

40H Motor count for time-out until motor is turned off

41H Disk status, indicating an error on the last diskette drive operation:

00H	No error	09H	Attempt to make DMA across
01H	Invalid drive parameter		64K boundary
02H	Address mark not found	0CH	Media type not found
03H	Write-protect error	10H	CRC error on read
04H	Sector not found	20H	Controller error
06H	Diskette change line active	40H	Seek failed
08H	DMA overrun	80H	Drive not ready

42H-48H Diskette drive controller status

Video Data Area 1

49H Current video mode, indicated by a 1-bit:

BIT	MODE	BIT	MODE
7	Monochrome	3	80×25 color
6	640×200 monochrome	2	80×25 monochrome
5	320×200 monochrome	1	40×25 color
4	320×200 color	0	40×25 monochrome

4AH–4BH Number of columns on the screen

4CH–4DH Size of the video page buffer

4EH–4FH Starting offset of the video buffer

50H–5FH Eight words for the current starting location for each of 8 pages, numbered 0–7

60H–61H Starting and ending lines of the cursor

62H Currently displayed page

63H–64H Port address of the active display (monochrome is 03B4H and color is 03D4H)

65H Current setting of the Video Mode Control register

66H Current color palette

System Data Area

67H–68H Data-edge time count

69H–6AH Cyclical redundancy check (CRC) register

6BH Last input value

6CH–6FH Timer, with time in reversed-byte sequence. Updated by one "tick" every 18.2 seconds (about 55 milliseconds). Dividing this value by 18.2 gives the actual seconds since midnight.

70H Timer overflow (1 if timer has passed midnight)

71H Ctrl+Break keys set bit 7 to 1

72H–73H Memory reset flag. If the contents are 1234H, pressing the Ctrl+Alt+Del keys causes a reboot.

Hard Disk Data Area

74H Status of last hard disk operation (details in Chapter 19)

75H Number of hard disks attached

Time-Out Data Area

78H–7BH Time-out for parallel ports (LPT1—LPT4)

7CH–7FH Time-out for serial ports (COM1—COM4)

Keyboard Data Area 2

80H–81H Offset address for start of keyboard buffer

82H–83H Offset address for end of keyboard buffer

Video Data Area 2

84H Number of rows on the screen (minus 1)

85H–86H Character height, in scan lines

87H Video information, according to bit:

   0 If 1, text mode emulation is enabled for cursor

3 If 1, video subsystem is inactive

6–5 Amount of video storage (11 means 256K or more)

7 Same as bit 7 of video mode number sent to INT 10H function 0

88H Miscellaneous video information

89H Miscellaneous flags, according to bit:

0 Bit = 1 means VGA is active

1 Bit = 1 means gray scale summing is enabled

2 Bit = 0 means color monitor, 1 means monochrome

3 Bit = 1 means default palette loading is disabled

4 and 7 define scan lines for text mode

BIT 4	BIT 7	MODE
0	0	350-line
0	1	400-line
1	0	200-line

Diskette/Hard Disk Data Area

8BH–95H Controller and error status

Keyboard Data Area 3

96H Keyboard mode state and type flags

BIT	ACTION	BIT	ACTION
7	Read ID in progress	3	Right Alt pressed
6	Last code was ACK	2	Right Ctrl pressed
5	Force NumLock if read ID and KBX	1	Last scan code was E0
4	Extended keyboard installed	0	Last scan code was E1

97H Keyboard LED Flags (bit 0 = ScrollLock, 1 = NumLock, and 2 = CapsLock)

Real-Time Clock Data Area

98H–A7H Status of wait flags

Save Pointer Data Area

A8H–ABH Pointers to BIOS Save Area. The first address (offset:segment) points to a video Save Pointer table.

Miscellaneous Data Area 2

ACH–FFH Reserved by the system for internal use

The following BIOS areas are in higher memory:

   A0000–AFFFF Video display graphics buffer

   B0000–B0FFF Monochrome video buffer

   B8000–B0FA0 Color text video buffer

   F0000–FFFFF ROM BIOS information area

INTERRUPT SERVICES

An interrupt operation suspends execution of a program so that the system can take special action. The interrupt routine executes and normally returns control to the interrupted procedure, which then resumes execution. BIOS handles INT 00H-1FH, whereas DOS handles INT 20H-3FH.

Interrupt Vector Table

When the computer powers up, the system establishes an Interrupt Vector Table in locations 000H–3FFH of conventional memory. The table provides for 256 (100H) interrupts, each with a related 4-byte offset:segment address in the form IP:CS. The operand of an interrupt instruction such as INT 05H identifies the type of request. Since there are 256 entries, each four bytes long, the table occupies the first 1,024 bytes of memory, from 00H through 3FFH. Each address in the table relates to a BIOS or DOS routine for a specific interrupt type. Thus bytes 0–3 contain the address for interrupt 0, bytes 4–7 for interrupt 1, and so forth. Following are some relevant table addresses:

INTERRUPT	OPERATION	INTERRUPT	OPERATION
0	Divide by 0	14	Serial port interrupt
1	Single step processing	16	Keyboard interrupt
2	Nonmaskable interrupt (NMI)	17	Printer interrupt
3	Breakpoint address	19	Bootstrap loader
4	Overflow	1A	Time of day
5	Print screen	1B	Control on keyboard break
8	Interval timer	1C	Control on timer interrupt
9	BIOS keyboard interrupt	1D	Video table address
E	Disk interrupt	1E	Disk table address
10	Video interrupt	1F	ASCII character address
11	Equipment check	21	DOS interrupt
12	Memory check	33	Mouse interrupt
13	Disk I/O		

Executing an Interrupt

An interrupt pushes onto the stack the contents of the Flags register, CS, and IP. For example, pressing Ctrl+PrintScrn causes BIOS to invoke the Vector Table address of INT 05H; the address is 0014H (05H × 4 = 14H). The operation extracts the 4-byte address from location 0014H and stores two bytes in IP and two bytes in CS. The address in CS:IP then points to the start of a routine in the BIOS area, which prints the Video Display Area. The interrupt returns via an IRET (Interrupt Return) instruction, which pops IP, CS, and flags from the stack and returns control to the instruction following the INT.

External and Internal Interrupts. An *external interrupt* is caused by a device that is external to the processor. The two lines that can signal external interrupts are the nonmaskable interrupt (NMI) line and the interrupt request (INTR) line. The NMI line reports memory and I/O parity errors. The processor always acts on this interrupt, even if you issue CLI to clear the Interrupt Flag in an attempt to disable external interrupts. The INTR line reports requests from external devices, namely interrupts 05H through 0FH, for the timer, keyboard, serial ports, fixed disk, diskette drives, and parallel ports.

An *internal interrupt* occurs as a result of the execution of an INT instruction or a divide operation that causes an overflow, execution in single-step mode, or a request for an external interrupt, such as disk I/O. Programs commonly use internal interrupts, which are nonmaskable, to access BIOS and DOS procedures.

BIOS INTERRUPTS

This section covers BIOS interrupts 00H through 1BH. Other operations not covered can be executed only by BIOS.

INT 00H: Divide by Zero. Invoked by an attempt to divide by zero; displays a message and usually hangs the system.

INT 01H: Single Step. Used by DEBUG and other debuggers to enable single-stepping through program execution.

INT 02H: Nonmaskable Interrupt. Used for serious hardware conditions, such as parity errors, that are always enabled. Issuing a CLI (Clear Interrupt) instruction does not affect these conditions.

INT 03H: Break Point. Used by debuggers to stop execution. DEBUG's Go and Proceed commands set this interrupt at the appropriate stopping point in the program; DEBUG undoes single-step mode and allows the program to execute normally up to INT 03H, whereupon DEBUG resets single-step mode.

INT 04H: Overflow. May be caused by an arithmetic operation, although usually no action takes place.

INT 05H: Print Screen. Causes the contents of the Video Display Area to print. Issuing INT 05H activates the interrupt internally, and pressing Ctrl+PrintScrn activates it externally. The operation enables interrupts and saves the cursor position. No registers are affected. Address 50:00 in the BIOS Data Area contains the status of the operation.

INT 08H: System Timer. A hardware interrupt that updates the system time and (if necessary) date. A programmable timer chip generates an interrupt every 54.9254 milliseconds, about 18.2 times a second.

INT 09H: Keyboard Interrupt.   Caused by pressing or releasing a key on the keyboard; described in detail in Chapter 10.

INT 0BH, INT 0CH: Serial Device Control.   Control the COM1 and COM2 ports, respectively.

INT 0DH, INT 0FH: Parallel Device Control.   Control the LPT2 and LPT1 ports, respectively.

INT 0EH: Diskette Control.   Signals diskette activity, such as completion of an I/O operation.

INT 10H: Video Display.   Accepts a number of functions in AH for screen mode, setting the cursor, scrolling, and displaying; described in detail in Chapter 9.

INT 11H: Equipment Determination.   Determines the optional devices on the system and returns the value at BIOS location 40:10H to AX. (At power-up time, the system executes this operation and stores AX in location 40:10H; see the earlier section "BIOS Data Area" for details.)

INT 12H: Memory Size Determination.   Returns in AX the size of base memory in terms of contiguous kilobytes.

INT 13H: Disk Input/Output.   Accepts a number of functions in AH for disk status, read sectors, write sectors, verify, format, and get diagnostics; covered in Chapter 19.

INT 14H: Communications Input/Output.   Provides bit stream I/O (that is, one bit at a time) to the RS232 serial port. DX should contain a code for the RS232 port (0–3 for COM1, 2, 3, and 4, respectively). A number of functions are established through the AH register.

Function 00H: Initialize Communications Port.   Set the following parameters in AL, according to bit number:

BITS/SEC	PARITY	STOP BIT	WORD LENGTH
7 – 5	4 – 3	2	1 – 0
100 = 1200	00 = none	0 = 1	10 = 7 bits
101 = 2400	01 = odd	1 = 2	11 = 8 bits
110 = 4800	10 = none		
111 = 9600	11 = even		

Here's an example that sets COM1 to 1200 bits per second, no parity, one stop bit, and 8-bit data length:

```
MOV   AH,00H          ;Request initialize port
MOV   AL,11100011B    ;Parameters
MOV   DX,00           ;COM1 serial port
INT   14H             ;Call interrupt service
```

The operation returns the status of the communications port in AX. (See function 03H for details.)

   Function 01H: Transmit Character.   Load AL with the character that is to be transmitted and DX with the port number. On return, the operation sets the port status in AH. (See function 03H.) If the operation is unable to transmit the byte, it also sets bit 7 of AH, although the normal purpose of this bit is to report a time-out error. Execute function 00H before using this service.

   Function 02H: Receive Character.   Load the port number in DX. The operation accepts a character from the communications line into AL. It also sets AH with the port status (see function 03) for error bits 7, 4, 3, 2, and 1. Thus a nonzero value in AX indicates an input error. Execute function 00H before using this service.

   Function 03H: Return Status of Communications Port.   Load the port number in DX. The operation returns the line status (from port 03FDH) in AH and modem status (from port 03FEH) in AL:

AH (LINE STATUS)	AL (MODEM STATUS)
7 Time out	Receive line signal detect
6 Transmit shift register empty	6 Ring indicator
5 Transmit hold register empty	5 Data set ready
4 Break error detect	4 Clear to send
3 Framing error	3 Change receive line signal detect
2 Parity error	2 Change in ring detector
1 Overrun error	1 Change in data set ready
0 Data ready	0 Change in clear to send

   Other INT 14H functions are 04H (Extended Initialize) and 05H (Extended Communications Port Control). Since INT 14H is limited to 9600 bps, it is best suited for experiments with transmitting data. A much faster but more complex method is to address the ports directly via INS and OUTS operations; a discussion is outside the scope of this book.

   INT 15H: System Services.   This elaborate operation provides for a large number of functions in AH, including the following:

21H Power-on self-testing	88H Determine extended memory size
43H Read system status	89H Switch processor to protected mode
84H Joystick support	C2H Mouse interface

   INT 16H: Keyboard Input.   Accepts a number of functions in AH for basic keyboard input; covered in Chapter 10.

   INT 17H: Printer Output.   Provides a number of functions for printing via BIOS; discussed in Chapter 20.

   INT 18H: ROM BASIC Entry.   Called by BIOS if the system starts up with no disk containing the system boot programs.

INT 19H: Bootstrap Loader.   If a disk(ette) device is available with the operating system programs, reads track 0, sector 1, into the boot location in memory at 7C00H and transfers control to this location. It is possible to use this operation as a software interrupt; it does not clear the screen or initialize data in ROM BIOS.

INT 1AH: Read and Set Time.   Reads or sets the time of day according to a function code in AH:

00H = Read system timer clock. Returns the high portion of the count in CX and the low portion in DX. If the time has passed 24 hours since the last read, the operation sets AL to a nonzero value.

01H = Set system timer clock. Load the high portion of the count in CX and the low portion in DX.

02H–07H. These functions handle the time and date for real-time clock services.

To determine how long a routine executes, you could set the clock to zero and then read it at the end of processing.

INT 1BH: Get Control on Keyboard Break.   When Ctrl+Break keys are pressed, causes ROM BIOS to transfer control to its interrupt address, where a flag is set.

INT 21H SERVICES

Following are DOS INT 21H services relevant to this book and which require a function code in AH.

01H: Keyboard Input with Echo.   (See Chapter 10.)

02H: Display Character.   (See Chapter 8.)

03H: Communications Input.   Reads a character from the serial port into AL; a primitive service, and BIOS INT 14H is preferred.

04H: Communications Output.   DL contains the character to transmit; BIOS INT 14H is preferred.

05H: Printer Output.   For printing single characters:

```
MOV  AH,05H   ;Request print
MOV  DL,char  ;Single character
INT  21H      ;
```

06H: Direct Keyboard and Display.   This rather bizarre operation can transfer any character or control code. There are two versions, for keyboard input and for screen output. For input, load 0FFH into the DL. If no character is in the keyboard buffer, the operation sets the Zero Flag and does not wait for input. If a character is waiting in the buffer, the operation loads the character in AL and clears the Zero Flag. The operation does not echo the character on the screen and does not check for Ctrl+Break or Ctrl+PrinttScrn. A nonzero value in AL represents a standard ASCII character, such as a letter or number. Zero in AL means that the user has pressed an extended function key such as Home, F1, or PageUp. To get its scan code in AL, immediately repeat the INT 21H operation. For screen output, load the ASCII character (not 0FFH) into DL.

07H: Direct Keyboard Input without Echo.   (See Chapter 11.)

08H: Keyboard Input without Echo.   (See Chapter 10.)

09H: Display String.   (See Chapter 8.)

0AH: Buffered Keyboard Input.   (See Chapter 10.)

0BH: Check Keyboard Status.   (See Chapter 10.)

0CH: Clear Keyboard Buffer and Invoke Input.   (See Chapter 10.)

0DH: Reset Disk Drive.   (See Chapter 18.)

0EH: Select Default Disk Drive.   (See Chapter 18.)

19H: Determine Default Disk Drive.   (See Chapter 18.)

1AH: Set Disk Transfer Area (DTA).   (See Chapter 18.)

1FH: Get Default Drive Parameter Block.   (See Chapter 18.)

25H: Set Interrupt Vector.   When a user presses Ctrl+Break or Ctrl+C, the normal procedure is for the program to terminate and return to the operating system. You may want your program to provide its own routine to handle this situation. The following example uses function 25H to set the address for Ctrl+Break in the Interrupt Vector Table (INT 23H) for its own routine, C10BREAK, which could take any necessary action.

```
            MOV  AH,25H        ;Request set table address
            MOV  AL,23H        ; for INT 23H
            LEA  DX,C10BREAK   ;New address
            INT  21H           ;Call interrupt service
            ...
  C10BREAK:                    ;Ctrl+Break routine
            ...
            IRET               ;Interrupt return
```

29H: Parse Filename.   (See Chapter 18.)

2AH: Get System Date.   Returns these binary values: AL = day of week (Sunday = 0); CX = year (1980–2099); DH = month (01–12); DL = day (01–31).

2BH: Set System Date.   Load these binary values: CX = year (1980–2099); DH = month (01–12); DL = day (01–31). On return, AL indicates a valid (00H) or invalid (FFH) operation.

2CH: Get System Time.   Returns these binary values: CH = hours, in 24-hour format (00-23, where midnight is 00); CL = minutes (00–59); DH = seconds (00–59); DL = hundredths of a second (00–99).

2DH: Set System Time.   Load these binary values: CH = hours, in 24-hour format (00–23, where midnight is 00); CL = minutes (00–59); DH = seconds (00–59); DL = hundredths of a second (00–99). On return, AL indicates a valid (00H) or invalid (FFH) operation.

2EH: Set/Reset Disk Verification.   (See Chapter 18.)

2FH: Get Address of Current Disk Transfer Area (DTA).   (See Chapter 18.)

31H: Terminate but Stay Resident.   (See Chapter 23.)

32H: Get Drive Parameter Block (DPB).   (See Chapter 18.)

3300H: Get Ctrl+C State.   If the Ctrl+C flag is off (0), causes the system to check for Ctrl+C only while handling character I/O functions 01H–0CH. If the flag is on (1), the system checks while handling other functions as well. To get the state, set subfunction 00H in AL. The value returned in DL is 00H = checking disabled or 01H = checking enabled.

3301H: Set Ctrl+C State.   If the Ctrl+C flag is off (0), causes the system to check for Ctrl+C only while handling character I/O functions 01H–0CH. If the flag is on (1), the system checks while handling other functions as well. To set the state, load subfunction 01H in AL, and load the state in DL as 00H = set checking off or 01H = set checking on.

3305H: Get Startup Drive.   Returns in DL the drive (1 = A, etc.) used to load the system files.

3306H: Get DOS.   Returns these values:

BL = major version number, such as n for version n.11

BH = minor version number, such as hex B (11) for version n.11

DL = revision number in bits 2–0

DH = DOS version flag (indicates whether the system is running in conventional memory, high-memory area, or ROM)

Although the SETVER command can fake the version number, function 3306H delivers the true version.

35H: Get Address of Interrupt Vector Table.   (See Chapter 23.)

36H: Get Free Disk Space.   (See Chapter 18.)

38H: Get/Set Country-Dependent Information.   Supports a number of functions concerning information specific to various countries, such as the symbol and format for the country's currency, separators for thousands and decimal places, and separators for the date and time. Load DX for the operation: FFFFH to set the country code that the system is to use until further notice, or any other value to get the country code currently in use.

39H: Create Subdirectory (MKDIR).   (See Chapter 18.)

3AH: Remove Subdirectory (RMDIR).   (See Chapter 18.)

3BH: Change Current Directory (CHDIR).   (See Chapter 18.)

3CH: Create File.   (See Chapter 17.)

3DH: Open File.   (See Chapter 17.)

3EH: Close File.   (See Chapter 17.)

3FH: Read File/Device.   (See Chapters 9 and 17.)

40H: Write File/Device with Handle.   (See Chapters 8, 17, and 20.)

41H: Delete File from Directory.   (See Chapter 18.)

42H: Move File Pointer.   (See Chapter 17.)

43H: Check/Change File Attribute.   (See Chapter 18.)

44H: I/O Control for Devices.   Supports an extensive set of subfunctions for checking devices and reading and writing data (See Chapter 18.)

45H: Duplicate a File Handle.   (See Chapter 18.)

46H: Force Duplicate of Handle.   (See Chapter 18.)

47H: Get Current Directory.   (See Chapter 18.)

48H: Allocate Memory Block.   (See Chapter 23.)

49H: Free Allocated Memory Block.   (See Chapter 23.)

4AH: Set Allocated Memory Block Size.   (See Chapter 23.)

4BH: Load/Execute a Program.   (See Chapter 23.)

4CH: Terminate Program.   The standard operation for ending program execution. (See Chapter 4.)

4DH: Retrieve Return Code of a Subprocess.   (See Chapter 23.)

4EH: Find First Matching Directory Entry.   (See Chapter 18.)

4FH: Find Next Matching Directory Entry.   (See Chapter 18.)

50H: Set Address of Program Segment Prefix (PSP).   Load BX with the offset address of the PSP for the current program. No values are returned.

51H: Get Address of Program Segment Prefix (PSP).   Returns the offset address of the PSP for the current program. (See Chapter 23.)

54H: Get Verify State.   (See Chapter 18.)

56H: Rename a File.   (See Chapter 18.)

57H: Get/Set File Date and Time.   (See Chapter 18.)

5800H: Get Memory Allocation Strategy.   (See Chapter 24.)

5801H: Set Memory Allocation Strategy.   (See Chapter 24.)

5802H: Get Upper Memory Link.   (See Chapter 23.)

5803H: Set Upper Memory Link.   (See Chapter 23.)

59H: Get Extended Error Code.   (See Chapter 18.)

5AH: Create a Temporary File.   (See Chapter 18.)

5BH: Create a New File.   (See Chapter 18.)

5DH: Set Extended Error.   Load DX with the offset address of a table of information on errors. The next execution of function 59H (Get Extended Error Code) is to retrieve the table. (See function 59H in Chapter 18 for details.)

62H: Get Address of PSP.   (Function 51H is an identical operation.)

65H: Get Extended Country Information.   Supports a number of subfunctions concerning information specific to various countries.

67H: Set Maximum Handle Count.   (See Chapter 23.)

68H: Commit File.   (See Chapter 18.)

6CH: Extended Open File.   Combines functions 3CH (Create File), 3DH (Open File), and 5BH (Create Unique File). (See Chapter 18.)

PORTS

A *port* is a device that connects the processor to the external world. Through a port, a processor receives a signal from an input device and sends a signal to an output device. Ports are identified by their addresses in the range of 0H–3FFH, or 1,024 ports in all. Note that these addresses are not conventional memory addresses.

The following lists some of the major port addresses:

020H–021H Ports for Programmable Interrupt Controller. Responds to external interrupts from such devices as keyboard, disk drives, and system clock. Requests from these devices interrupt the processor so that it acts on the request. The ports are

20H 8259 port address, which signals end of interrupt (EOI) when an operation sends the value 20H to it.

21H 8259 Interrupt Mask register, which indicates an interrupt is ended (0) or disabled (1). Bit numbers and IRQ are the same:

IRQ 0 System timer	IRQ 4 Serial port (COM1)
1 Keyboard	5 Parallel port (LPT2)
2 Secondary I/O channel	6 Diskette controller
3 Serial port (COM2)	7 Parallel port (LPT1)

040H–042H Ports for 8253 Programmable Interval Timer. Contains three ports that handle the following:

40H Channel 0 counter register, interrupts the system 18.2 times per second (counts 0 to 65,535 every 55 milliseconds) and updates the system clock.

41H Channel 1, interrupts direct memory access (DMA) controller to refresh memory. (RAM chips retain data for only a few milliseconds).

42H Channel 2, controls the speaker, connected via port 61H.

060H Keyboard. Handles the keyboard scan code.

061H Port for 8255 Interface Channel, which handles the following functions according to 0-bit values:

Bit 0 8253 Interval Timer (port 42H) clock disabled

Bit 1 Speaker disabled

Bit 4 RAM parity error enabled

Bit 6 Keyboard clicking off

Bit 7 Keyboard enabled

200H–20FH Game controller

278H–27FH Parallel printer port (LPT3)

2F8H–2FFH Serial port (COM2)

378H–37FH Parallel printer port (LPT2)

3B0H–3BBH Monochrome display port

3BCH–3BFH Parallel printer port (LPT1)

3C0H–3CFH VGA port

3DAH–3DFH VGA color CRT status register (read only)

3F0H–3F7H Disk controller

3F8H–3FFH Serial port (COM1)

Although the standard practice for input/output is to use INT operations, it is safe to bypass BIOS when accessing ports 21H, 40–42H, 60H, 61H, and 201H. For example, on bootup a ROM BIOS routine scans the system for the addresss of the serial and parallel ports. If the addresses are found, BIOS places the serial port addresses in its data area beginning at memory location 40:00H, and the parallel port addresses beginning at location 40:08H. Each location has space for four one-word entries. The BIOS table for a system with two serial ports and two parallel ports could look like this:

```
40:00  F803  COM1      40:08  7803  LPT1
40:02  F802  COM2      40:0A  7802  LPT2
40:04  0000  unused    40:0C  0000  unused
40:06  0000  unused    40:0E  0000  unused
```

For example, to use BIOS INT 17H to print a character, insert the printer port number in DX:

```
MOV  AH,00H    ;Request print
MOV  AL,char   ;Character to print
MOV  DX,0      ;Printer port 0 = LPT1
INT  17H       ;Call interrupt service
```

Some programs allow for printing only via LPT1. For a system with two printer ports installed as LPT1 and LPT2, the following partial program can be used to reverse (toggle) their addresses in the BIOS table. BIOSDATA defines the BIOS data area, and PARLPORT defines the first of the four word-size port addresses.

```
BIOSDATA    SEGMENT  AT 40H            ;BIOS data area
            ORG      8H                ;Printer port addresses
PARLPORT    DW       4 DUP(?)          ;4 words
BIOSDATA    ENDS
            ...
            ASSUME   DS:BIOSDATA
            MOV      AX,BIOSDATA        ;Init address of BIOS
            MOV      DS,AX              ;  data area in DS
            MOV      AX,PARLPORT(0)     ;LPT1 address to AX
            MOV      BX,PARLPORT(2)     ;LPT2 address to BX
            MOV      PARLPORT(0),BX     ;Exchange
            MOV      PARLPORT(2),AX     ;  addresses
            ...
```

The IN and OUT Instructions

The IN and OUT instructions can handle I/O directly at the port level. IN transfers data from an input port to AL if a byte and to AX if a word, whereas OUT transfers data to an output port from AL if a byte and from AX if a word. The formats are

[label:]	IN	accum-reg,port
[label:]	OUT	port,accum-reg

You can specify a port address either *statically* or *dynamically:*

Statically.   Use an operand from 0 through 255 directly as

```
Input    IN AL,port#     ;Input one byte from port
Output   OUT port#,AX    ;Output one word to port
```

Dynamically.   Use the contents of DX, 0 through 65,535, indirectly. You can use this method to process consecutive port addresses by incrementing DX. The following example uses port 60H:

```
MOV  DX,60H   ;Port 60H (keyboard)
IN   AL,DX    ;Get byte from port
```

Random Number Generator

The following program fragment can be used to generate random numbers from the 8253 Interval Timer:

```
MOV  AX,0     ;Interval timer
OUT  43H,AL   ;  via port 43H
IN   AL,40H   ;Make 2 accesses to
IN   AL,40H   ;  port 40H
```

The random number should now be in AL.

STRING INPUT/OUTPUT

The INSn and OUTSn string instructions can also transfer data, and work much like the string instructions covered in Chapter 11.

The INSn Instructions.   The instructions for the INSn operation are:

INSTRUCTION	EXAMPLE
INS (80286+)	INS ES:destination,DX
INSB (80286+)	REP INSB
INSW (80286+)	REP INSW
INSD (80386+)	REP INSD

The receiving data (or *destination*) is a "string" addressed by ES:DI, and DX contains the address of the input port. The normal practice is to use INSn with the REP prefix and

CX containing the number of items (bytes, words, or doublewords) to be received. If the Direction Flag (DF) is 0, DI is incremented by the size of each item received; if the DF is 1, DI is decremented.

The following example illustrates the INSn operation:

```
MOV   CX,no-bytes      ;Number of bytes
LEA   DI,destination   ;String destination (ES:DI)
MOV   DX,port-no       ;Receive bytes
REP   INSB             ;  via port
```

The OUTSn Instruction.   The instructions for the OUTSn operation are:

INSTRUCTION	EXAMPLE
OUTS (80286+)	OUTS DX,DS:*source*
OUTSB (80286+)	REP OUTSB
OUTSW (80286+)	REP OUTSW
OUTSD (80386+)	REP OUTSD

The sending data (or *source*) is a string addressed by DS:SI, and DX contains the address of the output port. The normal practice is to use OUTSn with the REP prefix and CX containing the number of items (bytes, words, or doublewords) to be sent. If the Direction Flag (DF) is 0, SI is incremented by the size of each item received; if the DF is 1, SI is decremented.

The following example illustrates the OUTSn operation:

```
MOV   CX,no-bytes   ;Number of bytes
LEA   SI,source     ;String destination (DS:SI)
MOV   DX,port-no    ;Send bytes
REP   OUTSB         ;  via port
```

GENERATING SOUND

The PC generates sound by means of a built-in permanent magnet speaker, which is connected to ports 42H, 43H, and 61H. The steps in operating the speaker are the following:

1. Get the status of port 61H and save it.
2. To turn on the speaker, send a bit string to port 61H with 11 in bits 0 and 1. The port activates the Intel 8255 Programmable Peripheral Interface (PPI) chip.
3. To turn off the speaker, send a bit string to port 61H with 00 in bits 0 and 1.

The partial program in Figure 24-1 generates a series of notes in ascending frequency. DURATION provides the length of each note, and TONE determines the frequency. The program initially accesses port 61H and saves the value that the operation delivers. The Interval Timer generates a clock tick of 18.2 ticks per second that interrupts execution of the program and causes the tone to wobble. A CLI instruction in the program clears the Interrupt Flag to enable a constant tone.

The contents of TONE determine its frequency; high values cause low frequencies and low values cause high frequencies. After the program plays each note, it increases

```
              .DATA
DURATION DW    10000              ;Length of tone
TONE     DW    512H               ;Frequency
;  -------------------------------------------
              .CODE
              ...
              IN    AL,61H         ;Get port status
              PUSH  AX             ;  and save
A20:          MOV   DX,DURATION    ;Set duration
A30:
              OR    AL,00000011B   ;Set bits 0 & 1
              OUT   61H,AL         ;Transmit to speaker
              MOV   CX,TONE        ;Set length
A40:
              LOOP  A40            ;Time delay
              OR    AL,00000010B   ;Set bit 1 on
              OUT   61H,AL         ;Transmit to speaker
              MOV   CX,TONE        ;Set length
A50:
              LOOP  A50            ;Time delay
              DEC   DX             ;Reduce duration
              JNZ   A30            ;Continue?
              SHL   DURATION,1     ;  no, increase length
              SHR   TONE,1         ;Reduce frequency
              JNZ   A20            ;Now zero?
              POP   AX             ;Reset
              AND   AL,11111100B   ;  port
              OUT   61H,AL         ;  value
              ...
```

Figure 24-1 Generating Sound

the frequency of TONE by means of a right shift of one bit (effectively halving its value). Because decreasing TONE in this example reduces how long it plays, the routine also increases DURTION by means of a left shift of one bit (effectively doubling its value).

The program ends when TONE is reduced to 0. The initial values in DURATION and TONE have no technical significance. You can experiment with other values and try executing the program without the CLI instruction.

You could use any variation of the logic to play a sequence of notes, in order, for example, to draw a user's attention.

KEY POINTS

- ROM resides beginning at location FFFF0H. Turning on the power causes the processor to enter a reset state, set all memory locations to zero, perform a parity check of memory, and set the CS register to FFFF[0]H and IP to zero. The first instruction to execute is therefore at FFFF:0, or FFFF0, the entry point to BIOS.

- On bootup, BIOS checks the various ports to identify and initialize devices that are attached. BIOS then establishes an Interrupt Vector Table, beginning at location 0 of memory, that contains addresses for interrupts that occur. Two operations that BIOS performs are equipment and memory size determination. BIOS accesses the first disk sector containing the bootstrap loader.

- BIOS maintains its own data area in lower memory beginning at segment address 40[0]H. Relevant data areas include those for serial port, parallel port, system equipment, keyboard, disk drive, video control, hard disk, and real-time clock.
- The operand of an interrupt instruction such as INT 12H identifies the type of request. For each of the 256 possible types, the system maintains a 4-byte address in the Interrupt Vector table at locations 0000H through 3FFH.
- BIOS interrupts range from 00H through 1FH and include print screen, timer, video control, diskette control, video display, equipment and memory size determination, disk I/O, keyboard input, communications, printer output, and bootstrap loader.
- DOS INT 21H handles such operations as keyboard input, display output, printer output, reset disk, open/close file, delete file, read/write record, terminate but stay resident, create subdirectory, and terminate program.
- Through a port, a processor receives a signal from an input device and sends a signal to an output device. Ports are identified by their addresses in the range 0H-3FFH, or 1,024 in all.
- The PC generates sound by means of a built-in permanent magnet speaker, which is connected to ports 42H, 43H, and 61H.

REVIEW QUESTIONS AND EXERCISES

24-1. Distinguish between an external and an internal interrupt.

24-2. Distinguish between an NMI line and an INTR line.

24-3. (a) What is the memory location of the entry point to BIOS? (b) On power-up, how does the system direct itself to this address?

24-4. On bootup, BIOS performs INT 11H, 12H, and 19H. Explain the purpose of each interrupt.

24-5. Where is the beginning location of the BIOS Data Area?

24-6. The following binary values were noted in the BIOS Data Area. For each item, identify the field and explain the significance of the 1-bits.
(a) 10-11H: 01000100 01100111   (b) 17H: 11101010
(c) 18H: 00000001   (d) 96H: 00011010

24-7. The following hex values were noted in the BIOS Data Area. For each item, identify the field and explain the significance of the value.
(a) 00-03H: F8 03 F8 02   (b) 08-0BH: 78 03 00 00
(c) 13-14H: 80 02   (d) 15-16H: 00 10
(e) 4A-4BH: 50 00   (f) 60-61H: 0E 0D
(g) 84H: 18

24-8. Identify the following BIOS INT operations: (a) Single-step mode, (b) communications I/O, (c) get equipment status; (d) print screen, (e) disk I/O, (f) keyboard input, (g) keyboard, (h) video display, (i) printer output, (j) read and set time.

24-9. Identify the functions for the following INT 21H services: (a) terminate but stay resident, (b) get address of Interrupt Vector Table, (c) create subdirectory, (d) get free disk space, (e) get address of PSP, (f) create new file, (g) get system time, (h) rename a file.

24-10. Identify the following INT 21H functions: (a) 05H, (b) 09H, (c) 0DH, (d) 19H, (e) 2BH, (f) 31H, (g) 36H, (h) 3AH, (i) 42H.

24-11. Refer to Figure 24-2 and revise the instructions so that the program reverses the addresses for COM1 and COM2.

24-12. Revise the program in Figure 24-3 for the following requirements: Generate notes that decrease in frequency; initialize TONE to 01 and DURTION to a high value. On each loop, increase the value in TONE, decrease the value in DURTION, and end the program when DURTION equals 0.

Chapter 25
Operators and Directives

Objective: To provide a detailed explanation of the assembly language operators and directives.

INTRODUCTION

The various assembly language features at first tend to be somewhat overwhelming. But once you have become familiar with the simpler and more common features described in earlier chapters, you should find the descriptions of the various type specifiers, operators, and directives in this chapter more easily understood and a handy reference. The assembly language manual contains a few other specialized features.

Note re Turbo Assembler: TASM can run either in MASM mode, which accepts the standard MASM specifications, or in Ideal mode, which in many cases uses somewhat different terms and rules and may not recognize the MASM specifications.

TYPE SPECIFIERS

Type specifiers can provide the size of a data variable or the relative distance of an instruction label. Type specifiers that give the size of a data variable are BYTE, WORD, DWORD, FWORD, QWORD, and TBYTE. Those that give the distance of an instruction label are NEAR, FAR, and PROC. A near address, which is simply an offset, is assumed to be in the current segment; a far address, which consists of a segment:offset address, can be used to access data in another segment.

The PTR and THIS operators, as well as the COM, EXTRN, LABEL, and PROC directives, use type specifiers.

OPERATORS

An operator provides a facility for changing or analyzing operands during an assembly. Operators are divided into various categories:

- *Calculation operators*: Arithmetic, index, logical, shift, and structure field name.
- *Macro operators*: Various types, covered in Chapter 21.
- *Record operators*: MASK and WIDTH, covered later in this chapter under the RECORD directive.
- *Relational operators*: EQ, GE, GT, LE, LT, and NE.
- *Segment operators*: OFFSET, SEG, and segment override.
- *Type (or Attribute) operators*: HIGH, HIGHWORD, LENGTH, LOW, LOWWORD, PTR, SHORT, SIZE, THIS, and TYPE.

Because a knowledge of these categories is not necessary, this chapter simply covers the operators in alphabetic sequence.

Arithmetic Operators.   These operators include the familiar arithmetic signs and perform arithmetic during an assembly. In most cases, you could perform the calculation yourself, although the advantage of using these operators is that every time you change the program and reassemble it, the assembler automatically recalculates the values of the arithmetic operators. Following is a list of the operators, together with an example of their use and the effect obtained:

SIGN TYPE	EXAMPLE	EFFECT
+ Addition	FLDA+25	Adds 25 to address of FLDA
+ Positive	+FLDA	Treats FLDA as positive
– Subtraction	FLDB-FLDA	Calculates difference between two offset addresses
– Negation	–FLDA	Reverses sign of FLDA
* Multiplication	value*3	Multiplies value by 3
/ Division	value/3	Divides value by 3
MOD Remainder	value1 MOD value2	Delivers remainder for value1/value2

Except for addition (+) and subtraction (–), all operators must be integer constants. The following related examples illustrate integer expressions:

```
value1 = 12 * 4       ;48
value1 = value1 / 6   ;48 / 6 = 8
value1 = -value1 - 3  ;(-8) - (3) = -11
```

A common use for arithmetic operators is for equate directives, covered in the section "Directives."

HIGH and HIGHWORD Operators.   The HIGH operator returns the high (leftmost) byte of an expression, and HIGHWORD (since MASM 6.0) returns the high word of an expression. (See also the LOW operator.) Here is an example:

```
EQUVAL   EQU   1234H
         ...
         MOV   CL,HIGH EQUVAL  ;Load 12H in CL
```

Index Operators. For indirect addressing of memory, an operand references a base or index register, constants, offset variables, and variables. The index operator, which uses square brackets, acts like a plus (+) sign. A typical use of indexing is to reference data items in tables. You can use the following operations to reference indexed memory:

- An immediate number or name in square brackets, coded as [*constant*]. For example, load the fifth entry of PART_TBL into CL (note that PART_TBL[0] is the first entry):

```
PART_TBL DB 25 DUP(?)          ;Defined table
         ...
         MOV CL,PART_TBL[4]  ;Get fifth entry (byte 6)
```

- Base register BX as [BX] in association with the DS segment register, and base register BP as [BP] in association with the SS segment register. For example, use the offset address in BX (as DS:BX), and move the referenced item to DX:

```
MOV DX,[BX] ;Base register DS:BX
```

- Index register DI as [DI] and index register SI as [SI], both in association with the DS segment register. For example, use the offset address in SI (as DS:SI), and move the referenced item to AX:

```
MOV AX,[SI] ;Index register DS:SI
```

- Combined index registers. For example, move the contents of AX to the address determined by adding the DS address, the BX offset, the SI offset, and the constant 4:

```
MOV [BX+SI+4],AX ;Base + index + constant
```

The first operand in the preceding example could also be coded as [BX+SI]+4. You may combine these operands in any sequence, but don't combine two base registers [BX+BP] or two index registers [DI+SI]. Only index registers must be in square brackets so that the assembler knows to treat it as an index operator.

LENGTH Operator. The LENGTH operator returns the number of entries defined by a DUP operator, as shown by the following MOV instruction:

```
PART_TBL  DW 10 DUP(?)
          ...
          MOV DX,LENGTH PART_TBL   ;Return length 10 to DX
```

If the referenced operand does not contain a DUP entry, the operator returns the value 01 (a limit to its usefulness). (See also the SIZE and TYPE operators.)

Logical Operators. The logical operators process the bits in an expression:

OPERATOR	USED AS	EFFECT
AND	*expression1* AND *expression2*	ANDs the bits
OR	*expression1* OR *expression2*	ORs the bits
XOR	*expression1* XOR *expression2*	Exclusive ORs the bits
NOT	NOT *expression1*	Reverses the bits

Here are two examples:

```
MOV   CL,00111100B AND 01010101B   ;CL = 00010100B
MOV   DL,NOT 01010101B             ;DL = 10101010B
```

LOW/LOWWORD Operators.   The LOW operator returns the low (rightmost) byte of an expression, and LOWWORD (since MASM 6.0) returns the low word of an expression. (See also the HIGH operator.) Here is an example:

```
EQU_VAL   EQU 1234H
          . . .
          MOV CL,LOW EQU_VAL   ;Load 34H in CL
```

OFFSET Operator.   The OFFSET operator returns the offset address of a variable or label. The operator is coded as OFFSET *variable/label*. The following MOV returns the offset address of PART_TBL:

```
MOV DX,OFFSET PART_TBL
```

Note that the instruction LEA DX,PART_TBL doesn't require OFFSET to return the same value:

MASK Operator.   See "RECORD Directive" in the later section "Directives."

PTR Operator.   The PTR operator can be used on data variables and instruction labels. It uses the type specifiers BYTE, WORD, FWORD, DWORD, QWORD, and TBYTE to specify a size in an ambiguous operand or to override the defined type (DB, DW, DF, DD, DQ, or DT) for variables. It also uses the type specifiers NEAR, FAR, and PROC to override the implied distance of labels.

The operator is coded as *type* PTR *expression*, where *type* is the new attribute, such as BYTE, and *expression* is a variable or constant. Following are unrelated examples of the PTR operator:

```
BYTEA   DB   22H
        DB   35H
WORDA   DW   2672H                  ;Data stored as 7226H
        . . .
        ADD   BL,BYTE PTR WORDA+1   ;Add second byte (26)
        MOV   BYTE PTR WORDA,05     ;Move 05 to first byte
        MOV   AX,WORD PTR BYTEA     ;Move two bytes (2235) to AX
        CALL FAR PTR[BX]            ;Call far procedure
```

A feature that performs a similar function to PTR is the LABEL directive, described later.

SEG Operator.   The SEG operator returns the address of the segment in which a specified variable or label is placed. Programs that combine separately assembled segments would most likely use this operator. The operator is coded as SEG *variable/label*.

The following unrelated MOV statements return the address of the segment in which the referenced names are defined:

```
MOV  AX,SEG WORDA     ;Get address of data segment
MOV  AX,SEG A10BEGIN  ;Get address of code segment
```

Segment Override Operator.   This operator, coded as a colon (:), calculates the address of a label or variable relative to a particular segment. The operator is coded as *segment:expression*. The *segment* can be any of the segment registers or a segment or group name. The *expression* can be a constant, an expression, or a SEG expression.

These next examples override the default DS segment register:

```
MOV  BH,ES:10H    ;Access from ES + 10H
MOV  CX,SS:[BX]   ;Access from SS + offset in BX
```

A segment override operator may apply to only one operand.

SHL and SHR Operators.   The operators SHL and SHR shift an expression during an assembly. The operator is coded as *expression* SHL/SHR *count*. In the following example, the SHR operator shifts the bit constant three bits to the right:

```
MOV BL,01011101B SHR 3 ;Load 00001011B
```

Most likely, the expression would reference a symbolic name rather than a constant value.

SHORT Operator.   The purpose of the SHORT operator is to modify the NEAR attribute of a JMP destination that is within +127 and −128 bytes. The operator is coded as JMP SHORT *label*. The assembler reduces the machine code operand from two bytes to one. This feature is useful for near jumps that branch forward, since otherwise the assembler initially doesn't know the distance of the jump address and may assume two bytes for a near jump.

SIZE Operator.   The SIZE operator returns the product of LENGTH times TYPE and is useful only if the referenced variable contains the DUP entry. The operator is coded as SIZE *variable*. See "TYPE Operator" for an example.

THIS Operator.   The THIS operator creates an operand with segment and offset values that are equal to those of the current location counter. The operator is coded as THIS *type*. The *type* can be BYTE, WORD, DWORD, FWORD, QWORD, or TBYTE for variables and NEAR, FAR, or PROC for labels.

THIS would typically be used with the EQU or equal sign (=) directives. The following example defines PART_REC:

```
PART_REC EQU THIS BYTE
```

The effect is the same as if you used the LABEL directive as

```
PART_REC LABEL BYTE
```

TYPE Operator.   The TYPE operator returns the number of bytes, according to the definition of the referenced variable. However, the operation always returns 1 for a string variable and 0 for a constant. The operator is coded as TYPE *variable/label*.

DEFINITION	NUMBER OF BYTES FOR NUMERIC VARIABLE
DB/BYTE	1
DW/WORD	2
DD/DWORD	4
DF/FWORD	6
DQ/QWORD	8
DT/TWORD	10
STRUC/STRUCT	Number of bytes defined by the structure
NEAR label	FFFFH
FAR label	FFFEH

The following examples illustrate the TYPE, LENGTH, and SIZE operators:

```
BYTEA     DB ?                          ;Define one byte
PART_TBL  DW 10 DUP(?)                  ;Define 10 words
          ...
          MOV AX,TYPE BYTEA      ;AX = 0001H
          MOV AX,TYPE PART_TBL   ;AX = 0002H
          MOV CX,LENGTH PART_TBL ;CX = 000AH (10)
          MOV DX,SIZE PART_TBL   ;DX = 0014H (20)
```

Because PART_TBL is defined as DW, TYPE returns 0002H, LENGTH returns 000AH (10) based on the DUP entry, and SIZE returns type times length, or 14H (20).

WIDTH Operator.   See "RECORD Directive" in the following section.

DIRECTIVES

This section describes most of the assembler directives. Chapter 4 covers in detail the directives for defining data (DB, DW, etc.), and Chapter 21 covers the directives for macro instructions, so they aren't repeated here. Directives are divided into various categories:

- Code labels: ALIGN, EVEN, LABEL, and PROC.
- Conditional assembly: IF, ELSE, and others, covered in Chapter 21.
- Conditional errors: .ERR, .ERR1, and others.
- Data allocation: ALIGN, EQU, EVEN, LABEL, and ORG. (DB, DW, DD, DF, DQ, and DT are covered in Chapter 4.)
- Listing control: .CREF, .LIST, PAGE, SUBTTL, TITLE, .XCREF, and .XLIST, covered in this chapter. (.LALL, .LFCOND, .SALL, .SFCOND, .TFCOND, and .XALL are covered in Chapter 21.)
- Macros: ENDM, EXITM, LOCAL, MACRO, and PURGE, covered in Chapter 21.

- Miscellaneous: COMMENT, INCLUDE, INCLUDELIB, NAME, &OUT, and .RADIX.
- Processor: .8086, .286, .286P, .386, .386P, etc.
- Repeat blocks: IRP, IRPC, and REPT, covered in Chapter 21.
- Scope: COMM, EXTRN, and PUBLIC.
- Segment: .ALPHA, ASSUME, .DOSSEG, END, ENDS, GROUP, SEGMENT, and .SEQ.
- Simplified segment: .CODE, .CONST, .DATA, .DATA?, .EXIT, .FARDATA, .FARDATA?, .MODEL, and .STACK.
- Structure/Record: ENDS, RECORD, STRUCT, TYPEDEF, UNION.

The following sections cover the directives in alphabetic sequence.

ALIGN Directive. The ALIGN directive causes the assembler to align the next data item or instruction on an address according to a given value. Alignment can facilitate the processor in accessing words and doublewords. The format is `ALIGN number`, where *number* must be a power of 2, such as 2, 4, 8, or 16.

In the following example, the location counter is at 0005 when the ALIGN 4 statement causes the assembler to advance its location counter to the next address evenly divisible by 4:

```
0005   ALIGN 4
0008   DBWORD DD 0  ;Align on doubleword boundary
```

If the location counter is already at the required address, it is not advanced. The assembler fills unused bytes with zeros for data and NOPs for instructions. Note that ALIGN 2 has the same effect as EVEN.

.ALPHA Directive. The .ALPHA directive, placed at or near the start of a program, tells the assembler to arrange segments in alphabetic sequence for compatibility with early assembler versions. You can also use the /A option on the assembler command line.

ASSUME Directive. ASSUME tells the assembler to associate segment names with the CS, DS, ES, and SS segment registers. Its format is

ASSUME	*segment-reg:segment-name* [, ...]

Valid *segment-reg* entries are CS, DS, ES, SS, FS, and GS. Valid *segment-name* entries are those of segment registers, NOTHING, GROUP, and a SEG expression. One ASSUME statement may assign up to four segment registers in any sequence. The simplified segment directives automatically generate an ASSUME.

In the following ASSUME statement, CODESEG, DATASEG, and STACK are the names the program has used to define the segments:

```
ASSUME CS:CODESEG,DS:DATASEG,SS:STACK,ES:DATASEG
```

Omission of a segment reference is the same as coding NOTHING. Use of the keyword NOTHING also cancels any previous ASSUME for a specified segment register: ASSUME ES:NOTHING. Suppose that you neither assign ES nor use NOTHING to cancel it. Then, to reference an item in the data segment, an instruction operand may use the segment override operator (:) to reference ES, which must contain a valid segment address for proper execution:

```
MOV  AX,ES:[BX]   ;Use indexed address
MOV AX,ES:WORDA   ;Move contents of WORDA
```

.CODE Directive.   This simplified segment directive defines the code segment. Its format is `.CODE [name]`, where *name* is optional. All executable code must be placed in this segment. For Tiny, Small, and Compact models, the default segment name is _TEXT. The Medium and Large memory models permit multiple code segments, which you distinguish by means of the *name* operand. (See also the .MODEL directive.)

COMM Directive.   Defining a variable as COMM (for common) gives it both the PUBLIC and EXTRN attributes. In this way, you do not have to define the variable as PUBLIC in one module and EXTRN in another. The format is

```
COMM   |   [NEAR/FAR] label:size[:count]
```

- COMM is coded within a data segment.
- The NEAR or FAR attributes may be coded or allowed to default to one or the other, depending on the memory model.
- The *label* is the name of the variable. Note that the variable cannot have an initial value.
- The *size* can be any of the type specifiers BYTE, WORD, DWORD, QWORD, and TBYTE, or an integer specifying the number of bytes.
- The *count* indicates the number of elements for the variable. The default is 1.

The following examples define items with the COMM attribute:

```
COMM  NEAR COM_FLD1:WORD    ;Word size with COMM attribute
COMM  FAR COM_FLD2:BYTE:25  ;25 bytes with COMM attribute
```

COMMENT Directive.   This directive can be used for for multiple lines of comments. Its format is

```
COMMENT delimiter [comments]
    [comments]
delimiter [comments]
```

The *delimiter* is the first nonblank character, such as % or +, following COMMENT. The comments end on the line on which the second delimiter appears. This example uses "+" as a delimiter:

```
COMMENT + This routine scans
            keyboard input for
       + invalid characters.
```

.CONST Directive.   This simplified segment directive defines a data (or constant-data) segment with the 'const' class. (See also the .MODEL directive.)

.CREF Directive.   This directive (the default) tells the assembler to generate a cross-reference table. It would be used following an .XCREF directive that caused suppression of the table.

.DATA and .DATA? Directives.   These simplified segment directives define data segments. .DATA defines a segment for initialized near data; .DATA? defines a segment for uninitialized near data, usually used when linking to a high-level language. For a standalone assembly program, you may also define uninitialized near data in a .DATA segment. (See also the .FARDATA and .MODEL directives.)

DOSSEG/.DOSSEG Directive.   There are a number of ways to control the sequence in which the assembler arranges segments. You may code the .SEQ or .ALPHA directives at the start of a program, or you may enter the /S or /A options on the assembler command line. The DOSSEG (.DOSSEG since MASM 6.0) directive tells the assembler to ignore all other requests and to adopt the DOS segment sequence—basically, code, data, and stack. Code this directive at or near the start of the program, primarily to facilitate the use of the CODEVIEW debugger for stand-alone programs.

END Directive.   The END directive is placed at the end of a source program. The format is END `[start-address]`. The optional *start-address* indicates the location in the code segment (usually the first instruction) where execution is to begin. The system loader uses this address to initialize the CS register. If your program consists of only one module, define a start-address. If it consists of a number of modules, only one (usually the first) has a start-address.

ENDP Directive.   ENDP indicates the end of a procedure, defined by PROC. Its format is `procedure-name` ENDP, where *procedure-name* is the same as the one that defines the procedure.

ENDS Directive.   This directive indicates the end of a segment (defined by SEGMENT) or a structure (defined by STRUC or STRUCT). Its format is `segment-name` ENDS, where *segment-name* is the same as the one that defines the segment or structure.

Equate Directives.   The two types of equate directives are Equal-Sign and EQU. Both are processed only at assembly time and do not generate any storage. Their purpose is to provide, for example, names for numeric constants and aliases for defined items. The directives should be defined in a program before they are referenced.

The Equal-Sign directive has the format `name = expression`, where *expression* is any integer value or numeric expression. The directive may assign a value to an item any number of times. Here are two examples:

Example 1: ROW = 12
            COL = 16
            MOV BX,ROW+COL
Example 2: SCREEN_LOCS = 25 * 0
            MOV CX,SCREEN_LOCS

The EQU directive is used to redefine a data name or variable with another data name, variable, or immediate value. The assembler replaces each occurrence of the name with the operand. The EQU directive may assign a value to an item only once in a program. The formats for numeric and string data differ:

Numeric equate: *name EQU expression*

String equate: *name EQU <string>*

Examples of the use of EQU with numeric data are:

```
COUNTER   DW   0
SUM       EQU  COUNTER   ;Another name for COUNTER
TEN       EQU  10        ;Numeric value
          . . .
          INC  SUM       ;Increment COUNTER
          ADD  SUM,TEN   ;Add 10 to COUNTER
```

Examples of the use of EQU with string data are:

```
PROD_MSG EQU    <'Enter product number:'>
BY_PTR   EQU    <BYTE PTR>
         . . .
MESSGE1  DB     PROD_MSG              ;Replace with string
         . . .
         MOV    SAVE,BY_PTR [BX]  ;Replace with string
```

The angle brackets make it easier to indicate a string operand.

.ERR Directives. These conditional error directives can help test for errors during an assembly:

DIRECTIVE	ERROR FORCED
.ERR	When encountered
.ERR1	During pass 1 of an assembly
.ERR2	During pass 2 of an assembly
.ERRE	By true (0) expression
.ERRNZ	By false (not 0) expression
.ERRDEF	By defined symbol
.ERRNDEF	By not defined symbol
.ERRB	By blank string
.ERRNB	By not blank string
.ERRIDN[I]	By identical strings
.ERRDIF[I]	By different strings

Since MASM 6.0, it is no longer necessary to refer to pass 1 (.ERR1) or pass 2 (.ERR2) of an assembly. You could use the preceding directives in macros and in conditional assembly statements. In the following conditional assembly statements, the assembler displays a message if the condition is not true:

```
IF      condition
        . . .
ELSE    .ERR
        %OUT [message]
ENDIF
```

EVEN Directive.   EVEN tells the assembler to advance its location counter if necessary so that the next defined data item or instruction is aligned on an even storage boundary. This feature facilitates processors that can access 16 or 32 bits at a time. (ALIGN 2 gives the same effect as EVEN.)

In the following example, BYTE_LOCN is a 1-byte field on an even boundary, 0016. The location counter is now at 0017. EVEN causes the assembler to advance the location counter one byte to 0018, where the next data item, WORD_LOCN, is defined:

```
0016   BYTE_LOCN   DB      ?
0017   EVEN                ;Advance location counter
0018   WORD_LOCN   DW      ?
```

.EXIT Directive.   You can use the .EXIT directive in the code segment to generate program termination code. Its format is .EXIT [*return-value*], where a *return-value* of 0 means no problem and 1 means an error terminated processing. The generated code is

```
MOV   AH,4CH
MOV   AL,return-value   ;Generated if return-value coded
INT   21H
```

EXTRN/EXTERN Directive.   The EXTRN (or EXTERN since MASM 6.0) directive informs the assembler and linker about data variables and labels that the current assembly references, but that another module (linked to the current one) defines. The format is EXTRN *name:type* [, ...], where *name* is an item defined in another assembly and declared in it as PUBLIC. The *type* can refer to either of the following:

- Data items: ABS (a constant), BYTE, WORD, DWORD, FWORD, QWORD, TBYTE. Code the EXTRN in the segment in which the item occurs.
- Distance: NEAR or FAR. Code NEAR in the segment in which the item occurs, and code FAR anywhere.

In the next example, the calling program defines CON_VALUE as PUBLIC and as a DW. The called subprogram identifies CON_VALUE (in another segment) as EXTRN and FAR.

Calling program:

```
DSEG1   SEGMENT
        PUBLIC CON_VALUE
        . . .
```

```
                    CON_VALUE DW   ?
                         . . .
                    DSEG1   ENDS
```

Called subprogram:

```
                    EXTRN CON_VALUE:FAR
             DSEG2   SEGMENT
                         . . .
                    MOV AX,WORD PTR CON_VALUE
                         . . .
                    DSEG2 ENDS
```

See Chapter 22 for examples of EXTRN.

.FARDATA and .FARDATA? Directives. These simplified segment directives define data segments. .FARDATA defines a segment for initialized far data, and .FARDATA? defines a segment for uninitialized far data. For a standalone assembly program, you may also define uninitialized far data in a .FARDATA segment. (See also the .DATA and .MODEL directives.)

GROUP Directive. A program may contain several segments of the same type (code, data, or stack). The purpose of the GROUP directive is to collect segments of the same type under one name, so that they reside within one segment, usually a data segment. The format is

name	GROUP	seg-name [, seg-name], ...

The following GROUP combines DATASEG1 and DATASEG2 in the same assembly module:

```
GROUPX     GROUP    DATASEG1, DATASEG2
DATASEG1   SEGMENT  PARA 'Data'
           ASSUME   DS:GROUPX
             . . .
DATASEG1   ENDS
;
DATASEG2   SEGMENT  PARA 'Data'
           ASSUME   DS:GROUPX
   . . .
DATASEG2   ENDS
```

The effect of using GROUP is similar to giving the segments the same name and the PUBLIC attribute.

INCLUDE Directive. If you have sections of assembly code or macro instructions that various programs use, you may store them in separate disk files, available for use by any program. Consider a routine that converts ASCII code to binary is stored in a file named CONVERT.LIB. To access the file, insert an INCLUDE statement such as

```
            INCLUDE path:CONVERT.LIB
```

at the location in the source program where you would normally code the ASCII conversion routine. The assembler locates the file on disk and includes the statements in your program. (If the assembler cannot find the file, it issues an error message.)

For each included line, the assembler prints a C (depending on version) in column 30 of the .LST file and begins the source code in column 33.

Chapter 21 gives an example of INCLUDE and explains how to use the directive only for pass 1 of an assembly.

LABEL Directive.   The LABEL directive enables a program to redefine the attribute of an instruction label or data variable. Its format is *name* LABEL *type-specifier*. For labels, LABEL may redefine executable code as NEAR, FAR, or PROC, such as for a secondary entry point into a procedure. For variables, *type-specifiers* BYTE, WORD, DWORD, FWORD, QWORD, or TBYTE, or a structure name may redefine data items and the names of structures, respectively. For example, LABEL enables a program to define a field as both DB and DW. The assembler does not advance its location counter.

The following example illustrates the BYTE and WORD types, assumed to begin at location 010H:

```
010    BYTE1    LABEL    BYTE      ;Define first byte as BYTE1,
010    WORD1    DW       2532H     ; first two bytes as WORD1,
012    WORD2    LABEL    WORD      ; third and fourth bytes as WORD2,
012    BYTE2    DB       25H       ; third byte as BYTE2,
013             DB       32H       ; fourth byte
       ...
       MOV      AL,BYTE1           ;Move 1st byte
       MOV      BX,WORD2           ;Move third and fourth bytes
```

The first MOV instruction moves only the first byte of WORD1. The second MOV moves the two bytes beginning at BYTE2. The PTR operator performs a similar function.

.LIST Directive.   The .LIST directive (the default) causes the assembler to list the source program. You may have a block of code that you don't need listed because it is common to other programs. In this case, you may use the .XLIST (or .NOLIST) directive to discontinue the listing and then use .LIST to resume the listing. Use these directives with no operand.

.MODEL Directive.   This simplified segment directive creates default segments and the required ASSUME and GROUP statements. Its format is .MODEL *memory-model*, where memory-models are the following:

Tiny. Code and data in one segment, for .COM programs.

Small. Code in one segment (<=64K), data in one segment (<=64K).

Medium. Any number of code segments, data in one segment (<=64K).

Compact. Code in one segment (<=64K), any number of data segments.

Large. Code and data both in any number of segments, no array >64K.

Huge. Code and data both in any number of segments, arrays may be >64K.

Flat. Unsegmented, runs in protected mode, with 32-bit addresses.

.NOLIST Directive.   (see .XLIST Directive)

ORG Directive.   Consider a data segment with the following definitions:

OFFSET	NAME	OPERATION	OPERAND	LOCATION COUNTER
00	WORD1	DW	2542H	02
02	BYTE1	DB	36H	03
03	WORD2	DW	212EH	05
05	BYTE2	DD	00000705H	09

Initially, the assembler's location counter is set to 00. Because WORD1 is two bytes, the location counter is incremented to 02 for the location of the next item. Because BYTE1 is one byte, the location counter is incremented to 03, and so forth. You may use the ORG directive to change the contents of the location counter and, accordingly, the location of the next defined item. Its format is ORG *expression*, where *expression* must form a two-byte absolute number and must not be a symbolic name.

Suppose the following data items are defined immediately after BYTE2 in the previous definition:

OFFSET	NAME	OPERATION	OPERAND	LOCATION COUNTER
		ORG	0	00
00	BYTE3	DB	?	01
01	WORD3	DW	?	02
03	BYTE4	DB	?	04
		ORG	$+5	09

The first ORG resets the location counter to 00. The variables that follow—BYTE3, WORD3, and BYTE4—redefine the memory locations originally defined as WORD1, BYTE1, and WORD2, respectively.

An operand containing a dollar symbol ($), as in the last ORG, refers to the current value in the location counter. The operand $+5 therefore sets the location counter to 04 + 5, or 09, which is the same setting as after the definition of BYTE2.

A reference to WORD2 is to a one-word field at offset 03, and a reference to BYTE4 is to a one-byte field also at offset 03:

```
MOV  AX,WORD2  ;One word
MOV  AL,BYTE4  ;One byte
```

When you use ORG to redefine memory locations, be sure to reset the location counter to the correct value and that you account for all redefined memory locations. Also, the redefined variables should not contain defined constants—these would overlay constants on top of the original ones. ORG cannot appear within a STRUC definition.

%OUT/ECHO Directive. This directive tells the assembler to direct a message to the standard output device (usually the screen). (Since MASM 6.0, the name is ECHO.) The format is `%OUT/ECHO message`. The ".ERR Directives" section gives an example.

PAGE Directive. The PAGE directive at the start of a source program specifies the maximum number of lines the assembler is to list on a page and the maximum number of characters on a line. Its format is `PAGE [[length],width]`. For example, PAGE 60,132 sets 60 lines per page and 132 characters per line.

The number of lines per page may range from 10 to 255, and the number of characters per line may range from 60 to 132. Omission of a PAGE statement causes the assembler to assume PAGE 50,80. To force a page to eject at a specific line, such as at the end of a segment, code PAGE with no operand.

PROC Directive. A procedure is a block of code that begins with the PROC directive and terminates with ENDP. Although technically you may enter a procedure inline or by a JMP instruction, the normal practice is to use CALL to enter and RETN or RETF to exit. The CALL operand may be a NEAR or FAR type specifier.

A procedure that is in the same segment as the calling procedure is a NEAR procedure and is accessed by an offset. Its format is *procedure-name* `PROC [NEAR]`. An omitted operand defaults to NEAR. If a called procedure is external to the calling segment, it must be declared as PUBLIC, and you should use CALL to enter it.

For an .EXE program, the main PROC that is the entry point for execution must be FAR.

Processor Directives. These directives define the processors that the assembler is to recognize. A processor directive may be placed at the start of a source program or at a point where you want a processor's features enabled or disabled. The default mode is .8086.

- .286, .386, .486, and .586 enable all the instruction sets up to and including the named processor. (For example, .386 enables .286 and .8086.)
- .286P, .386P, .486P and .586P enable all the instruction sets just cited, plus the processor's privileged instructions.

PUBLIC Directive. The PUBLIC directive informs the assembler and linker that the identified symbols in an assembly are to be referenced by other modules linked with the current one. Its format is `PUBLIC symbol [, ... ]`, where *symbol* can be a label, a number (up to two bytes), or a variable. See the "EXTRN Directive" section and Chapter 22 for examples.

RECORD Directive. The RECORD directive enables defining patterns of bits, such as color patterns and switch indicators as one bit or as multibit. Its format is

record-name	RECORD	*field-name:width[=exp] [, ...]*

The *record-name* and *field-names* may be any unique valid identifiers. Following each field name is a colon (:) and a *width* that specifies the number of bits. The range of the width entry is 1 to 32 bits. Lengths up to eight become 8 bits, 9 to 16 become 16 bits, and 17 to 32 become 32 bits, with the contents right adjusted if necessary. The following example uses the RECORD directive to define BIT_REC:

```
BIT_REC RECORD BITS1:3,BITS2:7,BITS3:6
```

BITS1 defines the first three bits of BIT_REC, BITS2 defines the next seven, and BITS3 defines the last six. The total is 16 bits, or one word. You may initialize values in a record as follows:

```
BIT_REC2 RECORD BITS1:3=101B,BITS2:7=0110110B,BITS3:6=011010B
```

Note that a RECORD definition does not actually generate any storage. Therefore, following a definition of RECORD in the data segment, you have to code another statement that allocates storage for the record. Define a unique valid name, the record name, and an operand consisting of angle brackets (the less-than and greater-than symbols):

```
DEF_BITS BIT_REC <>
```

The allocation for DEF_BITS generates object code AD9AH (stored as 9AAD) in the data segment. The angle brackets may also contain entries that redefine BIT_REC.

The partial program in Figure 25-1 defines BIT_REC as RECORD, but without initial values in the record fields. In this case, an allocation statement in the data segment as shown within angle brackets initializes each field.

Record-specific operators are WIDTH, shift count, and MASK. The use of these operators enables you to change a RECORD definition without having to change the instructions that reference it.

WIDTH operator.   The WIDTH operator returns a width as the number of bits in a RECORD or in a RECORD field. For example, in Figure 25-1, following the label A20 are

```
          .DATA
BIT_REC   RECORD BITSA:3,BITSB:7,BITSC:6   ;Define
DEF_BITS  BIT_REC <101B,0110110B,011010B> ;Initialize
          .CODE
          . . .
A20:                                  ;Width:
          MOV    BH,WIDTH BIT_REC ;  of record (16)
          MOV    AL,WIDTH BITSB   ;  of field (07)
A30:                                  ;Shift count:
          MOV    CL,BITSA         ;   hex 0D
          MOV    CL,BITSB         ;        06
          MOV    CL,BITSC         ;        00
A40:                                  ;Mask:
          MOV    AX,MASK BITSA    ;   hex E000
          MOV    BX,MASK BITSB    ;        1FC0
          MOV    CX,MASK BITSC    ;        003F
A50:                                  ;Isolate BITSB:
          MOV    AX,DEF_BITS      ;  get record
          AND    AX,MASK BITSB    ;  clear BITSA & 3
          MOV    CL,BITSB         ;  get shift 06
          SHR    AX,CL            ;  shift right
A60:                                  ;Isolate BITSA:
          MOV    AX,DEF_BITS      ;  get record
          MOV    CL,BITSA         ;  get shift 13
          SHR    AX,CL            ;  shift right
          . . .
```

Figure 25-1   Using the RECORD Directive

two examples of WIDTH. The first MOV returns the width of the entire record BIT_REC (16 bits); the second MOV returns the width of the record field BITS2 (7 bits), as shown by the object code to the left. In both cases, the assembler has generated an immediate operand for width.

Shift count. A direct reference to a RECORD field such as MOV CL,BITS2 does not refer to the contents of BITS2. Instead, the assembler generates an immediate operand that contains a shift count to help you isolate the field. The immediate value represents the number of bits that you would have to shift BITS2 to right adjust it. In Figure 25-1, the three examples following A30 return the shift count for BITS1, BITS2, and BITS3, respectively.

MASK operator. The MASK operator returns a mask of 1-bits representing the specified field and, in effect, defines the bit positions that the field occupies. For example, the MASK for each of the fields defined in BIT_REC is

FIELD	BINARY	HEX
BITS1	1110000000000000	E000
BITS2	0001111111000000	1FC0
BITS3	0000000000111111	003F

In Figure 25-1, the three instructions following A40 return the MASK values for BITS1, BITS2, and BITS3. The instructions following A50 and A60 isolate BITS2 and BITS1, respectively, from BIT_REC. A50 gets the record into AX and uses a MASK of BITS2 to AND it:

```
Record:              101 0110110 011010
AND MASK BITS2:      000 1111111 000000
Result:              000 0110110 000000
```

The effect is to clear all bits except those of BITS2. The next two instructions cause AX to shift 6 bits so that BITS2 is right-adjusted:

```
0000000000110110 (0036H)
```

The example following A60 gets the record into AX, and because BITS1 is the left-most field, the routine simply uses its shift factor to shift right 13 bits:

```
0000000000000101 (0005H)
```

SEGMENT Directive. An assembly module consists of one or more segments, part of a segment, or even parts of several segments. The format for a segment is

```
segment-name   SEGMENT    [align] [combine] ['class']
               . . .
segment-name   ENDS
```

The *align*, *combine*, and *class* operands are optional.

Align. This operand indicates the starting boundary for a segment:

BYTE   Next address
WORD   Next even address (divisible by 2)

DWORD	Next doubleword address (divisible by 4)
PARA	Next paragraph (divisible by 16, or 10H)
PAGE	Next page address (divisible by 256, or 100H)

PARA is commonly used for all types of segments. BYTE and WORD can be used for segments that are to be combined within another segment, usually a data segment.

    Combine. The *combine* operands NONE, PUBLIC, STACK, and COMMON indicate the way the linker is to handle the segment:

- NONE (default): The segment is to be logically separate from other segments, although it may end up physically adjacent to them. The segment is presumed to have its own base address.
- PUBLIC: LINK loads PUBLIC segments of the same name and class adjacent to one another. One base address is presumed for all such PUBLIC segments.
- STACK: LINK treats STACK the same as PUBLIC. There must be at least one STACK defined in a linked .EXE program. If there is more than one stack, SP is associated with the first stack.
- COMMON: If COMMON segments have the same name and class, the linker gives them the same base address. During execution, the second segment overlays the first one. The largest segment, even if overlaid, determines the length of the common area.
- AT paragraph-address: The paragraph must be defined previously. The entry facilitates defining labels and variables at fixed offsets within fixed areas of memory, such as the interrupt table in low memory or the BIOS data area at 40[0]H. For example, the location of the video display area is defined as

```
VIDEO_RAM SEGMENT AT 0B800H
```

The assembler creates a dummy segment that provides, in effect, an image of the memory locations.

    'class'. This entry can help the linker associate segments with different names, identify segments, and control their order. Class may contain any valid name contained in single quotes. The linker uses the name to relate segments that have the same name and class. Typical examples are 'Data' and 'Code'. If you define a class as 'Code', the linker expects that segment to contain instruction code. Also, the CODEVIEW debugger expects the class 'Code' for the code segment.

    The linker combines the following two segments with the same name (CSEG) and class ('Code') into one physical segment under the same segment register:

```
            CSEG    SEGMENT    PARA PUBLIC 'Code'
   module 1         ASSUME     CS:CSEG
                      . . .
            CSEG    ENDS
        ----------------------------------
            CSEG    SEGMENT    PARA PUBLIC 'Code'
   module 2         ASSUME     CS:CSEG
                      . . .
            CSEG    ENDS
```

To control the ordering of segments within a program, it is useful to understand how the linker handles the process. The original order of the segment names provides the basic sequence, which you may override by means of the PUBLIC attribute and class names. The following example shows two object modules (both modules contain a segment named DATASEG1 with the PUBLIC attribute and identical class names) before linking:

```
module 1   STACK      SEGMENT   PARA STACK
module 1   DATASEG1   SEGMENT   PARA PUBLIC 'Data'
module 1   DATASEG2   SEGMENT   PARA
module 1   CODESEG    SEGMENT   PARA 'Code'
module 2   DATASEG1   SEGMENT   PARA PUBLIC 'Data'
module 2   DATASEG2   SEGMENT   PARA
module 2   CODESEG    SEGMENT   PARA 'Code'
```

After the .OBJ modules are linked, the .EXE module looks like this:

```
module 1       CODESEG    SEGMENT   PARA 'Code'
module 2       CODESEG    SEGMENT   PARA 'Code'
modules 1 + 2  DATASEG1   SEGMENT   PARA PUBLIC 'Data'
module 1       DATASEG2   SEGMENT   PARA
module 2       DATASEG2   SEGMENT   PARA
module 1       STACK      SEGMENT   PARA STACK
```

You may nest segments provided that one nested segment is completely contained within the other. In the following example, DATASEG2 is completely contained within DATASEG1:

```
DATASEG1 SEGMENT
         ...        DATASEG1 begins
DATASEG2 SEGMENT
         ...        DATASEG2 area
DATASEG2 ENDS
         ...        DATASEG1 resumes
DATASEG1 ENDS
```

The .ALPHA, .SEQ, and DOSSEG directives and the assembler options /A and /S can also control the order of segments. (To combine segments into groups, see the GROUP directive.)

.SEQ Directive. This directive (the default), placed at or near the start of a program, tells the assembler to leave segments in their original sequence. You may also use the assembler command line option /A. (See also the .ALPHA and DOSSEG directives.)

.STACK Directive. This simplified segment directive defines the stack. Its format is .STACK [size], where the default stack size is 1,024 bytes, which you may override. (See also the .MODEL directive.)

.STARTUP Directive. You can use this directive at the start of the code segment to initialize DS, SS, and SP. See also the .EXIT directive.

STRUC/STRUCT Directive. The STRUC directive (STRUCT since MASM 6.0) facilitates defining related fields within a structure. Its format is

```
structure-name  STRUC/STRUCT
                ...
        [ defined fields ]
                ...
structure-name  ENDS
```

A structure begins with its name and the directive STRUC and ends with the name and the directive ENDS. The assembler identifies the defined fields one after the other from the start of the structure. Valid entries are DB, DW, DD, DQ, and DT definitions with optional field names.

In the partial program in Figure 25-2, STRUC defines a parameter list named PARAMLIST for use with INT 21H function 0AH to input a name via the keyboard. Note that, like the RECORD directive STRUC does not actually generate any storage. An allocation statement is needed to allocate storage for the structure, making it addressable within the program:

```
PARAMS PARAMLIST <>
```

The angle brackets (less-than and greater-than symbols) in the operand are empty in this example, but you may use them to redefine (or override) data within a structure.

Instructions may reference a structure directly by its name. To reference fields within a structure, instructions must qualify them by using the allocate name of the structure

```
          .DATA
PARAMLIST STRUC                      ;Parameter list
MAXLEN    DB      25                 ;
ACTLEN    DB      ?                  ;
NAMEIN    DB      25 DUP(' ')        ;
PARAMLIST ENDS

PARAMS    PARAMLIST <>               ;Allocate storage
PROMPT    DB      'What is the part no.?'
; -------------------------------------------------
          .CODE
          ...
          MOV     AH,40H             ;Request display
          MOV     BX,01
          MOV     CX,21              ;Length of prompt
          LEA     DX,PROMPT          ;Address of prompt
          INT     21H
          MOV     AH,0AH             ;Accept keyboard
          LEA     DX,PARAMS          ;  input
          INT     21H
          MOV     AL,PARAMS.ACTLEN
;         ...                        ;Length of input
```

Figure 25-2 Using a Structure

(PARAMS in the example), followed by a period that connects it with the field name, as, for example, MOV AL, PARAMS.ACTLEN.

You may also use the allocate statement (PARAMS in Figure 25-2) to redefine the contents of fields within a structure.

SUBTTL/SUBTITLE Directive.   The SUBTTL directive (SUBTITLE since MASM 6.0) causes a subtitle of up to 60 characters to print on line 3 of each page of an assembly source listing. You may code this directive any number of times. The format is SUBTTL/SUBTITLE *text*.

TEXTEQU Directive.   The format for this directive (introduced by MASM 6.0) is TEXTEQU [*text-item*]. The operand *text-item* can be a literal string, a constant preceded by %, or a string that a macro function has returned.

TITLE Directive.   The TITLE directive causes a title of up to 60 characters to print on line 2 of each page of a source listing. You may code TITLE once at the start according to the format TITLE *text*.

.XCREF/.NOCREF Directive.   The .XCREF directive (.NOCREF since MASM 6.0) tells the assembler to suppress the cross-reference table. Its format is .XCREF [*name* [,*name*] ...]. Omitting the operand causes suppression of all entries in the table. You may also suppress the cross-reference of particular items. Here are examples of .XCREF and .CREF:

```
        .XCREF                  ;Suppress all cross-references
        ...
        .CREF                   ;Restore all cross-references
        ...
        .XREF FIELDA,FIELDB     ;Suppress two cross-references
```

.XLIST/.NOLIST Directive.   You may use the .XLIST directive (named .NOLIST since MASM 6.0) anywhere in a source program to discontinue listing an assembled program. A typical situation would be where the statements are common to other programs and you don't need another listing. The .LIST directive (the default) resumes the listing. Use these directives with no operands.

Chapter 26

THE PC INSTRUCTION SET

Objective: To explain machine code and to provide a description of the PC instruction set.

INTRODUCTION

This chapter explains machine code and provides a list of symbolic instructions with an explanation of their purposes.

Many instructions have a specific purpose, so that a 1-byte machine language instruction code is adequate. The following are examples:

```
MACHINE       SYMBOLIC
CODE          INSTRUCTION     COMMENT
 40           INC AX          ;Increment AX
 50           PUSH AX         ;Push AX
 C3           RET (short)     ;Short return from procedure
 CB           RET (far)       ;Far return from procedure
 FD           STD             ;Set Direction Flag
```

None of these instructions makes a direct reference to memory. Instructions that specify an immediate operand, two registers, or a reference to memory are more complex and require two or more bytes of machine code.

Machine code has a special provision for indicating a particular register and another provision for referencing memory by means of an addressing mode byte.

REGISTER NOTATION

Instructions that reference a register may contain three bits that indicate the particular register and a *w-bit* that indicates whether the width is a byte (0) or a word (1). Also, only certain instructions may access the segment registers. Figure 26-1 shows the register notations. For example, bit value 000 means AH if the w bit is 0 and AX if it is 1.

Here's the symbolic and machine code for a MOV instruction with a one-byte immediate operand:

```
MOV  AH,00     10110 100 00000000
                |   |||
               w reg = AH
```

In this case, the first byte of machine code indicates a width of one byte (w = 0) and refers to AH (100). Here's a MOV instruction that contains a one-word immediate operand, along with its generated machine code:

```
MOV  AX,00     10111 000 00000000 00000000
                |   |||
               w reg = AX
```

The first byte of machine code indicates a width of one word (w = 1) and refers to AX (000). For other instructions, w and reg may occupy different positions. Also, the first byte of machine code may contain a *d-bit* that indicates the direction (left/right) of flow.

Machine Code Exercise. Try using a debugger for the following exercise in machine code. (For DEBUG, use the command A 100.) Enter instructions for MOV reg,0 in this sequence: AL, CL, DL, BL, AH, CH, DH, BH, AX, CX, DX, BX, SP, BP, SI, and DI. Note how the machine code increments from B0 through BF.

THE ADDRESSING MODE BYTE

The *mode* byte, when present, occupies the second byte of machine code and consists of the following three elements:

mod   A 2-bit mode, where the values 00, 01, and 10 refer to memory locations and
        11 refers to a register

General, Base, and Index Registers			Bits for Segment Registers	
Bits	w = 0	w = 1	000	ES
000	AL	AX/EAX	001	CS
001	CL	CX/ECX	010	SS
010	DL	DX/EDX	011	DS
011	BL	BX/EBX	100	FS
100	AH	SP	101	GS
101	CH	BP		
110	DH	SI		
111	BH	DI		

Figure 26-1   Register Notation

reg   A 3-bit reference to a register

r/m   A 3-bit reference to a register or memory, where *r* specifies which register and *m* indicates a memory address

In the following example of adding AX to BX

```
ADD   BX,AX      00000011   11 011 000
                 ||  || ||| |||
                 dw mod reg r/m
```

d = 1 means that *mod* (11) and *reg* (011) describe the first operand and *r/m* (000) describes the second operand. Since w = 1, the width is a word. Therefore, the instruction is to add AX (000) to BX (011).

The second byte of the object code indicates most modes of addressing memory. You can use DEBUG to check the example this way: Key in the machine code as E 100 03 D8 and unassemble it with U 100,101.

Mod Bits.   The two *mod bits* distinguish between addressing of registers and memory. The following explains their purpose:

00   r/m bits give the exact addressing option; no offset byte (unless r/m = 110).

01   r/m bits give the exact addressing option; one offset byte.

10   r/m bits give the exact addressing option; two offset bytes.

11   r/m specifies a register. The w-bit (in the operation code byte) determines whether a reference is to an 8-, 16-, or 32-bit register.

Reg Bits.   The three *reg bits,* in association with the w-bit, determine the actual width.

R/M Bits. The three *r/m (register/memory) bits,* in association with the mod bits, determine the addressing mode, as shown in Figure 26-2.

r/m	mod=00	mod=01 or 10	mod=11 w=0	mod=11 w=1
000	BX+SI	DS:[BX+SI+disp]	AL	AX
001	BX+DI	DS:[BX+DI+disp]	CL	CX
010	BP+SI	SS:[BP+SI+disp]	DL	DX
011	BP+DI	SS:[BP+DI+disp]	BL	BX
100	SI	DS:[SI+disp]	AH	SP
101	DI	DS:[DI+disp]	CH	BP
110	Direct	SS:[BP+disp]	DH	SI
111	BX	DS:[BX+disp]	BH	DI

Figure 26-2   The r/m Bits

Two-Byte Instructions

The following two-byte instruction adds BX to AX:

```
ADD AX,BX      0000 0011  11 000 011
               ||   ||  || ||| |||
               dw mod reg r/m
```

d = 1	reg plus w describe the first operand (AX), and mod plus r/m plus w describe the second operand (BX).
w = 1	The width is a word.
mod = 11	The second operand is a register.
reg = 000	The first operand is AX.
r/m = 011	The second operand is BX.

The next example multiplies AL by BL:

```
MUL BL         11110110  11 100 011
               |    ||  ||| |||
               w mod reg r/m
```

The width (w = 0) is a byte, mod (11) references a register, and the register (r/m = 011) is BL (011). Reg = 100 is not meaningful here. The processor assumes that the multiplicand is in AL if the multiplier is a byte (as in this example), AX if a word, and EAX if a double-word.

Three-Byte Instructions

The following MOV generates three bytes of machine code:

```
MOV mem-word,AX    10100011 mmmmmmmm mmmmmmmm
                   ||
                   dw
```

A move from the accumulator (AX or AL) needs to know only whether the operation is byte or word. In this example, w = 1 means a word, and the 16-bit AX is understood. (AL coded in the second operand would cause the w bit to be zero.) Bytes 2 and 3 contain the offset to the memory location. Using the accumulator register often generates a shorter instruction length and faster execution than the use of other registers.

Four-Byte Instructions

The following four-byte instruction multiplies AL by a memory location:

```
MUL mem-byte    11110110  00 100 110 mmmmmmmm mmmmmmmm
                |    ||  ||| |||
                w mod reg r/m
```

For this instruction, although reg is 100, the multiplicand is assumed to be AL (one byte, because w = 0). Mod = 00 indicates a memory reference, and r/m = 110 means a direct reference to memory; the two subsequent bytes provide the offset to the memory location.

The next example illustrates the LEA instruction, which specifies a word address:

```
LEA DX,memory     10001101  00 010 110 mmmmmmmmm mmmmmmmmm
                            ||  ||| |||
                  LEA   mod reg r/m
```

Reg = 010 designates DX; mod = 00 and r/m = 110 indicate a direct reference to a memory address; the next two bytes provide the offset to this location.

THE INSTRUCTION SET

This section covers the instruction set in alphabetic sequence, although closely related instructions such as conditional jumps are grouped together for convenience. The 80286 and later processors support a number of specialized instructions not covered here: ARPL, BOUND, CLTS, LAR, LGDT, LIDT, LLDT, LMSW, LSL, LTR, SGDT, SIDT, SLDT, SMSW, STR, VERR, and VERW. Instructions unique to the 80486 and later are BSWAP, INVD, WBINVD, and INVLPG, also not covered. A reference to a doubleword register or memory location implies a 80386 or later processor.

In addition to the preceding discussion of mode byte and width bit, the following abbreviations are relevant:

addr	Address of a memory location
addr-high	Rightmost byte of an address
addr-low	Leftmost byte of an address
data	Immediate operand (8-bit if w = 0, 16-bit if w = 1)
data-high	Rightmost byte of an immediate operand
data-low	Leftmost byte of an immediate operand
disp	Displacement (offset value)
reg	Reference to a register

Abbreviations for flags are the following: AF = Auxiliary, CF = Carry, DF = Direction, IF = Interrupt, OF = Overflow, PF = Parity, SF = Sign, TF = Trap, and ZF = Zero.

AAA: ASCII Adjust After Addition.

Corrects the sum (after an ADD) in AL of two ASCII bytes. If the value of the rightmost four bits of AL is greater than 9, or if the AF is set to 1, AAA adds 1 to AH, adds 6 to AL, and sets the AF and CF. Otherwise, the AF and CF are cleared. AAA always clears the leftmost four bits of AL.

Flags: Affects AF and CF. (OF, PF, SF, and ZF are undefined.)

Source code: AAA (no operand)

Object code: 00110111

AAD: ASCII Adjust Before Division

Adjusts an unpacked BCD value (dividend) in AX prior to division. AAD multiplies AH by 10, adds the product to AL, and clears AH. The resulting binary value in AX is now equivalent to the original unpacked BCD value and is ready for a binary divide operation.

Flags: Affects PF, SF, and ZF. (AF, CF, and OF are undefined.)

Source code: AAD (no operand)

Object code: |11010101|00001010|

AAM: ASCII Adjust After Multiplication

Adjusts the product in AL generated by multiplying two unpacked BCD digits. AAM divides AL by 10 and stores the quotient in AH and the remainder in AL.

Flags: Affects PF, SF, and ZF. (AF, CF, and OF are undefined.)

Source code: AAM (no operand)

Object code: |11010100|00001010|

AAS: ASCII Adjust After Subtraction

Adjusts the difference in AL (after a SUB) of two ASCII bytes. If the value of the rightmost four bits is greater than 9, or if the Carry Flag is 1, AAS subtracts 6 from AL, subtracts 1 from AH, and sets the AF and CF. Otherwise, the AF and CF are cleared. AAS always clears the leftmost four bits of AL.

Flags: Affects AF and CF. (OF, PF, SF, and ZF are undefined.)

Source code: AAS (no operand)

Object code: 00111111

ADC: Add with Carry

Typically used in multiword binary addition to carry an overflowed 1-bit into the next stage of arithmetic. ADC adds the contents of the Carry Flag (0/1) to operand1, and then adds operand 2 to operand 1, just like ADD. (See also SBB.)

Flags: Affects AF, CF, OF, PF, SF, and ZF.

Source code: ADC register/memory,register/memory/immediate

Object code: Three formats:

Reg/mem with reg: |000100dw|modregr/m|
Immed to accumulator: |0001010w|--data--|data if w=1|
Immed to reg/mem: |100000sw|mod010r/m|--data--|data if sw=01|

ADD: Add Binary Numbers

Adds binary values from memory, register, or immediate to a register, or adds values in a register or immediate to memory. Values may be bytes, words, or doublewords.

Flags: Affects AF, CF, OF, PF, SF, and ZF.

Source code: ADD register/memory,register/memory/immediate

Object code: Three formats:

Reg/mem with reg: |000000dw|modregr/m|
Immed to accumulator: |0000010w|--data--|data if w=1|
Immed to reg/mem: |100000sw|mod000r/m|--data--|data if sw=01|

AND: Logical AND

Performs a logical AND operation on bits of two operands. Both operands are bytes, words, or doublewords, which AND matches bit for bit. For each pair of matched bits that are 1, the 1-bit in the first operand is set to 1; otherwise, the bit is cleared. (See also OR, XOR, and TEST.)

Flags: Affects CF (0), OF (0), PF, SF, and ZF. (AF is undefined.)

Source code: AND register/memory,register/memory/immediate

Object code: Three formats:
Reg/mem with register: `|001000dw|modregr/m|`
Immed to accumulator: `|0010010w|--data--|data if w=1|`
Immed to reg/mem: `|100000sw|mod 100 r/m|--data--|data if w=1|`

BSF/BSR: Bit Scan Forward/Bit Scan Reverse (80386+)

Scans a bit string in operand 2 (16 or 32 bits) for the first 1-bit. BSF scans from right to left, and BSR scans from left to right. If a 1-bit is found, the operation returns its position (relative to bit 0 on the right) in the operand 1 register and sets the Zero Flag; otherwise it clears the ZF.

Flags: Affects ZF.

Source code: `BSF/BSR register,register/memory`

Object code: BSF: `|00001111|10111100|modregr/m|`
             BSR: `|00001111|10111101|modregr/m|`

BT/BTC/BTR/BTS: Bit Test (80386+)

Copies a specified bit into the Carry Flag. Operand 1 contains the bit string being tested and operand 2 contains a value that indicates its position. BT simply copies the bit to the CF. The other instructions also copy the bit but act on the bit in operand 1 this way: BTC complements the bit by reversing its value in operand 1; BTR resets the bit by clearing it to zero; BTS sets the bit to 1. References are to 16- and 32-bit values.

Flags: Affects CF.

Source code: BT/BTC/BTR/BTS register/memory,register/immediate

Object code: Two formats:
Immed to reg: `|00001111|10111010|mod***r/m|`
Reg/mem to reg: `|00001111|10***010|modregr/m|`
              `(*** means 100 = BT, 111 = BTC, 110 = BTR, 101 = BTS)`

CALL: Call a Procedure

Calls a near or far procedure. The assembler generates a near CALL if the called procedure is NEAR and a far CALL if the called procedure is FAR. A near CALL pushes IP (the offset of the next instruction) onto the stack; it then loads IP with the destination offset. A far CALL pushes CS onto the stack and loads an intersegment address onto the stack; it then pushes IP onto the stack and loads IP with the destination offset. On return, a subsequent RETN or RETF is used to reverse these steps.

Flags: Affects none.

Source code: CALL register/memory

Object code: Four formats:

Direct within segment:	`|11101000|disp-low |disp-high|`
Indirect within segment:	`|11111111|mod010r/m|`
Indirect intersegment:	`|11111111|mod011r/m|`
Direct intersegment:	`|10011010|offset-low|offset-high|seg-low|`
	`seg-high|`

CBW: Convert Byte to Word

Extends a 1-byte signed value to a signed word by duplicating the sign (bit 7) of AL through the bits in AH. (See also MOVSX.)

Flags: Affects none.

Source code: CBW (no operand)

Object code: `10011000`

CDQ: Convert Doubleword to Quadword (80386+)

Extends a 32-bit signed value to a 64-bit signed value by duplicating the sign (bit 31) of EAX through EDX.

Flags: Affects none.

Source code: CDQ (no operand)

Object code: `10011001`

CLC: Clear Carry Flag

Clears the CF so that, for example, ADC does not add a 1-bit. (See also STC.)

Flags: CF (becomes 0).

Source code: CLC (no operand)

Object code: `11111000`

CLD: Clear Direction Flag

Clears the DF, to cause string operations such as MOVS to process from left to right. (See also STD.)

Flags: DF (becomes 0).

Source code: CLD (no operand)

Object code: `11111100`

CLI: Clear Interrupt Flag

Clears the IF, to disable maskable external interrupts. (See also STI.)

Flags: IF (becomes 0).
Source code: CLI (no operand)
Object code: `11111010`

CMC: Complement Carry Flag

Reverses the CF bit values: 0 becomes 1 and 1 becomes 0.

Flags: CF (reversed).
Source code: CMC (no operand)
Object code: `11110101`

CMP: Compare

Compares the binary contents of two data fields. CMP internally subtracts operand 2 from operand 1 and sets/clears flags, but does not store the result. Both operands are byte, word, or doubleword. CMP may compare register, memory, or immediate to a register or may compare register or immediate to memory. (CMP makes a numeric comparison; see CMPS for string comparisons.) The results are the following:

	CF	SF	ZF
Operand 1 < operand 2	1	1	0
Operand 1 = operand 2	0	0	1
Operand 1 > operand 2	0	0	0

Flags: Affects AF, CF, OF, PF, SF, and ZF.
Source code: CMP register/memory,register/memory/immediate
Object code: Three formats:
   Reg/mem with register: `|001110dw|modregr/m|`
   Immed to accumulator: `|0011110w|--data--|data if w=1|`
   Immed to reg/mem: `|100000sw|mod111r/m|--data--|data if sw=0|`

CMPS/CMPSB/CMPSW/CMPSD: Compare String

Compares strings of any length in memory. A REPn prefix normally precedes these instructions, along with a maximum value in CX. CMPSB compares bytes, CMPSW compares words, and CMPSD (80386+) compares doublewords. DS:SI address operand 1 and ES:DI address operand 2. If the Direction Flag is 0, the operation compares from left to right and increments SI and DI by 1 for byte, 2 for word, and 4 for doubleword; if the DF is 1, it compares from right to left and decrements SI and DI. REPn decrements CX by 1 for each repetition. REPNE ends when the first match is found, REPE ends when the first nonmatch is found, or both end when CX is decremented to 0; DI and SI are advanced past the byte that caused termination. The last compare sets/clears the flags.

Flags: Affects AF, CF, OF, PF, SF, and ZF.

Source code: [REPnn] CMPSB/CMPSW/CMPSD (no operand)

Object code: `1010011w`

CMPXCHG: Compare and Exchange (80486+)

Compares the accumulator (AL, AX, or EAX) with operand 1. If equal, CMPXCHG copies operand 2 into operand 1 and sets the Zero flag; if unequal, CMPXCHG copies operand 1 into operand 2 and clears the ZF. Operands 1 and 2 are coded, whereas the accumulator, a third element, is not coded.

Flags: Affects AF, CF, OF, PF, SF, and ZF.

Source code: CMPXCHG register/memory,register

Object code: Hex `0F B0/r` or `0F B1/r`

CMPXCHG8B: Compare and Exchange (Pentium+)

Compares the 64-bit EDX:EAX with the operand. If equal, CMPXCHG8B loads EDX:EAX into the operand and sets the Zero flag; if unequal, it loads the operand into EDX:EAX and clears the ZF.

Flags: Affects ZF.

Source code: CMPXCHG8B register/memory (one operand, 64 bits)

Object code: Hex `0F C7`

CWD: Convert Word to Doubleword

Extends a one-word signed value to a signed doubleword in DX:AX by duplicating the sign (bit 15) of AX through DX, typically to generate a 32-bit dividend. (See also CBWDE and MOVSX.)

Flags: Affects none.

Source code: CWD (no operand)

Object code: 10011001

CWDE: Convert Word to Extended Doubleword (80386+)

Extends a one-word signed value to a doubleword in EAX by duplicating the sign (bit 15) of AX, typically to generate a 32-bit dividend. (See also CWD and MOVSX.)

Flags: Affects none.

Source code: CWDE (no operand)

Object code: `10011000`

DAA: Decimal Adjust After Addition

Corrects the result in AL after an ADD or ADC has added two packed BCD items. If the value of the rightmost four bits is greater than 9, or if the Auxiliary Flag is 1, DAA adds 6 to AL and sets the AF. Next, if the value in AL is greater than 99H, or if the Carry Flag is

1, DAA adds 60H to AL and sets the CF. Otherwise, the AF and CF are cleared. AL now contains a correct two-digit packed decimal result. (See also DAS.)

Flags: Affects AF, CF, PF, SF, and ZF. (OF is undefined.)

Source code: DAA (no operand)

Object code: `00100111`

DAS: Decimal Adjust After Subtraction

Corrects the result in AL after a SUB or SBB has subtracted two packed BCD items. If the value of the rightmost four bits is greater than 9, DAS subtracts 60H from AL and sets the Carry Flag. Otherwise, it clears the Auxiliary and Carry Flags. AL now contains a correct two-digit packed decimal result. (See also DAA.)

Flags: Affects AF, CF, PF, SF, and ZF. (OF is undefined.)

Source code: DAS (no operand)

Object code: `00101111` (no operand)

DEC: Decrement by 1

Decrements 1 from a byte, word, or doubleword in a register or memory and treats the value as an unsigned integer. (See also INC.)

Flags: Affects AF, OF, PF, SF, and ZF.

Source code: DEC register/memory

Object code: Two formats:

Register: `|01001reg|`
Reg/memory: `|1111111w|mod001r/m|`

DIV: Unsigned Divide

Divides an unsigned dividend in operand 1 by an unsigned divisor. DIV treats a leftmost 1-bit as a data bit, not a minus sign. Division by zero causes a zero-divide interrupt. (See also IDIV.) Here are the divide operations according to size of dividend:

Size	Dividend (Operand 1)	Divisor (Operand 2)	Quotient	Remainder	Example
16-bit	AX	8-bit reg/memory	AL	AH	DIV BH
32-bit	DX:AX	16-bit reg/memory	AX	DX	DIV CX
64-bit	EDX:EAX	32-bit reg/memory	EAX	EDX	DIV ECX

Flags: Affects AF, CF, OF, PF, SF, and ZF. (All undefined.)

Source code: DIV register/memory

Object code: `|1111011w|mod110r/m|`

ENTER: Make Stack Frame (80286+)

Creates a stack frame to facilitate a called procedure receiving passed parameters. Operand 1 gives the size of the stack frame in bytes; operand 2 denotes nesting level (0 for BASIC, C, and FORTRAN compilers). The operation pushes BP, moves SP to BP, and subtracts 4 from SP. (See LEAVE for the complementary instruction.)

> *Flags:* Affects none.
> *Source code:* ENTER size,nesting-level
> *Object code:* |11001000|--data--|--data--|

HLT: Enter Halt State

Causes the processor to enter a halt state while waiting for a hardware interrupt. When an interrupt occurs, the processor pushes CS and IP onto the stack and executes the interrupt routine. On return, an IRET instruction pops the stack, and processing resumes following the original HLT. (An STI operation must first set the IF to enable a hardware interrupt.)

> *Flags:* Affects none.
> *Source code:* HLT (no operand)
> *Object code:* 11110100

IDIV: Signed (Integer) Divide

Divides a signed dividend by a signed divisor. IDIV treats a leftmost bit as a sign (0 = positive, 1 = negative). Division by zero causes a zero-divide interrupt. (See CBW and MOVSX to extend the length of a signed dividend, and see also DIV.) Here are the divide operations according to the size of the dividend:

Size	Dividend (Operand 1)	Divisor (Operand 2)	Quotient	Remainder	Example
16-bit	AX	8-bit reg/memory	AL	AH	IDIV BH
32-bit	DX:AX	16-bit reg/memory	AX	DX	IDIV CX
64-bit	EDX:EAX	32-bit reg/memory	EAX	EDX	IDIV ECX

> *Flags:* Affects AF, CF, OF, PF, SF, and ZF.
> *Source code:* IDIV register/memory
> *Object code:* |1111011w|mod111r/m|

IMUL: Signed (Integer) Multiply

Multiplies a signed multiplicand by a signed multiplier. The operation treats the leftmost bit as the sign (0 = positive, 1 = negative). IMUL supports four formats:

1. The operation assumes the multiplicand is in AL, AX, or EAX, and takes its size from that of the multiplier. (See also MUL.) Here are the operations according to size:

Size	Multiplicand	Multiplier	Product	Example
8-bit	AL	8-bit register/memory	AX	IMUL BL
16-bit	AX	16-bit register/memory	DX:AX	IMUL mem-word
32-bit	EAX	32-bit register/memory	EDX:EAX	IMUL ECX

The other three formats reference any 16- or 32-bit general-purpose register; lengths of data items must be the same.

2. Operand 1 (a register) contains the multiplicand and is where the product is developed; operand 2 is an immediate value. Examples:

```
IMUL CX,32 and IMUL EBX,50
```

3. Operand 1 (a register) is where the product is developed; operand 2 (a register or memory location) contains the multiplicand; operand 3 is an immediate value. Examples:

```
IMUL CX,DX,25 and IMUL EBX,mem-dblword,100
```

4. Operand 1 (a register) contains the multiplicand and is where the product is developed; operand 2 (a register or memory location) contains the multiplier. Examples:

```
IMUL DX,mem-word and IMUL EBX,EDX
```

Flags: Affects CF and OF. (AF, PF, SF, and ZF are undefined.)

Source code (four formats).

1. `IMUL register/memory (all processors)`
2. `IMUL register,immediate (80286+)`
3. `IMUL register,register,immediate (80286+)`
4. `IMUL register,register/memory (80386+)`

Object code: |1111011w|mod101r/m| (first format)

IN: Input Byte or Word

Transfers from an input port a byte to AL, word to AX, or doubleword to EAX. Code the port as a fixed numeric operand (as IN AX,port#) or as a variable in DX (as IN AX,DX). Use DX if the port number is greater than 256. (See also INS and OUT.)

Source code: IN AL/AX,portno/DX

Flags: Affects none.

Object code: Two formats:
    Variable port: |1110110w|
    Fixed port: |1110010w|--port--|

INC: Increment by 1

Increments by 1 a byte, word, or doubleword in a register or memory and treats the value as an unsigned integer, coded, for example, as INC ECX. (See also DEC.)

> *Flags:* Affects AF, OF, PF, SF, and ZF (but not CF).
>
> *Source code:* INC register/memory
>
> *Object code:* Two formats:
> Register: `|01000reg|`
> Reg/memory: `|1111111w|mod000r/m|`

INS/INSB/INSW/INSD: Input String (80286+)

Receives a string (the destination) from a port. The destination is addressed by ES:DI, and DX contains the port number. INSn is commonly used with the REP prefix, with CX containing the number of items (as byte, word, or doubleword) to be received. Depending on the DF (0/1), the operation increments/decrements DI according to the item size. (See also IN and OUTS).

> *Flags:* Affects none.
>
> *Source code:* [REP] INSB/INSW/INSD (no operand)
>
> *Object code:* `|0110110w|`

INT: Interrupt

Interrupts processing and transfers control to one of the 256 addresses in the Interrupt Vector Table. INT performs the following: (1) pushes the flags onto the stack and resets the Interrupt and Trap flags; (2) pushes CS onto the stack and places the high-order word of the interrupt address in CS; and (3) pushes IP onto the stack and fills IP with the low-order word of the interrupt address. For the 80386+, INT pushes a 16-bit IP for 16-bit segments and a 32-bit IP for 32-bit segments. IRET is used to return from the interrupt routine.

> *Flags:* Clears IF and TF.
>
> *Source code:* INT number
>
> *Object code:* `|1100110v|--type--|` (if v = 0, type is 3)

INTO: Interrupt on Overflow

Causes an interrupt (usually harmless) if an overflow has occurred (the OF is set to 1) and performs an INT 04H. The interrupt address is at location 10H of the Interrupt Vector Table. (See also INT.)

> *Flags:* Affects IF and TF.
>
> *Source code:* INTO (no operand)
>
> *Object code:* `11001110`

IRET/IRETD: Interrupt Return

Provides a far return from an interrupt routine. IRET performs the following procedure: (1) pops the word at the top of the stack into IP, increments SP by 2, and pops the top of the stack into CS; (2) increments SP by 2 and pops the top of the stack into the Flags register. This procedure undoes the steps that the interrupt originally took and performs a return. For the 80386+, use IRETD (doubleword) to pop a 32-bit IP. (See also RET.)

Flags: Affects all.

Source code: IRET

Object code: `11001111` (no operand)

Jcondition: Jump on Condition

This section summarizes the conditional jump instructions that test the status of various flags. If the test is true, the operation adds the operand offset to IP and transfers control to the CS:IP address; if not true, processing continues with the next instruction in sequence. For the 8086–80286, the jump must be short (−128 to 127 bytes); for the 80386+, the assembler assumes a near jump (−32,768 to 32,767 bytes), but you may use the SHORT operator to force a short jump. The operations test the flags but do not change them. The source code is *Jcondition label.* All object codes are of the form `|distnnnn|--disp--|`, where *disp* bits are 0111 for short jumps and 1000 for near jumps.

In the first list, the instructions are typically used after a compare operation, which compares operand 1 to operand 2:

SOURCE CODE	OBJECT CODE	FLAGS CHECKED	USED AFTER COMPARISON
JA	`|dist0111|`	CF = 0, ZF = 0	Unsigned data, above/higher
JAE	`|dist0011|`	CF = 0	Unsigned data, above/equal
JB	`|dist0010|`	CF = 1	Unsigned data, below/lower
JBE	`|dist0110|`	CF = 1 or AF = 1	Unsigned data, below/equal
JE	`|dist0100|`	ZF = 1	Signed/unsigned data, equal
JG	`|dist1111|`	ZF = 0, SF = OF	Signed data, greater
JGE	`|dist1101|`	SF = OF	Signed data, greater/equal
JL	`|dist1100|`	SF not= OF	Signed data, lower
JLE	`|dist1110|`	ZF = 1 or SF not= OF	Signed data, lower/equal
JNA	`|dist0110|`	CF = 1 or AF = 1	Unsigned data, not above
JNAE	`|dist0010|`	CF = 1	Unsigned data, not above/equal
JNB	`|dist0011|`	CF = 0	Unsigned data, not below
JNBE	`|dist0111|`	CF = 0, ZF = 0	Unsigned data, not below/equal
JNE	`|dist0101|`	ZF = 0	Signed/unsigned, not equal
JNG	`|dist1110|`	ZF = 1 or SF not= OF	Signed data, not greater
JNGE	`|dist1100|`	SF not= OF	Signed data, not greater/equal
JNL	`|dist1101|`	SF = OF	Signed data, not lower
JNLE	`|dist1111|`	ZF = 0, SF = OF	Signed data, not lower/equal

In the second list, the instructions are typically used after a an arithmetic or other operation, which clears or sets bits according to the result:

SOURCE CODE	OBJECT CODE	FLAGS CHECKED	USED TO TEST
JC	|dist0010|	CF = 1	If CF set (same as JB/JNAE)
JNC	|dist0011|	CF = 0	If CF off (same as JAE/JNB)
JNO	|dist0001|	OF = 0	If OF off
JNP	|dist1011|	PF = 0	If no (odd) parity: odd number of bits set in low-order 8 bits
JNS	|dist1001|	SF = 0	If sign is positive
JNZ	|dist0101|	ZF = 0	If signed/unsigned data not zero
JO	|dist0000|	OF = 1	If OF set
JP	|dist1010|	PF = 1	If even parity: even number of bits set in low-order 8 bits
JPE	|dist1010|	PF = 1	Same as JP
JPO	|dist1011|	PF = 0	Same as JNP
JS	|dist1000|	SF = 1	If sign is negative
JZ	|dist0100|	ZF = 1	If signed/unsigned data is zero

JCXZ/JECXZ: Jump if CX/ECX Is Zero

Jumps to a specified address if CX or ECX contains zero. This operation could be useful at the start of a loop, although limited to a short jump.

Flags: Affects none.

Source code: JCXZ/JECXZ label

Object code: |11100011|--disp--|

JMP: Unconditional Jump

Jumps to a designated address under any condition. A JMP address may be short (−128 to +127 bytes), near (within + or -32K, the default), or far (to another code segment). A short or near JMP replaces IP with a destination offset address. A far jump (such as JMP FAR PTR label) replaces CS:IP with a new segment address.

Flags: Affects none.

Source code: JMP register/memory

Object code: Five formats:
    Direct within seg short: |11101011|--disp--|
    Direct within segment: |11101001|disp-low |disp-high|
    Indirect within segment: |11111111|mod100r/m|
    Indirect intersegment: |11111111|mod101r/m|
    Direct intersegment: |11101010|offset-low|offset-high|seg-low|seg-high|

LAHF: Load AH from Flags

Loads the low-order eight bits of the Flags register into AH. (See also SAHF.)

Flags: Affects none.

Source code: LAHF (no operand)

Object code: `10011111`

LDS/LES/LFS/LGS/LSS: Load Segment Register

Operand 1 references any of the general, index, or pointer registers. Operand 2 references two words in memory containing an offset:segment address. The operation loads the segment address in the segment register and the offset in the operand 1 register. Used for example as LDS DI,SEG_ADDRESS.

Flags: Affects none.

Source code: LDS/LES/LFS/LGS/LSS register,memory

Object code:
```
LDS: |11000101|mod reg r/m|
LES: |11000100|mod reg r/m|
LFS: |00001111|10110100|mod reg r/m| (80386+)
LGS: |00001111|10110101|mod reg r/m| (80386+)
LSS: |00001111|10110010|mod reg r/m| (80386+)
```

LEA: Load Effective Address

Loads a near (offset) address into a register.

Flags: Affects none.

Source code: LEA register,memory

Object code: `10001101`

LEAVE: Terminate Stack Frame (80286+)

Terminates a procedure's stack frame created by an ENTER operation. LEAVE reverses the action of the ENTER (moves BP to SP and pops BP).

Flags: Affects none.

Source code: LEAVE (no operand)

Object code: `11001001`

LES/LFS/LGS: Load Extra Segment Register (See LDS)

LOCK: Lock Bus

Prevents a numeric coprocessor from changing a data item at the same time as the processor. LOCK is a 1-byte prefix that you may code immediately before any instruction. The operation sends a signal to the coprocessor to prevent it from using the data until the next instruction is completed.

Flags: Affects none.

Source code: LOCK instruction

Object code: `11110000`

LODS/LODSB/LODSW/LODSD: Load Byte, Word, or Doubleword String

Loads the accumulator register with a value from memory. Although LODS is a string operation, it does not require a REP prefix. DS:SI address a byte (if LODSB), word (if LODSW), or doubleword (if LODSD, 80386+) and load it from memory into AL, AX, or EAX, respectively. If the Direction Flag is 0, the operation adds 1 (if byte), 2 (if word), or 4 (if doubleword) to the SI; otherwise it subtracts 1, 2, or 4.

Flags: Affects none.

Source code: LODS mem or LODS segreg:mem
                    LODSB/LODSW/LODSD (no operand)

Object code: `1010110w`

LOOP/LOOPW/LOOPD: Loop Until Complete

Controls the execution of a routine a specified number of times. CX should contain a count before starting the loop. LOOP appears at the end of the loop and decrements CX by 1. If CX is nonzero, LOOP transfers to its operand address (a short jump), which points to the start of the loop (adds the offset in IP); otherwise LOOP drops through to the next instruction.

LOOP uses CX in 16-bit mode and ECX in 32-bit mode. LOOPW is used for CX, and LOOPD (80386+) for ECX.

Flags: Affects none.

Source code: LOOPnn label

Object code: `|11100010|--disp--|`

LOOPE/LOOPZ/LOOPEW/LOOPZW/LOOPED/LOOPZD: Loop While Equal/Loop While Zero

Controls the repetitive execution of a routine. LOOPE and LOOPZ are similar to LOOP, except that they transfer to the operand address (a short jump) if CX is nonzero and the Zero Flag is 1 (zero condition, set by another instruction); otherwise the operation drops through to the next instruction. (See also LOOPNE/LOOPNZ.)

LOOPE and LOOPZ use CX in 16-bit mode and ECX in 32-bit mode. LOOPEW and LOOPZW are used for CX, and LOOPED and LOOPZD (80386+) for ECX.

Flags: Affects none.

Source code: LOOPnn label

Object code: `|11100001|--disp--|`

LOOPNE/LOOPNZ/LOOPNEW/LOOPNZW: Loop While Not Equal/Loop While Not Zero

Controls the repetitive execution of a routine. LOOPNE and LOOPNZ are similar to LOOP, except that they transfer to the operand address (a short jump) if CX is nonzero and the Zero Flag is 0 (nonzero condition, set by another instruction); otherwise the operation drops through to the next instruction. (See also LOOPE/LOOPZ.)

LOOPNE and LOOPNZ use CX in 16-bit mode and ECX in 32-bit mode. LOOP-NEW and LOOPNZW are used for CX and LOOPNED/LOOPNZD (80386+) for ECX.

Flags: Affects none.

Source code: LOOPNnn label

Object code: |11100000|--disp--|

LSS: Load Stack Segment Register (See LDS)

MOV: Move Data

Transfers data between two registers or between a register and memory, and transfers immediate data to a register or memory. The referenced data defines the number of bytes (1, 2, or 4) moved; the operands must agree in size. MOV cannot transfer between two memory locations (use MOVS), from immediate data to segment register, or from segment register to segment register. (See also MOVSX/MOVZX.)

Flags: Affects none.

Source code: MOV register/memory,register/memory/immediate

Object code: Seven formats:

Reg/mem to/from reg:	`|100010dw|modregr/m|`
Immed to reg/mem:	`|1100011w|mod000r/m|--data--|data if w=1|`
Immed to register:	`|1011wreg|--data--|data if w=1|`
Mem to accumulator:	`|1010000w| addr-low| addr-high |`
Accumulator to mem:	`|1010001w| addr-low| addr-high |`
Reg/mem to seg reg:	`|10001110|mod0sgr/m| (sg = seg reg)`
Seg reg to reg/mem:	`|10001100|mod0sgr/m| (sg = seg reg)`

MOVS/MOVSB/MOVSW/MOVSD: Move String

Moves data between memory locations. Normally used with the REP prefix and a length in CX, MOVSB moves bytes, MOVSW moves words, and MOVSD (80386+) moves doublewords. Operand 1 is addressed by ES:DI and operand 2 by DS:SI. If the Direction Flag is 0, the operation moves data from left to right into the operand 1 destination and increments DI and SI by 1, 2, or 4. If the DF is 1, the operation moves data from right to left and decrements DI and SI. REP decrements CX by 1 for each repetition. The operation ends when CX is decremented to 0; DI and SI are advanced past the last byte moved.

Flags: Affects none.

Source code: [REP] MOVSB/MOVSW/MOVSD (no operand)

Object code: 1010010w

MOVSX/MOVZX: Move with Sign Extend or Zero Extend (80386+)

Copies an 8- or 16-bit source operand into a larger 16- or 32-bit destination operand. MOVSX fills the sign bit into leftmost bits, and MOVZX fills zero bits.

Flags: Affects none.

Source code: MOVSX/MOVZX register/memory,register/memory/ immediate

Object code: MOVSX: |00001111|1011111w|modregr/m|

MOVZX: |00001111|1011011w|modregr/m|

MUL: Unsigned Multiply

Multiplies an unsigned multiplicand by an unsigned multiplier. MUL treats a leftmost 1-bit as a data bit, not a negative sign. The operation assumes the multiplicand is in AL, AX, or EAX, and takes its size from that of the multiplier. (See also IMUL.) Here are the multiply operations according to the size of the multiplier:

Size	Multiplicand	Multiplier	Product	Example
8-bit	AL	8-bit register/memory	AX	MUL BL
16-bit	AX	16-bit register/memory	DX:AX	MUL mem-word
32-bit	EAX	32-bit register/memory	EDX:EAX	MUL ECX

Flags: Affects CF and OF. (AF, PF, SF, and ZF are undefined.)

Source code: MUL register/memory

Object code: |1111011w|mod100r/m|

NEG: Negate

Reverses a binary value from positive to negative or from negative to positive. NEG provides the two's complement of the specified operand by subtracting the operand from zero and adding 1. Operands may be a byte, word, or doubleword in a register or memory. (See also NOT.)

Flags: Affects AF, CF, OF, PF, SF, and ZF.

Source code: NEG register/memory

Object code: |1111011w|mod011r/m|

NOP: No Operation

Used to delete or insert machine code or to delay execution for purposes of timing. NOP simply performs a null operation by executing XCHG AX,AX.

Flags: Affects none.

Source code: NOP (no operand)

Object code: 10010000

NOT: Logical NOT

Changes 0-bits to 1-bits and vice versa. The operand is a byte, word, or doubleword in a register or memory. (See also NEG.)

Flags: Affects none.

Source code: NOT register/memory

Object code: `|1111011w|mod 010 r/m|`

OR: Logical OR

Performs a logical OR operation on bits of two operands. Both operands are bytes, words, or doublewords, which OR matches bit for bit. For each pair of matched bits, if either or both are 1, the bit in the first operand is set to 1; otherwise the bit is unchanged. (See also AND and XOR.)

Flags: Affects CF (0), OF (0), PF, SF, and ZF. (AF is undefined.)

Source code: OR register/memory,register/memory/immediate

Object code: Three formats:
Reg/mem with register: `|000010dw|modregr/m|`
Immed to accumulator: `|0000110w|--data--|data if w=1|`
Immed to reg/mem: `|100000sw|mod001r/m|--data--|data if w=1|`

OUT: Output Byte or Word

Transfers a byte from AL, word from AX, or doubleword from EAX to an output port. The port is a fixed numeric operand or a variable in DX. Use DX if the port number is greater than 256. (See also IN and OUTS.)

Flags: Affects none.

Source code: Fixed port: OUT port#,AX
Variable port: OUT DX,AX

Object code: Fixed port: `|1110011w|--port--|`
Variable port: `|1110111w|`

OUTS/OUTSB/OUTSW/OUTSD: Output String (80286+)

Sends a string (the source) to a port. The source is addressed by DS:SI, and DX contains the port number. OUTSn is commonly used with the REP prefix, with CX containing the number of items (as byte, word, or doubleword) to be sent. Depending on the Direction Flag (0/1) the operation increments/decrements SI according to the item size. (See also IN and OUTS.)

Flags: Affects none.

Source code: [REP] OUTSB/OUTSW/OUTSD (no operand)

Object code: `0110111w`

POP: Pop Word/Doubleword off Stack

Pops a word or doubleword previously pushed on the stack to a specified destination—a memory location, general register, or segment register. SP points to the current word at the top of the stack; POP transfers it to the specified destination and increments SP by 2. A 32-bit operand denotes a doubleword value, and ESP is incremented by 4. (See also PUSH.)

Flags: Affects none.

Source code: POP register/memory

Object code: Three formats:
Register: `|01011reg|`
Segment reg: `|000sg111|` (sg implies segment reg)
Reg/memory: `|10001111|mod 000 r/m|`

POPA/POPAD: Pop All General Registers

POPA (80286+) pops the top eight words from the stack into DI, SI, BP, SP, BX, DX, CX, and AX, in that order. POPAD (80386+) pops the top eight doublewords from the stack into EDI, ESI, EBP, ESP, EBX, EDX, ECX, and EAX. The SP value is discarded rather than loaded. Normally, PUSHA/PUSHAD has previously pushed the registers.

Flags: Affects none.

Source code: POPA/POPAD (no operand)

Object code: `01100001`

POPF/POPFD: Pop Flags Off Stack

POPF pops the top word from the stack to the 16-bit Flags register and increments SP by 2. POPFD (80386+) pops the top doubleword from the stack to the 32-bit Flags register and increments SP by 4. Normally PUSHF has pushed the flags.

Flags: Affects all.

Source code: POPF/POPFD (no operand)

Object code: `10011101`

PUSH: Push Onto Stack

Pushes a word or doubleword onto the stack for later use. SP points to the current (double)word at the top of the stack. PUSH decrements SP by 2 or ESP by 4 and transfers a (double)word from the specified operand to the new top of the stack. The source may be a general register, segment register, or memory. (See also POP and PUSHF.)

Flags: Affects none.

Source code: PUSH register/memory
                PUSH immediate (80286+)

Object code: Three formats:
Register: `|01010reg|`
Segment reg: `|000sg110|` (sg implies segment reg)
Reg/memory: `|11111111|mod110r/m|`

PUSHA/PUSHAD: Push All General Registers

PUSHA (80286+) pushes AX, CX, DX, BX, SP, BP, SI, and DI, in that order, onto the stack and decrements SP by 16. PUSHAD (80386+) pushes EAX, ECX, EDX, EBX, ESP, EBP, ESI, and EDI and decrements SP by 32. Normally, POPA/POPAD subsequently pops the registers.

> *Flags:* Affects none.
>
> *Source code:* PUSHA/PUSHAD (no operand)
>
> *Object code:* `01100000`

PUSHF/PUSHFD: Push Flags onto Stack

Pushes the contents of the Flags register onto the stack for later use. PUSHF decrements SP by 2. PUSHFD (80386+) pushes the 32-bit Flags register and decrements SP by 4. (See also POPF and PUSH.)

> *Flags:* Affects none.
>
> *Source code:* PUSHF (no operand)
>
> *Object code:* `10011100`

RCL/RCR: Rotate Left through Carry/Rotate Right through Carry

Rotates bits through the Carry Flag. The operation rotates bits left or right in a byte, word, or doubleword in a register or memory. The operand may be an immediate constant or a reference to CL. On the 8088/86, the constant may be only 1; a larger rotate must be in CL. On later processors, the constant may be up to 31. For RCL, the leftmost bit enters the Carry Flag, and the CF bit enters bit 0 of the destination; all other bits rotate left. For RCR, bit 0 enters the Carry Flag, and the CF bit enters the leftmost bit of the destination; all other bits rotate right. (See also ROL and ROR.)

> *Flags:* Affects CF and OF.
>
> *Source code:* RCL/RCR register/memory,CL/immediate
>
> *Object code:* RCL: `|110100cw|mod010r/m|` (if c = 0, shift is 1;
> RCR: `|110100cw|mod011r/m|` if c = 1, shift is in CL)

REP: Repeat String

Repeats a string operation a specified number of times. REP is an optional repeat prefix coded before the string instructions MOVS, STOS, INS, and OUTS. Load CX with a count prior to execution. For each execution of the string instruction, REP decrements CX by 1 and repeats the operation until CX is 0, at which point processing continues with the next instruction. (See also REPE/REPZ/REPNE/REPNZ.)

> *Flags:* See the associated string instructions.
>
> *Source code:* REP string-instruction
>
> *Object code:* `11110010`

REPE/REPZ/REPNE/REPNZ: Repeat String Conditionally

Repeats a string operation a specified number of times or until a condition is met. REPE, REPZ, REPNE, and REPNZ are optional repeat prefixes coded before the string instructions SCAS and CMPS, which change the Zero Flag. Load CX with a count prior to execution. For REPE/REPZ (repeat while equal/zero), the operation repeats while the ZF is 1 (equal/zero condition) and CX is not zero. For REPNE/REPNZ (repeat while not equal/zero), the operation repeats while the ZF is 0 (unequal/nonzero condition) and CX is not zero. While the conditions are true, the operation decrements CX by 1 and executes the string instruction.

Flags: See the associated string instruction.

Source code: REPE/REPZ/REPNE/REPNZ string-instruction

Object code: REPNE/REPNZ: `11110010`
            REPE/REPZ: `11110011`

RET/RETN/RETF: Return from a Procedure

Returns from a procedure previously entered by a near or far CALL. The assembler assumes a near RET if it is within a procedure labeled NEAR and assumes a far RET if it is within a procedure labeled FAR. For near, RET moves the word at the top of the stack to IP and increments SP by 2. For far, RET moves the words at the top of the stack to IP and CS and increments SP by 4. A constant operand (an immediate value coded as RET 4) is added to SP.

    RETN and RETF are used to code a near or far return explicitly.

Flags: Affects none.

Source code: RET/RETN/RETF [immediate]

Object code: Four formats:
    Within a segment: `|11000011|`
    Within a segment with immediate: `|11000010|data-low|data-high|`
    Intersegment: `|11001011|`
    Intersegment with immediate: `|11001010|data-low|data-high|`

ROL/ROR: Rotate Left or Rotate Right

Rotates bits left or right in a byte, word, or doubleword (80386+) in a register or memory. The operand may be an immediate constant or a reference to CL. On the 8088/86, the constant may be only 1; a larger rotate must be in CL. On later processors, the constant may be up to 31. For ROL, the leftmost bit enters bit 0 of the destination; all other bits rotate left. For ROR, bit 0 enters the leftmost bit of the destination; all other bits rotate right. (See also RCL and RCR.) The rotated bit also enters the Carry Flag.

Flags: Affects CF and OF.

Source code: ROL/ROR register/memory,CL/immediate

Object code: ROL: `|110100cw|mod000r/m|` (if c=0 count=1;
           ROR: `|110100cw|mod001r/m|` if c=1 count is in CL)

SAHF: Store AH Contents in Flags

Stores the eight bits from AH in the low-order bits of the Flags register. (See also LAHF.)

> *Flags:* Affects AF, CF, PF, SF, and ZF.
> *Source code:* SAHF (no operand)
> *Object code:* `10011110`

SAL/SAR: Shift Algebraic Left/Shift Algebraic Right

Shifts bits to the left or right in a byte, word, or doubleword in a register or memory. The operand may be an immediate constant or a reference to CL. On the 8088/86, the constant may be only 1; a larger shift must be in CL. On later processors, the constant may be up to 31.

SAL shifts bits to the left a specified number and fills 0 bits in vacated positions to the right. SAL acts exactly like SHL. SAR is an arithmetic shift that considers the sign of the referenced field. SAR shifts bits to the right a specified number and fills the sign bit (0 or 1) to the left. All bits shifted off are lost.

> *Flags:* Affects CF, OF, PF, SF, and ZF. (AF is undefined.)
> *Source code:* SAL/SAR register/memory,CL/immediate
> *Object code:* SAL: `|110100cw|mod100r/m|` (if c=0 count=1;
> SAR: `|110100cw|mod111r/m|` if c=1 count in CL)

SBB: Subtract with Borrow

Typically used in multiword binary subtraction to carry an overflowed 1 bit into the next stage of arithmetic. SBB first subtracts the contents of the CF (0/1) from operand 1 and then subtracts operand 2 from operand 1, just like SUB. (See also ADC.)

> *Flags:* Affects AF, CF, OF, PF, SF, and ZF.
> *Source code:* SBB register/memory,register/memory/immediate
> *Object code:* Three formats:
> Reg/mem with reg: `|000110dw|modregr/m|`
> Immed from accumulator: `|0001110w|--data--|data if w=1|`
> Immed from reg/mem: `|100000sw|mod011r/m|--data--|data if sw=01|`

SCAS/SCASB/SCASW/SCASD: Scan String

Scans a string in memory for a specified value. For SCASB load the value in AL, for SCASW load it in AX, and for SCASD (80386+) load it in EAX. The ES:DI pair references the string in memory that is to be scanned. The operations are normally used with a REPE/REPNE prefix, along with a count in CX; use REPE to find the first nonmatch and REPNE to find the first match. If the Direction Flag is 0, the operation scans memory from left to right and increments the DI. If the DF is 1, the operation scans memory from right to left and decrements the DI. REPn decrements CX for each repetition. The operation ends on an equal (REPNE) or an unequal (REPE) condition or when CX is decremented to 0. The *last* compare clears/sets the flags. If the specified condition is not found, REP has decremented CX to 0; otherwise, DI and SI contain the address of the following item.

> *Flags:* Affects AF, CF, OF, PF, SF, and ZF.
>
> *Source code:* [REPnn] SCASB/SCASW/SCASD (no operand)
>
> *Object code:* `1010111w`

SETnn: Set Byte Conditionally (80386+)

Sets a specified byte based on a condition. This is a group of 30 instructions, including SET(N)E, SET(N)L, SET(N)C, and SET(N)S, that exactly parallel the set of conditional jumps (Jnn). If a tested condition is true, the operation sets the byte operand to 1, otherwise to 0. An example is

```
CMP  AX,BX ;Compare contents of AX to BX
SETE CL    ;If equal, set CL to 1, else to 0
```

> *Flags:* Affects none.
>
> *Source code:* SETnn register/memory
>
> *Object code:* `|00001111|1001cond|mod000r/m|`
> (cond varies according to condition tested)

SHL/SHR: Shift Logical Left/Shift Logical Right

Shifts bits left or right in a byte, word, or doubleword in a register or memory. The operand may be an immediate constant or a reference to CL. On the 8088/86, the constant may be only 1; a larger shift must be in CL. On later processors, the constant may be up to 31. SHL and SHR are logical shifts that treat the sign bit as a data bit.

SHL shifts bits to the left a specified number and fills 0 bits in vacated positions to the right. SHL acts exactly like SAL. SHR shifts bits to the right a specified number and fills 0 bits to the left. All bits shifted off are lost.

> *Flags:* Affects CF, OF, PF, SF, and ZF. (AF is undefined.)
>
> *Source code:* SHL/SHR register/memory,CL/immediate
>
> *Object code:* SHL: `|110100cw|mod100r/m|` (if c = 0, count = 1;
> SHR: `|110100cw|mod101r/m|` if c = 1, count in CL)

SHLD/SHRD: Shift Double Precision (80386+)

Shifts multiple bits into an operand. The instructions require three operands. Operand 1 is a 16- or 32-bit register or memory location containing the value to be shifted. Operand 2 is a register (same size as operand 1) containing the bits to be shifted into operand1 . Operand 3 is CL or an immediate constant containing the shift value.

> *Flags:* Affects CF, OF, PF, SF, and ZF. (AF is undefined.)
>
> *Source code:* SHLD/SHRD register/memory,register,CL/immediate
>
> *Object code:* `|00001111|10100100|modregr/m|`

STC: Set Carry Flag

Sets the CF to 1. (See CLC for clear CF.)

> *Flags:* Sets CF.
> *Source code:* STC (no operand)
> *Object code:* 11111001

STD: Set Direction Flag

Sets the DF to 1 to cause string operations such as MOVS to process from right to left. (See CLD for clear DF.)

> *Flags:* Sets DF.
> *Source code:* STD (no operand)
> *Object code:* 11111101

STI: Set Interrupt Flag

Sets the IF to 1 to enable maskable external interrupts after execution of the next instruction. (See CLI for clear IF.)

> *Flags:* Sets IF.
> *Source code:* STI (no operand)
> *Object code:* 11111011

STOS/STOSB/STOSW/STOSD: Store String

Stores the contents of the accumulator in memory. When used with a REP prefix along with a count in CX, the operation duplicates a string value a specified number of times; this is suitable for such actions as clearing an area of memory. For STOSB load the value in AL, for STOSW load the value in AX, and for STOSD (80386+) load the value in EAX. ES:DI reference a location in memory where the value is to be stored. If the Direction Flag is 0, the operation stores in memory from left to right and increments DI. If the DF is 1, the operation stores from right to left and decrements DI. REP decrements CX for each repetition and ends when it becomes 0.

> *Flags:* Affects none.
> *Source code:* [REP] STOSB/STOSW/STOSD (no operand)
> *Object code:* 1010101w

SUB: Subtract Binary Values

Subtracts binary values in a register, memory, or immediate from a register, or subtracts values in a register or immediate from memory. Values may be byte, word, or doubleword. (See also SBB.)

> *Flags:* Affects AF, CF, OF, PF, SF, and ZF.
> *Source code:* SUB register/memory,register/memory/immediate

Object code: Three formats:
    Reg/mem with register: `|001010dw|modregr/m|`
    Immed from accumulator: `|0010110w|--data--|data if w=1|`
    Immed from reg/mem: `|100000sw|mod101r/m|--data--|data if sw=01|`

TEST: Test Bits

Uses AND logic to test a field for a specific bit configuration, but does not change the destination operand. Both operands are bytes, words, or doublewords in a register or memory; the second operand may be immediate. The operation clears the ZF if any pair of matched bits are 1; else it sets the ZF. After its execution, you may use a Jnn instruction to test the flags.

    Flags: Clears CF and OF and affects PF, SF, and ZF. (AF is undefined.)

    Source code: TEST register/memory,register/memory/immediate

    Object code: Three formats:
        Reg/mem and register: `|1000010w|modregr/m|`
        Immed to accumulator: `|1010100w|--data--|data if w=1|`
        Immed to reg/mem: `|1111011w|mod000r/m|--data--|data if w=1|`

WAIT: Put Processor in Wait State

Allows the processor to remain in a wait state until an external interrupt occurs, in order to synchronize it with a coprocessor. The processor waits until the coprocessor finishes executing and resumes processing on receiving a signal in the TEST pin.

    Flags: Affects none.

    Source code: WAIT (no operand)

    Object code: `10011011`

XADD: Exchange and Add (80486+)

Adds the source and destination operands, stores the sum in the destination, and moves the original destination value to the source.

    Flags: Affects AF, CF, OF, PF, SF, and ZF.

    Source code: XADD register/memory,register

    Object code: `|00001111|1100000b|mod reg r/m|`

XCHG: Exchange

Exchanges data between two registers (as XCHG AH,BL) or between a register and memory (as XCHG CX,word).

    Flags: Affects none.

    Source code: XCHG register/memory,register/memory

    Object code: Two formats:
        Reg with accumulator: `|10010reg|`
        Reg/mem with reg: `|1000011w|mod reg r/m|`

XLAT/XLATB: Translate

Translates bytes into a different format, such as encrypted data. Load the address of a translate table in BX or EBX for 32-bit size, and then load AL with a value that is to be translated. The operation uses the AL value as an offset into the table, selects the byte from the table, and stores it in AL. (XLATB is a synonym for XLAT.)

> *Flags:* Affects none.
>
> *Source code:* XLAT/XLATB [AL] (AL operand is optional)
>
> *Object code:* `11010111`

XOR: Exclusive OR

Performs a logical exclusive OR on bits of two operands. Both operands are bytes, words, or doublewords, which XOR matches bit for bit. For each pair matched bits, if both are the same, the bit in the first operand is cleared to 0; if the matched bits are different the bit in the first operand is set to 1. (See also AND and OR.)

> *Flags:* Affects CF (0), OF (0), PF, SF, and ZF. (AF is undefined.)
>
> *Source code:* XOR register/memory,register/memory/immediate
>
> *Object code:* Three formats:
>
> | | |
> |---|---|
> | Reg/mem with reg: | `\|001100dw\|mod reg r/m\|` |
> | Immed to reg/mem: | `\|1000000w\|mod 110 r/m\|--data--\|data if w=1\|` |
> | Immed to accumulator: | `\|0011010w\|--data--\|data if w=1\|` |

Appendix A

CONVERSION BETWEEN HEXADECIMAL AND DECIMAL NUMBERS

This appendix provides the steps required to convert between numbers in hexadecimal and decimal formats. The first section shows how to convert hex A7B8 to decimal 42,936, and the second section shows how to convert 42,936 back to hex A7B8.

CONVERTING A HEXADECIMAL NUMBER TO DECIMAL

To convert a hex number to a decimal number, start with the leftmost hex digit, continuously multiply each hex digit by 16, and accumulate the results. Because multiplication is in decimal, convert hex digits A through F to decimal 10 through 15. The steps to convert A7B8H to decimal format are:

```
First digit: A (10)          10
Multiply by 16             × 16
                            160
Add next digit, 7          +  7
                            167
Multiply by 16             × 16
                           2672
Add next digit, B (11)     + 11
                           2683
Multiply by 16             × 16
                         42,928
Add next digit,          +    8
Decimal value            42,936
```

You can also use a conversion table. For A7B8H, think of the rightmost digit (8) as position 1, the next digit to the left (B) as position 2, the next digit (7) as position 3, and the leftmost digit (A) as position 4. Refer to Table A-1 and locate the value for each hex digit:

```
For digit 8 in position 1, column 1 =       8
For digit B in position 2, column 2 =     176
For digit 7 in position 3, column 3 =   1,792
For digit A in position 4, column 4 =  40,960
                          Decimal value 42,936
```

CONVERTING A DECIMAL NUMBER TO HEXADECIMAL

To convert decimal number 42,936 to hexadecimal, first divide 42,936 by 16; the remainder becomes the rightmost hex digit, 8. Next divide the new quotient, 2,683, by 16; the remainder, 11 or B, becomes the next hex digit to the left. Continue in this manner developing the hex number from the remainders of each step of the division until the quotient is zero. The steps proceed as follows:

OPERATION	QUOTIENT	REMAINDER	HEX
42,936/16	2683	8	8 (rightmost)
2,683/16	167	11	B
167/16	10	7	7
10/16	0	10	A (leftmost)

You can also use Table A-1 to convert decimal to hexadecimal. For decimal number 42,936, locate the number in the table that is equal to or next smaller than it. Note the equivalent hex number and its position in the table. Subtract the decimal value of that hex digit from 42,936, and locate the difference in the table. The procedure works as follows:

	DECIMAL	HEX
Starting decimal value	42,936	
Subtract next smaller number	-40,960	A000
Difference	1,976	
Subtract next smaller number	-1,792	700
Difference	184	
Subtract next smaller number	-176	B0
Difference	8	8
Final hex value		A7B8

Table A-1 Hexadecimal-Decimal Conversion Table

8		7		6		5	
Hex	Dec	Hex	Dec	Hex	Dec	Hex	Dec
0	0	0	0	0	0	0	0
1	268,435,456	1	16,777,216	1	1,048,576	1	65,536
2	536,870,912	2	33,554,432	2	2,097,152	2	131,072
3	805,306,368	3	50,331,648	3	3,145,728	3	196,608
4	1,073,741,824	4	67,108,864	4	4,194,304	4	262,144
5	1,342,177,280	5	83,886,080	5	5,242,880	5	327,680
6	1,610,612,736	6	100,663,296	6	6,291,456	6	393,216
7	1,879,048,192	7	117,440,512	7	7,340,032	7	458,752
8	2,147,483,648	8	134,217,728	8	8,388,608	8	524,288
9	2,415,919,104	9	150,994,944	9	9,437,184	9	589,824
A	2,684,354,560	A	167,772,160	A	10,485,760	A	655,360
B	2,952,790,016	B	184,549,376	B	11,534,336	B	720,896
C	3,221,225,472	C	201,326,592	C	12,582,912	C	786,432
D	3,489,660,928	D	218,103,808	D	13,631,488	D	851,968
E	3,758,096,384	E	234,881,024	E	14,680,064	E	917,504
F	4,026,531,840	F	251,658,240	F	15,728,640	F	983,040

4		3		2		1	
Hex	Dec	Hex	Dec	Hex	Dec	Hex	Dec
0	0	0	0	0	0	0	0
1	4,096	1	256	1	16	1	1
2	8,192	2	512	2	32	2	2
3	12,288	3	768	3	48	3	3
4	16,384	4	1,024	4	64	4	4
5	20,480	5	1,280	5	80	5	5
6	24,576	6	1,536	6	96	6	6
7	28,672	7	1,792	7	112	7	7
8	32,768	8	2,048	8	128	8	8
9	36,864	9	2,304	9	144	9	9
A	40,960	A	2,560	A	160	A	10
B	45,056	B	2,816	B	176	B	11
C	49,152	C	3,072	C	192	C	12
D	53,248	D	3,328	D	208	D	13
E	57,344	E	3,584	E	224	E	14
F	61,440	F	3,840	F	240	F	15

Appendix B

ASCII CHARACTER CODES

The term ASCII stands for "American Standard Code for Information Interchange." Table B-1 lists the representation of the entire 256 ASCII character codes (00H through FFH), along with their hexadecimal representations. The categories of character codes are:

00–1FH   Control codes for screens, printers, and data transmission, that are intended to cause an action.

20–7FH   Character codes for numbers, letters, and punctuation. (20H is the standard space or blank.)

80–FFH   Extended ASCII codes, foreign characters, Greek and mathematics symbols, and graphic characters for drawing boxes.

Here are control codes 00H through 1FH and their descriptions:

HEX	CHARACTER	HEX	CHARACTER	HEX	CHARACTER
00	Null	01	Start of header	02	Start of text
03	End of text	04	End transmission	05	Enquiry
06	Acknowledge	07	Bell	08	Back space
09	Horizontal Tab	0A	Line feed	0B	Vertical tab
0C	Form Feed	0D	Return	0E	Shift out
0F	Shift in	10	Data line escape	11	Device ctl 1
12	Device ctl 2	13	Device ctl 3	14	Device ctl 4

15	Neg acknowledge	16	Synch idle	17	End trans block
18	Cancel	19	End of medium	1A	Substitute
1B	Escape	1C	File separator	1D	Group separator
1E	Record separator	1F	Unit separator		

Table B-1 ASCII Character Set

Code	Chr	Code	Chr	Code	Chr	Code	Chr	Code	Chr	Code	Chr	Code	Chr	Code	Chr
00		20		40	@	60	`	80	Ç	A0	á	C0	└	E0	α
01	☺	21	!	41	A	61	a	81	ü	A1	í	C1	┴	E1	ß
02	●	22	"	42	B	62	b	82	é	A2	ó	C2	┬	E2	Γ
03	♥	23	#	43	C	63	c	83	â	A3	ú	C3	├	E3	π
04	♦	24	$	44	D	64	d	84	ä	A4	ñ	C4	─	E4	Σ
05	♣	25	%	45	E	65	e	85	à	A5	Ñ	C5	┼	E5	σ
06	♠	26	&	46	F	66	f	86	å	A6	ª	C6	╞	E6	µ
07		27	'	47	G	67	g	87	ç	A7	º	C7	╟	E7	τ
08		28	(	48	H	68	h	88	ê	A8	¿	C8	╚	E8	Φ
09		29	)	49	I	69	i	89	ë	A9	⌐	C9	╔	E9	θ
0A		2A	*	4A	J	6A	j	8A	è	AA	¬	CA	╩	EA	Ω
0B		2B	+	4B	K	6B	k	8B	ï	AB	½	CB	╦	EB	δ
0C		2C	,	4C	L	6C	l	8C	î	AC	¼	CC	╠	EC	∞
0D		2D	-	4D	M	6D	m	8D	ì	AD	¡	CD	═	ED	φ
0E		2E	.	4E	N	6E	n	8E	Ä	AE	«	CE	╬	EE	ε
0F		2F	/	4F	O	6F	o	8F	Å	AF	»	CF	╧	EF	∩
10	►	30	0	50	P	70	p	90	É	B0	░	D0	╨	F0	≡
11	◄	31	1	51	Q	71	q	91	æ	B1	▒	D1	╤	F1	±
12	↕	32	2	52	R	72	r	92	Æ	B2	▓	D2	╥	F2	≥
13	‼	33	3	53	S	73	s	93	ô	B3	│	D3	╙	F3	≤
14	¶	34	4	54	T	74	t	94	ö	B4	┤	D4	╘	F4	⌠
15	§	35	5	55	U	75	u	95	ò	B5	╡	D5	╒	F5	⌡
16	▬	36	6	56	V	76	v	96	û	B6	╢	D6	╓	F6	÷
17	↨	37	7	57	W	77	w	97	ù	B7	╖	D7	╫	F7	≈
18	↑	38	8	58	X	78	x	98	ÿ	B8	╕	D8	╪	F8	°
19	↓	39	9	59	Y	79	y	99	Ö	B9	╣	D9	┘	F9	·
1A		3A	:	5A	Z	7A	z	9A	Ü	BA	║	DA	┌	FA	·
1B		3B	;	5B	[	7B	{	9B	¢	BB	╗	DB	█	FB	√
1C	∟	3C	<	5C	\	7C	|	9C	£	BC	╝	DC	▄	FC	ⁿ
1D	↔	3D	=	5D	]	7D	}	9D	¥	BD	╜	DD	▌	FD	²
1E	▲	3E	>	5E	^	7E	~	9E	Pt	BE	╛	DE	▐	FE	■
1F	▼	3F	?	5F	_	7F	⌂	9F	ƒ	BF	┐	DF	▀	FF	

Appendix C
The DEBUG Program

The DOS DEBUG program is useful for writing very small programs, for debugging assembly programs, and for examining the contents of a file or memory. You'll find DEBUG.EXE under DOS in a directory named \DOS or under Windows 95/98 by requesting the Start menu and selecting the MS-DOS prompt. To print a copy of the display, a convenient approach is to run DEBUG in a window. Use the mouse to specify the area for copying to the clipboard; subsequently, you can paste it into Notepad or a word processor.

To initiate the program, key in the word DEBUG and press <Enter>. DEBUG should load from disk into memory. When DEBUG's prompt, a hyphen (-), appears on the screen, DEBUG is ready to accept your commands. (That is a hyphen, although it resembles the cursor.)

You may key in one of two commands to start DEBUG:

1. To create a file or examine memory, key in DEBUG with no filespec; or
2. To modify or debug a program (.COM or .EXE) or to modify a file, key in DEBUG with a filespec, such as DEBUG n:PROGC.COM.

The program loader loads DEBUG into memory, and DEBUG displays a hyphen (-) as a prompt. The CS, DS, ES, and SS registers are initialized with the address of the 256-byte (100H) program segment prefix (PSP), and your work area begins at PSP + 100H. Here is how DEBUG displays the Flags register, from left to right:

	Over- flow	Direc- tion	Inter- rupt	Sign	Zero	Auxiliary Carry	Parity	Carry
On	OV	DN	EI	NG	ZR	AC	PE	CY
Off	NV	UP	DI	PL	NZ	NA	PO	NC

A reference to a memory address may be in terms of segment:offset, such as DS:120, or offset only, such as 120. You may also make direct references to memory addresses, such as 40:17, where 40[0]H is segment and 17H is offset. Note that the data segment for .EXE programs begins at DS:0, whereas that for .COM program begins at DS:100.

DEBUG assumes that all numbers entered are hexadecimal, so you do not key in the trailing H. The F1 and F3 keys work this way: F1 duplicates the previous command one key at a time, whereas F3 duplicates the entire previous command. Also, DEBUG does not distinguish between uppercase and lowercase letters.

Following is a description of each DEBUG command, in alphabetic sequence.

A (Assemble).   Translates assembly source statements into machine code. The operation is especially useful for writing and testing small assembly programs and for examining small segments of code. The default starting address for code is CS:0100H. The format for the A command is A *[address]*, where *address* defaults to 100H.

DEBUG supports the following features:

- DB and DW can be used to define data items that the program needs to reference.
- An operand in square brackets, such as [12E], specifies a memory offset.
- The PTR operator can be used to specify byte or word, as INC BYTE PTR [12E].
- All forms of register-indirect operands are available, such as [BP+DI] and 25[BX].

The following example creates an assembly program consisting of five statements. You key in the instructions only; DEBUG generates the code segment (shown here as xxxx:) and an offset beginning at 0100H:

```
             A (or A 100) <Enter>      Explanation
xxxx:0100    MOV CX,[10D] <Enter>    ;Get contents at 10D
xxxx:0104    ADD CX,1A <Enter>       ;Add immediate value
xxxx:0107    MOV [10D],CX <Enter>    ;Store CX in 10D
xxxx:010B    JMP 100 <Enter>         ;Jump back to start
xxxx:010D    DW 2500 <Enter>         ;Define constant
             <Enter>                 ;End of command
```

Because of the size of the PSP, DEBUG sets IP to 100H, so that the statements begin at 100H. The last <Enter> (that's two in a row) tells DEBUG to end the program. You may now optionally use the U (Unassemble) command to examine the machine code and T (Trace) to trace program execution.

You may change any of the preceding instructions or data items, provided that the new length is the same as that of the old one. For example, to change the ADD at 104H to SUB, key in

```
                        A 104 <Enter>
          xxxx:0104    SUB CX,1A <Enter> <Enter>
```

When you reexecute the program, IP is still incremented. Use the register (R) command to reset it to 100H. Use Q to quit.

C (Compare).   Compares the contents of two areas of memory. The default register is DS. You may code the command with a length or a range:

1. C *start-from-addr length start-to-addr*. The following example compares 20H bytes beginning at DS:050 with bytes beginning at DS:200:

   ```
   C 050 L20 200 ;Compare using length of 20H
   ```

2. C *start-from-addr end-from-addr start-to-addr*

   This example compares bytes beginning at DS:050 through DS:70 to bytes beginning at DS:200:

   ```
           C 050 070 200 ;Compare using a range
   ```

   The operation displays the addresses and contents of unequal bytes.

D (Display or Dump).   Displays the contents of a portion of memory in hex and ASCII. The default register is DS. You may code the command with a length or a range:

1. D *[start-address [length]]*. You may specify *start-address* with an optional *length*. Omission of *length* causes a default to 80H (128 bytes). Here are some examples:

   ```
   D 200       ;Display 80H bytes beginning at DS:200H
   D           ;Display 80H bytes beginning at end of last display
   D CS:150    ;Display 80H bytes beginning at CS:150H
   D DS:20 L5  ;Display 5 bytes beginning at DS:20H
   ```

2. D *[start-addr end-addr]*. Here is an example:

   ```
   D 300 32C   ;Display the bytes from 300H through 32CH
   ```

E (Enter).   Enables keying in data or machine instructions. The default register is DS, and the format is E *address [list]*. The operation allows two options:

1. Replace bytes with those in a *list*, as shown next:

   ```
   E 105 13 3A 21      ;Enter three bytes beginning at DS:105H
   E CS:211 21 2A      ;Enter two bytes beginning at CS:211H
   E 110 'anything'    ;Enter character string beginning at DS:110H
   ```

   Use either single or double quotes for character strings.

2. Provide sequential editing of bytes; key in the *address* that you want displayed:

   ```
   E 12C               ;Show contents of DS:12CH
   ```

   The operation waits for input from the keyboard. Key in one or more bytes of hex values, separated by a space, beginning at DS:12CH.

F (Fill).   Fills a range of memory locations with values in a list. The default register is DS. You may code the command with a length or a range:

1. `F start-addr length 'data'`. Here is an example:
   ```
   F 210 L19 'Help!' ;Use a length of 19H (25) bytes
   ```
2. `F start-addr end-addr 'data'`. Here is an example:
   ```
   F 210 229 'Help!' ;Use a range, 210H through 229H
   ```

Both examples fill locations in memory beginning at DS:210H with bytes containing repetitions of 'Help':

G (Go).   Executes a machine language program that you are debugging through to a specified breakpoint. Be sure to examine the machine code listing for valid IP addresses, because an invalid address may cause unpredictable results. Also, set break points only in your own program, not in DOS or BIOS program modules. The operation executes through INT operations and pauses, if necessary, to wait for keyboard input. The default register is CS and the format is

```
G [=start-address] break-address [break-address ...]
```

The entry =*start-address* is optional. The other entries provide up to ten break-point addresses. The command G 11A tells DEBUG to begin executing all instructions from the current location of IP to location 11AH.

H (Hexadecimal).   Shows the sum and difference of two hex values, coded as `H value value`. The maximum length is four hex digits. For example, the command H 14F 22 displays the result 171 (sum) and 12D (difference).

I (Input).   Inputs and displays one byte from a port, coded as `I port-address`.

L (Load).   Loads a file or disk sectors into memory. A file may be "named" so that DEBUG recognizes it one of two ways: either by requesting execution of DEBUG with a filespec, or from within DEBUG by issuing the N (Name) command. There are two formats for the L command:

1. Load a named file: `L [address]`. Use the *address* parameter to cause L to load beginning at a specific location. Omission of *address* causes L to load at CS:100. To load a file that is not named, it should first be named (see the N command):
   ```
   N filespec  ;Name the file
   L           ;Load the file at CS:100H
   ```
   To reload the file, simply issue L with no address; DEBUG reloads the file and initializes registers accordingly.
2. Load data from disk sectors: `L [address [drive start number]]`.
   - *Address* provides the starting memory location for loading the data. (The default is CS:100.)
   - *Drive* identifies the disk drive, where 0 = A, 1 = B, etc.

- *Start* specifies the hex number of the first sector to load (relative number, where cylinder 0, track 0, sector 1, is relative sector 0).
- *Number* gives the hex number of consecutive sectors to load.

The following example loads beginning at CS:100 from drive 0 (A), starting at sector 20H for 15H sectors:

```
L 100 0 20 15
```

The L operation returns to BX:CX the number of bytes loaded. For an .EXE file, DEBUG ignores the address parameter (if any) and uses the load address in the .EXE header. It also strips off the header; to preserve it, rename the file with a different extension before executing DEBUG.

M (Move).   Moves (or copies) the contents of memory locations. The default register is DS You may code the command with a length or a range:

1. M *start-addr length end-addr*. Here is an example:
   ```
   M DS:50 L100 DS:400 ;Use a length for the move
   ```
2. M *start-from-addr end-from-addr start-to-addr*. Here is an example:
   ```
   M DS:50 150 DS:400 ;Use a range for the move
   ```

Both examples copy the bytes beginning at DS:050H through 150H into the address beginning at DS:400H:

N (Name).   Names a program or a file that you intend to read from or write onto disk. Code the command as N *filespec*, such as

```
N path:SAM.COM
```

The operation stores the name at CS:80 in the PSP. The first byte at CS:80 contains the length (0AH), followed by a space and the *filespec*. You may then use L (Load) or W (Write) to read or write the file.

O (Output).   Sends a byte to a port, coded as O *port-address byte*.

P (Proceed).   Executes a CALL, LOOP, INT, or repeat string instruction (REP) through to the next instruction. Its format is P *[=address] [value]*, where *=address* is an optional starting address and *value* is an optional number of instructions to proceed through. Omission of *=address* causes a default to the current CS:IP value. For example, if your trace of execution is at an INT 10H operation, just key in P to execute through the entire operation. See also G and T.

Q (Quit).   Exits DEBUG. The operation does not save files; use W for that purpose.

R (Register).   Displays the contents of registers and the next instruction. Its format is R *[register-name]*. The following examples illustrate the use of this command:

R   Displays all registers

R DX   Displays DX; DEBUG gives you an option:

 1. Press <Enter>, which leaves DX unchanged; or

 2. Key in one to four hex digits to change the contents of DX.

R IP   Displays IP. Key in another value to change its contents.

R F   Displays the current setting of each flag as a two-letter code. See the start of
        this Appendix for flag names.

S (Search).   Searches memory for characters in a list. If the characters are found,
the operation delivers their addresses; otherwise it does not respond. The default register
is DS. You may code the command with a length or a range:

 1. S *start-addr length 'data'*. The following example searches for the word
     "VIRUS" beginning at DS:300 with a length of 2000H bytes:
     ```
     S 300 L 2000 "VIRUS"
     ```

 2. S *start-from-addr end-from-addr start-to-addr*. The following example
     searches from CS:100 through CS:400 for a byte containing 51H:
     ```
     S CS:100 400 51
     ```

T (Trace).   Executes a program in single-step mode. Note that you should
normally use P (Proceed) to execute through INT instructions. The default registers are
CS:IP and the format is T *[=address] [value]*. The optional entry *=address* tells
DEBUG where to begin the trace, and the optional *value* gives the number of instructions
to trace. Omission of the operands causes DEBUG to execute the next instruction and to
display the registers. Here are two examples:

```
T     ;Executes the next instruction
T 10  ;Executes the next 10H (16) instructions
```

The T command attempts to execute anything, and an invalid instruction causes the processor to lock up, requiring a reboot.

U (Unassemble).   Unassembles machine instructions, that is, converts them into
symbolic code. The default registers are CS:IP and the format is

```
U [start-addr] or U [start-addr end-addr]
```

The area specified should contain valid machine code, which the operation displays as symbolic instructions. Here are three examples:

```
U 100     ;Unassemble 32 bytes beginning at CS:100
U         ;Unassemble 32 bytes since last U, if any
U 100 140 ;Unassemble from 100H through 140H
```

DEBUG does not properly translate some conditional jumps and instructions specific
to the 80286 and later processors, although they still execute correctly. (DEBUG represents
them as DB statements.)

W (Write).   Writes a file from DEBUG. The file should first be named (see N) if it
wasn't already loaded. The default register is CS and the format is

```
W [address [drive start-sector number-of-sectors]
```

Write program files only with a .COM extension because W does not support the .EXE format. (To modify an .EXE program, you may change the extension temporarily.) You may use DEBUG to write a program on disk under two circumstances:

1. To retrieve an existing program from disk, modify it, and then save it, follow these steps:
   - Load the machine language program into memory under its name: DEBUG `n:filename.ext`.
   - Use the D command to view the program and E to enter changes.
   - Use the W (Write) command to write the revised program.
2. To use DEBUG to create a very small machine language program that you now want to save, follow these steps:
   - Use the A (Assemble) and E commands to key in the source program.
   - Type N `filename.COM` to name the program. The program extension must be .COM.
   - Because only you know where the program really ends, insert in the BX:CX pair the size of the program in bytes. Consider this program example:
     ```
     xxxx:0100 MOV CL,42
     xxxx:0102 MOV DL,2A
     xxxx:0104 ADD CL,DL
     xxxx:0106 JMP 100
     ```
     Although you key in symbolic code, DEBUG generates machine code, and that is what you are going to save. Because the last instruction, JMP, is two bytes, the program size is 100H through 107H inclusive, or 8.
   - First use R BX to display BX (the high portion of the size), and enter 0 to clear it.
   - Next use R CX to display CX. DEBUG replies with CX nnnn (whatever value it contains), and you replace it with the program size, 8.
   - Key in W <Enter> to write the revised program on disk.

DEBUG displays a message, "Writing 8 bytes." If the number is zero, you may have failed to enter the program length; try again. Watch out for the size of the program because the value is hexadecimal, and the last instruction could be longer than one byte.

Appendix D
Reserved Words

The assembler recognizes some words as having a specific meaning; you may use these words only under prescribed conditions. Words that the assembler reserves may be classed into four categories:

1. Register names, such as AX and AH
2. Symbolic instructions, such as ADD and MOV
3. Directives (commands to the assembler), such as PROC and END
4. Operators, such as DUP and SEG.

If used to define a data item, many of the reserved words that follow may confuse the assembler or cause an assembly error. A particular assembler version may have reserved words in addition to those listed here.

Register Names

AH, AL, AX, BH, BL, BP, BX, CH, CL, CS, CX, DH, DI, DL, DS, DX, EAX, EBP, EBX, ECX, EDI, EDX, EIP, ES, ESI, FS, GS, IP, SI, SP, SS

Symbolic Instructions

AAA, AAD, AAM, AAS, ADC, ADD, AND, ARPL, BOUND, BSF, BSR, BTn, CALL, CBW, CDQ, CLC, CLD, CLI, CLTS, CMC, CMP, CMPSn, CMPXCHG, CMPXCHG8B, CWDn, DAA, DAS, DEC, DIV, ENTER, ESC, HLT, IDIV, IMUL, IN, INC, INSn, INT, INTO, IRET, JA, JAE, JB, JBE, JCXZ, JE, JECXZ, JG, JGE, JL, JLE, JMP, JNA, JNAE, JNB, JNBE, JNE, JNG, JNGE, JNL, JNLE, JNO, JNP, JNS, JNZ, JO, JP, JPE, JPO, JS, JZ,

LAHF, LAR, LDS, LEA, LEAVE, LES, LFS, LGDT, LGS, LIDT, LLDT, LMSW, LOCK, LODSn, LOOP, LOOPE, LOOPNEn, LOOPNZn, LOOPZ, LSL, LSS, LSS, LTR, MOV, MOVSn, MOVSX, MOVZX, MUL, NEG, NOP, NOT, OR, OUTn, POP, POPA, POPAD, POPF, POPFD, PUSH, PUSHAD, PUSHF, PUSHFD, RCL, RCR, REN, REP, REPE, REPNE, REPNZ, REPZ, RET, RETF, ROL, ROR, SAHF, SAL, SAR, SBB, SCASn, SETnn, SGDT, SHL, SHLD, SHR, SHRD, SIDT, SLDT, SMSW, STC, STD, STI, STOSn, STR, SUB, TEST, VERR, VERRW, WAIT, XADD, XCHG, XLAT, XOR

Directives

ALIGN, .ALPHA, ASSUME, BYTE, .CODE, COMM, COMMENT, .CONST, .CREF, .DATA, .DATA?, DB, DD, DF, DOSSEG, DQ, DT, DW, DWORD, ELSE, END, ENDIF, ENDM, ENDP, ENDS, EQU, .ERRnn, EVEN, EXITM, EXTRN, EXTERN, .FARDATA, .FARDATA?, FWORD, GROUP, IF, IF1, IF2, IFB, IFDEF, IFDIF, IFE, IFIDN, IFNB, IFN-DEF, INCLUDE, INCLUDELIB, IRP, IRPC, LABEL, .LALL, .LFCOND, .LIST, LOCAL, MACRO, .MODEL, NAME, ORG, &OUT, PAGE, PROC, PUBLIC, PURGE, QWORD, .RADIX, RECORD, REPT, .SALL, SEGMENT, .SEQ, .SFCOND, .STACK, STRUC, SUBTTL, .TFCOND, TITLE, TWORD, UNION, WORD, .XALL, .XCREF, .XLIST

Operators

AND, BYTE, COMMENT, CON, DUP, EQ, FAR, GE, GT, HIGH, LE, LENGTH, LINE, LOW, LT, MASK, MOD, NE, NEAR, NOT, NOTHING, OFFSET, OR, PTR, SEG, SHL, SHORT, SHR, SIZE, STACK, THIS, TYPE, WHILE, WIDTH, WORD, XOR

Appendix E

ASSEMBLING AND LINKING PROGRAMS

This appendix covers the rules for assembling, linking, generating cross-reference files, and converting .EXE programs to .COM format. The steps in converting a source program into an executable file are:

1. Assemble the source program. This step creates an object (.OBJ) file, an optional listing (.LST), and an optional file for use as a cross-reference.
2. Link the object file. This step creates an executable (.EXE) file, an optional map (.MAP), and a optional library (.LIB) file. (Linking may involve combining more than one object file into one executable file.)
3. Optionally convert the .EXE file into a .COM file.

The various assembler versions handle these steps differently and provide a seemingly endless array of options, not all of which can be covered here. This appendix covers the versions for Microsoft MASM 6.1, MASM 5.1, and Borland Turbo TASM.

The word *path* used in this appendix means file and directory for programs and files; you can substitute the appropriate value, such as C: or C:\subdirectory.

MICROSOFT MASM 6.1

The Microsoft MASM 6.1 assembler uses the ML command, but also accepts the MASM command for compatibility with earlier versions. The ML command allows you to assemble and link any number of programs into one executable module. The format for the ML command to assemble and link is

```
ML [options] filename.ASM [[options] filename.ASM] ... [/LINK options]
```

Command-line *options* are case-sensitive and begin with a slash (/) character. They include the following:

/AT Indicates a program using the Tiny memory model, which the command is to convert to .COM format

/c Assemble, do not link

/Fl Generate a listing (.LST) file

/Fm Generate a link map (.MAP) file

/Fr Generate a .SBR (cross-reference) file

/Sn Suppress listing of the symbol table

/Zd Include line number debugging information

/Zi Include symbolic debugging information (for CodeView)

Here are two examples:

```
ML /Sn /Fr program23.asm  (Assemble and link)
ML /AT /Zd program34.asm  (Assemble, link, generate .COM file)
```

A useful command is simply ML -?, which displays the complete command-line syntax and options.

You may also use the MASM command line, which acts like MASM 5.1. (See MASM 5.1 in the next section.)

.COM Programs.   If the source program uses the Tiny memory-model, the ML command generates a .COM program. If the program uses conventional segments, ML generates a .EXE file, and you have to use EXE2BIN to convert it to .COM format (see MASM 5.1 next).

Linking.   You may assemble without linking (use the /c option), assemble and link (the default), specify LINK in the command line, or run the LINK program separately. The format for LINK is

```
LINK [options] object-file(s), [exefile], [mapfile], [libraries]
```

For a display of all link options, key in LINK /?.

Cross-reference File.   The /Fr option on the ML command line generates a .SBR file; use the CREF program to convert it to a proper, sorted .CRF file:

```
CREF xreffile.SBR, refffile.REF
```

MICROSOFT MASM 5.1

This version requires separate steps for assembling, linking, and converting into .COM format. The format for the assembler's command line is

```
MASM [options] source-file[,object-file][,list-file][,xref-file]
```

- *Options* are explained later.
- *Source-file* identifies the source program. The assembler assumes the extension .ASM, so you need not enter it. You may also key in the path, such as C:\subdirectory\filename.
- *Object-file* provides for a generated .OBJ file.
- *List-file* provides for a generated .LST file that contains the source and object code.
- *Xref-file* provides for a .CRF cross-reference file containing symbols for a cross-reference listing.

Each file may have its own path and filename, which may be the same or different from the source. This example spells out all the files:

```
MASM prog-name,prog-name,prog-name,prog-name
```

The following shortcut command allows for defaults for the object and cross-reference files, both with the same name, but no listing file: MASM filename,,,. MASM *options* include the following:

/C Create a cross-reference table in the .LST file.

/L Create a normal listing (.LST) file. The command line also provides a path for this option.

/N Suppress generation of the symbol table in the .LST file.

/Z Display source lines on the screen for errors.

/ZD Include information on line numbers in the object file for CodeView.

/ZI Include line-number and symbolic information in the object file for CodeView.

The following example requests two options: MASM /L/Z filename. For a brief explanation of all options, type in MASM /H (for help) with no filenames or other options.

Cross-reference File.   The .CRF file is used to produce a listing of a program's labels, symbols, and variables. Use CREF to convert the .CRF file to a sorted cross-reference (.REF) file:

```
CREF xreffile,reffile
```

- *xreffile* identifies the cross-reference file generated by the assembler. The program assumes the extension, so you need not enter it. You can also specify a path.
- *reffile* provides for generating a .REF file. The path and filename may be the same as or different from those in the source.

The following example writes a cross-reference file named ASMPROG.REF on drive C: CREF C:ASMPROG,C:.

Linking.   The command line for linking a MASM 5.1 program is

```
LINK objfile,exefile[,mapfile][,libraryfile]
```

- *Objfile* identifies the object file generated by the assembler. The linker assumes the extension .OBJ, so you need not enter it. The path and filename may be the same as or different from those in the source.

- *Exefile* provides for generating an .EXE file. The path and filename may be the same as or different from those in the source.
- *Mapfile* provides for generating a .MAP file that indicates the relative location and size of each segment and any errors that the linker has found. Entering CON (for console) tells the linker to display the map on the screen so that you can view it immediately for errors.
- *Libraryfile* provides for the libraries option.

If the object file is to have the same name as that of the source, you need not repeat it; the reference to drive number or path is sufficient to indicate a request for the file. The following example links the object file A05ASM1.OBJ; the linker is to write the .EXE file on drive n:, display the map (CON), and ignore the library option: LINK n:A05ASM1,n:,CON.

If the source program was written for .COM requirements, the linker displays a message "Warning: No Stack Segment."

To link more than one object file into an executable module, combine them in one line like this: `LINK PROGA+PROGB+PROGC`.

If you intend to use CodeView, include the assembler's /ZI command-line option. For linking, use the /CO option as LINK /CO filename.

Converting MASM 5.1 Object Files to .COM Programs. The EXE2BIN program converts .EXE modules generated by MASM into .COM modules, provided that the source program was originally coded according to .COM requirements. Type in the following command:

```
EXE2BIN filename,filename.COM
```

The first operand always references an .EXE file, so do not code the .EXE extension. The second operand may be any valid filename with a .COM extension. If you omit the .COM extension, EXE2BIN assumes .BIN, which you have to rename subsequently as .COM in order to execute the program.

BORLAND TURBO ASSEMBLER (TASM)

Turbo Assembler lets you assemble multiple files, each with its own options, in one command line. You can also use wild cards (* and ?). To assemble all source programs in the current directory, key in TASM *. To assemble all source programs named PROG1.ASM, PROG2.ASM, and so on, key in TASM PROG?. You can key in groups (or sets) of filenames, with each group separated by a plus sign (+). The following command assembles PROG1 and PROG2 with the /L option and PROG3 with the /Z option:

```
TASM /L PROG1 PROG2+ /Z PROG3
```

Requesting the /L option causes TASM to generate a listing (.LST) file, and /Z causes a display of source lines with errors. Keying in TCREF with no command line displays the general format for the command and an explanation of its options. Ideal mode also has many additional features. Borland supplies two other assembler versions, TASMX and TASM32, for protected mode.

Cross-Reference Files.   A .XRF file is used to produce a cross-reference listing of a program's labels, symbols, and variables. Use TCREF to convert the listing to a sorted cross-reference file:

```
TCREF xreffile,reffile
```

The rules for the TCREF command are similar to those for MASM 5.1 CREF. The following example writes a cross-reference file named ASMPROG.REF on drive C: `TCREF C:ASMPROG,C:`.

Linking.   The command line for linking a TASM program is

```
TLINK objfile,exefile[,mapfile][,libraryfile]
```

The rules for the TLINK command are similar to those for MASM 5.1 LINK.

Converting Turbo Object Files to .COM Programs.   TLINK allows you to convert an object program directly to .COM format, provided that the source program was originally coded according to .COM requirements. Use the /T option:

```
TLINK /T objfile,comfile,CON
```

Debugging Options.   If you intend to use TurboDebugger, use the assembler's /ZI command-line option. For linking, use the /V option, as `TLINK /V filename`.

ASSEMBLER TABLES

Following an assembler .LST listing are a Segments and Groups table and a Symbols table.

Segments and Groups Table.   This table has a heading similar to the following:

```
Name   Length   Align   Combine   Class
```

- The *name* column gives the names of all segments and groups in alphabetic sequence.
- The *length* column gives the size, in hex, of each segment.
- The *align* column gives the alignment type, such as BYTE, WORD, or PARA.
- The *combine* column lists the defined combine type, such as STACK for a stack, NONE where no type is coded, PUBLIC for external definitions, or a hex address for AT types.
- The *class* column lists the segment class names, as coded in the SEGMENT statement.

Symbol Table.   A symbol table has a heading similar to the following:

```
Name Type Value Attribute
```

- The *name* column lists the names of all defined items, in alphabetic sequence.
- The *type* column gives the type, as follows:
  L NEAR or L FAR: A near or far label

N PROC or F PROC: A near or far procedure

BYTE, WORD, DWORD, FWORD, QWORD, TBYTE: A data item

ALIAS: An alias (or nickname) for another symbol

NUMBER: An absolute label

OPCODE: An equate for an instruction operand

TEXT: An equate for text

- The *value* column gives the hex offset from the beginning of a segment for names, labels, and procedures.
- The *attribute* column lists a symbol's attributes, including its segment and length.

MASM 6.1 also provides a Procedures, Parameters, and Locals table, which lists their names and attributes.

Appendix F

Keyboard Scan Codes and ASCII Codes

In the following lists, keys are grouped rather arbitrarily into categories. For each category, the columns show the format for a normal key (not combined with another key) and formats when the key is combined with the Shift, Ctrl, and Alt keys. Under the columns headed "Normal," "Shift," "Ctrl," and "Alt" are two hex bytes as they appear when a keyboard operation delivers them to the AH and AL registers. For example, pressing the letter "a" causes BIOS to deliver 1EH in AH for the scan code and 61H in AL for the ASCII character. When shifted to uppercase ("A"), the keyboard delivers 1EH and 41H, respectively. Scan codes 85H and higher are for the extended keyboard.

LETTERS	NORMAL		SHIFT		CTRL		ALT	
a and A	1E	61	1E	41	1E	01	1E	00
b and B	30	62	30	42	30	02	30	00
c and C	2E	63	2E	43	2E	03	2E	00
d and D	20	64	20	44	20	04	20	00
e and E	12	65	12	45	12	05	12	00
f and F	21	66	21	46	21	06	21	00
g and G	22	67	22	47	22	07	22	00
h and H	23	68	23	48	23	08	23	00
i and I	17	69	17	49	17	09	17	00
j and J	24	6A	24	4A	24	0A	24	00

k and K	25	6B	25	4B	25	0B	25	00
l and L	26	6C	26	4C	26	0C	26	00
m and M	32	6D	32	4D	32	0D	32	00
n and N	31	6E	31	4E	31	0E	31	00
o and O	18	6F	18	4F	18	0F	18	00
p and P	19	70	19	50	19	10	19	00
q and Q	10	71	10	51	10	11	10	00
r and R	13	72	13	52	13	12	13	00
s and S	1F	73	1F	53	1F	13	1F	00
t and T	14	74	14	54	14	14	14	00
u and U	16	75	16	55	16	15	16	00
v and V	2F	76	2F	56	2F	16	2F	00
w and W	11	77	11	57	11	17	11	00
x and X	2D	78	2D	58	2D	18	2D	00
y and Y	15	79	15	59	15	19	15	00
z and Z	2C	7A	2C	5C	2C	1A	2C	00
Spacebar	39	20	39	20	39	20	39	20

FUNCTION KEYS	NORMAL		SHIFT		CTRL		ALT	
F1	3B	00	54	00	5E	00	68	00
F2	3C	00	55	00	5F	00	69	00
F3	3D	00	56	00	60	00	6A	00
F4	3E	00	57	00	61	00	6B	00
F5	3F	00	58	00	62	00	6C	00
F6	40	00	59	00	63	00	6D	00
F7	41	00	5A	00	64	00	6E	00
F8	42	00	5B	00	65	00	6F	00
F9	43	00	5C	00	66	00	70	00
F10	44	00	5D	00	67	00	71	00
F11	85	00	87	00	89	00	8B	00
F12	86	00	88	00	8A	00	8C	00

NUMERIC KEYPAD	NORMAL		SHIFT		CTRL		ALT	
Ins and 0	52	00	52	30	92	00		
End and 1	4F	00	4F	31	75	00	00	01
DnArrow and 2	50	00	50	32	91	00	00	02

Key								
PgDn and 3	51	00	51	33	76	00	00	03
LtArrow and 4	4B	00	4B	34	73	00	00	04
5 (keypad)	4C	00	4C	35	8F	00	00	05
RtArrow and 6	4D	00	4D	36	74	00	00	06
Home and 7	47	00	47	37	77	00	00	07
UpArrow and 8	48	00	48	38	8D	00	00	08
PgUp and 9	49	00	49	39	84	00	00	09
+ (gray key)	4E	2B	4E	2B	90	00	4E	00
− (gray key)	4A	2D	4A	2D	8E	00	4A	00
Del and .	53	00	53	2E	93	00		
* (gray key)	37	2A	37	2A	96	00	37	00

TOP ROW	NORMAL		SHIFT		CTRL		ALT	
` and ~	29	60	29	7E			29	00
1 and !	02	31	02	21			78	00
2 and @	03	32	03	40	03	00	79	00
3 and #	04	33	04	23			7A	00
4 and $	05	34	05	24			7B	00
5 and %	06	35	06	25			7C	00
6 and ^	07	36	07	5E	07	1E	7D	00
7 and &	08	37	08	26			7E	00
8 and *	09	38	09	2A			7F	00
9 and (	0A	39	0A	38			80	00
0 and)	0B	30	0B	29			81	00
− and _	0C	2D	0C	5F	0C	1F	82	00
= and +	0D	3D	0D	2B			83	00

OPERATION KEYS	NORMAL		SHIFT		CTRL		ALT	
Esc	01	1B	01	1B	01	1B	01	00
Backspace	0E	08	0E	08	0E	7F	0E	00
Tab	0F	09	0F	00	94	00	A5	00
Enter	1C	0D	1C	0D	1C	0A	1C	00

PUNCTUATION	NORMAL		SHIFT		CTRL		ALT	
[and {	1A	5B	1A	7B	1A	1B	1A	00
] and }	1B	5D	1B	7D	1B	1D	1B	00
; and :	27	3B	27	3A			27	00
' and "	28	27	28	22			28	00
\ and |	2B	5C	2B	7C	2B	1C	2B	00
, and <	33	2C	33	3C			33	00
. and >	34	2E	34	3E			34	00
/ and ?	35	2F	35	3F			35	00

Following are the duplicate keys on the enhanced keyboard (the first entry (Slash) is an ASCII character, whereas the rest are command keys):

KEY	NORMAL		SHIFT		CTRL		ALT	
Slash (/)	E0	2F	E0	2F	95	00	A4	00
Del	53	E0	53	E0	93	E0	A3	00
DownArrow	50	E0	50	E0	91	E0	A0	00
End	4F	E0	4F	E0	75	E0	9F	00
Enter	E0	0D	E0	0D	E0	0A	A6	00
Home	47	E0	47	E0	77	E0	97	00
Ins	52	E0	52	E0	92	E0	A2	00
LeftArrow	4B	E0	4B	E0	73	E0	9B	00
PageDown	51	E0	51	E0	76	E0	A1	00
PageUp	49	E0	49	E0	84	E0	99	00
RightArrow	4D	E0	4D	E0	74	E0	9D	00
UpArrow	48	E0	48	E0	8D	E0	98	00

The following control keys also have identifying scan codes, although BIOS doesn't deliver them to the keyboard buffer:

CapsLock	3A	Shift (Right)	36
NumLock	45	Alt	38
ScrollLock	46	Ctrl	1D
Shift (Left)	2A	PrtScreen	37

INDEX